D0937162

THE
ANATOMY OF
BIBLIOMANIA

by

HOLBROOK JACKSON

FARRAR, STRAUS AND COMPANY
New York

Copyright 1950 by Farrar, Straus and Company.
All rights reserved, including the right to
reproduce this book or portions thereof.

010
J 13 a
82240

Manufactured in the United States of America
The Murray Printing Company, Wakefield, Massachusetts

CONTENTS

7

PART XI. A PAGEANT OF BOOKMEN

PART XII. HOW BOOKMEN CONQUER TIME AND PLACE

PART XIII. THE INFLUENCE OF BOOKS

PART XIV. BOOKS PHARMACEUTICALLY DISPOSED

THE AUTHOR TO THE READER

entle Reader, I presume thou wilt be very inquisitive to know
what antic or personate actor it is that so insolently intrudes
upon this common theatre to the world's view, arrogating, as
you will soon find, another man's style and·method: whence he is, why
he does it, and what he has to say. 'Tis a proper attitude, and the questions
clear and reasonable in themselves, but I owe thee no answer, for if the
contents please thee, 'tis well; if they be useful, 'tis an added value; if
neither, pass on, nor, in the observation of that wise Glanvill,[1] *hath any one
need to complain, since no one is concerned about what another Prints, further
than himself pleaseth; and since Men have the liberty to read our Books, or not,*
they should give us leave to write what we like, *or forbear*, which for the
most part they do.

Yet in some sort to give thee satisfaction, which thou hast a right to
demand, since I have caused my book to be printed and sold for money, I
will show a reason both of this usurped title and style. And first for the
name and form, which I have so freely adapted from Robert Burton his
Anatomy of Melancholy: lest any man by reason of it should be deceived,
expecting a pasquil, a scherzo, a burlesque, a satire, some humorous or
fantastic treatise (as I myself should have done, recalling that all parodies
are jests), I may at once undeceive him, for my intent is serious; I have
gleaned the crops of innumerable authorities scattered far and wide,
winnowing the chaff from the grain, and setting out the various species in
such an order that they may best contribute to our knowledge of books in
general and of *Bibliomania* in particular.

But should my treatise be deemed to have missed its mark as a piece of
science, I am content that it should have its niche as a pastiche, for then it
cannot be other than an entertainment, an extravaganza, a *Revue des Livres*
with all the stars in the cast, and a libretto sparkling with an infinite variety
of wit and wisdom, sense and nonsense, in prose and verse, epigram,
aphorism, tale, apophthegm, anecdote, history, etc.; sometimes authori-
tative, sometimes speculative; spiced with whims, paradoxes, fancies,
facts, the whole tending towards a harmony, which is mine own gift to
this Pageant of Books for Bookmen.

Books and the Man I sing:[2]

[1] *Essays.* (1676) Preface.   [2] Pope, *Dunciad.* (First Ed.) 1.

and since thou, Gentle Reader, art *ad unguem factus homo*, a polished man, of that bookish kind, for none but bookmen will understand, still less enjoy this assemblage, 'tis in part of thee. Thou thyself art the subject of my discourse; and I desire leave to inform you that shall become my readers, that I write not these things unto you because you know them not, but because you know them.

> Quicquid agunt homines, votum, timor, ira, voluptas,
> Gaudia, discursus nostri farrago libelli est.[1]

> What *Bookmen* do, vows, fears, in ire, in sport,
> Joys, wand'rings, are the sum of my report.

Thus my title and form become plain, for this treatise is an *Anatomy* of its subject: a fair analysis of books and their meaning for all kinds of men and women, with a particular relation of the madness engendered by them and for them in those extreme cases which I have explicated. My first purpose was to expound only this last, but in doing so I have wandered many times from my main theme in order that a true relation between sanity and dotage should be made clear; wherein I now find that I have incorporated as much of the one matter as of the other; so that if the centre or core of my dissertation remains *Bibliomania*, its environs extend far beyond it, as towns grow from a single citadel, institution or workshop, into a county, but remain towns. Examine the rest, therefore, in like sort, and you shall find a true picture of a book and all its relations and purposes: its joys, advantages, infirmities and offences.

But in the meantime, how does Burton concern me, or upon what reference do I usurp his style? I confess, indeed, that to compare myself unto him for aught I have yet said, were both impudency and arrogancy. I do not presume to make any parallel between my work and his, for what I have accomplished should be plain, even to the hurried passer-by, and if, posing myself deliberately as God posed him, I look awkward, ridiculous, strange, the fault is mine not his, which is too evident to need proof. And since I must not be over-confident of my own performance after him, it will be prudence in me to be silent, and let my treatise tell its own tale.

Yet I hope I may affirm, and without vanity or brag in any sort, that by acknowledging Burton my master, and by imitating him, I have excelled myself; and further, again as I hope without any suspicion of pride or self-conceit, that although I had not his advantage of a University life *as long almost*, he saith,[2] *as Xenocrates in Athens, ad senectam feré*,[3] penned up most part in his study, *ego in Arcadia vixi*, I have yet lived a silent, solitary, private life, *mihi Musis*, to myself and books, in the busy world. For I have been brought up a student in the university of affairs, the modern city, as

---

[1] Juvenal, *Satires*. I, 85–6.   [2] *Anat. of Melan*. (1904) i, 13.   [3] 'To old age almost.'

he was in *the most flourishing College of Europe*.[1] What he found concentrated in those rich warehouses of wisdom, the Bodleian and the Library of his own college, I have found dispersed in many places; and if he can brag with Jovius almost, *in ea luce domicilii Vaticani, totius orbis celeberrimi, per 37 annos multa opportunaque didici*;[2] for forty years and more I have had the use of as good libraries as ever he had; and at all times I have had books of my own, with no memory even of a time when I was bookless, for I am come from a bookloving tribe, and, like Mr. Lear,

> *I live* in a beautiful parlour
> With hundreds of books on the wall;

and I have used my books, perchance, with even greater gusto than Burton used his, for whereas he was a student by condition, I have remained one by waging constant warfare with opposing circumstances: every studious hour a victory over the tyranny of business; and as my *augustissimum collegium* has been books and the world, I would be, therefore, as loth as he was in his more concentrate and more learned amplitude, either by living as a drone to be an unprofitable or unworthy member of so diverse and operose a society, or to write in my hours of freedom that which should be any way dishonourable to such a momentous and manifold foundation.

And if I am so bold as to claim this slender kinship with him, seeming thus to honour myself over much, I am not blind to the differences between us. I frankly confess I am a scholar without scholarship, pursuing learning without attaining it, and kin to him by inclination rather than achievement.

In this light my treatise of *Bibliomania*, insofar as it is Burton *redivivus*, may be taken as an act of homage which I offer to his memory, *ab singulari amore*, as well I may, for constant companionship since first I met with his *Anatomy* nigh forty years ago. Thus in general; but from another point of view, such a work, in such a form, is as much of me as his of him.

Something I have done out of a running wit, *turbine raptus ingenii*,[3] product, as Burton confesses of himself, *of an unconstant unsettled mind*;[4] though in that both he and I are unjust to ourselves (*si parva licet componere magnis*), for inconstancy could never have sired his treatise, or mine. Put case that we are observers, lookers-on, *transmitters of ideas*,[5] commentators of the passing show, not actors in it, or playwrights; we create nothing,

---

[1] Christ Church in Oxford. [2] Praefat. *hist.* [3] Scaliger. [4] *Anat. of Melan.* i, 14.
[5] Sir William Osler divided writers into Transmitters, Transmuters and Creators: 'In the days when Sir Thomas Bodley concluded to set up his staff at the Library door at Oxford, there lived in this country the last of the great transmitters, Robert Burton; the first of the great modern transmuters, Francis Bacon; and the greatest of the world's creators, William Shakespeare.' *Proceedings*. Oxford Bibliographical Society. v. i. pt. 3. p. 216.

but allow everything to create a lively interest in the cosmos of ourselves, a curious courage before the *convictions of others*,[1] not taking our own too seriously, but willing enough to tilt in a joust with those who throw down the gage for the fun of it. Our patron saint is Democritus, as he frankly owned, and our final comment, a laugh, however we may set it forth with words; and I see a parable in this story of Democritus:[2] how he retired to Abdera, a town in Thrace, where he lived at last in a garden in the suburbs, wholly betaking himself to his studies, and a private life, saving that sometimes he would walk down to the haven, and laugh heartily at such variety of ridiculous objects which there he saw.

Such a one was Robert Burton, and he emulated his master both in what he wrote and what he did, for he would walk down to Folly Bridge at Oxford to recreate himself with laughter at what he saw and heard, and I, in our own time, have abundant opportunity to recreate myself with laughter when I taxi down to London Bridge or Piccadilly or the Strand, or such other notable gathering-places of people as my greater freedom of movement affords me; for *what is all this Life but a kind of Comedy, wherein men walk up and down in one another's Disguises, and Act their respective Parts, till the property-man brings 'em back to the Tyring House.*[3] But I am not always laughing, any more than they were: I sometimes rail with Carlyle, satirically tax with Shaw, lament with Schopenhauer, sometimes again *sum petulanti splene cachinno*,[4] and then again, *jecur urere bilis*,[5] I am much moved to see the abuse which I cannot mend. Our artistry is thus in an attitude, and if, in the main, it is like to die with us, but this not certain, it entertains us, and others perchance, while it lasts.

I am not ignorant that I might, as one friend (a notable poet and stiff-necked critic of himself as well as others) advised, have sorted out and co-ordinated my store of *analecta* on some plan more to the purpose of our own age and, indeed, more particular to myself. It was sage advice, *necessitati qui se accommodat, sapit*,[6] and I was, and am, so much enamoured of the tenent that each and every age should express itself in its own way, and not in that of the past, however excellent, for *composition is not there, it is going to be there and we are here*,[7] that I seriously gave my mind to the problem of re-casting the whole business; but it fell out otherwise, for I then discovered, what I should have known if I had given thought to the origin of my enterprise, that there is no modern method of literary mosaic. The art was perfected by Robert Burton and he remains its unapproachable master. Many have larded their lean books with the fat of his masterpiece,

[1] Whistler, *Gentle Art of Making Enemies*.   [2] *Anat. of Melan*. i, 13.   [3] Erasmus, *Praise of Folly*. Trans. Wilson. Clarendon Press Ed. 53.   [4] 'I am a laugher with wanton spleen.' *Persius*. i, 12.   [5] 'Gall burns my liver.' Horace, *Sat*. i, 9, 66.   [6] Epictetus, *Morals*. c. 18. 'He is wise that suits himself to the time.'   [7] Gertrude Stein, *Composition as Explanation*. 16.

but he has had no imitator till now, save Charles Lamb in an experiment which was never meant to be more than a fragment.[1] From this it may be argued still more stiffly that a literary form which has found no copiers in over three centuries must needs be out-moded, defunct, a wash-out. To this so specious an objection I have this to answer, that it would have been such had it been no more than a patchwork, a show or pattern of words and phrases, but the *Anatomy of Melancholy* is far more than that; and as a great part of this discourse is grounded upon the *Anatomy* I hold myself obliged to a short account of that supposal.

Robert Burton's ingenious treatise is a curiously wrought-out design. There are idle students and cavillers, who have advertised Burton as the creator of a peculiar anthologic maze, an amusing literary chaos, a farrago of quotations, a mere *olla podrida* of quaintness, a *pot pourri* of pleasant *delites*, a *florilegium* of elegant extracts, a tangled fardel of old-world flowers of thought, a faggot of odd fancies, quips, *facetiæ*, loosely tied, the creator, in short, of a book for a rainy day and a cosy corner. And I will not deny that he has made for the curious and more bookish of readers our greatest work in this kind. But particularly I say it was not his aim to be an entertainment, though he diligently sought to avoid being tedious. Burton wrote as a psychologist and a philosopher: inlaying to those ends his *tesseræ* of borrowed apophthegms and notions. He was so bold as to dispose himself scientifically without other authority or qualification than inclination, at the dawn of our era of deduction from observed phenomena, and although it was his disposition to admire and consider strange rather than common things, and to set too great a store upon the unfolding of learned and curious opinions, he sought to make his book as scientificl as Dr. William Harvey made his *De Motu Cordis* or Sir Isaac Newton his *Principia*; or, for the matter of that, and to come nearer home, as Charles Darwin the *Origin of Species*; and as philosophical as such notable works of our own time as *Die Welt als Wille und Vorstellung* or the *Evolution Créatrice*; and if he knew no better than to mingle science with philosophy, as I erewhile began to say, it is all for our own good, for in this dereliction of scientific duty he achieved wisdom without dullness, by means of which it comes to pass that his book survives in our affection as well as in our admiration. Yet, and here is an end of this business, for I am come at length to my point, he is a precursor not so much of these exact works as of those of such conspicuous co-ordinators of anthropological ideas and phenomena as Keane and Frazer, Krafft-Ebing and Havelock Ellis.

In these anticipations I am much in concert with him, and were I equally sympathetic with their style I should have preferred it to his, but since it was otherwise and I more enamoured of my Burton as a writer, and find-

[1] Lamb, 'Curious Fragments', *Miscellaneous Prose*.

ing my subject of bibliomania amenable to his method, with an affinity to its leisureliness and copious garrulity, I was therefore bold to imitate, to revive again, prosecute and finish, in this treatise. And for reasons which will become plain, if they are not so already, I found in the ample form and slow measure of his diction (which goes trippingly enough on occasion) a refuge from the dirt-track of civilization,

Safe in the hallowed quiets of the past.[1]

A large still book is a piece of quietness, succulent and nourishing in a noisy world, which I approach and imbibe with *a sort of greedy enjoyment*, as Marcel Proust those rooms of his old home whose air was *saturated with the bouquet of silence*.[2] From this enjoyment of so wide a calmness I found an inclination to reproduce it, and proceeded more by instinct than design, as though sauntering into a domain of unexplored tranquillity, wherein *I beheld the bright countenance of truth in the quiet and still air of delightful studies*,[3] and began, for gladness, to extend its bounds. This ancient manner, with its undulations and digressions, its dingles and coppices of verbiage, its elegant parterres of selected prose and verse, its sharp contrasts of grassy plots and arid places, is not, I am well aware, the fashion of these times when all men hurry and many torture us with noises which disrupt our thoughts and interrupt our lives.[4] I have taken pains to make it slow and long (against my custom), and the manner of it is often so tedious that it is apt to please only those who *study to be quiet*[5]—but that may be accounted a prime virtue in these times; for the rest I keep in the common path, aiming at neither simplicity nor subtlety. I saunter along, loitering when and where I will, taking my time, *I lean and loafe at my ease observing a spear of summer grass*;[6] there is no hurry (*Haste not, be at rest, this Now is eternity.*);[7] there is time to rest if we wish it, no good to be always rushing about. I like to do nothing, to escape from purpose: to brood, to think back and forth; *to sit by a fire in Winter, or in a garden in Summer; to loaf on a sea-beach with the sun on me; to hang over the wall of a pier-head watching the waves in their green and white tantrums; to sit in a brasserie on a Parisian boulevard with a common bock, and the people moving to and fro; to idle in parks or public squares, or in the quadrangles and closes of colleges, or the Inns of Court, or the great cathedrals; to forget haste and effort in old empty churches, or drowsy*

[2] J. R. Lowell, 'The Cathedral'.   [2] *Swann's Way*. Trans. Scott Moncrieff. i, 65. [3] Milton, *Reason for Church Government*. Intro. ii.   [4] 'Noise is the most impertinent of all forms of interruption. It is not only an interruption, but a disruption of thought. Of course, where there is nothing to interrupt, noise will not be so particularly painful.' Schopenhauer, 'On Noise', *Studies in Pessimism*. Trans. Saunders. 128.   [5] 1. *Thess.* iv, 11.   [6] Walt Whitman, 'Song of Myself', *Leaves of Grass*. 1. [7] Richard Jefferies, *The Story of My Heart*. (1898) 45.

*taverns; to rest by a road-side hedge, or in a churchyard where sheep browse; to
lie in a punt in the green shade of the willows; to sit on a fence—these things
please me well:*[1]

A poor life this if, full of care,
We have no time to stand and stare.[2]

So it is done, and as it cannot be helped or amended, make the best of it.
I descend, then, to the second prejudice, which may have been formed in
behalf of the objectors.

You have had a reason for the manner. If any man except against the
matter, and will demand a reason of it, I can allege more than one. I writ
of bibliomania, by being busy to avoid bibliomania. There is no greater
cause of bibliomania than bibliophilia inordinately pursued, no better cure
than study or adventurous and eventful reading, and, for some, writing,
to express and record such experiences, but of this I have discoursed elsewhere. Some have been afflicted with bibliomania through idleness, and
for them there is small hope of cure; others, and I count myself among
them, from excess of affairs. Many, like asses that wear out their time for
provender, are so buried in the minor and immediate tasks of earning a
living at to get *confounded promptly and permanently with the victims of com-
mercial ambition*,[3] whence it comes to pass that, slily and insensibly perverted, nerves frayed and brains dulled, they take to books as sick souls
take to drugs. They hoard at first against a time of leisure when they may
perchance read, and end by hoarding for the sake of hoarding, thus allying
themselves with those dizzards who wallow among possessions which they
cannot use, and who die before they have lived. *To husband a favourite
claret until the batch turns sour, is not at all an artful stroke of policy; and how
much more with a whole cellar.*[4] I writ, therefore, and busied myself in this
playing labour, first for mine own advantage, that I might avoid the tor-
por of business and the atrophy of the sensibilities which is the punishment
of those who enslave themselves in affairs, and next *otium in utile vertere
negotium*, to turn my leisure to good purpose:

Simul èt jucunda et idonea dicere vitae;
Lectorem delectando simul atque monendo,

at once to say both useful things and pleasant, to assemble these *fond
Crotchets of Philosophy*[5] which I have lighted on in the highways and byways of books, so as to please the reader, yet instruct; which if it be granted

---

[1] Holbrook Jackson, *Southward Ho! and Other Essays*. ii, 17.   [2] W. H. Davies,
'Leisure', *Collected Poems*. 19.   [3] Louise Imogen Guiney, 'The Precept of Peace',
Patrins. 124.   [4] R. L. Stevenson, 'Crabbed Age and Youth', *Virginibus Puerisque*. 94.
[5] Glanvill, *Witches and Witchcraft*. (1667) 60.

possible, 'tis sufficient for my defence; and the sum of my argument, whatever else this treatise may contain or mean, is that books are for our enjoyment and that pleasurable reading is the best prophylactic against bibliomania, and a sure solatium for their lovers.

Yea, but you will infer that this is *actum agere*, an unnecessary work, full of vain repetition, the again and again in other words; which I do not deny, for, I confess, *I love to renew a pleasure by relating it*;[1] but since this conceit is so much mine own affair, you may well ask, to what purpose? To which, among other things which might be suggested, I ask what is purpose? Many desirable things have no purpose whatsoever. And yet if it is possible to distribute as well as augment a pleasure by relating it, I am acting to some purpose, for I bequeath to you the freedom of my enjoyment without forcing its acceptance. Next, my work, you think, is superfluous because many excellent bookmen, critics, commentators, bibliographers, etc., have written just volumes and elaborate tracts of this *Bibliomania*; no news here. You may infer, again, that that which I have in great measure is stolen from others. I admit it, *dicitque mihi mea pagina, fur es.*[2] But if the severe doom of Synesius be true, that *it is a greater offence to steal dead men's labours than their clothes*,[3] what shall become of most writers? I hold up my hand at the bar amongst others, including my good master, for, although I have not privily rifled, I am addicted to larceny in this kind (as I shall anon explain), *habes confitentem reum*, I plead guilty, I am content to be condemned with the rest.

But why, it may still be urged, swell further this welter of repetition, and worse, if all that they say of plagiary be true? And if, indeed, I have done no more than echo and pilfer, *actum est de me*, it is all up with me, I am undone; to which implications 'twere enough to say, *ab abusu ad usum non valet consequentia*;[4] but I have attempted something more particularly, and claim propriety in my method and fair usage. Were it otherwise, it might have been charged against me that I have writ out of an incontinent penmanship, an itching humour, which is common enough in this scribbling age (and most ages, as the authorities agree, are no better), so that oftentimes it falls out (as Robert Burton taxed of old), a new book is no more than *some bauble or toy which idle fellows write, for as idle fellows to read*.[5] I have no wish to row in that galley, though I despise not idleness when I can get it, nor idle reading neither, which hath its place with the rest, *in virtute multi ascensus*,[6] there are degrees in virtue, as in vice.

That there is a vast chaos and confusion of books I have no doubt, and that our eyes ache with reading, our fingers with turning, I do not deny;

---

[1] Pliny, *Letters*. Trans. Melmoth. Loeb. Ed. vii, 24.   [2] 'And my page says to me, you are a thief.' Martial, i, 54, 12.   [3] *Epistles*, 142.   [4] 'The abuse of anything is no argument against its proper use.'   [5] *Anat. of Melan.* i, 21.   [6] Cicero.

nor can I deny that I have risked censure by becoming one of the mob of producers. I do not deny it, and I have only this to say for myself, as Burton said of his book,[1] *Omne meum, nihil meum*, 'tis all mine and none mine. As a bee gathers wax and honey out of many flowers, and makes a new bundle of all,

Floriferis ut apes in saltibus omnia libant,[2]

I was ever wont to intermix with mine own work some ornaments from the works of others, and I have laboriously collected this fardel out of divers writers, and like him, *sine injuria*, I have wronged no writers, but given every man his due; and thus citing and quoting mine authors, I am no thief, *sumpsi, non surripui*, I have taken, not stolen; and what Varro[3] speaks of bees, *minimè maleficae quod nullius opus vellicantes faciunt deterius*, that they are not malicious, because they cause no injury to the flowers which they rifle, on the contrary, they give more than they take, I can say of myself; whom have I injured? It would be as untrue to say of me, as Montaigne alleged might be said of him: *that here I have but gathered a nosegay of strange floures, and have put nothing of mine into it, but the thread to binde them.*[4] The matter is theirs most part and yet mine, and in some instances, especially of bibliomania proper, more mine than theirs, for the best of them are, as the saying is, at sea with that subject. I have tried to bring them safely into port; and if among so many borrowings I have been pleased to filch some, I have disguised and altered them to a new service, as Ragnar Ostberg, if I may compare my small building with his, plundered the architectural notions of all times and wove them into the fabric of that inimitable *pastiche*, the *Stadshus* of Stockholm. So I pick and choose, and *quicquid bene dictum est ab ullo, meum est*,[5] whatever has been well said by anyone is my property; but as nature doth the aliment of our bodies incorporate, digest, assimilate, *concoquo quod hausi*, I dispose of what I take; and such kind of borrowing, as Milton holds, cannot be accounted a plagiary;[6] so if I make them pay tribute, to set out this my *Macaronicon*,

Yet credit to the Artist will accrue,
Who in known things still makes th' appearance new;[7]

for, as Goethe holds, and I go some of the way with him, *the best sign of originality lies in taking up a subject and then developing it so fully as to make every one confess that he would hardly have found so much in it.*[8]

The theory, at least, is mine and the choice and arrangement of my collectanea of shreds and patches. I make no excuse: *qui s'excuse, s'accuse;*[9] and

[1] *Anat. of Melan.* 1, 22. [2] Lucretius. iii, 11· [3] *De Re Rust.* 3.16.7. [4] 'Of Phisiognomy', *Essays.* Ed. Seccombe, iii, 387. [5] Seneca, *Epistolae.* xvi, 7. [6] *Iconoclasts.* xxiii. [7] W. King, *Art of Cookery.* 61. [8] *Maxims and Reflections.* Trans. Saunders. 153. [9] Gabriel Meurier, *Trésor des Sentences.* 63. n. 2.

if this new farrago in an ancient manner is condemned because there were
giants of old in history and bibliography, then I say, with Didacús Stella,
Pygmaei Gigantum humeris impositi plus quam ipsi Gigantes vident,[1] a dwarf
standing on the shoulders of a giant may see farther than a giant himself:
so I may likely *adopt, adapt, improve*, as our Prince of Wales advises, and
also, see farther than my predecessors. Were it otherwise, as it may well be,
this method is not defenceless, for as Pliny saith, *alienis pedibus ambulamus,
alienis oculis agnoscimus, aliena memoria salutamus, aliena opera vivimus*,[2] we
walk with the feet of others, see a friend through another's eyes, salute him
by another recalling his name, live by the work of others, for, if you
believe the relation of that shrewd man, Samuel Butler, *all things which
come to much, whether they be books, buildings, pictures, music, or living beings,
are suggested by others of their own kind*.[3] This supposal may give a fairer and
more probable account of some of my actions.

It is no greater prejudice for me to indite after Burton, than for him
after others; and as he hath rescued many a passage from the oblivion of a
prosaic environment by giving it a witty setting, so may the dry bones of
such of my authorities as have hitherto slumbered in their own limbo,
awake to significance, and perchance to distinction (for I wish them no
harm), from the new contexts (whether witty or not) and distinguished
companions I have given them. Nor, perhaps, ought I to omit this other
argument, that I have resolved into my theme many of those clear circumstances of fact, which we find in well-attested and confirmed relations
of this kind; and I here avow that I have been scrupulous to observe the
rights of mine authorities in full propriety, citing with precision, so far as
I could, their own words, not only in matter but in form, out of a confessed regard for them, as Favorinus implied when he said: *si ex Platonis
oratione verbum aliquod demas mutesve atque id commodatissime facias, de
elegantia tamen detraxeris; si ex Lysiae, de sententia;*[4] no altering Plato, however skilfully, without disfiguring his style, nor Lysias without obscuring
his sense. I know nothing, therefore, to help me to imagine that I have
wronged anyone purposely.

If, then, as Donne feared for his *Biathanatos, in multiplicity of not necessary
citations there appear vanity, or ostentation, or digression*, my honesty must make
my excuse and compensation. I am not only with Pliny where he says
that to choose rather to be taken in a theft than to give every man his due,
is *obnoxii animi et infelicis ingenii*,[5] but can say, again with Donne, that
*every branch which is excerpted from other authors, and engrafted here, is not
written for the reader's faith, but for illustration and comparison*.[6] I solve it thus;

[1] In *Lucan.* x, 2. Qt. Burton, *Anat. of Melan.* i, 23. 　 [2] Pliny, *Hist. Nat.* 29. 　 [3] *Alps
and Sanctuaries.* 87. 　 [4] Aulus Gellius, *Noctes Atticae.* ii, 5. 　 [5] 'A mark of a diseased
mind and an ill-starred disposition.' 　 [6] Preface, *Biathanatos.* Nonesuch Ed. *Complete Poetry and Selected Prose.* 424.

and the conclusion from all these premises is, I hope, sufficiently demonstrated. For the rest, *jacta alea est*, the die is cast and you must take it or leave it.

As for those other faults of style, manner as distinct from matter and method, I am exposed to attack on all fronts, and most by comparison: I have missed my mark, fallen short, o'ershot it; out-Burtoned Burton here, vulgarized him there, and diluted him too often; I am barbaric, unscholarly, provincial, amateurish, sentimental, glib, garrulous, what you will; a dealer in tautologies, rhetoric, gusto, purple patches, rhapsodies, clichés, vogue words, *rags gathered together from several dunghills, excrements of authors, toys and fopperies confusedly tumbled out*, as he said of his own book,[1] *without art, invention, judgment, wit, learning, harsh, raw, rude, phantastical, absurd, insolent, indiscreet, ill-composed, indigested, vain, scurrile, idle, dull and dry*; and with him I confess all; few writers are more frequent in this kind of mischief. Thou canst not think worse of my performance than I do myself, for in the first place I have my vision of what it might have been, and in the second, any work in this kind must remain an effort rather than an achievement, and in that alone I am belike overbold in advancing it. But thou canst still say 'tis not worth reading; to which I reply again briefly and yet I hope sufficiently: the choice is thine; and if it is as bad as I have said, I yield it, I desire thee not to waste time in perusing so vain a work, I should be peradventure loth myself to read myself or thee so writing. But such arguers may please to consider that I have precedents; 'tis not the first usurpation of an author's style and method; others have done as much and not always as frankly, but the theme is mine, the whole discourse being a kind of picture of mine own disposition.

Well or ill, I have put myself upon the stage, and I must take all risks. I have laid myself open in this treatise, turned mine inside (or the bookish part of me) outward. I shall be censured, I doubt not, for to say truth with Erasmus, *nihil morosius hominum judiciis*, there's nought so peevish as men's judgements, yet this is some comfort, *ut palata, sic judicia*, our censures are as various as our palates;

> 'Tis with our judgments as our watches—none
> Go just alike, yet each believes his own:[2]

and never were there two opinions in the world alike, no more than two haires, or two graines. Diversity is the most universal quality;[3] and for every thought expressed there are many glosses and interpretations: *Plotinus believes only in philosophers; Fénelon, in saints; Pindar and Byron, in poets. To the Platonists all men who are not devoted to their shining abstractions are rats and mice.*

---

[1] *Anat. of Melan.* i, 24.   [2] Pope, *Essay on Criticism.* 9–10.   [3] Montaigne, 'To My Lady of Duras', *Essays*. Ed. Seccombe. ii, 657.

Pope and Swift *describe mankind around them as monsters*; Goethe and Schiller *are scarcely more kind*.[1] I could name many more instances, but refrain lest it be thought that I am opposed to critics, when, forsooth, I rejoice in them, and am so entertained an observer of the varieties and inconsistencies of the human mind that, in the language of our own day, I should with grave misgiving contemplate any attempt to rationalise it. I must confess to an eclectic habit of mind. I like my critics assorted, and am fortunate in this respect, for their variety has no end:

There's some Peculiar in each leaf and grain,
Some unmarked fibre, or some varying vein:[2]

One likes this, another that; he respects matter, thou art wholly for style; he loves to be amused, entertained, thou to be informed, uplifted; he is for tradition, thou for what is modern; one will draw upon authority, another upon expedient; this one demands what is personal, that one what is impersonal; and so they go on, *quot homines, tot sententiae*;[3] so many men, so many minds; that which thou condemnest he commends; that which is more pleasing to one is *amaracinum*, most harsh to another; scarce any conveyance so accurately penned by one which another will not find a crack in, or cavil at, and the meanest of them claw and prey upon one another as so many ravenous birds; 'tis *a war of opinions* which *has fallen out among the writers of all ages*;[4] so how shall I make any way through such prickly quiddities, or hope to express myself to each man's humour and conceit, still less, give satisfaction to all? I have not tried; *best leave such things to take their chance*,[5] for everything is desired according to our belief of its excellency: *Where I incline, there I entertaine myselfe, how soever it be, and am caried away by mine owne weight*.[6] I have implied as much several times: *de gustibus non est disputandum*. And when I have spread all my reasons out, it remains, and it must be plain to all perspicacious readers, that this treatise is writ for mine own exercise and satisfaction: *I have made a recreation of a recreation*,[7] to please myself, not in vanity, but as a game is played, and if you like not my game, go play something else, I shall not be offended.

As for the disciples of that *malignant deity called criticism*[8] (whose existence I doubt), I fear neither them that are old and sour, nor those *sucking critics, who would fain be nibbling ere their teeth are come*,[9] and who *mistake their own toy-trumpets for the trombones of fame*;[10] but for those who are with me in this enterprise, kin to me in taste, and who judge not altogether by the measure of popular and customary opinion, I hope I have graduated in their favour

[1] Emerson, *Representative Men*. (1850) 73.   [2] Pope, *Moral Essays*. i, 15–16.   [3] Ter. *Phorm*. 454.   [4] Dryden, *Dramatic Poesy*, Dedication.   [5] Euripides, *Electra*. 379.   [6] Montaigne, 'Raymond Sebond', *Essays*. Ed. Seccombe. ii, 346.   [7] Izaak Walton, *Compleat Angler*. Pref.   [8] Swift, *Battle of the Books*.   [9] Dryden, Pref., *All for Love*.   [10] Schopenhauer, *Art and Literature*. Trans. Saunders. 88.

by writing not only according to *jus et norma loquendi*,[1] but what is readable, for a readable book is a fair island full of flowers, birds, and trees, whereof we should thank God of His good grace. Whether I have writ such a book 'tis for my reader to pronounce; but that there are good things in it I am very apt to believe; and, I add out of the apology of Izaak Walton for his treatise of fishing, *that he that likes not the discourse, should like the pictures of the trout and other fish, which I may commend, because they concern not my self;*[2] for *I am a crow who have followed many ploughs;*[3] *a gatherer and disposer of other men's stuffe.*[4] I have trawled the seas of authorship; presumed to put my sickle in other men's corn. I have rifled gardens; picked pockets; dipped my bucket into friendly wells; charged my battery at others' dynamos; gone up and down the world of imagination, which without doubt can do wonderful things and beget strange persuasions; climbed *Parnassus*, roamed round *Helicon*, stared at *Olympus*; looked through

> Magic casements, opening on the foam
> Of perilous seas, in faery lands forlorn;[5]

hobnobbed with bards and philosophers by the proxy of *many a quaint and curious volume of forgotten lore*,[6] in

> The Muse-discovered World of Islands Fortunate,[7]

and gathered as I went rare thoughts and fine phrases,

> And words more sure and sweet than they,
> Love could not think, truth could not stay.[8]

I have perchance in some instances jumbled up these many good things immethodically, but not always; there is order in my chaos, nor do I beg pardon for those wild parts, for *unless you have chaos within you cannot give birth to a dancing star.*[9] Greater men have failed, how then shall I, that am *vix umbra tanti philosophi*, hope always to please? *No man so absolute*, Erasmus holds,[10] *to satisfy all, except antiquity*, and not, as it is managed in this age, even that. 'Tis the common doom of all writers: I must (I say) abide it; I seek not applause, enough

> If my slight Muse do please these curious days.[11]

---

[1] 'The law and correct usage of speech.' Hor. A.P. 72.   [2] *Compleat Angler.* Pref.
[3] Bernard Shaw, Pref., *Three Plays for Puritans.* xxxvi.   [4] Sir Henry Wotton, Pref., 'Elements of Architecture', *Reliquiae Wottonianae.* 195.   [5] Keats, *Ode to a Nightingale.*   [6] Poe, *The Raven.*   [7] Cowley, *Pindarique Ode.*   [8] Crashaw, *Hymn to St. Thomas.*   [9] Nietzsche.   [10] *Judic. de Sen.*   [11] Shakespeare, *Sonnets.* xxxviii.

Yet I am not coy of appreciation neither:

laudatus abunde
Non fastidus si tibi, lector, ero,[1]

but praise enough if you, gentle reader, do not despise me; greater praise if you enjoy my garden: *a man is really alive only when he delights in the goodwill of others.*[2] So whilst I fear the censure of wise men, and respect their assessment of my labours, I scorn the rest, for it is better that a man is willing to be what he is: *quod sis, esse velis.* What, therefore, I have said, *pro tenuitate mea,*[3] I have said.

One or two things I would yet say in anticipation of legitimate censure. I was desirous to have amended, if I could, concerning the manner of handling this my subject: to have polished and preened more, so that my style, which sometimes flows remissly, would have better mirrored that of my master, but the least said of that the soonest mended. I would also have added many more of those examples, aphorisms, stories, apophthegms, etc., which are still roving free in the ocean of letters, but I was constrained to stop, for there is no end to the testimony of books, and, at best, I could do no more than hope that I had adequately represented my theme in this treatise, even though it be an inadequate gallimaufry, an incomplete and often tangled medley, for *I am a lesse maker of bookes, then of anything else;*[4] hoping that you might buttress my edifice where it is frail, from your own quarry. In brief, and to have done with explanations, I confess it is neither as I would, nor as it should be. I would willingly add much, but 'tis too late. It was not in my power to end so large a subject, for I had done little more than advance upon its outposts when time bid me stop. In the meantime I have gathered enough, and if my argument is not plain, no additions could have made it plainer.

Last of all, and for final *apologia* in so writing, I give my belief that *the proper study of mankind is books,*[5] which was supported by the learned Dr. Donne when he claimed that *the world is a great volume, and man the Index of that Book.*[6] So, to cut the matter short, I presume of thy good favour, and gracious acceptance (gentle reader), and out of an assured hope and confidence thereof, I will close this prolegomenon, and begin.

---

[1] Ovid, *Trist.* I, 7, 31, 32.   [2] Goethe, *Maxims.* Trans. Saunders. 68.   [3] 'In my own poor fashion.'   [4] Montaigne, 'To my Lady Duras', *Essays.* Ed. Seccombe. ii, 654.   [5] Aldous Huxley, *Crome Yellow.* 304.   [6] *Sermons, Selected Passages.* L. P. Smith. 67.

Part I

OF BOOKS IN GENERAL

―――――――――⟨✠⟩――――――――――

I. OF BOOKS AND THEIR MOST EXCELLENT
QUALITIES

Books, the most excellent and noble creations of Man, *are*, saith one,[1] *for company, the best Friends; in doubts Counsellours; in Damps Comforters; Time's Prospective, the home Traveller's Ship, or Horse, the busie man's best Recreation, the Opiate of Idle Weariness, the Mindes best Ordinary, Nature's Garden and Seed-plot of Immortality.* He would have that Books are not only *more than riches*, but that they *challenge Pre-eminence above the World's admired fine things:*[2] they are *the Glasse of Counsel to dress ourselves by;* and summing up their benefits he well adds, *Books are Life's best business: vocation to these hath more Emolument coming in, than all the other busy terms of life. They are feeless counsellors, no delaying Patrons, of easy access, and kind expedition, never sending away empty any Client, or Petitioner, nor by delay, making their* δῶρα ἄδωρα, *Courtesies injurious.*[3]

Achieving, as they do, so much in the economy of life, it is no surprise to learn from Richard de Bury that their origin is divine: *all the glory of the world would be buried in oblivion, unless God had provided mortals with the remedy of books;*[4] and in many other parts of the same dissertation this most notable authority apostrophizes books in terms which outrace praise and exalt them beyond most mortal things, which I shall have occasion to cite. In the meantime let him relate how *they are masters who instruct us without rod or ferule, without angry words, without clothes or money,* and that *if you come to them they are not asleep; if you ask and enquire of them they do not withdraw themselves; they do not chide if you make mistakes; they do not laugh at you if you are ignorant;* they *give to all who ask* and *enfranchise* all who serve them faithfully;[5] *they are the treasured wealth of the world, the fit inheritance of generations and nations,*[6] *necessities of life.*[7]

Since they are of such great value, it is not unreasonable for John Lyly to resolve that it is *far more seemly to have thy Studie full of Bookes, than thy*

---

[1] Richard Whitlock, *Zootomia.* (1654) 248.   [2] *Ib.* 236.   [3] *Ib.* 246.   [4] *Philobiblon.* Trans. Thomas. 9.   [5] *Ib.* 9. 11–12.   [6] Thoreau, *Walden.* Scott Lib. 101.
[7] Theopompus, Qt. *Athenaeus.* Loeb. Ed. ii, 67.

Purse full of money.[1] All these appraisals I might largely prove in their particular instances (and will somewhat in succeeding parts), but it is not here needful, since those that deny them do so out of prejudice, or ignorance of my theme, or from a frank and honest apprehension that such opinions are absurd, forgetting that *literature is the Humanities,*[2] and, *except a living man nothing more wonderful*[3] than a book; for books are the cosmography of man, a world in themselves, as several credible relations do attest. 'Tis just, therefore,

> That I should here assert their rights, attest
> Their honours, and should, once for all, pronounce
> Their benediction.[4]

II. THE PRAISE OF BOOKS

The praise of books rings through the centuries, each age, nay, each year bodying forth rhapsodists; and such is the candour and integrity of succeeding ages that Thomas Carlyle, nearly five hundred years after Richard de Bury,[5] claims that books are the supreme member of the three most notable *visible and tangible products of the past,*[6] and he marshals his richest harmonies in their favour: *Wondrous indeed is the virtue of a true Book,* not like a dead city of stones, yearly crumbling, *yearly needing repair;* but *more like a tilled field, a spiritual field; a spiritual tree, let* him rather say, *standing from year to year, and from age to age (we have books that already number some hundred and fifty human ages); and yearly comes its new produce of leaves (Commentaries, Deductions, Philosophical, Political Systems; or were it only Sermons, Pamphlets, Journalistic Essays), every one of which is talismanic and thaumaturgic, for it can persuade men.* He exhorts the writer of a real book not to envy *him whom they name City-builder* and *inexpressibly to pity him whom they name Conqueror or City-burner! Thou too,* he advises the book-builder, *art a Conqueror and Victor; but of the true sort, namely over the Devil: thou too hast built what will outlast all marble and metal: and be a wonder-bringing City of the mind, a Temple and Seminary, and Prophetic Mount, whereto all kindreds of the earth will pilgrim.*[7]

Not less truly but with even more riot of fancy Richard le Gallienne exalts the glory of books in a dulcet panegyric. They are *nightingales* and *honeycombs, orchards, moonlit woods,* and such-like delicacies and delights: *Books,* he chants, *those miraculous memories of high thoughts and golden moods;*

---

[1] *Euphues.*   [2] Edward Dowden, *Fragments from Old Letters.* 3.   [3] Charles Kingsley.
[4] Wordsworth, *Prelude.* v, 216-18.   [5] The *Philobiblon* was finished in 1345 though not published until 1473.   [6] The other two are cities and tilled fields.   [7] *Sartor Resartus.* Bk. ii, ch. 8.

those magical shells, tremulous with the secrets of the ocean of life; those love-letters that pass from hand to hand of a thousand lovers that never meet; those honeycombs of dreams; those orchards of knowledge; those still-beating hearts of the noble dead; those mysterious signals that beckon along the darksome pathways of the past; voices through which the myriad lispings of the earth find perfect speech; oracles through which its mysteries call like voices in moonlit woods; prisms of beauty; urns stored with all the sweets of all the summers of time; immortal nightingales that sing for ever to the rose of life.[1] And there is a saying of a saint that seems to countenance these high modern opinions: *Take thou a book in thine hands,* Thomas à Kempis advises in his *Doctrinale Juvenum*, as *Simon the Just took the Child Jesus into his arms to carry him and kiss him. And when thou hast finished reading, close the book and give thanks for every word out of the mouth of God; because in the Lord's field thou hast found a hidden treasure.*

III. A CATALOGUE OF FOND SIMILITUDES

To descend more to particulars, they are likened to most of the admired and useful conditions and things known to man: to Guests, *welcome these three books as fellow-guests;*[2] to Companions, *a blessed companion is a book;*[3] Teachers, *it is books that teach us to refine on our pleasures when young: and which: having taught us: enable us to recall them with satisfaction when old;*[4] Masters, *after some whiles meditation,* I *walk up to my masters and companions, my books;*[5] Guides, *books are a guide in youth and an entertainment for age.*[6] Some are Directories *to Heavenly Wisdom;*[7] others Circulars, *for every book is, in an intimate sense, a circular-letter to the friends of him who writes it;*[8] they are Actions, *every great book is an action;*[9] Universities, *the true university of these days is a collection of books;*[10] Talismans and Spells, *books are not seldom talismans and spells;*[11] Proverbs, like them they *receive their highest value from the stamp and esteem of ages through which they have passed;*[12] Prophets, *in books we foresee things to come;*[13] Magicians, *Books: written words, are still miraculous Runes, the latest form!;*[14] Physic, *no mood to which a man may not administer the appropriate medicine at the cost of reaching down a volume from his bookshelf;*[15] Anaesthetics, *books are the blessed chloroform of the mind;*[16] Limbs, *the limbs of scholars;*[17] Windows, *through which the soul looks*

[1] *Prose Fancies.* (1894) 114.   [2] Cicero. *De Officiis.* iii, 33 (speaking to his son Marcus, of that work)   [3] Douglas Jerrold.   [4] Leigh Hunt.   [5] Joseph Hall, 'Epistle to Lord Denny'.   [6] Jeremy Collier, 'Of the Entertainment of Books.' *Essays.*   [7] Richard Whitlock, *Zootomia.* 236.   [8] R. L. Stevenson.   [9] Martin Luther.   [10] Thomas Carlyle, *Heroes.* 262.   [11] Cowper, *The Task.* vi.   [12] Sir William Temple.   [13] Richard de Bury.   [14] Carlyle, *Heroes.* 258.   [15] Lord Balfour, *Essays and Addresses.* 36.   [16] Robert Chambers.   [17] Rhodiginus, *Aist. Ludicra.* (1656) ix, 148.

out, for a home without them is like *a house without windows;*[1] Lamps, *Blessed be God that hath set up so many clear lamps in His Church;*[2] Flowers, as in the poet:

> But you were all choice flowers; all set and dressed
> By old sage florists, who knew the best;[3]

Riches, *Keep your books and do not despair of my making them mine some day; if I ever do, I shall be the richest of millionaires, and shan't envy any man his manors and meadows;*[4] Treasures, *these fathered treasures of time, the harvest of so many generations;*[5] Mines, *to which the wise man sends his son that he may dig out treasures.*[6] They are Legacies, *which genius leaves to mankind;*[7] Money, *the best viaticum I have yet found out for this human journey;*[8] Estates, *Cowper's 'task' is as good as an estate to every reading man.*[9] They are also militant: Battles, *a good book may be as great a thing as a battle;*[10] and Engines of War, *the weapons spiritual of the monks, as libraries are the magazines of the Church militant;*[11] *Claustrum sine armario quasi castrum sine armamentario.*[12]

That they are ornaments none will gainsay: ornaments of learning, wisdom, knowledge, art, science, manners, even *genteel ornaments,* as Lord Chesterfield claims;[13] and some writers, abandoning the exalted, descend to the commonplace, comparing them with familiar things such as Furniture, *The Best Furniture,* Richard Whitlock relates in a learned Discourse (*Zootomia.* 236-248), for Solomon *his Library, was not the least piece of his Magnificence: Such Furniture thought he necessary, and stately the* Queen of Sheba *thought it;* Sydney Smith well adds, *no furniture so charming as books, even if you never open them or read a single word* (which many support by practice); Couches, *can any couch be more delectable than the Elysian leaves of Books;*[14] Warehouses and Depositories, *good books are the warehouses of ideals,* saith one,[15] whilst another[16] marks them out as *the depository of everything that is most honourable to man.*

Lord Bryce denies that they are *mere vehicles of information,* but calls them rather Engines—*for the stimulation and training of the thinking power.* Others have it that they are ships, *which pass through the vast seas of time;*[17] and 'tis no strain upon our credulity to discover in this maritime connection that they are also Lighthouses, *erected in the sea of time.*[18] Sir William

---

[1] Henry Ward Beecher, *Sermons.*   [2] Joseph Hall, *Occasions and Meditations.*
[3] Henry Vaughan.   [4] Cicero, *Letters to Atticus.* Loeb. Ed. i, 4.   [5] Robert Southey.
[6] Richard de Bury, *Philobiblon.* Trans. Thomas. 12.   [7] Charles Gore.   [8] Montaigne.
[9] Robert Chambers, 'What English Literature Gives Us', *Chambers' Journal.*
[10] Benjamin Disraeli.   [11] Merryweather, *Bibliomania in the Middle Ages.* 50.
[12] 'A monastery without a library is like a castle without an armoury.' *Ib.* From letter of Gaufredi of St. Barbary to Peter Mangot, in Martene, *Thes. Nov. Anecd.* Tom. i, col. 511.   [13] *Letters.*   [14] Frank Carr.   [15] H. G. Wells.   [16] William Godwin.   [17] Bacon, *Advancement of Learning.*   [18] Edwin P. Whipple.

Davenant does not hesitate to call them Monuments, *the monuments of vanished minds*, and Horace will have it that the written word is more permanent than brass or stone:

> I've reared a monument, my own,
> More durable than brass;
> Yea, kingly pyramids of stone
> In height it doth surpass.[1]

Their gastronomic virtues have many witnesses; Richard de Bury gives out that they are *wells of living waters, delightful ears of corn, combs of honey, golden pots in which manna is stored*, and *udders of milk;*[2]

> By sucking you, the wise like bees do grow.[3]

Coleridge makes them out to be Fruit-trees, *an excellent book is like a well-chosen and well-tended fruit-tree;*[4] Oliver Wendell Holmes that they are Fruits, especially when first published, *new books are fruits of the world's age;* and Robert Southey says they are *not only the pride of my eye, and the joy of my heart, and the food of my mind*, but *more than metaphorically, meat, drink and clothes for me and mine;*[5] but I shall expound their gastronomy in my section of the *Bibliophagi*.

IV. OF BOOK-REVERENCE

For Charles Lamb, epicure of letters, books were *Spiritual repasts*, and he exclaims in wonderment that we say no grace before them, *a grace before Milton—a grace before Shakespeare—a devotional exercise proper to be said before reading the ' Fairy Queen'.*[6] Not alone was he in this pious wish, for not only did the learned monks of old exercise, as Merryweather observes,[7] the utmost care in the preservation of their *darling books*, but they supplicated the blessing of God upon their *goodly tomes* in various exhortations: *O Lord*, saith one, *send the virtue of thy Holy Spirit upon these our books; that cleansing them from all earthly things, by thy holy blessing, they may mercifully enlighten our hearts and give us true understanding; and grant that by thy teaching, they may brightly preserve and make full an abundance of good works according to thy will.*[8] Liu Tsung-Yuan so reverenced the poetry of his friend Han Yu, that, as Giles telleth,[9] he never opened his books without *first washing his hands in rose-water;* and Dibdin is so imbued with book-reverence that

---

[1] Horace, *Odes*. iii, 30.   [2] *Philobiblon*. 12.   [3] Henry Vaughan.   [4] Prospectus to a Course of Lectures.   [5] Letter to Bedford.   [6] 'Grace before Meat', *Essays of Elia*.   [7] *Bibliomania in the Middle Ages*. 17.   [8] Martene, *de Antiq. Eccl. Ritibus*. ii, 302.   [9] *Chinese Biog. Dict*. 255.

B

he would have illustrious copies ceremoniously transported from one
State to another: the Spaniards, he says,[1] *ought to have made a canopy of
their swords over* Sir John Tobin's copy of the *Ferdinand and Isabella Missal,*
as it left its *native soil.*

V. OF BIBLIANTHROPOMORPHISM

Books are anthropomorphized by many observers; they

> are men of higher stature,
> And the only men that speak aloud for future times to hear;[2]

this is no book, exclaimed Whitman of his *Leaves of Grass.*[3]

> Who touches this touches a man,
>
> .   .   .   .   .
>
> It is I you hold and who holds you,
> I spring from the pages into your arms—decease
>   calls me forth.
> O how your fingers drowse me,
> Your breath falls around me like dew, your pulse
>   lulls the tympans of my ears,
> I feel immerged from head to foot,
> Delicious, enough.

Swift advertises them as *children of the brain.*[4] Nothing made by man is so
like unto him: if they are alive, they go on living by a process of reproduction one from the other, they increase and multiply in varying degrees,
and bear other resemblances to their creators, as over-production and
sterility, youth, age, decay, and death. They suffer the same fate as men,
They share with us, Joseph Conrad says, *the great incertitude of ignominy or
glory—of severe justice and senseless persecution—of calumny and misunder-
standing—the shame of undeserved success. Of all the inanimate objects, of all
men's creations, books are the nearest to us, for they contain our very thought, our
ambitions, our indignations, our illusions, our fidelity to truth, and our persistent
leaning towards error. But most of all they resemble us in their precarious hold on
life.*[5]

The study of books is no traffic with dead things: the Elzevir classics are
pretty little pets, literary bantams;[6] Henry Bradshaw gives out that bibliography is *a branch of natural history* and that books have *genera* and *species;*[7]

[1] *Reminiscences.* ii, 972.   [2] E. B. Browning, *Lady Geraldine's Courtship.*   [3] 'So long!'
Leaves of Grass. 382.   [4] *Tale of a Tub.*   [5] *Notes on Life and Letters.* (1921) 5.
[6] J. Hill Burton, *Book-Hunter.* 60.   [7] Prothero, *Memoir of Bradshaw.* 365–6.

*books are to me, saith mine author, living organisms, I can only study them as
such.*[1] He studied books, said William Blades, much as *a botanist treats
plants or an entomologist insects.*[2] Coleridge has it that a library is *a living
world, and every book a man, absolute flesh and blood,* which is miraculous,
supporting Victor Hugo in his saying that a book is a miracle itself:
*Behold a book. I will nourish with it five thousand souls—a million souls—all
humanity. In the action of Christ bringing forth the loaves, there is Gutenberg
bringing forth books. One sower heralds the other. . . . Gutenberg is forever the
auxiliary of life.*[3] But most will be content with good Dr. Thomas Fuller
when, in his *Holy State,* he calls the occupants of his study *a company of
honest old fellows in leathern jackets,*[4] knowing well enough that those
jackets contain Souls, *the assembled souls of all that men held wise, imprisoned
until some one takes them down from a shelf and reads them;*[5] or even Ghosts,
not collections of printed pages;[6] and we shall agree with Cicero, who held
that *a room without books was as a body without a soul.*[7]

VI. MICROCOSMS THAT OUTLIVE MONUMENTS

Some would have them to be microcosmic, embracing all life: *the making
of Shakespeare's mind was like the making of the world.*[8] *Books,* said William
Wordsworth, *are a substantial world both pure and good.*[9] Leigh Hunt would
have that they are half of the known world, the globe we inhabit being
*divisible into two worlds: the common geographical world, and the world of
books;* and he holds further, they are *such real things,* that, *if habit and perception make the difference between real and unreal, we may say that we more
frequently wake out of common life to them, than out of them to common life.*[10]
Stéphane Mallarmé cries that *the world was made for nothing more than to
produce a beautiful book,* which some even among good bookmen may
account a heresy, and though I adventure to affirm nothing concerning the
truth and certainty of this supposition, yet I must needs say, it does not
seem to me unreasonable; and there are others also who would attribute to
books qualities which might fit them even for so great a destiny. James
Thomson upholds them as mediums of *the mighty dead,*[11] bridging eternities; *no past,* says Bulwer Lytton, *so long as books shall live,*[12] and that they

[1] *Ib.* 327.   [2] *Ib.* 363.   [3] Qt. *Book-Lovers' Anth.* 375.   [4] Davenant. *Gondibert.* ii.5.37.
[5] Samuel Butler, *Note Books.* 95.   [6] Alexander Smith, 'Books and Gardens'.
Dreamthorp. 249.   [7] Qt. Lubbock, *Pleasures of Life.* i, 56.   [8] William Cory,
'Table Talk' in M. E. Coleridge, *Gathered Leaves.* 323.   [9] *Personal Talk.*   [10] *Monthly
Repository.* Farewell address. (1828)   [11] 'Winter'. *The Seasons.* 431.   [12] *The Souls
of Books.*

do live is thus further supposed by the poet when he records of the books in his room:

> I feel your great hearts throbbing deep in quire,
> And hear your breathing round me in the gloom;[1]

which is again supported by Dean Swift, who felt, when reading a book, whether wise or silly, that it seemed to be *alive* and talking to him.[2] Bronson Alcott, in his *Concord Days*, calls them *living friends*, for they have both *voice and physiognomies, personality and complexion;* and with another poet 'tis not absurd to believe that

> They are not dead, but full of blood again,
> I mean the sense, and every line a vein.[3]

Some claim that they are richer than sentient beings, and *may last as long as the sun and moon and perish only in the general wreck of nature.*[4] Immortality itself is theirs: *Laws die, Books never;*[5]

> Not marble, not the gilded monuments
> Of princes, shall outlive this powerful rhyme;[6]

the *romance of 'Tom Jones'*, saith Gibbon,[7] *that exquisite picture of human manners, will outlive the Escurial, and the imperial eagle of the house of Austria;* and no greater testimony to their power of endurance has been paid to them than by our Lord Verulam,[8] who associates the knowledge which is to be found in books with that *immortality or continuance* to which *man's nature doth most aspire,* for *monuments of wit and learning are more durable than the monuments of power or of the hands. Have not the verses of Homer continued twenty-five hundred years, or more, without the loss of a syllable or letter; during which time infinite palaces, temples, castles, cities, have been decayed and demolished? It is not possible,* he argues, *to have the true pictures of Cyrus, Alexander, Caesar, no, nor of the kings or great personages of much later years; for the originals cannot last, and the copies cannot but leese of the life and truth. But the images of men's wits and knowledge remain in books, exempted from the wrong of time and capable of perpetual renovation;* which, Emerson in his *Spiritual Laws* would have, is dependent upon no effort friendly to them or hostile, but upon *their own specific gravity, or the intrinsic importance of their contents to the constant mind of man;*

> O blessed letters! that combine in one
> All ages past, and make one live with all.[9]

---

[1] Richard Le Gallienne, 'Confessio Amantis', *Volumes in Folio.* 60.   [2] 'Thoughts on Various Subjects.'   [3] Henry Vaughan, 'On Sir Thomas Bodley's Library'.   [4] Addison, *Spectator.* 166.   [5] Bulwer Lytton, *Richelieu.* i, 2.   [6] Shakespeare, *Sonnets.* lv.   [7] *Memoirs.* Ed. Hill. 5.   [8] *Advancement of Learning*, Bk. i, fin.   [9] Samuel Daniel, *Musophilus.*

VII. THEY ARE GOD-LIKE AND IMMORTAL

If Milton is to be believed, *a good book is the precious life-blood of a master-spirit, embalmed and treasured up on purpose to a life beyond life;*[1] for him a book is even more than that, more than the immortal reflex of man, master or otherwise, a book in this view, *ordinibus deorum*, leaps all worldly similitudes and becomes divine: *who kills a man kills a reasonable creature, God's image; but, he who destroys a good book, kills reason itself; kills the image of God, as it were, in the eye; he slays an immortality rather than a life;*[2] and this most high enthronement is supported by Plato: *books are the immortal sons deifying their sires,* as gods are created in the Poet:

> Where man is met
> The gods will come; or shall I say man's spirit
> Hath operative faculties to mix
> And make his gods at will?[3]

which translates the created into the creator, the gift of God into the maker of Gods. It makes the thing itself more potent than the writer himself, for *how often does the worm-eaten volume outlast the reputation of the worm-eaten author!*[4]

They are harbingers of heaven and evidences of immortality, for great souls live in them,

> I never yet the Living Soul could see,
> But in Thy Books and Thee.[5]

Nay, they do preserve as in a vial the purest efficacy and extraction of that living intellect which bred them.[6] Alexander Smith will have it that books are Heaven itself, *the true Elysian fields where the spirits of the dead converse, and into these fields a mortal may venture unappalled;*[7] and if some there are who cannot support him in this, as may well be, for Heaven is often a matter of taste, they may yet hold that books (some of them) are harbingers of that Kingdom of God which is situate in the cosmography of ourselves, *we carry with us the wonders we seek without us;*[8] but whatever their Heaven (and 'tis none of my business), it is their aim to get there sooner or later, and they cannot but rejoice that books are accredited instruments to that end, as acclaimed by so reliable a witness as Richard de Bury, Bishop of Durham, and High Chancellor of England, in that notable panegyric: *Ye are the tree of life and the fourfold river of Paradise, by which the human mind is nourished, and the thirsty intellect is watered and refreshed. Ye are the ark of Noah and the ladder of Jacob, and the troughs by which the young of those who*

---

[1] *Areopagitica.* [2] *Ib.* [3] Robert Bridges, *Achilles in Scyros.* 23, 552-5. [4] Thomas Hood. [5] Cowley, *Pindaric Odes.* 'To Mr. Hobs.' [6] Milton, *Areopagitica.* [7] 'Books and Gardens'. *Dreamthorp.* 249. [8] Browne, *Religio Medici.* xv.

look therein are coloured; Ye are the stones of testimony and the pitchers holding the lamps of Gideon, the scrip of David, from which the smoothest stones are taken for the slaying of Goliath. Ye are the golden vessels of the temple, the arms of the Soldiers of the Church with which to quench all the fiery darts of the wicked, fruitful olives, vines of Engadi, fig-trees that are never barren, burning lamps always to be held in readiness.[1]

All of which Thomas de Quincey hath made good in a laudation of Milton in which he claims that *Paradise Lost is not a book among books, not a poem among poems, but a central force amongst forces*; thus those words with which Sir Thomas Browne concludes his *Religio Medici* have a new meaning, for after claiming happiness to be only wherein God Himself and His Angels are happy, *in whose defect the Devils are unhappy*, he proceeds to argue that *whatsoever else the World terms Happiness*, is to him *a story out of Pliny, a tale of Boccace or Malizspini*, which would content many, though for him it be but a *neat delusion*. No marvel that *in the highest civilisation the book is still the highest delight*,[2] or that they beam eternally as beacons upon the sea of time:

> Bright books: the perspectives to our weak sights.
> The clear projections of discerning lights,
> Burning and shining thought, man's posthume day,
> The track of fled souls in their Milky Way,
> The dead alive and busy, the still voice
> Of enlarged spirits, kind Heaven's white decoys![3]

Well may Heinsius exclaim as he enters the library at Leyden, before even it was endowed with Scaliger's books: *In the very bosom of Eternity among all these illustrious souls I take my seat.*[4]

As long as we are ruled by wisdom and veneration towards these *Images of God*, regarding them as Angels, for they are of that constitution, which has been supported by the Sage of Concord: *Angels they are to us of entertainment, sympathy, and provocation.*[5] so shall we attain somewhat of their peace and joy, and escape all manner of incurable diseases of the mind which are the just and deserved punishment of our sins of bookish neglect, *for without books God is silent, justice dormant, natural science at a stand, philosophy lame, letters dumb, and all things involved in Cimmerian darkness.*[6] This is a great and evident truth, plainly manifested in all histories, both ancient and modern, thus exalting our reading or traffic with books as ministry or sacrament to *Liber Pater*, after whose image they are made. *Te quoque dignum finge deo.*[7]

[1] *Philobiblon.* Trans. Thomas. 12–13.   [2] Emerson, 'Quotation and Originality', *Letters and Social Aims.* 129.   [3] Henry Vaughan.   [4] *Great Book-Collectors.* Elton. 180.   [5] Emerson.   [6] Thomas Bartholin, 'De libris legendis'. *Dissertations.* Copenhagen. (1672)   [7] 'Make thyself worthy of God.'

VIII. THE BIBLIOMANIA OR MADNESS THEY ENGENDER

That madness should disturb so beneficent a gift is strange, but all the world, according to Burton[1] (and some learned observers as well) is mad or dotes in one or another member of itself: pragmatically mad or logically mad; ego-mad or mad in disposition: deranged, demented, cracked, and therefore stupid, angry, drunken, silly, sottish, sullen, proud, vainglorious, ridiculous, beastly, peevish, jealous, foolish, obstinate, fanatical, impudent, extravagant, grasping, avaricious, dry, doting, dull or desperate; harebrained or obsessed; crazy, frantic, lunatic; if not wholly morons, cretins, which no asylum can hold or physic help. So also with books and book-folk.

My purpose in the following work is to discourse of the nature, excellences, uses, and diseases of books, and particularly to anatomize this humour of *Bibliomania*, through all his parts and species, as it is an habit, or a disease; and philosophically and medicinally to show the causes, symptoms, signs, expressions, meanings, manifestations, eccentricities, vanities, impudences, and, where expedient, the cures, for 'tis plain to conceive that it is often a genial mania, less harmful than the sanity of the sane, and most happy when endemic with moderation in the constitution of a man.

In doing so, I have described and opened up, as by a kind of dissection, not only those peccant humours (some of them) which have given impediment to the proficiency of learning and occasion to the traducement of the love of books, but also those more robust passions which are proper to bibliophilia: wherein, if I have been too plain, it must be remembered, *fidelia vulnera amantis, sed dolosa oscula malignantis:*[2] to be true to any subject without frankness is impossible. These methods and motives at this present have induced me to make choice of the subject.

IX. OF THE PARTS NEXT TO BE SET OUT

Yet, before I proceed to discourse farther, I hold it not impertinent to make a brief digression of the body and faculties of books, for the better understanding of what is to follow; because there are many strange words, and strange connotations of unfamiliar words, which of the uninitiated (if any adventure with me in this treatise) will not so easily be perceived, what they are, how cited, and to what end they serve. Besides, it may peradventure give occasion to some men, to examine more accurately, search

---

[1] *Anat. of Melan.* (1904) i, 137. [2] 'Faithful are the wounds of a lover, but deceitful are the kisses of an enemy.' *Proverbs* xxvii, 6.

farther into this excellent subject, and thereupon with that Royal Poet[1] to
praise God, for a book, like a man, *is fearfully and wonderfully made, and
curiously wrought*, and for such matters as concern the knowledge of these
treasures, many are wholly ignorant or careless, they know not what the
body and soul of them are, how combined, of what parts and faculties they
consist, how one book differs from another, in format, character and
quality, and how these in turn differ infinitely within themselves, and of
their essence. To stir up, therefore, a more exact observation of books,
and to give some small taste or notice of the rest, I shall now, for your
better understanding, open up the parts with a consideration of their
physiology and morphology.

[1] *Psalms* cxxxix, 14, 15.

Part II

OF THEIR MORPHOLOGY AND DIMENSIONS

I. A GLANCE AT THEIR ANATOMY

It is not necessary to do more than point at the anatomy of the books themselves, since their physical constituents, except in the matter of form and appearance (and then from the point of view of taste alone), have no considerable or definite concern with bibliomania, either in its cause or cure. The parts of this subject which present themselves to my view, insomuch as they serve to nutrition or generation of the disease, will be revealed in their place; and you that are readers in the meantime must be content with a running account of the physical parts as a preparative to the exposition of those spiritual and intellectual excellencies which are the substance of succeeding sections of this treatise.

Of the parts of a book there are two main divisions: the *outward* and the *inward*. The chief outward parts are situate forward and backward, for they constitute the membrane or skin, whose office is to clothe or bind the rest for the protection of the inward and more delicate and perishable parts. They are of a firm or limp consistency according as they are composed of boards of wood, as in old times, or, in the manner of to-day, of stout cards fashioned out of pulped wood, straw, or hemp; there are also limp bindings fashioned of paper or boards of lighter weight. And as the binding is the membrane or epidermis of the book itself, so the boards have a skin for their own protection, which is often the subject of decoration, like the tattooing on the skins of primitive peoples; but of this I discourse apart, and shall here only recite the further parts as sides, back, spine, doublures, panels, bands, joints and edges (with their various letterings, toolings, gildings, pigmentation), labels, clasps, and finally wrappers or dust-jackets for the protection of the cover proper during the transit of the book from the publisher's office, through the shop, to the reader.

The inward parts comprise paper and print. The paper is the body of the book and may be thin or thick, according to purpose and ultimate form, whether that form is to be slim or fat, extended or concentrate. Papers are varied in size, consistency and colour. The sizes of the sheets are named variously, as Royal, Imperial, Foolscap, etc., and the book is designate by the number of folds made in the original state of the paper, called a sheet, as folio, duodecimo, octavo, quarto, which make up the leaves, each side of which is a page. The consistency or character of the paper is rough or smooth (also, as I have said, thick or thin), *laid* or *wove*, *watermarked* with semi-transparent lines or devices; straight or *deckle* edges, and fine or coarse in quality as it is made of pulped straw, wood, sisal, linen rags, or of old and used paper, as *shoddy* is composed of old and worn cloth. The sheets are printed and then folded in *gatherings* or *quires*, which in turn are sewn together by the binder, thus constituting the body or inward form of the book proper.

Typographically considered, a book is a world in itself, with a long history of varying methods and tastes, a complex technique, and an unbroken tradition from the days of the scribes who worked laboriously with stylus or pen, through those of the printer who designed and printed his pages, to those of the mechanized compositor of to-day who cannot design, working out the designs of the typographer who cannot print. Every type has its own character and range of sizes, and each printed page its particularities of design and layout, governing the making of a fair reading surface, and the whole so hedged about with technicalities expressed in their own jargon, that I shall leave it alone, and would only name these esoteric affairs to bring forward, at the outset, some general idea of the complexities upon which a book is built, as a preliminary to the ideas of bio-bibliology to be unfolded. The upshot of the matter being that the *corpus* or body of a book is no more than a design to an end, and that end is the convenient presentation of its essence or authorship to a reader. Decoration, rich trappings, or other ornamentation, may be added for delight or homage, or even vanity, as I shall show; but they are tolerable only insofar as they hold no check upon the purpose of a book, which is to be read. And now to our theme.

II. OF SIZE AND CONVENIENCE

According to Dr. Johnson,[1] the best books, for size, are those that can be held in the hand, and carried to the fireside, or to any other convenient place. Most who love books and use them lovingly are of the same opinion. *Fi des gros livres!* exclaims Jules Janin,[2] *nous ne voulons plus que de petit format qui marche avec nous:* a fig for big books! *In angulo, cum libello*, a little book in a cosy corner. It is all there, the whole case. A book should be small enough to hold in the hand, and large enough to engage the eye at a single glance; it is thus a friend and a companion. *A big book is as bad*

[1] *Johnsonian Miscellanies*. Hill. ii, 2.   [2] *Le Livre*. 109.

as a great misfortune,[1] and although he may have referred to the size of the work itself rather than to its *format*, which is the subject of my present discourse, it is only another objection to the same end: a book should not only be appropriate in style and matter, but, I say again, convenient in size; at the same time not all book-folk are of the same opinion. *I detest a quarto*, says Jane Austen;[2] but Horace Walpole prefers *quarto* to *octavo* because *a quarto lies free and open before one*, and he is surprised *how long the world was pestered with unwieldy folios*.[3] *No man*, said Dr. Johnson, *read long together with a folio on his table*.[4] Théophile Gautier, no book-lover, as I will show, has a greater dislike of *octavos* than of *folios*, because the *folios* could be used as presses or stools, but *octavos*, he claims, *the Devil take me, if I can derive the slightest benefit from them; I cannot imagine why they were ever made*.[5] But there is a place for each notwithstanding what I have said, and a medium in book-sizes, as even Walpole implies, when he sighs out: *what a pity it is I was not born in the golden age of Louis the Fourteenth, when it was not only the fashion to write folios, but to read them too*.[6]

Edward FitzGerald, a very fastidious bookman, preferred Shakespeare in *folio*, of which he had both the Second and Third; *one had need of a big book to remember him by, for*, he laments, *Shakespeare is lost to the theatre*.[7] Trevelyan records that Macaulay *read Plato in a ponderous folio, sixteen inches long by ten broad, and weighing within half an ounce of twelve pounds*. It was the edition of Marsilius Ficinus of Frankfort, 1602, and *it contained nearly fourteen hundred closely printed pages of antique Greek type, bristling with those contractions which are a terror to the luxurious modern scholar*.[8]

I myself have known, and still know, the delight of sprawling over an eighteenth-century *quarto*, or a small *folio* of Jacobean days, and even, on occasion, larger, as that great *folio* of 1604, which contains Philemon Holland's translation of Plutarch's *Moralia*, a goodly portly book and a corpulent, as ever there was: a well, into which you may dip your bucket without fearing that it will run dry, a sea upon which you can sail without shortage of adventure or dearth of things to look at. I would not have him smaller, being so fortunate as to possess him in all the pomp of his ancient and learned amplitude, for he is vast by nature, as a whale is, or an elephant, and who would wish a whale a minnow, or an elephant a mouse? Boswell's *Johnson* is more opulent, and nowhere so like unto himself as he is in the roomy pages of the first edition; Burton reads better in *folio*, but not later than 1638; and Sir Thomas Browne must be sipped in the vintage of 1686. Yet I have my regrets at times, for I cannot take them out

---

[1] Callimachus, Ath. iii, 72, *Fragment*. 359.   [2] *Memoir*, J. E. Austen-Leigh. 108.
[3] *Walpoliana*. 162.   [4] *Johnsonian Miscellanies*. Hill. ii, 2.   [5] Preface, *Les Jeunes-France*.   [6] *Letters*. Cunningham. ii, 62.   [7] *Letters and Literary Remains*. i, 26.
[8] *Marginal Notes of Lord Macaulay*. 54.

into the garden or nurse them in my armchair beside the fire; but this proves my case and Dr. Johnson's and that of all true bookmen, who, whatever their fad at particular moments, love best the book which can be read in hand anywhere and anywhen: *Books that you may carry to the fire and hold readily in your hand are the most useful after all.*[1]

Of these extremes of big and little I will speak briefly, for they are few among the multitude of books, and so foreign to the purpose of reading as to be, perhaps, the only veritable *biblia a-biblia*. Nor need I expatiate against them, for they have had their day and passed into limbo by reason of those same laws of the *survival of the fittest* which ordained the passing into fossildom of the Dinotherium and of the Icthyosaurus. The two *Brobdingnagian Choral Books*, measuring a yard in length and two feet wide, which Dibdin[2] saw in the library of the Duke of Sussex at Kensington Palace, are museum pieces, specimens, curiosities, recalling the books in the Library at Brobdingnag,[3] which Gulliver could read only after they had built for him *a kind of wooden Machine five-and-twenty Foot high, formed like a standing Ladder, the Steps being fifty Foot long*, which he would mount so that he could read the vast pages leaning open against the wall, beginning on the top step and so working his way downwards. The nearest approach to that great work were those *grand Aldines, enormous armfuls that require strong persons to handle*, or those volumes which contain the Denon collection of illustrations, which repose in the Escurial on *an elephantine lectern, weighing six tons, and moving on a pivot;* the volumes measure *six feet in height and four in breadth*; they are bound in the *famous yellow leather of Cordova*, and *heavily clasped and clamped with brass.*[4]

Elephant folio, which was once so popular for maps, engravings and Service Books, will rarely be used again because of the discovery of more ingenious methods of dealing with such material. The era of giant printed books has passed away as surely as that which produced MSS. as vast as the *Vernon*, in the Bodleian, whose written area alone measures $17\frac{1}{2}$ by $12\frac{1}{2}$ inches.[5] The last resort of the ancient passion for unwieldy books is the recurrent fashion for *Large Paper* copies, which are no encumbrance because they are show books and generally supplementary to reading copies, as show dogs and show cattle are supplementary to the normal. No one uses them: they are monuments, museum pieces, or, where useful, exaggerations which strain a point to point a strain. The best that can be said of *Large Paper* is that it is *not a good absolute and in itself, but only when it is beautiful and appropriate.*[6] A library of *Large Paper* copies would be a necropolis of books, a bibliomaniac's Père Lachaise or Kensal Green.

[1] *Johnson*, Hawkins. 197.   [2] *Reminiscences.* ii, 943.   [3] Swift, *Gulliver's Travels.*
[4] Percy Fitzgerald, *Book Fancier.* 142.   [5] Macray, *Annals of the Bodleian.* 144.
[6] Lang, *Library.* xiv–xv.

In the opposite class are those diminutive books which cannot be read without the aid of a magnifying glass. These are freaks, their only defence and justification being their littleness. They are the toy-terriers of books, bibliographical lap-dogs. How small they can be is incredible. W. T. Spencer had a *Bible*, dated 1660, which was so small that it *would not cover your finger nail*. A man once entered his shop bragging that he carried a library in his hand-bag. He proved his statement by opening the bag and revealing a collection of such miniatures.[1] *The book which has the reputation of being the smallest printed book in the world* is Galileo à Madame Cristina di Lorena, 1615; it was printed in Italy and measures 15 by 10 millimetres.[2] There is a copy of it in the British Museum in a miniature Chippendale bookcase containing a whole library of Lilliputian books. In the Harleian Collection there is a *Bible* small enough to go into a walnut shell. The earliest known miniature English book is the *Hours of the Blessed Virgin* (1500), it measures an inch and a half by one inch, and is printed in black-letter.

Many small books are produced by lithographic and photographic processes, and are therefore not examples of typography. Fine examples of printing from microscopic types are rare in our time, but notable specimens of the past came from England, France, and Italy. The finest and most legible of the foreign type are probably, says Davenport, the *Types Microscopiques* of Henri Didot (Paris, 1765–1852). Notable also among such midgets are those pocket volumes of the past, Pickering's *Diamond Classics*, and the like, which are pleasant enough, but still no more than pretty toys, though better than freaks. Mark Pattison, says Percy Fitzgerald,[3] *had a special fancy for the little antique Latin pocket volumes published in myriads a couple of centuries ago*. It is curious, he thinks, for scholars to have issued *their profoundest lugubrations* in volumes no bigger than *Pocket Testaments*; but it was then the fashion to squeeze into what was called *portable shape*, histories, as *Strada*, who is as long as *Hume* or *Smollett*, or even *Gibbon*. *Eyes in those days*, he concludes, *must have been stouter and clearer*.

But I must end this chapter lest it become tedious, and leave the monsters and midgets to their born lovers; *longe alia mihi mens est*, my own tastes are otherwise; *in medio virtus*, I take a middle course, and confess to a liking for a small and slender *folio* without prejudice to my love for an *octavo* or a *twelve*, or even a *quarto* when the mood dictates and the circumstances are appropriate; and I will conclude by observing that although there are big *Elzevirs* and little *Elzevirs*, those who have sung their praises have had the little rather than the big in mind. I am sometimes moved to believe that, in this matter, affection expands from a beginning among the *twelves* to an

---

[1] *Forty Years in My Bookshop.* xxxii.   [2] Davenport, *Byways among English Books.* 143.   [3] *Book Fancier.* 7.

ending among the *octavos*; but I shall not dogmatize, for the way of a man with a book is a mystery, yet I may infer, out of my own experience and that of my friends, that the quality of bibliophily proceeds in a *diminuendo*: one respects a *folio*, admires a *quarto*, and loves a *twelve*;

> For the row I prize is yonder,
>   Away on the unglazed shelves,
> The bulged and the bruised *octavos*,
>   The dear and the dumpy twelves;[1]

so let every bookman, in his own defence, set as good a face upon the business as he can.

III. OF LITERARY DIMENSIONS

Next to their physical size must be noted their measure as spiritual or intellectual entities. Here again there are diverse opinions, each proper to be considered; but it were superfluous to consider them all, though some few of greater importance I must point at. Dr. Johnson *was a great friend to books like* the French *Esprits d'un Tel* and *Beauties of Watts*, at which, he said, *a man will often look and be tempted to go on*,[2] when bigger books might have frightened him. *A big book*, says Myles Davies,[3] *is a scare-crow to the head and pocket of the author, student, buyer, and seller*; it is also *a harbour of ignorance*, and he attributes *the inexpugnable ignorance and superstition of the ancient heathens, degenerate Jews, and popish scholasters and canonists*, to the circumstances that they were *entrenched under the frightful bulk of huge, vast, and innumerable volumes*, among which he names the *great folio containing the celestial sciences that the Jewish rabbins fancied in a dream was given by God to his pupil Adam*, and the volumes of *Zoroaster*, entitled *The Similitude*, which is said to have taken up a space covered by 1260 hides of cattle.

 The *grossness and multitude* of the books of Aristotle and Varro were *both a prejudice to their authors, and an hindrance to learning, and an occasion to the greatest part of them being lost; the largeness of Plutarch's treatises is a great cause of his being neglected; Origen's 6000 volumes (as Epiphanius will have it) were not only the occasion of his venting more numerous errors, but also for the most part of their perdition*. On the other hand, he contends, Longinus and Epictetus, *in their pamphlet Remains, are everyone's companions*, and *young mathematicians, freshwater physicians, civilian novices*, and *les apprentices en la ley d'Angleterre, would be at a loss and stand, and total discouragement*, were it not for Euclid's *Elements*, Hippocrates' *Aphorisms*, Justinian's *Institutes*, and

---

[1] Austin Dobson, *Poetical Works*. 194. [2] *Johnsonian Miscellanies*. Hill. ii, 2.
[3] Qt. D'Israeli, *Curiosities of Literature*. ii, 95–6.

Littleton's *Tenures*, in *small pamphlet volumes*. One of the great advantages
the *Dispensary* has over *King Arthur* is its pamphlet size, and he commends
Boileau's *Lutrin*, in respect of Perrault's and Chapelain's *St. Paulin* and *La
Pucelle*, for the same reason, concluding that *these seem to pay a deference to
the reader's quick and great understanding: those to mistrust his capacity, and to
confine his time as well as his intellect*.

South, in his *Sermon Against long Extempore Prayers*, supported short
books for the good argument that *the reason of things lies in a little compass.
Most of the writings and discourses in the world are but illustration and rhetoric:
which*: he says, *signifies as much as nothing to a mind eager in pursuit after the
causes and philosophical truth of things*; and he wisely holds that there would
be no art or science could not *the mind gather the general natures of things out
of the heap of numberless particulars*, and bind them into *short aphorisms* and
propositions; made thus *portable to the memory* they are ready and at hand for
practical application and use as there shall be occasion. Addison[1] supports
Callimachus in his claim that *a book is a great evil*, and points out in
explanation of the cause of big books that authors of them have *established
it as a kind of rule that a man ought to be dull sometimes*, and so make allow-
ances for *many rests and nodding-places in a voluminous writer*. At the same
time he is all for brevity and quintessence, and no more *folios*. He would
have the works of an age concentrated in a few shelves and the millions of
superfluous volumes annihilated:

> Les longs ouvrages me font peur.
> Loin d'épuiser une matière
> Il faut n'en prendre que la fleur.[2]

The revolt against the big book developed to so great an extent in the
eighteenth century that some even resented the size of *Gibbon*, one of the
few big histories that no true bookman would shorten by so much as a
chapter. The original edition was in six *quarto* volumes, which appeared at
different times. It was Gibbon's custom to present by his own hand copies
as published to the Duke of Cumberland. Bringing the third volume to
him one day, *elated with pride at the delightful office, and imagining as he went,
what handsome things the duke would say to him*—all he got from His Royal
Highness was: *What? ah! another damned big square book, eh!*[3]

I hate all big Books, Edward FitzGerald told Quaritch,[4] and he confessed
he had given all his own away because of *unhandiness as well as want of
room*. All *verse*, he gave out,[5] should be in *a handy pocketable size*, and this
was not only an objection to corporeal bulk, for it was his habit to reduce

[1] *Spectator*. 124.   [2] 'Long works frighten me; far from exhausting a subject, one
should only skim the cream.' La Fontaine.   [3] William Davis, *Olio of Anecdotes*. 7.
[4] *Letters to Bernard Quaritch*. 80.   [5] *Letters to Bernard Quaritch*. 59.

the obesity of masterpieces by extracting pages, until they were slim enough for his fancy. I doubt not that he would have upheld Joubert's contention that *every work of genius, be it epic or didactic, is too long if it cannot be read in one day.*[1]

Notwithstanding so much may be alleged in favour of small books, scholars of former times regarded them with contempt. Isaac D'Israeli brings much evidence to support the statement.[2] Scaliger cavils at Drusius for the smallness of his books; and one of the famous printers of that time (Moret, successor to Plantin) complained to the learned Puteanus that his books were too small for sale, purchasers being scared away by their diminutive size. Puteanus referred him to Plutarch, whose works consisted of small treatises; but the printer took fire at the comparison, and turned him out of the shop for being so vain as to pretend that he wrote in any manner like Plutarch. Jurieu reproached Colomies for being *a great author of little books*. It was the humour of a certain Mæcenas (he quotes out of Addison),[3] who *cheered the lustre of his patronage with the steams of a good dinner*, to place his guests according to the size and thickness of the books they had published. At the head of the table sat those who had published in *folio, folissimo*; next the authors in *quarto*; then those in *octavo*. At such a table, he says, *Blackmore* would have had the precedence of *Gray*; which reveals his own opinion, supported out of Francis Osborne: *Huge volumes, like the ox roasted whole at Bartholomew Fair, may proclaim plenty of labour, but afford less of what is delicate, savoury, and well-concocted, than smaller pieces.*

But who shall decide the controversy? I shall not attempt it, beyond saying that in my experience authentic bookmen are insatiate, they want their favourites to be endless: *I love those large, still books*, said Tennyson of *Clarissa*;[4] which a modern bookman supports when he boldly announces that *novels of character must be long to be great*.[5] The fixed devotion of some of them to one book is no more than an aspiration to that end, unless it is in like case with those of short memory, who, like William Cory,[6] was made less poor in books since he could go to the few he possessed again and again *with a fair sense of discovery*. W. B. Yeats loves the long prose romances of William Morris. They are the only books he reads slowly so that he may not come too quickly to the end.[7] This is the plaint of the best of them, they would have, as who would not,

A linkèd sweetness long drawn out.[8]

A pleasure exhausted! sighs Maurice de Guérin,[9] after reading the last page of *Etudes de la Nature. It is one of those books*, he says, *which one wishes would*

---

[1] *Selections*. Trans. Lyttleton. 140. [2] *Cur. Lit.* ii, 96–8. [3] *Spectator*. 529. [4] Edward FitzGerald, *Letters and Literary Remains*. i, 419. [5] Viscount Grey, 'Pleasure of Reading', *Fallodon Papers*. 22. [6] *Letters and Journals*. 484. [7] Yeats, *The Trembling of the Veil*. 30. [8] Milton, *L'Allegro*. [9] *Journal*. Trans. Trebutien. 72.

never come to an end. All his life Mitford[1] *delighted in voluminous works.* He contemplated *very long, very big books* with *a sense of enjoyment,* and shrank with *aversion and horror from that invention of the enemy—an Abridgement.* Bruce's *Abyssinia* took such *possession* of him that *he named a whole colony of Bantams* after that traveller's Abyssinian princes and princesses; and he never felt *greater disgust than at seeing this magnificent work cut down to a thick, dumpy volume, seven inches by five.* He experienced a like feeling when he met Drinkwater's *Siege of Gibraltar,* where he had *first learned to tremble at the grim realities of war,* degraded from *a goodly quarto* into *a meagre pamphlet.*

Most of us would be as vexed as he was at the abridgement of a favourite, looking upon it as a desecration, the transformation of what is whole and virile into something meagre and contemptible, like a man into a eunuch. But this has little to do with my present theme, which is of the true-born reader's preference for big or little books; and I have sufficiently explicated these differences to show that, although of an insatiate appetite, good bookmen are at one whether they chew over a little book or browse at large over a big one. This only let me add here, for I return to the theme, that in some cases those hard censures of the one or the other must be taken *cum grano salis,* for the two opinions may alternate, or even exist side by side, in the same person. It is a question of mood or whim, and my own conviction is that no bibliophile was ever all out for books of any one size.

[1] *Recollections of a Literary Life.*

Part III

THE PLEASURE OF BOOKS

I. OF READING FOR ITS OWN SAKE

Of the reading of books there is no end, and no end to its delight:

> I never knew
> More sweet and happy hours than I employ'd
> Upon my books.[1]

I was so allured to read, Milton confirms,[2] *that no recreation came to me better welcome*; no exercise of mortals more agreeable, *what party*, asks Thomas Carlyle, *so good as reading Thucydides, Dante or Johannes von Müller?*[3] or more satisfying, whether for consolation or composure, *in omnibus requiem quaesivi*, said Thomas à Kempis, *sed non inveni nisi in angulis et libellis.*[4] *I too*, comments Robert Southey, *have found repose where he did, in books and retirement, but it was there alone I sought it; to these my nature, under the direction of a merciful Providence, led me betimes, and the world can offer nothing which should tempt me from them.*[5]

For amusement they are infallible; reading is not *necessarily study.*[6] Another authority holds that *the use of books for pleasure is the most satisfactory recreation; without having acquired the power of reading for pleasure*, he says, *none of us can be independent.*[7] Dryden never read anything but for pleasure, and books, whatever other purpose they serve, are always the idle man's best friend. Montaigne's works have been called the *Breviary of Idlers*;[8] it is an epithet which might qualify whole libraries, for no other works of man are more eligible to that end, *no apparatus, no appointment of time and place, being necessary for the enjoyment of reading*;[9] no class, condition, or age exempt. *Who is he*, enjoins Robert Burton,[10] *that is now wholly overcome with idleness, or otherwise involved in a labyrinth of worldly cares,*

[1] James Shirley, *The Lady of Pleasure*. Act ii, Sc. 1.   [2] *An Apology for Smectymnuus.*
[3] *New Letters.* i, 116.   [4] 'I have sought rest everywhere, and only found it in corners and books.' Qt. Herbert Rosweyd, Preface to *Imitatio*. Antwerp. (1617)   [5] Qt. in *Book-Lover's Enchiridion.* 162.   [6] Lubbock, *Pleasures of Life.* i, 56.   [7] Viscount Grey. 'Recreation', *Fallodon Papers.* 66.   [8] Isaac D'Israeli, *Miscellany of Literature.*
[9] John Aikin, in *Book-Lover's Enchiridion.* 126.   [10] *Anat. of Melan.* (1904) ii, 101.

troubles, and discontents, that will not be much lightened in his mind by reading of some enticing story, true or feigned, where (as in a glass) he shall observe what our forefathers have done, the beginnings, ruins, falls, periods of Commonwealths, private men's actions displayed to the life. etc.

Thus may books command their lovers and thus they do command and captain the soul of man. *Ut studiis se literarum a mortalitate vindicet,* seek in literature deliverance from mortality.[1] *All literature,* a recent observer claims, *springs from the ineradicable instinct in man to communicate good; and thus almost all books assure us that the soul is divine.*[2] So great this efficacy of books that Thomas Carlyle claims reading to be one of the *Rights of Man* and *a very cruel injustice if you deny it to a man,*[3] for, by their beneficence to readers in all times and stations, they are necessities of life to some and may yet be so to all. In the busy world they are respites and recreations, as I shall sufficiently make out; and, *because the soul of Man is not by its own Nature or observation furnisht with sufficient Materials to work upon,* books are essential to solitude, for it is only by a continual recourse to them that the soul can be replenished with *fresh supplies,* otherwise the solitary would *grow indigent, and be ready to starve without them.*[4] To which I add that which seems to me more probable, that without them, not only the solitary, but the social grow needy of mind and impoverished of spirit, for books are the granaries in which the harvest of mankind is stored; they are the best, readiest, surest way to choose inward riches which all wise men approve. In proof of this, Confucius owned that in the pursuit of knowledge he forgot not only his *food* and his *sorrows,* but *he did not even perceive that old age was coming on.*[5]

Yet, for mine own part, and in spite of what may seem otherwise, I scorn all special pleading for what should be evident, and I here say, and shall hint again and again, that reading is not a duty, and if it is not a pleasure it is a waste of time, and

Lectio, quae placuit, decies repetita placebit,[6]

what we read with pleasure we read again with pleasure, for *the desire of mind to mind is never satiated but rather continually increased by inter-communion;*[7] thus reading is justified. Whatever other purposes it may have, and there are many, it is its own reward. There are counsels and records to support this tenent, out of which, because every man cannot attend to read or peruse them, I will collect in this section some few of the more notable.

[1] Pliny, Qt. Walter Pater, *Marius the Epicurean.* i, 71.   [2] Garrod, 'How to Know a Good Book from a Bad', *Profession of Poetry.* 256.   [3] *New Letters.* i, 212. [4] Cowley, 'Of Solitude', *Essays.*   [5] Qt. Lubbock, *Pleasures of Life.* i, 54–5. [6] Horace, *A. P.* 365.   [7] Coventry Patmore. *Memoirs,* Champneys. i, 135.

II. PLEASURE A CONDITION BOTH PROFITABLE
AND HONEST

As he that is invited to a feast eats what is set before him, and looks for no other, enjoy then that thou hast at this banquet, and ask no more, forasmuch as it is sweet, or pleasant, for a man to read books, and be recreated by them. It is also an evident truth, that without both these sweetnesses or pleasures, or one of them at least, neither the felicity of books can be tasted nor their goodness be received, for *literature does not please by moralizing us; it moralizes us because it pleases:*[1]

No profit grows where is no pleasure ta'en;
In brief, sir, study what you most affect;[2]

which is no more than the intention of Jeremy Collier[3] where he says that *if books are well chosen, they neither dull the Appetite, nor strain the Capacity, but, on the contrary, they refresh the Inclination, and strengthen the Power, and improve under Experiment: And which is best of all, they Entertain and Perfect at the same time; convey Wisdom and Knowledge through Pleasure.* Enjoyment is taste untrammelled, it is the only test of predilection, for, as Dr. Johnson holds, *no man is a hypocrite in his pleasures,*[4] and that even for *general improvement, a man should read whatever his immediate inclination prompts him to,* for, *if we read without inclination, half the mind is employed in fixing the attention,* and only half left *to be employed on what we read.*[5] Lubbock is therefore right when he maintains *that we profit little by books which we do not enjoy.*[6] Therefore I accept pleasure, suavity, jocundity, and other terms of the like import, for one and the same thing in the rules of reading, as the Epicureans do in their rules of life.[7] The inference is exceeding plain, for if a book is not pleasurable it is unreadable and thus defeats its aim, which, as I have said, and will say again, is to be read. It is equally evident that this pleasure of books is widespread and diverse, for they not only *delight us to the marrow,*[8] profoundly move, or exalt us up to heaven, but they entertain the passing fancy, the light and evanescent whim; so *let every one take the view* (or the book) *which pleases him, and enjoy it.*[9]

There have not wanted some, chiefly in times past, who with great pomp and ostentation have discoursed of these pleasurable qualities in life no less than in the arts, as if they were evil in themselves. I say such infer-

---

[1] Garrod, 'How to Know a Good Book from a Bad.' *Profession of Poetry.* 264.
[2] *Taming of the Shrew.* i, 1.   [3] 'Of the Entertainment of Books.' *Essays.* ii, 97.
[4] *Life,* Boswell. Ed. Hill, iv, 316.   [5] *Ib.* iii, 43.   [6] *Pleasures of Life.* i, 63.   [7] Epicurus,
Morals. ii, 8.   [8] Petrarch, in Tatham, *Francesco Petrarca.* ii, 36.   [9] Longinus,
The Sublime. Trans. Prickard. 67.

ences are devoid of sense, as they are of charity and good taste: *the soul of sweet delight can never be defil'd;*[1]

Wherefore I assert:—if Reason's only function were
to heighten our pleasure, that were vindication enough.[2]

These moral cavillers, Chadbands, spoil-sports, impotent and resentful ones, whose chief profession is

all pleasure to destroy,
Save what is in destroying,[3]

are at one with those dull and incompetent teachers, still extant in some measure, who have so misused books in churches, chapels, little bethels, schools, colleges, seminaries, etc., as to make them unpalatable to the young, and so to promote bookshyness in maturity as a common distemper, which it still is in all lands. Dibdin gives an extreme instance in that of a schoolmaster of Suabia, who, for fifty-one years, *had superintended a large institution with old-fashioned severity,* and *in the course of his exertions* had given 911,500 *canings,* 121 *floggings,* 209,000 *custodes,* 136,000 *tips with the ruler,* 10,200 *boxes on the ear,* and 22,700 *tasks by heart;* and in addition he had made 700 boys *stand on peas,* 6000 *kneel on a sharp edge of wood,* 5000 *wear the fool's cap,* and 1700 *hold the rod.*[4].But I rove, I confess, and talk like a reformer (which I am not). *The wisest man preaches no doctrines; he has no scheme; he sees no rafter, not even a cobweb, against the heavens. It is clear sky.*[5] I am not my brother's keeper; and if there were still less readers than there are, and books still less accessible, I should be content, for every true reader will work out his own salvation with taste and affection his best guides.

What we most need is not more books or more readers, but more time for reading, although I would not lay too much stress on that point, for in the last resort we are the sires of our opportunities, and if *non cuivis homini contingit adire Corinthum,*[6] all have not the luck to visit Corinth, desire carries more thither than otherwise would be possible, good luck being the ratio between what we get and the constancy with which we desire it. So to this defence of the pleasure of books I shall bring no more support in this place than the high evidence of Wordsworth, who, in his young days by Windermere, read poetry with a friend, and gladness came upon them both because they were

[1] William Blake, *Marriage of Heaven and Hell.*   [2] Bridges, *Testament of Beauty.* i, 202–3.   [3] Milton, *Paradise Lost.* ix.   [4] *Bibliomania.* (1911) 375.   [5] Thoreau, *Week on the Concord.* Scott Lib. 60.   [6] Hor., i *Ep.* xvii, 36.

Lifted above the ground by airy fancies,
More bright than madness or the dreams of wine;
And, though full oft the objects of our love
Were false, and in their splendour overwrought,
Yet was there surely then no vulgar power
Working within us,—nothing less, in truth,
Than that most noble attribute of man,
Though yet untutored and inordinate,
That wish for something loftier, more adorned,
Than is the common aspect, daily garb,
Of human life. What wonder, then, if sounds
Of exultation echoed through the groves!
For images and sentiments, and words,
And everything encountered or pursued
In that delicious world of poesy,
Kept holiday, a never-ending show,
With music, incense, festival, and flowers![1]

After such words I am disposed to close this argument with Augustine
Birrell where he claims that *literature exists to please—to lighten the burden of
men's lives; to make them for a short while forget their sorrow and their sins, their
silenced hearths, their disappointed hopes, their grim futures*—and, as he well
adds, *those men of letters are the best loved who have best performed literature's
truest office*,[2] for, as Keats insinuated for his own clan:

they shall be accounted poet kings
Who simply tell the most heart-easing things.[3]

III. DELIGHT THAT VARIES WITH TIME AND PLACE

We may not all be bibliophiles of genius, all illustrious; still less, all serene
and rich in books, with time and capacity to enjoy them; but we are as
sufficient as we are various, and know our own food. We are as various
as our books and our love of them; and a piece of arras is composed of
several parcels, some wrought of silk, some of gold or silver, or embroidered of divers colours, all to serve for the exornation of the whole;
or as music is made of divers chords and keys, harmonies and cacophonies,
a total sum of many small numbers, so is the pleasure of books in its greatest corporeality, a library (whether big or little), of several inequal books

[1] *Prelude.* v, 567–83.   [2] 'The Office of Literature', *Collected Essays.* iii, 56.   [3] 'Sleep
and Poetry.'

and the faculty variously to relish them. One will like this, another that, as dishes are chosen at a feast, not for the good they do us but for the pleasure they give us, there being no greater good than enjoyment; *as to dine with H. B. Wheatley and to fondle his 'Drydens', was to sup with Atticus;*[1] such are the very words of their profession, and an exercise of logic which few bookmen would put to doubt in so rapt a relation.

The exquisite moment of joy, to be prolonged according to taste or skill (or both combined), is the object, as in the amorous poet,

Oh heaven of Love! thou moment of Delight![2]

Let every reader cite further examples from his own adventures; for my part I hold it fortunate that tastes are various; *jucundum nihil est, nisi quod reficit varietas,*[3] nothing is pleasant unless spiced with variety. *Let your book-cases and your shelves be your gardens and your pleasure-grounds. Pluck the fruit that grows therein, gather the roses, the spices, and the myrrh. If your soul be satiate and weary, change from garden to garden, from furrow to furrow, from sight to sight. Then will your desire renew itself and your soul be satisfied with delight;*[4] remembering, perchance, that

short retirement urges sweet return.[5]

But in the present matter, the effect of this consideration ought to be (and in this I find most content) that the greater the variety of tastes the greater the variety of desirable books, and the wider the opportunity of enjoyment.

It may be perhaps not impertinently added that this same argument holds good of that outward association with books peculiar to several collectors whose desire is not primarily to read. If all should be *Huths* and *Huntingtons* there would not be enough covetable copies to go round, and this extrinsic bibliophily would succumb in a bibliomaniacal brawl in which *Croesi* and *Darii* would continuously rage together over the shrinking treasure-trove of *rariora*, until the fall of that *Götterdämmerung* when *desirable copies* would cease to *occur*. Who should then fill his shelves, build his *bibliothèque intime*, make his several choice for bookish raiment? We should starve for company and sue at last to be as we were at first. But to this problem I shall return; in the meantime 'tis exceeding likely to conjecture, that God hath appointed this inequality to sublimate our pleasure by the tonic of effort; for it is not solely, except in some instances, that the books themselves bring pleasure; we bribe them to a revelation of

---

[1] Harold Child, 'Ego et Libri mei', *Bibliophile's Almanack.* (1927) 16.   [2] Rochester, 'The Perfect Enjoyment', *Poems of Affairs of State.* (1697) 12.   [3] Bacon, *Ornamenta Rationalia.*   [4] Judah Ibn Tibbon, in Abrahams, *Jewish Life in the Middle Ages.* 354–5.   [5] Milton, *Paradise Lost.* ix, 250.

their inward riches by a hint of our own quality of enjoyment. Books are to us what we are to them. *Nihil aliud necessarium ut sis miser* (saith Cardan[1]) *quam ut te miserum credas*, let thy fortune be what it will, thy mind alone makes thee poor or rich, miserable or happy; but being *nulli secundi*, a quintessence of the most sensitive minds, books vary with our intentions, our moods, and our years: they *change like friends, like ourselves, like everything; but they are most piquant in the contrasts they provoke . . . the vicissitudes of years are printed and packed in a thin octavo, and the shivering ghosts of desire and hope return to their forbidden home in the heart and fancy.*[2]

IV. POVERTY NO HINDRANCE, RICHES NO HELP

Nor is it the number possessed which so much commends them to their lovers. I myself have seen a man miserably dejected in a pleasant library, and yet again another well occupied and at good ease with a solitary book. *There is a great deal of difference between the eager man who wants to read a book, and the tired man who wants a book to read.*[3] I may yet add, therefore, a word or two for a corollary, for there are many rich collectors, I dare boldly say it, that lie amid *First Folios* and *Groliers*, *Clovis Eves* and *Samuel Mearns*, *Kelmscott 'Chaucers'* and *Doves 'Bibles'*; with *first editions, unique copies*, pampered every day, in their luxurious libraries, who live at less heart's ease, with more anguish than many a clerk who makes a lucky-dip in the twopenny box, or poor student who, as William Cobbett, spends his supper-money on a coveted volume.

George Gissing bought dozens of books with money which ought to have been spent upon *what are called the necessaries of life. Many a time*, he confesses, *I have stood before a stall, or a bookseller's window, torn by conflict of intellectual desire and bodily need*; and at the dinner hour, his stomach clamouring for food, he has been so held up by the tempting price of a long-coveted volume, that he has secured it with the *pangs of famine*. His copy of Heyne's *Tibullus* was thus grabbed from the stall of the old bookshop in Goodge Street for sixpence, when sixpence was all he had in the world; and although that sum would have purchased *a plate of meat and vegetables*, he dared not hope that the volume *would wait until the morrow, when a certain small sum fell due* to him. *I paced the pavement*, he recalls, *fingering the coppers in my pocket, eyeing the stall: two appetites at combat within me.* The book was bought, and as he made shift with *a dinner of bread and butter* he *gloated over the pages.*[4]

Let me conclude these citations with that familiar passage from *Elia*, which records how the essayist let a brown suit hang upon him until it

[1] *De consolat*. Lib. 3.   [2] Reference lost.   [3] G. K. Chesterton, *Charles Dickens*. 99.
[4] *Private Papers of Henry Ryecroft*. 31–32.

was threadbare because of *a folio Beaumont and Fletcher* which he *dragged home late at night* from Barker's in Covent Garden. He and his sister had *eyed* this volume for weeks, unable to make up their minds to buy it; then of a sudden comes decision near ten o'clock on a Saturday night, and Elia sets off from Islington to Covent Garden fearing it may be too late. The old bookseller grumbles, as he opens his shop, and *by the twinkling taper (for he was setting bedwards)* lights out the relic from among his dusty treasures. Elia secures the prize and lugs it home, *wishing it were twice as cumbersome. When you presented it to me,* his sister recalls, *and when we were exploring the perfectness of it . . . and while I was repairing some of the loose leaves with paste, which your impatience would not suffer to be left till daybreak —was there no pleasure in being a poor man? or can those neat black clothes which you wear now, and are so careful to keep brushed, since we became rich and finical, give you half the honest vanity with which you flaunted it about in that overworn suit—your old corbeau—for four or five weeks longer than you should have done, to pacify your conscience for the mighty sum of fifteen—or sixteen shillings was it?—a great affair we thought it then—which you had lavished on the old folio.*[1] The admonition, I think, is not unreasonable, for the rich can never own such delights, and it will fully answer any objections, so moralize this fable by thyself.

V. TREASURIES OF HAPPINESS NEVER EXHAUSTED

To these conjectures I may adventure to subjoin another, namely, that the fulness of this pleasure of books is, in the familiar saying, a gift, alike removed from other influences or conditions, and not common to all men. Only the congenital bookman discovers in the memory of reading in times past a treasury of present delight, as Hazlitt, when, after thirty years, the sight of his copies of *Paradise Lost* and the *Reflections on the French Revolution* recaptured the pleasure with which he first *dipped into them* at Shrewsbury School, where he had won them as prizes. *That time is past,* he mourns, *'with all its giddy raptures'*: but so sweet the recollection he is determined to preserve its memory, *'embalmed with odours'*;[2] just as he gloats on the recollection that his first meeting, as a boy, with *Tom Jones* in Cooke's *British Novelists* was *a dance through life, a perpetual gala-day.*[3]

Talk of the happiness of getting a great prize in the Lottery! Southey exclaims;[4] what is it to opening a box of books! He compares the delectable recreation of lifting the lid to what we shall feel when *Peter the Porter opens the door upstairs, and says, 'Please to walk in, Sir'.* Well may Thomas Love

[1] 'Old China', *Last Essays of Elia.*   [2] *The Plain Speaker.* 79.   [3] *Ib.* 69.
[4] In a letter to Coleridge, quoted in *Book-Lovers' Anthology.* 5.

Peacock claim that there is no place in which even the *outside of a book* is not *an innocent and becoming spectacle,*

> Not daily conned, but glorious still to view,
> With glistening letters wrought in red and blue,[1]

or John Aikin, that without books he had never been able to pass a single day to his entire satisfaction; for they are *at the head of all the pleasures which offer themselves to the man of liberal education; in variety, durability, and facility of attainment, no other can stand in competition with it; and even in intensity it is inferior to few;* and he supports his argument by the supreme fact that books give us the power *to call up the shades of the greatest and wisest men that ever existed, and oblige them to converse with us on the most interesting topics;* 'tis *an inestimable privilege,* he well says, and *superior to all common enjoyments;* and an added advantage that from this feast of the *choicest thoughts of the ablest men in their best dress,* we can exclude *dullness and impertinence,* and open our doors only to *wit and good sense.*[2]

Hazlitt merrily inculcates that reading is *the greatest pleasure in life,* and others come near to this opinion, as Leigh Hunt: *the most heart-felt of all our enjoyments;* and Southey: *old friends and old books are the best things this world affords.* The habit of reading, Anthony Trollope testifies,[3] *is the only enjoyment in which there is no alloy; it lasts when all other pleasures fade,* and will make *our hours pleasant* as long as we live. The *purest pleasures* Cobden ever knew were *intercourse with intelligent* minds and *communion with the departed great,* through books by his own fireside.[4] Milton, at the University, is so *allur'd to read, that no Recreation* comes to him *better welcome.*[5] Gibbon,[6] comfortably seated in his library, in his own easy chair, before his own fire, after a journey, rejoices in the feeling that he is *surrounded with a thousand old acquaintances of all ages and characters, who are ready to answer a thousand questions* which he is impatient to ask:

> And to hem yeve I feyth and ful credence,
> And in myn herte have hem in reverence
> So hertely, that ther is game noon,
> That fro my bokes maketh me to goon.[7]

So sweet the pleasure of reading that (saith Burton) *all those ornaments and childish bubbles of wealth are not worthy to be compared to them,*[8] and, *to me,* Leo Allatius well seconds him, *the light of the sun, the day, and life itself, would be joyless and bitter if I had not something to read;*[9] which Prospero in

---

[1] O. W. Holmes, 'The Study', *Poems.* [2] John Aikin, *Letters from a Father to his Son.* [3] Speech at Bolton, Dec. 7, 1868. [4] Address at Manchester Athenæum, Nov. 1847. [5] 'Apology Against Smectymnuus.' *Works.* (1697) 335. [6] *Autobiography and Correspondence.* 269. [7] Chaucer, *Legende of Goode Women.* Prologue. i, 29. [8] *Anat. of Melan.* (1904) ii, 104. [9] Qt. *Book-Lover's Ench.* 54.

The Tempest supports when he finds his library *dukedom large enough*, prizing certain volumes above his dukedom. Macaulay ventures even further, books becoming *everything* to him: *If I had at this moment any choice of life*, he says, *I would bury myself in one of those immense libraries* (at the Universities) and *never pass a waking hour without a book before me*.[1] But to leave all declamatory speeches and verses in their praise, I will confine myself to my present subject, which is to assert and show how they have given pleasure by the reading of them or by their presence.

Some are fully convinced that through them they enclose their desires in the security and satisfaction of their own minds, and I think that the arguments that are brought by a recent ingenious author are perpendicular to this point, when he makes Henry Wimbush recite his opinion that books promote superior pleasures to such desirable *human contacts* as love and friendship. These have been highly valued in the past because books *were scarce and difficult to reproduce*; but as *reading becomes more and more habitual and widespread, an ever-increasing number of people will discover that books will give them all the pleasures of social life and none of its intolerable tedium*.[2] There is support for this from many sources, but notably in the argument, often put forth, that books are sure protectors, not only against the ravages of Time, but against those of

Business, which the Muses hate,[3]

for they translate our leisure into quiet happiness, and if, as Dibdin[4] claims, it is a *fictitious* happiness, it is none the less *real, inasmuch as it produces positive sensations of delight*, and no happiness, real or unreal, can do more, so, he advises,[5] *build your book-nest to forget the world without, and the many wretched creatures that crawl upon its surface*, for, as I may buttress him out of Cowley,[6] *if once we be thoroughly engaged in the Love of Letters, instead of being wearied with the length of any day, we shall only complain of the shortness of our whole life:*

And, feeling kindly unto all the earth,
Grudge every minute as it passes by.[7]

VI. THE GOLDEN RULE FOR READERS

But to make an end of these controversies, and scatter them abroad, let me put out that reading hath many purposes, as many perchance as there are books and readers; and whatever their attitude, aim, object, readers, I say

[1] *Life*, Trevelyan (1909) i, 343.   [2] Aldous Huxley, *Crome Yellow*. 304.   [3] Cowley, *Pindaric Ode*.   [4] *Bibliomania*. (1811) 608-9.   [5] *Reminiscences*. ii, 946.   [6] 'Of Solitude', *Essays*.   [7] William Morris, 'An Apology', *Earthly Paradise*.

again, read best who read for their own delight; of which George Gissing[1] may be cited as a final and sufficient witness: *To what end do I read and remember? Surely*, he submits, *as foolish a question as ever man put to himself. You read for your own pleasure, for your solace and strengthening. Pleasure, then, purely selfish? Solace which endures for an hour and strengthening for no combat? Ay, but I know, I know. With what heart should I live here in my cottage, waiting for life's end, were it not for those hours of seeming idle reading?*

If that be deemed an insufficient argument and a stronger defence be required, take Montaigne: *I love no books but such as are pleasant and easy, and which tickle me, or such as comfort and counsel me, to direct my life and death; Logical* and *Aristotelian ordinances* held no attraction for one who only endeavoured to become *more wise and sufficient and not more witty and eloquent*; he does not busy himself to anatomize *death and voluptuousness*, for of these he understands only what is understandable. At the first reading of a book he seeks out good and solid reasons, that may instruct him how to sustain their assaults; he seeks neither *grammatical subtilties, nor logical quiddities, nor the wittie contexture of choice words, or arguments, and syllogismes*; these serve not his turn.[2]

Yet in these as in other affairs *the golden rule is that there are no golden rules*;[3] nothing against a good stomach, as the saying is; we must take our choice, refraining rather by experience of ill than by precept of good; live and learn, until good taste is formed, then you may with safety side with Philodemus when he sings:

> Philosopher, whom dost thou most affect,
> Stoics austere, or Epicurus' sect?
> Friend, 'tis my grave infrangible design
> With those to study, and with these to dine.[4]

Generally thus much we may conclude, with Bronson Alcott,[5] that *that is a good book which is opened with expectation and closed with profit*, provided we agree that *profit* may differ in kind with every good book, being sometimes a pearl of wisdom, at others a golden vision; sometimes the silver of happiness, anon the bronze of information; nor would I despise that most fickle of all profits, entertainment, when

> words themselves
> Move us with conscious pleasure;[6]

all the more so because, as Viscount Grey has it, the *deep and abiding pleasure* of reading not only *increases the more it is indulged*, but *actually*

---

[1] *Private Papers of Henry Ryecroft.* 55.   [2] 'Of Bookes.' *Essays.* Ed. Seccombe. ii.
[3] Bernard Shaw, 'Maxims for Revolutionists.' *Man and Superman.* 227.   [4] Trans.
Richard Garnett, *Idylls and Epigrams.* 59.   [5] *Table Talk.* i, 2.   [6] Wordsworth,
Prelude. v, 44–5.

refreshes and restores as well as entertains.[1] But apart from all high-minded arguments, amusement has its place. 'Tis better many times to be entertained than improved, and *dulce est desipere in loco*, to play the fool now and then is not amiss, for *it is just as well to be a little giddy-pated, if we are to feel at home on this teeming earth.*[2] There is time for all things.

[1] 'The Pleasure of Reading.' *Fallodon Papers.* 11.   [2] Logan Pearsall Smith, *Life and Letters.* (April 1930)

Part IV

THE ART OF READING

━━━━━━━━━━━━━━━━◄═►◄═►◄═►━━━━━━━

I. ÆSTHETICAL CONSIDERATIONS

A book is not complete until it has found a mate who can read and understand. *Pro captu lectoris habent sua fata libelli,*[1] for *'tis the good reader that makes the good book; in every book he finds passages which seem confidences or asides hidden from all else and unmistakably meant for his ear;*[2] *the profit of books is according to the sensibility of the reader; the profoundest thought or passion sleeps as in a mine, until it is discovered by an equal mind and heart.*[3] To accept a book for what it is—the triune creation of author, printer, and reader—is to accept these exalted opinions. Physically disposed, a book is an amalgam of paper, ink, and type; but mingled with these ingredients there is that which we call 'the author', and he in turn is mind, emotion, imagination, filtered through the senses and distilled into words and sentences, which only come fully to life at the magic touch of the reader, who must himself supply the forms, colours, sentiments, to which the writer's symbols correspond. *It will,* says Anatole France,[4] *depend on him whether these be dull or brilliant, hot with passion or cold as ice;* each word being no less than a *magic finger that sets a fibre of the brain vibrating like a harp-string,* and *so invokes a note from the sounding-board of the soul;* for, as Vernon Lee sums it up, *the words which are the writer's materials for expression are but the symbol of the ideas already existing in the mind of the reader.* The writer thus *playing on the Reader's mind, as the pianist, although his fingers touch only the keyboard, is really playing on the strings.*[5] There must, of course, be strings to play on. Small wonder that a great reader is almost as rare as a great writer. Sir Walter Raleigh held[6] that *there are only two or three real readers alive at any given time,* and Emerson claimed[7] that *there are not in the world at any time more than a dozen persons who read and understand Plato.*

---

[1] 'Books have their fate from the capacities of their readers.' Ter. Maurus. Qt. Thomas Wilson, *Maxims.* (1898) 9.   [2] Emerson, 'Success', *Society and Solitude.* (1870) 249.   [3] Emerson, 'Quotation and Originality', *Letters and Social Aims.* (1898) 143.   [4] *Garden of Epicurus.* Trans. Allinson. 42.   [5] *Handling of Words.* 41–44.   [6] *Letters.* i, 233.   [7] 'Spiritual Laws', *Essays.* (1885) 123.

Since writing, then, is *justly denominated an art*, reading should be permitted the same distinction. I will cite Sir Arthur Quiller-Couch as a chief patron of this notion. He boldly gives out that *Reading is an Art*,[1] if only because it depends so greatly upon *selection*, which is an art in itself: *Selection implies skilful practice. Skilful practice is only another term for art;*[2] and another observer as stiffly maintains that *it is almost as much an art as writing.*[3] To read *well, that is to read true books in a true spirit, is a noble exercise*; it requires training such as athletes undergo: *steady intention almost of the whole of life to this object; books must be read as deliberately and reservedly as they were written.*[4]

To receive with happy discrimination ideas adorned by the art of writing is *a task not less useful than writing.*[5] *It is a faculty to be acquired, not a natural gift,*[6] for *there is something which a reader himself must bring to the book.* He must bring himself, and *when a man says he sees nothing in a book, he very often means that he does not see himself in it.*[7] There may here be some defect sometimes in the author, and I hold with Logan Pearsall Smith, that *the great art of writing is the art of making people real to themselves with words.*[8] *All books*, Bulwer-Lytton will have, *grow homilies by time;*[9] but only, he ought to have added, by time conditioned by readers.

Nothing ever becomes real till it is experienced, Keats advises, *even a Proverb is no proverb to you till Life has illustrated it;*[10] *axioms in philosophy are not axioms till they are proved upon our pulses*; and he will have that though we read *fine things*, we *never feel them to the full until we have gone the same steps as the author.*[11] *To read a book in the true sense*, Leslie Stephen gives out,[12] *to read it, that is, not as a critic but in the spirit of enjoyment—is to lay aside for the moment one's own personality and to become a part of the author.* Several in general affirm this, Thoreau among them, who holds that the works of the great poets *have never yet been read. . . for only the great poets can read them.*[13] Crates contends that in order to appreciate the compositions of Heraclitus, a reader must be a cunning swimmer, lest the depth and weight of the learning should drown and swallow him up;[14] and Emerson argues that *one must be a great inventor to read well.*[15] So vast the field, so many mazes and perils, *that unless we be directed by some artist*, George Wither warns,[16] *we shall spend half our age before we can find authors which are worth our reading.*

All those of whom we hear bring evidence in support of these opinions,

[1] *On the Art of Reading.* 24.   [2] *Ib.* 26.   [3] Bernard Lintot, *End Papers.* 154. [4] Thoreau, *Walden*, Scott Lib. 99.   [5] Isaac D'Israeli, *Misc. Lit.* (1801) 173. [6] Frederic Harrison, *Choice of Books.* 24.   [7] A. W. and J. C. Hare, *Guesses at Truth.* 24.   [8] *Life and Letters.* (April 1930).   [9] Qt. *Book-Lovers' Anthology.* 24. [10] *Letters* (Ed. Forman. 1895). 305.   [11] *Letters* (Ed. Forman. 1895). 127.   [12] *Hours in a Library.* iv, 54.   [13] *Walden*, Scott Lib. 102.   [14] *Montaigne.* Ed. Seccombe. iii, Bk. 12.   [15] *The American Scholar.*   [16] *The Scholar's Purgatory.*

and the chains would be still more complete if we could add to it the testimonies of those innumerable readers who never speak out, but are content to be of that silent communion which is a most fruitful destiny of literature. There are records of great writers, but great readers who cómplete the circle of authorship live and die for the greater part in the privacy of their studies. *O quantum eruditorum aut modestia ipsorum aut quies operit ac subtrahit famae!*[1] Sometimes the gifts of reader and writer are united in one person; then we learn something about them, but in the main we depend upon the chance record of some chronicler or gossip woven into the story of his own life or times; the rest is a closed book. Yet, although we are disfurnished of much necessary knowledge, I hope to show in the following chapters that we are not finally ignorant of what readers have felt and thought about their art.

II. METHODS OF FAMOUS BOOKMEN

Dr. Johnson used to advise young people never to be without a book in their pocket, *to be read at bye-times when they had nothing else to do*,[2] claiming that he acquired all his own knowledge that way, except what he had picked up by running about the world with his wits ready to observe and his tongue ready to discuss. *Sir*, he said to Boswell, *in my early years I read very hard. It is a sad reflection, but a true one, that I knew almost as much at eighteen as I do now.*[3] Ill-health favoured him, as it has favoured many another reader; but he read always and at all times, though not continuously in any one book, for all need not be read from beginning to end: *A book may be good for nothing; or there may be only one thing in it worth knowing; are we to read it all through?*[4] *How few are there*, he warned Mrs. Thrale, *of which one ever can possibly arrive at the last page! Was there ever yet anything written by mere man that was wished longer by its readers, excepting* '*Don Quixote*', '*Robinson Crusoe*', *and* '*The Pilgrim's Progress*'?[5] He advised Boswell to have *as many books about* him *as he could: that he might read upon any subject upon which he had a desire for instruction at the time*;[6] *just as inclination prompted him which alone would do him any good; better go into company than read a set task.*[7] He prescribes five hours a day reading for a young man,[8] but books are no substitute for life: *books without the knowledge of life are useless*;[9] for as Lord Chandos[10] concurs, *though reading do*

---

[1] Pliny, *Epp.* vii, 25. 'What numbers of learned men does their own modesty or love of repose conceal and withdraw from the notice of the world!' (Melmoth)
[2] Mrs. Thrale, in *Johnsonian Miscellanies*. ii, 311.   [3] He was then fifty-four. *Life*.
Ed. Hill. i, 445.   [4] *Ib.* iv, 308.   [5] *Johnsonian Miscellanies*. i, 332.   [6] *Life*.
Hill. iii, 193.   [7] Boswell, *Letters*. Tinkler. i, 23.   [8] *Life*. Hill. i, 428.   [9] *Johnsonian Miscellanies*. i, 324.   [10] *Horae Subsecivae*.

furnish and direct a man's judgement, yet it doth not wholly govern it; at which few will demur, recalling Plutarch when he confessed that it was not so much by the knowledge of words that he came to understand things as that the experience of things did enable him *to follow the meaning of words.*[1] *Expression is what we want; not knowledge but a vent; men transformed by books become impotent praters;*[2] which, I doubt not, Henry Jackson had in mind when he advised Alfred Ollivant to *feed* his *imagination* and not worry about knowledge.[3] Every history yields examples.

Some would have it that books are to be taken slowly and piecemeal followed by much pondering,

> Learn to read slowly; all other graces
> Will follow in their proper places.[4]

To this the answer is evident from the words and experiences of adepts in the craft, and it is obvious that, with so many books to be read, and most readers would read many, speed is indispensable. Lubbock compromises by suggesting that it is better, *as regards by far the larger number.of books, to read quickly, dwelling only on the best and most important passages.*[5] But whatever the experts say, those readers who can will go the pace. Dr. Johnson seized *at once what was valuable in a book, without submitting to the labour of perusing it from beginning to end.*[6] He read Fielding's '*Amelia*' through without stopping,[7] and was an adept in that branch of the *art of reading* which, Hamerton says, *is to skip judiciously; whole libraries may be skipped*, he says, *in these days.*[8]

Many other authorities, I find, defend skipping, and with reason, for there is no other remedy for those who would keep pace, even in some small measure, with the multiplication of books and the subtraction of time. *There is but one art*, said Stevenson, *to omit*; if he knew how to omit, he would ask *no other knowledge*. A man who knew how to omit, he says, *would make an 'Iliad' of a daily paper*; and, he concludes, that the technique of omission is partial blindness. *Artistic sight is judicious blindness*. From this premise it would follow that selection after the book is chosen, as well as before, is essential. *The book that is wise in spots should be read in spots;*[9] to argue, he says, *that every book worth reading is worth reading straight through is no better than insistence upon eating a table-full every time one sits down to a meal.*[10] Emerson is so conscious of the lack of balance between the number of our books and the fewness of our years, that he would have us read by *proxy, if we had good proxies*; but in all times our skipping has been done

[1] *Plutarch*, Clough. v, 2.   [2] Emerson, in Cabot, *Memoir.* i, 293.   [3] *Henry Jackson*, O. M., A Memoir. Parru. 63.   [4] W. Walker, *Art of Reading.*   [5] *Pleasures of Life.* i, 62.   [6] *Life.* i, 71.   [7] *Ib.* iii, 43.   [8] *Intellectual Life.* 163.   [9] Richardson, *Choice of Books.* 130.   [10] Ibid., 127.

for us by anthologists and compilers of *elegant extracts*, though few would uphold such works as final substitutes for complete masterpieces. *In the end the reader finds himself alone: he has to decide for himself, to make up his own mind.*[1] Better skip for yourself, so long as you do not make skipping a habit; but better still master a few masterpieces than let many master you.

Southey *coursed from page to page with a greyhound's speed*, and in a few hours he *classified and arranged everything in a book which it was likely he would ever want;*[2] Napoleon read so fast that a book lasted him scarcely one hour, and at St. Helena, a servant *was kept busy carrying away armfuls of finished books which only a day before had been brought from the shelves;*[3] Sydney Smith galloped through a book *so rapidly*, that his family laughed *when he shut up a thick quarto as his morning's work*, charging him with having *looked at it, not read it*. But on being cross-examined it *was found that he knew all that was worth knowing in it*.[4] Macaulay would take in *at a glance* the whole of a printed page;[5] he read books *faster than other people skimmed them, and skimmed them as fast as any one else could turn the leaves*. One who had watched him said *he seemed to read through the skin*; nor was it speed at the cost of accurate memory, he read and remembered everything from the *most detestable trash that ever consumed ink and paper manufactured for better things*, to the noblest of masterpieces, looking upon misquotation as *a species of minor sacrilege*.

Laurence Sterne was against all such furious reading; he rebukes those of that *vicious taste, which has crept into thousands*, who read *straight forwards more in quest of adventures than of deep erudition and knowledge*. He would have it that the mind should *make wise reflections, draw curious conclusions, as it goes along*, and it was this habitude, he believed, which made Pliny the Younger affirm that *he never read a book so bad, but he drew some profit from it*.[6] Many, and they are wise, seek to read at a moderate pace (as Milton, who read *with selection*, and *meditated*, as Aubrey gives out),[7] absorbing leisurely, and pausing anon to roll a passage over the palate to taste its full flavour, or to fall into a dream upon a name, an incident, a rare description, purple patch or fine phrase; or perchance to share with another the treasures thus discovered, as I dilate in its place. Charles Lamb was of this kind; *a grace*, he urged, should be said before opening some great works, though others are of such *quick interest*, dependent upon *incidents*, that they *are for the eye to glide over only;*[8] of a like mind is Christopher Morley,[9] who has contrived a ceremonial for the reading of Thomas

[1] Herbert Read, *Bibliophile's Almanack*. (1928) 36.   [2] Dowden, *Southey*. 108.
[3] Ludwig, *Napoleon*. 622.   [4] Holland, *Memoir*. i, 112–13.   [5] *Life and Letters*, Trevelyan, i, 60–61.   [6] *Tristram Shandy*. Bk. I, Chap. xx.   [7] *Milton*, Pattison. 18.
[8] 'Detached Thoughts on Books and Reading.' *Last Essays of Elia*.   [9] *Thomas Hardy as a Poet*.

Hardy's *Poems*. *Grace yourself with quiet*, he advises: *take first a long swallow of open air, and have something burning beside you, even if only a candle; fire being element and symbol of sheer life*. *Then set away every irrelevant mirth or perplexity: be for an hour or so as passively aware as a sprawling dog*; and so with a *smell of earth and sky* and a *humble love of human beings*, you may explore our great modern explorer of the human heart. Montaigne was a persistent but desultory reader. When he met difficulties he did not fret himself, but if after one or two charges at them he failed to extract that pleasure which he stoutly demanded from all books, he circumvented them, for, saith he, *should I earnestly plod upon them, I should lose both time and myself, for I have a skipping wit*; he claimed to do nothing without blitheness and that *an over-obstinate continuation and plodding doth dazzle, dull, and weary the same*, and he would not have his sight thus confounded and diminished.[1]

Last of all to come to our students, who being searchers, enquirers, rather than readers *per se*, use books as the *media* of their craft, not solely to enjoy them. *We professionals*, Henry Jackson exclaimed,[2] *are no better than* '*damned scholiasts*', *too much occupied with unimportant difficulties to be able to enjoy the real thing*. For such as these, *a library is the great intellectual stratification in which the literary investigator works*; he examines its *external features, or perhaps drives a shaft through its various layers*, passing over this or that *stratum as not immediate to his purpose*, examining the rest with *minute attention* and *microscopic investigation*. For this work they have a special aptitude and develop a precise and particular sense, an instinct like a pointer's for the required fact or passage; *reading with the fingers*, as Basnage said of Bayle, with an *acuteness* which astonishes the unlearned.[3]

III. WHETHER TO READ QUICKLY OR SLOWLY

A book is a miracle of itself, but a wise book is the greatest wonder; *multi Thyrsigeri, pauci Bacchi*, many Bacchantes, but few Bacchuses; which Swift divides into three classes: *the superficial, the ignorant, and the learned*.[4] Fuller segregates from the rest some books that are only *cursorily to be tasted of*; they are: *voluminous books, that task a man's life to read them over; auxiliary books, only to be repaired to on occasions*; and, *such as are mere pieces of formality*.[5] Others throw a wider net, and would allow the reading at will of any book at any time for which we may have a fancy. Yet (and it is the quintessence and chief glory of the miracle of books that none is so mean as to lack admirers) the Bacchuses must be separated, segregated, sorted out from the Bacchantes, the geese from the swans, the sheep from the goats. But if few out of the millions of books command, or deserve to command,

---

[1] 'Of Books', *Essays*. Ed. Seccombe, ii, 112.   [2] *Memoir*, Parry. 199.   [3] J. Hill Burton, *Book-Hunter*. 115–16.   [4] *Tale of a Tub*. x.   [5] *Holy and Profane State*.

our whole hearts, those few become many in the multitudinous battalions
of the printed word, and the best of them eternities in print, for if *it takes
millenniums to make a Bible,*[1] it survives through eternity.

The reading of these great books alone, few though they be, is more
than enough, did we choose but them, for the shortness of our days, *tempus
fugit, et nunquam revertitur; a lifetime will hardly suffice to know, as they ought
to be known,* the *great masterpieces of man's genius.* Yet for all this we take
them, in the vulgar phrase, *as read,* although, as Frederic Harrison well
says,[2] they are never sufficiently read until they become our *daily mental
food.* For more to this purpose, read him, but it needs no defence, for, as
all agree, good seeketh what is good and dwelleth on it as a dog gnaweth
his bone; which is the same as the proverb advises: *Read a page, think an
age.* Pliny advises: *Pray remember to select with care the standard authors on
each subject, for, as the saying is, 'though we should read much, we should not
read many books'.*[3] This is good enough advice in a general comprehension,
but we must be curious to avoid a mistake here by accepting it as a final
piece, for, as Henry Jackson wisely gives out,[4] *reading slowly, and reading
quickly, are distinct arts, both of them valuable.*

A notable instance of varied reading occurs in the life of Dr. Johnson,
who in his youth as well as in later days roamed freely and broadly over
many book realms. *He might, perhaps,* says Boswell, *have studied more assiduously; but it may be doubted whether such a mind as his was not more enriched by
roaming at large in the fields of literature than if it had been confined to any single
spot.* Then drawing upon the analogy of mind and body, he suggests that
*as the flesh of animals who feed excursively is allowed to have a higher flavour
than those who are cooped up,* so there may be *the same difference between men
who read as their taste prompts and men who are confined in cells and colleges to
stated tasks.*[5]

Quintilian held that all reading should be slow and meditative: *not
delivered to the memory in its crude state, but sweetened and worked up by frequent repetition.*[6] *Reading furnishes the mind with materials of knowledge,* saith
Locke,[7] *it is thinking makes what we read ours. We are of the ruminating kind,
and it is not enough to cram ourselves with a great load of collections; unless we
chew them over again they will not give us strength and nourishment*; we must
meditate in solitude upon what we read as well as upon what we think,
for, as Cowley maintains,[8] *cogitation is the thing which distinguishes the
Solitude of a God from* that of *a wild Beast.*

Emerson is a prime example of this method, he read a book *for the*

---

[1] Emerson, 'Books', *Society and Solitude.* (1870) 185.   [2] Frederic Harrison, *Choice
of Books.* 84.   [3] 'Multum legendum esse, non multa.' *Letters.* Trans. Melmoth. Loeb
Ed. vii, 9.   [4] *Henry Jackson, O.M., A Memoir,* Parry, 47.   [5] *Life.* Ed. Hill. i, 57–8.
[6] *Inst. Or.* x, 1, 19.   [7] *Conduct of the Understanding.*   [8] 'Of Solitude', *Essays.*

lustres, the high-lights, at which he kindled his own thoughts. Books for him were, again, territories wherein he might find jumping-off places for the depths of himself; *his reading was for a touch of suggestion that might help to crystallize the thoughts that were floating within him;*[1] he had a *quick eye* for a phrase, epigram, or aphorism; pounced upon them, made them his own: they help *to make my top spin*, he said, and Cabot thinks that these discoveries were *all he cared to know of a book.*[2] A compatriot of Emerson's in our own time advertises a like method, seeking to establish from his reading *magnetic centres—live spots, which thrust out tentacles of association, and catch and draw to themselves their kind; for*, he says, there are few *joys in reading like the joy of the chase*, a joy which *comes largely through the action of these centres of association in your brain.*[3]

Keats believed[4] that *a man might pass a very pleasant life*, reading *on a certain day a certain Page of full Poesy or distilled Prose: let him wander with it*, he advises, *muse upon it, and reflect upon it, and bring home to it, and prophesy upon it, and dream upon it, until it becomes stale*, which will never be. For to a man of ripe intellect, *any one grand and spiritual passage* may serve as *a starting-post towards all 'the two-and-thirty Palaces'. 'Tis a happy voyage of conception, what delicious diligent Indolence! A doze upon a sofa does not hinder it, and a nap upon Clover engenders ethereal finger-pointings—the prattle of a child gives it wings, and the converse of middle-age a strength to beat them—a strain of music conducts to 'an old angle of the Isle', and when the leaves whisper it puts a girdle round the earth.* Nor is this *sparing touch of noble Books irreverent to their Writers*, for *the honours paid by Man to Man are trifles in comparison to the Benefit done by great Works to the 'Spirit and pulse' of good by their mere passive existence. Man should be content*, therefore, *with a few points to tip with the fine Web of his Soul, and weave a tapestry empyrean full of symbols for his spiritual eye, of softness for his spiritual touch, of space for his wandering, of distinctness for his luxury.* This is no other than what is enjoined as a duty by Emerson, in his Journal. His idea is this: Do not give us counters of base coin, but every word of real value, which must *warm* and *invite* the mind to desirable movement: *The essential mark of poetry is that it betrays in every word instant activity of mind;*[5] and Stevenson had the same idea when he declared that *in anything fit to be called by the name of reading, the process itself should be absorbing and voluptuous: we should gloat over a book, be rapt clean out of ourselves, and rise from the perusal, our mind filled with the busiest, kaleidoscopic dance of images.*[6]

I would apply the same test to all writing, which should be as a vehement flame-making fuel to consume the dross it meets in its way, so that

[1] Cabot, *Memoir of Emerson*. i, 291.   [2] *Ib*. i, 288–9.   [3] John Livingstone Lowes, *Of Reading Books*. 145.   [4] *Letters*. (Ed. Forman. 1895) 88.   [5] Cabot, *Memoir of Emerson*. i, 293.   [6] 'Gossip on Romance.'

it may warm and illuminate the rest. Whereunto may be added the wise testimony of Rabelais,[1] who stoutly recommended the dog-and-bone method to those of his disciples, and other *jolly fools*, who presumed to believe that his *Life of the Great Gargantua and Father Pantagruel* contained nothing but *jests, mockeries, lascivious discourse, and recreative lies*. In order to correct that impression he gives them a parable of a dog with a marrow-bone; *mark*, he says, with what devotion and *circumspectiveness he wards and watcheth it: with what care he keeps it: how fervently he holds it; how prudently he gobbets it: with what affection he breaks it: with what diligence he sucks it*. And all this labour to what end? What reapeth he? Nothing but a little marrow. But it is the marrow of his book Rabelais would have his disciples seek, and when he so much commends them to emulate a dog with a bone, I dare venture the opinion that he speaks for all good books and good readers, for what he advocates for his own books is equally sound for the rest. He is very frequent and confident in this particular: *It becomes you to be wise, to smell, feel and have in estimation, these fair, godly books, stuffed with high conceptions*; and further, you must, by a sedulous lecture, and frequent meditation, break *the bone and suck out the marrow*. In this allegorical sense and in these *Pythagorical Symbols* he proposes to lead his disciples to a well-advised and valiant reading of his own works, and so may all disciples of books and such jolly fools of ease and leisure who may adventure upon the art of reading, *find another kind of taste*, and be thus initiated into the most *glorious doctrines and dreadful mysteries*, for the marrow of a book is not less than these, but more.

IV. OF ASSIMILATION

It is more in this respect of assimilation that books feed soul as well as mind, for the two differ, as our modern science of psychology sets out. Long since it was acclaimed by James Howell[2] that *you must first assume and suck in the matter into your Apprehension*, thus making it your own, one with yourself, which must be retained by disputation (as the Greeks knew and practised), discourse (well known at all times), and meditation (as the monks of old knew and those older orders of Hindustan which are recorded and illustrated in the *Upanishads*, and especially the *Bhagavad-gítá*). Whether these be prophylactics or not in all cases, they are certainly preventatives of the *dyspepsias* common to those whom *sloth seduces* because they are too weak to bear

> The insupportable fatigue of thought,
> And swallowing, therefore, without pause or choice,
> The total grist unsifted, husks and all.[3]

[1] *Works*. Trans. Urquhart and Motteux. Prologue. Bohn Ed. i, 95.　[2] *Familiar Letters*. Tenth Ed. 205–6.　[3] Cowper, *The Task*. vi.

But this only by the way, for those who are chronically constipated by books are past cure: assimilation is essential. *It is not quantity so much that tells, as quality and thoroughness of digestion.*[1]

Literary matter must, therefore, *be well concocted,* Howell continues in the same place, *then it must be agglutinated, and converted to nutriment:* all this he reduces under two heads, *tenere fideliter,* and *uti faciliter,* two of the happiest properties in a student. Finally *good concoction* requires another act, *call'd the Act of Expulsion, which puts off all that is unsound and noxious:* such *expulsive virtue* is necessary because no science *but is full of such stuff* which by direction of the Tutor and the selection of good books *must be excern'd.* It is the same as Frederic Harrison argues,[2] that *to stuff our minds with what is simply trivial, simply curious,* or of *a low nutritive power,* is *to close our minds to what is solid and enlarging, and spiritually sustaining.* Jeremy Collier has a warning to the same end of books in general. *A man,* he says, *may as well expect to grow stronger by always eating, as wiser by always Reading. Too much overcharges Nature, and turns more into Disease than Nourishment. 'Tis Thought and Digestion which makes Books serviceable, and gives Health and Vigour to the Mind.*[3] Rabelais conjures the student not to confound himself with multiplicity of Authors, two being enough on any Science, *provided they be plenary and orthodox,* which some will consider parsimonious. Philosophy he orders for *substantial food,* and Poetry, *your banqueting stuff:* the former having more reality in it than any knowledge: the Philosopher being a wonder-worker, an engineer of the mind, an adventurer in high places who can *fathom the deep, measure Mountains, reach the Stars with a staff, and bless Heavens with a Girdle..*

The greater part of reputable opinion favours this slow and meditative method, yet there are two notable exceptions which I may give in a parenthesis, not as examples for procedure, but to indicate that special conditions require particular considerations. The first is that of Emily Eden,[4] who knew *almost by heart* Boswell's *Johnson,* the *Memoires de Retz, Shakespeare,* and a great part of the *Bible,* before she was eleven years of age, *so that there was not a thought left for* her to think upon manners or men, imagination or morals. Her *sentiments,* in later life, she took *by the lumps and in cwts.,* out of *Corinne* and Byron's *Poems;* consoling herself with the argument that since she never had thoughts of her own, and if she had they might have been *foolish thoughts,* it was as well to get a supply from reliable sources. The second is that of Charles Lamb. Undisturbed by the experiences of an *ingenious acquaintance* who gave up entertaining himself with the product of the brains of others, greatly to the *improvement of his originality,* he dedicated no inconsiderable amount of his own time to other

[1] Quiller-Couch, *Art of Reading.* 14.   [2] *Choice of Books.* 2.   [3] 'Of the Entertainment of Books', *Essays.* ii, 99.   [4] *Miss Eden's Letters.* 107–8.

people's thoughts, and boldly owned that he liked to dream away his life in others' speculations, to lose himself in other men's minds. *When I am not walking, I am reading*, he said; *I cannot sit and think. Books think for me.* He has no repugnances and few reservations. *Shaftesbury is not too genteel for me, nor Jonathan Wild too low. I can read anything which I call a book. I mean some day to attack Caryl on Job, some six folios.*[1]

Friedrich Nietzsche advises concentration, and fearlessly pushes the argument to its logical end, demanding the quantities small, an aphorism, a sentence, an axiom at a time, chewed over and over as a cow chews the cud. The books of the future will be aphoristic and readers masticators of thoughts and ideas. It was his ambition *to say in ten sentences what everyone else says in a whole book,—what everyone else does not say in a whole book; to create things on which time may try its teeth in vain*,[2] for *a good aphorism is too hard for the tooth of time;*[3] to practise *reading as an art*, the quality of *rumination* is essential: *it is necessary*, he says,[4] *to be a cow, and under no circumstances a modern man!* All of which was summed up by Horne Tooke when he said: *Read few books well; multum legere potius quam multa*, read much rather than many things; if they be hard books as well as good, which often happens, so much the better: *difficilia quae pulchra*; as one[5] said of *Tacitus, the second reading will please thee more than the first, the third more than the second.* All of which I would sum up in an injunction to *read between the lines*, for splendid as the surface is, in all great writing, there is more splendour in the deeps. But I could produce such arguments till dark night, so I pass on to the next phase, dropping the hint by the way that reading is not for all, it is not even for the majority who think themselves and would be thought readers. Pass them by. *No one who understands the real thing cares twopence about the dull student, except as a man and a brother. Drink with him, pray with him; don't read with him.*[6]

V. A DIGRESSION OF READING ALOUD

Many are those who have found in books the El Dorado of their dreams, treasure troves, Aladdin's caves, Ultima Thule, Havens of Rest, Utopias, Harbours of Refuge,

Ay, in the very temple of delight[7]

---

[1] 'Detached Thoughts on Books and Reading.'   [2] *Twilight of the Idols. Works.* xvi, iii.   [3] *Human, all-too-Human. Works.* vii, 83.   [4] *Genealogy of Morals. Works.* xiii, 13.   [5] 'A. B. To the Reader', in *The End of Nero*, etc. Tacitus, Histories, Bk. iv. Trans. Savile (1591)   [6] Sir Walter Raleigh, *Letters.* i, 265.   [7] Keats, 'Ode to Melancholy.'

they have their *sovran shrine*:

> A Book of Verses underneath the Bough,
> A Jug of Wine, a Loaf of Bread—and Thou
> Beside me singing in the Wilderness—
> Oh, Wilderness were Paradise enow![1]

What more delightful than to share our reading with a wise friend or *one better than wise being fair?*[2]

> There, obedient to her praying, did I read aloud the poems
> Made to Tuscan flutes, or instruments more various of our own;
> Read the pastoral parts of Spenser—or the subtle interflowings
> Found in Petrarch's sonnets—here's the book—the leaf is folded down.
>
> Or at times a modern volume,—Wordsworth's solemn-thoughted idyl,
> Howitt's ballad-verse, or Tennyson's enchanted reverie,—
> Or from Browning some 'Pomegranate', which, if cut deep down
>   the middle,
> Shows a heart within blood-tinctured, of a veined humanity.[3]

Thus read Paolo to Francesca:

> If thou art bent to know the primal root,
> From whence our love gat being, I will do
> As one who weeps and tells his tale. One day
> For our delight we read of Lancelot,
> How him love thrall'd. Alone we were, and no
> Suspicion near us. Ofttimes by that reading
> Our eyes were drawn together, and the hue
> Fled from our alter'd cheek. But at one point
> Alone we fell. When of that smile we read,
> The wished smile so rapturously kiss'd
> By one so deep in love, then he, who ne'er
> From me shall separate, at once my lips
> All trembling kiss'd. The book and writer both
> Were love's purveyors. In its leaves that day
> We read no more.[4]

Thus also Romeo to Juliet, Abelard to Héloïse, and thus have many other lovers *linked* themselves together with books.

Leigh Hunt's father *completed the conquest* of his mother's heart by reading *the poets and other Classics of England* to her *with his remarkably fine*

[1] *Rubaiyat of Omar Khayyam.* xi. FitzGerald.   [2] Sir William Watson 'Ode in May'.
[3] E. B. Browning, *Lady Geraldine's Courtship.*   [4] Dante, *Inferno.* Trans. Cary.
Canto v, 121–35.

74 THE ART OF READING

voice. which he modulated with great effect.[1] It was a custom he continued during his married life, when of an evening, *after brightening the fire and bringing in the coffee*, the poet's mother would listen with *satisfaction* whilst her husband read *Saurin and Barrow to her, with his fine voice and unequivocal enjoyment.*[2] Anne and Alexander Gilchrist, on their honeymoon, read joyously together such *improving* books as Carlyle's *John Sterling*, Herbert Spencer's *Social Studies*, Guizot's *Earth and Man*, Mariotti's *Italy in* 1848, and Mrs. Browning's *Casa Guidi Windows. The reward and crown of the day*, she says, is when her husband thus reads *earnest books* to her, she *working with the needle the while*;[3] and doubtless also we have another expression of love in the task imposed upon John Ruskin by his mother, who forced him to read the *Bible* aloud to her, *every syllable, hard names and all*, from *Genesis* to the *Apocalypse*, about once a year;[4] this faculty was acquired early by Stanley Baldwin, for by the time he was nine years of age he had read to an aunt the whole of *Guy Mannering, Ivanhoe, Red Gauntlet, Rob Roy, The Pirate*, and *Old Mortality*.[5]

What more delicious than Walter Pater's account of those exquisite boys, Marius and Flavian, reading together the *Golden Ass* of Apuleius in the old granary at *White Nights: the two lads were lounging together over a book, half-buried in a heap of dry corn, in an old granary—the quiet corner to which they had climbed out of the way of their noisier companions on one of their blandest holiday afternoons. They looked round: the western sun smote through the broad chinks of the shutters. How like a picture! and it was precisely the scene described in what they were reading, with just that added poetic touch in the book which made it delightful and select, and, in the actual place, the ray of sunlight transforming the rough grain among the cool brown shadows into heaps of gold. What they were intent on was, indeed, the book of books, the 'golden' book of that day, a gift to Flavian, as was shown by the purple writing on the handsome yellow wrapper, following the title. Flaviane! it said, Flaviane! lege feliciter!⌐ Flaviane! Vivas! Floreas! Flaviane! Vivas! Gaudeas! It was perfumed with oil of sandal-wood, and decorated with carved and gilt ivory bosses at the ends of the roller.*[6]

Such instances may be repeated from real life, as when Wordsworth *with a dear friend* walked early, *while the morning light was yellowing the hill tops*,

> By the still borders of the misty lake,
> Repeating favourite verses with one voice,
> Or conning more, as happy as the birds
> That round us chaunted.[7]

[1] Leigh Hunt, *Autobiography*. World's Classics. 20.   [2] *Ib.* 31.   [3] A. Gilchrist, *Life and Writings.* 36.   [4] *Fors Clavigera.*   [5] 'Books', *Our Inheritance.* 286.   [6] *Marius the Epicurean.* i, 40.   [7] Wordsworth, *Prelude.* v, 560–63.

Shelley read the whole of *English Bards and Scotch Reviewers*, and *all the notes*, with *fervid and exulting energy*, to Hogg, in the country outside London, whither they had walked after buying the book, then newly published, at a bookseller's in Oxford Street.[1] Swinburne and Meredith enjoyed FitzGerald's *Omar* for the first time, lying together on a *heathery knoll* on Box Hill in Surrey, *reading a stanza alternately, indifferent to the dinner bell, until a prolonged summons reminded* them of *appetite*.[2]

Nor are companions or any human audience always necessary, for there is joy in reading aloud for one's own ears, or for the benefit of those natural objects which are as near and often as dear to us as our own kind, as when the youthful Heine, in the Palace Garden of Düsseldorf, still unpractised in reading, pronounced every word of his favourite *Don Quixote* aloud, so that birds and trees, streams and flowers were able to hear everything;[3] or, more fantastically, when Luke Bird would go of a summer's evening to a little mound *that in May was always covered with cowslips*, with William Law's *Serious Call to a Devout and Holy Life* for company. *Mr.Mumby's herd of cows would feed about him*, says my authority,[4] *and sometimes a gentle beast would wander near to him and gaze at him with eyes of affection, and Luke would open his book and inform the creature what heaven was like: and read to it aloud a few pages in a mild manner*. Shelley read aloud on all occasions, with or without audience. *Gebir* was an early obsession: *he would read it aloud, or to himself sometimes, with a tiresome pertinacity*, which once so enraged Hogg that he snatched the book from him and threw it out of the window.[5]

Yet in the face of all this evidence of delight there are some few would have it that *books are not written to be read aloud* (this was asserted by Théophile Gautier), but they need not delay our argument, as so many writers of books refute them by their practice, delighting not only to read their own works but those of others to any willing listeners. Reading aloud needs no defence. There are some even who hold it to be the best way to explore the inwardness of certain works in theology and poetry. Profiat Duran advised Jewish students in the Middle Ages to read with both *eye and ear, read aloud*, he said, *do not work in silent poring*;[6] and there are living authorities who would have us catch the rhythm of poetry by the same practice. The Greek for reading means, Lang reminds us, *reading aloud*.[7] *Homer* was read in public places by the Rhapsodists, who wore a blue gown when they recited the *Odyssey* and a red one for the *Iliad*.[8] The

[1] T. J. Hogg, *Shelley*. London Library Ed. 179. This was Shelley's introduction to Byron.   [2] George Meredith, Ellis. 135.   [3] *Memoirs*, Ed. Gustav Karpeles, Trans. Cannan. i, 59.   [4] T. F. Powys, *Mr. Weston's Good Wine*. 186–7.   [5] Hogg, *Shelley*. London Library Ed. 127.   [6] Qt. Abrahams, *Jewish Life in the Middle Ages*. 355. [7] Intro. *Pleasures of Bookland*. Shaylor, xiv.   [8] Cuperus, *Apotheosis*, in Evelyn, *Memoirs*. ii, 265.

Romans so valued the method that their literary works were first read aloud, with a view to selling them, and readings were a recognised form of entertainment at many Greek and Roman feasts. It is not required of me that I should do more than name the reading of scriptures and other pious works which is common to all religions both in public and private, for these exercises of the art, whether enjoyable or not, are ceremonial rather than indulgent.

Pliny made reading aloud one of the regular means of entertaining his guests, on whom he often tried his own works. On one occasion he thus read for *two days successively*, and he held that *to be so confident of your friends' affection that you feel no dread of wearying them, is a sure indication of your own.*[1] In the ancient monasteries, says Merryweather,[2] books were read aloud to the brothers at mealtimes, or to the whole community when otherwise met together, and by this means a genuine communalisation of literature was accomplished. Sir Thomas More introduced the custom into his own home at Chelsea: *He used to have one read daily at his table, which, being ended, he would ask of some of them how they understood such and such a place, and so there grew a friendly communication, recreating all men that were present with some jest or other.*[3] King Alfred the Great was read to by his secretaries at all times, day and night, whenever he had respite from other occupations.

If more evidence from times past is demanded, read it in *Rabelais*,[4] where Grangousier orders Ponocrates to instruct his son, Gargantua, in a diversity of learning at all times of the day and during all functions. Thus was read unto him, at four o'clock in the morning, some chapter of the Holy Scripture, *whilst they were in rubbing of him*; at dinner *there was read some pleasant history of the war-like actions of former times, until he had taken a glass of wine.* Then: *if they thought good, they continued reading*, or held discourse together upon the virtue, propriety, efficacy and nature of all things served at the table: bread, wine, water, salt, fleshes, fishes, fruits, herbs, roots, and of their dressing, substantiating their arguments with learned passages from *Pliny, Athenaeus, Dioscorides, Heliodorus, Aristotle, Aelian*, and others, and in order to be more certain they caused the books of these authors to be brought to the table. Then he betook himself to athletics, running, riding, bathing, tilting, etc., climbing up trees like a squirrel and pulling down great boughs *like another Milo*, running up and down a wall like a rat (by the aid of two well-steeled daggers and two bodkins), casting the dart, throwing the bar, putting the stone, practising the javelin, the boar-spear, and the halbert; afterwards rubbing down, supper, and recapitulation of all he had heard read to him, in the manner

---

[1] *Letters*, Melmoth. Loeb. Ed. viii, 21.   [2] *Bibliomania in the Middle Ages*. 12.   [3] *Life*, Cresacre More. Ed. Hunter. 103–4.   [4] Book I, Chap. xxiii.

of the Pythagoreans, and so to bed, giving thanks to the Creator for His bounty, in which the praise of books and of reading aloud might properly have been included, of which, however, mine author says nothing.

In modern times the practice still has many devotees. Tennyson would entertain his friends by reading to them his own poems, particularly 'Maud', *in the deep melodious thunder of his voice . . . rather murmuring than mouthing, like the sound of a far sea or of a pine wood.*[1] On the 27th September, 1855, he read this poem to a small party at the Brownings'. Robert and Elizabeth were there, and Dante Gabriel Rossetti, who then made his famous sketch of the Laureate as he read with book close to eyes. *One of the pleasantest things which have happened to us here,* Mrs. Browning tells Mrs. Mitford, *is the coming down to us of the Laureate,* from Freshwater; he *dined with us, smoked with us, opened his heart to us (and the second bottle of port), and ended by reading 'Maud' through from end to end, and going away at half-past two in the morning. If I had a heart to spare,* she confesses, *certainly he would have had mine. He is captivating with his frankness, confidingness, and unexampled naïveté! Think of his stopping in 'Maud' every now and then— 'There's a wonderful touch! That's very tender! How beautiful that is!'* Yes, and it was *wonderful,* tender, beautiful, and he read *exquisitely in a voice like an organ, rather music than speech.*[2] Writers of books have ever indulged themselves by reading their manuscripts and printed works to select friends; instances are innumerable, but I will do no more than cite one or two, that of Thoreau reading parts of his newly-written *Week on the Concord* to Emerson seated *under an oak on the river bank,* when the listener was *invigorated* by the new work;[3] and that in which Blades went down to Cambridge to read his *Life of Caxton* to the University Librarian Bradshaw. *It was a fine warm afternoon, and after dinner—they dined earlier in those days—they went down, as Bradshaw was fond of doing, into the college garden. A bottle of wine was ordered out, and there and then, without moving from the place, Mr. Blades read the whole of the historical portion of the book to his willing listener, who frequently interposed criticisms and suggestions of the most useful kind.*[4] And I doubt not that writers enjoy (sometimes) hearing their own works read to them, as Dr. Johnson must have done on that occasion when his poem, *London,* was produced by Boswell during a jaunt to Greenwich, who read aloud *with enthusiasm* the lines on that *favourite scene.*[5]

Henry Crabb Robinson journeyed from London to Witham for the pleasure of reading *The Excursion* (then a new book) to Mrs. W. Pattison, to whom he also read the reviews of the poem in the *Eclectic* and the *Edin-*

---

[1] Hallam, Lord Tennyson, *Tennyson, A Memoir.* i, 202 and 194.   [2] *Letters.*
[3] Cabot, *Memoir of Emerson,* i, 284.   [4] Prothero, *Memoir of Bradshaw.* 73-4.
[5] *Life,* i, 460.

burgh;[1] Robert Southey counselled Grosvenor Bedford not only to buy Wordsworth's *Lyrical Ballads* but to read *aloud* the poems entitled *The Brothers* and *Michael*,[2] presumably to himself, for so also may the true flavour of poems be tested. Charles Dickens, on the other hand, wore himself out reading his novels to vast audiences; he told Miss Hogarth (in a letter from Dublin, 25.8.1858) that *everybody* was at *Little Dombey*, so great the crowd that people had to be *shaken into their seats; we could stay here a week with that one reading, and fill the place every night*; but more like a theatrical performance, this, than a reading.

Not so those quiet hours Dorothy Wordsworth devoted to reading to her brother, the poet, as on that occasion when he was tired out with working at his poem *The Pedlar*; they *made up a good fire after dinner, and William brought his mattress out, and lay down upon the floor*, and she read the *Life of Ben Jonson* to him;[3] or Mrs. Boyle's reading of *Tom Brown's Schooldays* to Barberina, Lady Grey;[4] or Lady Louisa Stuart reading *Coleridge* at Richmond to her family, or *Ivanhoe: they are making me read 'Ivanhoe' to them in the evening; in my mind few books gain so much as those* (meaning the *Waverley Novels*) *by being read aloud*; and Miss Berry (Horace Walpole's friend) was equally happy reading aloud or being read to by others; she entertained her friends with such diverse works as *Marmion*, Gell's *Ithaca*, and *Mr. Fox's Historical Works, in the beautiful large-paper copy which Robert Ferguson had given her*; and Lord Rosslyn read *Lara, Lord Byron's new tale*, on 20th August, 1814, and on an evening in the same year she heard the poet Campbell read a discourse on English poetry at Madame de Stael's.[5]

Reading aloud in the old days was one of the methods by which the tedium of long winters was combated. Madame de Sévigné was never happier than when her son Charles helped to while away the long evenings at Les Rochers by reading aloud some comedy of Molière's, or some pamphlet of Pascal's, or the latest books from Paris.[6] Miss Catherine Talbot writes, from Cuddesden, to her friend the 'learned' Mrs. Elizabeth Carter, that they have *happily fixed in a scheme of reading through all Sir Richard Steele's papers*, which would last them as long as they stayed in the country, and although they were familiar with these works, *this orderly and sociable way of reading gives novelty to them*; they were read thus every day *after breakfast and supper, ten o'clock is the hour that generally concludes them at both those times*;[7] she read Dr. Young's *Night Thoughts* to her aunt,[8] when *Clarissa* appeared she and her family *lived quite happy the whole* time they were reading it, and by reading only *en famille*, they made that time last as

[1] *Diary*. i, 245.   [2] *Letters*. (World's Classics) 48.   [3] *Journals of Dorothy Wordsworth*. 89.   [4] *A Family Chronicle*. 292.   [5] *Miss Berry's Journal*. Lewis. [6] *Letters*. i, xxxiii.   [7] Mrs. Elizabeth Carter, *Letters*. Pennington. i, 33.   [8] *Ib*. 217.

long as they could, reading at *set hours* and the rest of the day talking of it[1].
Mrs. Hemans had *the delightful talent of reading aloud well*, for the entertainment of her family circle, and *she could continue this even as she walked*.[2]
Mark Pattison records[3] that his father, *who read well, and liked doing so*,
took *Paradise Lost* one winter for his family reading. Reading aloud was
practised in the family of the poet, William Allingham, who remembers
how his Aunt Maryanne, a *voracious novel-reader*, would read the *Waverley
Novels* on a winter's evening at Ballyshannon: *my Grandmother in her arm-
chair by the fire, with close cap, knitting incessantly, her snuff-box on a little
table, an old cat called 'Norway' snoozing on the hearthrug and sometimes jumping into her lap; Aunt Bess also knitting, grave and silent*; and himself
with paper and pencil, drawing, and listening to the story at the same
time.[4]

Sir John Herschel records how the blacksmith of a certain village would
sit on his anvil of an evening reading *Pamela* to the villagers, and that when
*the happy turn of fortune arrived, which brings the hero and heroine together, and
sets them living long and happily according to the most approved rules, the congregation were so delighted as to raise a great shout, and procuring the church keys,
actually set the parish bells ringing*. Friedrich Nietzsche would read to his
sister and their intimate friends; once he read scenes from *Faust* to a party
of twelve friends on the summit of Mt. Brè, above the lake of Lugano,
*while our eyes wandered over the magnificent spring landscape, and grew intoxi-
cated with the overflowing riches of the world*;[5] Henry Bradshaw was devoted
to *Tennyson* during his Eton days, and when a new volume came out he
would take it home with him on his holidays and *read it aloud to his sisters*;[6]
and he liked to read *Dickens* to his friends at Cambridge;[7] Edward Fitz-
Gerald's sisters read Lyell's *Geology* to him of an evening, when he was a
young man, and when he was old and his sight growing dim, he would
hire a village boy to read to him every evening, who stumbled at *every
third word*, and got tired, so that he had to be renovated with cake and
sweet wine.[8] Another instance of youth reading to their elders is that of
Archdeacon Groome, who, as *a very small boy, read 'Gil Blas' to the cook
Lois Dowsing, and the sweetheart she never married, a strapping sergeant of the
Guards, who had fought at Waterloo*.[9] Tolstoy *read aloud very well*, and would
often read *something he had just written* to his family, or *something from the
works of other writers*.[10] I could go on adding to my instances without augmenting my thesis, that reading aloud is a proper practice, and on this
account 'tis as clear and reasonable in itself as solitary and silent reading;

---

[1] *Ib.* 204.   [2] *Memorials of Mrs. Hemans.* Chorley. i, 13.   [3] *Memoirs.* 11.   [4] *William
Allingham, A Diary.* 27.   [5] Frau Forster-Nietzsche, *The Young Nietzsche.* 245.
[6] Prothero, *Memoir of Bradshaw.* 14.   [7] *Ib.* 114.   [8] *Letters and Literary Remains.*
i, 40, 320.   [9] Francis Hindes Groom, *Two Suffolk Friends.* 12.   [10] *Life.* Maude.i, 361.

and those that speak other things about it seem to me to talk at random, and perfectly without book.

There are no written laws for this gentle and sociable art, but some that are unwritten and proper to be observed; the most acceptable being that which draws us towards reading which is unaffected and unposed. Choice of matter must also be considered, but here individual taste must remain the only reliable law-giver. Charles Lamb gives out that some poets, *Milton* and *Shakespeare* for instance, demand reading aloud *to yourself, or (as it chances) to some single person listening: more than one*, he adds, *and it degenerates into an audience*; but books of *quick interest, that hurry on for incidents*, such as novels, even of the better sort, are for the eye to slide over, not the voice, and *a newspaper read out is intolerable*.[1] Each one of his strictures could be hotly contested and his tastes are opposed by many examples in this digression. I shall not add further differences, for such problems settle themselves; but if the matter of choice is free, the manner is fixed. It will be unadorned by any pose or pretence. In reading aloud you are greatly privileged, first to consort with all that is noble and beautiful in thought and imagination, and then to give it forth again. You adventure among masterpieces and spread the news of your discoveries. No news better worth the spreading; few things better worth sharing, for its loveliness endureth for ever. But you must read with reverence, for you are the interpreter of genius; you add your mind to his; your vision to his; your voice to his: you become spokesman for him and intermediary. *The art*, said Dr. Johnson, *is to read strong, though low*.[2] Let, therefore, no voice of brass, insolence of mind, or arrogance of heart, cheapen or impede this traffic. Let your reading aloud be good talk, and shun elocution and histrionics as you would the plague.

[1] 'Detached Thoughts on Books and Reading.'   [2] *Life*. iv, 207.

Part V

·OF BOOKFELLOWSHIP

I. THEY ARE THE BEST COMPANY

The possession of no good can be wholly delightful without a companion: *Fellowship is life, lack of fellowship is death;*[1] and to all those who dote for select company, books are propitious, because they are friends whom we can associate with our *choicest thoughts.*[2] There are three kinds of companions, Sir John Davys claims (after a French writer): *men, women and books*, and the greatest of these is books, as the poet maintains,

> the women we deem that he chose for their looks,
> And the men for their cellars: the books were his friends:
> 'Man delights me not', often, 'nor woman', but books
> Are the best of good comrades in loneliest nooks.[3]

F. D. Maurice holds that the best books are friends and the best use of books to discover their friendship. The origin of every book that *is* a book is a man of genius who wants to share his genius with a reader: *he may be writing about a great many things*; but it is *a man who writes; and when you get acquainted with that man, you get acquainted with the book*, and, as he follow, it, the work is then no more *a collection of letters and leaves*, it is *a friend;*[4] and not only a friend but a rare friend, for, said Dr. Johnson,[5] *the best part of every author is in general to be found in his* book:

> This, Cicero, is thy heart;
> I hear it beating through each purple line.
> This is thyself, Anacreon—yet thou art
> Wreathed, as in Athens, with the Cnidian vine.
> I ope thy pages, Milton, and, behold,
> Thy spirit meets me in the haunted ground! . . .
> These *are* yourselves—your life of life! The Wise

---

[1] William Morris, *Dream of John Ball.* 29.   [2] Thoreau, *Week on the Concord.* Scott Lib. 240.   [3] Andrew Lang, in Gleeson White's *Book-Song.* 63.   [4] F. D. Maurice, *Friendship of Books.* 3.   [5] *Johnsonian Miscellanies.* Hill. ii, 310.

81

(Minstrel or Sage) *out* of their books are clay; . . .
Angels—that, side by side, upon our way,
Walk with and warn us.[1]

This sense of companionship which we receive from our love of books
is common to all bibliophiles. It is cousin-german to bibliomania, a concomitant condition, goes hand in hand with it, and is, by the testimony of
all bookfolk, cause and symptom both; but it is here set forth as a condition of book-love in its essence, as love of letters, their companionship,
friendliness, power to succour and console in solitude, either enforced or
voluntary.

Enforced solitariness is commonly seen in Monks, Friars, Anchorites,
that by their order and course of life must abandon all company, society
of other men, and betake themselves to a private cell. Monastic life com-
pels them, as Merryweather points out,[2] to *seek the sweet yet silent companionship* of friendly books, the willing companions *of everyone doomed to
lonely hours and dismal solitude*:

> I envy them, those monks of old;
> Their books they read, and their beads they told.[3]

Students in voluntary exile joyously apostrophise books, with Richard de
Bury, as celestial gifts of divine liberality, *descending from the Father of Light
to raise up the rational soul even to heaven!*[4] Such are those, some of them,
who *find shelter among books*.[5] I include also among them the sick of body
or soul, which I have dilated upon; but all, whether the companionship be
cause or effect, enforced or voluntary, come to love books for themselves,
they translate them by affection, and by a genial animism make them more
real, more alive than any other corporeal thing, entering into themselves,
becoming by the alchemy of association at one with their dearest intimacies. *If I were blind*, said Sylvestre de Sacy, *I would still take pleasure in
holding a beautiful book*:

> But whether it be worth or looks
> We gently love or strongly,
> Such virtue doth reside in books
> We scarce can love them wrongly.[6]

No better acquaintances, no truer friends, and *like living friends they have
their voices and physiognomies*.[7] Nothing in the world so accessible, so eager
for friendship. *They advise us and talk with us and treat us with a bright and*

[1] Bulwer Lytton, Qt. *Book-Lovers' Anthology*. 23.   [2] *Bibliomania in the Middle
Ages*. 9.   [3] G. P. R. James, *The Monks of Old*. [4] *Philobiblon*. Chap. 1. [5] Charles
Lamb, 'Poor Relations', *Last Essays of Elia*.   [6] Cosmo Monkhouse, 'De Libris',
in *Book-Song*. 91.   [7] A. Bronson Alcott, *Concord Days*.

witty familiarity; nor does each ingratiate itself by its own merit alone but suggests the names of more, one introduces Petrarch to *Marcus Varro, De Officiis* sends him to *Ennius*, and the *Tusculan Disputations* imbues him with a love of *Terence*, and fourteen more like instances, for he regarded books not as *musty parchments*, but as friends with whom, saith Tatham,[1] he could *freely converse under his own roof*; they were *men, not shadows*; books were no mere *storehouses of words and facts*, but the embodiment of *living writers*. So, nearer our time, Madame de Sévigné was reincarnate out of her *Letters* for Edward FitzGerald, the *companion* of his old age: *quite alive in the Room with him*;[2] he is astonished to find that when he looks into *Shakespeare* it is *not a Book, but People*, he says,[3] *talking all round me*; and Dr. Furnivall *lived on terms of personal friendship* with *Chaucer*.[4] They are thus our very familiars, we are on the best of terms with them, we enter into their lives and occupations,

> With Wordsworth paddle Rydal Mere,
> Taste rugged Elliott's home-brewed beer,
> And with the ears of Rogers at fourscore,
> Hear Garrick's buskined tread and Walpole's wit
> once more.[5]

Many know the characters in *Shakespeare, Sterne, Dickens* and *Thackeray* better than their own near friends. The people of Jane Austen's novels, the Dashwoods and Bennets, the Bertrams and Woodhouses, the Thorpes and Musgroves, *have been admitted as familiar guests to the firesides of many families*, where they are known *as individually and intimately as if they were living neighbours*.[6]

Even when they have served their turn as *tools* they remain *companions*. Sir Edmund Gosse looked upon his library as *the workshop* as well as the *playground of a man of letters; these books*, he says, *have been my tools and are still my companions*.[7] Mark Rutherford advised his friend Mrs. Colenutt to buy Ibsen's *Rosmersholm* and *keep it as a companion*.[8] To meet with the *Meditations* of Marcus Aurelius, Robert Louis Stevenson testifies,[9] is to touch a *royal hand*, to look into *brave eyes*, to make *a noble friend. Learned authors*, Joseph Hall attests in his *Letter* to Lord Denny, are the *most harmless*, the *sweetest companions*, a scholar lives in *Heaven*, for in one small room he can converse with *all the glorious martyrs and fathers*, can single out at pleasure *sententious Tertullian, or grave Cyprian, or resolute Hierome, or flowing Chrysostome, or divine Ambrose, or devout Bernard, or (who alone is all*

---

[1] *Francesco Petrarca*. ii, 36.　　[2] *Letters and Literary Remains*. i, 383.　　[3] *More Letters*. 53–4.　　[4] Alois Brandl, in Monro, *F. J. Furnivall*. 11.　　[5] Whittier, 'A Magnate in the Realm of Books'.　　[6] *Memoir of Jane Austen*, Austen-Leigh. 2.　　[7] *The Library of Edmund Gosse*. Cox. xxii.　　[8] *Letters to Three Friends*. 48.　　[9] 'The Influence of Books', *Art of Writing*. 84.

these) heavenly Augustine, talk with them, hear their wise and holy counsels, verdicts, resolutions, *yea,* he saith, *(to rise higher) with courtly Esau, learned Paul, all their fellow-prophets, apostles; yet more, like another Moses,* to talk with God Himself; and if there be any that think this riding too high, they may rise with Barry Cornwall as high at least as the angelic hosts, when he called his books *angels and seraphim;*[1] to both of which I have brought support already in my first chapter, for many bibliophiles are, and have been, of the same mind, particularly in those times when it was the height of appreciation to attribute all good things to the inspiration of God and His Angels, and if this which I have said will not suffice, see more in the *Philobiblon* of our devout Richard de Bury, Bishop of Durham, or William Ellery Channing, who pines for no other intellectual companionship, if, he says, *Milton will cross my threshold to sing to me of Paradise; and Shakespeare open to me the world of imagination and the workings of the human heart; and Franklin enrich me with his practical wisdom.*[2]

II. CONVERSING WITH BOOKS

When Oliver Goldsmith read an excellent book it was as if he had *gained a new friend,* and when he read a book over again it was like *meeting with an old one;*[3] *Béranger* and Eugene Field were *old cronies;*[4] *a pocket edition of Plato, of Plutarch, of Euripides, or of the Septuagint, was* Shelley's *ordinary companion.*[5] They are indeed *silent, eloquent companions;*[6] and, as in the poet, all the better for being

> Friends, not adopted with a schoolboy's haste,
> But chosen with a nice discerning taste.[7]

Bookmen would be inseparable from their books: *Walter Scott* was Cory's *lost childhood, his first great friend: I long for him,* he said,[8] *and hate the death that parts us.* Petrarch was desolate when removed from his comrade-books. Once this was brought about through the intervention of his friend Philippe de Cabassoles, Bishop of Cavaillon, who thought the poet was destroying his health by over-study; but it was a mistaken treatment, for Petrarch was immediately still more seriously distressed. The first day of absence from his books passed wearily, *seeming longer than a year*; on the second he had *a headache from morning till night,* and on the third he began to feel *symptoms of fever*; the good Bishop thereupon restored the keys to the book-room and Petrarch on the instant recovered.[9]

[1] *Autobiographical Fragment.*   [2] Qt. Richardson, *Choice of Books.* 20.   [3] *Citizen of the World.* lxxv.   [4] Eugene Field, *Love Affairs of a Bibliomaniac.* 103.   [5] Hogg, *Shelley.* London Lib. Ed. 84.   [6] Washington Irving, Qt. *Book-Lover's Enchiridion.* 196.   [7] Cowper, *Retirement.*   [8] *Letters and Journals.* 223   [9] Tatham, *Francesco Petrarca.* i, 362–77.

Many have given out that one of the precious qualities of this companionship is that it is silent; but there is as much evidence that, though silent, books are not dumb, that they hail their lovers and are ever ready to talk with them. Of an evening Machiavelli would go into his study and thus pass into *the antique courts of ancient men* to be *welcomed lovingly by them*. Such tender greeting encouraged him to speak with them without show, to learn the history and the motive of their lives, and these dead responded by reason of a common humanity; *for hours together*, he adds, *the miseries of life no longer annoy me, for I have transferred myself to those with whom I converse*.[1] Petrarch also, Tatham gives out,[2] loved to converse with his books: Cicero, Seneca and Augustine were *individuals in whom he discerned the reflection of his own personality*, and, as he read their works, *he held long and animated dialogues with them*, which he sometimes recorded on the margins of his books, and sometimes he talked to them in elaborate epistles, as in his *Letters to Dead Authors*. So also, as John Fletcher relates it, *the place that does contain my books, the best companions, is to me a glorious court*, wherein he *conversed* with the sages and philosophers of olden days; for Robert Southey,

> My never-failing friends are they,
> With whom I converse day by day;[3]

Cowley advertises that this is *the best and noblest conversation*;[4] and when old age comes, books are still willing to talk with us: *I have one more reason for reading*, said Dr. Johnson, *that Time has, by taking away my companions, left me less opportunity for conversation*;[5] thus our greatest talker found peace, when he could no longer talk with his mortal peers.

III. FRIENDS THAT CHANGE NOT YET ARE EVER NEW

Petrarch found[6] books friends whose society was *always delightful*; they are of all ages and countries, distinguished in affairs, in sciences, knowledge, easy to live with, they come at our call and retire when we desire them; *no distracting element about a book: leave it alone and it will leave you alone*.[7] Books are never out of humour; never envious or jealous; they answer all questions with readiness; they reveal the secrets of Nature, the events of the past; they teach us how to live and how to die; they dispel melancholy by their mirth, and amuse by their wit; they prepare the soul to suffer everything and desire nothing; they introduce us to ourselves; they uphold

---

[1] *Opere di Machiavelli*. 1813. v, 8.   [2] *Francesco Petrarca*. ii, 238.   [3] 'My days among the dead are passed.'   [4] *Pindaric Ode*.   [5] Croker's *Boswell*. 727. Qt. Hill. *Life*. iv. *n*. 218.   [6] Verse Letter to Bishop of Lopez. Qt. Tatham, *Francesco Petrarca*. ii, 67.   [7] F. Madan, *Ideal Bodleian*. 33.

the downcast, and restrain the conceited by warning that days are swift and life short; and all they ask in return is a quiet corner where they may be safe from the attacks of their enemies. *To divert at any time a troublesome fancy*, Fuller advises, *run to thy books; they always receive thee with the same kindness*.[1]

Pliny[2] also found his joy and solace in books, *no gladness they cannot increase, no sorrow they cannot lessen*; he flew to them as the *sole alleviators of his fears*: they helped him to understand his troubles better, his fears to bear more patiently; and Montaigne, in his *Tower of Learning*, is tranquilly disposed towards them, as all know: *commerce of Books* everywhere assisted him: *it comforts me in age, and solaceth me in solitariness: it easeth me of the burden of wearysome sloth: and at all times rids me of tedious companies*.[3]

> But what strange art, what magic can dispose
> The troubled mind to change its native woes?
> Or lead us willing from ourselves, to see
> Others more wretched, more undone than we?
> This, books can do; nor this alone; they give
> New views to life, and teach us how to live;
> They soothe the griev'd, the stubborn they chastise,
> Fools they admonish and confirm the wise:
> Their aid they yield to all; they never shun
> The man of sorrow, nor the wretch undone:
> Unlike the hard, the selfish, and the proud,
> They fly not sullen from the suppliant crowd;
> Nor tell to various people various things,
> But show to subjects what they show to kings.[4]

When Laurence Sterne's neighbours thought him alone he was *in company with more than five hundred mutes—each of whom, at my pleasure, communicates his ideas to me by dumb signs—quite as intelligibly as any person living can do by uttering words*; they keep their distance as he directs, or come to him when he pleases; he handles fifty of them in an evening as he likes, they never complain of ill-usage, and take no offence when dismissed, *though ever so abruptly*; such *convenience*, he maintains, *is not to be enjoyed—no such liberty to be taken—with the living*.[5] Jeremy Collier confirms this in a memorable essay,[6] where he argues that in *conversing with Books* we may not only choose our company but *disengage without Ceremony or Exception*, and further, we are free from the *Formalities of Custom and Respect*, we *need not undergo the Penance of a dull Story from a Fop of Figure*; but may *shake off*

[1] 'Of Books.' *The Holy State*.   [2] *Letters*. viii, 19.   [3] *Essays*. Ed. Seccombe. iii, 52. [4] Crabbe, *The Library*.   [5] *Works*. (1819) iv, 45.   [6] 'Of the Entertainment of Books', *Essays*. ii, 98.

the Haughty, the Impertinent, and the Vain, at Pleasure. Besides all this, *Authors, like Women, commonly Dress when they make a visit.* They polish up their thoughts *and exert the Force of their Understandings* out of *Respect to themselves,* far more than they would in *ordinary Conversation,* thus giving the reader the *Spirit* and *Essence* in *a narrow Compass,* which was *drawn off from a much larger Proportion of Time, Labour, and Expence.* He is *like an Heir: born rather than made Rich,* inheriting *a Stock of Sense, with little or no trouble of his own.*

Well may the poet[1] boast,

> All round the room my silent servants wait,
> My friends in every season;

and well may another claim that they are *the most mannerly of companions, accessible at all times, in all moods, frankly declaring the author's mind, without offence.*[2] We have now less cause to wonder that Charles Lamb's poor student *found shelter among books, which insult not; and studies, that ask no questions of a youth's finances.*[3] It is this coyness, this well-mannered diffidence, which makes them supreme for companionship, for they are as guiltless of a desire to obtrude as they are insensitive to neglect. Emerson *lived among his books and was never comfortable away from them, yet,* says Cabot,[4] *they did not much enter into his life; they were pleasant companions, but not counsellors—hardly even intimates*; but his books were not chagrined, they were content to serve and wait for an intimacy, and remain still faithful if it never came:

> A good book is a friend; the best of friends,
> That cannot be estranged or take offence
> Howe'er neglected, but returns at will
> With the old friendship.[5]

To *this warm and undying feeling of the friendliness of books,*[6] I could go on multiplying tributes *ad infinitum,* but will do no more than give you a handful of commendations gathered from various reliable authorities in support of this pleasant theme: books are *the best solitary company in the world;*[7] *cheering and soothing companions in solitude, illness and affliction;*[8] *he that loveth a book will never want a faithful friend;*[9] *they wind into the heart;*[10] they are *sweet unreproaching companions to the miserable;*[11] and *when all that is worldly turns to dross around us, these only retain their steady value*; when

[1] Barry Cornwall, *Autobiographical Fragment.*   [2] A .Bronson Alcott, *Concord Days.*
[3] 'Poor Relations', *Last Essays of Elia.*   [4] *Memoir of Emerson.* i, 292.   [5] W. J.
Linton, in *Book-Song.* 80.   [6] Richardson, *Choice of Books.* 17.   [7] Sir W. Waller,
Divine Meditations.   [8] W. E. Channing, *Self-Culture.*   [9] Isaac Barrow, *On Industry.*
[10] Hazlitt, *Lectures on Dramatic Literature.*   [11] Goldsmith, *Vicar of Wakefield.*

friends grow cold, books *only continue the unaltered countenance of happier days,* cheer with *true friendship,* which never *deceived hope nor deserted sorrow;*[1] for they *nourish youth; delight old age; adorn prosperity; afford a refuge and solace in adversity; forming our delights at home; anything but hindrances abroad; they are our nightly associates; our indoor and out-of-door companions.*[2]

The best of them all, and most rational, have said in this kind; but neither he, they, nor any one of them, gives his reader, to my judgement, that satisfaction which he ought, unless he claims, as Andrew Lang does,[3] that *a book is a friend whose face is constantly changing,* but ever remaining a friend, and all the more because the change is in us, to whom the book is a mirror, reflecting our moods, hopes, joys, and sorrows, *dies diem docet,* one day teacheth another, and books are the friendly legionaries in this great advance; it is every man as he likes; so many men, so many minds; so many days, so many moods, and by the help of books, all tending to good purpose, though each is different, after its own manner.

It will be a great delight to him *in the next world,* Robert Southey confesses, to revisit his books among the lakes of Cumberland, *and to tell them what excellent company* he found them, for *I exist more among the dead than the living, and think more about them, perhaps feel more about them. Coleridge is gone to Devonshire,* he tells G. C. Bedford, *and I was going to say I am alone, but the sight of Shakespeare, and Spenser, Milton, and the Bible, on my table, and Castanheda, and Barros, and Osorio at my elbow, tell me I am in the best of all possible company. What were days without such fellowship?* asks A. B. Alcott, and he answers that we are *alone in the world without it.*[4]

Ye dear companions of my silent hours;[5]

I call myself a solitary, but sometimes I think I misapply the term. No man sees more company than I do. I travel with mightier cohorts around me than ever did Timour or Genghis Khan on their fiery marches.[6]

There is room for all; those who know and enjoy the companionship of the patricians of intellect and imagination by conversation with them and those who know by outward contact, for many are joyful merely in rubbing shoulders with nobility, but

While you converse with lords and dukes,
I have their betters here—my books.[7]

Others are fain not only to be in the great tradition, but to be of it by right of possession, as Frederick Locker when he confessed, *I seem to be*

[1] Washington Irving, *The Sketch Book.*   [2] Cicero, *Pro Archia.* Qt. Dibdin, *Reminiscences.* ii, 957.   [3] *The Library.* Second Ed. 15.   [4] *Tablets.* Qt. *Book-Lovers' Anthology.* 6.   [5] Leigh Hunt.   [6] Alexander Smith, *Dreamthorp.* 249.   [7] Thomas Sheridan.

*nearer to Shakespeare when I have his volume of 'Sonnets' (edition 1609) open
before me,*[1] as well he may; for the rest, everyone to his taste, and estate, for
as Oliver Wendell Holmes rightly gave out, they are well-mannered
companions,

> Each knows his place, and each may claim his part
> In some quaint corner of his master's heart.[2]

*Every reader who holds a book in his hand is free of the inmost minds of men past
and present; their lives both within and without the pale of their uttered thoughts
are unveiled to him; he needs no introduction to the greatest.*[3]

> He may hear the voice of Demosthenes, Homer, or *Roman Virgil,*
>   Wielder of the stateliest measure ever moulded
>   by the lips of man.[4]

He may hear Burke perorate at Westminster, Johnson dogmatise in Fleet
Street, Socrates argue, Rabelais laugh, Augustine confess, Swift scoff,
Pepys gossip, Donne preach, Carlyle scold, Ruskin lecture, Taylor pray,
Scott yarn, Herrick sing, Whitman sound his *barbaric yawp,*[5] Shelley *beat
in the void his luminous wings in vain,*[6]

> Or sweetest Shakespeare, Fancy's child,
> Warble his native wood-notes wild.[7]

And as the chattering of the world dies down books will sing to him un-
heard melodies and whisper eloquence *born of the very sigh that silence
heaves;*[8] *Quando omnes loquuntur et deliberant, optimum a mutis et mortuis est
consilium. Homines quoque si taceant, vocem invenient libri, et quae nemo dicit,
prudens suggerit antiquitas:*[9] When all men talk and deliberate, the best
counsel is from the silent dead; if men are silent, then books will find a
voice; what no one says, the wisdom of the ages will suggest; and even
voluble love is best heard in the voice of silence,

> O let my books be then the eloquence
> And dumb presagers of my speaking breast;
> Who plead for love, and look for recompense,
> More than the tongue that more hath more expressed.
> O learn to read what silent love hath writ: ·
> To hear with eyes belongs to love's fine wit.[10]

---

[1] *My Confidences.* 189.   [2] 'The Study.'   [3] Frederic Harrison, *Choice of Books.* 7.
[4] Tennyson, 'To Virgil'.   [5] 'Song of Myself', *Leaves of Grass.* 78.   [6] Matthew
Arnold, 'Shelley'. *Essays in Criticism.*   [7] Milton, *L'Allegro.*   [8] Keats, 'I stood tip-
toe'.   [9] Inscription Guelferbylanae Bibliothecae.   [10] Shakespeare, *Sonnets.* xxiii.

Part VI

OF THE READING OF BOOKS

I. READING WITH PURPOSE

In every age there are high-minded mentors who never tire of preaching that books are not lightly to be approached without an earnest purpose: *the golden key to knowledge, a key that will only fit its own proper doors, is purpose;*[1] *every book that we take up without a purpose is an opportunity lost of taking up a book with a purpose;*[2] *let your reading have a practical bearing,* commands Fénelon, *let it tend to the correction of your faults, reading for reading's sake is one of the worst and commonest and most unwholesome habits.*[3] They that thus scorn are kith and kin to those fanatics of the past (and sometimes even of the present) who see in pleasures only the seductions of the Devil.

Addison is opposed to solitary and self-absorbed studies; book knowledge to a *recluse man* is as a *lantern* hiding him who carries it and serving only to pass him through *secret and gloomy paths of his own*; but *it is a torch in the hand of one who is willing and able to show those who are bewildered the way which leads to prosperity and welfare.*[4] Brother Agnellus of Pisa, the first Franciscan Missionary to Oxford, found the Monks in the library of the school he had set up *bestowing their time on frivolous learning*, to so great an extent, he thought, as to lead them to debate the existence of God, which he one day found them doing. *Woe is me! Woe is me!* he burst forth, *the simple brethren are entering heaven, and the learned ones are debating if there be one*; and he made a donation of £10 sterling to buy a copy of the *Decretals,* that the Friars might study it and be weaned from their *frivolities.*[5]

Sir Walter Scott's old librarian, Dominie Sampson, in *Guy Mannering,* though no monk, had a monastic fear of frivolous literature, and he tossed indignantly aside even *belles lettres*, poems, plays and memoirs, as belonging to that forbidden class. *Whether novels, or poetry, or history be read,* says John Ruskin, *they should be chosen not for what is out of them, but for what is in them*; and Bulwer-Lytton asserts that more is gotten from one book *on which the thought settles for a definite end in knowledge* than from whole

[1] Richardson, *Choice of Books,* 130.   [2] Harrison, *Choice of Books.* 15.   [3] *Ib.* 6.
[4] *Spectator.*   [5] Elton, *Great Book-Collectors.* 33.

libraries *skimmed over by the wandering eye*; which is confirmed by Miss Eden, who strove to bring herself to *a high state of cultivation by studying fifteen books at a time; no saying*, she admits, *how much I shall read, or how little I shall remember*.[1] She was no better off in the end than young Waverley in Scott's romance, who *drove through the sea of books like a vessel without pilot or rudder*. He that reads many books must *compare one opinion or one style*, argues Dr. Johnson, *must distinguish, reject, and prefer*. Books for such folks must be uplifting, serious, purposeful in their morality; they must be good books, great books, that could be defended against their depreciators:

> Books that purify the thought,
> Spirits of the learned dead,
> Teachers of the little taught,
> Comforters when friends are fled.[2]

II. BOOKS MORALLY APPROACHED

Some distinguish between good and bad books; others even give out that books are profane or vulgar, for gentle or for simple. Sir Richard Colt Hoare told John Nichols that he had *a great treat in Dibdin's ' Tour'*, which was *quite a Gentleman's Book*. This *pregnant brevity* Dibdin approved as the warmest eulogy of his book.[3] Others will have that there are week-day books and Sunday books. When Dibdin[4] was for a time incapable of attending to his duty as Vicar of St. Mary's, Bryanston Square, he *cast about* to suit his reading to the *day*, and conceived the idea of a portable *Sunday library*, composed of *a collection of Discourses by eminent Churchmen*. Of this type are those who believe that there are secular and sacred books, one class ordained by circumstance and the other by God Himself. Henry Crabb Robinson resolved to devote his Sundays to books *of a religious character*;[5] William Cory *dragged* himself through *Paradise Lost* because he *thought it a good thing to do on Sunday afternoons*;[6] Henry Bradshaw also set about *Paradise Lost* for his Sunday reading, and was *charmed with the first two books*;[7] and James Howell exhorts his student cousin not to forget *unicum necessarium: on Sundays and Holidays let Divinity be the sole object of your speculation, in comparison whereof all other knowledge is but Cobweb-learning; prae qua quisquiliae caetera*.[8] But this disposition is long since outmoded, and there is no such reluctancy among modern readers, who read now on Sundays what they like, and to so little hurt that younger folk

---

[1] *Miss Eden's Letters*. 108–9.   [2] William Barnes.   [3] *Reminiscences*. ii, 679.   [4] *Ib*. 860.
[5] *Diary*. i, 404.   [6] 'Table Talk', *Gathered Leaves*. M. E. Coleridge, 317.   [7] Prothero, *Memoir of Bradshaw*. 39.   [8] *Familiar Letters* (Tenth Ed.) 206.

wonder at that superstition which made Sundays hideous to our forebears. Lord Macaulay, who in one year read a Greek play every Sunday,[1] gave out that *the absurd superstition of Sunday reading* was, in his time, *one of the curses of England*;[2] but such evidence is now happily impertinent to my purpose, and I omit further reference to it.

Richard de Bury,[3] lover of all books, would sustain all who uphold and prefer religious books: *Certes, thou hast placed thy tabernacle in books, where the Most High, the Light of lights, the Book of Life, has established thee. In that book everyone who asks is received, everyone who seeks finds, and to everyone who knocketh boldly it is speedily opened; the cherubim spread out their wings, that the intellect of the student may ascend and look from pole to pole, from the east and west, from the north and from the south.* And greater still, for therein *the mighty and incomprehensible God Himself is apprehensively contained and worshipped,* the nature of things celestial, terrestrial and infernal is revealed, laws of state discerned, offices of the celestial hierarchy distinguished, and the tyranny of demons described, *such as neither the ideas of Plato transcend, nor the chair of Crato contained.* He finds supporters in every age. Richard Whitlock[4] will have that *most usefull Books are the Comments on one of God's Books: that Hieroglyphicall one of Nature and the Creatures; or that precious book of Life, that Verbum Dei (to be esteemed next to Verbum Deus, that was pleased to be bound up in the coarse Cover of Humane Nature), that written Epistle of the Creatour to the Creature; In qua quicquid docetur Veritas, praecipitur Bonitas, promittitur Felicitas. Now what Benefit Readers, what Glory Authors may reap from such Labours in comparison of any other Labour under the Sun is demonstrated to those prudent Chapmen of the World that know the just value of Things.* Nothing so sweet, saith Eugénie de Guérin,[5] *as those saintly voices that speak to us of God; nothing so beautiful as what God inspires*; to the understanding of this all reading, say they, should be directed.

All that a University, or final highest school can do for us is to teach us to read;[6] and by reading is here meant that which contributes to our virtue, or strength of character. Gellius felt nothing but disgust for those *worthless books, nihil ad ornandum iuvandumque usum vitae pertinentes*, which contribute nothing to the enrichment or profit of life;[7] and of all men perchance, Harrison insists, *the book-lover needs most to be reminded that man's business here is to know for the sake of living, not to live for the sake of knowing*;[8] as John Milton, in his riper years, was led by study from the *laureat fraternity of poets* to the *shady spaces of philosophy*, and chiefly to the *divine volumes of Plato, and his equal Xenophon*, where he *learnt of chastity and love*,

---

[1] *Life.* i, 392–3.   [2] Journal, 8.iv.1849. Qt. *The Times*, 7.xii.1928.   [3] *Philobiblon.* Trans. Thomas. 8–9.   [4] *Zootomia.* 236.   [5] *Letters.* Trans. Trebutien. 141.   [6] Carlyle. *Heroes and Hero-Worship.* (1841) 262.   [7] *Attic Nights.* (Loeb Ed.) ix, 4.   [8] *Choice of Books.* 20–1.

and how to distinguish between her *whose charming cup is only virtue, which she bears in her hand to those who are worthy*, and that *thick intoxicating potion, which a certain sorceress, the abuser of love's name, carries about.*[1]

III. OF EPHEMERAL AND SHALLOW WORKS

To purge the world of literary rubbish will require some monster-taming Hercules, a ruthless Cæsar, or a Mussolini; but no persuasion, no terror, no persecution can divert those

> Who hunger, and who thirst for scribbling sake;[2]
>   Tenet insanabile multos
>   Scribendi cacoethes.[3]

This scribbling itch is an incurable disease, and Montaigne's *common rabble of scribblers and blur-papers* a constant menace to be circumvented, since cure is beyond hope. It is an ordinary thing for us to account of value those books which have outstripped time, and to press them forward is a prime means of side-tracking the *remorseless cataract of daily literature,*[4] which is no better than so much incontinently discharged waste paper. But to sift the good from the bad in the daily onset taxes all our wit, and in the end our efforts are a *non ens*, a mere flash, a ceremony, a toy, a thing of nought; no use battling against such a stream; all the shouting, the crying and spluttering of all times, have not arrested it, nor will they, for rubbish is necessary to the *profanum vulgus*, light amusement their prerogative: *panis et circenses*:

> Authors hear at length one general cry,
> Tickle and entertain us, or we die![5]

Such ephemeral matter is the *chopped straw* of the circulating library,[6] or those news-sheets, magazines, the trivia of commerce, whether fiction or articles, notes on passing events; read to-day, forgotten to-morrow,

> Sons of a Day! just buoyant on the flood,
> Then number'd with the puppies in the mud;[7]

thistle-down blown hither and thither by the wind and settling nowhere, or, if anywhere, where least wanted, weeds, litter, matter out of place, dust of the mind; *as general and vulgar as a smell.*[8]

---

[1] *Apology for Smectymnuus.* (1697) 336.   [2] Pope, *Dunciad.* i, 50.   [3] Juvenal, *Sat.* vii, 52–3.   [4] Harrison, *Choice of Books.* 16.   [5] Cowper, *Retirement.* [6] Harrison, *Choice of Books.* 28.   [7] Pope, *Dunciad.* ii, 307–8.   [8] Sir Walter Raleigh, *Letters.* i, 233.

Yet midst this tide of unpropitious time,
Quacks advertise, and paltry poets rhyme;
Book-makers ply their trade—booksellers puff,
And, urged by avarice, vend the vapid stuff.[1]

Nothing so dwarfs the mind as *to debauch it by frivolous reading, and by the moral dram-drinking of sensational rubbish,*[2] or to pamper it with peptonised pap; but such penurious stuff,

Abstracts, abridgements, please the fickle times.[3]

There are books to be *perused,* says John Aikin,[4] and books to be *possessed. Of the former you may find ample store in every subscription library. Such books the world swarms too much with,*[5] so that, as Wither says, *[6]those that desire knowledge are still kept ignorant; their ignorance increaseth their affection to vain toys; their affection makes the stationer to increase his provision of such stuff: and at last you shall see nothing to be sold amongst us but Curranto's 'Bevis of Southampton' or such trumpery.* The warehouses are full of *quack-salving receipts, false propositions, in artificial rhymings, of which last,* he ingenuously confesses, *they have some of mine there, God forgive me!* 'Tis a vicious circle. Dr. Johnson (read his *Idler,* No. 85) has some such a notion when he claims for an ignorant age that it had too many books, and Lord Chesterfield the same when he exhorts his son to throw away none of his time *upon those trivial futile books, published by idle or necessitous authors, for the amusement of idle or ignorant readers: such sorts of books swarm and buzz about one every day; flap them away,* he commands, *they have no sting;*[7] and Harrison[8] had them in mind when he *could almost reckon the printing press as among the scourges of mankind.*

Beneath the word *Finis,* in one such stupid book, an unknown wit wrote:

Finis! an error, or a lie, my friend!
In writing foolish books there is no end;[9]

which Sir Thomas Browne stiffly supports; there are too many books in the world, he says, and he would with patience behold the urn and ashes of the Vatican, could he recover, with a few others, *the perished leaves of Solomon.* It was not *a melancholy Utinam* of his own, but the desire of better heads, that instead of attempting to *unite the incompatible differences* of religion, they should *form a general Synod* for the benefit of learning, to reduce it as it lay at first, *in a few, solid authors; and to condemn to the fire*

---

[1] *The Craniad.* 8.   [2] S. Laing, *Modern Science and Modern Thought.*   [3] George Crabb, *The Library.*   [4] *Letters from a Father to his Son.*   [5] Thomas Fuller.   [6] *The Student's Purgatory.*   [7] *Letters to his Son.* cclxxx.   [8] *Choice of Books.* 5.   [9] Qt. William Davis, *An Olio of Anecdotes.* (1814) 6.

those swarms and millions of 'Rhapsodies', begotten only to distract and abuse the weaker judgements of Scholars, and to maintain the trade and mystery of Typographers.[1] Good and serious men, lovers of books, scholars and the like, have always thought as much. There is too much writing and printing, 'tis an overdone business, and in all times a menace. *Were all books,* Addison taxeth,[2] *reduced to their quintessence, many a bulky author would make appearance in a penny pamphlet, and there would be scarce any such thing in Nature as a Folio.* Millions of volumes would be *utterly annihilated* and the *works of an age contained on a few shelves*; which is no more than Coventry Patmore argued in our own time when he announced that, *of the forty miles of shelves in the Museum, forty feet would contain all the real literature of the world.*[3] Fuller argues that[4] *foolish pamphlets prove most beneficial to the printers,* and he quotes the story of Rabelais, whose printer was *utterly undone* by printing his solid and serious work concerning physic and was recompensed when Rabelais wrote his *jesting scurrilous work, which repaired the printer's loss with advantages*:

So the worst books some knave will still defend;[5]

not that I, and some others, would condemn Rabelais.[6]

Possibly the endless multiplication of books makes for contempt, encouraging that bibliophobia which is the common lot. *People in general do not willingly read, if they can have any thing else to amuse them,* said Dr. Johnson.[7] *Mankind, as a rule, detests literature,* says Lang.[8] *What an inestimable price would a Virgil or a Homer, a Cicero or an Aristotle bear, were their works, like a statue, a building, or a picture, to be confined only in one place, and made the property of a single person!*[9] Yet I will go on and say that if it be true that *the public which reads, in any sense of the word worth considering, is very, very small,* and that *the public which would feel no lack if all book-printing ceased to-morrow is enormous,* the production of great books is unaffected. What boots it to complain, as he does, that *many of the most valuable books slowly achieve the sale of a few hundred copies,* and that if we gathered from all the ends of the British Empire those men and women who regard fine books as a necessity of life, they could be assembled comfortably in the Albert Hall?[10] The good bookman is not disturbed if *the Reading of most men is like a Wardrobe of old Cloaths that are seldom used.*[11] He can gnaw his own bone.

---

[1] *Religio Medici.* i, 24.   [2] *Spectator.* 124.   [3] *Memoirs,* Champneys. i, 68.
[4] *The Holy State and the Profane State.*   [5] J. Taylor, *An Arrant Thief.*
[6] Coleridge said: 'I could write a treatise in praise of the moral elevation of Rabelais' work, which would make the church stare, and the conventicle groan, and yet would be the truth, and nothing but the truth.'   [7] *Life.* Hill. iv, 218.
[8] Intro., *Pleasures of Bookland,* Shaylor. xvi.   [9] Addison, *Spectator.* 166.   [10] Gissing, *Private Papers of Henry Ryecroft.* 60.   [11] Halifax, 'Thoughts and Reflections', *Character of Charles II, etc.* 148.

That there are not many of his kind is no disparagement. With a few fine
books he is safe, even from fools, for in the presence of great writers they
would seek to hide their faults, so Seneca promises[1] and Montaigne
approves.[2] Bibliophiles are not reformers or proselytisers; they are not out
to defend or propagate ideas or wisdom: *diffused knowledge immortalises
itself,*[3] and only the loveless advocate love,

cras amet qui nunquam amavit quique amavit cras amet.[4]

A good book never lacks lovers, and they in turn will reject trivial consolations, ordinary speeches, popular appeals. Known persuasion in this
behalf will be of small force; what can a man say that hath not been said?
To what end are such phrenetic discourses? You may as soon remove the
Matterhorn as alter some men's affections. And though, as Montaigne
holds,[5] *there are divers bookes profitable by reason of their subjects of which the
author reapeth no commendations at all*; it *is not to be remedied*, as my Lord of
Verulam hath it, *by making no more books, but by making more good books,
which*, as he supports again and most wisely, visualising a beneficent cannibalism, like *the serpent of Moses, might devour the serpents of the enchanters.*[6]
In all ages there have been those who see nought but triviality or even
evil in romances, plays, novels and the like. *I never heard of any plays fit for
a Christian to read*, Parson Adams objects, *but 'Cato' and 'The Conscious
Lovers'*; yet he must own that *in the latter there are some things almost solemn
enough for a sermon.*[7] *I never read a novel*, says Thoreau,[8] *they have so little
real life and thought in them*. Dibdin records[9] that Ludovicus Vives has *strung
together* in a *saucy philippic* a long list of popular romances, calling them
ungracious books; they are, he protests, books written by idle men and *set
all upon filth and viciousness*; that men delight in them proves *that vice
pleaseth them so much*. There is no shadow of learning in them and they are
full of *plain and foolish lies: One killeth twenty himself alone, another killeth
thirty; another, wounded with a hundred wounds, and left dead, riseth up again;
and on the next day, made whole and strong, overcometh two giants, and then
goeth away laden with gold and silver and precious stones*. 'Tis madness, he
warns us, to have pleasure in such books; *there is no wit in them, but a few
words of wanton lust; which be spoken to move her mind with whom they love,
if it chance she be steadfast*. If they be read for this, make an end of it by
making *books of bawds' crafts*; he *never heard man say that he liked these books,
but those that never touched good books*. In Hazlitt's day *only young ladies from*

[1] *Epist.* xi.   [2] *Essays.* Ed. Seccombe. i, 313.   [3] Sir James Mackintosh, *Vindiciae
Gallicae.*   [4] 'To-morrow shall be love for the loveless, and for the lover to-
morrow shall be love.' *Pervigilium Veneris.* Loeb Ed. 349.   [5] *Essays.* Ed. Seccombe.
iii, 217.   [6] Bacon, *Advancement of Learning.* ii, 103.   [7] *Joseph Andrews.* Fielding.
iii. chap. 9.   [8] *Week on the Concord.* Scott Library Ed. 61.   [9] *Bibliomania.* (1811) 201.

OF EPHEMERAL AND SHALLOW WORKS

the boarding school, or milliners' girls, read all the new novels that come out,[1] but nowadays such books are more widely appreciated.

Journalism has been denounced and devoured in all ages; it is a common thing among those who would have a definite purpose in reading to rail against the popular press, and, like as not, they are the same that condemn romances and novels, as Thoreau;[2] *blessed are they who never read a newspaper, for they shall see Nature, and, through her, God*; and when he was forced to read one of the condemned sheets, he *counterbalanced* the act with a dose of *Herodotus* or *Strabo*. Some object to newspapers because they compete with more permanent writing: *when a nation reads its newspapers it does not read its books.*[3] M. Swann, in *A la Recherche du Temps Perdu,*[4] is of the same opinion: *The fault I find with our journalism is that it forces us to take an interest in some fresh triviality or other every day, whereas only three or four books in a lifetime give us anything that is of real importance.* They forget, however, that much of our best literature rose from the ranks of journalism. On the other hand, there are some few, as Lord Orrery,[5] the friend of Swift, who find newspapers a great relief to a man who leads a solitary life. At his country retreat at Marston, he generally reserved them as a *Feast for night* and passed some of the long evenings *speculating on the advertisements over a Dish of Coffee.* By this means he learnt who sells *the infallible electuary,* and many curious things of other lands, the doings of Stanislaus, and the pronunciation of Polish names.

This collection of opinions is wild, and there is inconsistency in several of the varieties, which need not be more than noted, for *opinion in good men is but knowledge in the making.*[6] To attack them were a waste of time, for they represent a confusion common in one form or other in all periods, and may therefore be looked upon as an idiosyncrasy of the human mind, which cannot affect those who are capable of forming their own tastes. The rest do not count. But I may conclude with some words from Coleridge which indicate that even writers of supreme genius may be afflicted with the same moral squint. Coleridge would not even dignify the reading of these rejected books with the name of reading: *call it rather,* he advises, *a sort of beggarly day-dreaming, during which the mind of the dreamer furnishes for itself nothing but laziness and a little mawkish sensibility;* while the whole *material* and imagery of the dose is supplied *ab extra* by a mental *camera obscura* manufactured at the printing office, which *pro tempore* fixes, reflects and transmits *the moving phantasms of one man's delirium, so as to people the barrenness of an hundred other brains afflicted with the same*

[1] 'On Reading New Books', *Sketches and Essays.* (1839)   [2] *Essays and other Writings.* Scott Lib. 254.   [3] Edmond and Jules de Goncourt.   [4] *Swann's Way.* (Du Côté de chez Swann) Proust. Trans. Scott Moncrieff. i, 32.   [5] *Orrery.* 124-5.   [6] Milton, *Areopagitica.*

trance of suspension of all common sense and all definite purpose. It is but an attempt to reconcile *two contrary yet co-existing propensities of human nature: indulgence of sloth and hatred of vacancy.* The reading of such books he classes with *gaming; swinging or swaying on a chair or gate; spitting over a bridge; smoking; snuff-taking; tête-à-tête quarrels after dinner between husband and wife; conning word by word all the advertisements of the daily advertisers in a public house on a rainy day, etc., etc.*[1]

To this I answer, that although those who read thus lose greatly thereby, for they take the shadow for the substance, yet 'tis their fashion to do so; they like it and no great harm comes to them. Perchance they are thus saved from a worse evil: themselves. Yet none will say that they are wise who prefer a dull and shallow print to a work composed of all graces, elegancies, imagination, an absolute piece, *for beautiful words are, in a real and special sense, the light of thought.*[2]

IV. AGAINST IDLE AND DESULTORY READING

Difficult works only are advocated by many earnest authorities, who hold, with Musonius, that *remittere animum quasi amittere est*,[3] to relax the mind is to lose it, and that books are primarily a means of mental exercise, literature a gymnasium for the intellect. *Reading is to the mind what exercise is to the body, health is preserved, strengthened, and invigorated by the one, virtue (which is the health of the mind) is kept alive, cherished, and confirmed*[4] by the other. *In the sweat of the brow is the mind as well as the body to eat its bread. Nil sine magno Musa labore dedit mortalibus; it is wholesome and bracing for the mind to have the faculties kept on the stretch; like the effect of a walk in Switzerland upon the body.*[5] They would have us read only books with a sting, records of the profundities, books in which to burrow, mole-like, or to gnaw at as the beaver gnaws his log.

Another argument which may be derived from the precedent is that *the use of reading is to aid us in thinking.*[6] Nicholas Breton meant as much when he let his scholar assert that *wordes are without substance, when they are layed for easie beleevers.*[7] Coventry Patmore[8] also puts in a caveat against easy reading, giving out that *to anyone who seeks more in reading than the merest amusement*, it is not *the less pleasant because the way is somewhat rough, and there be many great boulders and even craggy hills which he must avoid and go*

[1] Coleridge, *Biographia Literaria.*   [2] Longinus, *The Sublime.* Trans. Prickard. 55. [3] Qt. Aulus Gellius, *Noct. Att.* xviii, 2.   [4] Steele, *Tatler.* 147.   [5] A. and J. C. Hare, *Guesses at Truth.* 458.   [6] Edward Gibbon.   [7] 'The Angle's Conference with the Scholler'. *Works.* Ed. Kentish; Wright. i, 60.   [8] *Religio Poetate, etc.,* 'On Obscure Books'.

round instead of over; on the contrary, *the way often sparkles with gems of forgotten novelty*, and if you do not understand *one-tenth* of a treatise by Aristotle, St. Augustine, St. Thomas Aquinas, Swedenborg, or Hegel, *what you do comprehend remains engraved in your memory like a precious intaglio*, because you have been learning *things* and not gossip *about* things. Not to follow such precepts, they argue, is to destroy both mind and taste. A generation which reads rubbish, or even, as Harrison[1] expostulates, *Zola's seventeenth romance, can no more read Homer than it could read a cuneiform inscription*. There is no *creative* or *moral value* in the *sewage out-fall* produced by them that have made literature a *mere trade*; to read such stuff is no real enjoyment; *non ragioniam di lor, ma guarda e passa*. *To be addicted to it, is a vice; to manufacture it is a crime. They are not books, these things. To imbibe this compound is not to read.*

Some believe that culture and reading are one: *culture is reading*, Matthew Arnold contends;[2] not, he warns us, any kind of reading, but only that *with a purpose to guide it, and with a system*; and he contends that *a man's life each day depends for its solidity and value on whether he reads during that day, and, far more still, on what he reads during it.*[3] Lord Chesterfield was so much of this way of thinking that he never tired of advising his son to unite the manners of a courtier with the knowledge of a scholar, *to join, what is seldom joined in any of my countrymen, Books and the World;*[4] and he counselled Lord Huntingdon to suspend his classical studies, during the Grand Tour, and to divide his time *between reading the State of Europe from Charlemagne downwards*, and *learning the present world by seeing it* with his own eyes; but although it is necessary to observe life, to *read men and women unbound*, still *the best companions are the best books.*[5]

Ben Jonson[6] laid down that *as it is fit to read the best authors to youth first*, they should be of the *openest and clearest*, as *Livy before Sallust, Sidney before Donne*. He warned against *letting them taste Gower or Chaucer first, lest, falling too much in love with antiquity, and not apprehending the weight, they grow rough and barren in language only*. When their judgement grows firm they can read both old and new, but he would have them take heed that they be not corrupted by *their new flowers and sweetness*; advice which Frederic Harrison extols: *idle reading debilitates and corrupts the mind for all wholesome reading;*[7] but this is only half true, for in many instances corruptible minds are already corrupted.

Sir W. Waller expostulates[8] against desultory reading, *running from one book to another, as birds skip from one bough to another, without design; it is no marvel if they get nothing but their labour for their pains, when they seek nothing*

---

[1] *Choice of Books.* 28, 66, 70, 79.   [2] Preface, *Literature and Dogma.* (1883) xxvi.
[3] *Culture and Anarchy.*   [4] *Letters to his Son.*   [5] *Letters to Lord Huntingdon.* 3.
[6] *Timber.* cxvi.   [7] *Choice of Books.* 6.   [8] *Divine Meditations.*

but change and diversion: they that ride post, he says, *can observe but little.* He
would therefore fix his study solely upon those books that are of most
importance to fit him for action, *which is the true end of all learning,* and
avoid, with Frederic Harrison,[1] *the misuse of books, the debilitating waste of
brain in aimless, promiscuous, vapid reading,* which is of like kind with the
poisonous inhalation of literary garbage and bad men's worst thoughts. In their
Guesses at Truth, Augustus and Julius Hare have an equally notable invective against such reading, which they account mischievous because it turns
the memory into *a common sewer for rubbish of all sorts to float through,* and
by relaxing attention destroys those powers which should be most
improved by it.

Opposing these extremes, some fortify themselves with Pliny the Elder:
Nullus est liber tam malus, qui non ex aliqua parte prosit,[2] which was copied by
Cervantes when he made his bachelor in *Don Quixote*[3] claim *no book so
bad but something good may be found in it.* Laurence Sterne never read any
book without drawing profit from it; so also Elizabeth Barrett Browning,
as she claims in *Aurora Leigh*:

> I read books bad and good—some bad and good
> At once (good aims not always make good books).

John Hill Burton was of this same opinion: *it is difficult, almost impossible,
to find a book in which something either valuable or amusing may not be found,
if the proper alembic be applied;* books known to him were curious and
amusing, even from *their very badness;*[4] and Lord Sherbrooke was so bold
as to tell the students at the Croydon Science and Art Schools, in 1869,
that any reading which amused created a taste for reading, therefore he
commended novels, and even *frivolous books.* I find support for this theory
in the experience of Hughlings Jackson, a notable practitioner in the art of
trivial reading when he had a mind to it, or, rather, no mind for better
stuff, for he was an admirer of Dr. Johnson, Jane Austen, Trollope and
Dickens. In such moods he would read the most *trivial rubbish* and the
effect would be beneficial, for he would return *to his serious writing with
added zest and spirit.*[5] In fact, he found these works not only restful but
fertile. *He could throw a novel or ' Tit-Bits' aside and proceed at once to record
any recondite speculations which had flashed into his mind.* This sort of reading
was a form of rest, for *the moment his brain felt tired he betook himself to his
novel again.*[6]

There is so little danger from alleged bad books, or good books with
some presumed bad in them, that so safe a guide as John Ruskin would let

---

[1] *Choice of Books.* 1.   [2] In Pliny, *Epp.* Bk. iii, 5.   [3] Pt. ii, Chap. 3.   [4] *The Book-
Hunter.* 152–3.   [5] James Taylor, 'Memoir', in *Neurological Fragments.* Hughlings
Jackson. 20.   [6] Sir Jonathan Hutchinson, 'Recollections of Jackson', *op. cit.* 32.

a young girl *loose in the library as you do a fawn in a field*, to browse at will upon knowledge as the fawn upon herbage: risking ill weeds, *it knows the bad weeds twenty times better than you; and the good ones too, and will eat some bitter and prickly ones, good for it, which you had not the slightest thought were good*;[1] which recalls again Lord Sherbrooke, who advises us to *form a habit of reading at all costs*, not minding what: the taste for *better books will come when you have a habit of reading the inferior*. Thence all is well, for *aquila non captat muscas*, as Glanvill reminds us,[2] the Eagle flies not but at noble game; and a young Alexander *will not play but with monarchs. He that hath been cradled in Majesty, and used to Crowns and Scepters, will not leave the Throne to play with beggars at Put-pin, or be fond of Tops and Cherry-stones: neither will a Spirit that dwells with Stars, dabble in this impurer Mud; or stoop to be a Play-fellow and Copartner in delights with Creatures that have nought but Animal*. All of which arguments are summed up by Milton[3] where he says that *a wise man will make better use of an idle pamphlet, than a fool will do of sacred Scripture*; like a *good refiner* he will *gather gold out of the drossiest volume*, whilst *a fool will be a fool with the best Book, yea without a Book*, for as Nietzsche advises, *no one can draw more out of things, books included, than he already knows*;[4] so that since, as Shaftesbury advises,[5] *read we must, let writers be ever so indifferent*, there is no need to deprive wise men of their chance of wisdom, in order to keep fools from that which is no hindrance to their folly.

V. VAIN AND PEDANTIC READING CONDEMNED

Some read to think,—these are rare; some to write,—these are common; and some to talk,—and these form the great majority.[6] There are others, and many of them, that eschew all reading except for vainglory,

> Who read huge works to boast what ye have read,[7]

to disport their second-hand stock of ideas and information, *for a fading greedy glory, to cousin and delude the foolish world*;[8] to peacock themselves at large, like Æsop's daw in borrowed feathers. Among them are others who

> Affect all books of past and modern ages,
> But read no further than the title-pages.[9]

They prate: Plato said this, Aristotle that; this from Nietzsche, that from

[1] *Sesame and Lilies*. ii.   [2] *Scepsis Scientifica*. (1885) 211–12.   [3] *Areopagitica*. Ed. Holt White. 74.   [4] *Ecce Homo*. Trans. Ludovici. 57.   [5] *Characteristics*. (1744) i, 239.   [6] Colton, *Lacon*.   [7] Crabbe, *The Library*.   [8] Montaigne, *Essays*. Ed. Seccombe. iii, 388.   [9] S. Butler, *Satire upon Imperfection and Abuse of Human Learning*.

Croce, t'other from Shaw. But what say they themselves? Nothing. It is
all idle prattle. A parrot would say as much as these psittacists,

> We have threshed a stock of print and book, and
>   winnowed a chattering wind
> And many a soul wherefrom he stole, but his
>   we cannot find.[1]

Such readers, if so I dare name them, are no better than the pretender
stigmatised by Earle as a mere *nomenclator of authors, which he has read in
general in the Catalogue, and in particular in the Title, and goes seldom so far as
the Dedication. He never talks of anything but learning, and learns all from
talking;*[2]

> As Roman noblemen were wont to greet,
> And compliment the rabble in the street,
> Had nomenclators in their trains, to claim
> Acquaintance with the meanest by his name,
> And by so mean contemptible a bribe
> Trepanned the suffrages of every tribe;
> So learned men, by authors' names unknown,
> Have gained no small improvement of their own,
> And he's esteemed the learnedest of all others
> That has the largest catalogue of authors.[3]

Some, says Montaigne, went even farther, by having in their retinue tame
pedants to prompt them, should they at any time move among friends
who desired to speak on matters pertaining to scholarship. Then came the
pedants' chance; they were rushed up to fill learning's breach: *some with
discourse, some with a verse of Homer, othersome with a sentence, each one
according to his skill or profession.* These rich Romans persuaded themselves
that all such learning was their own because it was contained in their servants' minds: *whose sufficiencie is placed in their sumptuous libraries.* When
asked what they know, they *will require a book to demonstrate the same;* one
*durst not tell me that his posteriors are scabious, except he turne over his 'lexicon'
to see what posteriors and scabious is.* They take the opinions and knowledge
of others into their protection, and that is all; such knowledge is not
enfeoffed and made their own, as it should be. They recall one who, having
need of fire, goes to his neighbour's house rather than light his own.
*What availes it us to have bellies full of meat, if it be not digested? If it be not
transchanged in us? except it nourish, augment, and strengthen us?* Would

---

[1] Kipling, 'Tomlinson', *Barrack-Room Ballads.* 199.   [2] 'A Pretender to Learning',
Microcosmography. xlv.   [3] S. Butler, *Satire upon Imperfection and Abuse of Human
Learning.*

Lucullus, whom learning made so great a captain, have acted thus? We rely too much on other men's arms, and so disannul our own strength. *Will I arm myself against the feare of death? it is at Seneca's cost: will I draw comfort either for myselfe, or any other? I borrow the same of Cicero.* He loves not this *begged-for sufficiencie: sure I am,* he stiffly concludes, *we can never be wise, but by our own wisdom,*[1] for to remember too much is to forget all, to be no better than a *bibliolathas* or book-forgetter, as Didymus the Grammarian, who had written so many books, some say as many as 3500, that he could not recall the names of half of them.[2]

> *There are multitudes who read merely to qualify themselves for the world;*[3]
> > Man has a natural desire to know,
> > But the one half is for interest, the other show;[4]

they are small fellows, *reading coxcombs,* in Mallet's phrase:

> Grave sons of idle Industry and Pride,
> Whom learning but perverts, and books misguide.[5]

John Earle rightly calls them Pretenders to Learning,[6] *Scholar-mountebanks,* and their art a *delusion*; and he marks one down as *oftener in his study than at his Book,* delighted for you *to deprehend him: yet he hears you not till the third knock, and then comes out very angry as interrupted. His table is spread with some Classick Folio, which is as constant to it as the carpet, and hath lain open in the same page this half year. His pocket is seldom without a Greek Testament or Hebrew Bible, which he opens only in the Church, and that when some stander-by looks over. He has sentences for company, some scatterings from Seneca and Tacitus, which are good upon all occasions. If he read anything in the morning, it comes up all at dinner; and as long as that lasts, the discourse is his. He is a great Plagiary of tavern wit, and comes to Sermons only that he may talk of Austin. His Parcels are the mere scrapings from company, yet he complains at parting what time he has lost.* Bliss[7] as frankly reproves such *sottish and idle enthusiasts,* who call learning but a *splendidum peccatum.*

Such coxcombs and mountebanks are numerous and familiar in all ages. They are satirised by Young:

> Unlearned men of books assume the care,
> As eunuchs are the guardians of the fair;[8]

and Hazlitt sees them, *hanging like a film and cobweb upon letters, or like the dust upon the outside of knowledge;*[9] but we are well content if, as Earle adds,

---

[1] *Essays.* Ed. Seccombe. i, 156-7.   [2] *Athenaeus.* Loeb. Ed. iv, 139.   [3] J. Butler, *Sermons.* Preface.   [4] S. Butler, *Satire on the Imperfection and Abuse of Human Learning.* [5] Qt. *Book-Lovers' Anth.* 152.   [6] *Microcosmography.* xlv.   [7] Qt. *Microcosmography.* Ed. Irwin. Note. 15.   [8] *The Love of Fame.*   [9] *On the Conversation of Authors.*

those who have taken pains to be asses, though not to be scholars, are *at length discovered and laughed at.*[1] Dr. Johnson recognized that it was common *for people to talk from books, to retail the sentiments of others*; but he exonerates himself and Boswell from that vice: *You and I*, he said, *do not talk from books.*[2] That pretenders to learning are not extinct is advanced by a later writer,[3] who condemns them as liars, equalling gamblers, and perchance even *anglers*, in this *branch of depravity.* Yet he himself was once of their kind, with *good results* in the esteem of his fellow-readers; but happily *the greying years have almost cured him of the sin.*

Reading may make a full man, but is no guarantee that he will be wise, or even bright. *You, poor fool, must have learned your letters backwards; books have turned your life upside down. You have gabbled your silly philosophy to earth and heaven, which pay no heed whatever to your words.*[4] *Salmasius was a man of enormous reading and no judgment;*[5] Andrew Kippis, according to Robert Hall, *laid so many books upon his head that his brains could not move.*[6]

> And in sad cadence, as the bands condense,
> The curfew tolls the knell of *parting Sense.*[7]

Macaulay[8] insinuates as much in his tale of the young fellow in the Oxford coach who read a novel, *The Hungarian Brothers*, the whole way; the coach stopped for the party to dine in the High Street, and *this youth*, who had *passed half an hour in the midst of that city of palaces, looked down about him with his mouth open as he re-entered the coach, and all the while that we were driving away past the* Ratcliffe Library, the Great Court of All Souls, Exeter, Lincoln, Trinity, Balliol, and St. John's. When about a mile on the road, the youth, who had not hitherto spoken, said: *That was a pretty town enough. Pray, sir, what is it called?* Macaulay could not answer for laughing, but the youth *seemed unconscious of his own absurdity.*

When books distract a man from the proper observation of life they do nothing but *generate a learned folly.*[9] *Simia est simia, etiamsi purpura vestiatur,* an ape is an ape, though clad in scarlet.[10] Sir W. Waller feared above most things connected with study such vain acquisition of knowledge; *take me off from the curiosity of knowing only to know,* he prayed, *from the vanity of*

---

[1] 'A Pretender to Learning', *Microcosmography.* xlv.   [2] *Tour.* Hill's Boswell. vi, 378.
[3] Arnold Bennett, in *Evening Standard.* 9.xii.26.

[4] ἐπαρίστερ ἔμαθες, ὦ πόνηρε, γράμματα·
  ἀνέστροφέν σου τὸν βίον τὰ βίβλια·
  πεφιλοσόφηκας γῇ τε κοὐρανῷ λαλῶν,
  οἷς οὐδέν ἐστιν ἐπιμελὲς τῶν σῶν λόγων.

Theognetus, in *Athenaeus.* Loeb. Ed. iii, 104.   [5] Mark Pattison, *Milton.* 106.
[6] *Life of Hall*, Gregory.   [7] Mathias, *Pursuits of Literature.* 180.   [8] *Life*, Trevelyan.
i, 249.   [9] Channing, *Self-Culture.*   [10] Greek Proverb. Qt. Erasmus, *Praise of Folly.* Oxford Ed. 33.

knowing only to be known, and from the folly of pretending to know more than I do know.[1] Others in all times have shared his fears: *if I had read as much as other men*, bragged Hobbes, *I should have been as ignorant as others*; and Elizabeth Barrett Browning confessed in a letter to R. H. Horne that if she had *not read half as much* she would have had *stronger and better faculties*, for reading is the *ne plus ultra of intellectual indolence.*

The like may be said of any faculty. It is our own fault if we permit our books to become *sepulchres of thought*,[2] and I would therefore rather conclude with our politic Francis Bacon, who, in his treatise *Of the Advancement of Learning*, admits such evils (and many more), that *if any man be laborious in reading and study and yet idle in business and action, it groweth from some weakness of body or softness of spirit; such as Seneca speaketh of: Quidam tam sunt umbratiles, ut putent in turbido esse quicquid in luce est; and not of learning*, or (I say) of true and legitimate reading, for, as Hazlitt rightly holds, *books are but one inlet of knowledge, and the powers of the mind, like those of the body, should be left open to all impressions.*

VI. OLD *v.* NEW BOOKS

Even if the precedent cautions are accurately kept, the objections are not ended, for those who seek to formulate plans to instruct the young and the unwary in their traffic with books have several opinions *pro* and *con* on the virtues of old and new writings. Old books have many supporters: *some will only read old books, as if there were no valuable truths to be discovered in modern publications*, says Isaac D'Israeli;[3] Hazlitt[4] *cannot understand the rage manifested by the greater part of the world for reading new books*, and he is amazed that so many people *would as soon think of putting on old armour as of taking up a book not published within the last month, or year at the utmost*; and Samuel Rogers[5] frankly confesses that *when a new book comes out, he reads an old one.*

Never read any book that is not a year old. Never read any but famed books. Never read any but what you like, advised Emerson.[6] Only in science, another will have are the newest books to be read, in literature the oldest: *the Classics are always modern*;[7] *they have attained, they are at rest.*[8] Yet Lord Beaconsfield was not afraid to admit that he preferred a new book, *even if bad, to a classic*;[9] and Hamerton contends[10] that a man who never read any-

[1] *Divine Meditations.* See also Chesterfield's *Letters.* cxlii.   [2] Longfellow, 'Wind over the Chimney'.   [3] *Literary Miscellanies.* (1801) 183.   [4] 'On Reading New Books', *Sketches and Essays.* (1839)   [5] Hayward, *Biog. and Crit. Essays.* i, 106.
[6] *Society and Solitude.* 'Books.'   [7] Bulwer-Lytton, *Caxtoniana.*   [8] Lionel Johnson, *Post Liminium.* 212.   [9] *Maxims.* 16.   [10] *Intellectual Life.* 384.

thing but the classic authors *would live in an intellectual monastery*, and *would not even understand the classic authors themselves*, for we judge the past by the present. *Do you want to get at new ideas?* Lord Lytton asked his son, and answered, *read old books; do you want to find old ideas? read new ones.*[1] There is no novelty, even in novels, for they

> (witness every month's review)
> Belie their name and offer nothing new.[2]

Nothing so old as a new book, Mark Pattison enjoins,[3] and he quotes out of De Quincey that *one of the misfortunes of life* is *that one must read thousands of books only to discover that one need not have read them.* Long since Bacon[4] knew this when he deprecated such *flashy things,* comparing them to *distilled water,* and 'tis the same tenet which Dr. Johnson holds. Modern writers are but *the moons of literature,* shining with reflected light borrowed from the ancients. Greece appeared to him *to be the fountain of knowledge* and Rome of *elegance.*[5] In this present age Rudyard Kipling[6] contends in a like case, that if we devote ourselves exclusively to modern literature we get to think the world is progressing when it is only repeating itself; and the sum of it all is in the satiric poet:

> Old musty tomes transform'd to volumes new,
> Pens, paste, and shears, eternal toil pursue.[7]

Montaigne was not greatly affected to new books, because ancient authors, in his judgement, were *more full and pithy;*[8] for that reason, belike, those books which have survived from past days, are, as Emerson states,[9] the only ones that have deserved to last. Hazlitt was another who always read an old book when a new one was published: *I hate to read new books. There are twenty or thirty volumes that I have read over and over again, and these are the only ones that I have any desire ever to read at all. One would imagine,* he adds,[1] *that books were like women, the worse for being old; that they have a pleasure in being read for the first time; that they open their leaves more cordially; that the spirit of enjoyment wears out with the spirit of novelty; and that, after a certain age, it is high time to put them on the shelf.* Dr. Johnson dilates at large in his essays, conversation, letters (read his copious *Idlers* and *Ramblers*), on the *superfœtation, this teeming of the press in modern times;* and although he gives us to understand that *we must read what the world reads at the moment,* doing so is *prejudicial to good literature,*[10] because, as Haz-

---

[1] Qt. *Times Litt. Supp.* 19.x.1906.   [2] Cowper, *Retirement.*   [3] 'Books and Critics', *Fortnightly Review.*   [4] *Essays.* 'Of Studies.'   [5] *Life,* iii, 332–3.   [6] *A Book of Words.* 79.   [7] *The Craniad.* 8.   [8] *Essays.* Ed. Seccombe. ii, 112.   [9] 'Spiritual Laws', *Essays.*   [10] 'On Reading New Books', *Sketches and Essays.* (1839)   [11] *Life.* iii, 332.

litt will have,[1] *the taste for literature becomes superficial as it becomes universal and is spread over a larger space.* Rather than follow in the train of *the insatiable monster of modern reading,* Charles Lamb would *forswear his spectacles, play at put, mend pens, kill fleas, stand on one leg, shell peas, or do whatsoever ignoble diversion you shall* set him to. *Alas!* he expostulates, *I am hurried on in the vortex, I die of new books, or the ever-lasting talk about them. I faint of Longman's. I sicken of the Constables. Blackwood and Cadell have me by the throat;* and he relieves himself *with honest John Bunyan, or Tom Brown,* or *Tom anybody, so long as they are not of this whiffling century.*[2] *This literary prurience after new print,* says Harrison, *unmans us for the enjoyment of the old songs chanted forth in the sunrise of human imagination.*[3]

There is *a fashion in reading as well as in dress, which lasts only for a season,*[4] and many read new books without discrimination, from vanity, to say they have read them, to be in the swim. It is a mania with some to read only those books which have lately come from the press for the sole reason that they are new, and *of all odd crazes,* says Birrell, *the craze to be for ever reading new books is one of the oddest.*[5] Many lesser men are full of such relations, agreeing with the learned Chinese bibliographer, Chi Yun, who catalogued the Imperial Library at Pekin, when he declared that everything worth saying had been said, if we only knew where to find it;[6]

> For out of the old fieldes, as men saithe,
> Cometh al this new corne from yere to yere,
> And out of old bookes, in good faithe,
> Cometh all this new science that men lere.[7]

More ado, saith Montaigne[8] *to interpret interpretations, than to interpret things; and more bookes upon bookes, than upon any other subject;* commentaries swarm, but of *authors* there is *great penury.* None the less, looking round upon his books, among which are, willy-nilly, several such echoes and distillations, he confesses, with a glint in his wise eye, that he may *presently borrow from a number of such botcherly-patchcotes* (men that he plods not much upon), wherewith to *enamel* his treatise of *Physiognomie.*[9]

When the Earl of Dudley[10] heard of a new poem, he asked himself first, whether it was superior to Homer, Shakespeare, Ariosto, Virgil, or Racine, and next whether he had all these at his *fingers'* ends, and then answering himself in the negative, he inferred that it was better to devote what time he had to the reading of *Homer, Ariosto & Co.,* than to newer

[1] *Op. cit.*   [2] 'The "Lepus" Papers', *Miscellaneous Prose.* 322.   [3] *Choice of Books.* 29.
[4] Hazlitt, 'On Reading New Books', *Sketches and Essays* (1839)   [5] 'Books Old and New', *Coll. Essays.* iii, 137.   [6] Giles, *Chinese Biog. Dict.* 122.   [7] Chaucer. 'Assembly of Fowles.' 22.   [8] 'Of Experience', *Essays.* Ed. Seccombe. iii, 407.
[9] *Ib.* 388.   [10] Qt. *Book-Lovers' Anthology.* 73.

writers. The good poet Gray[1] (writing to Benjamin West, May 8, 1742) exonerates himself from sending news of the present because he converses (as usual) *with none but the dead*, his *old friends*, who almost make him long to be with them; and, he goes on with a relish: *I have finished the Peloponnesian War, much to my honour, and a tight conflict it was . . . I have drunk and sung with Anacreon for the last fortnight, and am now feeding sheep with Theocritus*, and, quitting his figure because it is foolish, *I have run over Pliny's 'Epistles', and Martial . . . not to mention Petrarch*. James Russell Lowell[2] finds not only a *sense of security* in old books but a *feeling of seclusion* in having a *double wall of centuries* between them and the heats and clamours of contemporary books, and he dilates luxuriously on the sensuous delights of ripe old authors, tasting them as a connoisseur tastes a rare old vintage: *How limpid* (he rejoices) *seems the thought, how pure the old wine of scholarship that has been settling for so many generations in those silent crypts and Falernian amphoræ of the Past*. The voices of the past come from the *morning fields* rather than the *paved thoroughfares* of thought; old books *have sucked colour and ripeness from the genial autumns of all the select intelligences that have steeped them in their love and appreciations; these quaint freaks of russet tell of Montaigne; these stripes of crimson fire, of Shakespeare; this sober gold, of Sir Thomas Browne; this purpling bloom, of Lamb: in such fruits we taste the legendary gardens of Alcinous and the orchards of Atlas*.

New books, objects Austin Dobson,[3] *have* (for the time being) *neither part nor lot in our past of retrospect and suggestion. Of what we were, of what we like or liked, they know nothing; and we—if that be possible—know even less of them. Whether familiarity will breed contempt, or whether they will come home to our business or bosom, are things that lie on the lap of the Fates*. Old books, on the other hand, are memorable by *length of tenure, propinquity*, even by *patience under neglect*. We may never read them, but it would be a wrench to part with them, as all good bookmen know; for, as Lionel Johnson has well said,[4] *we live in time, and the past must always be the most momentous part of it. 'Peace, for I loved him, and love him for ever! The dead are not dead but alive*,' he quotes out of Tennyson, and infers that *what is true of loved humanity is true also of loved humanities, the high expression of man's mind. As Augustine said of the Christian faith, here is a beauty both old and new; only a starveling imagination is so hampered by the accidents of any ancient excellence that it cannot discern the essence which is dateless*.

And so they go on with a sense of the sacredness of authorship and a lively reverence for that which is beautiful with the *patina* of the ages, as many more have done in all times, and not least Alfonso of Aragon, who, as Bacon records in his *Apophthegms*, was wont to say in commendation of

---

[1] *Poems and Letters.* (1820) 151-2.   [2] *A Library of Old Authors.*   [3] *De Libris.* 3-4.
[4] *Post Liminium.* 211.

what is ripe with age that this quality appeared to be best in four things: *Old wood to burn, old wine to drink, old friends to trust, and old authors to read,* and in this quaternary of desirable old things we may well leave a subject which common experience so universally acclaims, and our William Shakespeare himself has summed up in three words: *Ripeness is all.*[1] That is what they all mean when they claim that there is no joy, no comfort, no sweetness, no pleasure in the world like that of a good book, and that all these are augmented if that book be old as well as good, for none but a zany of learning would set a value upon age *per se.* Against such folly Tacitus warned when he said that *we extol the productions of the ancients but are wholly unmindful of contemporary merit*; and Montaigne also when he argued against the folly that makes us run after *strange and scholastic examples,* deeming *truth to be nothing wiser by being more aged. But is it not,* he asks, *that we rather seek the honour of allegations, than the truth of discourses? As if it were more to borrow our proofs from the shop of Vascosan or Plantin, than from that we daily see in our village;*[2] a pitfall into which no bookman this side of bibliomania would slip did he remember also that in no sense can antiquity *privilege an error* or novelty *prejudice a truth.*

John Ruskin came near the truth when he said *all books are divisible into two classes, the books of the hour, and the books of all time,*[3] and Oliver Goldsmith meant no less when, in the *Citizen of the World,* he reckoned up that *the volumes of antiquity, like medals, may very well serve to amuse the curious, but the works of the moderns, like the current coin of a kingdom, are much better for immediate use.* The visits we pay to the former are like those we pay to the great; but our acquaintance with modern books is familiar, giving more inward satisfaction, like sitting with a friend; which, doubtless, is what they all intend when they advise, expound, expostulate and argue upon this theme: *lux longe alia est solis et lychnorum.*[4] There is good and bad in all books whether old or new, and Hamerton detects[5] *jealousy* in the persistence with which contemporaries belittle the older writers, yet he holds that for knowledge *the best authors are always the most recent,* that *our methods have gained in precision since Milton's time,* and that although Shakespeare and Milton can *still fill our imagination richly,* modern writers can do as much.

Hazlitt again would sum up the matter in an irony hinting that survival is a test of merit: *I do not think altogether the worse of a book for having survived the author a generation or two,* he argues,[6] yet *I have more confidence,* he confesses, *in the dead than in the living.* I am not entirely with him in that,

[1] *King Lear.* v, 2.   [2] *Essays.* Ed. Seccombe. iii, 426.   [3] *Sesame and Lilies.* i.
[4] 'There is a wide difference between the light of the sun and that of a lamp.'
Cicero. Coel. 28.   [5] *Intellectual Life.* 382–3.   [6] 'On Reading Old Books', *The Plain Speaker.* 1826. ii, 64.

though I would say with Lionel Johnson,[1] *take me with you in spirit, Ancients of Art, the crowned, the sceptred, whose voices this night chaunt a 'gloria in excelsis', flooding the soul with a passion of joy and awe*; for, as he explains, *the voices of the day must wait for their consecrate authority and confirmed applause till Time, the just, shall please*: books being living things must ripen, and they ripen best, like buildings and the greater trees, in the spaces of time; even the mediocrities of the past, he says, are more tolerable than those of the present: *the blunders of the dead are over and done, harming no one; the blunders of the living are a danger and a nuisance*: which is as it should be, *de mortuis nil nisi bonum*. But who can speak of all, or account for all times and what may happen in them? Great writers have been born and become classics, since many of my authorities upheld the past, each in his time, and no one shall say what the future may hold: *there is more day to dawn, the sun is but a morning star*;[2] and although it may well be *an economy to read old and famed books*, as Emerson advises,[3] the *company of the masters is a roll long closed and complete, the gates which lead to the Elysian fields may slowly wheel back, on their adamantine hinges, to admit some new and chosen modern.*[4] *Ab uno disce omnes*, take this for a taste, and look out for the best: *Speak of the moderns without contempt, and of the ancients without idolatry; judge them all by their merits, but not by their ages.*[5]

VII. SUBSTITUTES FOR LIFE

There are, as all know, many paths by which we may search out powers and faculties of human nature, consider its wants, survey its inclinations, propensities and desires, ponder its intuitions, proposals and ends, examine the causes and fitness of its attitudes and ambitions, the worth of them all, their general excellency. Books are but one, and they are better as instruments of life than substitutes for life. Even good bookmen, like John Burroughs, ask for *few books and plenty of real things*.[6] *Everything*, says Epictetus,[7] has *two handles, the one by which it may be borne, the other* by which it cannot. It is in our choice to take and leave what we will, and in our own power, as they say, to make or mar ourselves. *By Jupiter*,[8] Calvisius Taurus exclaimed, *one man actually asks to read Plato, not in order to better his life, but to deck out his diction and style, not to gain in discretion, but in prettiness.*

We may study the same things with diverse results, for palates vary according to their constitution and the ends at which they aim, so let

[1] *Post Liminium.* 217–18, 213. [2] H. D. Thoreau, *Walden.* Scott Lib. 331.
[3] *Society and Solitude.* (1870) 163. [4] Frederic Harrison, *Choice of Books.* 23.
[5] Chesterfield, *Letters to his Son.* cxlii. [6] *Indoor Studies.* 244. [7] *Enchiridion.*
Trans. Elizabeth Carter. [8] Aulus Gellius, *Attic Nights.* Loeb. Ed. i, 9.

experience determine. Jeremy Collier held that *to take Measures wholly from Books, without looking into Men and Business, is like travelling in a Map, where though Countries and Cities are well enough distinguished, yet Villages and private Seats are either overlooked, or too generally marked for a stranger to find; therefore he that would be a Master must Draw from the Life, as well as copy from Originals, and joyn Theory and Experience together.*[1] The learned and pious Dr. Henry More confessed that he *very sparingly so much as read any books,* seeking *a more near Union with a certain Life and Sense than the Driness of mere Reason, or the Wantonness of the trimmest Imagination,* however much those may be *useful Instruments for some to draw them to Good.* He read not all, but the most *Useful Writings,* holding *Ille Intellectus qui Plura intelligit non est Nobilior, sed qui Digniora*; that understanding is the noblest which knows not the most but the best things. He bragged that he was no *Wholesale Man,* for the more we attended to things *ad extra,* the less we did to those *ad intra*; his motto: *Claude Fenestras, ut Luceat Domus,* shut the window that the house may be lit, intimates *that we must turn our eyes inwards, if we would behold the shining truth in our own minds*;[2] or upwards, as some hold,

> he who receives
> Light from above, from the fountain of light,
> No other doctrine needs, though granted true;[3]

but 'tis all one if, as some would agree, *the Kingdom of God is within,* and he

> who reads
> Incessantly, and to his reading brings not
> A spirit and judgment equal or superior,
> (And what he brings, what needs he elsewhere seek?)
> Uncertain and unsettl'd still remains,
> Deep verst in books and shallow in himself,
> Crude or intoxicate, collecting toys,
> And trifles for choice matters, worth a spunge;
> As children gathering pebbles on the shore.[4]

The earth has had to forget its books, says F. D. Maurice, *that it might recover its men.*[5] Men come first, and when the world has recovered them, they produce books, which do not crush manhood: they call it forth, showing what men have been and what they may be; they show what a divine discipline has been at work to form men; *they teach us that there is such a discipline at work to form us into men*; that is the test, he urges, to which all books must at last be brought: *if they do not bear it their doom is fixed.*

[1] *Essays on Several Moral Subjects.* ii, 100.   [2] *Life,* Ward. xii.   [3] Milton, *Paradise Regained.* iv, 288–90.   [4] *Ib.* 322–30.   [5] *Friendship of Books.* 62.

They may be light or heavy, penny sheet or vast folio; *they may speak of things seen or unseen; Science or Art; what has been or what is to be; they may amuse or weary us, flatter or scorn us*: but if they do not help to *make us better and more substantial men*, they only provide fuel for *a fire larger, and more utterly destructive, than that which consumed the Library of the Ptolemies.*[1] But I will urge these cavilling and contumelious arguments no farther, yet before I conclude I will add a relation out of the *Centuries of Meditations* of our wise Traherne,[2] what he hath said tending to this purpose: *He that knows the secrets of nature with Albertus Magnus, or the motions of the heavens with Galileo, or the cosmography of the moon with Hevelius, or the body of man with Galen, or the nature of diseases with Hippocrates, or the harmonies in melody with Orpheus, or of poesy with Homer, or of grammar with Lilly, or of whatever else with the greatest artist; he is nothing, if he knows them merely for talk or idle speculation, or transient and external use. But he that knows them for value, and knows them his own shall profit infinitely.* Many besides might I reckon up in this wise, but I have set out that which I intended, *et sic demonstratur, quod erat demonstrandum,* which is to the same purpose as that tenet of Lord Balfour: *Fill a dull man to the brim with knowledge and he will not become less dull.*[3]

The mind nauseates the thought of processions of learned dunces and dullards: schoolmasters, professors, dons, clerics, popes of knowledge, morosophi, wise fools, who

> Turn Caxton, Wynkyn, each old Goth and Hun,
> To rectify the reading of a pun.
> Thus, nicely trifling, accurately dull,
> How one may toil, and toil,—to be a fool![4]

tyrants of information, crammed, packed full of learning, but lifeless, stupid, repellent, *men who have piled such a load of books on their heads, their brains have seemed to be squasht by them:*[5]

> The bookful blockhead, ignorantly read,
> With loads of learned lumber in his head.[6]

They have neither lived wisely nor read wisely. *They regard knowledge as a kind of capital—not revenue. They sit on the bag: It's the credit of knowing they care for: and the discredit of not knowing they fear.*[7] They are neither big readers nor little readers. They are worse than those who, according to Sir W. Waller,[8] affect rather to look upon books, than in them; thus missing their grace and glory. They have purchased unto themselves nought but

---

[1] *Friendship of Books.* 91.   [2] xli, 189.   [3] *Essays and Addresses.* 10.   [4] D. Mallet. Qt. *Book-Lovers' Anth.* 152.   [5] A. and J. C. Hare, *Guesses at Truth:* (1889) 149. [6] Pope, *Essay on Criticism.* 612–13.   [7] Sir Walter Raleigh, *Letters.* i, 266. [8] *Divine Meditations.*

tediousness, which they too fondly communicate to others, for if, as Swift asserts,[1] wit without knowledge is *a sort of cream, which gathers in a night to the top, and by a skilful hand may be soon whipped into froth, but once scummed away, what appears underneath will be fit for nothing, but to be thrown to the hogs,* what shall we say of knowledge without wit? *Quid enim est tam furiosum quam verborum vel optimorum atque ornatissimorum sonitus inanis, nulla subiecta sententia nec scientia?*[2] What they both advance is that a balance between judicious learning from books and from experience should be our aim, an idea well put by Jeremy Collier when he wrote that *He who depends only upon his own Experience, has but a few Materials to work upon. He is confined to narrow Limits both of Time and Place: And is not fit to draw a large Model, and to pronounce upon Business which is complicated and unusual.* He sees the same difference between a *Man of meer Practice* and a man of *Learning* as between an *Empirick* and a *Physician. The first,* he says, *may have a good Receipt, or two; and if Diseases and Patients were very scarce, and all alike, he might do tolerably well. But if you enquire concerning the Causes of Distempers, and the Constitution of Human Bodies, the Danger of Symptoms, and the Methods of Cure, upon which the Success of Medicine depends, he knows little of the Matter.*[3] For the rest, as Lord Chesterfield advises, *wear your learning like your watch, in a private pocket; and do not pull it out, and strike it, merely to show that you have one*; which is no more than he intends when he says *if you happen to have an Elzevir classic in your pocket, neither show it nor mention it.*[4] I shall leave it at that: *verbum satis sapienti.*

---

[1] *Battle of the Books,* Preface.   [2] 'For what so mad as the sound of empty words, however well chosen and elegant, if there be no basis of sense or sagacity?' Cicero, *De Oratore.* i, 51.   [3] 'Of the Entertainment of Books', *Essays.* ii, 99–100.
[4] *Letters to his Son.* cxlii.

Part VII

STUDY AND BOOK-LEARNING

I. THE FASCINATION OF STUDY

In any catalogue of the uses of books, high place must be given to the *delight of knowledge and learning*, which, as some point out, *surpasseth all other in nature*, for in all *other pleasures there is satiety, and after they be used, their verdure departeth; which showeth well they be but deceits of pleasure, and not pleasures: and that it was the novelty which pleased, and not the quality; therefore we see that voluptuous men turn friars, and ambitious princes turn melancholy. But of knowledge there is no satiety, satisfaction and appetite* being *interchangeable*.[1] *To most kind of men it is an extraordinary delight to study*, says Robert Burton,[2] *for what a world of books offers itself, in all subjects, arts, and sciences, to the sweet content and capacity of the Reader!* It is, indeed, a world of endless exploration and uncountable adventures, full of strange countries, peoples, animals; wonders, beauties, terrors, astonishments; it has treasures and riches; curiosities, freaks, fantasies, monsters, hobgoblins, fays, gnomes, satyrs, nymphs; trees, flowers.

> With buds, and bells, and stars without a name,
> With all the gardener Fancy e'er could feign,
> Who breeding flowers, will never breed the same;[3]

a world without end, for *all that Mankind has done, thought, gained, or been is lying as in magic preservation in the pages of Books*.[4]

Books are the universe in print, nay, eternity; the sure preservatives of events:

> Troy owes to Homer what whist owes to Hoyle:
> The present century was growing blind
> To the great Marlborough's skill in giving knocks,
> Until his late Life by Archdeacon Coxe.[5]

And if, as George Herbert attests (in *Jacula Prudentum*), *the years know more than books*, which needs no defence, without books the years would have less significance, for books are the reading-glasses of time, and *Knowledge*,

---

[1] Bacon, *Advancement of Learning*. Bk. i.   [2] *Anat. of Melan.* (1904) ii, 102.   [3] Keats, Ode to Psyche'.   [4] Carlyle, *Heroes and Hero-Worship*. (1841) 259.   [5] Byron, *Don Juan*. xc.

the Quarry out of which these Jewels (Books) are digged;[1] *haurit aquam cribris qui vult sine discere libris,*[2]

> Who, without Books, essays to learn,
> Draws water in a leaky urn;[3]

they reflect the present and *summon up remembrance of things past.*[4] A book itself, as I have quoted out of Carlyle, is a university; Gibbon's Autobiography *supplied the place of a college* for Mark Pattison,[5] not only giving advice, but inspiring him to follow it.

What *magic casements* are opened by them on all the wonderlands of Knowledge: Mathematics, Sociology, Biology, Chemistry, Astronomy, Psychology, Medicine, Geology, Anthropology, etc., of which so many and such elaborate treatises are of late written: in Mechanics and Manufactures, Crafts and Trades, and their mysteries; Military matters, Aeronautics, Navigation, Riding of Horses, Fencing, Cricket, Racing, Swimming, Golf, Billiards, Tennis, Hunting, Motoring, Fishing, Fowling, etc., with exquisite pictures of all sports and games, and what not! In Music, Art, Poetry, Philosophy, Philology, Heraldry, Bibliography, Genealogy, Topography, Geography, etc., they afford great tomes; or of those studies of Antiquity: Archæology, Ethnology, Paleontology, History and the like: what so speculative, what so pleasant? What vast tomes are extant on Law and Divinity, for profit, pleasure, practice, or speculation! The names of books alone fill whole volumes: all manner of authors of all manner of kinds offering endless feasts to suit all palates.

Some take an infinite delight to study the very languages wherein these books are written, Greek, Latin, Hebrew, French, German, Italian, Syriac, Sanscrit, Chaldaic, Arabic, etc. Methinks it would please any man to peruse those excellent books of Travel put out by Cook, Mungo Park, Wallace, Waterton, Marco Polo, Shackleton, Bruce, Scott, Hakluyt, Richard Burton, Mary Kingsley, Nansen, Dampier, Sven Hedin, Doughty: to go with them to the ends of the earth and never go forth the limits of his study; to read those exquisite descriptions of cities, temples, pictures, monuments of Ruskin, John Addington Symonds, Walter Pater, Arthur Symons, Pierre Loti, Sacheverell and Osbert Sitwell; those famous histories of Herodotus, Thucydides, Cæsar, Livy, Tacitus, Suetonius, Gibbon, Napier, Macaulay, Grote, Mommsen, Green; those natural histories of Pliny, Linnæus, Buffon, Cuvier, Darwin, Faber, Hudson; those accurate diaries and curious confessions of Benvenuto Cellini, Evelyn, Pepys, Sully, Rousseau, Marie Bashkirtseff, Blunt, Barbellion; those pleasant epistles of

---

[1] Richard Whitlock, *Zootomia*. 238.   - [2] Motto on Lord de Tabley's bookplate.
[3] Austin Dobson, *A Bookman's Budget*. 188.   [4] Shakespeare, *Sonnets*. 30.   [5] Pattison, *Memoirs*. 130.

Cicero, Pliny, Walpole, Lamb, Madame de Sévigné, Edward FitzGerald, Keats, Cowper, Lady Mary Montagu, making us privy to their familiar affairs, tastes, ambitions, aspirations, etc.; the curious itineraries of Johnson, Boswell, Davidson, Edward Lear, Richard Le Gallienne, Hilaire Belloc, Aldous Huxley, Lady Duff Gordon, Dufferin; and all the essays, poems, novels, tales, that make up this multi-coloured and multitudinous world *flowing with milk and honey.* To see well-cut Herbals, Entomologies, Ornithologies, Conchologies, expressed in their proper colours to the life; to see birds, beasts, and fishes of the sea, spiders, gnats, scorpions, serpents, flies, living and extinct monsters, etc., all creatures set out by the same art, or by photo-engraving, lithography, collotype, stencil, etc., and truly expressed in lively colours, with an exact description of their natures, virtues, qualities, etc., as hath been accurately performed by various cunning artificers of past and present times: what more pleasing studies can there be than these?

Such is their excellency that (I say with Burton) all those ornaments and childish baubles of wealth are not worthy to be compared with them. I could live and die with them, as he saith, and take more delight, true content of mind in them than thou hast in all thy wealth and sport, whoever and how rich soever thou art. And, as Cardan[1] well seconds him, *Honorabile magis est et gloriosum haec intelligere quam provinciis praeesse, atque juvenem esse*: it is more honourable and glorious to understand these truths than to govern provinces, and to be young. *To most persons books are but an amusement, an interlude between the hours of serious occupation*, but *the scholar is he who has found the key to knowledge, and knows his way about in the world of books.*[2] So sweet is the delight of Study, the more learning he has the more he covets to learn (as he that hath a dropsy, the more he drinks the thirstier he is), and the last day is the pupil of its predecessor, *prioris discipulus*; the longer he lives the more he is enamoured of the Muses: *the zeal of learning is never out of date; the example—were there no more—burns before one as a sacred fire, for ever unquenchable*;[3] and well it may, *for there is no treasure so much enriches the mind of man as learning; for learning nature acknowledgeth a reason, by leaving industrie to finish her unperfect work; for without learning conceyte is like a fruitfull soyl without tilling, the memorie like a storehouse without wares, the will like a shippe without a rudder.*[4] I may therefore boldly conclude as I began this chapter, with Francis Bacon[5] and that which hath *rationem totius*: which is, that learning *disposeth the constitution of the mind not to be fixed or settled in the defects thereof, but still to be capable and susceptible of growth and reformation.*

[1] Qt. Burton, *Anat. of Melan.* (1904) ii, 104.   [2] Mark Pattison, *Milton.* 110.
[3] Gissing, *Private Papers of Henry Ryecroft.* 37.   [4] 'A. B. To the Reader', in *The End of Nero, etc.* Tacitus. Hist. iv. Trans. Savile. 1591.   [5] *Advancement of Learning.* Bk. i.

II. WHAT SEEK THESE STUDIOUS ONES?

In the other extreme or defect of this love of learning, studies, knowledge, scholarship, I know there are such as err in kind and quantity, bookworms, misers of knowledge, moles of print, eternally burrowing in musty tomes without purpose, pedants, missing the sweetness and the light of life. Cousin-german to them are those pretenders of learning, literate fools who sit in wise men's seats, whom the common people hold learned, grave and wise; and those other vain students *whose learning* Roger Ascham described as *gotten in a summer heat, and washed away with the Christmas snow again.*[1] But before I can come to treat of these several errors and obliquities, their causes, symptoms, affections, which I do apart, I must say something of the object, joys, and allurements of the scholarly passion.

What seek they who study with so much avidity, with such absorption? I speak not of those who study for position, occupation or preferment in profession or trade—Milton, in his trade of poetry, retired to Horton, as he told Diodate: consuming· five years of solitude in reading ancient writers as a preparation for the writing of *Paradise Lost,*

Et totum rapiunt me, mea vita, libri—[2]

but of those who love study for its own sake, who glory in that *felicitous studiousness* and that *studious felicity* which Richard de Bury[3] attributes to *the all-powerful eunuch,* who, we are told in the *Acts,* was *so mightily kindled* by the prophetic books that he ceased not to study on his long journey, *banished all thought of the populous palace of Queen Candace,* and *forgot even the treasures of which he was keeper,* ignoring alike the incidents of his journey and the chariot in which he rode; those who know Learning, as Nicholas Breton so eagerly proves and firmly demonstrates, *the darling of wisdom and the delight of wit, unpleasing to none that knows her, unprofitable to none that loves her,* making *age honourable, youth admirable, the virtuous wise and the wise gracious: the nurse of nature, with that milk of reason that would make a child of grace never lie from the dug.*[4]

In the fervour of learning they find wisdom, which is joy, ecstasy; whether they seek it or not, it is bliss, for the *Round of Knowledge is like the great and exemplary Wheels of Heaven.*[5] *Happy is the man that findeth wisdom, and the man that getteth understanding. For the merchandise of it is better than the merchandise of silver, and the gain thereof than fine gold* (Proverbs iii, 13–14). The scholar and the poet are related, in Joubert's opinion, because they

[1] *The Schoolmaster.* i.   [2] 'And I am wholly captivated by my books, which are my life.' Milton, *Ad Carolum Diodatum.* 26.   [3] *Philobiblon.* Trans. Thomas. 96–7.
[4] *Characters upon Essays, Moral and Divine.*   [5] Sir Thomas Browne, *Pseudodoxia Epidemica.* Pref. Works. i, 115.

become such, more for pleasure than by labour; they are *impelled* or *restrained* not *by their ambition but* by *their genius*.[1] They will not be denied; no temptations powerful enough to draw them from their studies; riches, honours, rewards, love, adventures, have no manner of purchase for them. *I would rather*, Alexander told Aristotle,[2] *be first in learning than in wealth and power*. Nor can threats, intimidations, or dangers affect them. There are many examples: Richard de Bury (*Philobiblon, ix*) relates of Taurus the Philosopher (out of *Aulus Gellius*), how the Athenians, hating the people of Megara, decreed that any of them entering Athens should be put to death; but despite that decree Euclid, himself a Megarean, was so determined to hear the lectures of Socrates that he disguised himself as a woman and thus had his wish, travelling from Megara to Athens each night, a distance of twenty miles. The learned fervour of Archimedes was so *imprudent and excessive* that the same study which saved his life deprived him of it; for *assuming as much glory in saving Archimedes, as in destroying Syracuse*, Marcellus, after his great Sicilian victory, commanded the soldiers to spare the life of the philosopher; but while Archimedes was making geometrical figures near his home, his eyes fixed upon the ground, a soldier entering his house, bent on plunder, asked him who he was. The philosopher was so intent that he made him no direct answer, but pointing to the figure, he said, *Have a care not to spoil this circle*. Thereupon the soldier, feeling that the victor of the Empire had been slighted, drew his sword and cut off the philosopher's head, *blending his blood with the lineaments of his art*.[3]

If learning is denied to men because of their station in life, they will get it all the same, as those two Chinamen[4] in the fourth century B.C., who, being servants in a school, picked up their education by inscribing exercises on the palms of their hands and on their bare legs, and transcribing them at night when they got home; or on the other side, Cheng Hsuan, to whom Confucius appeared in a vision, who was rich and so fond of wine that he is said to have been able to take three hundred cups without *losing his head*, yet he lived so much for learning that his very slave girls were highly educated, and inlarded their conversation with quotations from the *Odes*, like Sir Maurice Meanwell's servants in *The Female Virtuosos*, who became so learned after the example of the heroine of that play, that even his *little boy cannot turn the spit without a Pharamond or a Cassandra in his hand*, and if he calls for drink, the butler brings him a *Spenser* or a *Ben Jonson*. Giles tells also how K'uang Heng, a famous minister of the time of the Emperor Yuan Ti, being born in poverty,

---

[1] *Selected Thoughts*, Trans. Lyttleton, 176.   [2] Aulus Gellius, *Attic Nights*. Loeb. Ed. xx, 5.   [3] Q. V. Maximus, *Romae Antiquae Descriptio*. Eng. trans. (1678) 399.
[4] Giles, *Chinese Biog. Dict.* 27.

entered the service of a wealthy man as a wageless menial, for the sole chance of being within reach of books; he had no candles, so at night time bored a hole in the wall between his own and a neighbour's house, and was thus able to filch enough light to carry on his studies with success.[1]

No labour in the world too great for them that love learning, and if those labours in our times are reduced by the preservation of books, and their general accessibility, in ancient times knowledge was gathered with difficulties which none but the heroic could surmount. Printing not being in use, as Thomas Hearne points out,[2] scholars were forced very often to travel into other countries, if they desired, as they did, *advantage of any book*. Pythagoras travelled into Egypt and *stayed there many years before he could be admitted to a knowledge of their mysteries*, returning a complete scholar and philosopher. For aught I know, Hearne continues, he might have understood all those inscriptions which are reported to have been upon the Pyramids. That which made the ancients more ready and expert was the art with which they used to strengthen their memories.

When they were particularly in love with any author, *they not only read him over and over*, but would be at the pains of transcribing him several times. Demosthenes so admired Thucydides, that *he writ him over eight times with his own hand*; and we have other notable instances, as that of Petrarch when on a visit to Liège. Finding a good company of books, he transcribed one oration of Cicero with his own hand and had another written out by a colleague, under great difficulties, for *in that fair city of the barbarians it was very difficult to get any ink*, and what he did get was *as yellow as saffron*;[3] and nearer our own time, Dr. Henry Aldrich used often to transcribe the authors he read, especially when he was to print anything. But to such as are well informed, this passion for study is common knowledge; most of them can augment its history from their own reading or observation, and they will each make answer in like case that it is a stimulation in youth, a consolation in age, whatever misadventures affect its less fortunate devotees.

But have I not yet sufficiently answered mine own question: To what end? There may be no answer, study being an end in itself. I should be well content with that conclusion, for can we be in better condition than happy? Yet some ask more of study, and some have found more, as I have shown. Some have gone so far as to find in learning the key of life and an assurance of immortality. When Dante, in the seventh Circle of his *Inferno*, addresses Brunetto Lattini as

---

[1] *Chinese Biog. Dict.* 386.   [2] *Herneanae.* Ed. Bliss. 85.   [3] Qt. Elton, *Great Book-Collectors.* 43.

La cara e buona imagine paterna
Di voi, quando nel mondo ad ora ad ora
M' insegnavate come l' uom s' eterna:[1]

The dear, benign, paternal image, such
As thine was, when so lately thou didst teach me
The way for man to win eternity,[2]

he is referring, Tatham reminds us,[3] to *the new secular learning*, to which Brunetto's work had introduced him, awakening in him the desire for that earthly fame which should make his name immortal; 'tis a common humour, incident to all men, to applaud and flatter themselves with the notion of earthly fame and heavenly bliss, and I doubt not that Dante was among the rest in this business, for men have not, even in our time, learnt to live without reward or purpose, for the joy of living, as they say, or if some have, and I know some have, they are shy in admitting it, fearing, as they well may, the resentment of the venal and the purposeful.

But I grow tedious and must make an end, for I have said enough to the observant, and *a nod is as good as a wink to a blind horse*; howbeit, if a purpose you would have for your studies beyond that of the immediacy of your trade (on which matter I would not trespass, for it is not my business), take the words of Francis Bacon again (I know none better), where he argues that *as both heaven and earth do conspire to contribute to the use and benefit of man*; so the end ought to be *to separate and reject vain speculation; whatsoever is empty and void*, and *to preserve whatsoever is solid and fruitful: that knowledge may not be as a courtesan, for pleasure and vanity only, or as a bonds-woman, to acquire and gain to her master's use; but a spouse, for generation, fruit, and comfort;*[4] and let us remember, as Goethe advises, after Socrates, *not to indulge in empty speculation*, but to *live and do*.[5]

III. STUDIES AND OLD AGE

No labour in the world is like unto study, for no other labour is less dependent upon the rise and fall of bodily condition; and, although learning is not quickly got, there are ripe wits and scholarly capacities among men of all physical degrees, whilst for those of advancing years study is of unsurpassed advantage, both for enjoyment and as a preventative of mental decay. *Old men retain their intellects well enough*, said Cicero, then on the full tide of his own vigorous old age, *if only they keep their minds active and*

[1] *Inferno*. xv, 83–5.   [2] *Ib*. Trans. Cary. i, 65.   [3] *Francesco Petrarca*. ii, 20.
[4] *Advancement of Learning*. Bk. i.   [5] *Maxims*. Trans. Bailey Saunders. 161.

fully employed;[1] and Dr. Johnson holds the same opinion: *There must be a diseased mind,* he said, *where there is a failure of memory at seventy.*[2] Cato (so Cicero tells us) was a tireless student in old age; when past sixty he composed the seventh book of his *Origins,* collected and revised his speeches, wrote a *treatise on augural, pontifical, and civil law,* and studied Greek to keep his *memory in working order;* he held that such studies were *the training grounds of the mind,* and prophylatics against consciousness of old age.[3] Isaac D'Israeli[4] has several instances of the pursuit of studies into advanced age: how Socrates learnt to play on musical instruments when an old man, Cato *thought proper* to learn Greek and Plutarch Latin, when the one had reached his eightieth year and the other was approaching it; Theophrastus began his *Characters* at ninety; Izaak Walton wrote his Life of Bishop Sanderson at eighty-five; the great Arnauld was studying rigorously at eighty-two; Ronsard applied himself late to books, and Boccaccio was thirty-five before he commenced his studies in *polite literature;* Sir Henry Spelman began to *cultivate the sciences* at fifty; Colbert returned to his Latin and Law studies at sixty; Tellier, Chancellor of France, learned Logic in order to dispute with his grandchildren; Dr. Johnson *applied himself* to the Dutch language a few years before his death; Ogilby, the translator of *Homer* and *Virgil,* knew little Latin or Greek till he was past fifty; Franklin did not begin his *philosophical pursuits* until he was nearly the same age; and I have heard it said that Queen Victoria took up Hindustani when past seventy.

Michelangelo was so proud of his capacity for study in extreme old age, that he is said to have invented the device representing an old man in a go-cart bearing an hour-glass and the inscription *Ancora imparo,* I am still learning. Ludovico Monaldesco, at the extraordinary age of 115, wrote the Memoirs of his times, and La Casa bragged, in a letter to a friend, that he would go on making sonnets twenty-five or thirty years after his death: *Io credo ch' io faro Sonnetti venti cinque anni, o trenta, poi che io saro morto.* As this may be no more than a fantastic boast, I shall resolve this chapter with Adam Smith, who contends that *of all the amusements of old age, the most grateful and soothing is a renewed acquaintance with the favourite studies of youth,* and as he said it *Sophocles* and *Euripides* lay open before him for proof. How many such encomiums I might add out of the histories of scholars and learned men is so well known to all experienced readers, that I need not examine further particulars, for there are few who will dispute that the intellect and the soul require support as well as the body, *for they are like lamps: unless you feed them with oil, they too go out from old age.*[5]

---

[1] *De Senectate.* 22. Trans. E. S. Shuckburgh. 38. [2] *Life.* Ed. Hill. iii, 191. [3] *Op. cit.* 61–2. [4] *Cur. Lit.* i, 171–5. [5] Cicero, *De Senectute.* 22. Trans. Shuckburgh. 63.

IV. A DIGRESSION OF CAPACIOUS MEMORIES

If a people can be *destroyed for lack of knowledge* (*Hosea* iv, 6), a man, in spite of the belief that *a good memory is an essential element of genius*,[1] may be destroyed or translated into a dolt of learning, a dizzard, a mere zany of words, by excess of it. As the athlete may become muscle-bound, or a glutton pot-bellied, so may an incontinent scholar become memory-bound, pot-headed: remembering all, knowing nought: no more than a *walking encyclopædia*;

> Pox on't, quoth *Time* to *Thomas Hearne*,
> Whatever I *forget* you learn.[2]

Yet great industry in study and capacious memory have often accompanied practical ability, as when Mithridates learned the two and twenty several tongues current within his dominions, in order to address his army and discourse with his people without intermediaries, and that other Persian king, Cyrus, found it convenient to remember the names of all his soldiers;[3] and it is said of Themistocles *could call by name the 20,000 citizens of Athens*.[4] But to such as are judicious, and immune from dotage, the dangers of excessive memory are easily avoided or remedied, so out of humane authors I shall take a few examples which, though curious in themselves, may serve as cautions (some of them) to those in danger of remembering too much. Bookmen of capacious memories are common to all lands. In China, Chang Fang-p'ing committed the *Three Histories* to memory, Ch'en T'uan could remember anything read over once, and that *precocious student*, Chang An-shih, was able so exactly to repeat the contents of *three boxes of books*, which were missing, *that on recovery of the books they were found to tally exactly with his description*.[5] Niebuhr, *the historian, restored from recollection a large book of accounts that had been accidentally destroyed in one of the public offices of Denmark*;[6] and in our own land, Ben Jonson could repeat *all that he had ever written and whole books that he had read*;[7] Dr. Sanderson, Bishop of Lincoln, had so matchless a memory that he could recite all the *Odes of Horace*, all Tully's *Offices*, and much of *Juvenal* and *Persius, without book*;[8] the Rev. John Beale, the scientifical Rector of Yeovil in Somerset and sometime Chaplain to King Charles II, could memorize the contents of any book after a single reading; Richard Heber was ever *ready and copious in long quotations from Politian, Sannazarius, Vida*, etc., and Dibdin and Drury once heard him repeat Canning's *Iter ad*

---

[1] J. F. Nisbet, *Insanity of Genius*. 255.   [2] Qt. Dibdin, *Bibliomania*. Ed. 1811. 445.
[3] Q. V. Maximus, *Romae Antiquae Descriptio*. 401.   [4] Nisbet, *op. cit.* 255.   [5] Giles, *Chinese Biog. Dict*. 21, 105, 8.   [6] Nisbet, *op. cit.* 255.   [7] *Ib.*   [8] *Life of Sanderson*, Isaak Walton.

Meccam from beginning to end, apparently without a single trip; his memory, saith mine author,[1] was only exceeded by that of Porson, which he had often heard him call *almost divine.* Dr. George Hakewill claims that one of the most famous for memory among the ancients was Seneca, the father, *who reports of himself that he could repeat two thousand names, or two hundred verses, backward or forward;* but, mine authority adds, out of *Muretus,* a young man of Corsica *far exceeds it,* for *he could recite thirty-six thousand names in the same order as they were delivered, without any stay or staggering, as readily, as if he had read them out of a book.*[2]

Nathaniel Wanley[3] gives twenty-nine instances for the most part of men who have benefited themselves and others by their power of retention of books, laws, figures, names, etc., of which I may cite as relevant those notable examples of Joseph Scaliger, who committed to memory the whole of *Homer* in twenty-one days; Franciscus Suarez, who had St. Augustine's works by heart; and Dr. Raynolds, who had memorized not only all *St. Augustine,* but *also all classical authors,* becoming, as he may well add, *a living library. Carmidas a Grecian,* or *Carneades,* as *Cicero* and *Quintilian* call him, *was of so singular a memory, that he was able to repeat by heart the contents of most books in a library,* as if he read *immediately out of the books themselves;* Portius Latro had so great a memory that *he needed not the assistance of books;* the famous Bishop Jewel could *repeat anything he had penned after once reading it,* and anything he had once read, no matter what difficulties it contained, barbarous or hard words, as Welsh or Irish, he could repeat *both forwards and backwards without hesitation.* Lord Bacon once read to him the last clauses of ten lines in Erasmus's *Paraphrase* in *a confused and dismembered manner,* but after a small pause he rehearsed *all those broken parcels of sentences the right way,* without stumbling. Neoptiamus, cousin of Heliodorus the Bishop, by continual reading *made his bosom a Christian library,* so that in disputation and familiar conference, if any man *cited a testimony, he could straight know from whence it was,* this from Tertullian, that Cyprian's, another from Lactantius; Theodorus Metochites was another *living library and, as it were, an oracle, where a man might know all he desired;* our own Thomas Fuller had so great a memory that he could name *in order all the signs on both sides the way from the beginning of Paternoster Row at Ave-Maria Lane, to the bottom of Cheapside,* and he could *dictate to five several writers at the same time, on as many different subjects,* a faculty which many might envy in the hurrying days of these later times.

But they in some measure are all exceeded by the account of Jerome of Prague, *the same that was burnt alive in the council of Constance,* who after three hundred and forty days *in the bottom of a stinking and dark tower,*

---

[1] Dibdin, *Reminiscences.* i, 431–2.   [2] *Apologie.* (1630) 225.   [3] *Wonders of the Little World.* (1806) i, 151–60.

where *he could neither read nor see*, yet alleged so many testimonies from the most learned and the wisest persons in favour of his tenets, cited so many fathers of the Church, as might have sufficed had he had their books with him. Of Magliabecchi the librarian of Florence, of whom I shall speak more opportunely in another place, he discourses at length, but I shall only name here that reference he makes to his head, which became *an universal index of both titles and matter*. As a final example, I may conclude with that account of Lipsius, who remembered the whole of *Tacitus*, and pledged himself to recite word for word any passage required of him, consenting to allow a person to stand by him with a dagger, and to plunge it into his body should he fail to repeat the exact words. And now may it please your good worships to find, if you desire them, more of such marvels in *Wanley*.

V. OF LETTER FERITS AND BOOK SOTS

I have sufficiently illustrated the power and fascination of study, and have also done so more at large in my sections of Reading and Readers. Many will not believe all such stories to be true, but laugh commonly, and deride them when they read them, but let these men consider with themselves how many marvels are recounted daily, nay hourly, throughout the world in the popular press, and that every day it is being proved to them that there are more things in Heaven and Earth than are dreamt of in their philosophy. But what more marvellous than that, as I have already hinted, so beneficent a faculty as study should not be wholly good, so many several ways are we plagued by ill-seeming and ill-usage, that even faculties excellent in themselves may become vanity and vexation of spirit.

The testimony of Montaigne[1] may not unfitly be added, for he has a whole essay *Of Pedantisme*, the chief defect of scholarship, and in his *vulgar Perigordin-speech doth verie pleasantly term such selfe-conceited wisards*, or pedants, *letter-ferits*, book-struck men, to whom *letters have given a blow as with a mallet*. The shoemaker and the plain husbandman simply and naturally plod on their course, speaking only of what they know, and no farther: *whereas the letter-puft pedants, because they would faine raise themselves aloft, and with their literall doctrine which floteth up and downe the superficies of their braine, arme themselves: they utter loftie words, and speake golden sentences, but so that another man doth place, fit, and applie them*; all theory, no practice; *they are acquainted with Galen but know not the disease*; their heads are stuffed with Laws, but they cannot handle the case. *If Books*, Lucian[2] admonished such a student, *have made you what you are, you ought of all things to avoid*

[1] *Essays*. Ed. Seccombe. i, 158–9.   [2] Qt. Elton, *Great Book-Collectors*. 5.

them; for, as Bacon[1] reckons it up, *to spend too much time in studies is sloth; to use them too much for Ornament is affectation.*

Hobbes bragged that his own reading was inconsiderable, but *if he had spent as much time in reading as other men of learning, he should have been as ignorant as they.*[2] Petrarch is of the same opinion. He reproves a professor of Bologna for roving through volumes which are strange to him in order to insert extracts in his lectures, so that, *stunned by the names of countless writers,* his pupils think him *omniscient*; but real scholars, he warns us, are not to be deceived, *they can tell what is borrowed or begged or stolen, and know the difference between a deep draught from any writer and a passing sip.*[3] Such a letter-ferret, or thief of phrases, lives by making apophthegms *serve him for wit,* seldom making any joke, says John Earle,[4] *but which belonged to some Lacedemonian or Roman in Lycosthenes; he is like a dull carrier's horse, that will go a whole week together, but never out of a foot pace*; so that *he that sets forth on the Saturday shall overtake him.* He is no more than a *Pretender to Learning,* a scholar-mountebank, *who never talks anything but learning, and learns all from talking,* like Sir Thomas Overbury's pedant,[5] who *never had meaning in his life, for he travelled only for words,* a Heteroclite wanting *the plural number, having only the single quality of words.*

A true scholar, philosopher, man of letters, will not *pester his brains with idle punctilios and cavils,*[6]

Old puns restore, lost blunders nicely seek,
And crucify poor Shakespeare once a week;[7]

such *superfine, curious sort of learning signifies no more than a splendid foppery, to no manner of purpose,* and we are no better for *studies that furnish us with unactive thoughts, and useless discourse.*[8] Students of this sort are mere parrots of scholarship, ossified academics, who miss the blossoms in a hedge of prickles. *They cannot see the wood for trees. How many have I seene in my daies,* exclaims Montaigne,[9] *by an over-greedy desire of knowledge, become as it were foolish?* by which means, as Joseph Glanvill follows it (read his *Scepsis Scientifica,* xvii),[10] their *vain Idolizing of Authors* and *the silly vanity of impertinent citations, inducing Authority in things neither requiring, nor deserving it,* produces *ridiculous fooleries.* 'Tis an inglorious acquist, he supposes, *to have our heads or Volumes laden, as were Cardinal Campeins his Mules, with old and useless luggage. Methinks 'tis a pitiful piece of knowledge, that can be learnt from an Index; a poor ambition,* he well says, *to be rich in the Inventory of another's Treasure. To boast a memory (the most that these Pedants can aim at) is but an*

---

[1] *Essays,* 'Of Studies'.　[2] D'Israeli, *Cur. Lit.* ii, 179.　[3] Tatham, *Francesco Petrarca.* ii, 32–3.　[4] *Microcosmography,* 'A Plodding Student'.　[5] *Characters,* Overbury.　[6] W. de Britaine, *Human Prudence.* 2.　[7] Pope, *Dunciad.* i. First Ed.　[8] W. de Britaine, *op. cit.*　[9] *Essays,* Ed. Seccombe. i, 199.　[10] Ed. John Owen. 120–2.

humble ostentation. He desires, rightly, to be a *Fountain* rather than a *Hogshead,* and claims that 'tis better to own a Judgement, though but with a *curta supellex* of coherent notions, than a memory, like *a Sepulchre, furnished with a load of broken and discarnate bones.* And he concludes with *what is more perpendicular to his discourse, that if we impartially look into the remains of Antique Ages, we shall find but little to justify so groundless a Tyranny as Antiquity hath impos'd on the enslaved world.*

VI. A CURE FOR PEDANTRY

Pedantry is the dotage of knowledge: *much learning doth make thee mad.*[1] The remedy is to mingle your knowing with being; to lose yourself in your book, not for the sake of the losing but for the sake of the discovery, or rediscovery of a self replenished with vitality, by reason of its experience. Such adventures re-acquaint us with ourselves new furnished by our rich experiences, rapt beyond ourselves yet more ourselves because we have gone forth into others, whether better or worse than we are is no matter so long as they are alive. *What we should read is not the words,* says Butler, *but the man whom we feel to be behind the words.*[2] The words are nothing in themselves. The letter killeth. Words, like facts, observations, etc., are expedients, and a book (whatever other purpose it may have, and I shall show many) is, in this context, a doorway which you open, going out or in as needs be: sallying forth upon an adventure or homing to the same end, for whether we go back or forth, out or in, we come back to the same spot—the citadel of ourselves. Learning can do no more than point at the harbour, it cannot bring us into port, or, for that matter, get us out; understanding only can do that:

> Knowledge is proud that he has learn'd so much;
> Wisdom is humble that he knows no more.[3]

To make books, therefore, the mere and sole tools of knowledge is to misuse them. That way lies pedantry. The best that is in a book comes out to us only when we enter into its spirit; and in a bookish jurisdiction the spirit of letters is an essence of life; if we have the luck to meet it on equal terms we come near to living, so

> Let's even compound, and for the Present Live,
> 'Tis all the Ready Money Fate can give.[4]

---

[1] *Acts.* xxvi, 24.   [2] *Note-Books.* 94.   [3] Cowper, *The Task.* 94–5.   [4] Cowley, 'To Dr. Scarborough.'

All of which was summed up by Antisthenes when he replied to one who asked him what learning was most necessary for man's life: *To unlearn what is nought*.[1] Therefore, that which Bacon said at the opening of his essay *Of Studies* may be for ever applied to the correction of pedantry and all those defects of scholarship upon which I have dilated: *Studies serve for Delight, for Ornamentation, and for Ability. Their chief use for Delight is in Privateness and Retiring; for Ornament is in Discourse; and for Ability, is in the Judgment and Disposition of Business*, of which he himself was a chief instance, *nihil quod tetigit non ornavit*.

When we confer with masterpieces, exchange, compare our ideas with theirs, we get most out of them, not by absorbing them wholly, or by following them implicitly, but by remaining ourselves in all our traffic with them, only better, fuller, stronger for the association. You might *read all the books in the British Museum* and remain *illiterate*, Ruskin warns, but *read ten pages of a good book with real accuracy*, and *you are for evermore in some measure an educated person*;[2] and this is what James Rhoades meant when he gave out to his students that *if they could really master the ninth book of 'Paradise Lost', so as to rise to the height of its great argument and incorporate all its beauties in themselves, they would at one blow, by virtue of that alone, become highly cultivated men*.[3] Any noble passage will serve us as well, and we could not be served better. *Masterpieces*, Quiller-Couch advises, *serve us as prophylactics of taste*, they *help us to interpret the common mind of civilisation. But*, he holds, *they have a third and yet nobler use. They teach us to lift our own souls*.[4]

This is what Montaigne[5] had in mind when he argued that study and plodding on books was a *languishing and weake kinde of motion*, which *healeth and earnesteth nothing*; whereas, *conference doth both learne, teach and exercise at once*. He only is wise *qui disciplinam suam non ostentationem scientiae, sed legem vitae putet quique obtemperet ipse sibi, et decretis suis pareat*,[6] whose learning is not an ostentation of knowledge, but a rule of life, which he himself obeys, doing what is decreed. Which brings us back to the central object of all endeavour, viz., how to live; and, clearly, if study is mere repetition of the ideas and sayings of others, as it was in the Middle Ages, when *the ultimate foundations of knowledge rarely went beyond knowing what somebody had said about something*,[7] then it is but a pretty game, and if so recognized, 'tis no great harm. But to know what somebody has said about something is to acquire knowledge, not wisdom, which is the end of the matter. And in this problem of study it is wisdom to know a writer rather than his commentator. A man who has made a great book is an artist, and

---

[1] Bacon, *Apophthegms*. 177.　　[2] *Sesame and Lilies*. i.　　[3] Qt. Quiller-Couch, *Art of Reading*. 215.　　[4] *Ib*. 226.　　[5] *Essays*. Ed. Seccombe. iii, 192.　　[6] Cicero, *Tusc*. ii.
[7] Rashdall, *Universities of the Middle Ages*. i, 433.

his book is a piece of life. A pedant is a *bookish sot*,[1] and they and their kind are to be avoided, for too many have been *frightened away from the fairest realms of poetry* (and prose) *by the fences of these grim guardians*,[2] who *aim as a rule at acquiring information rather than insight*,[3] without which learning can never be distilled into our lives.

---

[1] Montaigne, *Essays*. Ed. Seccombe. i, 159.   [2] Hamerton, *Intellectual Life*. 385.
[3] Schopenhauer, 'On Men of Learning', *Art of Literature*. Trans. Saunders. 49.

Part VIII

OF THE USES OF BOOKS

―――――――――――᚛◇᚜―――――――――

I. SOME ADVENTITIOUS USES

Many and sundry are the uses to which bookmen, students, and others put their books. All manner and conditions of folk use them for all manner of purposes. Some sell them for money, as others publish, and yet more write them or write about them to the same end. Some use them as a currency of exchange, as Gibbon, who gave a copy of the *Decline and Fall* for a hogshead of Madeira;[1] Tolstoy, in his youth, would use Tatishef's *Dictionaries* as tests of endurance, by holding them in his outstretched hand for five minutes at a time, though the feat caused him *terrible pain*;[2] George Wyndham *played* with his books and so *defied the North East wind*;[3] in the United States of America books are up-held as a means of adding to the attractiveness of women: *Any woman who knows something of literature and science, of travel and biography, will find herself becoming more and more attractive.*[4] In some lands Holy Books are used for the taking of oaths; and, in an emergency, a secular book has been used for a sacred purpose, as on that occasion, recorded by Festing Jones, when an engineer in Central America, lacking a *Bible*, married a couple of coloured folk, who spoke no English, with *Tristram Shandy*, out of which he read a chapter.[5] Others again collect books, hoarding them as men gather around them postage stamps or defunct coins, blown eggs or dead butterflies, but I have anatomized these inferior faculties in subsequent sections; so also those, of whom again there is more elsewhere, who beg, borrow, steal or even buy them to read, thus giving them their due homage and putting them to their proper service:

Pro captu lectoris habent sua fata libelli.[6]
The reader's fancy makes the fate of books.

At the same time they are not solely for reading; even when they are read, they are tools, companions, consolers, guides, entertainments (Field-

---

[1] Letter to Lord Sheffield. 31.xii.1791.   [2] *Life*. Maude. i, 31.   [3] *George Wyndham*. Gatty. 36.   [4] From an advertisement in the *Atlantic Monthly*. February 1927. p. 31.   [5] *Samuel Butler: A Memoir*. 155 i, 136–7.   [6] Terentianus Maurus.

ing called the novel a *pocket-theatre*), doctors, teachers; kill-times and life-preservers; substitutes for thought; all of which uses have been touched upon briefly or at large; escapes from inconveniences, such as going into the country. Sir Leslie Stephen loved the country *best in books*.[1] The *rationale* of their utility in these respects remaineth *jucundum et anceps subjectum*, a pleasant, but a doubtful subject (as one terms it), and with brevity to be discussed. Many erroneous opinions held are about the use of books, not alone among the profane, if among that sort at all, for they would hesitate to ascribe any useful purpose to literature, or, if any, not, as they say, for *the likes of them*; rather would I impute this limitation to one or, at most, two purposes, such as study or reading, among the learned. The uses of books are much more varied, as I have noted and shall proceed further to dilate.

Mohammedans are in the habit of scrutinizing any printed or written piece of paper lying upon the ground, not knowing but it may contain some piece of their *Koran*. It was owing to the possession of a like habit that Addison was able to search out many uses for books which might else have been overlooked, *for*, as he wisely saith, *no mortal author, in the ordinary fate and vicissitude of things, knows to what use his works may some time or other be applied*. Thus a man may often meet with *very celebrated names in a paper of tobacco*. He admitted having lighted his pipe more than once *with the writings of a prelate* (a use which other books have served many times, as when Carlyle ordered Edward FitzGerald *to read, or light pipes with*, a book which he had given him[2]); and he had a friend who was ingenious enough to convert *the essays of a man of quality into a kind of fringe for his candlesticks*; he remembered in particular, *after having read over a poem of an eminent author on a victory*, meeting with several fragments of it *upon the next rejoicing day*, employed in *squibs and crackers*, thus celebrating its subject in a double *capacity*. He once met with a page of *Mr. Baxter under a Christmas Pie*. This discovery had a notable result, for *whether the pastry-cook had made use of it through chance or waggery, for the defense of that superstitious viand*, he knew not; but *upon the perusal of it he conceived so good an idea of the author's piety* that he bought the *whole book*. He often profited by such accidental readings, coming across many pieces either out of print or not to be met with in the bookshops; and on the shelves of his library, among the *folios*, were two *band-boxes lined with deep erudition and abstruse literature*.[3]

The habit of using the pages of books for packing parcels was at one time popular. John Rawlinson, who bequeathed his collection to the Bodleian, *rescued* from the grocers, chandlers, etc., many rare documents, including *originals* from My Lords Bolingbroke, Oxford, Ormond, Straf-

---

[1] 'Country Books', *Hours in a Library*. iv, 102.   [2] FitzGerald, *More Letters*. 149.
[3] *Spectator*. 85.

ford, the Electress of Hanover, Prior, etc., and on another occasion documents formerly belonging to Sir John Cooke. They were sold by his nephew's widow *to support pyes, currants, sugar, etc.*[1] Macaulay went so far as to prophesy that some of *the well-puffed fashionable novels* of 1829 would *hold the pastry* of 1830, and others, then *extolled in language almost too high-flown for the merits of 'Don Quixote'*, would *line the trunks* of 1831.[2] When Duke Humphrey's Library at Oxford was pillaged by *anti-popish vandalism*, MSS. *were sold to tailors for their measures, to bookbinders for covers and the like*;[3] these uses have several records: on the day that M. Duvergier de Hauranne, abbé of Saint-Cyran, came out of the dungeon of Vincennes, he was having himself measured for a suit of clothes, which he badly needed, when he observed that the tailor had cut out his *bandes sacrilèges* from the works of St. Augustine on *grand papier, que le cardinal Richelieu avait fait saisir dans la prison de son diocese.*[4] Read in *Isaac D'Israeli*[5] how ancient Manuscripts have been used for covering the drums of battledores, patching clothes, bookbinding, etc., for there is no end to their ingenious uses in the service of man, some of which I shall now set out.

II. BOOKS AS FURNITURE

As furniture they have been widely esteemed in divers places, through many ages: *ils meublent mieux que tout.*[6] People *decorate their rooms with the furniture that was intended to be an ornament of the soul, as if they were bronzes and statues*;[7] they employ them as the accessories of a *Chippendale suite, which is glorified by the presence of these mute embodiments of brainwork and energy;*[8] *some covet to have libraries in their houses, as ladies have cupboards of plate in their chambers, only for show; as if they were only to furnish their rooms, and not their minds.*[9]

> The lettered fop now takes a larger scope,
> With classic furniture, designed by Hope,
> (Hope, whom upholst'rers eye with mute despair,
> The doughty pedant of an elbow chair).[10]

We know *the gaudy volumes that repose at all the points of the compass*[11] on the drawing-room tables of apartment houses, in the rooms of doctors and dentists where *patients bide their time sadly*. Some books are *intended for ornament*, manufactured for decoration, born furniture, destined for show;

[1] *Annals of the Bodleian.* Macray. 239–40.   [2] 'Mr. Montgomery's Poems.' *Essays.*
[3] Macray. *Op. cit.* 13.   [4] Janin, *Le Livre.* 464–5.   [5] *Cur. of Lit.* i, 34–5.   [6] 'They furnish better than anything.' Octave Uzanne, *Zigzags d'un Curieux.* 205.   [7] Petrarch, *On Fortune.* Qt. Elton. *Great Book-Collectors.* 45.   [8] *Book-Lore.* 139.   [9] Waller, *Divine Meditations.*   [10] Ferriar, *Bibliomania.* 112–15.   [11] P. Fitzgerald, *Book Fancier.* 123.

but even then *no furniture so charming as books*, claims Sydney Smith,[1] *even if you never open them, or read a single word*; and when they are *not made for furniture, nothing else to beautifully furnishes a house*, the plainest row of cloth or paper-covered books is *more significant of refinement than the most elaborately-carved* étagère *or sideboards*. Another will have *a house furnished with books rather than furniture*;[2] John Bright prefers a room well *stocked with books* to any *decoration which the highest art can supply*.[3]

Some range them with bric-à-brac, knick-knacks, articles of *virtu*, in domestic collections; others with ornaments, setting them on the tops of pianofortes, in parlour windows, on tables (there was once a curious trade in *table books* specially wrought for this purpose), as those Ladies of Llangollen, Lady Eleanor Butler and Miss Sarah Ponsonby, at Plas Newydd, where they lived together for fifty years without going away for a single night, surrounded, as Lockhart found, when he visited them with Sir Walter Scott, by *bijouterie*, cabinets and glass-cases, books, *whirligigs of every shape and hue*; among the books they were gratified to find illustrated copies of Scott's poems. But much as *the Ladies* delighted to have books among their *bric-à-brac*, they were sedulous readers.[4]

I speak it not to detract from such as are so virtuous and noble as to revere books for their content rather than their seeming, for I hold firmly with Sir Edmund Gosse that books are *the furniture of the mind*,[5] and do much respect and honour students and bookmen; but this desire for books as furniture, to have them about on shelves, tables, window-sills, whatnots, overmantels, sideboards, etc., is in the nature of praise, symbolical, an inverted homage. At the same time there are strenuous opponents of this view. Seneca, for example, would have none of it. He was for reading books, not looking at them, and contemplating the luxurious unread collections of Lucullus and Mithridates, he rejoiced at the conflagration at Alexandria: *Our idle book-hunters know about nothing but titles and bindings; their chests of cedar and ivory, and the book-cases that fill the bath-room, are nothing but fashionable furniture.*[6] Young supports him in his satire *The Love of Fame*:

> Thy gaudy shelves with crimson bindings glow,
> And Epictetus is a perfect beau.
> How fit for thee bound up in crimson too,
> Gilt, and like them, devoted to the view!
> Thy books are furniture. Methinks 'tis hard
> That science should be purchased by the Yard,
> And T——n, turned upholsterer, send home
> The gilded leather to fit up thy room.

[1] *Memoir*. Holland. i, 241.   [2] H. W. Beecher, *Sermons*.   [3] *Speech*, at opening of Birmingham Library.   [4] Ponsonby, *English Diaries*. 241–6.   [5] *The Library of Edmund Gosse*. xiv.   [6] Qt. Elton, *Great Book-Collectors*. 5.

Nevertheless, the taste is widespread, and the commerce of book-selling is ready to meet it, even in so great a seat of learning as Oxford: *We can offer*, so runs the advertisement of a dealer in books in the famous High Street of that illustrious city, *a quantity of well-bound Books, suitable as Furniture, at the following Clearance Prices: Sizes: 8vo, cr. 8vo, post 8vo, Half Calf, 1/6 per vol.; Whole Calf, 2/– per vol. Lists of Titles on application.*[1] I doubt not that such collections go to furnish those *fine houses*, of which Oliver Wendell Holmes has records, *where a library is a part of the uphol-stery*,[2] and such booksellers (in this respect) *little more than upholsterers*, as Horace Walpole told Sir David Dalrymple, who sell *sets* and *bodies* of arts and sciences *for furniture*, and the purchasers, he was very sure they were not readers, *but only in that view*, and although he *never thought there was much merit in reading*, he rightly argues it is *too good a thing to be put upon no better footing than damask or mahogany*.[3]

The learned Dr. Routh, President of Magdalen College, Oxford, for over sixty years editor of the *Reliquiae Sacrae*, knew better than to decorate his cupboard doors with sham books, as some do; he lined all his walls with real books: dining-rooms, drawing-room, corridors, even staircase and hall, as *Mercurius Rusticus* himself saw on his tour of research into the cause of bibliophobia, in 1830, and was gratified to note that the doctor's house *contained the same goodly book-furniture as of old—outvying, in intrinsic worth, all the velvet and silk and chintz hangings of the proudest Palace in Christendom.*[4] In this wise doubtless Charles Lamb thought on his *cheerful dining-room* in Colebrooke Row near Sadler's Wells Theatre, *all studded over and rough with books.*[5] Magliabecchi, in his great passion for books, went even further: he lived in a cavern of books, slept on them, wallowed in them; they were his bed and board, his only furniture, his chiefest need. For sleep he spread an old rug over a heap of them and so composed himself; or he would cast himself, fully clothed, among the books which covered his couch.[6] In the same manner it is recorded[7] of a bibliomaniac of the early days of the last century whose collection was *choice, costly, and copious*, that no man loved more *to embed himself* amongst them: his pillow-case, Columbus's *Letter* of 1493, stitched to the original *Challenge* of Crichton; his counterpane, the large paper *Hearnes*, formerly in Dr. Mead's library, *still glittering in their primitive morocco attire*; his mattress, large paper *Dugdales*; his bed-curtains, *slips of the original Bayeux Tapestry!* I know what can be said against these extravagances, and record them not for argument, still less for condemnation, but to show further how every man uses books for his own ends.

[1] *Catalogue*. Sanders & Co., Oxford. May 1927. p. 13.   [2] *The Poet at the Breakfast Table.*   [3] *Letters*. Cunningham. iv. 177.   [4] Dibdin, *Bibliophobia*. 79.   [5] *Charles Lamb.* P. Fitzgerald. 163.   [6] *The Book Fancier.* P. Fitzgerald. 3.   [7] Dibdin, *Bibliophobia*. 50.

III. A DIGRESSION OF DUMMY BOOKS

To assume a virtue if you have it not is a maxim with some, and there are others who conjure the outward bearing and aspect of books with *counterfeit presentment* on shelves that are not shelves but the fancy panels of doors, and the like, as that upper shelf in a lady's library, described by Addison,[1] which was stuffed with *counterfeit books carved in wood*, serving only to fill up, *like faggots in the muster of a regiment.* I have known in my time such panels of deception, one in a Piccadilly mansion nigh to Apsley House, and another, more vastly pretentious, in the Royal Automobile Club, a third in the Gallery of the British Museum Reading Room. How many country mansions are so decorated with dummy books I know not, but that there were many at one time cannot be gainsaid, for the sixth Duke of Devonshire, *desiring to construct a door of sham books, for the entrance of a library staircase at Chatsworth*, invites the help of Tom Hood in the matter of inscriptions for his *unreal folios, quartos, and 12mos*, because his own inventiveness in so delicate an engagement had failed, and he was tired of the *Plain Dealings, Essays on Wood*, and *Perpetual Motion on such doors*; on one he had seen the names of *Don Quixote's Library and other impossibilities*, as *Virgilii Odaria, Herodoti Poemata*, Byron's *Sermons* etc. From Hood he *ventured to hope for more attractive titles*,[2] and he received from him, says Percy Fitzgerald,[3] such titles as *Malthus's Attack on Infantry, Lamb's Reflection on Suet, John Knox on Death's Door, Boyle on Steam, On Sore Throat and the Migration of the Swallow, Johnson's Contradictionary, Cursory Remarks on Swearing, The Scottish Boccaccio by D. Cameron*, and many more in this punning strain. Fitzgerald gives examples of *simulacra* in the same manner covering a door in Sir Thomas Acland's library, where the dummy books bore such titles as *Friend's Right of Entrance, Trap on Fictitous Entries*, and, more wittily, near the hinges, *Squeak on Openings, Bang on Shutting*, and *Hinge's Orations*.

In the Sheraton room at Marlborough House there is (or was) a dummy library with such titles as *Lever on Lifts, An Actor on Falling Stars, The Newcomers, Superficial Knowledge, Tiresome Tomes, Nine Tails by a Cat, Constable's Notes on Motoring, Lochs and Quays of England. The Male Coach, Bleak Houses*, and the *Story of the Greek Kalends.* On a door in the Army and Navy Club Library, in Pall Mall, *are, or were, to be found quips in the same spirit*, as *The Rape of the Lock, The Art of Turning, by Handle, Le Livre Fermé* and *Tréatise sur les Sorties Imprévues*. Charles Dickens had a collection of sham books at Gad's Hill for which John Forster devised such titles as

---

[1] *Spectator.* 37.   [2] *Memorials of Thomas Hood.* (1860) i, 30–1.   [3] *The Book Fancier.* 126–7.

The Corn Question by John Bunyan, Dr. Kitchener's *Life of Captain Cook,* Mr. J. Horner on *Poets' Corner, Savage on Civilisation,* and so on. Aldous Huxley gives an account of the dummy library at Crome.[1] In the middle of one of the walls of the library was a door *ingeniously upholstered with rows of dummy books* concealing a cupboard where rested, among a pile of letter-files and old newspapers, the *mummy-case* of an *Egyptian* lady, brought back by the second Sir Ferdinando on his return from the Grand Tour. From a distance the books looked genuine, and bore ingenious titles, as Caprimulge's *Dictionary of the Finnish Language; A Biographical Dictionary* in parts; *Biography of Men who were Born Great, Biography of Men who Achieved Greatness, Biography of Men who had Greatness thrust upon Them,* and *Biography of Men who were Never Great at All;* then there were Thom's *Works and Wanderings,* in ten vols.; *Wild Goose Chase, a Novel,* in six vols., and seven volumes of *The Tales of Knockespotch.*

Many a briefless barrister has used dummy books to give an air of established prosperity to his chambers, and so too doctors of medicine have garnished their consulting-rooms. Maurice Hewlett dreamed once of a fair library of tall tomes, but was awakened from his pleasant adventure when he took down a volume as *big* and *hefty* as *Liddell and Scott* and found it only a box to hold papers with nothing in it but a wire clip.[2] Others use them as boxes for pamphlets, as *camouflage* for chess boards, which can be conveniently folded and stowed away on shelves. But what shall we say of those ghouls, chiefly in France, who scour the auction rooms, the booksellers' shops and the stalls, for choice and ancient bindings which they turn into boxes by gluing the pages together, cutting out the type area, and so translating books into receptacles for cigarettes, cigars, liqueurs, jewels, chocolates, *bon-bons,* or note-paper? And what of those who encourage this ghoulish trade? They are no better than body-snatchers, desecrators of the temple, vain, tawdry, callous, whether sellers of such monuments of destruction or buyers of them, biblioclasts and dolts to boot, necrophils of a sort; beside them the *naïfs* who use dummy books are princes of intelligence, nay, bibliophiles of the blood, though dizzards, for they would fox their fellows, if that be their aim, by making boxes to look like books rather than books like boxes, as in that singular library at Warsenstein, near Cassel in Germany, where the books are boxes made of wood, as he[3] records, each a specimen from a different tree with its bark for the spine. The outsides are polished examples of the timber, and the insides contain specimens of the tree's fruit, seeds, leaves, the moss which grows upon its trunk and the insects which feed upon it. But I rage and roam. Let us to our theme.

[1] *Crome Yellow.* xiv, 146–7.   [2] *Extemporary Essays.* 118.   [3] P. Fitzgerald, *The Book Fancier.* 127.

IV. THEIR USE AS TOOLS ETC.

As tools they need no explication; that is their business: *they are not creative powers in any sense, merely helps, instruments, tools;*[1] and when bookmen alight upon those true, moving works, which *make them happy and wise*, they do well to name their books *bridges or ships* because they have carried readers safely over *dark morasses and barren oceans, into the heart of sacred cities, into palaces and temples.*[2] In like measure they are *engines of war*, fighting men's battles in place of armies:

> The King to Oxford sent his troop of Horse,
> For Tories own no argument but force;
> With equal care to Cambridge books he sent,
> For Whigs allow no force but argument.[3]

Sir Edward Burne-Jones argued that books were of no use to a painter save *to prop up models in difficult positions*, and for that purpose he acclaimed their value;[4] so also have they been used as stools to sit upon and to raise the height of chairs. Gautier had no other use for *Plutarch* in folio than as a press for creased and crumpled engravings, or to *put under children* who would not otherwise be able to sit at table.[5] Coventry Patmore received from his father one of the *greatest rebukes* he could remember, for taking from its place *a thick old Bible to enable* him *to sit more conveniently at dinner*.[6] They have been used as presses from early times; but most of all for pressing flowers either as souvenirs or for scientific purposes. Samuel Pepys visited John Evelyn at Deptford and was shown his '*Hortus Hyemalis'; leaves laid up in a book of several plants kept dry, which preserve colour, however, and look very finely, better than any Herball.*[7]

Samuel Butler, the nimble-witted author of *Erewhon*, made careful researches into their use as writing-desks in the Reading-room of the British Museum, a sloping desk being necessary to his habit of composition. For weeks he experimented with *sundry poetical and philosophical works*, without finding his *ideal desk*; at length, *more by luck than cunning*, he lit upon Frost's *Lives of Eminent Christians*, which he found the perfection and *ne plus ultra* of *everything that a book should be*. But ill-fate befell him, for when next he visited the Museum the book had disappeared and he could not write until he had found a substitute. He tried various books: Migne's *Complete Course of Petrology*, but abandoned it because it was in several volumes of varying thicknesses and he could never remember the

---

[1] J. S. Blackie, *Self-Culture.*   [2] Emerson, *Society and Solitude.* 'Books.'   [3] Sir W. Browne. Qt. *Book-Lovers' Anthology.* 113.   [4] *Memorials of Edward Burne-Jones.* i, 130.   [5] Preface. *Les Jeunes-France.*   [6] *Memoirs.* Champneys. ii, 41.   [7] *Diary.* Wheatley. v, 137.

volume he had used; *Bede* in Giles's *Anglican Fathers*, although in four volumes, was not open to this objection, yet, for some unstated reason, inadequate; he turned, therefore, to Mather's *Magnolia*, which promised well, had not the binding displeased him. Cureton's *Corpus Ignatianum* was too thin; Baxter's *Church History of England*, Lingard's *Anglo-Saxon Church*, and Cardwell's *Documentary Annals*, though none so good as *Frost*, were deemed of *considerable merit*. Norton's *Genuineness of the Gospels* he did not like taking as it was *just possible someone may be wanting to know whether the Gospels were true or not, and be unable to find out because* he *had got Mr. Norton's book;* in the end he found Arvine's *Cyclopædia of Moral and Religious Anecdote* to be the one book in the room coming within *measurable distance of Frost*, which was fortunate for posterity, for unless he had found some successor he must have given up writing altogether.[1]

V. THEIR BELLIGERENT USEFULNESS

After a long and tedious discourse of these numerous material uses to which books have been put, and their several varieties, which are comprehended under Furniture, Tools, Operations, etc. I am come now at last to *horrida bella*, or that kind of purpose which is procured only by *ultima ratio regum*, the arbitrament of the sword, or gun, of which there are several records. Many fear the power of books, as I have shown under *Influence*, and that they have proved a *casus belli* is well known; but such cavillers will belike find less to censure in this record of their armigerous use as the munitionment of war. C. and M. Elton, in their description of book-collecting in Ireland,[2] make mention, amongst other matters, of the dispute over the copying of St. Finnen's *Psalter* by St. Columba, *who was passionately devoted to books*. St. Finnen claimed the copy as his, and when St. Columba appealed to King Diarmid, at the Court of Tara, the King upheld St. Finnen's claim on the ground that to every mother-book belongs the child-book, as to the cow belongs her calf. St. Columba was so enraged that he went over the wild mountains and raised the tribes of Tyrconnel and Tyrone and a great battle was fought in which King Diarmid was defeated. When Columba went to Iona he took his *Psalter* with him and bequeathed it to the chieftain of the tribe of Tyrconnel. It was then called the *Book of the Battle*, and if they carried it three times round the enemy in one day, they were certain of victory.

Their value as life-preservers against projectiles and other engines of war hath sundry instances. Many stories tell how books have stopped bullets in their swift and deadly course, and turned the points of swords.

[1] S. Butler, 'Quis Desiderio', *Essays on Life, Art, and Science*. 1904. 3–11.   [2] *Great Book-Collectors*. 17.

But it would seem that only Holy Books, and of our own Faith, are thus to be relied upon. I have no documentary evidence in support of such stories, nor have I discovered any one among my acquaintances who could give me an authentic instance out of his own experience in the Great War, which had such a profusion of marvels, so I shall do no more than record the rumour, which is as persistent as a legend, and as readily believed by many. That experienced observer Dr. Rosenbach is not among them, in spite of the fact that so many *bullet-hole Bibles* have been offered to him that his rest has been broken by dreams of armies charging him, *each soldier wearing a protecting copy of the Holy Scriptures over his heart.*[1]

Whether they have proved successful as armour or not, they are no despicable munitionment of war in other respects. As weapons they have *done their bit*, most effectively, as when Dr. Johnson knocked Osborne down with a folio, because that notorious bookseller had blamed his learned and diligent employee for negligence. The historic volume, so Sir Leslie Stephen records, a copy of *Biblia Graeca Septuaginta*, 1594, was in the possession of a Cambridge bookseller as late as the year 1812. Few will dispute with Stephen when he urges that so desirable an *association* copy *should have been placed in some safe author's museum.*[2] Another instance of the use of books as weapons is recorded by Anthony Trollope, whose father often knocked him down with a *great Folio Bible* as a punishment for youthful idleness.[3] As missiles they are widely appreciated, lending themselves as they do both by reason of their size and shape to sudden precipitation at an offending head. Another Johnson, William (Cory), used them in this manner. He threw a book at any boy in his class at Eton who was either *flagrantly unoccupied or suspiciously absorbed*;[4] and it is reported that William Morris hurled a fifteenth-century quarto (which was so precious that he would allow no one to touch it) at the head of a person who had irritated him, and with such force that in the course of its militant career it knocked the panel out of a door.

Even in warfare on a larger scale they are of proved value, as Wilfrid Scawen Blunt discovered when attacked by the Senussi in the Egyptian desert, whither he had journeyed in the hope that he might find among that remote tribe *something of the better traditions of Islam* which he could not find in *more civilised Mohammedan lands*. But the Senussi, believing him to be a spy, attacked, captured, and robbed his caravan, and it was only by adopting passive tactics, until he could advise the Sheiks of his English nationality, that he was permitted to escape with his life. He attributes this manœuvre to Doughty's *Arabia Deserta*, which he had been reading on the journey.[5]

---

[1] *Books and Bidders.* 239.   [2] L. Stephen, *Johnson* 27.   [3] *Autobiography.* World's Classics Ed. 14.   [4] In *Lit. Anec. of 19th Cent.* ii, 400.   [5] W. S. Blunt, *My Diaries.* i, 273.

VI. CHARMS, AMULETS AND FORTUNE-TELLERS

Amulets and things to be borne about for luck, or to charm a life by warding off the blows of Fate, Chance, the Evil Eye, or the Devil himself, I find prescribed in histories; and although their efficacy is taxed in these times by some, it is approved by others, but often by deed rather than by word, as many a trinket semi-jocularly worn can attest. The medicinal value of amulets is now generally denied by civilized people, who have transferred their faith to drugs and serums, and their allegiance to vaccinations, operations, and therapeutical religious ceremonies.

The power of books to charm is, however, well known, and they have largely taken the place of amulets. In times past amulets were included in the medical equipment of all classes. Samuel Pepys carried a *hare's foot* against the colic; although he sometimes doubted whether that amulet relieved him or whether he should attribute *the relief of taking every morning of a pill, of turpentine, or to having left off wearing of a gown*.[1] His doubts were set at rest later when, on January 20th, 1665, he brought home a hare and Mr. Batten showed him that it was necessary to carry a hare's foot that *hath not the joynt to it*, assuring him that he himself had *never had his cholique since he carried it about him. It is strange*, says Pepys, *how fancy works, for I no sooner almost handled his foote but my belly began to be loose and to break wind, and whereas I was in some pain yesterday and tother day and in fear of more to-day, I became very well, and so continue.* Next day he was *mighty well* and attributed it to his *fresh hare's foot*. But he was again in doubt on March 26th, when he *never was better in his life*, though the winter had been hard, and he had gone lightly clad *wearing only a doublet, and a waist-coate cut open on the back; abroad, a cloake, and within doors a coate I slipped on. I am at a losse*, he admits, *whether it be my hare's foot which is my preservative against wind*; but he continues to carry it.

Robert Burton[2] gives several curious instances. Precious stones are useful for most diseases; a wolf's dung borne with one helps the cholick, a spider is good for an ague, a ring made of the hoof of an ass's right forefoot carried about has recognized medical value, and he gives instances which he contends, with Renodeus,[3] are not altogether to be rejected. And he recounts how Levinus Lemmius set down certain amulets, herbs, and precious stones, which have marvellous virtues all *profligandis daemonibus*, to drive away Devils and their illusions. He agrees, however, with Philes, who flourished in the time of Michael Palaeologus, that *a sheep or a kid's skin, whom a wolf worried,*

Haedus inhumani raptus ab ore lupi,[4]

[1] *Diary.* 31.xii.1664.   [2] *Anat. of Melan.* (1904) ii, 289–90.   [3] *Pharmacopœia.* lib. i. 12,
[4] 'A goat snatched from the jaws of a cruel wolf.' *Martial.* x, 48, 14.

ought not at all to be worn about a man, because it causes palpitation of the heart, not for any fear, but a secret virtue which amulets have; and he doubted his mother's ability to cure an ague by an amulet of *a spider in a nutshell lapped in silk.* She had excellent skill in chirurgery, but of all experiments he thought this one most *absurd and ridiculous.* He could see no warrant for it, till at length rambling amongst authors (as he often did) he found this very medicine in *Dioscorides,* approved by Matthiolus, repeated by *Aldrovandus, cap. de aranea, lib. de insectis,* and so *began to have a better opinion of it.* But he still believed that such medicines are *to be exploded that consist of words, characters, spells, and charms, which can do no good at all, but out of strong conceit, as Pompanatius proves; or the Devil's policy, who is the first founder and teacher of them.*

Whether he would include books in this castigation is not set forth, but perhaps not, for books have so many strange powers that no one so wise as mine author would dispute their magic, even as amulets, for as such they have been and still are used. There are many instances of the efficacy of the *Bible,* the *New Testament,* and the *Koran* against perils, accidents, and diseases, and among the Norsemen, Lubbock reports, *runes were supposed to be endowed with miraculous powers.*[1] I find a memorable modern instance of book-magic in the chronicle of *Lawrence in Arabia,* by Lowell Thomas. Nearly all Arabs, he says, carry some sort of good-luck charm, and the belief in *jinn* and *genii* is still common; the talisman worn by Auda, a great Bedouin Chief, *was probably one of the most extraordinary to be found in all Arabia.* It was a diminutive copy of the *Koran,* no more than one inch square, for which he had paid the sum of £200. Auda used it as his sole protection against snake bites, the only danger which fills a Bedouin with fear. He displayed his treasure with great pride to Lawrence, who discovered it had been printed in Glasgow and published for eighteenpence.[2]

Sortilege, the casting of Lots, has been promiscuously performed by nearly all peoples at most times; and, notwithstanding cavils and objections, many writers both ancient and modern do much approve of it, and they are stiffly supported by primitive peoples as well as by cultured sects in London, New York, Paris, and elsewhere, who seek news of their fate by gazing into *crystals,* casting of *horoscopes,* fortune-telling, *Palmistry, Phrenology, table-rapping, handwriting, Mediums,* and the like; as from all time men have practised *Haruspication,* or divination by entrail-gazing; *Scapulomancy,* by the shoulder-blade or *scapula; Angang,* from meeting with ominous animals; and *Astrology* from the stars, consulting them as Plato and Pythagoras did when they left their country to confer with those wise *Egyptian Priests,* and as Apollonius travelled in Ethiopia and Persia to

[1] *Pleasures of Life.* i, 54.   [2] *With Lawrence in Arabia.* 195.

consult with the *Magi, Brachmanni,* and *Gymnosophists.* The Queen of Sheba thus came to visit Solomon; and many others, so Hierome records,[1] went a thousand miles to behold eloquent Livy, as countless pilgrims still journey to Rome and Mecca, and some of our own contemporaries, as Edward Carpenter and Annie Besant, have journeyed to sit at the feet of *Gurus* in Ceylon and *Mahatmas* in Hindustan.

For divination they have sought out many inventions and curious enterprises. Homer's heroes prayed to the Gods when they cast *Lots* in *Agamemnon's cap,* and Mopsus *divined* with sacred *Lots* when the Argonauts embarked. Pliny decided to repair and enlarge the Temple of Ceres, which stood upon his estate in Tuscany, *in compliance with the advice of the Haruspices,* or entrail-gazers.[2] The Emperor Julian took public part in the ceremonies of Haruspication: *Amidst the sacred but licentious crowd of priests, of inferior ministers, and of female dancers, who were dedicated to the service of the temple, it was the business of the Emperor to bring the wood, to blow the fire, to handle the knife, to slaughter the victim, and, thrusting his bloody hands into the bowels of the expiring animal, to draw forth the heart or liver, and to read, with the consummate skill of an Haruspex, the imaginary signs of future events.*[3] Tacitus recounts how the Germans invoked the Gods by small pieces of wood cut from a fruit-bearing tree conjointly with the auguries of birdsong or flight. Horses, too, were mediums (read *Herodotus* iii, 84, for the neighing of King Darius his horse) or, as Tacitus hath it: *kept at the public expense in these same woods and groves are white horses, pure from the taint of earthly labour. These are yoked to a car and accompanied by a priest and the king or chief of the tribe, who note their neighings and snortings. No augury so trusted by priests or people. The priests are the ministers of the Gods, and the horses are acquainted with their will.*[4]

Similarly *dice* are thrown for purposes of *sortilege.* The *astragali* or knucklebones, used of old times in children's games, were first instruments of divination. In Polynesia the *coco-nut* is spun like a *teetotum* to discover a thief.[5] They hope by sorcery, spells, incantations, etc., to *dip into the future,* to expound the mysteries of life, to receive guidance when the way is dark. They *read* all these *charms, totems, talismans, amulets,* as we now read books, for they were the precursors and progenitors of books. I think Sir James Frazer is wise in his inference that Joseph *piqued himself on his power of detecting a thief by means of his divining cup;*[6] though how he did it we know not. But people have *read* the mysteries in cups as in crystals, and this mode of divination is still practised in Egypt, where it is associated, thus supporting my contention, with the written word, as some of our own simple

---

[1] Praefat. bib. vulgar.   [2] 'Haruspicum monitu', *Letters.* Melmoth. Loeb Ed. ix, 39.
[3] Gibbon, *Decline and Fall,* xxiii.   [4] *Germania.* Trans. Donne. 48.   [5] *Encyclopædia Britannica.* VIII, 333.   [6] *Folk-Lore in the Old Testament.* ii, 426.

womenfolk think of what is written or what may be written when they essay to read the dregs left in their tea-cups.

The Greeks made predictions by *Hydromantia* or the reading of water. In Egypt this same process is still called the *Magic Mirror*, and Frazer cites,[1] out of *Klunzinger*, how it is employed in our days: *A pure innocent boy (not more than twelve years of age) is directed to look into a cup filled with water and inscribed with texts, while under his cap is stuck a paper, also with writing on it, so as to hang over his forehead; he is also fumigated with incense, while sentences are murmured by the conjurer.* Anon the boy claims to see images of persons on the water as in a mirror. He is then ordered to make demands of these spirits, to set up a tent, bring coffee and the like, and after a while to command from the *vasty deep* of the cup (for vast and deep it is, being a mystery) any person living or dead. This he proceeds to attempt.

Nearer to *book-magic*, to which I am proceeding, is that substitution of ink for water which was poured into the diviner's hand and thus used for detection of the living, or for *Necromancy*. The only good diviners from ink are pure young boys, black female slaves, or pregnant women, but boys are most commonly employed. *A magic square is drawn with ink in the palm of his hand, and in the centre of the square a little pool of ink serves as the magic mirror. While the diviner gazes in it, incense is burnt, and pieces of paper with charms written on them.* When Kinglake was in Cairo (Frazer relates out of *Eothen* xviii) he asked a Magician, a stately old man with flowing beard, vast turban and ample robes, to exhibit his skill. This he set out to do by employing a boy to gaze into *a blot of ink in his palm and there* to descry the image of any person the Englishman might name. Kinglake would have Keate, his old Eton master, *a ferocious dominie of the ancient school, short in figure and in temper, with shaggy red eyebrows and other features to match*, to appear. In response to this call, the youthful diviner professed to see in the inky mirror the image of a fair girl, golden-haired, blue-eyed, pallid of face and rosy of lip. Kinglake's laughter so discomfited the Magician that, *perceiving the grossness of his failure*, he declared *the boy must have known sin (for none but the innocent can see truth), and accordingly kicked him down stairs.*[2] But why do I digress? If you desire to know more, particularly of what this *Magic* is, how it influences, how it fascinates (for, as all hold, it still does fascinate both men and women), read it in Frazer, his *Golden Bough*, Rivers, Perry, etc., etc.

Somewhat different are the *omens* to be drawn from books and the method of drawing them. Divination by books is called *Bibliomancy*,[3] and is reckoned by many a branch of *Necromancy*. It was much practised in the Middle Ages, as Scott and Tennyson have recorded in the *Lay of the Last Minstrel* and the *Idylls of the King*. Alphonsus of Aragon, saith Bacon

[1] *Ib.* ii, 427–8.   [2] *Eothen.* (1852) xviii, 188.   [3] Rogers, *Manual for Bibliography.* 161.

(*Apophthegms*), *was wont to say of himself that he was a great necromancer, for that he used to ask counsel of the dead: meaning books.* The British Museum Reading-room is *a city of necromancers*, an *Heraclea*, in which they raise the dead, says Bulwer-Lytton.[1] *Do I want to speak to Cicero? I invoke him. Do I want to chat in the Athenian market-place, and hear news two thousand years old? I write down my charm on a slip of paper, and a grave magician calls me up Aristophanes, etc.; it is a world beyond the grave, a land of ghosts.* A library, according to Henry Ward Beecher,[2] is but *the soul's burial-ground, the land of shadows*; which George Crabbe supports in his poem of *The Library*:

> With awe, around their silent walks I tread;
> These are the lasting mansions of the dead.

A book is never a masterpiece, it becomes one. Genius is the talent of a man who is dead,[3] and when a lover of books sits in his library, he is conscious of the company of friendly geniuses who speak to him out of the grave; as Whittier's magnate among his books:

> The old, dead authors thronged him round about,
> And Elzevir's grey ghosts from leathern graves looked out.

Joseph Hall, in his *Occasional Meditations*, disclaims *all offence of Necromancy* when he indulges in the happiness of calling up *ancient worthies, whether human or divine*; and Dr. Johnson agrees with Alphonsus of Aragon that *dead counsellors are safest*, because *death puts an end to flattery and artifice*, so that *the information we receive from books is pure from interest, fear and ambition*.[4] But from early times they have consulted these dead—

> My days among the dead are past—[5]

hoping to divine something of the hereafter, or guidance in some present dilemma:

> Studious let me sit,
> And hold high converse with the mighty dead.[6]

Many books have been used for magical purposes, but chiefly the *Bible*, *Homer*, and *Virgil*. In all the intercourse of man with books nothing is more remarkable than the *Sortes Virgilianae*, which I essay apart, but there is a temptation, an instinct, towards *sortes bibliothecae*, in all bookmen.

> Therefore will I turn my Magic books,
> And strain out Necromancy to the deep.[7]

The love of *lucky dipping* into books promotes an involuntary observation of coincidences and chances in textual openings, which attract the interest

[1] *The Caxtons*.   [2] *Star Papers*, 'The Bodleian Library'.   [3] Edmond and Jules de Goncourt.   [4] *Adventurer*. 137.   [5] Southey, *Occasional Pieces*. xviii.   [6] James Thomson, *The Seasons*. 430–31.   [7] R. Greene, *Honourable History of Friar Bacon and Friar Bungay*.

even of those least inclined towards magic. *In going into a great library*, Professor Playfair told Miss Berry,[1] *it often occurs to me to take up some remarkable book, open it by chance, and observe what turns up, as the truths thus carelessly suggested live long in the memory*. That day in the University Library he took up the *Theatrum Cometicum*, and the first sentence was: *Causa cometarum maxime universalis est Deus*.[2] The *truism* was all he got for his pains, and it was the only piece of instruction he was likely to carry away from Cambridge; but he consoled himself by thinking *some have perhaps gone away with less*. If Maurice Hewlett[3] had wished to try the *sortes* not of Fate but of Conduct, *Montaigne* would have been his oracle. *Here*, he says, *is a reflection which should have been found by unhappy Habsburg or Hohenzollern in* 1914; '*C'est le déjeuner d'un petit ver, que le cœur et la vie d'un grand et triomphant Empereur*.' *God*[4] *knows what the digestion of that might have saved us*.

Spartianus, in his *Life* of the Emperor Hadrian, discourses of the custom of the ancients to inquire after Futurity by the haphazard opening of the leaves of Homer and Virgil. Afterwards the Christians, *retaining some remnants of the Pagan superstition*, thought to be mighty clever in preserving the custom of making the *Holy Scriptures*, especially the *Psalms*, take the place of the Pagan classics; *and what is more surprising, if we may credit Agrippa* (c. 4 of his *Vanity of the Sciences*), several members of the Sorbonne in his time approved of this *two-fold piece of impiety*. The custom spread to France in the days of the early kings, when three books of the *Bible*: the *Prophets*, the *Gospels* and the *Epistles of St. Paul*, were first placed on the altar, or the shrine of some Saint, and they *maturely considered* those parts of the text revealed at a first opening which were germane to their wishes. This custom was abolished by Louis the Debonair, Art. 46, *ut nullus in psalterio, vel evangelio, vel aliis rebus sortiri praesumat, nec divinationes aliquas observare*.[5] Thus far in general; I now turn to more particular instances.

VII. HOW PANTAGRUEL EXPLORES THE SORTES VIRGILIANAE

In three admirable chapters of *Rabelais*,[6] the illustrious Pantagruel excogitates the whole business of the *sortes* bearing upon the prophetic virtues of both *Homer* and *Virgil* in the matter of Panurge's desire for marriage.

---

[1] *Miss Berry's Letters*. Lewis II, 294–5.   [2] 'The most universal cause of comets is God.'   [3] *Extemporary Essays*, 121.   [4] 'The heart and the life of a great and triomphant Emperor are nothing but the breakfast of a little worm.'   [5] 'That no one shall presume to draw lots in the Psalms, or the Gospel or anywhere else, nor observe any divinations.'   [6] *Works*. Bohn Ed. Trans. Urquhart and Motteux. iii, 10–12.

These cogitations, and those of the precedent chapter, are an epitome of the frailty and bewilderment of human reason, for with the best will to deny the *sortes*, those who are experienced of the world, and honest withal, cannot but see that there are arguments *pro* and *contra* in every case, whether taken *a posteriori* or *a priori*. This is seen to no better advantage than in the famous joust where Panurge, after fetching from the bottom of his heart a very deep sigh, took counsel of his lord and master, Pantagruel, whether he should marry, yea or nay. In the great discourse which succeeds, marriage, its joys and sorrows, trials and tribulations, tricks, dangers, sorties, caprices, as well as its conveniences, pleasantries, and comforts, are so laid bare by disquisition and ratiocination, that, although Pantagruel advises him *to it*, and concludes his final tilt, after swaying this way and that way after every encounter, with: *Marry then, in the name of God!* Panurge is still bewildered. *Your counsel,* quoth he, *under your correction and favour, seemeth unto me not unlike to the song of Gammer Yea-by-nay: full of sarcasms, mockeries, bitter taunts, nipping bobs, derisive quips, biting jerks, and contradictory iterations, the one part destroying the other.* But divining that he had resolved to make a trial of the state of marriage, Pantagruel told him that there was nothing now for Panurge to do but bow his head, kiss the ground, put the business to a venture and give it a fair hazard, *recommending the success of the residue to the disposure of Almighty God.* It was not in his power to give any other assurance, or otherwise to certify what should ensue on the undertaking. *Nevertheless, if it pleases you,* Pantagruel advises, *this you may do. Bring hither Virgil's 'Poems' that after having opened the book, and with our fingers severed the leaves thereof several times, we may according to the number agreed upon between ourselves, explore the future hap of your intended marriage. For frequently, by a Homeric lottery, have many hit upon their destinies.*

How they would cast their *Virgilian Lots* caused further argument. Panurge was for abandoning the book and finding a more expedite adjustment of destiny by the chance of three fair dice-throws. Pantagruel would have none of that, for *that sort of lottery is deceitful, abusive, illicitous, and exceeding scandalous.* Furthermore it had been forbidden by his father, Gargantua, over all his kingdoms and dominions. He argued that the fortunate cast of Tiberius, within the fountain of Appona, at the oracle of Gerion, was one of *those baited hooks by which the devil attracts and draweth unto him the foolish souls of silly people into eternal perdition.* But to satisfy Panurge's humour in some measure, he will compromise by throwing three dice upon the table, the number of spots cast up marking the verse of that page which in the setting open of the book he shall have hit upon. They proceeded according to this decision.

Panurge was attacked by nervous fears, when the *Works of Virgil* were brought in, his heart beat with violence and his pulse so quickened that he asked Pantagruel if he would not hold it expedient, before they proceeded farther, to invoke Hercules and the Tenetian goddesses who are said to rule over Lots. *Neither him nor them*, answered Pantagruel, *only open the leaves of the book with your fingers and set your nails to work.* He did so. The dice cast up sixteen, and at the sixteenth line of the disclosed page Panurge encountered the following verse:

Nec Deus hunc mensa, Dea nec dignata cubili est.

The God him from his table banishèd
Nor would the Goddess have him in her bed.[1]

This response, quoth Pantagruel, *maketh not very much for your benefit or advantage: for it plainly signifies and denoteth, that your wife shall be a strumpet, and yourself by consequence a cuckold.* And he continues in the following deductions: That the Goddess whom Panurge shall not find propitious nor favourable unto him is Minerva, a most redoubtable and dreadful Virgin, a powerful and fulminating Goddess, an enemy to cuckolds and effeminate youngsters, to cuckold-makers and adulterers, and much more lusty stuff of the kind, until he bids him try his fortune for the second time, when he falls upon this verse:

Membra quatit, gelidusque coit formidine sanguis.

His joints and members quake, he becomes pale,
And sudden fear doth his cold blood congeal.[2]

This importeth, quoth Pantagruel, *that she will soundly bang your back and belly. Clean and quite contrary*, answered Panurge, *it is of me that he prognosticates, in saying that I will beat her like a tiger, if she vex me. Sir Martin Wagstaff will perform that office, and in default of a cudgel, the devil gulp him, if I should not eat her up quick, as Candaules the Lydian King did his wife, whom he ravened and devoured.* Thereafter did he hit, at the third opening of the book, upon this verse:

Femineo praedae et spoliorum ardebat amore.

After the spoil and pillage, as in fire,
He burnt with a strong feminine desire.[3]

This portendeth, quoth Pantagruel, *that she will steal your goods and rob you. Hence this, according to these three drawn lots, will be your future destiny. I clearly see it,—you will be a cuckold, you will be beaten, and you will be robbed.*

[1] *Eclogues.* iv, 63.   [2] *Aeneid.* iii, 30.   [3] *Ib.* xi, 782.

But since they were nowise in agreement, and as a last refuge and in the hope of a surer remedy, Pantagruel claimed that they should abandon their expounding of the *Virgilian Lots*, bend their course another way and try a new sort of divination. *Of what kind?* asked Panurge. *Of a good and authentic fashion*, answered Pantagruel, *it is by dreams*, the efficacy of which is clearly described by Hippocrates, Plato, Plotinus, Iamblichus, Synesius, Aristotle, Xenophon, Galen, Plutarch, Artemidorus, Valdianus, Herophilus, Q. Calaber, Theocritus, Pliny, Athenaeus, and others, but *de his satis*, read him in Book III of *Rabelais*, where he treats *Of the Heroic Deeds and Sayings of the Good Pantagruel*, a most delectable excursion.

VIII. OF THE *SORTES* IN ANCIENT AND MODERN TIMES

Give me but a little leave, and I will set before your eyes a fair number of examples common to the ancients and those nearer our own times which go further to prove how men have resorted to books for purposes of divination. One, which many will recall, recounts what befell during the visit of King Charles I to the Bodleian in 1642, and is given by Macray[1] out of Welwood's *Memoirs*. The King being at Oxford during the Civil Wars, went one day to see the Public Library, where he was shown, among other Books, a Virgil nobly printed and exquisitely bound. The Lord Falkland, to divert the King, would have his Majesty make a trial of his fortune by the *Sortes Virgilianae*, which everybody knows, and I have shown, was a usual kind of augury some ages past. Whereupon the King opening the book, the period which happened to come up was that part of Dido's imprecation against Aeneas:

At bello audacis populi vexatus et armis,
Finibus extorris, complexu avulsus Iuli,
Auxilia imploret, videatque indigna suorum
Funera; nec, cum se sub leges pacis iniquae
Tradiderit, regno aut optata luce fruatur,
Sed cadat ante diem mediaque inhumatus arena.[2]

Yet let a race untam'd, and haughty foes,
His peaceful entrance with dire arts oppose
Oppress'd with numbers in th' unequal field,
His men discourag'd, and himself expell'd,

[1] *Annals of the Bodleian.* 96–7.   [2] *Aeneid.* iv, 615 *seq.*

Let him for succour sue from place to place,
Torn from his subjects, and his son's embrace.
First let him see his friends in battle slain,
And their untimely fate lament in vain:
And when at length the cruel war shall cease,
On hard conditions may he buy his peace.
Nor let him then enjoy supreme command,
But fall untimely by some hostile hand,
And lye unburied in the common sand.[1]

It is said King Charles seemed concerned at this accident, and that the Lord Falkland observing it, would likewise try his own fortunes in the same manner, hoping he might fall upon some passage that could have no relation to his case, and thereby divert the King's thoughts from any impression the other might have made upon him. But the place that Falkland stumbled upon was yet more suited to his own destiny than the other had been to the King's, for it contained the exclamations of Evander upon the untimely death of his son Pallas:

Non haec, O Palla, dederas promissa parenti,
Cautius ut saevo velles te credere Marti!
Haud ignarus eram, quantum nova gloria in armis
Et praedulce decus primo certamine posset.
Primitiae juvenis miserae! bellique propinqui
Dura rudimenta![2]

O Pallas, thou hast fail'd thy plighted word,
To fight with reason, not to tempt the sword.
I warned thee, but in vain, for well I knew
What perils youthful ardor would pursue;
That boiling blood would carry thee too far,
Young as thou wert in dangers, raw to war.
Oh! curst essay of arms, disastrous doom,
Prelude of bloody fields and fights to come.[3]

No copy of *Virgil*, says Macray, answering the description of this volume is now in the Bodleian, and Archbishop Bancroft, in one of his MS. *Note Books* in the Bodleian Library (Li. 29), assigns Windsor as the *locale* of the story. *There goes a story that Charles I a little before the Rebellion, being at Windsor, the company agreed to take their lots out of Virgil.* The King's was this:

At bello audacis populi vexatus et armis, etc.

[1] Dryden, *Aeneid.* iv, 881.   [2] *Aeneid.* xi, 152 *seq.*   [3] Dryden, *Aeneid.* xi, 230.

A third report, vouched for by Aubrey, *the gossip-monger*, would have that the casting took place at Paris, and the Prince of Wales, not the King, was chief party to it.

So much for history, but it is all one, whether King or Prince, Oxford, Windsor, or Paris, for all three cities and many princes have resorted to Virgil, Homer, etc., when their destinies were at stake; as those of more humble station in most ages, like Robert Herrick, in *The Ebb Tide*,[1] would roam about his South Sea Island with *Virgil* his only companion. He would dip into the *Aeneid*, seeking *sortes; and if the oracle* (as is the way of oracles) replied with no very certain or encouraging voice, *visions of England at least would throng upon the exile's memory: the busy schoolroom, the green playing-fields, holidays at home, and the perpetual roar of London, and the fire-side, and the white head of his father. For it is the destiny of those grave, restrained and classic writers, with whom we make enforced and often painful acquaintance at school, to pass into the blood and become native in the memory; so that a phrase of Virgil speaks not so much of Mantua or Augustus, but of English places and the student's own irrevocable youth.*

In like manner, as may be imagined, the *Bible* has been the medium of prophecy for many good men, notably St. Augustine, for when he was a young man in some distress of spirit, not knowing which way to turn for comfort, he heard a mysterious voice say unto him: *Take up and read, take up and read.* After a while, finding no human origin for this command, he presumed it came from God and gat him to the Apostle's book in the presence of his friend Alypius, where he opened and read: *Not in rioting and drunkenness, not in chambering and wantonness, not in strife and envying: but put ye on the Lord Jesus Christ; and make not provision for the flesh, to fulfil the lusts thereof.*[2] No further would he read, nor needed he. For, *instantly even with the end of the sentence, by a light as it were of confidence now darted into my heart, all the darkness of doubting now vanished away.*[3] He then shut up the book, and discovered all this unto Alypius, who confessed that a like revelation was wrought in his own heart, and he requested to see what Augustine had read, and looking further found these words following: *Him that is weak in faith, receive;*[4] which he applied to himself, and with it was strengthened. This reading established the saintliness of Augustine, for he *sought no more after a wife, nor any other hopes in this world.*

Of the Homeric and Virgilian lotteries, several instances from classical times are given by Pantagruel;[5] many have thus hit upon their destinies, as is testified in the person of Socrates, who whilst he was in prison, hearing in a dream the recitation, by a beautiful woman, of this verse of Homer, said of Achilles in the Ninth of the *Iliad*,[6]

[1] By Robert Louis Stevenson. 2.　[2] *Rom.* xiii, 13.　[3] *Confessions.* Trans. Watts. viii, 12.　[4] *Rom.* xiv, 1.　[5] Rabelais. iii, 10.　[6] 363.

ἤματί κε τριτάτῳ ϕθίην ἐρίβωλον ἱκοίμην

The third day, I at Pthia might arrive;

thereby foresaw that on the third subsequent day he was to die. Of the truth whereof he assured Crito; as Plato, *in Critone*, Cicero *in primo De Divinatione*, Diogenes Laertius, and others, have to the full recorded. The like is also witnessed by Opilius Macrinus, to whom, being desirous to know if he should be the Roman Emperor, befell by chance of lot this sentence in the Eighth of the *Iliad*,[1]

ὦ γέρον, ἦ μάλα δή σε νέοι τείρουσι μαχηταί,
σὴ δὲ βίη λέλυται, χαλεπὸν δέ σε γῆρας ὀπάζει.

Dotard, new warriors urge thee to be gone,
Thy life decays, and old age weighs thee down.

In fact, he being somewhat ancient, had hardly enjoyed the sovereignty of the empire for the space of fourteen months, when by Heliogabalus, then both young and strong, he was dispossessed thereof, thrust out of all, and killed.

Brutus bears witness to another experiment of this nature. He was willing, through this exploratory way of lot, to learn what the event and issue should be of the Pharsalian battle, wherein he perished, and casually encountered on this verse, said of Patroclus in the Sixteenth of the *Iliad*,[2]

ἀλλά με μοῖρ᾽ ὀλοὴ καὶ Λητοῦς ἔκτανεν υἱός.

Fate and Latona's son have shot me dead.

Accordingly 'Apollo' was the field-word in the dreadful day of that fight. Divers notable things of old have likewise been foretold and known by casting of Virgilian lots, and, in matters of no less importance than the obtaining of the Roman Empire, as it happened to Alexander Severus, who, trying his fortune at the said kind of lottery, did hit upon this verse written in the Sixth of the *Aeneid*,[3]

Tu regere imperio populos, Romane, memento.

Know, Roman, that thy business is to reign.

Within very few years thereafter he was effectually and in good earnest created and installed Roman emperor.

A semblable story thereto is related of Adrian, who, being hugely perplexed within himself out of a longing humour to know in what account he was with the emperor Trajan, and how large the measure of that

[1] 102-3.   [2] 849.   [3] 85⁓

affection was which he did bear unto him, had recourse, after the manner above specified, to the Maronian lottery, which by haphazard tendered him these lines out of the Sixth of the *Aeneid*:[1]

> Quis procul ille autem ramis insignis olivae,
> Sacra ferens? Nosco crines, incanaque menta
> Regis Romani;

> But who is he, conspicuous from afar,
> With olive boughs, that doth his offerings bear?
> By the white hair and beard I know him plain
> The Roman king.

Shortly thereafter was he adopted by Trajan, and succeeded to him in the empire. Moreover, to the lot of the Emperor Claudius befell this line of Virgil, written in the First of his *Aeneid*,[2]

> Tertia dum Latio regnantem viderit aestas,

> Whilst the third summer saw him reign a king
> In Latium.

And in effect he did not reign above two years. To the said Claudian also, enquiring concerning his brother Quintilius, whom he proposed as a colleague with himself in the empire, happened the response following, in the Sixth of the *Aeneid*,[3]

> Ostendent terris hunc tantum fata,—

> Whom fate just let us see,
> And would no longer suffer him to be.

And so it fell out; for he was killed on the seventeenth day after he had attained unto the management of the imperial charge. The very same lot also, with the like misluck, did betide the Emperor Gordian the younger. To Claudius Albinus, being very solicitous to understand somewhat of his future adventures, did occur this saying, which is written in the Sixth of the *Aeneid*,[4]

> Hic rem Romanam, magno turbante tumultu
> Sistet; eques sternet Poenos, Gallumque rebellem.

> The Romans boiling with tumultuous rage,
> This warrior shall the dangerous storm assuage;
> With victories he the Carthaginian mauls,
> And with strong hand shall crush the rebel Gauls.

[1] 809.   [2] 265.   [3] 870.   [4] 858.

Likewise when the Emperor D. Claudius, Aurelian's predecessor, did with great eagerness research after the fate to come of his posterity, his hap was to alight on this verse in the First of the *Aeneid*,[1]

> Hic ego nec metas rerum nec tempora pono.

> No bounds are to be set, no limits here.

Which was fulfilled by the goodly genealogical row of his race. When Peter Amy, the friend of Rabelais, did in like manner explore and make trial, if he should escape the ambush of the hobgoblins,[2] who lay in wait all-to-bemaul him, he fell upon this verse in the Third of the *Aeneid*,[3]

> Heu! fuge crudeles terras, fuge littus avarum!

> Ah flee the bloody land, the wicked shore!

which counsel he obeying, forthwith avoided all their ambuscades.

Were it not well to shun prolixity, I could enumerate a hundred such like adventures, which, conformable to the dictate and verdict of the verse, have by that manner of lot-casting befallen the curious researchers of them. Do not you nevertheless imagine, lest you should be deluded, that I would, upon this kind of fortune-telling, infer an uncontrollable and not-to-be-gainsaid infallibility of truth. I say no more than that it has comforted men in all ages since the birth of books. Among our own people, and others, *pricking the Bible* for luck or prophecy has been an old wives' custom this long time. And among those who go down to the sea in ships and seek business in great waters the *sortes* are still consulted out of any handy volume. One such instance has been given me by a sailor from his own observation, in which the crew of a ship cast lots for treatment *all round* to strong drink, by stabbing the pages of a book with a knife, the one cutting at an agreed letter nearest the first A on the left-hand page paying for the drinks.

The latest recourse to the *sortes* I can find in times present is recorded of Mr. Stanley Baldwin, when Prime Minister.[4] He confessed to having himself used the *Oxford Dictionary* for this purpose, finding in it much enlightenment on Cabinets and politics, as where *Cabinet councils* are defined as *a remedy worse than the disease*. But after events proved the inefficacy of this form of prophecy, when the *Dictionary* told him that girls are *naturally timid, prone to dependence, but born Conservatives*, for at the next election the Conservative Party was given its quietus, if all I read be true, by the girls he himself had enfranchised, who were so bold and independent as to vote

---

[1] 278.   [2] i.e. Cordeliers. *Rabelais*. Bohn Ed. *n.* i, 522.   [3] 44.   [4] Speech at the Dinner on the completion of the *New English Dictionary*. Goldsmiths' Hall. 6.vi.1928. *Times*, 7.vi.1928.

for the revolutionaries. I have thus far digressed and may certainly conclude my account of this strange conceit or superstition by declaring it *astrum hominis*, and if books are thus made the rudder of our ship, which most argue reason should steer, it is no more than a further tribute to the immemorial tradition of their power, the *medium deferens* of that faith by whose means they have worked and produced prodigious effects. As such phantasies are more or less intended or remitted, and their humours disposed, so does the soul of man move, more or less, and take deeper impression of life and time.

Part IX

OF THE BIBLIOPHAGI OR BOOK-EATERS

I. A DIET OF BOOKS CONSIDERED

Diet, Διαίτημα, *Victus*, or Living, is concomitant with all functions, whether *natural* or *artificial*; and if some, as they say, *live to eat*, we must all *eat to live*,

> We may live without poetry, music and art;
> We may live without conscience, and live without heart;
> We may live without friends; we may live without books;
> But civilized man cannot live without cooks.[1]

The argument holds, whether we are concerned for the preservation of the body, the mind, or the soul, for cook and poet are alike: *the art of each lies in his brain*.[2] Each must be nourished on a proper diet for the retention of its form and the maintenance of its condition in the first place, and the increase or expansion of its power in the second.

> The things we eat by various Juice controul
> The Narrowness or Largeness of our Soul.
> Onions will make ev'n Heirs or Widows weep,
> The tender Lettice brings on softer Sleep.
> Eat Beef or Pye-crust if you'd serious be:
> Your shell-fish raises Venus from the Sea:
> For Nature that inclines to Ill or Good,
> Still nourishes our Passions by our Food;[3]

and following our poet, that renowned authority, Brillat-Savarin, laid it down that it was part of the business of gastronomy to consider *how food may influence the moral nature of man, his courage and his perceptions, whether awake or asleep, in action or repose*.[4]

I have read many treatises to this purpose, but nowhere do I find any

---

[1] Owen Meredith, *Lucile*. i, 2.

[2] οὐδὲν ὁ μάγειρος τοῦ ποιητοῦ διαφέρει.
ὁ νοῦς γάρ ἐστιν ἑκατέρῳ τούτων τέχνη.

Euphron, in *Athenaeus*. Loeb Ed. i, 7–8.   [3] King, Art of Cookery. 71.   [4] *Physiologie du Goût*. Trans. Anderson. 32.

serious study of the dietetics of literature, or any evidence of research into this curious subject. All references are *en passant*, as in Peignot his *Diction- naire de Bibliologie*, where a *Bibliophage* is noted as signifying *celui qui mange des livres*, and with this bare recognition he passes on. *We are not*, Hill Bur- ton complains,[1] *favoured with any examples explanatory of the kind of books most in demand by those addicted to this species of food, nor of the effect of the different classes of books on the digestive organs*; but he does not attempt to remedy the defect, and as no other authority has done so, I have therefore adventured upon this section, bringing together my notes, specimens and deductions for the benefit of those who would understand more clearly the dietetic relationship of books to men. I shall assemble many observa- tions to show that books are food, libraries *so many dishes of meat, served out for several palates*,[2] and that we eat them from love or necessity, as other foods, but most from love, and for that reason the bibliophagi may be ranked among the first of bibliophiles.

Perhaps it is easier than Voltaire believed *to pass from people kissing to people eating one another*,[3] for, as James Thomson gives out, cannibals may be the only *real lovers of their fellow-men*,[4] and on this basis the bibliophagi may be the best lovers of their fellow-books. We may contemplate the idea with fortitude, since the performance up to now has been, in the main, of a metaphorical character, or, if it is more tangible than that, there being no smoke without fire, the will has not yet discovered a way to- wards a more precise interpretation of the passion. Which is well, especi- ally for our *rariora*, although there is fodder enough in the commoner sort of contemporary books; but since these might not be deemed edible, it is fortunate that the practice has not been pressed to its logical conclusion, for, as Voltaire said of cannibalism, *if we were allowed to eat our neighbours, we should soon eat our countrymen, which would be rather unfortunate for the social virtues*.[5]

Joseph Hall would take books and *imitate the skilfullest cooks, which make the best dishes from manifold mixtures*;[6] and Fletcher supports him with the picture of a hungry book-eater:

> If all thy pipes of wine were filled with books,
> Made of the barks of trees, or mysteries writ
> In old moth-eaten vellum, he would sip thy cellar
> Quite dry, and still be thirsty. Then for 's diet,
> He eats and digests more volumes at a meal,
> Than there would be larks (though the sky should fall)
> Devour'd in a month in Paris.[7]

[1] *Book-Hunter*. 207.   [2] Burton, *Anat. of Melan.* (1904) ii, 102.   [3] *Philosophical Dictionary*, 'Cannibals'.   [4] *Poems, Essays, and Fragments.* 260.   [5] *Op. cit.*   [6] 'Epistle, to Lord Denny', Qt. *Book-Lover's Ench.* 41.   [7] *The Elder Brother.* i, 2.

Whether the inscription on the portal of the Library at Alexandria was, as Diodorus reports, *The Medicine of the Mind*, or as some others would have, *The Nourishment of the Soul*, it is all one, as who shall estrange soul from mind, or say in what finally body differs from either, for we are constituents of the whole of life as well as sum-total in ourselves. *The analogy between body and mind is very general*, says Boswell,[1] *and the parallel will hold as to their food, as well as any other particular*, for, as the poet infers,

> Poets and Pastry Cooks will be the same,
> Since both of them their Images must frame.
> Chimeras from the Poet's Fancy flow,
> The Cook contrives his Shapes in real Dough.[2]

Our traffic with books is not one but many; as much gustation as devotion. At the very beginning of our pilgrimage through life we are book-fed, for, as Anatole France holds, *Grammars are but feeding bottles*.[3] *A book*, Gibbon told Lady Sheffield, *takes more time in making than a pudding*; the *Ciceros* of Leyden, Paris and Geneva are *long standing dishes*;[4] every book *a feast of reason and a flow of soul*: a *Banquet of Wit*;

> Were Horace, that great Master, now alive,
> A Feast with Wit and Judgment he'd contrive;[5]

or more particularly that *Bachelars Banquet*, published in 1603, *wherein is prepared sundrie dainties to furnish their table*. Readers should approach literature as gourmets approach good food, for *a good dinner is brother to a good poem*.[6] After a preliminary taste of the *Bibliographical Decameron*, Isaac D'Israeli advised Dibdin that *fruits and comfits have been the 'goûter' as yet; but I shall sit down soon to a solid meal*.[7] The bibliophagi note fragrance, flavour, it is *the first flavours that make or unmake taste*;[8] whether edible, digestible; they revel in them at table as at a meal:

> But who is he, in closet close y-pent,
> Of sober face, with learned dust besprent?
> Right well mine eyes arede the myster wight,
> On parchment scraps y-fed, and Wormius hight.[9]

They devour them anywhere, as I will show. Plutarch *browsed on literature and thought*, secreting the *most valuable constituents*;[10] Hazlitt describes a human bookworm who *browses on the husk and leaves of books, as the young*

---

[1] *Life of Johnson*. Ed. Hill. i, 57–8.   [2] King, *Art of Cookery*. 131.   [3] *Pierre Nozière*. Trans. May. 119.   [4] Dibdin, *Bibliophobia*. 72.   [5] King, *Art of Cookery*. 129. [6] *Apician Morsels*. 105.   [7] Dibdin, *Reminiscences*. ii, 636.   [8] Joubert, *Selections*. Trans. Lyttleton. 173.   [9] Pope, *Dunciad*. iii, 185–8.   [10] Tucker, Intro. *Select Essays of Plutarch*, 15.

fawn browses on the bark and leaves of trees;[1] Rosenbach records that *very young children eat their books, literally devouring their contents,* and he gives this as one reason for the scarcity of first editions of *Alice in Wonderland* and other favourites of the nursery.[2] Librarians of old, says another authority,[3] *ate books,* and the colour of the food *showed through,* like the green grass consumed by small green caterpillars, but in *a sort of general brown, faded colour, a little undusted around the edges;* and for writers they are nourishing, as Joseph Glanvill sufficiently declares, in his *Essay concerning Preaching,*[4] where he advises young Divines, when writing their sermons, to make use of *notions* met with in their reading, not by tying themselves to the *words of the Author,* but by digesting them into their *store of thoughts, as the various juyce of flowers is by the industrious Bee,* and so *making them enjoyable and agreeable.*

When Meric Casaubon visited the Bodleian, over three hundred years ago, what great content he had to see the numerous students *revelling at their banquet;*[5] recalling, as like as not, Cicero's claim that studies are the *aliment of youth;*[6] or, perchance, Timon of Phlius, who dubbed the Museum at Alexandria, where the great library was housed, *a bird-cage,* in order to ridicule *the philosophers who got their living there because they are fed like the choicest birds in a coop.*[7] Paterson, the bibliographer, was *highly feasted* on certain favourite passages in the *Bibliotheca Croftsiana* (1783);[8] *hungry bibliographers meet, at sales, with well-furnished purses,* saith mine author,[9] *and are resolved upon a sumptuous fare.* Books for Robert Southey were *more than metaphorically meat, drink, and clothing.*[10]

Well may some go so far as to argue that books are edible, and to serve their purpose must be eaten: *you must eat the book, you must crush it, and cut it with your teeth and swallow it;*[11] they are food and drink, accessible to the culinary art, creators of appetite, satisfiers of hunger, as Robert Herrick, the beachcomber in *The Ebb-Tide,* found his *Virgil,* which he failed to exchange *against a meal,* but which *often consoled him in his hunger,* as *Robinson Crusoe* had consoled Coleridge at Christ's Hospital, where the food was so bad that the boys' appetites *were damped, never satisfied:* the starved young poet would *crumple himself up in a sunny corner and read, read, read; fixing himself on Robinson Crusoe's Island, finding a mountain of plum cake, and eating a room for himself, and then eating it into the shapes of tables and chairs—hunger and fancy;*[12] thus supporting Tom Hood's con-

---

[1] 'On the Conversation of Authors.' *The Plain Speaker.* (1826) i, 96. [2] *Books and Bidders.* 186. [3] Gerald Stanley Lee, *Lost Art of Reading.* 201. [4] p. 67. [5] *Great Book-Collectors,* Elton. 125. [6] 'Haec studia adolescentiam alunt.' Cicero, *Pro Archia.* 7. [7] Qt. *Athenaeus.* Loeb Ed. i, 22. [8] Dibdin, *Bibliomania.* (1811) 526. [9] *Ib.* 517. [10] In a letter to G. C. Bedford. [11] Dr. John Brown, 'With Brains Sir!', *Horae Subsecivae.* [12] *Letters.* Ed. E. H. Coleridge i, 20. n.

tention that they even *atone for a meagre diet; rich fare on the paper for short commons on the cloth.*[1]

Long absence from bookish fare creates bookish hunger, which Gibbon discovers after prolonged abstention from reading during his service with the Militia, *amid the perpetual hurry of an inn, a barrack, or a guard-room,* he records,[2] *all literary ideas were banished from my mind;* but after this long *fast,* the longest he had ever known, he *tasted* once more the pleasures of reading, and the *hungry appetite* with which he opened a volume of *Tully* remained long in his memory. George Gissing provided against a like calamity by keeping a number of appetising books on shelves where he could get at them readily when he hungered for them.[3] Dr. Johnson was always hungry for books. At Mr. Dilly's, on 15th April, 1778, Boswell mentions[4] how he seized upon Charles Sheridan's *Account of the Late Revolution in Sweden,* and *seemed to read it ravenously, as if he devoured it;* during dinner he kept the book *wrapped up in the table-cloth in his lap, from the avidity to have one entertainment in readiness when he should have finished another;* resembling, he says, *a dog who holds a bone in his paws in reserve, while he eats something else which has been thrown to him.*

II. VARIETIES OF BOOK-EATERS

Bibliophiles are gastronomes, gourmets, gourmands, epicures; Elton calls Du Fay *an epicure of learning;*[5] Leigh Hunt had a dainty gusto *like an epicurean over a choice dish,* he tasted his books with a *doting* and *succulent relish.*[6] Narcissus Luttrell was *voracious in his bibliomaniacal appetites,*[7] and in the pathological stage they are *helluones librorum,* book-gluttons like Matthias Corvinus, King of Hungary, who had the largest library in Europe, and was derided for *a mere gourmandiser of books,* voracious, of indiscriminate appetite. Bookmen taste, chew, masticate, nibble, ingustate, devour, gorge, cram; they are subject to appetite and repletion; starving, over-eating, the one reacting upon the other, and thus precipitating indigestions and dyspepsias. Richards notes such a result from a *condition of poetic starvation,* where the sufferer *swallows* all the poetry he can *for a while, hoping that it will do him good, and improve his taste;*[8] but gorging, whether of poetry or puddings, induces bad digestion, not good taste. *Critics,* Arnold Bennett observes, *have been known to contract mortal 'occupational diseases' of the mind from a steady diet of bad books.*[9] Better be selective and moderate, for thus

[1] *Letter to the Manchester Athenæum.* 1843.   [2] *Memoirs,* Hill. 140.   [3] *The Private Papers of Henry Ryecroft* 145.   [4] *Life,* Hill. iii, 284, 285.   [5] Elton, *The Great Book-Collectors.* 197.   [6] Percy Fitzgerald, *Charles Lamb.* 17.   [7] Dibdin, *Bibliomania.* (1811) 426.   [8] *Practical Criticism.* 312.   [9] *Evening Standard.* 21.viii.1930.

only is safety to be found. *Taste is still conditioned by the palate*, says Garrod, and *a safe diet makes a clean palate. Shakespeare and Milton and Wordsworth are*, he says, *a clean diet*.[1] *Do not overfeed us with Anecdotes of Books*, a friend warned Dibdin when he began his *Reminiscences*;[2] too much book-food over-charges Nature, saith Jeremy Collier,[3] *and turns more into disease than Nourishment*. 'Tis Thought and Digestion which makes Books serviceable, giving health and vigour to the mind:

> Who readeth much, and never meditates,
> Is like a greedy eater of much food,
> Who so surcloys his stomach with his cates,
> That commonly they do him little good;[4]

as Edward in *Waverley*, who, like *the epicure who only deigned to take a single morsel from the sunny side of a peach*, read only so long as a book amused him, and then on to another, and so nibbling, until *the passion for reading, like other strong appetites, produced by indulgence a sort of satiety*. Francis Osborne[5] advocates a few books *thoroughly digested* rather than *hundreds but gargled in the mouth*; John Locke[6] counsels as much: it is necessary to be of the *ruminating kind; not enough to cram ourselves with a great load of collections, unless we chew them over again, they will not give us strength and nourishment*; Quintilian supports him in this when he gives out[7] that only the best writers are to be read, and that when a *volume is finished, it is to be gone through again from the beginning*. For the rest we may ignore those testy and choleric cavillers whom Sir John Harrington so well confutes out of *Martial*:

> The readers and the hearers like my books,
> And yet some writers cannot them digest;
> But what care I? for when I make a feast,
> I would my guests should praise it, not the cooks.[8]

For the most part authors of books will agree with him, but all critics are not literary dyspeptics, some, and they as like as not among the best, are peptonisers of otherwise tough works; the book-tasters, or *reviewers*, of Saxony and Pomerania, in Richter's times were called *praegustatores* because they *eat a mouthful of every book beforehand, and tell the people whether its flavour be good*.[9] They roll fine phrases over the palate as they would any other dainty: *no morsel more delicious than a ripe book*;[10] better taste it kindly, than gulp it down freely. Poetry for them is like wine with

---

[1] *Profession of Poetry*. 265.   [2] Dibdin, *Reminiscences*. Preface v.   [3] 'Of the Entertainment of Books', *Essays*.   [4] J. Sylvester, *Tetrasticha*.   [5] *Advice to a Son*.   [6] *Conduct of Understanding*.   [7] *Inst. Or*. x, 1, 20.   [8] *Epigrams*. ix, 82.   [9] *Analecta from Richter*, De Quincey.   [10] A. B. Alcott, *Concord Days*, 'Books'.

fragrance and *bouquet* in its fine vintages; these are true *gourmets*, and among them stand most notable Charles Lamb and Leigh Hunt, who *both literally feasted on books*, they desired *the taste of certain delicious volumes to linger on their palates, as the memory of sweet dishes does on that of other men's. They enjoyed the flavour of a rare passage of poetry with an exquisite relish, as though it were a morsel of ripe and juicy fruit.*[1]

Some books are tough, others tender (how many a tender ballad have young lovers devoured!); some green, others ripe; some hot, others cold; some raw, but most are cooked, fit for all manner of dishes; and so let the bookman *rove, like a bee, from flower to flower,*[2] sipping what is sweet, picking and tasting where he will, according to whim, inclination, as Lipsius approves, *delibare gratum de quocunque cibo, et pytissare de quocunque dolio jucundum,* to taste of every dish and sip of every cup, which, saith Montaigne, was well performed by Aristotle and his own learned country-man, Adrian Turnebus, or as Elizabeth Barrett Browning, when a child, ransacked and ravaged a garret-room *piled high* with cases of books:

> Like some small nimble mouse between the ribs
> Of a mastodon, I nibbled here and there.[3]

That indiscriminate book-eating exists in all ages I have no doubt, and the learned historian, Guglielmo Ferrero, holds[4] that in times present *a wolfish, insatiable hunger for printed paper and reading matter is the scourge of our civilisation.* Yet when bookmen overfeed is not easily decided: where one starves another waxes fat: *if a diet of contemporary sonnets leaves you hungry,* Lionel Johnson prescribes[5] Drayton's *Polyolbion*; that some eat more than others is inevitable, but what sufficiency one discommends another approves. John Hill Burton expostulates[6] against *a course of reading* which is no more than *a course of regimen for dwarfing the mind, like the drugs which dog-breeders give to King Charles spaniels to keep them small.* Anthony Wood called Robert Burton *a devourer of authors*; it was necessary, another gives out, that the Mendicant Friars, in the Middle Ages, should be *devourers* of books if they were, as they wished, to become *monopolists of learning*;[7] but at all times bookmen have been good trenchermen at the literary table, especially and more properly in their young days, as healthy youths with other viands. John Stuart Mill thus *devoured treatises on Chemistry,* especially that of *his father's early friend and schoolfellow, Dr. Thomson.*[8] When a youth, Sir Edmund Gosse was employed as a *transcriber* in the Printed Book Department of the British Museum, and in those days *great laxity prevailed among the assistants and the librarians,* so

[1] Percy Fitzgerald, *Lamb.* 195–6.   [2] Dibdin, *Bibliomania.* (1811) 73.   [3] *Aurora Leigh.*   [4] *Ancient Rome and Modern America.* 56.   [5] *Post Liminium.* 215.   [6] *The Book-Hunter.* 120.   [7] Elton, *Great Book-Collectors.* 31.   [8] *Autobiography.* 17.

that among the younger clerks cricket was practised *in remoter galleries* whilst *less audacious spirits cultivated the pencil and the jews'-harp*. Young Gosse did not join in these excitements: his diversion was *ceaseless devouring of the printed page*.[1]

Cato, says Petrarch, had an *insatiable hunger for books*, to which Cicero bears witness in his *Letters to Atticus*; and Petrarch himself had a like appetite: *one unquenchable longing has the mastery of me, which hitherto I neither would nor could repress; 'tis an insatiable craving for books, although, perhaps, I already have more than I ought*;[2] but whether his hunger constituted a bulimy or inordinate appetite, as that which men, as Nicholas Wood,[3] have for viands, is not stated; some others have come nearer to a Gargantuan reading, as Heber, who had a *book-appetite* of *cormorant-capacity*,[4] whilst Magliabecchi, whose chronic book-hunger I dilate apart, was truly called *the Glutton of Books*;[5] in this there is as little virtue as in any other form of gluttony, as in the satiric poet:

> Large Justice Greedies, who will gormandize
> At city feasts, till they can barely rise!
> Or drink strong wines, till off their seats they fall
> Flat on the floor,—and cannot rise at all![6]

But it may be (as R. L. Stevenson states) that in books as in viands, it is only *in a chosen few that any man will find his* appointed food.[7] *He who eats too much, knows not how to eat*;[8] he who reads too much knows not how to read.

III. THE PHYSIOLOGY OF BOOK-EATING
GOURMETS *v.* GOURMANDS

Bibliophagi should be *gourmets* rather than *gourmands*, they must eat to live, and avoid the condition of those of whom he[9] said *in solo vivendi causa palato est*,

> Men whose sole bliss is eating, who can give
> But that one brutal reason why they live,

for, as Brillat-Savarin rightly holds, *in compelling man to eat that he may live, Nature gives appetite to invite him, and pleasure to reward him*.[10] *It needs a strong head to bear that diet*, says Emerson, of all good books; and, again,

---

[1] *The Library of Edmund Gosse*. xv. [2] Tatham, *Francesco Petrarca*. ii, 36–7. [3] *The Great Eater of Kent*, John Taylor. 1630. [4] Dibdin, *Bibliophobia*. 93. [5] *The Book Fancier*, Fitzgerald. 3. [6] *The Craniad*. 27. [7] 'The Influence of Books', *The Art of Writing*. 89. [8] Brillat-Savarin, *Physiologie du Goût*. Trans. Anderson. xxxvi. [9] Juvenal. [10] *Physiologie du Goût*. Trans. Anderson. xxxvi.

that, although we expect a great man to be a good reader, *assimilating power* should be in proportion to *spontaneous power*.[1] Dryden's aphorism to the same end supposes it *impossible even for a good Wit to understand the proprieties and delicacies* of English, without *the help of a liberal Education, long Reading, and digesting of those few good authors we have amongst us*.[2] Books (argues the Critic in Petrarch's treatise *on Fortune*) *have led some to learning and others to madness, when they swallow more than they can digest*; for sometimes the best of them are sweet in the mouth but bitter in the belly, as St. John the Divine found after he had *ate up* that little book which he took from the open *hand of the Angel which standeth upon the sea and upon the earth*.[3] Jeremy Collier demonstrates[4] with a solid argument in a just essay that *a Man may as well expect to grow stronger by always Eating, as wiser by always Reading. Too much over-charges Nature, and turns more into Disease than Nourishment. 'Tis Thought and Digestion which makes Books serviceable, and gives Health and Vigour to the Mind*; it was sound of Neoptolemus, in *Ennius*, to advise *ex philosophia cenet, non in eam ingurgitandum*, tasting better than gorging, for

> Knowledge is as food, and needs no less
> Her Temperance over appetite, to know
> In measure what the mind may well contain;
> Oppresses else with surfeit, and soon turns
> Wisdom to folly, as nourishment to wind.[5]

You must, in a phrase, *read, mark, learn and inwardly digest*, for, as Mary Coleridge well said, *the fruits of the tree of knowledge are various*, and *he must be strong indeed who can digest all of them*; she herself only learnt this after *vainly endeavouring to get* her *teeth through the sour apple of science, to crack the hard nuts of philosophy*, when all that she was fit for was *to gather up the stray blossoms that fell in the spring*.[6]

Dr. Johnson was able to *gorge books, tear the hearts out of them*, as Leslie Stephen[7] records, with small risk of dyspepsia; Milton, *the most learned of our poets, from his childhood upwards was a devourer of Greek and Latin books, of the romances of the Middle Ages, of French and Italian poetry, above all of the Hebrew Scriptures*;[8] Leigh Hunt was *a glutton of novels*,[9] and survived to an advanced age; Hazlitt *fell early upon French Romances and devoured them tooth and nail*,[10] and, he adds, *I made many a dainty repast of the 'New Eloise'*. Dibdin, always a mighty eater of books, *fell upon* Warton's *History of*

---

[1] 'Quotation and Originality', *Letters and Social Aims*. 130.   [2] *Sylvae*. Pref.
[3] *Revelation*. x, 9–10.   [4] 'Of the Entertainment of Books', *Essays*. ii, 199.   [5] *Paradise Lost*. vii, 126.   [6] *Gathered Leaves*. 8–9.   [7] *Samuel Johnson*. 6.   [8] F. D. Maurice, *Friendship of Books*. 14.   [9] *Life*, Monkhouse. 35.   [10] ' On Reading Old Books', *Plain Speaker*. ii, 71.

English Poetry, absolutely devoured it, and then took Ellis's *Specimens of English Poetry* as *a lighter or second course in the intellectual banquet;*[1] Mark Pattison gobbled Gibbons's *Autobiography,*[2] with great content; and Washington Irving observed readers in the British Museum falling upon *ponderous tomes, tooth and nail with famished voracity.*[3]

Grant Duff regarded Lord Acton as a mere *Helluo librorum,* but Henry Jackson found that learned nobleman capable of forming *a keen, sound and independent judgment* on all he *saw, heard or read.*[4] Edward FitzGerald was a hearty though temperate book-eater, he would gourmandise only off certain books, or when time with a favourite was short, as when he was staying with a friend in Bedford, he took up Boswell's *magical book,* a dish he delighted in, and *could have sat down and read it all through right on end,* but being at that house for two days, he *could only devour two days' worth of it;*[5] but he believed that heavier fare was necessary in certain circumstances, as when marooned in an unfamiliar place, away from one's own books; a goodly row of the *Annual Register,* which, he asserts, *may be found in every country town,* is not amiss; 'tis not easily exhausted, *so long as there is appetite, there is food: and of that plain substantial nature which, Johnson says, suits the stomach of middle life.*[6]

The Rev. Frederick Ekins tells Dibdin[7] that although he is enjoying the *Bibliographical Tour in France and Germany,* he does not *gulp his food* but takes it *quietly like a good boy;* George Hibbert, on the other hand, takes delight in *a solitary and gluttonous monopoly,* of the same book.[8] But lesser men only imitate the vagaries of genius at their peril. A varied diet, moderately taken, is indicated by those who have brought great knowledge and wide experience to bear upon this theme, as John Hill Burton:[9] *Even Gibbon's Decline and Fall, luminous and comprehensive as its philosophy is, and rapid and brilliant the narrative, will become deleterious mental food if consumed straight through without variety;* relieve it with Boston's *Fourfold State,* or Hervey's *Meditations,* or Sturm's *Reflections,* or *Don Juan,* or Ward's *History of Stoke-upon-Trent.* But those who may consider the remedy worse than the disease will prefer to agree with Heath when he sings in his *Praise of Books:*

> A few good books, digested well, do feed
> The mind; much clogs, or doth ill humours breed.

Let us digest them! otherwise they enter our memory, but not our mind;[10] James Howell, in his *Familiar Epistles,* subscribes to this opinion, where he dis-

[1] Dibdin, *Reminiscences.* i, 224–5.   [2] *Memoirs.* 129.   [3] 'Art of Bookmaking', *Sketch Book.*   [4] *Henry Jackson, O.M., A Memoir,* Parry. 124.   [5] *Some New Letters of Edward FitzGerald.* 129–30.   [6] *Letters and Literary Remains.* i, 72.   [7] *Reminiscences.* ii, 686.   [8] *Reminiscences.* ii, 679.   [9] *The Book-Hunter.* 111.   [10] Seneca, *De Tranq. An.* 9. *Book-Lover's Ench.* 5.

commends gorging yourself with *multiplicity of authors: two*, he claims, *is enough upon any science, provided*, he saith, *they be plenary and orthodox* (which is more than needs, too much orthodoxy is nought); Thoreau[1] relates as much of the transcendental philosophy of Carlyle, which *needs the leaven of humour to render it light and digestible*; the same may be said of theology, which is not easily assimilated, especially by the young, as Edmund Gosse knew, his father causing him much pain by cramming him with *theological meat* which it was impossible for the lad to digest.[2] But they are all agreed that nothing pesters the mind so much as to be stall-fed, to eat and ingurgitate beyond all measure, as many do, and, if rightly understood and favourably interpreted, would support a further claim that Philosophy should be your substantial food, Poetry your banqueting stuff. So let us take by proxy those Gargantuan feasts or monotonous repasts, being ready, on occasion, as Joubert advises, even *to breathe Plato* rather than *feed upon him*.[3]

A correspondent of Birkbeck Hill assured him that on their first appearance he *lived on* Mrs. Browning's *Sonnets from the Portuguese*,[4] and Charles Lamb confessed to Landor that he lived upon *Rose Aylmer* (a poem of only two verses) *for weeks*;[5] nor is a whole book or a complete poem required at all times for sustenance; many have kept body and soul together, as the saying is, on a sentence or other concentrated passage, as Edward Fitz-Gerald, who found the *last sentence* of J. M. Kemble's article on the *Government of Russia*, in the *British & Foreign Review* (1840), *meat and drink* to him *for a fortnight*.[6] But, in the end, it is the manner rather than the matter that counts: *est quiddam gestus edendi*.[7] Lockhart's *Scott* made Stevenson ill,[8] and Thomas Hood, wisest and wittiest of the bibliophagi, recounts that when on a journey in Germany his good English stomach revolted against such coarse food as they set before him, but he suffered not at all so long as he could get his *Peregrine Pickle*, and though he did not yearn *towards calf's head à la tortue or sheep's heart*, he could still relish *Head à la Brunnen and' The Heart of Midlothian'*.[9] All are *contenti in hac animi voluptate, quam pascunt per volumina varia divagando et liguriendo*:[10] happy in the luxury which they nourish by ranging and browsing among the diverse volumes of an abundant store of books; so may we approve without desiring to emulate Hazlitt, who sought to browse like a sheep or a rabbit, preferably on folios, revelling in pastures rich with *fat and large* tomes which he had

---

[1] 'Carlyle and his Works', *Essays*. Scott Lib. Ed. 161.   [2] Gosse, *Father and Son*. 90.
[3] *Selected Thoughts*. Trans. Lyttleton. 181.   [4] *Talks about Autographs*. 85.   [5] *Letters*.
Everyman. ii, 305.   [6] *Letters and Literary Remains*. i, 67.   [7] 'There is much in one's mode of eating.' Ovid, *Ars Amatoria*. iii, 755.   [8] *Letters*. Ed. Colvin. i, 301.
[9] Letter to the Manchester Athenæum. 1843.   [10] Geyler, *Navicula sive Speculum Fatuorum*. 1511. B. iiij. rev. Qt. Dibdin, *Bibliomania*. (1811) 651.

scarcely strength to lift, folios as solid as they were heavy, and if dull, full of matter;[1] but others prefer to feast, perchance, upon such books as the *Anecdotes of Painting* and the *Castle of Otranto*, which Horace Walpole sent on Christmas Eve, 1764, to George Montagu as *food* for his fireside,[2] and if we cannot always avoid excess, we may recall with advantage that, as Cicero observes, it is the distinction of man to seek ever for a law of good taste, a measure for his words and deeds;[3] as it is in the invitation of the poet:

> What neat repast shall feast us, light and choice,
> Of Attic taste. . . .[4]

IV. A DISSERTATION UPON APPETITE

In reading, as in eating, an appetite is half the feast,[5] but Isaac D'Israeli argues that there is a literary appetite which the author can no more impart than a skilful cook can give appetency to the guests at a banquet;[6] and well he may, for books are their own appetisers. They need no sauce, not even so great a masterpiece as that one invented by Chirac, *with which*, it is said, *it might be held excusable for a man to eat his own father.*[7] He is no true bookman who has to be wheedled into reading, as Homeric heroes were tempted to drink by grating cheese and onion into their wine[8] Bibliophiles need no synthetic appetite. When Thackeray was a boy his hunger for books was keen and insatiable: *It may be the tart was good; but how fresh the appetite was!*[9] *I need no allurement for sauce*, said Montaigne, *my stomach is good enough to digest raw meat.* He disparages all preliminary forcing of the appetite; such *preparatives, flourishes, preambles*, etc., have a contrary effect on him: *they thinke to sharpen my taste, or stir my stomacke*, but *they cloy and make it wallowish.*[10] Appetite is keen, even when the dish is familiar, as William Hazlitt testifies:[11] *when I take up a work I have read before (the oftener the better) I know what I have to expect; satisfaction is not lessened by being anticipated*; but a new book arouses suspicion like *a strange dish.* He would *turn and pick out a bit here and there*, doubtful of the composition: *there is a want of confidence and security to second appetite*, but with old familiar books he knows his *palate* will not be *nauseated.*

A grace, as Charles Lamb affirmed, might be appropriate before a literary feast, but extraneous *apéritifs* are not necessary as for a coarser diet

---

[1] Qt.*Book-Lover's Ench.* 181.   [2] *Letters*, Cunningham. iv, 306–7.   [3] *De Officiis.* i, 4.
[4] Milton, *Sonnets.* xx.   [5] Anon. Qt. *In Praise of Books.* 4.   [6] *Misc. of Lit.*   [7] T. L. Peacock, 'Gastronomy and Civilization', *Works.* ix, 391.   [8] *Iliad.* xi, 639.   [9] *Roundabout Papers.*   [10] 'Of Bookes', *Essays.* Ed. Seccombe. ii, 119.   [11] 'On Reading Old Books', *The Plain Speaker.* ii, 65.

· where the gastronomic engines must be tuned up by cocktails. A healthy reader needs no *Martinis* (dry or sweet), *Manhattans, Bronxes*, or such-like *tickle-tastes*. Books are their own *apéritifs*. Appetite comes with reading, as Angeston declared of eating.[1] Petrarch ordered his brother to *ransack Tuscany* for books *to appease (or shall I say) to whet my thirst*;[2] and so true bookmen devour book after book *with appetite whetted to a swallowing-point perfectly gluttonous*.[3] Dr. William King complains to a friend who has advised him of the publication of Lister's treatise, *De Condimentis et Opsoniis Veterum*, without sending him a copy, that *you have made my mouth water, but have not sent me wherewithal to satisfy my appetite*;[4] and when William Blades saw the title-pages of the poems of Taylor, *the Water Poet*, in the album of a biblioclast, they made his *mouth water for the books themselves*.[1] George Wyndham, says Gatty,[5] *loved nothing better than to browse among the pages of his facsimile First Folio; the sight of the old type whetted his appetite for the intellectual feast*; and after *wallowing in the sixteenth century*, and *hankering after the thirteenth*, like an *archaistic barbarian*, he developed *a still ruder relish for the pagan horseflesh of the Sagas*;[6] and, some, as Landor, are made keen by a reverse process:

> After Byron's peppery dishes
> Matho's mild skim milk goes down.[7]

Yet too much pepper is condemned by some authorities, as Henry Jackson,[8] who recognised that there are *some people whose palates require pepper* for such a book as *Tess*, but, he says, *indulgence in such things has blunted their sensibility to less violent impressions, for, as saith the wise man, Excellens sensibile corrumpit sensum*; but for himself he complained that *Jane Austen* required *pepper, salt and mustard*.[9]

Books never pall on him, relates Petrarch in his *Epistolae de Rebus Familiaribus*,[10] their piquant familiarity is their own stimulant, *not only does each book inspire the sense that it belongs to its readers, but it also suggests the names of others, and one begets the desire of the other*. Thus also Roger Ascham: *my book hath been so much my pleasure, and bringeth daily to me more pleasure and more, that in respect of it, all other pleasure, in very deed, be but trifles and troubles unto me*.[11] They are supported by Colley Cibber:[12] he had read a volume of *Sir Charles Grandison*, and asked for more (in a letter to Samuel Richardson, the author of it, 6.vi.1753): *The delicious meal I made of Miss Byron on Sunday last, has given me an appetite for another slice of her, off from*

[1] *Rabelais*. Bohn Ed. i, 113.   [2] Tatham, *Francesco Petrarca*. ii, 37.   [3] M. A. C., in *Book-Lore*. v, 59.   [4] *Art of Cookery*. 2.   [5] *The Enemies of Books*. 113.   [6] *George Wyndham, Recognita*. 44.   [7] Intro. to *Essays of George Wyndham*. viii.   [8] Landor, 'Sent with Poems'. *Works*. (1876) viii, 113.   [9] *Henry Jackson, O.M., A Memoir*, Parry. 179.   [10] *Ib*. 172.   [11] Qt. *Book-Lover's Ench*. 9.   [12] *Works*, Giles. v, 3.

the spit, before she is served up to the public table. Alcott goes farther, arguing that the test of a ripe book is that its *flavour is as refreshing at the thousandth tasting as at the first,*[1] which Henry Bradshaw supported in his admission to a friend that *he devoured Kingsley's Saints' Tragedy, during all his undergraduate Mays with fresh pleasure each time,*[2] and he read Wordsworth's *Excursion over and over again, finding it wholesome food.*[3] Find more examples of this kind where I record the exploits of great readers. The conclusion is, books are a condiment in themselves, and, unlike other foods, even when excessively consumed, need none of *those additional Sauces, which Physitians of old found out to restore the deprav'd Appetites of such great men as had lost their Stomachs by an excess of luxury.*[4]

V. OF CUISINE

Some will have that books are *fruit*—Alcuin *filled* his students with *the fruits of grammatical lore*[5]—or, as Coleridge,[6] *fruit trees* to which *we may recur year after year* to find a supply of *the same nourishment* so long as we return with *the same healthful appetite.* And well they may, for the mouth of the bibliophile *waters* at the sight of them, even of a *catalogue.* The catalogue of the sale of his kinsman Sir Robert Gordon's library made Francis Jenkinson's *mouth water.*[7] King James I visited Bodley's Library in 1605; he looked at the well-stocked cases, and said that although he had proofs of the fruits of ability of the University, he had never before seen the garden where those fruits were gathered.[8] It was such a garden that our good Alcuin would have cultivated at Tours, where, being short of *books of Scholastic learning,* he intreated Charlemagne to send into England for some of the books which were so much desired, and thus *to transplant into France the flowers of Britain, that they may fructify and perfume, not only the garden at York, but also the Paradise of Tours,* so that they may say in the words of the song: *Let my beloved come into his garden and eat his pleasant fruit.*[9] Galileo compared the *Orlando Furioso* to a *melon field,* good in it *but not all good.*[10] Books were fruit also to Dibdin, for when visiting the Library at Lambeth Palace he told himself that he could gladly linger in such a *book-domain* through the four seasons of the year, *and gather fruit at every quarter;*[11] and when at Oxford. Dibdin found *Henry's history the sort of 'Hortus Adonidis'* from which he *strove to gather ripe and unperishing fruit;*[12]

[1] *Concord Days,* 'Books'. [2] Prothero, *Memoir of Bradshaw.* 42. [3] *Ib.* 51. [4] King, *Art of Cookery.* 141. [5] Merryweather, *Bibliomania in the Middle Ages.* 122. [6] *Literary Remains.* [7] *Francis Jenkinson,* Stewart. 22. [8] Macray, *Annals.* 31. [9] Merryweather, *op. cit.* 122. [10] Spence's *Anecdotes.* (1858) 76. [11] *Bibliophobia.* 55–6. [12] *Reminiscences.* i, 90.

and he refers to his own *Bibliographical Tour in France and Germany* as *an apple, juicy and well-flavoured*.[1] This recalls a Frenchman[2] who was asked if he preferred his books in *folio*.[3] '*No*,' he replied, '*I like them in fructu*.'[4] A taste widespread and shared by Mark Rutherford, who delighted in Cobbett's *Rural Rides* because he found it *so juicy*;[5] books nourish by their excellence, fruitiness, etc., and those who are under-fed on books are no better than the beasts that perish: *Sir, he hath never fed on the dainties that are bred in a book; he hath not eat paper, as it were; he hath not drunk ink; his intellect is not replenished; he is only an animal, only sensible in the duller parts*.[6] The miracle of books is a miracle of nourishment:

> He ate and drank the precious words,
> His spirit grew robust;[7]

it is not the quantity but the quality, and the head is not unlike the belly in this respect, for if the belly listens to no precepts, but demands and calls aloud, it is not, as Seneca discovered, and most authorities of to-day would agree, *a troublesome creditor*, demanding but a small amount *provided you give it what you ought, not what you can*,[8] so the head may be satisfied with a little so long as it be good.

In that renowned scriptorium of the Abbey of St. Martin at Tours, Alcuin said that he dealt out *the honey of the Scriptures* to some, others he excited with *the ancient wine of Wisdom*, and still others he filled with *the fruits of grammatical learning*.[9] And Richard de Bury recounts[10] how, in his search for books abroad, he entered the places where the mendicants had their convents, and found in their *fardels and baskets not only crumbs falling from the master's table for the dogs, but the shew-bread without leaven and the bread of angels having in it all that is delicious*: the *garners of Joseph full of corn*, as well as *all the spoil of the Egyptians*, and *the very precious gifts which the Queen of Sheba brought to Solomon. The Psalms are the Manna of the Church*, says Donne,[11] like *Angels' food contenting every man's delight, and agreeing to every man's taste*,[12] but for Eugénie de Guérin *good books are the manna of the people of God, the celestial food of souls on their journey to Heaven*.[13]

James Granger, the biblioclast, *eagerly devoured* Walpole's *Anecdotes on Painting*, and hoped *by reading them over a second time to* digest them.[14] Thomas Gray told West (in a letter, 27.vi.1742) that his life was like Henry the Fourth's supper of Hens—*Poulets à la broche, poulets en ragoût, poulets en hâchis, poulets en fricassées . . . nothing but books with different sauces*; Lord

[1] *Ib*. ii, 662.   [2] *Walpoliana*. (1800) 162.   [3] 'In the leaf.'   [4] 'In the fruit.'   [5] *Letters to Three Friends*. 38.   [6] *Love's Labour's Lost*. iv, 2, 24.   [7] Emily Dickinson, *Life: A Book*.   [8] *Epist*. 21.   [9] Elton, *Great Book-Collectors*. 24.   [10] *Philobiblon*. viii· [11] *Sermons*, 'Selected Passages', L. P. Smith. 23.   [12] *Wisdom of Solomon*. xvi, 20. [13] *Letters*. 141.   [14] *Letters*. Ed. Malcolm. 5–6.

Byron *supped full of horror in two cantos of darkness and dismay;*[1] Macchiavelli bragged that when he passed into his study he fed upon the food which was his own, and for which he was born;[2] Glycion tells Eusebius,[3] *After meat, I have a collation of learned stories*; Lord Keeper North, said Dibdin,[4] *used to make his meals upon some one entertaining Law-volume or another; breakfast upon 'Stamford', dine upon 'Coke', and sup upon 'Fitzherbert'*, and so insatiable was his appetite that, unsatisfied with this *lean* fare, he would *regale himself with a well served-up course of the Arts, Sciences, and the Belles-Lettres!*

Walter Bagehot in his early years found Keats and Shelley *delicious*, and Wordsworth and John Henry Newman were his *daily food;*[5] John Burroughs *lived* for a year on Johnson's *Rambler* and *Idler*, and for a whole summer he *fed upon* Emerson's *Essays;*[6] George Moore *for months fed on the mad and morbid literature that the enthusiasm of 1830 called into existence;*[7] Coventry Patmore was helped to survive a course of theological reading which occupied *four hours a day for five months* by an occasional *peg into the roast beef of Shakespeare;*[8] William Cory when at Eton *dined on a grilled fowl, talking foreign policy with Northcote expeditiously,* and *read a very amusing part of the 'Odyssey' by way of pudding;*[9] Lafcadio Hearn enjoyed *Kipling,* who was *like Paul Bourget boiled into thin soup.*[10] Hester Piozzi said she was always ready *for a bit of Old Stilton, as Dr. Johnson called profane History.*[11] Nor was she alone in finding books a substitute for cheese, for Edward FitzGerald once confessed to Frederick Tennyson[12] that he was about *to take down a Thucydides, to feed on: like a whole Parmesan*; and Robert Louis Stevenson calls *Herman Melville a howling cheese.*[13]

Behold *the heir apparent of a Ducal Coronet,*[14] sedulously sitting down to master volumes, exclaims Dibdin:[15] *His morning tiffin is alternately Aelian and Thomas Magister: his petit souper Porphyrius and Terentianus Maurus; while Sidonius Apollinaris, Manilius, and Mercurius Trismegistus he has in sundry little pocket editions, wherewith he delights himself as he wanders along the buttercupped meadows.* John Donne was a devout member of the bibliophagi: dining off the *Scriptures* with gusto, he liked the *Psalms of David* for a first course and the *Epistles of St. Paul* for a second, and he was supported in this *diet* by St. Augustine's protestation that he loved those books for the particular reason that they were *Scriptures*, written in such forms as he had been most accustomed to: *Saint Paul's being Letters, and David's Poems; for*

[1] Letter to Samuel Rogers. 27.vi.1814.   [2] Opere di Macchiavelli. (1813) vol. viii. Qt. *Book-Lover's Ench.* 18.   [3] Erasmus, 'Old Men's Dialogue', *Colloquies.* [4] *Bibliomania.* (1811) 407–8.   [5] *Life*, Barrington. *Works.* x, 8.   [6] *Indoor Studies.* Riverside Ed. *Works.* viii, 245–7.   [7] *Confessions of a Young Man.* (1904) 72. [8] *Memoirs*, Champneys. i, 252.   [9] *Letters and Journals.* 114.   [10] *Life and Letters.* Bisland. ii, 84.   [11] *Intimate Letters.* 220.   [12] *Letters and Literary Remains.* i, 84. [13] *Letters.* ii, 115.   [14] That of the Duke of Devonshire.   [15] *Bibliophobia.* 95–6.

God gives us, not only that which is merely necessary, but that which is convenient too; He does not only feed us, but feeds us with marrow and with fatness.[1]

Queen Elizabeth was also a gastronome of *Holy Writ*, as she records in a copy of Thomson's version of the *New Testament* (now in the Bodleian Library),[2] which she bound in a covering of her own make: *I walke manie times* (her words are on the fly-leaf of the volume) *into the pleasant fieldes of the Holye Scriptures, where I pluck up in the goodlie greene herbes of sentences by pruning, eate them by reading, chewe them up musing, and laie them up at length in the hie seate of memorie by gathering them together; that so having tasted thy sweeteness I may the lesse perceive the bitterness of this miserable life.*

VI. DISHES AND TASTES PARTICULARISED

We all know that the human body can be nourished on a great variety of foods, but how great that variety is we do not always realize. Aulus Gellius[3] tells of a dainty people in *farthest India* with bodies covered with feathers, *spiritu florum naribus hausto victitantem*, who live by inhaling the perfume of flowers; and, in the other extreme, a trustworthy observer[4] gives out that a native of Earl Soham in Suffolk *loved to catch* young frogs and *let them leap down his throat, when he would stroke his stomach,* observing that they were *Beautifully cool!* Well may Thoreau reckon that *there is not one kind of food for all men;*[5] for his own part he was not *unusually squeamish,* and could, if put to it, *eat a fried rat with a good relish.*[6] Human beings are the most omnivorous of all creatures. They can eat anything, even each other, and find nourishment in all manner of unpalatable stuff, even though, as Emerson[7] argues, it were *boiled grass and the broth of shoes.*

In Greenland they eat half-putrid whale and seal, and in England game birds and venison in the same state; the Laplanders relish bear and reindeer, and the Esquimaux and Samoiedes walrus, beaver, otter and fox, as well as decaying fish; the Calmuc Tartars eat horse and ass, preferably putrid, whilst fresh horse-flesh is a regular food in Germany, France and Italy; the Chinese, bad eggs, salted earthworms, smoked fish, sharks' fins, birds' nests, maggots, caterpillars, cats, dogs and rats; in Pegu, Aracan and Siam serpents and mice are delicacies, and the natives of the Ladrone Islands subsist on roots, fruit and fish; Hindoos are vegetarian; Persians enjoy wild ass flesh, and in olden times they ate camels and ostriches; the aborigines of Australia feed upon kangaroos, rats, opossums, bandicoots and rabbits, and they have an inborn taste for various insects and reptiles; reptile eating is

---

[1] *Donne's Sermons,* L. P. Smith. 21–2.   [2] Macray, *Annals of the Bodleian.* 65.   [3] *Noct. Att.* ix, 4.   [4] Groome, *Two Suffolk Friends.* 16.   [5] *Letters.* 2.vi.1848.   [6] *Walden.* Scott Lib. 216.   [7] *The American Scholar.*

still practised in Europe, where the French eat frogs and the English assess turtle a delicacy; Hottentots eat putrid buffalo, caterpillars, ants, grass-hoppers and snakes; Western Europeans eat shrimps and crabs; Melane-sians eat lice; Kaffirs enjoy lion flesh when they can get it, as well as elephant; Moors and Gipsies like hedgehog; the French and the English enjoy snails, the former preferring the land and the latter the sea varieties such as whelks and periwinkles; Red Indians eat rattlesnakes; crocodiles and inguanas are eaten in South America and the West Indies; the sloth is a dainty in Peru, and the tapir and armadillo in Brazil; centipedes are a delicacy in Central America, and shrimps, prawns, crayfish and lobsters in North America and most European countries; the Ottameques of the Orinoco, the Indians of the Mackenzie, the Peruvians and the Javanese, eat various kinds of earth and clay, a custom not unknown to Europe, for there have been earth eaters in Germany, Sweden, Russia, and Turkey, and in Germany the wood of various trees has been converted into a *nutritious substance*, and the *barke-brod* of the Norwegians is made from the bark of trees.[1]

The manner of eating these various foods is as varied as the foods them-selves. The flesh is eaten either raw, cooked, dried, salted or pickled; it is boiled to a pulp or burnt to a cinder; roasted, fried, baked, grilled or stewed; but in some instances the food is relished only when it is alive. The insect-eaters of the South Seas and the oyster-eaters of Western civili-zations have this particularity in common; but this taste reaches its finest expression in Abyssinia, where the cow or bull which is to be the main course of the feast is led to the table and carved alive in the presence of the diners;[2] in Sumatra, where it was the custom to dine off the bodies of condemned criminals or prisoners of war, the victim was brought alive to the table, and tied to a stake; but although the guests selected and carved each his own slice, which might be eaten raw, it was sometimes grilled and served with a seasoning of chili pepper and salt.[3]

The bibliophagi are no less varied in taste and range of choice, and their cuisine is equally varied. *Much reading is like much eating, wholly useless without digestion;*[4] for that reason books, *like salt fish, should be a good while soaking before being served.*[5] Books are as varied as dishes, infinite in their variety: *Great libraries full well furnished, like so many dishes of meat, served out for several palates;*[6] *some to be tasted*, Lord Bacon argues, *others to be swallowed, and some few to be chewed and digested,*[7] for according to Hierome, *as mastication is to meat, so is meditation to that which is read*; some, again,

---

[1] Most of these facts are taken from *Illustrations of Eating* (1847), where many of the sources are cited.   [2] Bruce, *Abyssinia*.   [3] *Illustrations of Eating*. 41–2.   [4] Robert South, *Sermons*. Qt. *Book-Lover's Ench*. 97.   [5] Anon. Qt. *In Praise of Books*. Swan. 4.   [6] Burton, *Anat. of Melan*. (1904) ii, 102.   [7] 'Of Studies', *Essays*.

declares Dr. Oliver Wendell Holmes,[1] must be read *tasting*, every word of them turned on the palate, especially such as *Tennyson, Milton, Gray*, for they themselves tasted every word in the making of their books, *as Ude or Careme would taste a potage meant for a king or a queen.*

Some are like great joints to cut at and come again; for *meat*, Hilaire Belloc knows no equal to *Gibbon*, and he sets the *Decline and Fall* above all literary dishes for permanent delight;[2] others are dainties, entrées, side-dishes, to support the main course; notable among these are the writings of Horace Walpole, which, in the opinion of Macaulay, *rank as high among the delicacies of intellectual epicures as the Strasbourg pies among the dishes described in the 'Almanach des Gourmands'.*[3] Some again are no better than slops, as *Robert Buchanan*, who is *Scotch gruel*,[4] or *cold collations*, as that volume of his verses which Austin Dobson inscribed to George Saintsbury:

> Here, with little variation,
> Comes another 'Cold collation'.[5]

There is a great variety of stews, réchauffés, hot-pots, salmagundies, jussels, olios, ragouts, fricassees, gallimaufries, hashes, forced meats, minces, good enough when the ingredients are sound and the cooking exquisite,

> Judgment provides the Meat in Seasons fit,
> Which by the Genius drest, its Sauce is Wit,[6]

but not those mixtures, *books distilled from books*,[7] messes of odd scraps, stale leavings, plate scrapings, crumbs fallen from the rich man's table (which none but Lazarus would eat), done up into a fardel to look fresh and new. Certain *newfangled books*, according to Hazlitt,[8] resemble *made dishes*, being little else than *hashes* and *rifaccimentos* of what has been *served up entire and in a more natural state at other times.* Such kickshaws are the common productions of those who live mainly upon literary *food*; better for them to take Isaac D'Israeli's advice to Magliabecchi, and *dress some dishes of* their *own invention, or at least some sandwiches to* their *own relish*:[9]

> Not but that books and Poets still were free,
> To use their Pow'r in nice Variety;[10]

but to dish up a company of obsolete sentences and stale phrases, for no other purpose than to make a book for profit, is to do no better than to make a stew of table-scraps and leavings and offer them as food in a public eating-house. Macaulay discommends those other *rifaccimenti, harmonies*,

[1] *The Autocrat of the Breakfast Table.*   [2] 'Gibbon', *New Statesman.* 18.ii.1928.
[3] 'Horace Walpole', *Essays.* (1872) 267.   [4] George Moore, *Confessions of a Young Man.* (1904) 80.   [5] Dobson, *Poetical Works.* 471.   [6] King, *Art of Cookery.* 131.
[7] Walt Whitman.   [8] 'On Reading Old Books', *The Plain Speaker.* ii, 65.   [9] *Cur. Lit.* ii, 179.   [10] King, *Art of Cookery.* 55.

abridgements, expurgated editions, commuted for queasy stomachs, but which, he stiffly holds, *no man of taste can endure.*

Cory recognizes one class of books as no better than *confectionery,*[1] and such as these have no more nourishment than those empty luxurious tomes put out by cunning publishers to tempt vain spenders, *their lusciousness puts many palates out of taste, so that they can never after relish any solid or wholesome writers:*[2]

> Luxury gives the mind a childish cast,
> And while she polishes, perverts the taste;[3]

as that, perchance, of Cleopatra, who had whole boars and sheep served up at her table at once, drank jewels dissolved, 40,000 sesterces in value; but to what end?

Other books are *hors d'œuvres, smorgosbord, Aufschnitte,* as anthologies, good for all sound stomachs, or savouries, which by their piquancy and brevity serve as culinary toys. Such *delicatessen* are for the idle moment or the preliminaries of the feast, when light talk, raillery, *brilliance,* badinage, etc., come into the game. They must be taken frugally, as also those delicious *entremets* and *glaces, trifles,* light as air, hot or cold, or both (as *soufflé surprise, Macédoine de fruits,* etc.). *Novels are sweets,* says Thackeray,[4] *all people with healthy appetites love them*; others there be who prefer

> To suck the sweets of sweet philosophy.[5]

Warton's edition of the minor poems of Milton, according to Leigh Hunt,[6] is *a wilderness of sweets*; and so on to *friandises* and dessert. Dibdin classed Ferriar's *Bibliomania* with the latter;[7] and when he dined with Dr. Butler at Shrewsbury School, after visiting the Library, he notes that there lurked, in an adjoining cupboard, which they could see *during snatches of savoury viands, and especially during the migrations of the glass, a dessert—in the shape of an ancient Greek MS.*;[8] walnuts and wine, salted almonds, the *frills and furbelows* of the repast, dainty, graceful, trivial, good in their place, but, like art in the poet, not to be indulged in *ad libitum*:

> Good to kiss and flirt with
> But marry if you dare![9]

Nor would the *judicious reader* indulge his palate or try his digestion overmuch with those works of the *captious critics* who *cut up their authors into chops, and by adding a little crumbled bread of their own, and tossing it up a little, present it as a fresh dish; you are to dine upon a poet;—the critic supplies the garnish.*[10]

[1] 'Table Talk', in *Gathered Leaves.* M. E. Coleridge. 303.   [2] Fuller, *Holy and Profane State.*   [3] Cowper.   [4] *Roundabout Papers.*   [5] *Taming of the Shrew.* i, 1.   [6] 'My Books', *Essays.* Camelot Ed. 300.   [7] *Reminiscences.* i, 272.   [8] *Ib.* ii, 971.   [9] Richard le Gallienne.   [10] Hannah More, *Memoirs.*

Part X

OF BOOK-DRINKERS

——————————⊷⦿⊶——————————

I. OF THEIR LIQUEFACTION AND PROPENSITIES PROPER TO DRINKING

To this gastronomic catalogue I must add a little, for I have not yet said all. Books are also beverages: *I never drink but in my breviary;*[1] so there is still to account for those numerous instances wherein they have quenched thirst and satisfied our Dionysian needs. When Mr. Grobe turned from Mr. Weston's Good Wine to his bookcase, he saw that *Good wine was there too. Good wine that had never yet failed him. Good wine that had ever given a deep drink of the proper colour and taste to the gentle reader.*[2] Many bookmen sit down to read as though at a banquet or a merry feast: *They taste styles, as some discreeter palates do wine;*[3] relish that delicious beverage which they have swallowed so thirstily from the magical cup of literature.*[4] Emerson observes as much in his parallel of *the insect world,* for whoever looks at it *must have remarked,* he relates,[5] *the extreme content they take in suction,* and *if we go into a* library, *we see the same function on a higher plane, performed with like ardour, with equal impatience of interruption, indicating the sweetness of the act.* I need not support him with more than two examples: one of Mrs. Hemans, *drinking in high thoughts and glorious images,*[6] and the other of Francis Thompson imbibing *the effluence of particular passages* of Shakespeare.[7]

> I love my books as drinkers love their wine;
> The more I drink, the more they seem divine;
> With joy elate my soul in love runs o'er,
> And each fresh draught is sweeter than before:[8]

and as connoisseurs of wine pride themselves on their palate and their staying power, so the three-bottle bookman likes a man who can carry his

[1] *Rabelais.* Bohn Ed. i, 111.   [2] T. F. Powys, *Mr. Weston's Good Wine.* 248.   [3] Earle, 'A Critic', *Microcosmography.* xlv.   [4] D'Israeli, *Curiosities of Literature.* i, 7.
[5] 'Quotation and Originality', *Letters and Social Aims.* 129.   [6] Chorley, *Memorials of Mrs. Hemans.* i, 20.   [7] *Life.* Everard Meynell. 11.   [8] Francis Bennoch, 'My Books', *The Storm and other Poems.*

bookish liquor; but the amateur of literary vintages prefers one who senses the subtleties of letters, their *bouquet*, fragrance, flavour, etc.; he feels as Erasmus did, *an impatient irritation at the thought and in the presence of those who* have *not drunk of their wisdom and undergone their discipline.*[1]

A nameless pamphleteer of the eighteenth century, in *A Project for the Destruction of Printing and Bookselling*, was so bold as to argue in favour of the liquefaction of books: barrel and bottle them off, he advises, and they will be more acceptable: *a cellar of books would be more invitingly absorbable than a library.* His discoverer[2] imagines *Mr. Birrell at the Athenæum Club, sipping his* 1791 *Boswell, critically appreciative of the vintage edition,* and younger members trifling with the club cocktail, *a piquant mixture of 'Punch' and the 'War Cry', blended from a recipe used in the family of a bishop for very many years.* Oliver Wendell Holmes[3] not only believed that books were capable of liquefaction, but that *society* was no more than *a strong solution of books*; it drew the virtue out of what was best worth reading, as hot water the strength of tea-leaves. *If I were a prince,* he adds, *I would hire or buy a private literary teapot, in which I would steep all the leaves of new books that promised well, that the infusion* would suffice *without the vegetable fibre.* He was supported, in anticipation, by Douce, the antiquarian, who gives out, in a letter to Dibdin,[4] that *bohea of a better quality than imperial souchong* may be *sipped* from *prick-songs, poetry, and anthems.* The lesser sort of books which circumstances compelled Beloe to *drink* for the purposes of his anecdotes, were *smaller, though not less pellucid and refreshing streams.*[5] Edward FitzGerald[6] held that there was an *infusion* of *Xenophon* in *Sophocles*, as compared with *Aeschylus*, who was a *dilution*; and Addison gives as a recipe for an essay writer that he *must practise in the chemical method and give the virtue of a full draught in a few drops,*[7] a method evidently adopted by Ben Jonson, who, John Addington Symonds[8] says, *held the prose writers and poets of antiquity in solution in his capacious memory*; and a young writer of the 'nineties has a friend who was *suckled from Dante, and weaned on Goethe.*[9]

Apuleius, in his *Florida*,[10] recalls the wise man's saying regarding the libations of the table: *the first cup for thirst, the second for mirth, the third for delight, the fourth for madness,* and finds no such *descensus* in the *Goblet of the Muses*, which the more unmixed it is and the oftener it is drained, *the more it conduces to soundness of mind.* The first cup takes away ignorance, the second instructs in science, and the third arms with eloquence. *Thus far,* saith he, *most people drink. But I have drunk other cups at Athens; the cup of*

[1] Lionel Johnson, *Post Liminium.* 164–5.   [2] W. G. Clifford, *Books in Bottles.* 15. [3] *The Autocrat of the Breakfast-Table.* (1902) 57.   [4] *Reminiscences.* ii, 889.   [5] Beloe, *Anecdotes.* ii, 372.   [6] *Letters and Literary Remains.* i, 190.   [7] *Spectator.* 124.   [8] *Ben Jonson.*   [9] Malcolm Macmillan. *Letters.* 34.   [10] Bohn. xx, 402.

Poetry, the inventive; of Geometry, the limpid; of Music, the sweet; of Dialectics, the roughish; and of Universal Philosophy, the never-satiating, nectarious cup. For Empedocles gives us verses; Plato, dialogues; Socrates, hymns; Epicharmus modulations; Xenophon, histories; Xenocrates, satires: your Apuleius, he concludeth, *all these together,* for he has *cultivated the Nine Muses with equal assiduity if with more good will than capacity.*[1] Well may Joubert discover that *when once the mind has tasted the sap of words, it can no more do without it,* for *it drinks thought there.*[2]

II. THEY RAISE AND QUENCH THIRST AND ARE POTENT BEVERAGES

I thirst for Mr. Burke's Reflections on the Revolution in France, says Gibbon, and he asks Cadell to *intreat Elmsley to dispatch it to Lausanne with care and speed, by any mode of conveyance less expensive than the post;*[3] Dibdin was *violently seized* with *the thirst for black letter literature,* which was somewhat quenched with a copy of More's *Utopia* of 1551;[4] Hazlitt *drank of the stream of knowledge* and *eagerly slaked* his *thirst of German sentiment* with Goethe's *Sorrows of Werther* and Schiller's *Robbers;*[5] it was late in life that Cicero became acquainted with Greek literature, absorbing it with avidity as though *yearning to quench a long-continued thirst.*[6] But many authorities agree that in any condition approaching bibliomania, this thirst is not so easily stayed, 'tis, in short, an *unquenchable thirst for possession.*[7] So *insatiable is the thirst of men*[8] for books, that they take delight in a vinous denomination for their favourites, as Pasquin, in his *Palinodia,* called a piece *A Pleasant Pint of Poetical Sherry.* Leigh Hunt[9] cried out for a *Literaria Hilaris Gaudens* in a score of volumes, to have at hand, like a *cellar of good wine,* against dull and rainy days: Fielding should be *port,* Farquhar, *champagne,* Sterne, *malmsey;* whenever the possessor cast eye upon such a collection he would know that he had *a choice draught for himself after a disappointment, or for a friend after dinner,—some cordial extract of Parson Adams, or Plume, or Uncle Toby, generous as heart could desire, and as wholesome for it as laughter for the lungs.* Sir Henry Savile, in the *Dedication*[10] of his *Tacitus* to Queen Elizabeth, likens that history to *wine* and his translation to the *lees,* but since her Highness had held the former in most worthy account she would not disdain the latter, for he hoped that it might peradventure pleasure her

---

[1] *App.* Bohn. xx, 402.   [2] *Selected Thoughts.* Trans. Lyttleton. 147.   [3] In a letter, 17.xi.1790.   [4] *Reminiscences.* i, 267.   [5] *Plain Speaker.* ii, 75.   [6] *On Old Age.* Trans. Shuckburgh. 50.   [7] R. M. Field. Intro. *Love Affairs of a Bibliomaniac,* Eugene Field. vii.   [8] Fuller, *The Holy State and the Profane State.*   [9] 'Cheerful Poets.'   [10] *The End of Nero, etc.* [Tacitus.] (1591)

though by change from vessell to vessell having taken winde and lost his pleasing taste to the palate, yet retaining somewhat of his former strength. So a library is a cellar stored with wines, spirits, and other rich beverages.

Dr. John Brown looked upon Stevenson's *Travels with a Donkey* as *a new liquor, fresh and aromatic;*[1] the poems of Catulle Mendès were sweet as *a smooth perfumed yellow wine* to George Moore;[2] Edward FitzGerald lamented[3] that the songs which Tennyson *stuck between the cantos of the 'Princess'* had none of *the old champagne flavour* of his earlier songs, and that *Gil Blas* was *too thin a wine* for him, *all sparkling with little adventures, but no one to care about;*[4] Froude always carried a collection of *pocket classics* on a journey, for *Greek and Latin literature is wine which does not spoil by time;*[5] Coventry Patmore found reading theology like *living on brandy and soda-water,*[6] and he liked to *consume the spirit* of his favourite books *diluted* with his *own thoughts, not with those of other people;*[7] for Joubert, *Voltaire was clear like water, Bossuet clear like wine;*[8] Edmund Gosse records that to put *Tom Cringle's Log* into the hands of a youth is like *giving a glass of brandy neat to some one who had never been weaned from a milk diet.*[9] Tom Hood was *little grieved* when reduced through ill-health to the *drink that drowns kittens,* because he could still quaff such rare liquors as the *champagne of Molière,* the *Monte Pulciano of Boccaccio,* the *hock of Schiller,* and the *sherry of Cervantes;* depressed bodily by *the fluid that damps everything,* he got *intellectually elevated* with *Milton,* a *little merry* with *Swift, rather jolly* with *Rabelais,* whose *Pantagruel* he found *equal to the best gruel with rum in it;*[10] and Robert Lang, the *Meliadus* of Dibdin's *Decameron,* though devoted to a fine table, *his beautiful house and beautiful bookcases* having *witnessed many a scene of delightful conviviality,* placed *Verard* above *Johannisberg,* and *Micel Le Noir* beyond *Champagne.*[11]

Some reliable witnesses will have that books are cordials:

> Who let me taste that more than cordial dram,
> The sharp, the rapier-pointed epigram.[12]

T. Edwards told Samuel Richardson[13] that as people kept their cordials for the winter, so, too, he now fled to his, which were *Pamela* and *Clarissa;* and what more characteristic of the power of potent liquor than Emerson's[14] testimony to that *miraculous force* which proceedeth from them, when after we have gone forth musing into a night of gloom where *no constella-*

[1] *Letters.* 338. [2] *Confessions of a Young Man.* (1904) 79. [3] *Letters and Literary Remains.* i, 200. [4] *Ib.* i, 370. [5] Froude, *Oceana.* 24. [6] *Memoirs.* Champneys. i, 252. [7] *Ib.* ii, 106. [8] *Selected Thoughts.* Trans. Lyttleton. 185. [9] *Father and Son.* Pop. Ed. 210. [10] Letter to the Manchester Athenæum. 1843. [11] Dibdin, *Reminiscences.* i, 372-3. [12] Keats, 'Epistle to Charles Cowden Clarke', *Letters.* Ed. Forman. (1895) 64-5. [13] Barbauld, Letter. 19. xii.1737. [14] *Thoughts on Modern Literature.*

tion shines, no muse descends, the stars are white points, the roses brick-coloured dust, the frogs pipe, mice peep, and wagons creak along the road, we return and take up *Plutarch* or *Augustine,* and lo! *the air swims with life; the front of heaven is filled with fiery shapes; secrets of magnanimity and grandeur invite us on every hand.* No other cordial has such power to restore the depressed soul of man; books are ever ready, it is always *tempus aptum* with them, always opportune, they are ever willing, and when other potions flag and fail it is they that uphold us. *I tried to cheer myself by thinking over the joys of our human lot. But there wasn't one of them for which I seemed to care a button—not Wine, nor Fame, nor Friendship, nor Eating, nor Making Love, nor the Consciousness of Virtue;* then he[1] thought of reading, and *the nice and subtle happiness of reading* was enough: *this joy not dulled by Age, this polite and unpunished vice, this selfish, serene, life-long intoxication.* And unlike all other liquors the barrel never runs dry, the bottle is never empty; a good book is always on tap; it may be decanted and drunk a hundred times, and it is still there for further imbibement: *My Aristophanes is nearly drained: that is, for the present first reading: for he will never be dry, apply as often as I may.*[2]

III. BIBLIOBIBACITY WITH A DIGRESSION OF ECSTASY

I may not deny but that there is some folly approved, a divine fury, a holy madness, a spiritual drunkenness, a rich ecstasy, in these book-struck men, familiar to saint or artist, which causeth many times a divine ravishment, a kind of *enthusiasmus,* and is, as all know, the inseparable companion, for however brief a time, of any creative act: *a divine drunkenness* is *given to them for their encouragement, surpassing the gift of the grape.*[3]

Euripides implies as much in the *Bacchae,* where he relates how Dionysus, *the good God, who bestoweth cheerfulnesse upon men, and youth unto aged men, and who layeth and aswageth the passions of the minde,*[4] is born of the ecstasy of Semelê by the mysterious flash of light which was the answer to her prayer that she should be visited by Zeus:

> Behold, God's Son is come into this land
> Of Thebes, even I, Dionysus, whom the brand
> Of heaven's hot splendour lit to life, when she
> Who bore me, Cadmus' daughter Semelê,
> Died here.[5]

[1] Logan Pearsall Smith, *Trivia.* 143.   [2] Edward FitzGerald, *Letters and Literary Remains.* i, 39–40.   [3] Hamerton, *Intellectual Life.* 45.   [4] Montaigne, 'Of Drunkennesse', *Essays.* Ed. Seccombe. i, 20.   [5] *Bacchae.* 1–4. Trans. Gilbert Murray. (*Athen. Drama.* iii, 79.)

Dionysus himself becomes *a God of Intoxication, of Inspiration, a giver of superhuman or immortal life,* and when his religion of ecstasy is displaced by Orphism, the priests of the new religion promise the faithful a hereafter of *eternal ecstasy* or *perpetual intoxication,* as Plato satirically calls it.[1] But whether it is one or the other, or whether there is any difference between drunkenness and ecstasy, once you are in either condition, the authorities (as usual) cannot agree; yet 'tis well known that to be well whittled with nectar was the prerogative and pleasure of the Gods. The wizard drunkenness, which Keats reckons up in his *Ode to the Nightingale,* where he yearns to be ravished into bliss by a tot of such witty liquor as might have been distilled by Bacchus himself, is a descendant of the true Dionysian frenzy:

> O for a draught of vintage, that hath been
>   Cool'd a long age in the deep-delvèd earth,
> Tasting of Flora and the country green,
>   Dance, and Provençal song, and sunburnt mirth!
> O for a beaker full of the warm South,
>   Full of the true, the blushful Hippocrene,
> With beaded bubbles winking at the brim,
>   And purple-stainèd mouth;
> That I might drink, and leave the world unseen,
> And with thee fade away into the forest dim.

But although we must not consider these adventures meet for common men, ecstasy in some degree is opportune to all, for we may be wrought up to it in love or war, in a theatre or in a church, in a crowd or in solitude, by all manner of circumstances, often trivial. Crowds are subject, as we know, to *frenzy,* and addicted to *collective hallucinations,*[2] which affect those who mingle with them; *solitude affects some people like wine,* says Mary Coleridge, *they must not take too much of it; for it flies to the head, and they become intoxicated;*[3] Horace Walpole was *intoxicated by his appointment to act as poet-laureate on the occasion of a visit of the Princess Amelia to Stowe;*[4] and Thoreau will have[5] *there are infinite degrees of drunkenness,* with as many causes and direct promoters; *even,* he says, *music may be intoxicating* (as musicians generally agree), but *of all ebriosity, who,* he asks, *does not prefer to be intoxicated by the air he breathes?* There are many also who hold that there is no better tipple than water, and there was a spring in Paphlagonia and a river near Erigon to which the natives resorted for a tipple,[6] as in later times connoisseurs have taken to the *mountain water*[7] of Swift.

Brillat-Savarin is tempted to couple the search for immortality and the

---

[1] *Id. Athen. Drama.* iii, Notes 165 *et seq.*   [2] Gustave le Bon, *The Crowd.* 46.
[3] *Gathered Leaves.* 223.   [4] Leslie Stephen, *Hours in a Library.* ii, 114.   [5] *Walden.*
Scott Library. 216.   [6] *Athenaeus.* ii, 42.   [7] Sir Walter Raleigh, *Letters.* i, 234.

search for strong drink as *the two attributes of man* which distinguish him from the *lower animals*, and he observes how savages have been ever restless in their search for fermented liquors, *they have soured the milk of their domestic animals; they have extracted the juice of different fruits, roots,* etc.,[1] in search of those *intimations of immortality* which Wordsworth found in the heart of a child or in the contemplation of natural objects; for what is ecstasy but a glimpse of eternity? There are no two answers to this question, even from those kill-joys who smell evil in all strong drink, yet one need not emulate the tosspot to discover these ecstasies, as many stout moralists have allowed, yea, even, as Montaigne gives out,[2] *some of the Stoickes deeme it not amisse for man sometimes to take his liquor roundly, and arinke drunke thereby to recreate his spirits.* John Addington Symonds infers[3] the same when he winces with world-weariness. What remedy is there for nerve-racked men but the anodyne of intoxication? All other antidotes fail before the anguish of the soul, *the cypress of knowledge springs, and withers when it comes in sight of Troy; the cypress of pleasure likewise if it has not died already at the root of cankering Calvinism; the cypress of religion is tottering, the axe is laid close to its venerable stem*; the only remedies for modern men are the anodyne of art, for artists; science, for the scientific; but music is *the best anodyne of all*, and next to it H*a*sheesh, *of one sort or another*, especially that which comes from books. *We can dull the pangs of the present by living the past again in reveries or learned studies, by illusions of the fancy and a life of self-indulgent dreaming. Take down the perfumed scrolls,* he advises, *open, unroll, peruse, digest, intoxicate your spirit with the flavour. Behold, there is the Athens of Plato, in your narcotic visions; Buddha and his anchorites appear; the raptures of St. Francis; and the fire-oblations of St. Dominic; the phantasms of mythologies, the birth-throes of religions, the neurotism of chivalry, the passion of past poems; all pass in your Maya-world of hasheesh, which is criticism. Nought,* therefore, *that Bacchus gives should be rejected.*[4] But I digress and roam about, so come we to our theme again.

Words, as I have sufficiently shown, have this potency: we are rapt out of ourselves by them, which is all some readers seek. *The great business of* Dr. Johnson's life *was to escape from himself.*[5] By words *we are shaken and lifted out of our ordinary state of consciousness,* says a reliable authority:[6] they enhance our faculties, give us *keener perceptions; more than our normal stock of penetrative sympathy*; and *another effect of the drug is that, while it is acting strongly, the whole adventure of mankind upon the earth gains, in our sight, a new momentousness, precariousness and beauty.* Of all ancient and modern opin-

---

[1] *Physiologie du Goût.* Trans. Anderson. 98-9.   [2] *Essays.* Ed. Seccombe. ii, 15.
[3] *John Addington Symonds, a Biography.* H. F. Brown. 243-4.   [4] οὐδὲν ἀπόβλητον
Διονύσιον, οὐδὲ γίγαρτον. Simonides. Qt. Athenaeus. i, 32.   [5] *Life,* Ed. Hill. i, 145.
[6] C. E. Montague, *A Writer's Notes on his Trade.* 246.

ions concerning the liquescency of books I find some more apt than those which refer their disposition in this kind to that ecstasy which is the immemorial prerogative of wine; for, as Wordsworth held, men are *stirred to ecstasy* by *glittering verse*,[1] and as Longinus was never tired of saying, *every bold experiment in language finds a solvent and a specific in deeds and passions which approach frenzy*.[2] The very words have in them the elements of these passionate experiences,

> Visionary power
> Attends the motions of the viewless winds,
> Embodied in the mystery of words,[3]

as those *gurus* and *yogi* of the East well know, and as Tennyson learnt when he threw himself into an ecstasy by repeating his own name[4] when *consciousness of individuality seemed to dissolve and fade away into boundless being,* which made him kin with the Buddhists who work themselves into a divine rapture by the rhythmical reiteration of the mystic monosyllable *Om* which prefaces the hymns of the *Vedas* and is for them the symbol of God, each letter having a sacred significance.[5]

How much more efficacious in their ebriosity are words when disposed rhetorically, whether as auto-intoxicants or applied inebriators, is well known. Lord Beaconsfield went so far as to charge Mr. Gladstone with being *inebriated with the exuberance of his own verbosity*;[6] and orators, from the rhetoricians of ancient Greece to the *spell-binders* of modern America —Demosthenes or Billy Sunday, it is all one—practise the same art on their audiences, *they dulcify the voice, modulating, smoothing, intoning* (or, in our times, shouting, stamping and thumping), *till the hearer is carried away with a perfect intoxication*.[7] It is known also that writers have induced this state of ecstasy in order to facilitate their creative work, or to relieve them of the burden of mundane cares, and so release their creative energies. Thus Thomas de Quincey and Coleridge composed masterpieces under the influence of opium, and according to Chamæleon, Aeschylus *wrote his tragedies when drunk*.[8] But whether they are drunk on mortal drink or not, makes no difference: they must get out of themselves before they can get into their art. *All good poets compose their beautiful poems not as works of art, but because they are inspired and possessed*; they are no more *in their right mind* when they compose than the *Corybantian revellers when they dance*.[9] Many authorities in all times have said as much, but I shall cite no other opinion than that of Macaulay, who deems, out of *Shakespeare*, that

[1] *Prelude*. v, 590–1.   [2] *The Sublime*. Trans. Prickard. 70.   [3] Wordsworth, *Prelude*. v, 595–7.   [4] Lang, *Tennyson, a Memoir*. i, 320.   [5] *Vishnu Parána*. Wilson. 273. n. 4.
[6] *Speech in the House of Commons*, 1878.   [7] Plutarch, *Select Essays*. Tucker. 165.
[8] Athenaeus. i, 22.   [9] Plato, *Ion*. Jowett. i, 247–8.

frenzy, amounting to *a partial derangement of the intellect*, is essential to poetry.[1]

Some even fly to books to escape the temptation of more potent fluids, as a Scottish philosopher, who *instead of having recourse to those gross stimulants*, by which *worn* men of both high and low degree are tempted, took down his *Sophocles*, or his *Plato*, his *Goethe, Dante, Shakespeare, Shelley, Wordsworth*, or *Tennyson*, and found the jars and discords of nerves cease and *physical exhaustion rise by degrees into consciousness of power.*[2] There are some authorities, I know, who would set liquor above literature as an inebriant,

> Oh many a peer of England brews
> Livelier liquor than the Muse,
> And malt does more than Milton can
> To justify God's ways to man;[3]

at the same time, my poet is brave enough to admit that the pleasures produced by malt are ephemeral; and they are wise, therefore, who like nothing better than to get drunk on books,

> Not charioted by Bacchus and his pards,
> But on the viewless wings of Poesy;[4]

the *reading of poetry* being, as some hold, no more than *self-intoxication*, and *artfully-ordered words, substitutes for the wine-flask.*[5] *Ne'er a line of* Aretino but is *able to make a man drunken with admiration.*[6] Some, I find, go even farther, giving out that it is not only possible to get drunk on poetry and on the *idle fumes and intoxicating fancies* of the bawdy play-books and romances reviled by Baxter,[7] but on the *Holy Scriptures*, as those good brothers in the monastic house of St. Martin, whom Alcuin *inebriated* with the *study of ancient wisdom.*[8]

That books have a like effect upon many of the more sensitive of their devotees is well known, in spite of Charpentier's scepticism when Heinsius announced that *Plato operated upon him like the intoxication produced by swallowing ten bumpers of wine.*[9] Dibdin has several instances. He himself, accidentally becoming the possessor, when a youth, of an odd volume of *Shakespeare*, was *excited almost to delirium*,[10] whilst the *Iliad* took *entire possession of the very strongholds of imagination and reason.*[11] Isaac D'Israel confesses that Dibdin's *Bibliomania* had *infected* him *with the most exquisite*

---

[1] 'Milton', *Essays.* (1872) 4.   [2] T. W. Robertson, *Lectures and Addresses.*   [3] A. E. Housman, *A Shropshire Lad.* lxii.   [4] Keats, 'Ode to a Nightingale'.   [5] Hamerton, *Intellectual Life.* 44.   [6] Thomas Nash, Qt. *Book of English Prose.* Ed. Henley and Whibley. 198.   [7] *Christian Directory.* i, 16.   [8] Merryweather, *Bibliomania in the Middle Ages.* 122.   [9] Qt. *Book-Lover's Ench.* 82.   [10] Dibdin, *Reminiscences.* i, 64–5.   [11] *Ib.* 73.

inebriation,[1] and some time after he tells its author that he is *not yet recovered from the delightful delirium*.[2] When the *Bibliographical Decameron* was published it *nearly turned the head* of Alexander Chalmers;[3] and Dibdin believes[4] that if ever he visited the Advocates' Library at Edinburgh, he might need *David Laing, Esq., the erudite and able secretary, to help him up in case* he fell, *or was taken with too long a swooning fit of delirious rapture.*

When we come to times present I find the same news. Anatole France records that men get *drunk with reading*; but Joubert will have that *the best literary work does not intoxicate—it enchants*,[5] which is not supported by the evidence I have collected from either past or present times. Thoreau gives out[6] that Mir Camar Uddin Mast experienced the pleasure of intoxication after he had *drunk the liquor of the esoteric doctrines*; Frederick Myers was intoxicated by *Sappho*;[7] Meredith's *Love in the Valley* makes Stevenson *drunk like wine*;[8] Hamerton has seen *a young poet intoxicated with the love of poetry*;[9] Edmund Gosse when a youth was *thrown into a temporary frenzy by the epic poetry of Scott*;[10] *Mdlle. de Maupin* made George Moore see *with delightful clearness and with intoxicating conviction, that by looking without shame and accepting with love the flesh*, he might *raise it to as high a place within as divine a light as even the soul had been set in*;[11] when C. E. Montague was a boy these lines out of *Scott*,

> Yet the lark's shrill fife may come
> At the day-break from the fallow,
> And the bittern sound his drum,
> Booming from the sedgy shallow,

made him *so drunk with delight* that he *had to walk up and down empty compartments of trains, saying them over and over again, as incapable as a bluebottle either of sitting quiet or ceasing to hum*;[12] and Proust notes those *intellectuals worshipping art with a big A, who, when they can no longer intoxicate themselves upon Zola, inject themselves with Verlaine, and become etheromaniacs out of Baudelairian devotion*.[13]

Henry Jackson escapes the *intoxicating* effects of Swinburne's *Atalanta* because, *unluckily*, he admitted, *I don't like getting drunk*.[14] Even when reading is impossible, the presence of books acquired by passionate devotion to them produces such an ecstasy that *the buying of more books than one can peradventure read* is nothing less than the soul *reaching towards infinity*, and

[1] *Ib.* 307.   [2] *Ib.* 306.   [3] *Ib.* ii, 650.   [4] *Ib.* i, 473.   [5] *Selected Thoughts*. Trans. Lyttleton. 174.   [6] *Walden*. Scott Lib. 97–8.   [7] Myers, *Fragments of Prose and Poetry*. 18.   [8] *Letters*. ii, 324.   [9] *Intellectual Life*. 44.   [10] *Father and Son*. (1909) 239.   [11] *Confessions of a Young Man*. (1909) 67.   [12] *A Writer's Notes on his Trade*. 244.   [13] *Cities of the Plain*. Trans. Scott Moncrieff. ii, 141.   [14] *Henry Jackson, O.M. A Memoir*. Parry. 239.

that this passion is *the only thing that raises us above the beasts that perish*,[1] an argument which some have used in defence of the giddy raptures invoked by wine.

I cannot deny that something may be said in defence of raptures by which a bookman may become no less than one of *Homer's gods drunk with Nectar and Nepenthe*;[2] so that it be discreetly and moderately done, it shall not be amiss to anyone, least of all himself; and if, as some will contend, he abide in a fool's paradise, he has an advantage in his folly unknown to those who are always sensible, and I could here tax many virtues, proprieties, moralities, respectabilities amongst us which are less kind and more properly to be condemned for the inconvenience they give and the pain they cause for the sake of principle, or the glory of God; there are many such, *quae nunc in aurem susurrare non libet*.[3] But I must take heed, *ne quid gravius dicam*, that I do not overshoot myself. I am forth of my element, as you peradventure observe.

[1] A. E. Newton, *A Magnificent Farce*. 78.   [2] Erasmus, *Moriae Encomium*. Trans. Wilson. 7.   [3] 'Which would give offence now even to whisper in the ear.'

Part XI

A PAGEANT OF BOOKMEN

―――――――――――――⟨◆⟩――――――――――――

I. BOOKFOLK DEFINED

In other sections mention is made, among many comfortable objects, of the usefulness, purpose, and pleasures which proceed from books. I shall now set out divers common experiences of bookmen of different times and several lands, which will inform how universal, profound and varied is the love of reading, so as to inculcate the final lesson of all my researches into this branch of the subject, namely: that the best books for you are the books you like best, and that in any catalogue of bookish preferences tastes cancel out. Books are like people, few suit all palates, all arouse dislike in some; and the best books, those that have survived the test of time and the slings and arrows of critics and lovers, remain closed to most people, bookfolk being a distinct, though scattered class, if not even more specifically to be differentiated, as I shall later discuss. Here again, however, let me observe that I find no fault with the crowds of men and women who read no books, or only *biblia a-biblia*; it is their nature, and they do very well in their several kinds and methods of life. Reading is a matter of taste, not morality.

Besides the reverence we owe to the wisest and most profound books, there are several considerable arguments I could allege to render it exceeding probable that the meaning of great books is dimmed or distorted by crowds, and in this respect it is better that books and crowds should remain apart; and, since crowds are powerful, it may be wise for us to bear with them *in their amusements, that they, in return, may shew indulgence to ours,*[1] for all the true bookman asks is to be left alone with the books of his own choosing, to escape alike the interference of moral meddlers and the noises raised by the propagandists and distributors of ready-made culture.[2] For

[1] 'Demus alienis oblectationibus veniam, ut nostris impetremus.' Pliny, *Letters*. Melmoth. Loeb Ed. ix, 17.   [2] 'Art is upon the Town!—to be chucked under the chin by the passing gallant—to be enticed within the gates of the householder—to be coaxed into company, as a proof of culture and refinement.' Whistler, *Ten o'clock*. (1888) 7.

the rest, those who are bookfolk, and they come from all classes, just as the vulgar herd is not confined to poor and untutored people, that which one omits another may haply see, that which one condemns another may uphold. There are chances for all, and the choice is yet free for those who care to exercise their own predilections.

There are some, even, and among them notable connoisseurs of books, whose curiosity is so intense that all print proves irresistible to them. J. C. Squire confesses that he is *one of those who can never help reading any odd piece of printed paper which comes into their hands accidentally.* For instance, he mentions, *odd sheets which shroud parcels sent by booksellers or publishers; fragments found amid the seaweed, straw, wood, bottles and corks on a beach; and pieces impaled by my stick when out walking.*[1] I note these differences and vagaries in passing, to clear the air, so that henceforward it should not be hard to describe what are the proper indications of a good reader. I shall now, therefore, get down to the facts and so make more familiar and easy his tastes, whims, eccentricities, for every one's capacity, which is a chief end of my discourse.

This part, then, is a fardel of general bookish experiences, chiefly *adventures among masterpieces,*[2] with many peculiar instances and examples, to be considered as preparatory to the understanding of this great faculty, which has been of such value to so many otherwise diverse men, and will still mean much, perchance more, in the years to come, for in the mechanisation and mass-rule which are upon us, books may well be our last line of defence, and reading our *loophole of retreat.*[3] But I hasten to my instances.

II. MONTAIGNE AND PETRARCH AS TYPES OF GOOD BOOKMEN

No better examples of good bookmen can be found or put up than those of Montaigne and Petrarch, and I set their names here as typical of all great readers, worthy to be masters and leaders in our adventuring. Montaigne swings eloquently to my purpose as a true indication of sanely varied and self-centred book-taste. He was (it appears by his own words) both a good and bad reader according to those authorities who would ever be sorting us out into moral equations, which most times is no more than attempting to make two straight lines enclose a space or parallel lines meet. He read for pleasure, and found profit in doing so, as all do whose inclinations are healthy. He was not much addicted to Greek books, but

[1] *Life at a Mermaid.* 101.   [2] Anatole France, *Life and Letters.* Preface. First Series. vii.
[3] Cowper.

set a high value upon *Plutarch* and *Seneca; both*, he says, *having this excellent commodity for my humour, that the knowledge I seeke in them is there so scatteringly and loosely handled, that whosoever readeth them is not tied to plod along upon them, whereof I am incapable.* He was not a regular, laborious reader, but loved, like our own Dr. Johnson, to sip here and sample there; to roam and browse and chew the cud. He frankly admits a preference even for desultory and idle reading, which so many are apt to condemn, but which has its place, to my thinking.

He sets uppermost in his picked hierarchy the poets, *Virgil, Lucretius, Catullus* and *Horace*, especially Virgil in the *Georgics*; and among the modern books *merely pleasant*, he esteemed Boccaccio his *Decameron, Rabelais*, and the *Kisses* of John the Second; but Cicero's *manner of writing* was very tedious to him, as all *such-like stuffe, for his prefaces, definitions, divisions, and Etymologies, consume the greatest part of his Works, and whatsoever quick, wittie, and pithie conceit is in him, is surcharged, and confounded by those his long and far-fetcht preambles*; as for *Amadis* and *such like trash of writings*, they had never the credit so much as to allure his youth to delight in them. But I have no complaint, his tastes were his own, and his whims were tastes, revealing him to himself and to us; for more, read his essay *Of Bookes*, where he discourseth at large on these matters; and compare if you will Petrarch, a great reader of another kind, who as the herald of the Renaissance of Ancient Literature, made the Greek and Latin Classics his close friends, *Virgil, Ovid, Seneca, Aristotle* and *Valerius Maximus* closest of all, despising for the most part the works of the Fathers, whose dominance he helped to end.

Into the midst of this galaxy of Pagan stars he brought St. Augustine's *Confessions, bubbling over with tears*, which he read *continuously for forty years*;[1] he loved the *Confessions* with passion and fidelity, it was his Bible, and dearer to him than the dearest of his beloved Classics; *few things in the history of literature are more touching than this spiritual comradeship—Petrarch clasping hands with St. Augustine across the Lethe of nine mediæval centuries, the last man of the classic age and the first man of the modern mingling their souls in sympathy and sentiment*;[2] for more see his *Letters*, more particularly that to Friar Dionisio Roberti of Borgo San Sepolcro.[3] Montaigne read to be companionable with himself; Petrarch to be companionable with himself and with others; and all bookmen approximate to the one or the other, and by so doing arrive at the essence of this business of reading, whatever other purpose it may have.

---

[1] Tatham, *Francesco Petrarca*. i, 306.   [2] J. A. Symonds, *Essays Speculative and Suggestive*. 297–8.   [3] Epistolae. Fracassetti (Florence, 1859) iv, 1.

III. VARIOUS TASTES OUTLINED

Let us peep a little farther into this mystery of variable tastes, to see if there be at least a common measure of bookishness, which I dare to say in advance it will not be difficult to prove. At the same time I know well that all readers, even the most omnivorous, do not at all times love or even like all books; this I sufficiently show in several places; but instances of the kind are countless, and as each has its particular cause and application, I may here cite a handful in order to clinch and bring home my present argument. Coleridge loved poetry, romance and mystical theology, and loathed rational philosophy; he went to Durham to study *Duns Scotus* in the Chapter's Library, and he told Southey that he meant to put this old writer *on his feet again,* and *in order to wake him out of his present lethargy,* he said, *I am burning Locke, Hume, and Hobbes under his nose. They stink worse than feather or asafoetida;*[1] Macaulay, who could and did read almost everything with enjoyment, had so small a liking for the work of Horace Walpole that he believed *none but an unhealthy and disorganised mind could have produced such literary luxuries;*[2] my father, said J. S. Mill, *never was a great admirer of Shakespeare, the English idolatry of whom he used to attack with some severity;*[3] after reading *Rossetti,* Edward Dowden longed for *blown sea-breezes in verse and sea-smells to restore* his *vigour;*[4] John Burroughs found *something gruesome about Swinburne's poetry, like clammy and rapidly growing fungi;*[5] Coventry Patmore thought George Eliot an improper novelist,[6] Hazlitt *a flashy and second-rate writer, with a certain gift of the gab,* suggesting genius,[7] and *Aurora Leigh* reminded him of *an ill-conditioned child jumping at the stars and stamping on the flowers;*[8] William Cory considered it necessary to recommend Johnson's *Lives of the Poets* as an *antidote for a love of Shelley;*[9] Dr. Johnson thought *Akenside a superior poet* to *Gray;*[10] Froude, in later life, found *Ovid wearisome and effeminate, an atheistical epicurean with neither Horace's humour nor Lucretius's grandeur to make up for his objectionable creed;*[11] Robert Louis Stevenson *would not give a chapter of old Dumas (meaning himself, not his collaborators) for the whole boiling of the Zolas,* which were no more to him than *romance with the smallpox;*[12] and W. B. Yeats so dislikes modern realistic plays that he condemns *Rosmersholm* for its *stale odour of spoilt poetry;*[13] to Aldous Huxley *Spenser* is

[1] *Letters.* Ed. E. H. Coleridge. i, 358.   [2] 'Horace Walpole', *Essays.* (1872) 267.
[3] *Autobiography.* 16.   [4] *Fragments from Old Letters.* 28.   [5] *Indoor Studies,* 251.
[6] *Memoirs.* Champneys. i, 363.   [7] *Ib.* ii, 265.   [8] *Ib.* ii, 186.   [9] 'Table Talk', in *Gathered Leaves.* Mary E. Coleridge. 334.   [10] *Life.* Ed. Hill. iii, 32.   [11] *Oceana.* 24.
[12] Stevenson, *Letters.* i, 234.   [13] *Trembling of the Veil.* 158,

no more than *a man with the conjuror's trick of extracting perfectly rhymed stanzas by the hundred out of an empty mind.*[1]

At the same time that which is more observable is the versatility of most bookfolk, despite grumbles and distempers, as I shall now proceed to exhibit. Benjamin Disraeli found Henry Bulmer's *France very amusing*, at a time when he was re-reading *Heine*, and Raumer's *Historical Illustrations very curious, especially about Mary Queen of Scots*; and he rejoiced, as a young man, when Sir William Molesworth gave him *Hobbes* in eighteen volumes;[2] John, Earl of Orrery, tells Major Clelland that he is enjoying *Bussy, Rabutin, Palison, Voiture, Les Lettres Galantes etc. etc. etc.*;[3] Thomas Gray complains to Dr. Wharton that there are many *flimsy articles* in the great *Encyclopedia* which the French have just finished in seventeen volumes; that there are now thirteen volumes of Buffon's *Natural History*, and he is not yet come to the monkeys, *who are a numerous people*, and that although the *Life of Petrarch* has entertained him, it is not well written.[4]

Robert Burns reads assiduously to purpose, no bibliophile he, no dilettante. The inspired peasant sought knowledge, understanding, learning; thus as a boy he read the *Life of Hannibal*, and the *History of Sir William Wallace*; the first giving his *ideas such a turn that he used to strut in rapture up and down after the recruiting drum and bagpipes, and the second poured a Scottish prejudice into his veins which will boil till the flood-gates of life shut in eternal rest*. Then came adventures among such masters as Shakespeare and Pope, as well as Addison and Steele and others of their shining company, commingled with Tull and Dickson on *Agriculture*, Justice's *British Gardener's Directory*, *The Pantheon*, Locke *On the Human Understanding*, Stackhouse's *History of the Bible*, Boyle's *Lectures*, Allan Ramsay's *Works*, Taylor's *Scripture Doctrine of Original Sin*, and Hervey's *Meditations*: all of which proves that a poet is born, not made, *poeta nascitur non fit*, and that even *biblia a-biblia* cannot unmake him. He also read, more to his poetic purpose, *A Select Collection of English Songs* (which I have noted in its place); so he went on until his twenty-third year. *Vive l'amour, et vive la bagatelle*, are now his sole principles of action, so he is greatly pleased by the addition to his library of Sterne's *Tristram Shandy* and Mackenzie's *Man of Feeling*.[5] At this time also he was *taken tooth and nail to the Bible . . . a really glorious book*,[6] and he celebrated his joy by procuring an *octavo* copy in sheets, *the best paper and print in town*, which he ordered his bookbinder to bedeck *with all the elegance of his craft*. His omnivorous bookappetite is proved by his orders to Peter Hill, the Edinburgh bookseller, from whom he demands works by Smollett, Otway, Ben Jonson, Dryden, Congreve, Wycherley, Vanbrugh, Cibber, Macklin, Garrick, Foote, Col-

[1] Huxley, *Jesting Pilate*. 57.   [2] *Correspondence with his Sister*. 232.   [3] Orrery. 105, 45.
[4] *Poems and Letters*. (1820) 317.   [5] *Letters*. Scott Lib. 66-9.   [6] *Ib*. 94.

man, Sheridan; and Molière, Racine, Corneille and Voltaire, in the French tongue; and, to end this list, an *Index* to the Excise Laws and an Abridgement of all Statutes *now in force* by Jellinger Symons.[1] Well may he advance that: *In the matter of books* he is *very profuse*.[2]

William Cowper admitted to Lady Hesketh that in three months he had read Savart's *Travels into Egypt*, Fenn's *Original Letters*, Madan's *Letters to Priestley*, the *Mémoires du Baron de Tott*, and those of Henri de Lorraine and the Duc de Guise; the *Letters* of Frederick of Bohemia, Barclay's *Argenis*, which he declares is *the best romance that ever was written*; and after all this rambling among now overgrown by-paths he concludes: *I am a great reader;*[3] and so he was, sucking the marrow even out of dull books, though he abstained from politics, which was his *abhorrence, being always hypothetical, fluctuating, and impracticable*, and Philosophy did not *suit him*.[4] In 1781, he told the Rev. William Unwin that he had read no poetry for thirteen years,[5] and he considered it an advantage, being *pretty much addicted to the writing of it*.[6] Yet he knew the bright books also, found consolation in them all like a true Epicurean, and even faced the approach of inclement winters without concern, though *a passionate lover of fine weather* (as who is not) *and the pleasant scenes of summer; but the long evenings have their comforts too, and there is hardly to be found upon earth*, he supposes, *so snug a creature as an Englishman by his fireside in the winter*, especially if one lives in the country, for in London one is not free from intrusion. *I have two ladies to read to, sometimes more, never less* (showing the wisdom that was his when his insanity was in abeyance). *At present we are circumnavigating the globe*, and he asks Joseph Hill to send him more voyages, books like Foster's, *to make the winter pass merrily*.[7]

Sir Philip Sidney doted on *Plutarch*, which so many have done and still do, and when in Venice (in 1573) he implored Hubert Languet to send him a copy in French from Vienna by some trader, for which he *would gladly* have given *five times the value*. He offers to send Languet *L'Historia del Mondo* of Tarchagnota, *Lettere de Principi*, *Lettere de Tredici Illustri Homini*, *Imprese* of Girolamo Ruscelli, and *Il Stato de Venezia*, by Contarini and Donato Gianotti, all of them *interesting books*.[8] Such reading is proper for the student, and especially the patrician and the ambassador, though time marks many changes in the garden of history.

William Morris found time for reading as for everything else. Weaver, printer, designer, politician, poet, story-teller, he still read his favourite books: *Chaucer* and *Froissart*, old French *Romances*, Icelandic *Sagas* and the *Ring of the Niblungs*; Carlyle's *Past and Present* and *Latter-Day Pamphlets*,

---

[1] *Ib.* 246–7. [2] *Ib.* 11. [3] *Letters of William Cowper*. Frazer. ii, 129. [4] *Ib.* i, 262.
[5] *Ib.* 158. [6] *Ib.* 262. [7] *Letters of William Cowper*. Frazer. i, 250–1. [8] *Correspondence of Sidney and Languet.* 9–10.

and Ruskin's *Nature of Gothic*, which he thought in future days would be considered *one of the very few necessary and inevitable utterances of the century;*[1] he revelled in *Dickens* (wanted to print him at the Kelmscott Press), *George Borrow, Surtees; Uncle Remus* and *Huckleberry Finn;* William Cobbett's *Rural Rides,* which he had almost by heart, and the novels of Thomas Love Peacock; all of which took up little of that time which he valued as his most precious possession, for, like Dr. Johnson and Lord Macaulay, *he tore the heart from a book with remarkable speed.*[2]

Thomas Carlyle, making an enjoyment of being annoyed at life, vexed himself with the reading of all varieties of books for recreation and condemnation. In his early years he read and grumbled incessantly. *It is not books that I want now,* he wrote to his brother (Dr. Carlyle) in 1836,[3] *but good sense and good spirits to make use of what I have* (three hundred volumes); *and I all biliousness and fret, and palpitating haste and bewilderment!* Out of *a considerable quantity of garbage* which he *allowed himself to devour,* he can name only Crabbe's poems as *worthy of being read;*[4] *Cicero de Officiis* read in comparison with *Chesterfield's Advice* should make us *blush for the eighteenth century;*[5] he could read but a volume of *Gibbon:* his style *too flowery; his sarcasms wicked; his notes oppressive, often beastly;*[6] *Byron* and *Scott* are to his liking, but still (in 1814) he prefers *Campbell* among modern poets; Hoole's *Tasso,* Dr. William Wilkie's now forgotten Epic, the *Epigoniad,* Wieland's *Oberon,* Savage's *Poems,* Miss Porter's *Scottish Chiefs,* and *Waverley* passed through the *tribulum* of his reading without censure;[7] but he sat up till four o'clock in the morning battering himself into luxurious indignation over Matt. Lewis's *Monk: the most stupid and villainous novel that I have read for a great while; considerable portions of it* being *grossly indecent, not to say brutish.*[8] He approved the *weightier kind of books:* Histories, Philosophies; *Homer* and all the Greeks and Romans; *Dante; Goethe;* but in old age his reading became *desultory, discontinuous, and insignificant;* he fed his spleen on Swift's *Gulliver and certain of his Essays and Poems,* all entertaining except *the Horse and Yahoo department,* which he found *extremely dirty and dull;*[9] the only book he read in October 1874 was Spedding's *Bacon,* and he found it *far from a seductive one!*[10] and nearer the end, the year before his flaming spirit was drenched out by death, he found peace in *Shakespeare* and Boswell's *Hebrides.*[11]

Lord Byron,[12] a tireless reader, though never *seen* reading; always seemed *idle and in mischief, or at play;* but the *truth is,* he confesses, *I read eating, read in bed, read when no one else reads;* he is also a choleric reader: he

[1] *Nature of Gothic.* 'Introduction.' (1899)   [2] *William Morris.* Holbrook Jackson. 54–5.   [3] *New Letters.* i, 3.   [4] *Early Letters.* xii, 35.   [5] *Ib.* vi, 17.   [6] *Ib.* xx.   [7] *Ib.* iii. [8] *Ib.* xviii.   [9] *New Letters.* ii, 337.   [10] *Ib.* ii, 308.   [11] FitzGerald, *Letters to Fanny Kemble.* 170.   [12] *The Ravenna Journa.* 82.

reads to scold and scorn, amusing himself mightily; he has no patience with the *sort of trash* his publisher sends out to him in Italy, except Scott's novels and *three or four other things*; never saw such works: *Campbell is lecturing, Moore idling, Southey twaddling, Wordsworth drivelling, Coleridge muddling, Joanna Baillie piddling, Bowles quibbling, squabbling, and snivelling: No more modern poesy, I pray, neither Mrs. Hemans, nor any female or male Tadpole of Poet Wordsworth, nor any of his ragamuffins: No more Keats, I entreat:—flay him alive; if some of you don't I must skin him myself: there is no bearing the drivelling idiotism of the Mankin.*[1]

The very worthy, industrious and curious[2] Mr. Samuel Pepys, diarist and man of affairs, confesses his bookish peccadilloes as frankly as those others which fell to his adventurous lot in old Rowlie's times: *To my bookseller's, and there bought Hooker's 'Polity', the new edition, and Dugdale's 'History of the Inns of Court', of which there was but few saved out of* the Fire of London, and *Playford's new 'Catch-book', that hath a great many new fooleries in it;*[3] William Penn's ' *Truth Exalted*' was *a ridiculous nonsensical book* (so he wrote on October 12th, 1668) *so full of nothing but nonsense, that I was ashamed to read it;*[4] discussed *a new book of drollery*[5] with Mr. Battersly to such good effect that he must *needs go find it out, and met with it at the Temple* (for 2s. 6d.). *But when I come to read it, it is so silly an abuse of the Presbyter Knight going to the wars that I am ashamed of it; and by and by meeting at Mr. Townsend's at dinner I sold it to him for 18d.;*[6] in less than six weeks, *it being certainly some ill-humour to be so against that which all the world cries out to be the example of wit;* he hies him to a bookseller in the Strand and buys another copy, *resolved once more to read him;*[7] towards the end of that same year (1662) he goes abroad to Paul's Church Yard, and *there looked upon the second part,* which he cautiously borrows, *to see if it be as good as the first, which the world cry so mightily up, though it hath not a good liking in me, though I had tried by twice or three times reading to bring myself to think it witty;*[8] twelve days pass and once more Mr. Pepys to his bookseller and thereat buys the new part, *the book now in greatest fashion for drollery,* though he cannot, he confesses, *see enough where the wit lies,*[9] but he will be in the fashion in books as in most other things. Nor could he see aught but what was ridiculous in the *History of My Lord Newcastle, wrote by his wife, which shews her to be a mad, conceited, ridiculous woman, and he an asse to suffer her to write what she writes to him, and of him;*[10] he studies *Selden* and *Grotius* so that he may the better write *something about our making strangers to strike to us at sea;*[11] and his love of what is fine in books is so great that one Sunday at Sir Philip Warwick's, as he sat in *a low room* reading *Erasmus de Scribendis*

---

[1] *Letters and Journals.* xxii.   [2] Evelyn, *Diary.* 26.v.1703.   [3] Pepys, *Diary.* Wheatley. iv, 273.   [4] *Ib.* viii. 122.   [5] Butler's *Hudibras.*   [6] *Diary,* ii, 425.   [7] *Ib.* iii, 32. [8] *Ib.* iii, 361.   [9] *Ib.* iii, 370-1.   [10] *Diary.* Wheatley. vii, 368.   [11] *Ib.* vii, 368.

Epistolis, he was tempted to *tear out two leaves* which pleased him mightily
—but, says he: *I forbore it.*[1] Nothing but the loss of his sight could absolve
him from the passion for books and reading: *So to bed,* he writes on March
18th, 1668, my eyes very bad; *and I know not how in the world to abstain
from reading;* little more than twelve months later his sight so fades that he
has to close his beloved *Diary: which is almost as much as to see myself go into
my grave, for which, and all the discomforts that will accompany my being blind,
the good God prepare me!*[2]

IV. OF BIBLIA A-BIBLIA

I must here insert some few further words on preferences, for, as I have
already shown, the literary taste has an uneven surface, and there is a wide
disparity between the predilections of readers, ranging from an enthusiastic universalism on the one part to a niggardly particularism on the
other. *What any man can write, surely I may read,* said Lamb,[3] but even for
him there are things in the shape of books which he *cannot allow for such.*
Among *these books which are no books—biblia a-biblia—*he includes Court
Calendars, Directories, Pocket Books; Draught Boards, bound and lettered on the back; Scientific Treatises, Almanacks, Statutes at Large; the
works of Hume, Gibbon (in which few will support him), Robertson,
Beattie, Soame Jenyns, and generally, all those volumes which *no gentleman's library should be without:* the Histories of Flavius Josephus (*that learned
Jew*), and Paley's Moral Philosophy. *With these exceptions* (he repeats) *I can
read almost anything:*[4] and he did, and none to better effect. He even read
books which were given to him (a thing which Oliver Wendell Holmes
said never happened).[5] He distilled the essence of books, following his
whim, seeking ever the gleam of exquisite writing, adoring and fondling
fine phrases and purple patches, quip, crank, oddity of style: euphuisms,
fine shades, nice meanings; thus he came as an explorer in neglected realms
upon the Elizabethans and the old Dramatists; revelled in *Shakespeare*
before the days of bardolatry, and rediscovered *Izaak Walton* and *Robert
Burton. Among all your quaint reading,* he asks Coleridge, *did you ever light
upon Walton's 'Complete Angler'? . . . it breathes the very spirit of innocence,
purity and simplicity of heart.*[6] Well may he bless his stars for *a taste so
catholic, so unexcluding,*[7] thus supporting Southey's claim that *your true
lover of literature is never fastidious;* for *a fastidious taste is like a squeamish*

---

[1] *Ib.* vi, 149.   [2] May 31st, 1669.   [3] *Letters.* Everyman. i, 340.   [4] 'Detached
Thoughts on Books and Reading.'   [5] *Autocrat of the Breakfast Table.*   [6] *Letters*
Everyman. i, 44.   [7] Lamb, 'Detached Thoughts', *Last Essays of Elia.*

appetite; the one has its origin in some distemper of the mind, as the other has in some ailment of the stomach.[1]

Your true reader, as like as not, is what Leigh Hunt[2] calls *a universalist,* he puts up *with difference of opinion, by reason of his own very difference,* a right upheld in *a spirit of universal allowance,* not as *a privilege arrogated by conceit;* he loves all books because he is *a thorough human being.* The more you read the more you want to read: *pluris facio quum relego: semper ut novum, et quum repetivi, repetendum.*[3] Books stimulate the appetite which reading seeks to appease, and readers would have it so; all's fish that comes to their net, and as the born reader can read anywhere he can read anything, even *biblia a-biblia,* which are a matter of taste, whim, fancy, for, in the last resort, every man has his own *biblia a-biblia* as well as his *biblia.*

Théophile Gautier maintained that the *Dictionary* was the best reading for a poet; so enamoured was King Henry VIII of Roger Ascham's book on *Shooting* that he gave him a living for it;[4] when that good ambassador and scholar, Sir Henry Wotton, was at Venice, *ad annum* 1609, he found *the then principal subject of discourse* in Italy *our good Master's*[5] excellent work *(Apologia pro Juramento Fidelitatis), which the devil fain would hurt,* although France openly abused and Spain refused it.[6] Sir Thomas Bodley was prejudiced against plays, proclamations and almanacks, and he argued with Dr. James (his first Librarian) against these coming into his Library at Oxford, calling them *riffe-raffe* and *baggage bookes;* and there were *many pamphlets, not worth the custody in suche a Librarie;*[7] some plays, he thought, might be worth keeping, *but hardly one in fortie,* and having those few, *(suche is the nature of malicious reporters) would be mightily multiplied by suche as purpose to speake in disgrace of the Librarie;* if he erred in that opinion he thought he would *erre with infinit others.*[8]

Thomas Frognall Dibdin read, during his later years, little save title-pages and bibliography, for the purpose of his vast books in that science; but at college he read with gusto in many diverse authors, favouring history for the most part, as Rushworth's *Collections; Henry's History was a sort of 'Hortus Adonidis',* always on his table, *his authorities by the side of him;* Hume was his *sofa companion,* and, *strange as may seem the juxtaposition,* Burton's *Anatomy* and Gibbon's *Decline and Fall were frequently lying upon the same sofa and table.*[9] Macaulay *was contented, when the humour took him, to amuse his solitary hours with such productions as Percival Stockdale's Memoirs, and the six volumes of Miss Anna Seward's Letters.*[10] On that curious tour in the Hebrides Dr. Johnson and Boswell read enthusiastically little but what

[1] Southey, *Doctor.* xvii.   [2] *A Book for a Corner.* Introductory.   [3] Lipsius of *Epictetus.* [4] Ascham, *Letter to Queen Elizabeth.* Mumby. 5–6.   [5] James I.   [6] *Life and Letters of Wotton.* Smith. i, 462.   [7] *Letters to Thomas James.*   [8] *Ib.* 222.   [9] *Reminiscences.* i, 88–90   [10] Trevelyan, *Marginal Notes by Lord Macaulay.* 5.

we should account *biblia a-biblia*, such as Ogden's *Sermons on Prayer*, Bishop Gastrell's *Christian Institutes*, Derham's *Physico-Theology*, Drummond's *Travels*, Daille *On the Fathers*, Lucas *On Happiness*, Gregory's *Geometry*, Gatakar *On Lots* and on the *Christian Watch* (*a very learned book*, comments Boswell, to which Johnson assents, describing it *as a treasure*), More's *Dialogues*, and other works now pretty generally forgotten or accounted dull and unreadable; but enjoy them as they did they were not averse from dipping into Ovid's *Epistles*, Burnet's *History of Our Own Times*, and *The Bible*.[1] Samuel Pepys, as I have shown, could not make up his mind whether *Hudibras* was dull or bright, but Charles II had no doubts, and *used to carry in his pocket a copy* of that work given him by Buckhurst.[2]

There are, as we know, those who seek to lay down the law in this matter of dullness, but all those who so vigorously take sides do no more than add to the confusion. Even sound and reliable bookmen are not agreed upon an acceptable definition of *biblia a-biblia*. I have shown up Lamb, now let us look at some modern authorities. *I call nothing a book*, says Garrod, *which does not address a large part of its appeal to imagination and emotion*. Consistently with this formula he rules out all books, *however important to mankind*, which aim at *instruction and information rather than at delight and edification*; thus he sweeps aside Newton's *Principia* and Darwin's *Origin of Species*, together with the logarithmic tables, books of dates, spelling books and Latin grammars.[3] This opinion would blend with Thoreau's contention that *dullness is but another name for tameness*, for it is wildness which attracts us: *It is the uncivilised free and wild thinking in 'Hamlet' and the 'Iliad', in all the Scriptures and Mythologies, not learned in the schools, that delight us.* He goes even farther by declaring that as *the wild duck is more swift and beautiful than the tame*, so is *the wild—the mallard—thought*; a *truly good book* (excellence being tested by brightness) *is something as natural, and as unexpectedly and unaccountably fair and perfect, as a wild flower discovered on the prairies of the West or in the jungles of the East.* But the excellence which he approves in wild and unexpected words and themes is the excellence of genius, which, as he sets it out, is the sole preventative of dullness. *Genius*, he advertises, is *a light which makes the darkness visible, like the lightning's flash, which perchance shatters the temple of knowledge itself*.[4]

Arnold Bennett may now be invited to bring this argument out of the empyrean and restore it to earth. *The test of a first-rate work*, he holds, *and*, he adds, *a test of your sincerity in calling it a first-rate work, is that you finish it.* If you cannot stay the course, the book is *either dull or tiresome*, and *all dull books are bad, and all tiresome books are either bad or maladroit or both*.[5] On the

---

[1] *Life*. Ed. Hill. v, 294.   [2] Louise Imogen Guiney, *Patrins*. 308.   [3] *Profession of Poetry*. 254.   [4] *Essays*. Scott Lib. 19.   [5] *Things that have Interested Me*. 90-1.

other hand, ·and I would have you concentrate upon this, Sir Leslie
Stephen, and some other good witnesses, advance the plea that dullness is
not absolutely and irrevocably dull, but may, on occasion and not seldom,
be so capricious as to be bright and dull at one and the same time. *Nobody*,
says Stephen, *ever wrote a dull autobiography*, and even if he did *the very dullness would be interesting*.[1] Robert Louis Stevenson went farther still, for, in
certain moods, he preferred to read dull books. At such times he revelled
in the two large folios of *Fountainhall*, which is *all dreary, and all true, and
all as terse as an obituary; and about one interesting fact on an average in twenty
pages, and ten of them unintelligible for technicalities*.[2] Many, he points out,
find Dostoieffsky's *Crime and Punishment* dull. Henry James could not
finish it; but Stevenson thought it *the greatest book he had read in ten years*,
although reading it *nearly finished him, it was like having an illness*.[3] But he
was not always revelling in the leviathan dullness of genius, nor yet indulging in dullness for its own sake: sometimes he plodded through deserts
of prose in the hope of reaching an oasis where he could rest amid the
palms and slake his thirst, as with those unreadable romances *The Cavalier*
and *Morley Ernstein*, which he found in the Franklin County Library at
Saranac. He read the first with *indescribable amusement*; it *was worse than he
had feared*, yet *somehow engaging*. The second, to his surprise, was better
than he had dared to hope: *a good, honest, dull, interesting tale*, with *a
genuine old-fashioned feeling for the English language*, which *awoke appetite*.[4]
Despite, however, these diverse opinions and experiences I find no mystery in this problem, and very little problem, for, as I have shown, and
shall show again from more than one angle, we read into books what is in
ourselves, reading being as much a process of digging ourselves out,
developing ourselves as chemicals develop a photographic plate, as a process for digging out the author or his ideas and fancies. *We find little in a
book but what we put there*;[5] for, as Vernon Lee discovers, in *literature, the
pattern is made of us; not merely of our own soul's motions, but of our memory's
contents*.[6] The greater the book the more room it will find for the reader.
Dullness is a mutable condition, in books as in persons (including ourselves); it varies as we do; changes with our attitudes. So if there are many
dull books, the dullest of them, as a later writer observes, *may become
potential Ophirs and Golcondas, if we are looking for something as we read*.[7] No
country is dull if the hunting is good. Voltaire, says Joubert, *would have
patiently read through thirty or forty folio volumes to find one small irreligious
joke*;[8] he would have enjoyed the task. Which explains Stevenson's
appetite, and allows me to proceed to my next point.

[1] *Hours in a Library*. iv, 185.   [2] *Letters*. ii, 299.   [3] *Ib*. 20.   [4] *Ib*. 95.   [5] Joubert,
Selected Thoughts. Trans. Lyttleton. 190.   [6] *Handling of Words*. 83.   [7] John Livingstone Lowes, *Of Reading Books*. 147.   [8] *Op. cit*. 177.

Montaigne found *Cicero* dull because he engaged in rhetoric for its own sake. Plutarch's '*Lives*' *were his Bible, as far as he had any Bible,*[1] in which preference he hath several companions, but I can find few among ancient bookmen who share his dislike for *Cicero*; yet it is unnecessary to proceed with examples of such preferences, for the unendurable in literature is relative; what is dull and what is bright in reading, as in so many other things, is according to taste; one likes this, another that. *This will never do!* exclaimed Jeffery when he opened Wordsworth's *Excursion,*[2] but Coventry Patmore thought that work *the greatest poem in our language, if not in any, not excepting that of the 'Divine Comedy'.*[3] So, in times present, those who revel in *Edgar Wallace* and *Elinor Glyn* wilt under *Ulysses* and *Pruefrock*; to the reader of *East Lynne, Point Counter Point* is unreadable; *Jude the Obscure* is dull to the devotees of *Far from the Madding Crowd*; to some *The Egoist* is obscure and to others *Anna Livia Plurabelle* is lucid; Dickensians and Proustians speak different languages; the generation which could not enjoy *Keats* and *Shelley* revelled in Zimmerman *On Solitude* and Dodderidge *On Death*; the *Proverbial Philosophy* was a bible in early Victorian parlours; *Festus* was popular when *Blake* was neglected; *Leaves of Grass* and *Bradshaw's Railway Guide*, wrongly approached, are equally unintelligible and uninteresting; many who like Bernard Shaw's *Plays* loathe his *Prefaces*; *Sitwells* and *Monros* do not mix; *Ezra Pounds* and *Richard Le Galliennes*, produced ever so far, do not meet. Macaulay[4] would walk for miles out of Cambridge to meet the coach bringing in the latest Waverley novel. *Waverley* itself made Scott's fortune and thousands of novel readers content; yet, Arnold Bennett[5] argues, *not one in a hundred could read it to-day*, and if he himself were asked to re-read it he would demand a fee of *fifty guineas for the feat*.

How the principles underlying this faculty of reading are distinguished and connected is (up to now) beyond human capacity to explain. Reasons in support of one side or the other do no more than buttress prejudices or idiosyncrasies. *The measure of choosing well is*, as Sir William Temple discovers in his essay '*Upon the Gardens of Epicurus*', *whether a man likes what he has chosen*. I shall hold on to that supposal, and end, therefore, with the most charitable advice I can give to my erring brethren (if such a charge can be brought against any of them): it is, to follow your whim, *gnaw your own bone*, as Thoreau enjoined, and let fancy decide, as Montaigne did: *I love no books*, he confessed, *but such as are pleasant and easie, and which tickle me, or such*, he added, *as comfort and counsell me, to direct my life and death*,[6]

[1] Edith Sichel, *Montaigne.* 58.   [2] *Edinburgh Review*, Nov. 1814.   [3] *Memoirs.* Champneys. ii, 98.   [4] Trevelyan, *Macaulay.* ii, 458.   [5] *Evening Standard*, 6.i.27.
[6] *Essays*. Ed. Seccombe. i, 311.

tacitum silvas inter reptare salubres
Curantem quidquid dignum sapiente bonoque est.[1]

Silently creeping midst the wholesome wood
With care what's for a wise man and a good.

And in his essay *Of Bookes*, he makes no pompous pose: *There is nothing I will trouble or vex myselfe about, no not for science it selfe, what esteem soever it be of. I do not search and tosse over Books, but for an honest recreation to please, and pastime to delight my selfe.* And if he studies, it is only to find out the knowledge of himself, or, as aforesaid, to instruct himself how *to die well, and how to live well.* The man of *robust and healthy intellect,* says Southey, *who gathers the harvest of literature into his barns, threshes the straw, winnows the grain, grinds it at his own mill, bakes it in his own oven, and then eats the true bread of knowledge,* is on the right track, and, *if he bake his loaf upon a cabbage leaf, and eat onions with his bread and cheese, let who will find fault with him for his taste—not I!*[2] In the last resort all proper bookmen are of his opinion, and they can exclaim out of *Horace,* with Archdeacon Wrangham, *stretching himself at length in his Elizabethan chair, in the midst of his Plantins and Elzevirs.*[3]

Sit bona librorum et provisae frugis in annum
Copia, neu fluitem dubiae spe pendulus horae.
Sed satis est orare Iovem, quae ponit et aufert,
Det vitam, det opes; aequum mi animum ipse parabo.[4]

V. BOOKS PREFERRED ABOVE ALL THINGS

Julius Scaliger[5] was so much affected with Poetry, that he declared he had rather be the author of twelve verses in *Lucan,* or such an ode (*Lib.* iii, *Ode* 9) in *Horace,* than Emperor of Germany, much as our General Wolfe exclaimed to his officers in the boat as they crossed the St. Lawrence River to the storming of the Heights, that he would sooner be the author of Gray's *Elegy* than take Quebec.[6] Nicholas Gerbelius is so much ravished with a few Greek authors, then recently restored to light, that he believes, *Arabibus atque Indis omnibus erimus ditiores,* we shall be richer than all the

[1] Horace, *I. Ep.* iv. 4.   [2] *Doctor.* xvii.   [3] Dibdin, *Reminiscences.* i, 394–5.
[4] *I. Ep.* xviii, 109–12. 'Let me have good store of books and assured food supply for the year, nor live in a flutter of doubtful hopes. 'Tis enough to pray to Jove for those things which he grants and takes away—the gift of life, of wealth: a contented mind I will get for myself.'   [5] Qt. Burton, *Anat. of Melan.* (1904) ii, 104.
[6] Timbs, *Anecdotes.* 309.

Arabian or Indian Princes; Seneca prefers *Zeno* and *Chrysippus,* two *doting Stoicks,* before any Prince or General of an Army; and Orontius the Mathematician so far admires *Archimedes,* that he calls him *divinum & homine majorem*; yet I say with Burton, I stand not upon this nor any praise likening authors to Gods or demi-Gods; the delight is what I aim at: the obvious great pleasure, the certain, sweet content. *When I was literally starving in London,* Gissing[1] confesses, *when it seemed impossible that I should ever gain a living by my pen, how many days have I spent at the British Museum, reading as disinterestedly as if I had been without a care!* *Quod cibus corpori, lectio animae facit,*[2] as meat to the body, so is reading to the soul.

Literature proved both an *entertainment* and a *consolation* to Pliny; there was no *pleasure* he would prefer to it.[3] and he *was glad to devote the leisure to literature* which others *throw away on idle employment.*[4] Pope would rather be employed in reading than in the most agreeable conversation;[5] Gibbon would not exchange his *invincible love of reading* for *the treasures of India.*[6] *When I open a noble volume,* Hamerton testifies,[7] *I say to myself, 'Now the only Croesus that I envy is he who is reading a better book than this'.* Some go so far as to acclaim books the superiors of life: *People say that life is the thing, but I prefer reading.*[8] To be at leisure without books is another Hell, and to be buried alive, but to be opportunely buried in books is Heaven:

I will bury myself in books, and the Devil may pipe to his own.[9]

King James, in 1605, when he came to our University of Oxford, and, amongst other edifices, went to view that famous Library, renewed by Sir Thomas Bodley, at his departure said, *If I were not a King, I would be an university man; and if it were so that I must be a prisoner, if I might have my wish, I would desire to have no other prison than that Library, and to be chained together with so many good authors et mortuis magistris.*[10] Heinsius, the keeper of the Library at Leyden, in Holland, was mewed up in it all the year long, and that which should have bred a loathing caused in him a great liking: *I no sooner* (saith he) *come into the Library, but I bolt the door to me, excluding lust, ambition, avarice, and all such vices, whose nurse is idleness, the mother of ignorance, and Melancholy herself, and il the very lap of eternity, amongst so many divine souls, I take my seat, with so lofty a spirit and sweet content, that I pity all our great ones, and rich men that know not this happiness.*[11] So do great readers rise to great heights: pitying rich and powerful men, seeing

---

[1] *Private Papers of Henry Ryecroft.* 45.   [2] Seneca.   [3] *Letters.* Melmoth. Loeb Ed. viii, 19.   [4] 'Per hos dies libentissime otium meum in litteris colloco quos alii otiosissimis occupationibus perdunt.' *Letters.* Melmoth. Loeb Ed. ix, 6.   [5] Spence, *Anecdotes.* (1858) 208.   [6] *Memoirs.* Ed. Hill. 38.   [7] *Intellectual Life.* 192.   [8] Logan Pearsall Smith, 'Afterthoughts', *Life and Letters.* Aug. 1930.   [9] *Maud.* Tennyson.   [10] Qt. Burton. *Anat. of Melan.* (1904) ii, 105.   [11] *Ib.*

nothing in them but poverty and lack of happiness. *Of all the human relaxations which are free from guilt*, exclaims that capacious reader, Sir Egerton Brydges,[1] *none so dignified as reading.*

Nothing so precious, for such as are *fracti animis*, troubled in mind, to ease them, over-toiled on the one part, to refresh: over-idle on the other, to keep themselves busied. How many of the masters of the world have solaced their leisure with books! *Among the great men of action, we recall Frederick's love of letters and Napoleon's travelling library; among statesmen we think of Pitt's sofa with its shelf of thumbed classics; and of Fox, a far more ardent lover of books, exchanging them and his garden for the House of Commons almost with tears; and of Gladstone's Temple of Peace.*[2] Books were Napoleon's solace throughout life; in his subaltern days he sacrificed all thought of luxuries so that he could buy books. To avoid comment from his brother officers, he tells Caulaincourt,[3] *I lived alone like a hermit, in a little room with my books—then my only friends. What strict economy it required even in the necessaries of life before I could allow myself the pleasure of purchasing them! When I had managed to save up two crowns by dint of stern self-denial, I wended my way to the bookseller's as pleased as a child, and I examined his shelves long and anxiously before my purse would allow me to gratify my desires.* Among the books he read at this time—*pen in hand*, saith Fournier, *and making copious notes*—were Duvernet's *History of the Sorbonne*, William Cox's *Travels in Switzerland*, Dulaure's *History of the Nobility*, Le Noble's *Esprit Gersons*, Machiavelli's *Florentine History*, Meissner's *Alcibiades*, Duclos's *Government of Louis XIV and XV*, Bernardin de St. Pierre's *Indian Tales*, Marmontel's *Incas*, Ariosto's *Orlando Furioso*, and Voltaire's *Essai sur les mœurs et l'esprit des nations.*

Of statesmen who have stored their minds and consoled their leisure with books, Lord Rosebery[4] has several examples. Harley was a collector rather than a reader, a bibliomane perchance; Bolingbroke claimed to be a book-lover, and spent his exile in the study of history; Stanhope, Sunderland, and Grenville formed great libraries; Canning was a bookman; Melbourne a great reader, though he only left behind him *a library of odd volumes*; Peel, *a brilliant specimen of Oxford scholarship*; Disraeli, who was cradled among books, was more bookish than Gladstone *in early, and less in later life*; Salisbury was a bookman from early days. *When I was a child*, Lord Rosebery recounts, *I was taken to see Hatfield. In the library we saw a tall thin figure carrying a huge volume. The housekeeper paused, saying with awe, 'That is Lord Robert Cecil'.* That bookish figure afterwards became Lord Salisbury and Prime Minister. I can complete Lord Rosebery's tale out of common knowledge, by naming himself as a bookman, among

---

[1] *The Ruminator.* No. 24.   [2] Lord Rosebery, *Appreciations and Addresses.* 168.
[3] Qt. Fournier. i, 33, out of *Coston.* i, 189.   [4] *Appreciations and Addresses.* 152–7.

succeeding Prime Ministers, together with Lord Balfour, Lord Oxford and Mr. Baldwin. Benito Mussolini finds little time for reading in his busy days, but such as he does find he devotes to serious books. *Novels are seldom included,* he confesses, but he enjoys *reading again and again the classics, philosophy, and books on economics or philosophy.*[1]

Well may Cardan call a Library the Physick of the soul; *for divine authors fortify the mind, make men bold and constant; and* (as Hyperius adds) *godly conference will not permit the mind to be tortured with absurd cogitations.*[2] All this variety of sense is intended by the fancy of that responsible witness, Francis Bacon,[3] where he proclaims that, *Reading maketh a full man; Conference a ready man; and Writing an exact man;* so *if a man Write little, he had need have a great memory; if he Confer little, he need have a present wit; and if he Read little, he had need have much cunning to seem to know that he doth not. Histories make men wise, Poets witty, the Mathematicks subtil, Natural Philosophy deep, Moral grave, Logick and Rhetorick, able to contend. Abeunt studia in Mores; Nay there is no Stand or Impediment in the wit, but may be wrought out by fit Studies.* But whether for study or dalliance there is no difference: books command their lovers, and when they tell over to themselves tales of what they have read, it is as sweet music. In pursuance of this truth, Izaak Walton records of Bishop Sanderson[4] that the repetition of one of the *Odes of Horace* to himself *was to him such music, as a Lesson on the Viol was to others, when they played it to themselves or friends.*

VI. THE GENESIS OF BOOKMEN

The claims of education, as a cause of bookishness, may justly be challenged; even the accidental presence of books in small or great numbers is no inducement except when opportunity and inclination coincide. Bookishness arises mysteriously out of the hidden consciousness, from some unknown predisposition which our psychologists have not yet explained. Nor shall I adventure in those uncertain realms; rushing in where Angels fear to tread is not my humour: I risk no such abandonment. This treatise is reasonably developed from example and precedent to inference and conclusion; yet I am well aware that this matter of early reading is germane to my purpose, for the child is father of the man, and it is no fault of mine if the argument ends in the paradox that one man's meat is another's poison,

What porridge had John Keats?[5]

---

[1] *Daily Express.* 17.i.27.   [2] Qt. Burton. *Anat. of Melan.* (1904) ii, 107–8.   [3] *Essays.* 'Of Studies.'   [4] *Life of Dr. Sanderson.*   [5] Browning.

We cannot answer, nor can we answer what porridge makes great readers.

This much, however, I can say and shall prove, namely, that they begin young and not necessarily with children's books; nor yet are they attracted by those religious works which have consoled so many grown men and women. Doubtless the young, like so many of their elders, have an inclination against books which they ought to read, and it perchance was in irony that Henry Fielding[1] made young Joseph Andrews a devoted reader of the *Bible*, the *Whole Duty of Man*, *Thomas à Kempis*, and *as often as he could, without being perceived*, that *great book which lay open in the hall window*, wherein he learnt *how the devil had carried away half a church in sermon-time, without hurting one of the congregation; and how a field of corn run down a hill, with all the trees upon it, and covered another man's meadow*; which sufficiently assured Parson Adams that the good book meant could be no other than Baker's *Chronicle*.

Not all readers remember how they came to read, for reading is learnt rather than taught, and the ease with which so many acquire it proves it one of mankind's most natural endowments. Men must be reading. Before books were they read the stars, the winds, movements of birds and beasts; beginning early, moved by instinct as much as or even more than by brain. So with books. There are many examples of early bookish instincts, but I will only point at some of the chiefest, as that of Hsiao Tsung, eldest son of the founder of the Liang dynasty in China, who is reported to have learnt the *Classics by heart* before he was five years old.[2] But for notable examples we need not wander beyond our own frontiers, or times present.

Take then, as a first instance, the extraordinary example of John Stuart Mill,[3] who must have read books in his cradle, for he began to learn Greek at three years old: Aesop's *Fables* his first book and the *Anabasis* his second. He had no Latin until he had reached the advanced age of eight, and by that time he had been through the whole of *Herodotus*, Xenophon's *Cyropaedia* and *Memorials of Socrates*, some of the lives of the philosophers by Diogenes Laertius, part of *Lucian*, the *Iliad*, *Isocrates ad Demonicum* and *Ad Nicoclem*, the *first six dialogues (in the common arrangement) of Plato, from the Euthyphron to the Theaetetus inclusive*, but, he doubts not, the last *would have been better omitted, as it was totally impossible I should understand it*. Between the ages of four years and seven he would take daily walks with his father *before breakfast, generally in the green lanes towards Hornsey*, and with his earliest recollections of *green fields and wild flowers, is mingled that of the account* he gave his father of what he had read the day before; and to the best of his remembrance this was *a voluntary rather than a prescribed*

---

[1] *Joseph Andrews*. iii.   [2] Giles, *Chinese Biog. Dict.* 283.   [3] *Autobiography*. Passim.

exercise; he made notes on *slips of paper* while reading and took up his tale from them. The books thus read and discussed were *chiefly histories*, of which he had absorbed *in this manner a great number: Robertson, Hume, Gibbon*, and *Burnet*, among them; but his greatest delight was Watson's *Philip II and III. The heroic defence of the Knights of Malta against the Turks, and of the revolted Provinces of the Netherlands against Spain, excited in him an intense and lasting interest.* Next to *Watson* his favourite was Hooke's *History of Rome*; of Greek history he had up to then little knowledge save of *school abridgements* and *Rollin*; but he read with *great delight* Langhorne's *Plutarch*; that he was still young is evident in some measure from his confession that in *Burnet* his main interest was *wars and battles.* His father borrowed from Mr. Bentham copies of the *Annual Register* from the beginning to about 1788, and the young scholar felt a lively interest in Frederick of Prussia and Paoli of Corsica, but his tender years asserted themselves again, for he gives out that when he came to the American war, *I took my part, like a child as I was (until set right by my father) on the wrong side, because it was called the English side.*

His father also made him read books which might not have interested him otherwise, as Millar's *Historical View of the English Government*, Mosheim's *Ecclesiastical History*, McCrie's *John Knox*, and *even* Sewell and Rutty's *Histories of the Quakers.* He was also encouraged to read *books which exhibited men of energy and resource in unusual circumstances*, as Beaver's *African Memoranda*, Collins's *New South Wales*, and he never wearied of *Anson's* and *Hawkesworth's Voyages*; but of *children's books, any more than of playthings*, he had *scarcely any*, except *an occasional gift* from a relative or acquaintance, notable among them, *Robinson Crusoe*, which delighted him throughout his boyhood. It was no part of his *father's system to exclude books of amusement*, so long as they were used *sparingly*; and owning none himself, he borrowed, and the boy thus came to possess happy memories of the *Arabian Nights*, Gazotte's *Arabian Tales*, *Don Quixote*, Miss Edgeworth's *Popular Tales*, and Brooke's *Fool of Quality*; and so he goes on, but, for further details, read him.

Many instances could be cited in support of the argument that great readers start early: *Even from my infancie*, says Montaigne, *Poesie hath had the vertue to transpierce and transport me*;[1] and sometimes so early that they forget the time. Abraham Cowley, a notable prodigy of book-love, confessed[2] that, when a very young boy at school, *instead of running about on Holy-daies* and playing with his fellows, he was wont to steal away from them, *and walk into the fields*, either *alone with a Book, or with some one companion*, if he could find one *of the same temper.* Very early he became acquainted with the poets, so that their *characters* were *engraved* in him,

[1] 'Of Cato the Younger', *Essays*. Ed. Seccombe. i, 292.   [2] *Essays*. 'Of Myself.'

like *Letters cut into the Bark of a young tree*; but he cannot tell how this love came to be produced in him so early. In the meantime he recalls the *particular little chance* that filled his head with the *Chimes of Verse*. When he began to read, and to take some pleasure in it, there was wont to lie in his Mother's Parlour (*I know not by what accident*, he says, *for she herself never in her life read any Book but of Devotion*) a copy of Spenser's *Works*. He happened to fall upon the book, and was first *infinitely delighted* with the stories of Knights, Giants, Monsters, etc., and later *by degrees with the tinkling of the Rhyme and the Dance of the Numbers, so that*, he concludes, *I think I had read him all over before I was twelve years old.*

William Morris must have been able to read as an infant: for neither he nor any member of his family knew exactly when he learnt; at four he was deep in the *Waverley Novels* and at seven he had devoured *Scott*, most of *Marryat*, and Lane's *Arabian Nights*.[1] So also his contemporary William Allingham who says, *I could read fluently at a very early age, and I remember nothing of being taught.*[2] Andrew Lang was a *bookworm from babyhood, almost.*[3] Edmund Gosse was slow in learning to speak, and he was told that, having resisted all attempts to make him say *papa* and *mama*, he one day caught hold of a volume and said *book* with *startling distinctness*; he learned to read at four, and could not recall a time when *a printed page of English was closed* to him;[4] but it was not until his eighth year that he was initiated into *the magic of literature*. This experience came whilst his father was reading the *Bible* to him. *I was incapable of defining what I felt*, he says, *but I certainly had a grip in the throat, which was in its essence a purely aesthetic emotion.*[5] The magic casement of poetry was opened by Virgil some few years later. One evening his father took down *Virgil*, and began to murmur, oblivious of the lad's presence, some of *the adorable verses by memory*

tu, Tityre, lentus in umbra
Formosam resonare doces Amaryllida silvas.[6]

The boy *listened as if to a nightingale*. The lines meant nothing to him, *but a miracle had been revealed to* him, *the incalculable, the amazing beauty which could exist in the sound of verses*. His prosodical instinct *was awakened on that instant: Verse, 'a breeze mid blossoms playing', as Coleridge says, descended from the roses as a moth might have done, and the magic of it took hold of his heart for ever.*[7]

Henry Bradshaw could read at the age of three or four years, and when still a boy at Eton, he was already *a lover of books* with a library of five hundred which included works *not often found in a boy's library, such* as the *Officium Beatae Mariae* (Antwerp, 1564), a *Bede* printed at Cologne in

[1] *Morris.* Jackson. 11.　[2] *Diary.* 13.　[3] Intro., *Pleasures of Bookland*, Shaylor. xviii.
[4] Gosse, *Father and Son.* (1909) 19.　[5] *Ib.* 89.　[6] *Eclogues.* i, 5.　[7] *Ib.* 168–9.

1501, and the *Odes* of Horace (Amsterdam, 1686). At the age of fourteen he remembered going to Durham and being locked in Bishop Cosin's library in that city, where he worked all day at *Strabo* or any books he could find on the geography of the Crimea.[1] He spent the greater part of his playtime at Eton in the Hawtrey's Library, *one of the most delightful reading-rooms in the world*. Bibliography and philology already interested him and he explored *Dibdin* and *Ducange*; he worked at divinity too, filling the margins of his *Bible* with careful references. But his chief study was our English literature, and in one year he read through all the standard poets, including the whole of *Spenser* and *Chaucer*, finding time also for some of the moderns, particularly *Tennyson*.[2]

Harriet Martineau knew *Paradise Lost* almost by heart at the age of seven;[3] Swift *could read any chapter of the Bible before he was three;*[4] Maurice Hewlett read the *Faerie Queene* when nine years old;[5] Walter Scott would pore over *Shakespeare* in his shirt by the fire at night after his parents had left him in bed;[6] Lord Byron read perpetually from the age of five, and the *moment he could read* his *grand passion was history;*[7] Thackeray when young revelled in *Scott*, recalling joyously in after life *the type and the brownish paper of the old duodecimo 'Tales of My Landlord'*, and he longed for the old joy of a half-holiday, a quiet corner and *those books again*; [8]Samuel Rogers had read enthusiastically *The Minstrel* of Beattie at the age of eight; when he was twelve, Gray's *Poems* and *Letters* captivated him, and a few years later he *walked to business* with a volume of Gray's poems in his hand, and he could repeat them all;[9] Coventry Patmore had read and studied *critically, all the standard poetry and much of the best secular prose in our language.*[10] before the age of fifteen; and *Waller, Spenser*, and *Dryden, were Mr. Pope's great favourites, in the order they are named, in his first reading till he was about twelve years old.*[11]

Alexander Ireland, the compiler of the *Book Lover's Enchiridion*, tells us that when a boy he was so delighted with the *Natural History of Selborne*, that *in order to possess a copy of his own he actually copied out the whole work.*[12] Charles Dickens has recounted in *David Copperfield* how books consoled and upheld him during his neglected boyhood; how *Roderick Random, Peregrine Pickle, Humphrey Clinker, Tom Jones, the Vicar of Wakefield, Don Quixote, Gil Blas, Robinson Crusoe, the Arabian Nights and Tales of the Genii, a glorious host, kept him company, kept alive his fancy and his hope, beyond that time and place*. Goethe was interested in books from early child-

---

[1] Prothero, *Memoir*. 9–10.   [2] *Ib*. 13–14.   [3] *Autobiography*. 1, 42.   [4] *Swift*. Leslie Stephen, 3.   [5] *Extemporary Essays*. 118.   [6] *Life*. Lockhart. i, 49.   [7] *The Ravenna Journal*. 29, 82.   [8] *Roundabout Papers*.   [9] Clayden, *Early Life of Samuel Rogers*. 57–8.   [10] *Memoirs*. Champneys. ii, 43.   [11] Spence, *Anecdotes*. (1858) 6.   [12] Lubbock, *Pleasures of Life*. i, 60.

hood, and when he passed out of the age of picture-books he discovered Ovid's *Metamorphoses*, the first parts of which he *studied carefully*; but these *somewhat coarse and questionable antiquities* were replaced by Fénelon's *Télémaque; Robinson Crusoe* was *added betimes*, and then the *Island of Felsenberg* and Anson's *Voyage Round the World*; he has enthusiastic memories of how he and his brothers and sisters revelled in the *Volksbücher*, or, as we say, *Chap-books, precious survivals from the Middle Ages*; they were printed from *stereotypes* on *hideous absorbent paper* and *barely legible*, but these were advantages, for when they had read, *worn out, or otherwise damaged* the *Eulenspiegel, Fair Melusina*, the *Wandering Jew*, and the rest, they could easily procure more and renew a feast which they preferred to sweetmeats.[1]

Wordsworth as a child was an omnivorous reader, devouring such books as *Tom Jones, Don Quixote, Gil Blas, Gulliver's Travels* and *The Tale of a Tub*;[2] and between nine and ten years of age he first tasted the flavour of poetry:

> Twice five years
> Or less I might have seen, when first my mind
> With conscious pleasure opened to the charm
> Of words in tuneful order, found them sweet
> For their own sakes, a passion, and a power;
> And phrases pleased me chosen for delight,
> For pomp, or love.[3]

At six years old, Frederick W. Myers read *Virgil* with the help of an interlinear translation given him by his father;[4] he never forgot the experience; the scene was stamped on his mind: *the ante-room at the Parsonage with its floor of bright matting, and its glass door into the garden, through which the flooding sunlight came, while I pored over the new revelation with awe-struck joy*;

> Musa, mihi causas memora, quo numine laeso—[5]

this *early burst of admiration for Virgil* was followed by a *growing passion for one after another of the Greek and Latin poets*; from ten to sixteen he *lived much in the inward recital of Homer, Aeschylus, Lucretius, Horace and Ovid*; the reading of Plato's *Gorgias* at fourteen was a *great event*, but the study of Plato's *Phaedo* at sixteen effected upon him *a kind of conversion*; the discovery of *Sappho*, at seventeen, *brought an access of intoxicating joy*; but he always returned to *Virgil*, of whose mind he ever was *the most intimate and adoring disciple*.[6]

---

[1] *Poetry and Truth* (Dichtung und Wahrheit). Trans. M. S. Smith. i, 23–5.
[2] *Memoirs of Wordsworth*, by Christopher Wordsworth. (1857) i, 10.   [3] *Prelude*.
v, 552–8.   [4] Myers, *Fragments of Prose and Poetry*. 6.   [5] Virgil, *Aen.* i, 8.   [6] Myers, *Fragments of Prose and Poetry*. 17–18.

At the age of seven Francis Thompson *was reading poetry, and, over-whelmed by feelings of which he knew not the meaning, had found his way to the heart of Shakespeare and Coleridge;*[1] at the age of nine Stanley Baldwin had read Malory's *Morte d'Arthur* and knew *Peter Simple* and *Midshipman Easy* by heart;[2] Eugene Field coveted the books in his grandmother's case when he was seven, *and*, he says, *I had learned to read I know not when*, but at that age he was familiar not only with the *Hymns* of Watts and Wesley, but with the *Annual Reports* of the American Tract Society.[3] John Addington Symonds read and was deeply moved by Shakespeare's *Venus and Adonis* at the age of ten;[4] from the time he was three years old Macaulay read incessantly at all times and places, becoming, perhaps, the world's greatest reader; as a child he loved to read lying on the rug before the fire, his book on the rug, and a piece of bread and butter in his hand; *a very clever woman who then lived in the house* [at Clapham] *tells how he used to sit in his nankeen frock, perched on the table by her as she was cleaning the plate, and expounding to her out of a volume as big as himself.* Books were his toys, and when taking a walk he loved to expound to mother or nurse, in language far above his years, what he had been reading.[5] John Ruskin, on the other hand, like John Stuart Mill, was trained to books by his parents; they read to him and he to them. His mother trained him in the Bible: chapter by chapter of every book, year by year; and his father read to him *Shake-speare, Scott, Don Quixote, Pope*, and *Byron*, and most English classics; and *at five he was a bookworm.*[6]

Leigh Hunt[7] was a reader at an early age, but he disliked the *Classics*, had no regard for *Ovid*, knew nothing of *Horace*, regarded *Homer* with *horror*, but was inclined to admire *Demosthenes*. His real loves were the *Arabian Nights*, the *Canterbury Tales*, *Paradise Lost* and *Rasselas*; like Cow-ley, he preferred the company of books to that of his schoolfellows, and even his games were literary: *I drew my sports as much as possible out of books, playing at Trojan wars, chivalrous encounters with coal-staves, and even at religious mysteries.*[8] Sydney Smith was discovered by *a man of considerable eminence, reading Virgil under a tree, when all his schoolfellows were at play: 'clever boy! clever boy!'* said his eminence, giving the lad a shilling, *'that is how to conquer the world.'*[9] Shelley also preferred books to games; although at Eton he *neglected the rules of school-attendance, he translated half of Pliny's 'Natural History' into English*, and he adventured enthusiastically into the literature of *magic* and *witchcraft*.[10] Coleridge took little pleasure in boyish

[1] Everard Meynell, *Francis Thompson*. 6.   [2] 'Books', *Our Inheritance*. 288–92.
[3] *Love Affairs of a Bibliomaniac*. 7.   [4] *Biography*. H. F. Brown. 10.   [5] *Life and Letters*. Trevelyan. i, 39.   [6] *Encyclopædia Britannica*. Eleventh Ed. xxiii, 858.
[7] *Leigh Hunt*. Monkhouse. 35.   [8] 'My Books', *Essays*.   [9] *Memoir*. Holland. i, 8.
[10] *Life*. Hogg. London Lib. Ed. 33–5.

games when at school, *but read incessantly*. His aunt kept a small shop at Crediton, and there he read through the stock of *gilt-covered little books, and likewise all the uncovered tales of Tom Hickathrift, Jack the Giant-Killer, etc.*; at the age of six he had read *Belisarius, Robinson Crusoe*, and *Philip Quarles*, and then he found the *Arabian Nights*, one tale of which (*that of a man who was compelled to seek for a pure virgin*) caused him to be so haunted with spectres whenever he was alone in the dark, that his father took the book and burnt it.[1]

Dr. Johnson could read at three: *when he was a child in petticoats*, his mother put the book of *Common Prayer* into his hands, and, pointing to the Collect for the day said: *Sam, you must get this by heart*. She then went upstairs, leaving him to study it, but before she had reached the second floor Sam followed her and *repeated it distinctly, though he could not have read it more than twice*.[2] He read so *very hard* in his youth that he claimed to have known as much at eighteen as he did at fifty-four. *As soon as the use of speech had prepared my infant reason for the admission of knowledge*, saith Gibbon, *I was taught the arts of reading, writing and arithmetic. So remote is the date, so vague is the memory of their origin in myself, that, were not the error corrected by analogy, I should be tempted to conceive them as innate*;[3] between the ages of nine and eleven he had mastered Pope's *Homer*, Dryden's *Virgil*, and Ovid's *Metamorphoses*, deriving more pleasure from this last than from the others, *especially in the fall of Phaethon, and the speeches of Ajax and Ulysses*.[4] Like him, Montaigne also was early impressed by Ovid: *The first taste or feeling I had of bookes, was of the pleasure I tooke in reading the fables of Ovid's 'Metamorphoses': for, being but seven or eight years old, I would steale and sequester myselfe from all other delights, only to reade them.*[5] Petrarch could enjoy the music of prose long before he could understand its meaning, when older boys were *yawning over Prosper and Aesop*, he says,[6] *I applied myself to the books of Cicero. I could understand nothing; simply the sweetness and harmony of the language enchained me, so that whatever else I heard or read sounded to me harsh and even discordant.*

Kinglake tells in *Eothen* how his mother taught him in earliest childhood *to find a home in his saddle, and to love old Homer, and all that Homer sung*. He pored over the *Odyssey* as over a story-book, but the *Iliad, line by line*, he *clasped to his brain with reverence as well as with love*. He was told by the writer of the *Preface* in the *towering folio* that *the works of men's hands were folly and vanity, and would pass away like the dreams of a child, but that the kingdom of Homer would endure for ever and ever*. He assented with all his soul: *I read, and still read; I came to know Homer.*[7] When but eleven years old that sturdy reformer, William Cobbett, attracted by the title of *The Tale*

---

[1] *Letters*. Ed. E. H. Coleridge. i, 11–12.   [2] Boswell, *Life*. Ed. Hill. i, 40.
[3] *Memoirs*. Hill. 31.   [4] *Ib*. 38–9.   [5] *Essays*. Ed. Seccombe. i, 217.   [6] Qt. *Francesco Petrarca*. Tatham. i, 96.   [7] *Eothen*. iv.

of a Tub, displayed in a shop window at Richmond, bought it in place of his supper for threepence, his whole fortune: *so impatient was I to examine it*, he tells, *that I got over into a field at the upper corner of Kew Gardens, and sat down to read, on the shady side of a haystack . . . I read on till it was dark without any thought of supper or bed. When I could see no longer, I put it into my pocket, and fell asleep beside the stack, till the birds awakened me in the morning; and then I started off: still reading my little book. I could relish nothing beside; I carried it about with me wherever I went, till, when about twenty years old, I lost it in a box that fell overboard in the Bay of Fundy.*[1]

Herbert Spencer was prompted to read by *Sandford and Merton*, but he learned to read late in boyhood;[2] so also Mark Pattison, who consistently forgot what he read until his youth was ended; his early passion was for natural history, and *Gilbert White* his favourite; but by the time he entered Oxford at nineteen he *had read Sallust through, about a dozen speeches of Cicero, twenty books of Livy, Virgil through, Horace through, Juvenal through, Persius through, Caesar through, Terence through: in Greek, the Gospels and Acts, Xenophon's 'Anabasis', Herodotus, Thucydides, some six or seven Orations of Demosthenes, Homer's 'Iliad', Pindar, Sophocles, Aeschylus, Porson's four plays of Euripides, seven plays of Aristophanes—all these*, he says, *not in scraps, but through.*[3] *Don Quixote* was the first book read by Heinrich Heine when he was only *in some measure acquainted with the alphabet*;[4] there is no record of early or unusual reading on the part of Tolstoy, but up to the age of fourteen he had been *influenced* by the story of *Joseph* from the *Bible*, the 'Forty Thieves' and 'Prince Kamaralzaman' from the *Arabian Nights*, Poushkin's *Tales* and his poem *Napoleon*, and Pogorelsky's *Black Hen*.[5] Benjamin Disraeli, who claimed to have been *born in a library*, was an early and swift reader; when he had a new book at school, he shared it with his friend, Jones, and they read together; but Jones was still in the middle of the page when Ben had run through it. He had read so much and heard so much talk of books from his father, that no difficulties held him up. Little Jones would sigh at this, says Maurois, and guessing his distress, Benjamin smiled and said with great kindness: *I can wait*.[6] When Napoleon had forced Blucher to retreat near Briauncy, he recognized a tree near by under which he had sat as a boy of twelve reading *Tasso*.[7] I could continue these instances *ad infinitum* almost, but since it is necessary to stop somewhere, lest we should run to infinity, it is best to stop where, as in this instance, the theme is sufficiently expounded, and the contention which I began with, namely, that great readers show by the early symptoms of their capacity, that they are born not made, is proved.

[1] Qt. *Book-Lovers' Anthology*. 184.   [2] *Autobiography*. i, 77.   [3] *Memoirs*. 62.
[4] *Memoirs*. Ed. Karpeles. i, 58.   [5] *Life*. Maude. i, 31.   [6] *Disraeli*. ii, 10.
[7] Ludwig, *Napoleon*. 457.

VII. READERS WHO NEVER WEARY

Every historian of bookmen has examples of tireless readers, and in this section I will briefly speak of some which may be worthily reckoned amongst those already given in my preceding chapters. Benjamin Robert Haydon *read seventeen hours a day at 'Clarissa'*;[1] John Addington Symonds, in a brief space, consumed 20,000 *odd lines of golden Ariosto, Tasso, Dante, Tassoni, and more modern singers*;[2] Samuel Johnson read in Boswell's *Journal* of their *Tour in the Hebrides* and wished it twice as long;[3] John Keats found Charles Wentworth Dilke *up to his ears in Walpole's letters*;[4] Henry Crabb Robinson[5] acclaims Carlyle's French Revolution: *a history in flashes of lightning*, to be taken only in small doses and not too frequently, a book to buy, to muse over and spell, rather than to be read through; which bears out what Thomas Carlyle himself records of a Rev. Alexander Scott who had *read the French Revolution over four times, every word of it!*[6] Lord Chesterfield implores his son to *read frequently, with the utmost attention, nay get by heart* that incomparable chapter in Cicero's *Offices* upon *Decorum*;[7] the Duke of Wellington, according to Benjamin Disraeli,[8] never reads anything but the *Commentaries* of Caesar; and a hundred years earlier Thomas Hearne,[9] Bodley's librarian, laments that *nothing is now hardly read but Burnet's romance or libel, call'd, 'The History of his Own Times'. 'Tis read by men, women and children. Indeed it is the common table-book for ladies as well as gentlemen, such as are friends to the revolution scheme.*

Most agree that books worth reading are worth reading more than once: *Repetitio est mater studiorum. Any book that is at all important*, says Schopenhauer, *ought to be at once read through twice*; partly because on a second reading the connection of its parts will be better understood, and *partly because we are not in the same temper and disposition on both readings.*[10] *Every good book*, says another,[11] *is worth reading three times at least*, and Benjamin Jowett held that all sensible persons were in the habit of reading *Pickwick Papers* at least twice a year. There is record also of a society *for which a twenty-fifth reading of 'Esmond' was the necessary qualification of membership.*[12] Gibbon when a young man was a tireless reader of a great variety of books; he *indulged himself in a second and even a third perusal of Terence, Virgil, Horace, Tacitus*, etc., and later in life he read the *Provincial Letters* of Pascal *almost every year with new pleasure.*[13] Ford Madox Brown gave Anne

[1] *Autobiography*. i, 223.   [2] *Biography*. H. F. Brown. 268.   [3] Boswell, *Life*. Ed. Hill. v, 307.   [4] *Letters*. Ed. Forman. (1895) 258.   [5] *Diary*. ii, 216.   [6] *New Letters*. i, 109.   [7] Scoones, *Four Centuries of English Letters*. 224.   [8] *Correspondence with his Sister*. 27.   [9] *Remains*. Bliss. iii, 125.   [10] *Art of Literature*. Trans. Saunders. 83.   [11] Charles Bray. Qt. *In Praise of Books*. Swan. 13.   [12] *The Times*. 27.xii.1928.   [13] *Memoirs*. Hill. 93, 97.

Gilchrist a copy of Walt Whitman's *Leaves of Grass* and she told W. M. Rossetti (the editor of the volume) that she could read no other book: *it holds me entirely spellbound, and I go through it again and again with deepening delight and wonder.*[1] Madame de Maintenon asks Mdlle. de L'Enclos to send her compliments to M. de la Rochefoucauld, and to tell him that the Book of *Job* and the Book of *Maxims* are the only things she ever reads;[2] Madame de Sévigné read *Corneille* again and again;[3] the Prince Regent was one of the earliest admirers of Jane Austen's novels, *he read them often, and kept a set in evry one of his residences;*[4] Miss Collier and other friends of Samuel Richardson were so enamoured of that author's novels that they despised all others, and she herself read *Clarissa* four times, once aloud to her parents.[5]

Macaulay was never tired of *Gil Blas*,[6] and Birkbeck Hill wished neither it nor *Robinson Crusoe* would ever come to an end; he did not know how many times he had read *Gil Blas* and *always with delight,*[7] and when *Maud* was first published it was always with him: *either in my hand or pocket or by me at night;*[8] Anthony Trollope wonders *how many dozen times* he had read *The Prairie* by Fenimore Cooper;[9] Edward FitzGerald read his old favourites *over and over again,*[10] and he was inseparable from *Don Quixote* and the works of George Crabbe, whom he cut and concentrated in choice excerpts for the delectation of himself and his friends; *I have been reading slowly Don Quixote,* so Dr. John Brown in a letter to Coventry Dick,[11] *I don't think that I ever enjoyed anything more; do read it and write me four sonnets upon it;* Lord Rosebery knew Jane Austen *by heart,* and *he read all Scott's novels every year;*[12] Henry Jackson could not remember how many times he had read the tales of Gaboriau, and he read the *Meno* of Plato thrice, the *Euthyphro* five times, and the *Laches* more times than he could say, in fifteen years.[13]

Oscar Wilde called Pater's *Studies in the History of the Renaissance* his *Golden Book; I never travel anywhere without it,* he said;[14] William Cory never wearied of *Jane Eyre* and he records[15] that he read it *straight through at a sitting* on two occasions, once in his *home drawing-room* and again on the rocks at Bude; R. L. Stevenson complained that he could not get enough *Sagas,* he wished *there were nine thousand* of them;[16] he read '*Boswell*' daily *by way of a Bible; I mean to read 'Boswell' now,* he said, *until the day I die;*[17]

[1] A. Gilchrist, *Life and Writings.* 177.   [2] *Letters of Mme de Maintenon, etc.* Eng. Ed. (1753) 27.   [3] *Letters.* i, 158.   [4] *Memoir of Jane Austen.* Austen-Leigh. 118.   [5] Barbauld, *Correspondence of Richardson.* ii, 89.   [6] *Life and Letters.* Trevelyan. ii, 44.   [7] G. B. Hill, *Letters.* 256–7.   [8] *Ib.* 58.   [9] *Autobiography.* World's Classics. 14.   [10] *Letters and Literary Remains.* i, 130.   [11] *Letters.* Nelson Ed. 108.   [12] An Old Friend, *Sunday Times.* 26.v.1929.   [13] *Henry Jackson, O.M., A Memoir.* Parry. 173–95.   [14] W. B. Yeats, *The Trembling of the Veil.* 20.   [15] *Letters and Journals.* 188.   [16] *Letters.* ii, 255.   [17] *Ib.* i, 116.

and we have it on the authority of John Chamberlain, that when Lord Chancellor Bacon sent his *Instauratio Magna* to King James I, *he wisht his majestie might be as long in reading it as he hath been in compiling it*, which was well near thirteen years;[1] James Boswell records[2] that *the learned Cunninghame*, critic upon Horace, *read Homer and Ariosto through every year*; W. C. Hazlitt never *waxed tired* of *conning over* Bayle St. John's *Montaigne the Essayist*, Thoreau's *Walden*, Howell's *Venetian Life* or *Italian Journeys. Cuique suum*: there are those, he says,[3] *who never let the sun set without dipping into Burton's 'Anatomy of Melancholy', or who have some pet volume with which they renew their intimacy every year, as Francis Douce did with 'Reynard the Fox'*.

Isaac D'Israeli gives out of *Maurice*, that Sir William Jones *invariably read through every year the works of Cicero*, and that *the famous Bourdaloue reperused* every year, not only *Cicero*, but *St. Paul* and *St. Chrysostom* as well; if, Burton comments, Bourdaloue began at the age of twenty-two and continued until his death, fifty years later, *he must have done it over fifty times: the tortures of the classic Hades, and the disgusting inflictions courted by the anchorites of old, and the Brahmins of later times*, saith mine author, *do not approach the horrors of such an act of self-torture;*[4] but he speaks for himself, the good Bourdaloue doubtless enjoyed his task, even if it was a penance. Lord Chatham read his folio *Bailey's Dictionary* twice;[5] Robert Louis Stevenson read *The Egoist* five or six times and meant to read it again;[6] Samuel Rogers read Marivaux's *Vie de Marianne* through six times;[7] and Edward FitzGerald read *Clarissa Harlowe* for the fifth time at the age of fifty-four.[8]

Coleridge argued[9] that there were few books which might be read *repeatedly at different times*, but among them he upheld the *Pilgrim's Progress*, which he read many times, *each time with a new different pleasure*: once as a *theologian*, once with *devotional feelings*, and once as a *poet*. Dibdin read Hume's *Reign of Elizabeth four times at the least*,[10] and he records that T. de Ocheda, an Italian scholar whom he met in Lord Spencer's Library, at Althorp, had read the *Fathers* through twice.[11] Mark Pattison[12] when a youth read Gilbert White's 'Natural History of Selborne' *over and over* until he *knew it by heart*, and later on he read Gibbon's *Autobiography* until he could *repeat whole paragraphs*. No use to argue, then, whether there are few or many books worth repeated reading, since repetitive reading has been a habit in all times, and sometimes so persistent that books have been worn out in the process. Some such fear may have been in the mind of

---

[1] *A Jacobean Letter-Writer*. 187.   [2] *Tour*. Hill. v, 373.   [3] *Book-Collector*. 100.
[4] *Book-Hunter*. 112.   [5] Timbs, *Anecdotal Biography*. 7.   [6] 'The Influence of Books', *Art of Writing*. 87.   [7] Dobson, *De Libris*. 142.   [8] *Letters and Literary Remains*. i, 393.
[9] *Table-Talk*. 89.   [10] *Reminiscences*. i, 90.   [11] *Ib*. ii, 593.   [12] *Memoirs*. 33, 129–30.

John Price, Bodley's librarian, in the reign of King George III, who encouraged a reader to keep Cook's *Voyages* (which had been given by the King to the *Rector* of Lincoln), telling him that the longer he kept it the better it would be, for if the book *was known to be in the library he should be perpetually plagued with enquiries after it.*[1]

Whether this repeated reading is good or bad taxeth opinion; still, where it gives pleasure, it may be accounted a good and sole justification, as when John Stuart Mill read Pope's *Homer* through *twenty or thirty times,*[2] Taine, the *Chartreuse de Parme* of Stendhal, and Dr. Arnold (of Rugby), *Humphrey Clinker,* each fifty times;[3] but it is less justifiable as a means of inculcating knowledge or understanding, as Laurence Sterne hinted,[4] when he recorded that Avicenna and Licetus read Aristotle's *Metaphysics forty times through apiece, and never understood a single word.* Whether this be wise or not, most will support them that advertise the advantages of reading over many times the great unfathomable masterpieces of literature, as *Homer,* at *the fiftieth reading* of whom, in Harrison's estimation,[5] *one never wearies, just as one can listen to Beethoven, or watch the sunrise or the sunset day by day with new delight;* he himself could read the *Antiquary, Bride of Lammermoor, Ivanhoe, Quentin Durward,* and *Old Mortality, at least once a year. A man, he holds, can hardly be said to know the 12th Mass or the 9th Symphony, by virtue of having once heard them played ten years ago; he can hardly be said to take air and exercise because he took a country walk once last Autumn. And so, he argues, he can hardly be said to know Scott or Shakespeare, Molière or Cervantes, when he once read them since the close of his schooldays, or amidst the daily grind of his professional life. The immortal and universal poets of our race, he concludes, are to be read and re-read till their music and their spirit are a part of our nature; they are to be thought over and digested till we live in the world they created for us.*[6]

VIII. SINGLE BOOK DEVOTEES

So, too, there are readers who find a library in a single book. They are sometimes suspect: *and it is most true which Seneca hath, as well in reading as eating, in books as dyet, varietas delectat, certitudo prodest, variety is delightful, but certainly more usefull and profitable.*[7] Joubert gives reasons for this when he says that *books which absorb our attention to such an extent that they rob us of all fancy for other books are absolutely pernicious,* because *they only bring*

[1] Macray, *Annals of the Bodleian.* 207. [2] J. S. Mill, *Autobiography.* 10. [3] Dobson, *Bookman's Budget.* 16. [4] *Tristram Shandy.* iv, 10. [5] Frederic Harrison, *Choice of Books.* 71. [6] *Ib.* 78. [7] George Hakewill, *Apologie.* (1630) 229.

fresh crochets and sects into the world.[1] *The 'homo unius libri' is proverbially formidable in all conversational figurantes.*[2] *Woe to him that reads but one book.*[3] quotes George Herbert, yet for himself,

> Not a word or look
> I affect to own,
> But thy book,
> And Thy book alone.[4]

Dr. Johnson saw the poet William Collins in his poor lodgings at Islington with a *New Testament* in his hand: *I have but one book,* he said, *but it is the best.*[5] When St. Thomas Aquinas was asked in what manner a man might become learned, he replied: *by reading one book,* meaning the *Bible*; when Sir Walter Scott was near his end he asked Lockhart to take him into the library at Abbotsford and place him near the window so that he might look once more upon the Tweed, and this being done he asked Lockhart to read to him, and when asked what book, he said: *Need you ask? There is but one.*[6] *It is our duty to live among books,* said John Henry Newman, *especially to live by one book, and a very old one;*[7] Hyperius holds that by means of this book *the mind is erected from all worldly cares, and hath much quiet and tranquillity;* for, as Austin hath it, it is *scientia scientiarum, omni melle dulcior, omni pane suavior, omni vino hilarior:* the supreme knowledge: sweeter than all honey, pleasanter than all bread, more cheering than all wine; *for neither,* as Chrysostom well adds, *those boughs and leaves of trees which are plashed for cattle to stand under, in the heat of the day, in summer, so much refresh them with their acceptable shade, as the reading of the Scriptures doth recreate and comfort a distressed soul, in sorrow and affliction;* no songs, for Milton, *comparable to the songs of Sion; no orations equal to those of the Prophets;* and for Coleridge, *Homer* and *Virgil* are *disgustingly* tame and *Milton scarcely tolerable* after *Isaiah* or St. Paul's *Epistle to the Hebrews,* though neither he nor Milton was *homo unius libri;* but *non nostrum tantas componere lites,* as Sir W. Waller,[8] who adventured among many books but ever came back to his *Bible: Write Thy law in my heart,* he prayed, *and I shall become the best book here.*

In the opposite extreme are those who attach themselves to a given book from among the infinite variety of general writings:

> Variety I ask not: give me one
> To live perpetually upon.[9]

Among profane or secular adherents there are enthusiasts like Parson Adams, in *Joseph Andrews,* who read only in a copy of *Aeschylus,* and

---

[1] *Selected Thoughts.* Trans. Matthew Arnold. 178.   [2] Southey, *The Doctor.* 164.
[3] *Jacula Prudentum.*   [4] 'Discipline.'   [5] *Lives of the Poets.* (1781) iv, 329.   [6] *Life of Scott.* Lockhart.   [7] *Tracts for the Times.*   [8] *Divine Meditations.*   [9] Cowley, 'Manna.'

Boffin, in *Our Mutual Friend*, who doted on Gibbon's *Decline and Fall of the Roman Empire*; these two may be taken as indicative of the rest, and that their concentration is justified will be amply shown both here and in that section where I recall many instances of readers who, without confining themselves to one book, return to their favourites again and again with cumulative delight, as Hilaire Belloc, in our own time, finds no book so readable as *Gibbon*; he can *pick him up at any moment*, open where he will, *read him for ten minutes or half an hour or half a day, and lay him down delighted*; not a *dull line in the enormous work, certainly not a dull page*; and one can take it up *at any period of one's life and so delight in it*; he himself has read *Gibbon* in this fashion for thirty-five years, *you can go back to him as often as you like*, read the same passage *over and over again, each time within a few days of the last*, and suffer no more fatigue than you suffer from *the prospect of a familiar and satisfying landscape;*[1] so great a devotion might have marked him out for a one-book-man, and thus observing him I may say there but for the grace of God goes Boffin; but 'tis a miracle of books as of all masterpieces of art, that no familiarity can *stale their infinite variety*, for like the *happy melodist* in the poet[2] they are, in their separate and individual entities

For ever piping songs for ever new.

Malherbe, *the father of French poetry*, had for sole favourite *Horace*, whom he called his *breviary; Horace* was his companion when out walking, and he laid him on his pillow at night;[3] Keats was *very near agreeing with Hazlitt that Shakespeare* was *enough for us*; he thought he would *never read any other Book much*;[4] and the Duke of Buckingham would have only *Homer*:

> Read Homer once, and you can read no more;
> For all books else appear so mean, so poor:
> Verse will seem prose, but still persist to read,
> And Homer will be all the books you need.[5]

Legend no less than history has records of such-like concentrate readers; as that one from whom Merlin got his magic book:

> little glassy-headed hairless man,
> Who lived alone in a great wild on grass;
> Read but one book, and ever reading grew
> So grated down and filed away with thought,
> So lean his eyes were monstrous.[6]

[1] 'Gibbon', *New Statesman*. 18.ii.1928.   [2] Keats, 'Ode on a Grecian Urn'.
[3] J. Roger Rees, *Diversions of a Bookworm*. 243.   [4] *Letters*. Ed. Forman. (1895) 19.
[5] These lines, according to Beloe (*Anecdotes*, i, 103), are inscribed in a copy of the Turnebus Homer in the Cracherode Col.   [6] Tennyson, 'Merlin and Vivien', *Idylls of the King*.

Dibdin tells[1] of a man *who declared that there were only two books in the world: the 'Bible' and 'Euclid'*, and, adds mine author, he *was not so far out of the way as would at first seem*; William Roberts[2] notes several *who appear, for the most part, to have made a constant companion* of some particular book, or who have favoured some single class of books: St. Jerome slept with a copy of Aristotle under his pillow; *Lord Clarendon had a couple of favourites, Livy and Tacitus; Lord Chatham had a good classical library, with an especial fondness for Barrow; Kant who never left his birthplace, Königsberg, had a weakness* for *books of travel*, and *Sir William Jones loved his Caesar*. Of this kind, too, was the Earl of Lonsdale, who told John Wilson Croker that he was *a worshipper of Arthur Young's*; he sang his praises, as though he were a God, and thought him *the most truthful writer and fuller of information upon any subject than any other author. In his* 150 *volumes that he wrote and edited, like Shakespeare and 'another book'* [the *Bible*, peradventure], *you find everything, or something à propos to every subject.*[3] This Earl kept duplicate copies of Young's works at his Town mansion in London and at Lowther Castle, and odd copies at his places at Barnes and Whitehaven, so that he could always practise his bibliolatry.

Tristram Shandy gives out in his *Life and Opinions*,[4] if you will permit this further piece of evidence from fiction, that his father was a most notable instance of the one-book-enthusiast, his anchorage being Slawkenbergius on *Noses; every page of him was a rich treasure of inexhaustible knowledge to my father;—he could not open him amiss; and he would often say, in closing the book: That if all the arts and sciences in the world, with the books which treated of them, were lost,—should the wisdom and policies of governments, he would say, through disuse, ever happen to be forgot; and all that statesmen had wrote or caused to be written upon the strong or the weak sides of courts and kingdoms, should they be forgot also,—and Slawkenbergius only left, —there would be enough in him in all conscience, he would say, to set the world agoing again.* Well may he treasure this *institute of all that was necessary on noses, and everything else*; he was inseparable from that notable work, *at matin, noon and vespers was Hafen Slawkenbergius his recreation and delight*; 'twas ever in his hands, and *so worn, so glazed, so contrited and attrited was it with fingers and with thumbs in all its parts, from one end even unto the other*, that you would have sworn it had been a *canon's prayer-book*.

It will be seen from these examples that any single book may serve the end of a whole library for those who are disposed by nature to one book, and, in final proof, I may yet cite the instance of Sir Walter Elliot, of Kellynch Hall, in Somersetshire, as a man who, *for his own amusement, never took up any book but the Baronetage; there he found occupation for an idle*

[1] *Reminiscences.* ii, 890.   [2] *Book-Hunter in London.* xv–xvi.   [3] *The Croker Papers.* iii, 201–2.   [4] Sterne, *Tristram Shandy.* iii, 42.

hour, and consolation in a distressed one; there his faculties were roused into admiration and respect, by contemplating the limited remnants of the earliest patents; there any unwelcome sensation, arising from domestic affairs, changed naturally into pity and contempt, as he turned over the almost endless creations of the last century; and there, if every other leaf were powerless, he could read his own history with an interest that never failed.[1]

IX. READING MANY BOOKS AT ONCE

Resembling these readers who focus their attention upon particular works, are others who revel in many books at one time, flitting from one to another as bees or butterflies from flower to flower, pollen gatherers these, honey-makers, dippers: and they are augmented by Robert Southey, who frankly advised those who seek knowledge *to have two or three books in course of reading at the same time,*[2] which the learned Elizabeth Carter would have upheld at special moments, such as that recorded by her[3] when, *overcome by a solitude in London . . . where there is not so much as a view of the sun, moon, and stars to entertain one,* she avoids the vapours by hedging herself in with *all manner of books, drawings, work-bags, and authors in all languages,* reading only the prefaces of some books and the conclusions of others. This is, perhaps, more to be encouraged than the habit of a Chinese scholar, Chia Shan, who in the second century before Christ, scampered over books *as a huntsman over the fields,—all breadth, and no depth,*[4] or Denis, in *Crome Yellow*[5] (p. 35), who in five years read twenty or thirty tons of *great thick books about the universe and the mind and ethics,* or Dr. William King, author of *The Art of Cookery,* who entered Christ's College in 1681, at the age of eighteen, and *prosecuted his studies with so much intenseness* that he was 8 *years standing,* and in that period read over and remarked upon *twenty-two thousand odd hundred books and manuscripts;*[6] or Shelley, who employed two-thirds of every day in reading; *it is no exaggeration,* Hogg affirms, *that out of the twenty-four hours, he frequently read sixteen.*[7]

Some read through a whole continent of books, giving their passion leave to rove from one book to all the books of a single author and all the books derived from them by a process of expansion similar, in its own realm, to that adopted by the extra-illustrator in his; others adventure freely among all the books in one definite class or upon one subject. Such readers have devoted whole lives to Shakespeare, Homer, Dante, who are continents in themselves; but lesser realms will suffice. Lionel Johnson,

---

[1] Jane Austen, *Persuasion*. i.   [2] *Letters.* To Henry Taylor.   [3] *Letters.* Pennington, i, 226.   [4] *Chinese Biog. Dict.* Giles. 129.   [5] By Aldous Huxley.   [6] Johnson. *Lives of the Poets.* ii, 271.   [7] Hogg, *Shelley.* London Lib. Ed. 84.

whose reading was as vast as it was varied, contracted an inordinate passion for *Newman* and revelled in the thirty-six volumes of that writer, *from the most splendid and familiar passage down to the slightest and most occasional note*; until he became better acquainted with him than with any *literature or language*.[1] The American scholar, Dr. Schelling, boasted of having read *every old play in our literature*;[2] and S. R. Gardiner, the historian of the Civil War, spent all his spare time in the British Museum Reading-room for nearly fifty years, and took in the stride of his vast reading *all the 23,000 tracts in the Thomason collection*.[3] Charles James Fox, says Lord Rosebery,[4] preferred *Homer*, but he would also read *all the novels he could get hold of. In conversation he would range over almost the whole field of literature with zest and passion, without apparently once straying into politics. A friend tells how in a day he would discuss Homer and Virgil, Aeschylus and Euripides, Milton and Massinger, Pope and Addison, Gibbon and Blackstone, Sophocles and Shakespeare, Metastasio, Congreve, Vanbrugh, Cowper, Fielding and Burns*; and there was a time

> When Gladstone, bluest of the blue,
> Read all Augustine's folios through.[5]

X. PREFERENCES NO BAR TO FURTHER ADVENTURES

To return again from this digression to a further account of my repetitious adventurers, I must crave leave to add a few more examples, to prove that the traversing of a particular realm of letters many times is no objection to frequent excursions elsewhere; determined readers are as happy when they rove in search of fresh pastures as when they browse in those that are familiar; and those who chew the cud of a single book are kin to those others who are forever sampling new nourishment. Most persistent and notable among them was Macaulay, who seemed to Henry Jackson, *not historian, nor orator, nor politician, but the book-lover*,[6] and as such to be respected; and Macaulay confesses himself a bibliophile first and last in every page of his life, and not least by his devotion to favourite books: *I have no pleasure from books*, he says, *which equals that of reading over for the hundredth time great productions which I almost know by heart*;[7] and he gave proof of this insatiable appetite in many a confession to his friends. He

---

[1] *Post Liminium*. 303.   [2] Newton, *A Magnificent Farce*. 62.   [3] G. F. Barwick, *Reading-room of the British Museum*. 113.   [4] *Appreciations and Addresses*. 157-8.
[5] William Cory, *Ionica*. 'Hersilia.' Third Ed. 193.   [6] *Henry Jackson, O.M., A Memoir*. Parry. 132.   [7] *Life*, Trevelyan. ii, 23.

would read through the Greek dramatists from end to end every year;[1] when writing his own *History of England*, he twice read through most of the works of Burke,[2] thinking them *admirable*, and Burke *the greatest man since Milton*.

In the early days of his stay in India he read almost continuously with a frenzied appetite for big and little masterpieces. Casting up his *reading account* from the time he unpacked his books in Calcutta, at the end of November, 1834, to December 30, 1835, he tells Ellis (in a letter)[3] that he read *Aeschylus, Sophocles, Pindar, Plautus, Theocritus, Terence*, and *Lucretius*, twice each; and in addition: *Herodotus, Thucydides, Euripides, Callimachus, Apollonius Rhodius, Quintus Calaber; almost all Xenophon's works, almost all Plato; Aristotle's 'Politics', and a good deal of his 'Organum', besides dipping elsewhere in him; the whole of Plutarch's 'Lives'; about half of Lucian; two or three books of Athenaeus; Catullus, Tibullus, Propertius, Lucan, Statius, Silius Italicus, Livy, Velleius Paterculus, Sallust, Caesar*, and he was then nearly through *Cicero* and at the same time deep in *Aristophanes* and *Lucian*, and full of shame that he had not read Lucian's *Dialogues of the Dead* since he was thirteen years of age. Five months later he gives a further account[4] to the same friend showing that bookish appetite is stimulated by what it devours. Since Christmas he had read *Aristophanes* twice through, and once again *Herodotus* and *Thucydides*; then he turned to the Latin writers, *Cicero* and the two *Senecas*, father and son, and *several third-rate and fourth-rate writers, as one does read such stuff: Valerius Maximus, Annaeus Florus, Lucius Ampelius*, and *Aurelius Victor. I have also gone through Phaedrus*. But he is *now better employed* deep in Tacitus his *Annals*, and *at the same time* (so he saith) *Suetonius*; all of which is but an account of his reading over a certain time, but all times were the same, differing only in the energy with which he pursued his passion. He read during all waking hours; how else could he have devoured so much? *Plautus* six times in twenty-four years,[5] and so on; but the tale of his reading is too long; *sufficit*.

Such multiple reading is a test of the quality of a book, as Miss Catherine Talbot well knew when lamenting to Mrs. Elizabeth Carter the scarcity of new books, *not a new book has shewed its head this century* (the eighteenth century was then forty-five years of age); but she had little cause for complaint, for there was *full as much pleasure in reading a very excellent book the fifth or sixth time, as if one had it fresh from the press*; curiosity at first is too eager, leisure is needed to dwell upon its beauties, and when one has *a general idea of the whole one can stop at what particular part one pleases*, which is true, but there is another kind of pleasure: *in life one is unwilling to part with an agreeable moment because one knows it will never come again*, but it is

---

[1] *Ib.* ii, 420.   [2] *Ib.* ii, 318.   [3] *Ib.* ii, 318.   [4] *Ib.* i, 389–90.   [5] *Ib.* i, 409.

otherwise with books: *by turning back to a full passage* one may recall the pleasure of the first moment at will.[1]

Because of this humour to turn back, dip into the past, many good bookmen are full of regrets, knowing as they do that opportunity to repeat old bookish adventures rarely comes. *Ah! the books that one will never read again*, sighs George Gissing:[2] *they gave delight, perchance something more; they left a perfume in the memory; but life has passed them by forever*. He has but to muse when one after another past adventures rise before him in a ghostly fantasy: *books gentle and quieting; books noble and inspiring; books that well merit to be pored over, not once but many a time*. Never to read them again, the years pass too quickly, and are too few, and he dreams that when he awaits the end *those lost books* may perchance *come wandering into his thought* and he will remember them as friends are remembered. This nostalgia for old favourites is an effect of the literary *wanderlust*, the desire to roam over too wide an area of books, and for those who suffer from it the best remedy is concentration, to find comfort with a few tried companions, as Coventry Patmore, who *limited* his reading *almost wholly to the few great books from which the world derives all its knowledge*.[3]

Friedrich Nietzsche was a purposeful reader, inasmuch as books, with music, were the raw materials of his deductions. He believed only in French culture, and it is *to a small number of old French authors* that he returns *again and again. I almost always take refuge in the same books*, he says: *altogether their number is small; they are the books which are precisely my proper fare*. It is not in his *nature to read much, and of all sorts*: a library makes him ill. His old French books were, *Montaigne, Pascal, Molière, Corneille* and *Racine*. Among the moderns he is particularly fond of Guy de Maupassant, and confessed, *between ourselves*, that he preferred the generation of Paul Bourget, Pierre Loti, Gyp, Meilhac, Anatole France and Jules Lemaitre *to its masters, all of whom were corrupted by German philosophy*.[4]

None among great readers has enjoyed more deliberately the *linked sweetness long drawn out* of our more spacious writers, those long, leisurely books which rove and meander, saunter, and lounge through their lives in an eternity of their own, than Mark Rutherford. Familiarity with those old books breeds affection for them, not contempt. He loved the *slow pages*[5] of the *Spectators* of Addison and Steele, and the *slow walking pace* of *Clarissa, which allows us to see everything by the way, never hurrying past anything of interest, turning back to look at it again is delightful*.[6] He read through the *Bible* once in every two or three years, *an hour daily before breakfast*, and found it *profitable beyond almost any other book*;[7] and Wesley's *Journal*,

---

[1] *Letters*. Pennington. i, 84.   [2] *Private Papers of Henry Ryecroft*. 145.   [3] *Memoirs*. Champneys. ii, 105.   [4] Nietzsche, *Ecce Homo*. Trans. Ludovici. 37–8.   [5] *Letters to Three Friends*. 256.   [6] *Ib*. 95–6.   [7] *Ib*. 92–4.

Carlyle's *Frederick the Great*, Spenser's *Faerie Queene*, Doughty's *Dawn in Britain* and *Arabia Deserta*. *Frederick* was for him *the great modern epic*,[1] and he read it more than once; so too the *Faerie Queene*, which on re-reading he was *prepared more eagerly than ever to champion against all fools*; Doughty's *Daw in Britain*, despite its six volumes of blank verse, *did not for a minute* tire him;[2] Boswell's *Life of Johnson* and his *Tour in the Hebrides* made him wonder why he should ever read a new book; such works have the peculiar merit of being inexhaustible; *each successive reading, if you repeat the first twenty times, will be profitable*;[3] which many another confirms, as Benjamin Robert Haydon nearly one hundred years earlier: *no resisting Boswell's Life*;[4] and to conclude this matter Mark Rutherford, letting us into his secret of slow reading and long-drawn familiarity, confesses that he goes over the old books, *Bacon, Shakespeare, Milton*, and those others, *again and again*, because he is gotten into their ways, *become tuned to them*, responding to them as to the known, tried, approved; the new is foreign; it has no roots and may be forgotten to-morrow: in the reading of it, therefore, there is no profit.[5] He is no mere *passéist* seeking the antique on principle; he could appreciate the new, as when he announced to Philip Webb, in a burst of praise, that he had read J. M. Synge's *Aran Islands* twice and *must read it again*; it held him, clutched him, would not let him go, and, recalling the tragedy of the author's early death, he took comfort from the thought that, dying young, Synge was saved from becoming literary;[6] but the reasons of such devotion are not to my present purpose.

XI. IN THE GARDEN OF EPICURUS

If less esteemed by the more serious of students, not less wise are those for whom books are toys of leisure, pleasant companions, retreats from boredom, arbours of content, feasts of fancy, cosy corners, *Pills to Purge Melancholy*, hones for the wit, memorisers, *magic casements*, tickle-palates, pastimes, *sanctuaries*, sedatives, palliatives, *panis et circenses* for the rebellious soul, etc., as Thomas Gray, who wished ever to be lying on sofas reading *eternal new novels by Crébillon and Marivaux*.[7] Such are condemned by high-brows, and the strenuously purposeful folk who would have us always bargaining with God, life or destiny for, in the common saying, *services rendered*, as Frederic Harrison,[8] who condemns for *literary dandyism* all *pursuit of letters without social purpose or any systematic faith*, and derides the use of books as *sedatives*, or as the *means of exciting a mild intellectual*

[1] *Ib.* 66–7.　[2] *Ib.* 295.　[3] *Ib.* 373.　[4] *Autobiography.* i, 97.　[5] Rutherford, *Op. cit.* 194–5.　[6] *Ib.* 393.　[7] Leigh Hunt, 'My Books', *Essays.*　[8] *Choice of Books.* 88.

titillation; he is all for *bracing the mind to think*, and not without good reasons, even if, in the meantime, he protests too much.

There is a medium, even among books, a time for play as well as work, for relaxation as well as strenuousness: thinkest *because thou art* cultured, *there shall be no more cakes and ale?* 'Tis as good sometimes to loaf with books as to labour with them, to *damn braces* and *bless relaxes*, as Blake advises.[1] Cicero, as I remember, in an epistle to his dear friend Atticus, confessed that he was so in love with idleness during his retirement, that he could not tear himself from it, and books aided and abetted the mood: *Itaque libris me delecto, quorum habeo Anti festivam copiam*,[2] I enjoy myself with my books, of which I have a good company at Antium. *My interests*, Alexander Smith declared, *are divided between my geraniums and my books*;[3] and Edward FitzGerald shamelessly dawdled with books, *as ladies work: to pass the time away*[4]—the partner of his idleness, as like as not, his *complete Voltaire*.[5]

High amongst those who know how to relax stands our prince of dilettantes, Horace Walpole. He lived in *Epicurean ease*, and made reading one of the instruments of his cosiness, preserving his sensations, impressions, fancies, in nearly four thousand letters (*gossiping gazettes*, he called them) to his friends. Historian, gossip, printer, poet, antiquary, this virtuoso was as book-born as he was well-born, and he read for dalliance, to gratify his whim, his taste, or his malice. Reading was the final decoration to his days; he distilled his books into his life and his life into his books. When he was not peering at the world through the window of art, he was peeping at it through the keyhole of letters. The story of Phaeton in the *Metamorphoses* was a picture of his beloved Twickenham: *Ardet Athos, taurusque Cilix, etc.; mount Richmond burns, parched is Petersham; Parnassusque biceps, dry is Pope's grot, the nymphs of Cliveden are burning to blackmoors, their faces are already as glowing as a cinder, Cycnus is changed into a swan: quodque suo Tagus anne vehit, fluit ignibus aurum; my gold fishes are almost molten.*[6]

He enjoys life and laughs at it, and he is no miser of laughter: *I desire to die when I have nobody left to laugh with me*, he tells George Montague.[7] My dandy Democritus has never seen or heard any serious things that were not ridiculous: *Jesuits, Methodists, philosophers, politicians, the hypocrite Rousseau, the scoffer Voltaire, the encyclopedists, the Humes, the Lyttletons, the Grenvilles, the atheist tyrant of Prussia, and the mountebank of history, Mr. Pitt, all are to* him *but impostors in their various ways*—fame or interest their object; and he regards the ploughman who *reads his almanack, and believes the stars so many farthing candles*, as wiser and more rational and *honester*

---

[1] *Marriage of Heaven and Hell.*   [2] *Ad Atticum.* Loeb Ed., 125. ii, 6.   [3] *Dreamthorp.* 248.
[4] *Letters and Literary Remains.* i, 49.   [5] *Ib.* i, 238.   [6] Walpole to George Montague, *Letters.* Cunningham. iv, 11.   [7] *Ib.* iv, 441.

than any of them. Oh! he cries, *I am sick of visions and systems*, for he sees in them no more than an eternal recurrence of things that *shove one another aside* to reappear like *the figures in a moving picture*. As he sees more of the world Rabelais *brightens up* to him, teaching him to laugh at it all rather than hate it. And in that *Histoire Philosophique et Politique du Commerce des Deux Indes* writ by the Abbé Raynal, which the Parliament of Paris condemned to be burnt and its author imprisoned, he found a cosmography much to his liking. *It tells one everything in the world;—how to make conquests, invasions, blunders, settlements, bankruptcies, fortunes, etc.; tells you the natural and historical history of all nations; talks commerce, navigation, tea, coffee, china, mines, salt, spices; of the Portuguese, English, French, Dutch, Danes, Spaniards, Arabs, caravans, Persians, Indians, of Louis XIV and the King of Prussia; of La Bourdonnais, Dupliex, and Admiral Saunders; of rice, and women that dance naked; of camels, ginghams, and muslin; of millions of millions of livres, pounds, rupees, and cowries; of iron cables and Circassian women; of Law and the Mississippi; and against all governments and religions*; such a largesse in the first two volumes that he cannot conceive what is left for the four others: *all is so mixed, that you learn forty new trades, and fifty new histories, in the single chapter.*[1]

Walpole is sedentary, a stay-at-home; travels by the proxy of books; they are his magic carpets, they carry him to the ends of the earth: *I read nothing but American voyages and histories of plantations and settlements*, he tells Bentley;[2] but most he loves to read gossiping histories such as he himself would write, and, like all hedonistic readers, the *Letters* of Madame de Sévigné; *there is scarce a book in the world I love so much*;[3] and after Madame, the gallant Count Grammont: *I am Grammont mad*, he tells Montague.[4] *Oh, madam, madam, madam* (he is now addressing Lady Hervey), *what do you think I have found? I am out of my wits! Never was anything like my luck; it never forsakes me! I have found Count Grammont's picture! I believe I shall see company upon it, certainly keep the day holy.*[5] Montesquieu's *Letters* are so agreeable that he cannot *go to bed till he has finished them at nearly three in the morning*;[6] Fulke Greville's *Maxims and Characters* is *a wonderful book by a wonderful author*;[7] Lord Clarendon's *Life entertains him more than any book he ever read*;[8] Gibbon's *Rome* lifts him up:[9] *Lo, there is just appeared a truly classic work: a history, not majestic like Livy, nor compressed like Tacitus; not stamped with character like Clarendon; perhaps not so deep as Robertson's 'Scotland', but a thousand degrees above his 'Charles'; not pointed like Voltaire, but as accurate as he is inexact; modest as he is tranchant, and sly as Montesquieu without being so recherché*; the style is *smooth as a Flemish picture*, muscles concealed, not exaggerated as in Michelangelo to exhibit the painter's skill

---

[1] *Letters.* Cunningham. v, 421.   [2] *Ib.* ii, 402.   [3] *Ib.* ii, 181.   [4] *Ib.* ii, 268.
[5] *Ib.* iv, 442.   [6] *Ib.* v, 52.   [7] *Ib.* iii, 6.   [8] *Ib.* iii, 273-4.   [9] *Ib.* vi, 310-11.

in anatomy, *nor composed of the limbs of clowns of different nations, like Dr. Johnson's heterogeneous monsters.*

He sits up all night reading Lord Chesterfield's *Letters to his Son*, and to his surprise finds them *really written from the heart, not for the honour of the author's head*; he thinks they do as little honour to the last as show feeling in the first: his lordship *was sensible what a cub he had to work on, and whom two quartos of licking could not mould, for cub he remained to his death.*[1] He sends Erasmus Darwin's *Botanic Garden* to Hannah More, extolling the author *a great poet* whose *powerful talent* has been wasted on descriptions in verse which have to be explained by essays in prose; belike she will be surprised at meeting *a Truffle converted into a Nymph . . . inhabiting a palace studded with emeralds and rubies like a saloon in the Arabian Nights.*[2] He revels in the *Lives of Leland, Tom Hearne, and Antony Wood*, and thinks it *the most delightful book in the world.*[3] He is no admirer of Richardson, who *wrote those deplorably tedious lamentations, 'Clarissa' and 'Sir Charles Grandison', pictures of high life as conceived by a Methodist teacher;*[4] '*Tristram Shandy*' is the *dregs of nonsense*[5] and *a very insipid and tedious performance;*[6] Boswell is a *jackanapes,*[7] his *Tour* a *most absurd enormous book . . . the story of a mountebank and his zany,*[8] and his *Life of Dr. Johnson* would be more readable *were it reduced from two volumes to one*; which censures few would support, but we have no cause to complain; *nowt so queer as folks*, as they say in my native Lancashire; nothing so amusing as opinions, and in the broad parterres of the garden of books there are blossoms and posies to suit all tastes, so for false fears, as all such objections must be, and all other inconveniences in this kind, not to get excited is best, but to be amused as he is when *Rousseau insists that the north and south blow at the same time.*[9] But I rove.

There are many more notable examples of readers who have fluttered from book to book as bees from flower to flower gathering honey, but, unlike the bees, for the pleasure of the taste rather than for sustenance, and of all the rest I admire most Edward FitzGerald, who lived for himself, possessed his soul, harmed no man, and died easily, bequeathing, by chance not design, the fragrant memory of a fastidious life among books and friends, and a set of verses, a bundle of letters and a dialogue, which will ever stand

Against the dark and Time's consuming rage.[10]

I am almost of opinion that he was incomparably beyond them all in his exquisite appreciation of books. He read like an artist, idled with genius, and found his *visionary inactivity* better than the *mischievous activity* of so

[1] *Letters.* Cunningham. vi, 74.   [2] *Ib.* ix, 177.   [3] *Ib.* v, 394.   [4] *Ib.* iv, 305–6.
[5] *Ib.* iii, 382.   [6] *Ib.* iii, 298.   [7] *Ib.* ix, 49.   [8] *Ib.* ix, 24.   [9] *Ib.* iv, 453.   [10] Daniel.

many he saw about him, if not better than the *useful and virtuous activity of a few others.*[1]

Idleness was the art he professed, he was an amateur in everything else: *I have been all my life apprentice to this heavy business of idleness, and am not yet master of my craft; the Gods are too just to suffer that I should.*[2] *Here I live with tolerable content,* he relates, *perhaps with as much as most people arrive at, and what if one were grateful one would perhaps call perfect happiness. Here is a glorious sunshiny day: all the morning I read about Nero in Tacitus lying at full length on a bench in the garden: a nightingale singing, and some red anemones eyeing the sun manfully not far off. A funny mixture all this: Nero, and the delicacy of Spring; all very human, however. Then at half-past twelve lunch on Cambridge cream cheese: then a ride over hill and dale; then spudding up some weeds from the grass: and then coming in I sit down to write to you, my sister winding red worsted from the back of a chair, and the most delightful little girl in the world chattering incessantly. So runs the world away. You think I live in Epicurean ease; but this happens to be a jolly day; one isn't always well, or tolerably good, the weather is not always clear, nor nightingales singing, nor Tacitus full of pleasant atrocity. But such is life, I believe I have got hold of a good end of it.*[3] So he idles busily and reads for delight, *dolce far niente,* flying from the grossness and the slag of life ·as he flew from Carlyle's *raving book about heroes,* taking refuge in the *Tale of a Tub* and *Tristram Shandy,* Shakespeare, and *Horace Walpole,* Burton's *Anatomy,* the *Letters* of Madame de Sévigné, *Voltaire* and *Cervantes.*

He roves over many pastures, sounds deep seas, takes pleasure even in what he does not *wholly understand, just as old women like sermons,* which is *of a piece with an admiration of all Nature around us;* so he is able to enjoy the charm in *the half meanings and glimpses of meaning that come in through Blake's wilder visions.*[4] His taste is catholic yet fastidious; he will look into any book, taste all with subtle and discriminating palate; any good is book that *notes down facts alone, especially about health*; he *wishes we had diaries of the lives of half the unknown men that have lived;*[5] he could not help *liking even a Cookery Book.*[6] He *sunned* himself with *Dickens,*[7] and made *a kind of Summer* in his room with *Boccaccio;*[8] W. F. Pollock tells him to read *Clarendon* and obediently he does so, liking him much: *delightful to read his manly, noble English after Lord Brougham's spick and span Birmingham ware in the 'Edinburgh';*[9] he is respectfully astonished at *Carlyle,* bored by *Browning,* contemptuous of *Mrs. Browning; George Eliot* he could not *relish at all;*[10] but he reads her and the rest of his antipathies for the pleasure of grumbling; dives with as cheerful a complaint into the *five thick volumes,*

[1] *Letters and Lit. Remains.* i, 202. [2] *More Letters.* 20. [3] *Letters and Lit. Remains.* i, 50.
[4] *Ib.* i, 23. [5] *Ib.* i, 22. [6] *Letters to Fanny Kemble.* 90. [7] *Ib.* 62. [8] *Ib.* 118.
[9] *More Letters.* 8. [10] *Letters to Fanny Kemble.* 171.

five hundred pages apiece of the *dull Letters* of Mrs. Delaney,[1] as he basks appreciatively in the sun of *George Crabb.* He toys with the magazines, flirts with novels from Mudie's, especially *A Woman in White,* and threatens to make readable *that aggravating Book, Clarissa Harlowe,* with a *pair of scissors;*[2] but when old age comes upon him he *recoils from making new Acquaintances in Novels,* and *retreats upon his Old Friends, in Shakespeare, Cervantes, and Sir Walter.*[3]

In this mode are many: take William Cory at Eton reading the *most sublime thing in literature,* Edward Irving's *Journal: window open, sun burning, a cock crowing on the other side of the street;* and to his surprise (and delight) Jeff, his Virginian nightingale, begins to sing: *what a puddle life is, what an ocean Irving's life was;*[4] the *Walter-Scott world is the best world, the true golden world;*[5] he relishes Virgil as the *founder of historical romance,* the *Aeneid* being the *real forerunner* of the *Lay of the Last Minstrel, more so of Waverley;*[6] he rests with John Henry Newman's *Poems,* then *a new book, full of oldness—old sacredness, old mystery, and the romance of theology;*[7] he is puzzled whilst enjoying Victor Hugo's novels: *Les Travailleurs de la Mer* is a *very pretty, noble book,* if you *skip resolutely;*[8] the *Misérables* is a *pathological work, almost a synoptic view of human suffering, which he compares with Job,* with the *Inferno,* with *Lucretius;*[9] but what a *fool* is Balzac *in his jingles* —'*Liberty is Peace', 'Congress is Progress'.* Cory appeals to *law-books, memoir-books, Plato, Butler,* to *save us from such delusions.*[10] Like FitzGerald and Horace Walpole, he is fastidious, but less catholic in choice; *Balzac* leaves a bitter taste in his mind which is cleansed away by a dose of *Octave Feuillet;*[11] he realizes his power, but does not *praise him as our fanatics praise* Shakespeare, because he has *hardly any dramatic skill, a dreadfully heavy hand, bad touch, morbid love of horrors:* and *insincere admiration of Catholicism and Royalism;*[12] George Eliot is *very noble, wise, sublime,* but *her human beings don't live with him for life;*[13] he is uncertain about *Shelley,* will only abide him in extracts, but *heartily* admires *Swinburne;*[14] abhors Ruskin's *rant about economics,* and *goes steadily year after year to his great books;*[15] *Wilhelm Meister* is *absolute bosh,*[16] and the *Epic of Hades below the standard of Eton boys' compositions.*[17]

Dr. John Brown, the author of *Rab and his Friends,* does nothing but eat and read;[18] his book-fare, Southey's *Bunyan,* the *Elixir of the Devil,* and *The Doctor;* lots of Shakespeare's *Poems* and the third volume of Carlyle's *French Revolution; it is glorious; and now I am regaling myself in 'Midshipman Easy'* ... *and then I mean to have the 'King's Own'.* Some retain their hedon-

---

[1] *More Letters.* 63.   [2] *Ib.* 77.   [3] *Letters to Fanny Kemble.* 15.   [4] *Letters and Journals.* 225.   [5] *Ib.* 184.   [6] *Ib.* 451.   [7] *Ib.* 215.   [8] *Ib.* 176.   [9] *Ib.* 391.   [10] *Ib.* 374.   [11] *Ib.* 270.   [12] *Ib.* 389.   [13] *Ib.* 420.   [14] *Ib.* 454.   [15] *Ib.* 351.   [16] *Ib.* 355.   [17] *Ib.* 294,   [18] Letters. 59

ism in the midst of household cares, as Dorothy Wordsworth at Grasmere: *Sauntered a good deal in the garden, bound carpets, mended old clothes, read 'Timon of Athens', dried linens; read Boswell in the house in the morning, and after dinner under the bright yellow leaves of the orchard.* She would soothe her bardic brother with *Shakespeare,* or with equal delight listen to him reading his own poems, hot from creation. She records with a glow how she and William and Mary sat round the fire on Christmas Eve (1801) reading *Chaucer,* and, with a different and more wistful glow, how one summer's day (June 10, 1802) Coleridge comes over the hills by Grisedale with *a sack full of books, etc., and a branch of mountain ash,* the more romantic for having been attacked on the way by a cow.[1] William Cowper was another of our good loiterers, he looked forward to the visit of his *dearest coz,* Lady Hesketh, and for the enjoyment of great books in the retreat in his orchard, the best winter-walk in all the parish, sheltered from the east, from the north-east, and open to the sun, except at his rising, all the day: *Then we will have Homer and Don Quixote,* he says, *and then we will have saunter and chat, and one more laugh before we die,* and the delectable orchard is alive with *creatures of all kinds:* poultry of *every denomination, and pigs, the drollest in the world.*[2]

Maurice Hewlett cherished biography and history. He could *pick up* and *browse happily* upon *The Lives of the Poets* as upon the *life of a grocer's boy, if it were printed. Anybody's life is interesting,* he well says, *or anybody's letters;* but *outdated* history, as *Robertson and Hume,* is *mainly unreadable;* not so *Motley and Prescott, Macaulay, Carlyle, and Michelet, though you need not believe a word they say.* He could always read *Gibbon* until a friend bade him notice how nearly every sentence in him ended with a *possessive case.* It was *horribly true,* and killed his pleasure, for henceforward he only read *to find out how true it was,* which is not reading but *a dreary game of Patience.*[3]

In such wise have men and women of taste and leisure added richness to their days by entrancing their idle moments with the magic and mystery of illustrious words; and finding in them keys to charm

> Magic casements, opening on the foam
> Of perilous seas, in faery-lands forlorn;[4]

and discovering also that in such dalliance they are procurers of

> A sweet content
> Passing all wisdom, or its fairest flower.[5]

---

[1] *Journals of Dorothy Wordsworth.*   [2] *Letters.* Ed. Frazer. ii, 196.   [3] *Extemporary Essays.* 119–20.   [4] Keats, 'Ode to a Nightingale'.   [5] R. H. Horne, *Orion.* iii, 2.

XII. THE TWILIGHT OF THE BIBLIOPHILE

The passion for books continues and even increases to the end. Anthony Trollope looked for happiness in his closing years first to his work, then to the love of those who loved him, and then to his books.[1] But many bibliophiles, when the shadows draw out, find consolation in books alone: *as the years go by, I value books more and more*, said Henry Jackson;[2] but as they grow older they roam less and less from one book to another, *for the books we plan to read in our old age are something like the places where we should wish to grow old*.[3] *Come*, cried George Gissing,[4] towards the close of his life, *once more before I die I will read 'Don Quixote'*. Montaigne confessed that *this old and heavie-paced minde of mine, will no more be pleased with Aristotle, or tickled with good Ovid*. The *quaint inventions* which *ravished him in the past now scarcely entertain* him; but he turns to Virgil, Lucretius, Catullus, and Horace again with joy. Charles Lamb thanks Payne Collier for the gift of a fine copy of the *Decameron* which came *just as he was wanting something of the sort*, and he confesses that he takes *less pleasure in books than heretofore*, preferring *books about books*; Dr. Johnson's *ardour for literature never failed*;[5] in his seventy-fourth year he *read all Virgil through*, and was reading and discussing *Homer* as well;[6] Walter Savage Landor, on the eve of his eighty-third year, reads little, chiefly *Punch* and *Household Words; I want*, he says, *amusing ideas not serious ones*;[7] and was thus unlike the old bachelor in Crabbe's *Tales of the Hall*:

> My books were changed; I now preferred the truth
> To the light reading of unsettled youth;

but although *novels grew tedious*, by *choice or chance*, he *still had interest in the wild romance*.

Edward FitzGerald was faithful to his old friends, the classics of Greece and Rome, France and England, throughout his life, but when he was nigh on sixty years, he implored Quaritch not *to waste his learned Catalogues* on him, for he now bought nothing but *Mudie's Secondhand Memoirs* —an exaggeration, as his letters to his illustrious bookseller themselves prove;[8] as he grew still older he sought out in books, as he told Sir Samuel Laurence, *People, Places, and Things, which I don't and can't see*; when one gets *old and dry*, he said, one *thirsts* for what is *delightful* rather than profound;[9] but to the end of his life he never tired of *Sir Walter Scott* and *Don*

[1] *Autobiography*. World's Classics. 335.   [2] *Henry Jackson, O.M., A Memoir*. Parry. 132.   [3] Joubert, *Selected Thoughts*. Trans. Lyttleton. 174.   [4] *Private Papers of Henry Ryecroft*. 244.   [5] Boswell. *Life*. Ed. Hill. i, 446.   [6] *Ib*. iv, 218.   [7] *Letters and Unpublished Writings*. 118–19.   [8] *Letters to Bernard Quaritch*. 10.   [9] *Letters and Literary Remains*. i, 378.

Quixote, who with his *blessed Sévigné, Crabbe and John Wesley*, were his *last and great hobbies*.[1] Carlyle, when over eighty, *kept on reading assiduously, sometimes till past midnight, in spite of all endeavours to get him to bed*, and during the spring of 1879 (his eighty-fourth year) he read *through all Shakespeare*;[2] *of late years putting aside the Latin classics*, says Anthony Trollope,[3] *I have found my greatest pleasure in our old English dramatists*; Coventry Patmore, in his seventy-third year, could no longer read *consecutive thinkers on Spiritual matters*, they made him feel as if he were *going mad*, and he became *impatient of all reading except novels*, which he *devoured eagerly*, gaining from them *spiritual apprehensions* which were of *great value* to him.[4]

Benjamin Disraeli found consolation in books, and during his last few days at Hughenden he would read the *History of the Venetian Republic, Lucian, Horace*, and *Virgil*, of whom he grew more and more fond;[5] Lord Grenville, Prime Minister of England and bibliophile, loved books all his days; a friend who used to visit him gives a picture of him in his old age, *sitting summer and winter on the same sofa with his favourite books on the shelves just above his head; Roger Ascham among them; Milton always within reach. He, at any rate in his sixty-sixth year, was clear as to the choice between literature and politics. A Minister leaves him to go to his office.* '*I would rather he was there than I*,' says Grenville. '*If I was to live my life over again*,' he continued, '*I should do very differently*.' Lord Rosebery gives out that Sir Robert Walpole in his retirement was desolate because he had never cultivated *the divine solace of books*. Seeing a friend reading in the library at Houghton, Walpole said: *I wish I took as much delight in reading as you do; it would be the means of alleviating many tedious hours in my present retirement, but, to my misfortune, I have no pleasure in such pursuits*. And to Henry Fox he said: *You can read. It is a great happiness. I totally neglected it when I was in business, which has been the whole of my life, and to such a degree that I cannot now read a page—a warning to all Ministers*.[6] Reading needs practice as much as any other art, otherwise the technique becomes atrophied, as taste itself may die or degenerate from other causes. Charles Darwin, for instance, was so immersed in scientifical research that, in later life, he *lost all pleasure in poetry of any kind, including Shakespeare*.[7] Hazlitt firmly supports early and continuous reading in his *Advice to a Schoolboy: Reading*, he says, *is perhaps the greatest pleasure you will have in life; the one you will think of longest, and repent of least*, and if his life had been *more full of calamity* than it had been, he confesses he would live it over again, in order to read the books he read in his youth.[8] But he was an exception among book-lovers in one

[1] *Letters to Fanny Kemble*. 186. [2] FitzGerald, *Letters and Literary Remains*. i, 441.
[3] *Autobiography*. World's Classics. 335. [4] *Memoirs*. Champneys. ii, 164. [5] *Disraeli*.
Maurois. Trans. Miles. Bk. iii, Chap. xi. [6] Qt. Lord Rosebery, *Appreciation and Addresses*. 152-7. [7] *Life and Letters*. F. Darwin. i, 33. [8] Hazlitt, *Conduct of Life*.

respect, for towards the end of his days, he confesses,[1] books in a great measure lost their power over him; and although the reading of *Mr. Keats's 'Eve of St. Agnes'* made him regret he was not young again, the *beautiful and tender images there conjured up* moved him no longer, they merely flitted across his fancy: *The sharp luscious flavour, the fine aroma is fled, and nothing but the stalk, the bran, the husk of literature is left.*

He that will know, therefore, how to use books so as to get out of them full measure of content, let him learn how the happiest readers have read at all times; how they have made books at one with their days, and thus found peace at the end. *To the end I shall be reading*, bragged Gissing,[2] and he meant to the end he would be happy, but not as those who flirt with books in their youth and then abandon them, and so, like grasshoppers, whilst they sing over their cups all summer, they starve in winter. Cicero implored Atticus[3] not to promise his library to anyone, *quamvis acrem amatorem inveneris*, however passionate a wooer, for he himself was *saving up*, as they say, to buy the books *ut subsidium senectuti*, as a prop for his old age. Macaulay never ceased to read in all his days. Towards the end he loved best to browse among his books, nibbling choice morsels as he roved: *I read miscellaneous trifles from the back rows of my books*,[4] Nathan's *Reminiscences of Byron*, Colman's *Broad Grins*, Strange's *Letters to Lord Bute*, Gibbon's *Vindication*, and his answer to Warburton about the Sixth *Aeneid*, Swift's *Polite Conversations* and Arbuthnot's *John Bull*; a few weeks before his death he began Nichol's '*Literary Anecdotes': a ponderous row of nine volumes, each containing seven or eight hundred closely printed pages. He searched and sifted this vast repertory of eighteenth-century erudition and gossip with a minute diligence such as few men have the patience to bestow upon a book which they do not intend to re-edit*; he read at the rate of a volume a week, finishing and annotating the entire work between the 17th day of October and the 21st of December, 1859.[5] A week later the greatest reader of all time was found dead seated at the table in his library with an open book before him.[6]

Thus would all good bookmen wish to die, as soldiers in action, as men of affairs at their work, as sailors at sea, amid their appropriate surroundings doing their work, shining to the end, rather than rusting out; and if regret will not be absent, *for the pain of parting with our happiness still rises in proportion to the length of its continuance*.[7] yet many a bookman has been able to make a happy end *holding in his hands a particular beloved volume*.[8] John Donne was so enamoured of his books that when he observed that

---

[1] 'On Reading Old Books', *The Plain Speaker*. ii, 74–5. [2] *Private Papers of Henry Ryecroft*. 46. [3] *Ad Atticum*. i, 10. [4] *Life and Letters*. Trevelyan. ii, 325. [5] *Life and Letters*. ii, 401. [6] *Ib*. ii, 405. [7] 'Fruendis voluptatibus crescit carendi dolor.' Pliny, *Letters*. Melmoth. Loeb Ed. viii, 5. [8] Field, *Love Affairs of a Bibliomaniac*. 169.

there was a vault under his study he hoped to *die reading; since* his *book and a grave are so near.*[1] And so happily have many of them passed in the midst of that life which was their sole passion, the world of books:

Lying dead among thy books,
The peace of God in all thy looks![2]

Giovanni Lami, the great Italian librarian and collector, whose memory is still preserved in the Greek collection which he gave to the University of Florence, spent his life among books and *died with a manuscript in his arms;*[3] and so died Magliabecchi, in his old cane-chair, book in hand, books around him; Grolier, *the Prince of book-collectors,* died as he would have wished, *surrounded by his books,* in his elegant mansion in the Rue de Bussy, Paris.[4]

Petrarch died alone in his library at Arqua, his head resting on an open book, the manuscript of his *Life of Caesar* unfinished before him, as Plato is said to have died long before with his head on Sophron's *Jests;* Fenton, the poet, died, in 1730, at Lady Trumbal's house at Easthampstead, among his *books and papers;*[5] Leibnitz died in a chair with the *Argenis* of Barclay in his hand;[6] when Sir William Osler was near his end, he asked to have Milton's *Nativity* read to him *from his precious first edition;*[7] Francis Thompson's final companions were Jacobs's *Many Cargoes* and a prayer-book;[8] Henry Bradshaw, our great bibliographer, was found dead by his servant in his room at Cambridge, sitting at his table, with *a little Irish book* in front of him.[9] Leigh Hunt lived for books, and, like Donne, prayed to die among them: *if fortune turns her face once more in kindness upon me before I go, I may chance, some quiet day, to lay my overbeating temples on a book, and so have the death I most envy.*[10] Père Jacob, in his treatise on famous libraries, tells of his journey to Ferrara, where he visited the tomb of Coelius, who was *buried among his books, at his own desire,* not, as he says, *like a miser in the midst of his riches,* but like a lover among the treasures of his heart.[11] And methinks 'tis not altogether unfit that when these true lovers depart this life, they should thus pass away among the *dear creations of the brain,* confident belike that they will take up their joy, renew their old companionships, for as the poet sings:[12]

O then the bliss of blisses, to be freed
From all the wants by which the world is driven;
With liberty and endless time to read
The libraries of Heaven!

[1] Letter to Sir H. G. (*c.* 1608).   [2] 'Bayard Taylor', Longfellow.   [3] *The Great Book-Collectors.* Elton. 73.   [4] *Ib.* 147.   [5] *Ib.* 77.   [6] W. Roberts, *Book-Hunter in London.* xv.   [7] *Life.* Cushing. ii, 684.   [8] *Life.* Meynell. 350.   [9] Prothero, *Memoir of Henry Bradshaw.* 322.   [10] 'My Books', *Essays.* Camelot Ed. 303.   [11] *Ma République.*   [12] Rot. Leighton.

Part XII

HOW BOOKMEN CONQUER TIME AND PLACE

━━━━━━━━━━(◦◦)━━━━━━━━━━

I. THE PROPER TIME FOR READING

The time to read is any time: *no apparatus, no appointment of time and place, is necessary.*[1] It is the only art which can be practised at any hour of the day or night, *whenever the time and inclination comes, that is your time for reading;*[2] in joy or sorrow, health or illness. *The mood for a book sometimes rushes upon one, either one knows not why, or in consequence, perhaps, of some trifling suggestion.*[3] Gissing tells how one day at dusk he was out walking when the sight of an old farmhouse, with the doctor's gig waiting at the door and a light in an upper window, put him so strongly in mind of *Tristram Shandy* that he must hurry home to *plunge into* the book, which he had not opened for twenty years. Nothing gave him greater pleasure than the thought that there were times when he could *sit reading, quietly reading all day long;* 'tis a common dream of them all whether it comes true or not, they would be reading *a mane ad noctem usque.*[4]

Yet it is folly to wait upon opportunity. The time to read is now, not hereafter. We must make time or miss our joy, as that friend of Hamerton's who *indulged in wonderful illusions about reading, collected several thousands of volumes, all fine editions, but died without having cut their leaves.* Well may Hamerton say that reading is the most *illusory* of all the tasks *we propose to ourselves,* nothing easier than the intention to read the *vastest literatures* in the *indefinite future,* and to be defeated by time.[5] Never put off till to-morrow the book you can read to-day.

Milton was *up and stirring, in Winter often 'ere the Sound of any Bell awake Men to Labour, or to Devotion; in Summer as oft with the Bird that first rouses, or not much tardier to read good Authors, or cause them to be read, till the Attention be weary, of Memory have his full Fraught;*[6] but Dr. Johnson, in the other extreme, could not remember the time since he left Oxford that he rose

[1] John Aikin, *Letters from a Father to his Son.*   [2] C. F. Richardson, *Choice of Books.* 44.   [3] Gissing, *Private Papers of Henry Ryecroft.* 144–7.   [4] 'From morning till night.   [5] Hamerton, *Intellectual Life.* 147.   [6] 'Apology for Smectymnuus.' *Works.* (1697) 333.

early except when he was writing the *Rambler*;[1] and Burton's *Anatomy of Melancholy* was *the only book that ever took him out of bed two hours sooner than he wished to rise*.[2] Samuel Pepys rose at four o'clock in the morning to read Cicero's *Second Oration*; Macaulay, when in Calcutta, read ancient literature every morning from five to nine; on September 9th, 1850, he was up soon after six reading *Cobbett with admiration, pleasure, and abhorrence*, and every now and then, *on an idle afternoon*, he read one of Plutarch's *Lives*;[3] Coleridge was a matutinal reader, and once announced that *Southey* and *Bowles* were his *only morning companions*;[4] but he confessed that he could read Beaumont and Fletcher's *Beggar's Bush* from *morning to night*.[5] Stevenson could read early and late, but *Virgil* was *not good fun on an empty stomach*.[6]

Others prefer to read late in the day, and far into the night, keeping themselves awake by wet towels and vinegar compresses applied to the head; copious draughts of coffee; hard chairs, etc. The Chinese scholar, Sun Ching, always tied his pig-tail *to a beam overhead to prevent himself from dozing over his books*.[7] Ringelbergius opposed the demands of sleep by sleeping transversely on two boards so that he might waken betimes and resume his reading. But with many notable readers such devices are unnecessary. St. Anselm's zeal was so *excessive* that the *time of meals* frequently passed by unnoticed, and *he applied himself to his literary enquiries* far into the night,[8] and Magliabecchi read all day and as far into the night as possible, and when exhausted fell asleep among his books.[9]

Milton's genius was revealed in his *impetuosity in learning*, which, the poet himself admitted, *seized him with such eagerness* that after his twelfth year he *scarce ever went to bed before midnight*;[10] in Huysman's *A Rebours*,[11] Des Esseintes sits up all night brooding over that old Latin poem *De Laude Castitatis*, written in the reign of Gondebald, by Avitus, Bishop Metropolitan of Vienna, and when he looked at his watch and found it was three o'clock, he simply lit a ·cigarette and *plunged* into it once again. Henry Crabb Robinson devoured a great part of *Waverley* after dinner; E. B. Cowell, who taught Edward FitzGerald Persian, *constantly*, says our English Omar,[12] *reads Miss Austen at night after his Sanscrit Philology is done: it composes him, like Gruel: or like Paisiello's Music, which Napoleon liked above all other, because he said it didn't interrupt his thoughts*; Dibdin read *early and late*;[13] Isaac D'Israeli was the *companion* of his *evening hours and lone musings beyond midnight*, when he was at Oxford: *I once*, he says, *saw the*

[1] *Johnsonian Miscellanies*. Hill. i, 16.   [2] *Life*. Ed. Hill. ii, 121.   [3] *Life and Letters*. i 385.   [4] *Letters*. Ed. E. H. Coleridge. i, 107.   [5] *Table Talk*. 212.   [6] *Letters*. Ed. Colvin. ii, 126.   [7] Giles, *Chinese Biog. Dict*. 688.   [8] *St. Anselm*. Möhler. Trans. Rymer. 9, 19.   [9] Buck, *Anecdotes*. i, 246.   [10] Pattison, *Milton*. 5.   [11] Chap. vi, 100. [12] *Letters and Literary Remains*. i, 335–6.   [13] Dibdin, *Reminiscences*. i, 281.

gothic battlements outside my window streaked with the dappled light of the morning, as I retired to rest closing the 'Curiosities of Literature'.[1]

Dr. Johnson read a book of the *Aeneid every night, so it was done in twelve nights, and,* he said, *I had great delight in it*;[2] Lord Chesterfield (in a letter, 26.xii.1749) records that he often read through the night, going to bed at six in the morning; I *should certainly have read very little* (between the ages of twenty and forty), *if I had not been up when my acquaintances were in bed*; which recalls Cicero (*Pro Archia Poeta*) on Seneca: *when others loitered, and took their pleasure, he was continually at his books*; and when Lord Chesterfield was old and *cut out of living company* by his deafness, he had recourse to the dead, *whom alone I can hear*, and he assigned them their stated hours and audience: *Solid folios are the people of business, with whom I converse in the morning. Quartos are the easier mixed company, with whom I sit after dinner*; and he passed his evenings in *the light, and often frivolous, chit-chat of small octavos and duodecimos.* Lord Orrery read consistently and late: *'Clarissa' kept us up till two in the morning. 'Roderick' will keep us up all night, and he, I am told, is to be succeeded again by 'Clarissa', whom I left, adorable girl, at St. Albans*;[3] and some years later Lady Orrery reveals a like habit of her lord, complaining of a *horrid headache* through *reading so much of 'Amelia' last night till it was very late*.[4] Benjamin Robert Haydon hurt his eyes by reading Stone's *Chronicles* late into the night; Hazlitt loved *luxuriating in books*, and remembered sitting up half the night to read *Paul and Virginia*, which he had *picked up at an inn at Bridgewater, after being drenched in the rain all day*;[5] Robert Southey wrote all day and read in the evening: *My after-supper book at present is Erasmus's 'Letters'*; Walter Scott sends him *The Lady of the Lake*,[6] which notwithstanding his obstinate habit of getting to bed early, he could not rest until he had finished, and the evening *Rokeby* arrived, he tells Scott, *I did not go to bed till I had read the poem through*;[7] Francis Jenkinson was a late reader on occasion, and one night he records how he killed slugs in his garden for an hour and then read *Hain* till nearly one o'clock.[8]

There are, John Hall thinks (*Horae Vacivae*), *unseasonable times of study* which are *very obnoxious, as after meals, when nature is wholly retired to concoction; or at night times: when she begins to droop for want of rest*; hence he argues, *so many rheums, defluxions, catarrhs*, etc., and Burton repeats the same:[9] *hard students are commonly troubled with gouts, catarrhs, rheums, cachexia, bradypepsia, bad eyes, stone, and colick, crudities, oppilations, vertigo, consumptions, and all such diseases as come by overmuch sitting; they are most part lean, dry, ill-coloured, spend their fortunes, lose their wits, and many times*

[1] *Ib.* 87–8.   [2] *Life.* iv, 218.   [3] *Orrery.* ii, 23.   [4] *Ib.* ii, 285.   [5] *On Going a Journey.*
[6] Southey, *Letters.* World's Classics. 179.   [7] *Ib.* 210.   [8] *Francis Jenkinson*, Stewart.
116.   [9] *Anat. of Melan.* 1904. i, 350–1.

their lives, and all through immoderate pains and extraordinary studies. But in our times, though some may wreck their health and even their lives for books, such immoderate reading is no longer common, and good light and fair print have so added to the amenities of the studious and the hedonist alike, that no great harm can come to them.

> Whence is thy learning? Hath thy toil
> O'er books consumed the midnight oil?[1]

Electricity and the Daylight Saving Act have turned the point of the old gibe. There still are more than enough of dull writers and stupid readers, but we can no longer blame the *midnight oil*.

Day-light or electric-light, it is now all one: readers will read, no matter what the hour, place, or season, though I find some differences here. Charles Lamb could not read much in the summer;[2] with the poet he prefers taper-time when the year wears chill:

> How pleasing wears the wintry night,
> Spent with the old illustrious dead![3]

They are supported in our own days by many, one even[4] claiming winter the time of the year for reading, *par excellence*; poets and essayists are then *all the more delightful* because they may transport us to *verdant lawns, blossoming trees, budding flowers, blue skies*, etc., when all is *cold and wet outside*.

> But when the skies of shorter days
> Are dark and all the ways are mire,
> How bright upon your books the blaze
> Gleams from the cheerful study fire,
>
> On quartos where our fathers read,
> Enthralled, the book of Shakespeare's play,
> On all that Poe could dream of dread,
> And all that Herrick sang of gay.[5]

Edward FitzGerald thought Southey's *Life of Cowper* not suitable for *every man to read at the fall of the leaf*,[6] that there was some *rocococity* in a gentleman reading *Seneca* in the *middle of February*, in a *remarkably damp cottage*,[7] and he was convinced that *Theocritus* harmonized with the *opening of fine weather*;[8] in the summer of 1866 he had *a sort of craze* for *Sophocles*,[9] but it was his *Sévigné* who always returned to him in the spring: *fresh as the Flowers*, he said,[10] and *Crabbe* came as naturally to him

[1] Gay, Intro. to *Fables.*   [2] *Letters.* Ed. Lucas. ii, 912.   [3] Mark Akenside.
[4] W. Davenport Adams, *Rambles in Book-Land.* 169.   [5] A. Lang, 'To F. L.', *Books and Bookmen.* 38–9.   [6] *Letters and Literary Remains.* i, 34.   [7] *Ib.* 125.   [8] *Ib.* 41.
[9] *More Letters.* 79.   [10] *Letters to Fanny Kemble.* 221.

at the fall of the leaf.[1] Henry James thought the *Mystical Romances* of Le Fanu *ideal reading for midnight at a country house*; Lionel Johnson believed that even *Beattie on Truth* could *be read in fine weather*;[2] Edward Dowden recommended *Chaucer* for summer reading *when you are not in an intense or a heroic mood*,[3] and Leigh Hunt *the Arabian Nights for all seasons*;[4] but when we have weighed each opinion, most bookmen will agree with Sir Walter Raleigh that *there is no time so good to read a book as when you have just bought it and brought it home*.[5] So if, as among men of affairs, statesmen, and others who are so much occupied that their days are partitioned into several sections each reserved for its particular duty, they will prepare a space for reading, my problem is solved. So I end as I began, the proper time is any time.

II. OF READING PLACES

True readers are not to be kept from books, despite those who argue otherwise, as that meticulous Jewish grammarian, Profiat Duran, who advised students to *read in a pretty well-furnished room* where the eye may be relieved by *beautiful objects; beauty*, he said, *must be everywhere, in your books and in your house*.[6] Charles Lamb expostulates that much depends on *when* and *where* you read; no one, he says, would take up the *Fairy Queen* during *the five or six impatient minutes* before dinner, or, as such a *stop-gap*, a volume of Bishop Andrewes' *Sermons*; and *Milton almost requires a solemn service of music before you enter upon him*.[7] More recent support comes from Maurice Hewlett,[8] who could not read every kind of book while waiting, even in a library; odd that, in such circumstances, he could take down *Dante* or *Homer, open anywhere and be occupied*, but would rather *twiddle* his thumbs than attempt *Paradise Lost. You seem to need*, he reckons, '*the consecration and the poet's dream' for the one, and not for the other*. Stevenson found *Horace* unsuitable for reading *under the open heaven*,[9] but he read Zola's *Bête Humaine in Noumea, listening the while to the strains of the convict band*.[10] Lionel Johnson, who could and did read in any condition or place, believed that special books were appropriate to be read in particular places, as Walter Pater, the *constant cordiality* of whose writings makes them books to be read with equal pleasure *under the garden trees* or *by the fire*.[11] Sir Walter Raleigh, on the other hand, doubts whether books can be read in wild places. ' *Social' books won't stand the criticism of the Atlantic Coast*,[12] and Charlotte Brontë's *Shirley* in such a place *was merely half-baked and unreal and*

---

[1] *Ib.* 55.   [2] *Post Liminium.* 215.   [3] *Fragments.* 123.   [4] *A Jar of Honey from Mount Hybla.* xiii.   [5] *Letters.* i, 144.   [6] Abrahams, *Jewish Life in the Middle Ages.* 355.   [7] 'Detached Thoughts', *Last Essays of Elia.*   [8] *Extempory Essays.* 119.   [9] *Letters.* Ed. Colvin. i, 65.   [10] *Ib.* ii, 195.   [11] *Post Liminium.* 28.   [12] *Letters.* ii, 587.

ignorant. Leigh Hunt would seem to prescribe definite times and places for reading this or that book; *How can I take Juvenal into the fields,* he enquires, *or take Valcarenghius' 'De Aortae Aneurismate' to bed with me?* How could he expect *to walk before the face of nature with the one* or to tire his *elbow properly with the other;* how could he *stick up Coke or Littleton against something on the dinner-table,* his taste divided between *a fresh paragraph and a mouthful of salad?*[1]

Charles Lamb preferred to read indoors, although he could read in the open air on occasions, as shall be mentioned in its place, but he stiffly maintained the necessity for harmony between the reader and his surroundings, and would not himself like to have been *caught in the serious avenues of some cathedral alone, reading Candide;*[2] but he could never *contemplate without affection* those impecunious readers of the open-air who *not having the wherewithal to buy or hire a book, filch a little learning at the open stalls,* under the jealous eyes of the bookseller. He gives an instance of one who got through two volumes of *Clarissa* in this wise, before the stall-keeper *damped his laudable ambition, by asking him whether he meant to purchase the work;* the thief of reading *admitted that under no circumstances of his life did he ever peruse a book with half the satisfaction which he took in those uneasy snatches.*[3] A still more notable instance is that of John Beale, a seventeenth-century scientist and divine who wrote on the Orchards of Herefordshire; the bookstalls were his main library; at them he would browse indifferent to the tempestuous glances of the bookseller, memorizing exactly for future reference the contents of whole volumes.

All this I doubt not; but it is plain also that few circumstances are too strange or difficult for the enjoyment of a book; nothing so common as invincible and indomitable readers; place, conditions, etc., are nothing in this case. Bookmen dictate their own terms to vandal time. Giles has a pretty story of a Chinese poet and alchemist, whose mental powers were so quick that he could remember any book after reading it over once, and who was taught by supernatural beings the *art of hibernating like an animal,* enabling him to sleep for one hundred days at a time, yet he *was never seen without a book in his hands.*[4]

This is only one of many instances I could cite (and shall do so) to prove that the born reader reads anywhere, anywhen, by day or night, by the light of the moon and the stars, or even, so I have heard, by lightning or the *aurora borealis;* by sunlight and candlelight, gaslight or electricity; on land or sea, walking or riding, standing or sitting or lying in bed; on chairs or sofas, on couches, in hammocks, in baths and at stool; on board ships, in punts, rowing-boats, and canoes; up trees; on ladders; on omni-

[1] 'My Books', *Essays*. Camelot Ed. 297. [2] 'Detached Thoughts', *Last Essays of Elia*. [3] *Ib.* [4] *Chinese Biog. Dict.* 105–6.

buses, or bicycles, in railway trains, or automobiles, cabs, carriages, tram-way cars, jaunting cars, buggies, balloons, airships or aeroplanes, or any other vehicle for sea, land or air; in hospitals, penitentiaries, prisons; in kitchens, parlours, caves, arbours, etc.; on the backs of horses, camels, mules, asses, elephants; in hot or cold climates, in all countries and all places; in houses, hotels, theatres, mines, concert halls, submarines, bar-parlours, saloons, billiard-rooms, turkish baths, sun-boxes, pastry cooks', barbers' shops, waiting-rooms at railway stations; in the ante-rooms of Ministers of State, and the waiting-rooms of physicians, surgeons, den-tists, etc.; in churches during service, surreptitiously and not always the *Holy Word*; in law courts; in streets walking or standing or leaning against a wall; in fields or forests; on the *Underground* in London, the *Overhead* at Liverpool and the *El* at New York, regardless of noise; during air raids and bombardments, wars, revolutions and pestilences; in joy and sorrow, health and sickness.

No end to reading and readers as there is no end to books, and I say again, no particular time or place is essential to reading. Every place a library or study to your true reader; undergraduates at Oxford and Cam-bridge make a pleasant study of a punt or a canoe while gliding along the green tunnels of the Cherwell or between the willows and lawns and under the bridges of the cool Granta. *In the very Court itself before the Senate fill'd, Cato would be reading Greek books;*[1] Ben Jonson rested from his work as a bricklayer in Lincoln's Inn Fields to read a book, and he was thus dis-covered deep in *Horace, by the great Camden, who sent him to the University at Cambridge.*[2] Place and position are matters of taste, some for one, some for another. Dr. Johnson was once discovered by Boswell, reading the *'Mémoires de Fontenelle', leaning and swinging upon the low gate into the court,* of Mrs. Thrale's house, *without his hat.*[3] Many observers of bookfolk could recount such incidents out of their own experiences; I have a record of G. K. Chesterton being espied on Ilkley Moor, in Yorkshire, one cold day in spring, *leaning in the rain against a budding tree, absorbed in the pages of a little red book;*[4] and I heard that same author tell how once, whilst riding in a hansom cab, reading one of his own admirable essays, he observed a commotion in the street through which the cab was passing and, to his astonishment, discovered that his situation had been strangely and suddenly translated, for instead of being seated comfortably reading in the cab, the cab was upside down and he sat beneath it in the road, still reading. But this may be a tale: so I proceed. Sir Joshua Reynolds, coming home from Italy, found Johnson's *Life of Savage* the book of the hour, and *knowing*

[1] Q. Valerius Maximus. *Romae Antiquae Descriptio.* Eng. Ed. (1678) 368.
[2] Spence, *Anecdotes.* n. p. 4.   [3] *Life.* iii, 247.   [4] Holbrook Jackson, 'G. K. Chesterton', *Romance and Reality.* 141.

nothing of the author, for it was published anonymously, he *began reading it while he was standing with his arm leaning against a chimney-piece*, and was *unable to lay the book down until he had finished it*, so that when he attempted to move, *he found his arm totally benumbed.*[1]

Shelley *was to be found, book in hand, at all hours; reading in season and out of season; at table, in bed, and especially during a walk; not only in the quiet country, and in retired paths; not only at Oxford, in the public walks, and High Street, but in the most crowded thoroughfares of London.*[2] Leigh Hunt hated *to read in public, or in strange company,*[3] but he would have done either (I say) rather than be deprived of books, which were his *staff of life*. Matthew Prior had other tastes, for he read his master, *Horace*, in the Rhenish Tavern, where he was found by the Earl of Dorset, who so marvelled at his skill in Latin that he gave him an education in literature.[4] James Agate tells how at a performance of Sacha Guitry's *Nono*, William Archer, who sat next to him, slept *through almost the entire performance, waking up in the intervals to draw from his pocket and peruse a volume of Gibbon's 'Decline and Fall'.*[5]

And now, the case being put, I shall proceed to show their variety and what difference there is between them, and to enumerate notable examples in support of my claim that books may be enjoyed at any time or in any circumstance; but, since which is the best place hath many opinions, I will not dictate. Lest, however, some cavillers complain that I have remembered every condition but the normal, I must not forget mine own fireside (and yours), for all of us, bookmen, students, scholars, etc., have known its delight as a vantage point for the attack upon a book. Macaulay[6] defined a scholar as *a man who can read Plato with his feet on the fender*; and what better place could he have? I need not waste time upon an answer.

III. THE ASSOCIATION OF BOOK AND PLACE

Many there are of the more romantic sort that seek to read their favourite authors under particular circumstances or in places associated with the theme of the book or with its writing. Thus they will take out *Dante* at Florence, *Shakespeare* at Stratford, *Rabelais* at Chinon, *Gibbon* among the ruins of the Forum at Rome, where he first imagined his mighty history, or at Lausanne where he wrote it; *Wordsworth* at Grasmere or Rydal, *Keats* at Hampstead, *Dickens* at Rochester or in Lincoln's Inn Fields, *Lamb* in the sparrow-haunted quadrangles of the Temple, *Goethe* at Weimar, *Rousseau* on the islet which bears his name at Geneva, *Emerson* at Concord,

[1] Boswell's *Johnson*. Ed. Hill. i, 165.   [2] Hogg, *Shelley*. London Lib. Ed. 84.
[3] 'My Books', *Essays*. Camelot Ed. 289.   [4] Bickley, *Life of Prior*. 13-15.   [5] *Sunday Times*. Review of Three Plays, by William Archer.   [6] *Life*, Trevelyan. i.

Thoreau beside Walden Pond, *Tennyson* where he lived at Freshwater Down, *Meredith* on Box Hill in Surrey, where he loved to breast the south-west wind, *Byron* at Venice and *Shelley* on the shores of the Bay of Spezzia, where his body was burnt after the sea had given it up.

To read *Wordsworth* on Westminster Bridge, *Browning* in Venice, *Omar Kháyyám* at Naishapur, *Gray* in the meadows at Eton, *Matthew Arnold* on Cumnor Hill or beside the 'stripling Thames' at Bablock Hythe, *William Morris* at Kelmscott, *Anatole France* on the Quai Voltaire, *Yeats* at Coole, *Rupert Brooke* at Grantchester, *Henry Newbolt* on Plymouth Hoe, *Belloc* on the Sussex Downs, *Lionel Johnson* at Winchester, *Richard le Gallienne* in the Strand, *John Davidson* in Fleet Street, *Ernest Dowson* in Soho, *Austin Dobson* in Queen Anne's Gate, *Walt Whitman* on *fish-shaped Paumanok*, or *Kipling* in Simla—these are accounted experiences.

Some are for historic spots and are brisk to read them to themselves or aloud amid the ruins of Pompeii; in the portico of the Parthenon at Athens, or in the shadows of the baths of Caracalla at Rome; on the Pyramids of Egypt or beside the great Sphinx; in York Minster, Notre Dame of Paris, St. Peter's at Rome, Monreale near Palermo; in the Teatro Greco at Syracuse or Taormina, etc.

For Macaulay, journeys to famous places were excuses for reading books about them. Thus, in Italy, his *journey lay over the field of Thrasymene, and as soon as the sun rose* he read *Livy's description of the scene,* wishing he *had brought Polybius too;*[1] Samuel Rogers and his sister read the *concluding passages* of the *Decline and Fall* on *the very spot where they were written;*[2] and Malcolm Macmillan *lay down against a fragment in the Forum and read Horace* to a friend who was making *architectural notes.*[3]

William Beckford, on his journey in Portugal, proposed to read his *favourite pocket companions, Monteiro and Manoel Maria Bocage,* in a *little cavern hewn out of a pumice rock, blessed with a little spring, and mantled all over with the deliciously-scented flowers of the Lonicera tribe in wild profusion— exactly the sort of grotto described by Gil Blas as the resort of Algerian pirates.* He longed to read in *total solitude,* and thus share *the deep reveries* of his *intellectual and Cowley-like poets;* but *fate* denied him *such dreamy happiness.*[4]

For my part I am not so romantically affected in my choice of reading places. I can read anywhere, but am not indifferent to that *genius loci,* which is not in the place itself but is brought there by recollection, experience, association:

> a sunset-touch,
> A fancy from a flower-bell, someone's death,
> A chorus-ending from Euripides.[5]

[1] *Life.* Trevelyan. ii, 31.   [2] Rogers, *Table Talk.* 198.   [3] *Letters.* 89.   [4] *Excursion to the Monasteries of Alcobaça and Batalha.* 31-2.   [5] Browning, 'Bishop Blougram's Apology', 182-4, *Men and Women.*

George Wyndham was moved by such feelings and he left to Charles Gatty *a legacy of places glorified by such experiences: the end of the garden at Derwent where he read to me Patmore's Ode to the Blessed Virgin, the smoking-room at Derwent where he and Alfred Lyttleton and myself chose passages in turn from a Globe Shakespeare, and I read the Duke of Exeter's description to the King of the death of York and Suffolk on the field of Agincourt.*[1]

There are those that are especially affected as much and more from the reading of books in particular places, for it cuts both ways: one would read a passage or a whole work in the place of its inspiration, another will read a book in some place not associated with its authorship or its theme, and ever afterwards hold that place in memory as the scene of a capital experience. The sum is this: that varieties of association are excellent good for books as well as bookmen.

IV. VARIOUS READERS AND THEIR READING PLACES

Happy the bookman who can read anywhere, secure in his book from all common annoyances: the tumult of traffic in cities, noise of trains, omni-buses, aeroplanes, automobiles, motor-cycles and pneumatic road-drills, with their vibrant oscillations. But not all can train themselves to endure such inconveniences: some cannot read in public or amidst noise; and who does not prefer quietude?

> The love of learning, the sequestered nooks,
> And all the sweet serenity of books.[2]

Books are born *of the very sigh that silence heaves*,[3] they are the voice of silence and quiet time, the colonizers of solitude; *true reading demands seclusion, leisure, freedom from the crowd*,[4] what is gregarious is foreign to it.

To walk or loaf with a book among orchards, gardens, bowers, parks, and arbours, artificial wildernesses, is most sweet; or in wild places, green thickets, copses, oases in the desert, lawns (with rivulets, fountains), and such-like pleasant places as *Antiochian Daphne so deeply bosomed in a thick grove of laurels and cypresses that it formed in the most sultry summers a cool and penetrable shade*, where *a thousand streams of the purest water, issuing from every hill, preserved the verdure of the earth and the temperature of the air;* where the senses *were gratified with harmonious sounds and aromatic odours; and the peaceful grove was consecrated to health and joy, to luxury and love;*[5] or those

---

[1] Charles T. Gatty, *George Wyndham, Recognita.* 11–12.　　[2] Longfellow, 'Morituri salutamus'.　　[3] Keats, 'I stood tip-toe upon a little hill'. 12.　　[4] Lang, Intro. *Pleasures of Bookland*, Shaylor. xiii.　　[5] Gibbon, *Decline and Fall.* xxiii.

Quincuncial, or other geometrical or reticulated gardens of the ancients, so enviously dilated upon by Sir Thomas Browne, in his *Garden of Cyrus*; or that garden at Athens where Epicurus passed his whole life studying and teaching philosophy, in comparison with which *no other abode seems to contribute so much to both the tranquillity of mind and indolence of body, which he made his chief end.*[1] It is a delectable recreation, for *how much better one's books read in country stillness, than amid the noise of wheels, crowds, etc.*[2] But we need not seek out such pleasant delights in ancient times or distant places, for in our own age in our own dear England they have been tasted, and still are. *I should like very well to be shut up in a garden for a whole summer with no literature but the 'Faerie Queen',* says Hamerton, and once he *nearly realized that project, but publishers and postmen interfered with it.*[3] Many of the most fortunate of bookmen have rich memories of Christ Church Meadows in Oxford, and those adorable *Backs* of Cambridge

> Where Arthur, Alfred, Fitz, and Brooks
> Lit thought by one another's looks,
> Embraced their jests and kicked their books,
> In England's happier times,[4]

loving them and reading them none the less, as is well known, and I do not find a more pleasant environment for reading than such places, soberly and opportunely used.

But when all is said, it is the greatest of good fortune to be able to defy the world and retreat into a book at any time or place. Many bookmen have done so and still do, by reason of that detachment which, properly disposed, all good books engender. It is the very same faculty which enabled John Wesley to read through Martin Luther's *Comment on the Epistle to the Galatians* and the tenth *Iliad* of Homer and many other profound works, on horseback during his great mission of evangelization: *having other employment at other times. How is it,* he asks, *that no horse ever stumbles while I am reading?* Because, he answers, when reading 'tis his custom to throw his rein on the horse's neck, and, *in riding above an hundred miles, he scarce ever* remembers *any horse (except two, that would fall head over heels anyway) to fall, or make a considerable stumble while he rode with a slack rein.*[5] ·This I record by the way, for the benefit of those about to follow his example. For further evidence of such feats take that of Colonel Lawrence, riding across the Arabian Desert on a camel at the head of his Bedouins, reading *Aristophanes* in the original when there was nothing else to be done.[6]

[1] Sir William Temple, *Upon the Gardens of Epicurus.*   [2] Edward FitzGerald, *Letters and Literary Remains.* i, 160.   [3] *Intellectual Life.* 147.   [4] William Cory, *Ionica,* 'Hersilia'. Third Ed. 193.   [5] Wesley, *Journal.* 21.iv.1770.   [6] *With Lawrence in Arabia.* Lowell Thomas. 153.

So sensitive a poet as Petrarch could read in all circumstances: *Whether I am being shaved, or having my hair cut, whether I am riding on horse-back or taking my meals. I either read myself or get someone to read to me;*[1] and on the table where he dined, and by the side of his bed, he kept all the materials for writing, out of an instinctive desire to lose no chance of adding to the world's store of delectable books. His favourite, the *Confessions of St. Augustine*, accompanied him everywhere, even on that adventure when he and his brother climbed Mt. Ventoux.[2]

Because he was so great a reader, Sydney Smith[3] called Macaulay a *book in breeches*. He read anything and remembered everything;[4] no place or time inappropriate for the practice of his bookishness. He would read the *Classics* while walking, *Plato* on the Heath at Tunbridge Wells, *Plautus* in the thickets at Bonchurch, sitting down here and there to read the *Poenulus*; and consuming the last five books of the *Iliad* at a stretch, walking over the hills at Malvern; in the train between London and Bangor (16 viii. 1849) he read the *Lives of the Emperors*, from Maximin to Carinus inclusive, in the Augustan History; and on another occasion he was so greatly amused and moved that he *was at last forced to turn into a by-path, lest the parties of walkers should see* him *blubbering for imaginary beings, the creations of a ballad-maker who has been dead two thousand seven hundred years.*[5] Yet not in the country alone does he walk and read: such feats are common enough, even to ordinary bookmen. He could thread the crowded streets of London with his eyes fixed upon a book, *walking as fast as other people walked, and reading a good deal faster than anybody else could read.*[6] He is eminent even among those peripatetic readers who, by instinct or long practice, I know not which, have acquired a sense of direction in which the eye plays but a secondary part, as Thomas Ballard, the painter friend of Samuel Butler, who *was always reading in the streets, and by long practice steering in and out among the passengers on the pavement in a most skilful manner;*[7] and that Unitarian Minister observed by Charles Lamb walking down Snow Hill reading *Lardner* so skilfully that it was a wonder how *he sidled along, keeping clear of secular contacts.*[8] Shelley was no less *absorbed by the volume that was open before him, in Cheapside, in Cranbourne Alley, or in Bond Street, than in a lonely lane, or a secluded library;*[9] and to show that this curious and useful gift is yet extant, there are many Londoners who remember having seen Dr. Furnivall on fine days *quietly walking along bareheaded, reading a book, in all the bustle of Oxford Street.*[10]

---

[1] *Famil. Ep.* lxxii. Qt. Merryweather, *Bibliomania in the Middle Ages.* 73.   [2] Tatham, *Francesco Petrarca.* i, 323.   [3] *Memoir.* 363.   [4] *Life and Letters,* Trevelyan. i, 129. [5] *Ib.* ii, 187.   [6] *Ib.* i, 118.   [7] *Butler.* Festing Jones. i, 139.   [8] 'Detached Thoughts on Books and Reading', *Last Essays of Elia.*   [9] Hogg, *Shelley.* London Lib. Ed. 84.   [10] Jessie Currie in Monro, *F. J. Furnivall.* 31.

Thomas Frognall Dibdin delighted to stroll about Camden Hill in company one day with *Erasmus, Scaliger, Casaubon, and Lipsius,* another with *a volume of old English Divinity, scoring the more striking passages—to be afterwards inserted in a common-place book;*[1] again he mentions sitting on a *grass hillock in the green fields of North End contiguous to Gloucester Lodge, with a volume of Baillet in one hand and a Schelhorn in another,* and *Spizelius, Bauer* and *De Bure* close by;[2] with *Johnson and Boswell* he used to sit *hour after hour, and day after day,* in *the groves and gardens* of Oxford, during his college days;[3] and when seeking respite from the labour of compiling his *Bibliotheca Spenceriana,* he went down to Ramsgate, *that most interesting of all watering places,* he says,[4] where under *a blue and serene sky,* he *strolled abroad, now with Pope, now with Dryden, and now with Milton.* Mark Rutherford, another peripatetic bookman, *wandered about London streets at 6 o'clock in the morning reading Tennyson's 'Maud';*[5] Leigh Hunt never walked without a book, regarding nature *chiefly as a reading-room out of doors, a place to lie down in, under a tree or a haystack, for the better enjoyment of a book;*[6] for he knew, as Petrarch before him, that to carry books into the fields was good, for silence suits them better than the noise of cities; as John Wilson, a London bookseller, has it:

> O for a booke and a shadie nooke,
>   Either in-a-door or out,
> With the greene leaves whisp'ring overhede,
>   Or the streete cries all about,
> Where I may Reade all at my ease,
>   Both of the Newe and Olde,
> For a jollie goode Booke whereon to looke,
>   Is better to me than golde.

This sentiment hath many exponents, as Richard Hooker, that notable prelate of our Church, who, when vicar of Drayton-Beauchamp, in Buckinghamshire, was discovered, Izaak Walton records, by two of his pupils, reading *Horace* while he tended *his small allotment of sheep in a common field, for that his servant had gone home to dine and assist his wife to do some necessary household business.*[7] Benjamin Robert Haydon retired to *the windmill beyond Kilburn,* where he *lounged on the grass* reading Allan Cunningham's *Lives of the Painters;*[8] Keats would read and loaf on Hampstead Heath with a friend, as John Hamilton Reynolds, whom he invites to go with him and enjoy his *black-letter Chaucer* of 1596;[9]

---

[1] *Reminiscences.* i, 221–2.   [2] *Ib.* i, 282.   [3] *Ib.* i, 87.   [4] *Ib.* ii, 509–10.
[5] Dorothy V. White, *The Groombridge Diary.* 93.   [6] Cosmo Monkhouse, *Life.* 39.
[7] Walton's *Lives.* Ed. Henley. 123.   [8] *Autobiography.* ii, 247.   [9] *Letters* Ed. Forman. (1895) 125.

Then I went indoors, brought out a loaf,
Half a cheese, and a bottle of Chablis;
Lay on the grass and forgot the oaf
Over a jolly chapter of Rabelais;[1]

in his youthful days Edmund Gosse made a reading place of the *turfed hillock* at the root of an elm in his father's garden; this, he says, *was long my summer reading-desk; for I could lie stretched on the lawn, with my head and shoulders supported by the elm-tree hillock, and the book in a fissure of the rough turf.*[2]

Henry Crabb Robinson walked to Clapton reading *Colonel Jack*;[3] Macaulay roamed the Pontine Marshes with Bulwer's *Alice*, and was more affected by it than by any novel *these many years;*[4] when he visited Angers, in 1843, he enjoyed the *scenery and a book* and was sorry when a Frenchman engaged him in talk;[5] Edward FitzGerald *sauntered in the fields* with the *Anthology* of Stobaeus.[6] Felicia Dorothea Hemans as a young girl would take her Shakespeare up into the branches of an apple-tree in the orchard of her Welsh home, near Abergele, and there study him in shade and quietness,[7] which is a habit much cultivated by young girls, and I may cite a more recent instance in that of Lady Lugard, who in her young days found studious seclusion perched in the branches of a tree, where she remembered reading Carlyle's *French Revolution*, which made her a Democrat.[8] Dorothy Wordsworth read *Henry V* in the orchard at Grasmere while William *lay on the seat*;[9] and William Wordsworth read to her his poems, *Peter Bell* and *Joanna*, on the roadside beside the Rothay;[10] in *The Prelude* he tells how as a young man he would go out for a day's fishing, but lay reading all day: though

a soft west wind
Ruffled the waters to the angler's wish,
For a whole day together, have I lain
Down by thy side, O Derwent! murmuring stream,
On the hot stones, and in the glaring sun,
And there have read, devouring as I read,
Defrauding the day's glory, desperate![11]

William Cory read *straight through 'Jane Eyre' on the black gnarled, wreathed rocks of Bude when there was a lowering storm-cloud and a sunset on a distant sail, and a hollow roar in the reefs, and the reading broken off by a queer*

[1] Browning, 'Sibrandus Schafnaburgensis', *Dramatic Romances and Lyrics.*   [2] *Father and Son.* Pop. Ed. (1909) 250.   [3] *Dairy.* i, 170.   [4] *Life.* Trevelyan. ii, 42–3. [5] *Ib.* ii, 131.   [6] *Letters and Literary Remains.* i, 310.   [7] Chorley, *Memorials of Mrs. Hemans.* i, 17.   [8] *The Times.* 28.i.1929.   [9] *Journals.* 119.   [10] *Ib.* 119. [11] *Prelude.* v, 481–7.

rattle of shingle which turned out to be a sheep fallen from the cliff;[1] George Moore read the *dazzling stanzas* of Shelley *by the shores of a pale green Irish lake;*[2] Lionel Johnson, at Winchester, refused to work at his studies when the heat was *visible and tangible . . . burning away to the heart of the world,* preferring *Lucretius* or *Hugo,* in the sunshine;[3] Newman Flower, the biographer of *Handel,* remembers reading *The Trumpet Major, sitting on a bank,* in Hardy's own shire of Dorset, whilst *waiting for an idle ferret to disturb a dilatory rabbit,* and when he later came to London he finished all Hardy's books *sitting under a gas-lamp after office hours on the Embankment.*[4]

It is recorded that David Blondel, a Protestant minister in the seventeenth century, would lie on the ground with the books he required for his studies all around him;[5] Isaac D'Israeli[6] tells of the biographer of Cujas, who would also study *lying prostrate* on a carpet; and one of Macaulay's earliest memories[7] is of lying on the hearth-rug, eating bread and butter and reading a book; at least two other of our statesmen have indulged a similar reading habit in their boyhood: Mr. Gladstone read *Ivanhoe* when he was nine years old, *I devoured it,* he said, *lying on my stomach on the hearth-rug;*[8] and Mr. Stanley Baldwin confessed in a discourse to the English Association that as a small boy he read Scott's novels in the same manner.[9] Prothero gives out that, when a child, the floor was Henry Bradshaw's *favourite place of study,* and once a friend found the infant bibliographer *lying under the table with a sheet of 'The Times' open before him, by the aid of which he was learning to read.*[10]

Francis Thompson could read anywhere; the noisier the environment the more absorbed he became. He found seclusion in the street, the market-place and the tavern. *Already* as a boy, says Everard Meynell,[11] *seeking the highway and the highway's seclusion, he would carry his book to the stairs, away from the constraint of chairs and tables and the unemotional flatness of the floor.* Thomas Gray wished to be always lying on sofas reading *eternal new novels of Crébillon and Marivaux.* Dominie Sampson, Walter Scott[12] tells us, *often opened a volume when half way up the library-steps, fell upon some interesting passage, and, without shifting his inconvenient posture, continued immersed in the fascinating perusal until the servant pulled him by the skirts, to assure him that dinner waited;* Mark Pattison records[13] how his father when at Oxford was caught one night by his tutor, Hodson, reading his favourite *Aristophanes,*

[1] Cory, *Letters and Journals.* 188.   [2] *Confessions of a Young Man.* (1904) 4.   [3] *Some Winchester Letters.* 210.   [4] *Sunday Times.* 15.i.28.   [5] Buck, *Anecdotes.* i, 246. [6] *Curiosities of Literature.* iii, 330–1.   [7] *Life and Letters.* Trevelyan. i, 39.   [8] Neville G. Lyttleton, Letter to *The Times.* 29.x.1927.   [9] 'Books', *Our Inheritance.* 285. [10] *Memoir of Henry Bradshaw.* 4.   [11] *Life* of Francis Thompson. 7.   [12] *Guy Mannering.*   [13] *Memoirs.*

on the back of Cain and Abel, and when asked what he did there replied

Ἀε ροβατῶ καὶ περιφρονῶ τὸν ἥλιον[1]

Shelley delighted to read, sitting naked on the rocks at the Bagni di Lucca, before bathing: *My custom*, he tells Peacock,[2] *is to undress, and sit on the rocks, reading Herodotus, until the perspiration has subsided, and then to leap from the edge of the rock into this fountain—a practice in the hot weather excessively refreshing.* Robert Burns *pored over A Select Collection of English Songs*, which was his *vade mecum*, whilst driving his cart, or walking to work, *song by song, verse by verse; carefully noting the true, tender, or sublime, from affectation and fustian*, and he is convinced that he owes to this practice much of his *critic-craft, such as it is;*[3] so also his compatriot of a later time, Robert Louis Stevenson, roamed the country with a notebook in one pocket and a reading-book in the other, playing *the sedulous ape*, as he admits, to his masters. And I have it on the evidence of Malcolm Macmillan, that when he was in Athens he met a learned German, who, he was credibly informed by *a very amusing lady*, was *supposed to have a Homer printed on indiarubber, to read during his bath.*[4] But I grow troublesome. Let this discourse have what ends it can; the use I make of these instances is but to pretend a reason for my belief that readers can read anywhere, and to entitle you to believe what I have proved to mine own satisfaction by personal experience, but could not prove to you but by these examples.

V. BOOKS ON BATTLEFIELDS

I have advanced enough instances to close my argument that books triumph over all discomforts, yet, if more are necessary, let this chapter give them. Hitherto my examples of an extraordinary kind have told mainly of discomforts, but these are toys to the stories of those who have refused to permit even warfare to arrest their reading, which I now come to relate. Some will say that those who tell such tales draw the long bow, but it is a general resolve and no private opinion how Alexander carried the *Iliad* to the wars enshrined in a precious casket; how Julius Cæsar swam with *a book in one hand, a sword in the other;*[5] how Charles the Bold had with him at the Battle of Nancy his favourite *Cyclopaedia;*[6] how Sunderland, the Cavalier and chivalrous lover of Sacharissa, *read in his tent when besieging Gloucester;*[7] how Napoleon devoured books during the lull of

[1] 'I tread the air and speculate on the sun.' Aristophanes, *Clouds.* 225.   [2] *Letters.* Camelot Ed. 227.   [3] *Letters.* Scott Lib. 66–79.   [4] *Letters.* 170.   [5] Joseph Hall, *Horae Vacivae.*   [6] Elton, *Great Book-Collectors.* 95–6.   [7] Cory, *Letters and Journals.* 459.

battles, speeding from front to front, and throwing the volumes out of the window of his carriage as he finished them, so that he left behind him *a trail like that of a paper-chase*;[1] and how, in our own time, Lawrence of Arabia went into battle (almost) reading *Aeschylus*.

Famous is that remark of Napoleon, during the Peace of Amiens, when a young English officer, named Lovelace, was presented to him: *I perceive your name, Sir*, said the First Consul, *is the same as that of the hero of Richardson's Romance*! This so pleased Hazlitt, who had the story from the young officer's uncle, that he gives it out as a prime reason for liking Buonaparte. *Here was a Consul*, he adds,[2] thrilled by the bookish allusion of a soldier who many times proved that he would not let the God of Battles hold up his engagements with the God of Books. When about to start on his campaign in Russia, Napoleon ordered the proof-sheets of a forthcoming book, about which the press censors disagreed, to be placed in his carriage, so that he might decide for himself what was to be suppressed: *Je m'ennuie en route*, he said; *je lirai ces volumes, et j'écrirai de Mayence ce qu'il y aura à faire*.[3] The volumes thus chosen *to beguile the imperial leisure* contained Madame de Deffand's letters to Horace Walpole.[4]

Sir Adam Ferguson, another bonny fighter, read *The Lady of the Lake* to himself and to his comrades in the lines at Torres Vedras; the *canto* about the stag-hunt was *the favourite*, he told Sir Walter Scott, *among the rough sons of the Fighting Third Division*;[5] *Horace* accompanied Gibbon, when a captain of Militia, *on every march, in every journey: always in my pocket, often in my hand*;[6] Stendhal, who accompanied Napoleon's armies during *the horrors of the retreat* from Moscow, in 1812, *abstracted from one of the deserted palaces* during the burning of the city a *finely bound* copy of the *Facéties* of Voltaire, which helped *to divert his mind as he lay crouched by the camp-fire through the terrible nights that followed*; but as his companions disapproved of anyone who could smile over *Akakia and Pompignan in such a situation*, he found it expedient to leave *the red-morocco volume behind him in the snow*.[7]

But to come to recent times: in the war of 1870 Anatole France, laying down the pen for the sword, tells how, during the battle of the 2nd of December, he was among those troops held in reserve beneath the fortress of Faisanderie, and there, amid the roar of shells which burst around and dropped into the waters of the Marne, he read through the *Silenus* of Virgil, a picture, says his biographer,[8] *which recalls Chateaubriand reading*

---

[1] Ludwig, *Napoleon*. 335.   [2] *The Plain Speaker*. ii, 78.   [3] 'I am bored by the journey; I will read these volumes, and will write from Mayence what is to be done.'   [4] Lytton Strachey, *Books and Characters*. 77.   [5] Lockhart, *Life of Scott*. Chandos Ed. 197.   [6] *Memoirs*. Ed. Hill. 142.   [7] Lytton Strachey, *op. cit.* 260.
[8] J. Lewis May, *Anatole France*. 72.

Homer beneath the walls of Thionville. Wilfrid Scawen Blunt read Doughty's *Arabia Deserta* on his caravan journey to the Senussis in the Egyptian desert,[1] and Colonel Lawrence carried the *Oxford Book of English Verse*, Malory's *Morte d'Arthur, Aeschylus* and *Aristophanes* all through his campaign of king-making and Turk-harassing, from Jeddah to Damascus; *Shelley* also and *Wordsworth* were his desert companions, and he would read them *squatted on a prayer-rug* in his tent like an Arab reading the *Koran*,[2] whilst the Emir Feisal, whom Lawrence made King of the Hedjaz, refreshed himself between battles with the Arabic poetry of his favourite Imr el Kais, the renowned bard who lived and sang about *Camels, the desert, and love*, before the days of Mohammed.[3]

In the Great War, books played their part, being mobilised for service like other munitions of war, and where so many fought there were many readers on all fronts, in camps, canteens, messes, trenches, redoubts, fortresses; on sea and land; and not least on the *home front* during air raids and bombardments. Dr. Johnson himself, from *his abode where the eternal are*,[4] would look with joy on that heroic Mrs. Dyble, wife of a soldier and keeper of the great lexicographer's house in Gough Square, who, during a bombardment from the air by Germans, scorned to *take cover* in a cellar while her husband was *at the front*, so mounted to the immortal attic where the *Dictionary* was compiled, and there read *Boswell* until the enemy had departed.[5]

VI. BOOKS IN PRISON

Servitude, loss of liberty, imprisonment, are no such miseries as they are held to be, if books may be read or written. Many captive men can prove it. One eminent authority[6] holds that it is only in prison that *the acid test of what is readable is to be found*, whilst Gilbert Wakefield's incarceration in Dorchester Gaol opened up for him a new era of study. *I am so wholly immersed in my studies,* he told Fox, *that my spirits are entirely recovered*; and he used his confinement *to combat some of that severe and unkindly reading, in authors of less gaiety and elegance, which, in a happier situation, would have been contended with more tardily and reluctantly, if contended with at all.*[7] When Sir Thomas More was a prisoner in the Tower of London, he occupied his time reading and writing, until they *took from him all his books, ink and paper, which being done, he applied himself wholly to meditation, keeping his chamber windows fast shut, and very dark,* and when they asked him why he

[1] *My Diaries*. i, 273.   [2] *With Lawrence in Arabia*. Lowell Thomas. 108.   [3] *Ib*. 53–4.
[4] Shelley, *Adonais*.   [5] A. Edward Newton, *A Magnificent Farce*. 243–4.   [6] Sir Edward Cook, *More Literary Recreations*. 1.   [7] *Correspondence with C. J. Fox*. 102.

did so, he replied: *when all the wares are gone, the shop windows are to be shut up.*[1]

Boëthius, emprisoned at Pavia, consoled himself with the thought of his library *decked with ivory and glass: nec bibliothecae potius comtos ebore ac vitro parietes, quam tuae mentis fidem requiro* (L. i, pros. v.),[2] and with the composition of the *Consolatio*. By this means he was enabled calmly to await his cruel execution, when a cord was tied round his head until *his eyes were almost forced from their sockets,* and he was afterwards beaten *with clubs until he died.*[3] In the prison of Seville, Cervantes planned *Don Quixote,* Sir Walter Raleigh wrote his *History of the World* in the Tower of London, John Bunyan *Pilgrim's Progress* in prison at Bedford; Surrey, Lovelace, Southwell, Prior, and Leigh Hunt, all suffered imprisonment and found books and the composition of poems their sweetest consolation, and, in our own time, Oscar Wilde wrote *De Profundis* whilst he was in Reading Gaol.

The golden day for Napoleon at St. Helena, says Ludwig,[4] was that on which the ship arrived bringing him a case of books. During his exile he accumulated some 8000 volumes, which he devoured with great speed, throwing each book on the floor as he finished it. The happiest of captive men are, indeed, those who have sought in books freedom from the prison walls. James Howell[5] when in the Fleet Prison thanked his friend, Benlowes, for enlarging his quarters *among those melancholy walls* by a gift of *a whole Isle to walk in,* meaning Phineas Fletcher's *delicate 'Purple Island'* ... *where I met with Apollo himself* (he adds) and all his daughters, with other excellent society, and where he also *stumbled upon* himself, *growing better acquainted with what I have within me and without me.*

That unfortunate parson, William Dodd, compiler of the *Beauties of Shakespeare,* found in books his greatest consolation whilst waiting for death in Newgate Prison:

> Their magic power they lose not; still the same,
> Of matchless influence in this prison-house,
> Unutterably horrid; in an hour
> Of woe, beyond all fancy's fictions drear.[6]

Lord Ferrers, the night before he was hanged for the murder of his valet, *made one of his keepers read Hamlet to him after he was in bed,* and *half an hour before the sheriffs fetched him, corrected some verses he had written in the Tower in imitation of the Duke of Buckingham's epitaph,* 'dubius sed non improbus

---

[1] *Life.* Cresacre More. Ed. Hunter. 253.   [2] 'Nor do I more miss the walls of my library, decked with ivory and glass, than the loyalty of thy heart.'   [3] Langford, *Prison Books and their Authors.* 13.   [4] *Napoleon.* 622.   [5] *Familiar Letters.* 392.
[6] Dodd, *Thoughts in Prison.*

vixi'.[1] Chastelard, that incorrigible romantic, condemned to death by Mary Stuart because of his tempestuous and inconvenient passion for her, would accept no spiritual consolation on the scaffold, but walked boldly to the block reading with great devotion Ronsard's *Hymn on Death*. Turning to the Queen's apartments, he exclaimed: *Farewell fairest and most cruel Princess in the World!* after which *he submitted to the stroke of justice, with the courage of a Rinaldo or an Orlando*.[2] When M. le Comte de Corbières, Minister of Charles X of France, was condemned to life-long imprisonment in the Château de Ham, in Picardy, Jules Janin records,[3] *il emporta dans sa prison ses grands amis: La Fontaine and Fénelon, Montaigne and Rabelais; plus tard, quand il fut libre enfin, grace au bon roi Louis-Philippe, il revint doucement à ses livres, et ne quitta plus sa librarie*.[4]

Writers were the constant visitors of Leigh Hunt, in Surrey Gaol, Byron, Moore, Keats, and they brought him books with which he solaced his lonely hours, turning his cell into a library, and Paul Verlaine,[5] when imprisoned at Mons, prepared for the press his *Romance sans Paroles* and taught himself English by much reading of volumes in that *Tauchnitz Collection* which has helped myriads of travellers to turn the prison of a Continental railway compartment into a pleasant study. When Oscar Wilde was in Reading Gaol Arthur Humphreys sent him books, and the companionship of these silent friends, he wrote, saved him mentally and physically, *each book was the hand of a friend, it lifted me out of the mire of despair and pain where I had for a whole year been lying*.[6]

But lest you think I am overstating my case, I will tell you a story, out of Macaulay,[7] of the opposite extreme, wherein reading proved a punishment harder to bear than the galleys. There was at one time a criminal in Italy who was condemned to choose for punishment between *Guicciardini* and the galleys. He chose the *History*. But the war of *Pisa* being too much for him, he changed his mind, and became a slave of the oar. And, in an opposite case, how the tedium of the monk in his cell has been relieved by reading is well known. That this practice has divine sanction is supported by the story of the miraculous reappearance of a lost book in the cell of Thomas à Kempis in answer to his prayer.[8] But I am o'erstepping the mark. What I am proving needs no proof. Solitude has but one greater ally than a book, namely, a self-possessed man, for I hold with Montaigne

---

[1] Walpole, *Letters*. Ed. Cunningham. iii, 314.   [2] Ferriar, *Illustrations to Sterne*. 37–8.   [3] *Le Livre*. 399.   [4] 'He took into his prison his great friends, La Fontaine and Fénelon, Montaigne and Rabelais; later on, when at last he regained his freedom, thanks to the good King Louis-Philippe, he returned peacefully to his books, and did not again leave his library.'   [5] *Life*. Lepelletier. Chap. xii. [6] Qt. Spencer, *Forty Years in My Bookshop*. 254–5.   [7] 'Burleigh and his Times', *Essays*.   [8] Lang, *Letters on Literature*. 113.

that *the greatest thing of the world, is for a man to know how to be his own.*[1] At the same time it is the prime virtue of books properly used that they readily and generously augment the most precious and inalienable of our riches, self-possession. In my few examples I have pointed somewhat at this belief, and could assemble more, but such are enough, being as good as a feast, and far better than a surfeit.

VII. READING ON A JOURNEY

As travelling companions books have no corrivals. If they lacked other purpose or defence, this alone would justify them before men. How many hours they have scattered pleasantly on lone and long journeys; what limitless tedium they have relieved or circumvented, how they have filled the waking hours, or composed the weary brain for sleep, every reader can support; and it is well known that scholars and bookmen are under no compulsion to be chained to desks or libraries: desk or library is wherever they are. All ages produce instances, as Pliny, Erasmus, Petrarch, Samuel Johnson, Macaulay, John Addington Symonds.

Some have gone so far as to construct travelling libraries for themselves, like Sir Julius Cæsar, Master of the Rolls in the reign of King James I. His library went wherever he did. It was arranged in a box, shaped like a *folio volume*, covered with olive-green morocco, finely tooled in an elaborate pattern. On the inside lid was a catalogue of the forty-four books which comprised the library, together with the arms of Sir Julius and two of his three wives, with other decorations. The books were bound in vellum tooled in gold, and furnished with variously coloured ribbons, to indicate whether they were theological, philosophical, historical, or poetical works.[2] This ingenious device is now preserved in the British Museum. Napoleon had a shelf for books fitted in his coach. Pliny the Elder looked upon journeys as opportunities of escape from the tedium of affairs into the more agreeable world of books. A shorthand writer attended him in his chariot, and when in Rome he always used a 'sedan' chair so as to continue reading or dictating.[3] The passage in *Cicero* which gave Leigh Hunt most pleasure was that where he says: *books delight us at home, and are no impediment abroad*; the period being rounded off to the same purpose: *Delectant domi, non impediunt foris; peregrinantur, rusticantur.*[4] He did not care *to be anywhere without having a book at hand*, and like Dr. Okeborne in the *Camilla*, he would *stuff the coach* or *post-chaise with them* whenever he travelled.[5]

[1] 'Of Solitarinesse', *Essays*. Ed. Seccombe. i, 305.   [2] Horne, *Binding of Books.* 188.
[3] Pliny, *Letters.* iii, 5.   [4] 'They go abroad, they go into the country.' *Pro Archia.* 7.   [5] 'My Books', *Essays*. Camelot Ed. 294.

Some dilate upon the number and kind of books suitable for a journey. Lubbock advised *two or still better three* for a long railway journey, one of them to be of *an amusing character,* so that possible tedium could be avoided by ringing the changes, the traveller thus *coming back again and again to each with renewed zest, and hour after hour would pass pleasantly away.*[1] There is some wisdom here, but it all depends on the book. The right book annihilates time wherever you are; but we are not always in luck, we cannot always guarantee the coincidence of the right book, mood and moment, so a few general experiences may be considered. In the first place, then, read what Aldous Huxley has lately written on this subject.[2] A *travelling-book* is one, he says, that you can open anywhere and be sure of finding *something interesting* which does not require *continuous attention* or *prolonged mental effort.* He gives as specimens any good anthology of verse (his own choice being Edward Thomas's *Pocket Book of Poems and Songs for the Open Air*); volumes of aphorisms, particularly *La Rochefoucauld* (a copy of which, in *sexto-decimo,* he always carries in his *upper left-hand waistcoat pocket*), or one of Nietzsche's aphoristic works; Boswell's *Johnson*; and, finally, any volume of the *Encyclopaedia Britannica* in the twelfth edition, which is half the old size, on india paper: *I never pass a day away from home without taking a volume with me,* he confesses; *it is·the book of books.* To all of which he brings good argument, and I do not oppose him.

Nor do I argue against the taste of Petrarch, who carried with him wherever he went, by sea or land, a copy of St. Augustine's *Confessions* small enough to go into a pocket, which Father Dionisio had given him;[3] or with Dr. Johnson, who made Cocker's *Arithmetick* his companion on his tour in the Hebrides, and who explained to Boswell, *if you are to have but one book with you upon a journey, let it be a book of science,* for *when you have read through a book of entertainment, you know it, and it can do no more for you; but a book of science is inexhaustible;*[4] he put this theory into practice on a visit to Lord Bute's seat at *Luton Hoe* with Boswell and Mr. Charles Dilly. *He talked little to us in the carriage, being chiefly occupied in reading Dr. Watson's second volume of 'Chemical Essays', which he liked very well;* but he alternated his reading on this journey with *his own 'Prince of Abyssinia', on which he seemed to be intensely fixed.*[5] Doubtless George Moore was moved by some such idea when he made a volume of *Kant* his travelling companion, into which he would dip, even whilst waiting for his carriage to take a party of *tarts* and *mashers* to the Derby.[6] Sir Edward Cook advises[7] that if a book is to make a good travelling companion, *it must not only be*

[1] *Pleasures of Life.* i, 61-2.   [2] *Along the Road.* 65-70.   [3] Tatham, *Francesco Petrarca.* i, 306.   [4] *Tour.* Ed. Hill. *Life.* v, 138. n.   [5] Boswell, *Life.* Ed. Hill. iv, 118-19.   [6] *Confessions of a Young Man.* (1904) 14.   [7] *More Literary Recreations.* 22.

readable and portable, it must also within its range be a full book, and he hints that the selecting is not easy: *no test of real liking for a book so searching as the choice of a travelling companion.*[1] But when, they have all said their say, the best travelling-book is that which you like best. That it should be portable needs no defence, and 'tis no obstacle in these days of pocketable volumes. I know of no other rule. For myself I can read any kind of book, except *light reading for travel* or *holiday books,* on any sort of journey, except at sea in a storm.

It is the same with all those happy readers who take the book of their choice in the place chance dictates, regardless of rules and advice. Picture Henry Crabb Robinson outside the Bury Coach on a mid-January day devouring Goethe's '*Autobiography*' *with great pleasure*[2] and Madame de Sévigné reading alternately her *Breviary* and *Corneille* in the carriage on her journeys from Paris to her country seat in Brittany;[3] Dr. Johnson with *Pomponius Mela de Situ Orbis* in the stage-coach *en route* for Harwich, and *very intent upon ancient geography,* as Boswell notes;[4] Edward FitzGerald[5] communing with *Sophocles, Virgil, Don Quixote, Montaigne* and *Boccaccio,* in his fishing-boat off Lowestoft; Ramsay Macdonald passing the time with *Hazlitt* when flying from London to his native Lossiemouth; John Addington Symonds travelling from London to Florence reading *Guicciardini* all the way, regardless (says Maurice Hewlett) of the *growing attractiveness of the journey and increasing gravity of the book*: a man, he well adds, who could read that book on a journey to Italy *could read Milton on top of a motor 'bus;*[6] Symonds could have done even that, for he was a trained and hardened reader, imperturbable amid noise and movement; it was his constant habit *to do a considerable amount of hard study while travelling,* and he found it difficult to enumerate how many *heavy German and Italian books on history, biography, and criticism, how many volumes of Greek poets, and what a library of French and English authors* had been *slowly perused* by him in *railway stations, trains, steamers, wayside inns, and Alpine chalets.*[7]

Of all travel-places, a railway compartment is most familiar and accessible to modern men. Wherever there are trains there are readers. *A long railway journey affords a first-rate opportunity for reading.*[8] Even those who look upon reading as a waste of time read in railway trains, where time seems to them so plentiful that they can afford to waste it. And next to railway trains, what more appropriate place for reading than on shipboard, on a long voyage, for good 'sailors', or even bad ones when the weather is fair. *What,* asks Froude, *did passengers do on long voyages when there were no*

[1] *Ib.* 2.   [2] *Diary.* i, 246.   [3] *Letters.* i, 150.   [4] *Life.* Hill. i, 465.   [5] *Letters and Literary Remains.* i, 101, 307.   [6] Hewlett, *Extemporary Essays.* 119.   [7] 'A Page of my Life', *Fortnightly Review.* December 1889.   [8] Viscount Grey, 'Pleasure of Reading', *Fallodon Papers.* 14.

novels? They must bless the man that invented them, he says; but, on his voyage to Australia, he re-read the classics, discovering that *in the absence of outward distractions one can understand and enjoy these finished relics of the old world.*[1] It was on his voyage to India, in 1834, that Macaulay performed the greatest of his *herculean feats as a man of books,*[2] making the passage a bookman's holiday and his ship a reader's paradise; his power of *finding amusement without companions was pretty well tried,* and it stood the trial, as he knew it would: *I read insatiably* (he tells Thomas Flower Ellis, in a letter from Ootacamund, I. vii. 1834),[3] the *Iliad* and *Odyssey, Virgil, Horace,* Cæsar's *Commentaries,* Bacon's *De Augmentis, Dante, Petrarch, Ariosto, Tasso, Don Quixote,* Gibbon's *Rome,* Mill's *India, all the seventy volumes of Voltaire,* Sismondi's *'History of France',* and the seven thick folios of the *'Biographia Britannica';* and as he devoured he brooded, comparing authors and impressions of previous readings, liking the *Iliad* a little less and the *Odyssey* a great deal more than heretofore (a preference he shares with Tennyson),[4] more than ever charmed with *Horace;* not quite so much with Virgil: *The want of human character, the poverty of his super-natural machinery, struck me very strongly. Can anything be so bad as the living bush which bleeds and talks,* he asks, *or the Harpies who befoul Aeneas's dinner? It is all, he thinks, as extravagant as Ariosto, and as dull as Wilkie's 'Epigoniad'.* So he waxeth eloquent on this great theme, liking Virgil in his last six books, *which he had not fully corrected,* better than his first six; he liked him best on his Italian ground, preferring his local and national enthusiasm; his allusions to his own country, its history, its antiquities and its greatness; and finding over all a resemblance to Sir Walter Scott, though no true mental affinity. The *Georgics* pleased him better; the *Eclogues* best, the second and tenth best of all; but he thought the five lines beginning:

'Sepibus in nostris parvam te roscida mala'[5]

the finest lines in the Latin language, and is amused to find Voltaire pronouncing them the finest Virgil.

Others have tasted identical delights, as Alexander never travelling without *those admirable poems of Homer in his company;*[6] Napoleon, making *Werter* and *Ossian* his *inseparable companions* on his voyage to Egypt;[7] Samuel Butler reading *Gibbon very carefully* on his way out to New Zealand;[8] John Wilson Croker treasuring Crabbe's *Tales* on a sea voyage.[9] Many have read with great content on lakes and rivers: *wonderful,* says A. Edward Newton,[10] *how conducive to reading I found the stuffy smoking-*

---

[1] J. A. Froude, *Oceana.* 234.   [2] Rosebery, *Appreciations and Addresses.* 146.   [3] *Life.* Trevelyan. i, 329–30.   [4] Hallam, *Lord Tennyson, Memoir.* i, 279.   [5] *Eclogue.* viii, 37.   [6] Sir William Temple, *Of Poetry.*   [7] Ludwig, *Napoleon.* 19.   [8] *Life of Butler.* Festing Jones. i, 97.   [9] *The Croker Papers.* i, 146.   [10] *Amenities of Book-Collecting.* ix.

room of the little steamers that dart like water-spiders from one landing to another on the Italian Lakes; picture William and Dorothy Wordsworth and Coleridge reading poems on Grasmere, *letting the boat take its own course* towards Loughrigg;[1] Samuel Pepys in his barge between London and Barne Elms with John Evelyn's *late new book against solitude;*[2] William Beckford, with Gargantuan appetite, buying Gibbon's library *to have something to read* when passing through Lausanne, shutting himself *up for six weeks from early in the morning until night, only now and then taking a ride; the people thought* him *mad,* as he *read* himself *nearly blind.*[3] *One of the slender volumes* of Matthew Arnold's verse had been Lord Morley's *cherished companion on many a journey; it takes little compass, and in it anybody who is for a short interval a traveller away from the hurry of the world's rough business, may well find beauty to refresh, wisdom to quiet, associations to remind and collect.*[4]

Others, again, in the opposite extreme, and they are the greater number, look upon travel as a time for light reading, or they would escape from its solitariness by means of magazines, newspapers and such like *ephemera.* To serve them, newsagents and booksellers have fixed bookstalls in railway stations, and on most harbours, piers, jetties, landing stages, used by travellers. In past times those who went on a journey carried all the books they might need with them perforce, nowadays the bookstalls are our travelling libraries, and *Tauchnitz* has girdled Europe with English literature; but whether reading be idle or studious, frivolous or profound, travel, in so mutable and kinetic an age as ours, offers a golden opportunity for the enjoyment of books or other printed matter, which, I observe, most travellers take, for few move about printless.

VIII. READING AT THE TOILET

Reading during the ritual of the toilet, especially that part of it devoted to the coiffing, has a long but mostly unrecorded history. Look for examples in any barber's shop or hairdressing saloon, for they are among the traditional news-centres of our common people and the focus of gossip. It is the custom not only to exchange news and views in such resorts, but to read the papers while waiting your turn, as the saying is, or during the operation itself. Every bookman (and most ordinary men) knows how fruitful in meditation are the solitary moments of the toilet when we are faced only by our own soapy visages. George Wyndham committed Shakespeare's *Sonnets* to memory while shaving,[5] and many others have

---

[1] *Journals of Dorothy Wordsworth.* 44.   [2] *Diary.* Wheatley. vi, 337–8.   [3] *William Beckford.* Melville. 180.   [4] *Recollections.* i, 132.   [5] *George Wyndham, Recognita.* Gatty. 2–3.

found this operation productive of literary memories, which are a kind of reading by proxy of the imagination, for to remember is as profitable as to re-read.

On Salome's dressing table in Aubrey Beardsley's picture[1] of her toilet and its ritual are copies of Zola's *Nana*, *The Golden Ass* of Apuleius, *Manon Lescaut*, *Fêtes Galantes*, and the *Works* of the Marquis de Sade, which are clearly his personal choice of books for such a lady at such a time. Although Helen[2] does not read before that toilet-table which was so like the Altar of Notre Dame des Victoires, the omission was surely an oversight on the part of Beardsley, for the scene was most appropriate for dalliance with such books as he provided for Salome. She should have toyed with *Apuleius* as the coiffeur Cosmé *was caring for her scented chevelure, and with tiny silver tongs, warm from the caresses of the flame, making delicious* intelligent curls fall as lightly as a breath about her forehead and over her eyebrows, to cluster finally like tendrils round her neck; or she might have fluttered appropriately the fragrant pages of an eighteenth-century edition of *Dorat* as her *three favourite girls, Pappelarde, Blanchemains, and Loreyne,* attended her with *perfume and powder in delicate flacons and frail cassolettes, and held in porcelain jars the ravishing paints prepared by Chatelaine for those cheeks and lips that had grown a little pale with anguish of exile.* She might have assessed the shameless confidences of *Aretino* as her *three favourite boys, Claud, Clair, and Sarrisine, stood amorously about with salver, fan and napkin,* and *Millamant held a slight tray of slippers,* and *Minette some tender gloves,* and *La Popelinière—mistress of the robes—a frock of yellow and white,* and *La Zambinella the jewels,* and *Florizel some flowers,* and *Amadour a box of various pins,* and *Vadius a box of sweets; whilst her doves, ever in attendance, walked about the room that was panelled with the gallant paintings of Jean Baptiste Dorat, and some dwarfs and doubtful creatures sat here and there, lolling out their tongues, pinching each other and behaving oddly enough.*[3] But I am forth of my subject again and must return from this baroque paradise.

More to the point is Mrs. Balfour's account of a lady who was reading to a party of two or three the seventh volume of *Clarissa, whilst her maid curled her hair, and the poor girl let fall such a shower of tears upon her lady's head, that she was forced to send her out of the room to compose herself.* On being asked why she cried, she answered, *to see such goodness in distress,* whereupon *a lady followed her out of the room, and gave her a crown for that answer.*[4] Or there is that classical reference to Pliny the Elder having books read to him while he was being *rubbed and wiped in the bath.*[5] Samuel Pepys records (see his *Diary* under December 22nd, 1662) that having reached home and *presently shifted* himself, *so had the barber come, and my wife and*

---

[1] Wilde, *Salome*. [2] Beardsley, *Under the Hill*. [3] *Ib.,* 14–15. [4] *Correspondence of Richardson.* Barbauld. IV, 305. [5] Pliny, *Letters.* iii, 5.

I to read Ovid's *Metamorphoses*, which that night he had brought home for her from St. Paul's Churchyard.

IX. READING AT MEALTIMES

Reading at mealtimes has innumerable precedents, and much may be said in support of it, in spite of those who would hold fast to the conviction that eating is an art in itself which tolerates no rival; or those others, more medically disposed, who give out that any exigent concern at table, by obtruding itself upon ingestion, which is the main object, sets up a disaffection of the inward parts and ends in dyspepsias and other gastric derangements. But their arguments are none too sound, and, if true, would rule out conversation and music, and all those other amenities which add so much to the pleasure of dining; this parallel I would urge because it is well known that content of mind is a notable peptonizer, and it would follow that whatsoever is conducive to it, whether it be music, talk or books, may accompany any feast. But the dissenters need no confutation, for every reader can support me out of his own experience, yet I shall cite a few precedents to confound the captious and console the rest.

Dr. Johnson, Byron, Charles Lamb, Shelley, Leigh Hunt, and, in our own day, Robert Louis Stevenson and Bernard Shaw, are all confessed table-readers. In past times it was the delight of cultured banqueters to have reading aloud numbered among the courses: at *Favorinus's table*, Aulus Gellius records,[1] *when he dined with friends, there was usually read either an old song of one of the lyric poets, or something from history, now in Greek and now in Latin*, as on that *mild day in Autumn* when he and Julius Celsinus were *entertained very pleasantly with vegetables and fruits* and the reading at table of the *Alcestis* of Laevius, by Julius Paulus, at his little place *in agro Vaticano*.[2] Peter Daniel Huet had someone to read to him at mealtimes: *neither the heat of youth, nor a multiplicity of business, nor the love of company, nor the hurry of the world, has ever been able to moderate my love of study;*[3] our own High Priest of Bibliophiles, Richard de Bury, *every day while at table would have a book read to him, unless some special guest were present;*[4] whilst Carneades, that *laborious and diuturnal soldier of Wisdom's*, even at the age of ninety years, Quintus Valerius Maximus relates,[5] *so addicted himself to the works of learning, that when he sat down to eat, busie in his thoughts, he would forget to reach his meat*, and would have starved had not Melissa, *whom he kept as a Wife, fed him*.

'Tis with us as it was of old, with this difference: books being more

[1] *Attic Nights*. Loeb Ed. ii, 22. Favorinus was a philosopher of the time, born in Gaul; he was greatly admired by Gellius.   [2] *Attic Nights*. Loeb Ed. xix, 7.   [3] Qt. *Book-Lover's Ench.* 94.   [4] *Philobiblon*. King's Classics Ed. Pref. xi.   [5] *Romae Antiquae Descriptio*. Eng. Ed. (1678.) 368.

easily got at, more makes them accessories to the feast. I dare boldly say that few of our later bookmen would scruple to feed at once mind and body; most indulge thus with great content and no hurt. I could speak for myself in this case, for it has always been my habit to read during meals unless inclination bade me engage in talk, and I have no acquaintance with dyspepsia—but I must on to my instances. Trevelyan knew of no society that Macaulay *would have preferred at breakfast or at dinner to the company of Sterne, Fielding, Horace Walpole,* or *Boswell,* and *there were many less distinguished authors with whose productions he was very well content to cheer his repasts;* not even a Brillat-Savarin could make eating predominate over reading for Macaulay, who lived to read and read to live. All books, however, were not appropriate to any meal: *Henderson's* Iceland was *a favourite breakfast book;* but *some books which I never should dream of opening at dinner please me at breakfast and vice versa.*[1] He was fastidious and a gourmet, it voracious, walking with the heavies, breakfasting with the dull, and (*dined at my inn, reading Cooper's 'Pathfinder'*)[2] dining with the light; but, appetite still unsatisfied, he complained that *except while dressing and undressing* he got *no reading at all.*[3]

Charles Lamb found *Milton* a good supper book. *If,* he wrote to Coleridge, *you find the Miltons in certain parts dirtied and soiled with a crumb of right Gloucester blacked in the candle (my usual supper), or peradventure a stray ash of tobacco wafted into the crevices, look to that passage more especially: depend upon it: it contains good matter.*[4] William Hazlitt sat down to a volume of the *New Eloise,* at the Inn at Llangollen, *over a bottle of sherry and a cold chicken;*[5] Leigh Hunt would read the booksellers' catalogues at tea or dinner, ticking favourite books and enjoying *the pure imagination of buying them, the possibility being out of the question;*[6] Benjamin Disraeli read at mealtimes, and in his old age at Hughenden brought a book to table and read for ten minutes after every course.[7] Campbell confesses that *reading Homer at breakfast has become, by long habit, necessary* to his *existence;*[8] Stevenson read Aikman's *Annals* at breakfast and *almost forgot* to drink his tea and eat his egg;[9] but of all these instances I admire most J. A. Symonds's relation of how he enjoyed *nothing more* than *to sit in a bar room among peasants, carters, and postillions, smoking with a glass of wine beside him, and a stiff work on one of the subjects* he was bound to *get up,*[10] because it reminds me how I once saw Cecil Chesterton standing in the middle of a crowded London tap-room with a tankard of ale in one hand and a book in the other, chuckling over the page, unconscious of the din and reek of the place.

[1] *Life.* Trevelyan. ii, 394.   [2] *Ib.* 193.   [3] *Ib.* 68.   [4] *Letters.* Ed. Lucas. i, 255.
[5] *On Going a Journey.*   [6] *Retrospective Review.* 1837.   [7] Disraeli, *Maurois.*
Chap. x.   [8] Qt. R. N. Carew Hunt, *The Times.* 17.ix.1930.   [9] *Letters.* Ed.
Colvin. i, 17.   [10] 'A Page of My Life', *Fortnightly Review.* December 1889.

X. READING IN BED

But how many are there who neither wait to get up to read nor go to bed without reading; a notable instance is the Oxford scholar in Chaucer's *Canterbury Tales*:

> For him was lever han at his beddes heed
> Twenty bokes, clad in black and reed,
> Of Aristotle and his philosophy,
> Than robes riche, or fithele, or gay sautrye.

Certain philosophers have even gone to bed to think. Descartes used to lie in bed sixteen hours every day, curtains drawn, windows shut, imagining that he had more command over his mind in that situation; and some others, as Malebranche and Mezerai, meditated and studied with drawn blinds or by candlelight.[1] Many readers favour the night for the pursuit of their passion, the record for this kind of reading being held, according to Osler,[2] by Sir Kenelm Digby, but I doubt whether he was a greater practitioner in this art than Liu Hsun,[3] that notable Chinese student who was so enamoured of his books that he scarcely ever left them; he would read *all night*, and to make sure that he did not fall asleep, he had *a lighted twist of hemp arranged in such a way as to burn his hair if he began to nod from drowsiness*.[4] Some are more temperate, reading a little every night before sleep, as a *popular* Lord Mayor of Dublin, in *Yeats*,[5] who bragged *that he never went to bed at night without reading at least twelve pages of* '*Sappho*'; but on the other hand, some resent the overtures of unconsciousness, warding off sleep as they would an enemy, as the poet, Lionel Johnson,[6] who would rather read than sleep,

> Sleep wins me not: but from his shelf
> Brings me each wit his very self;
> Beside my chair the great ghosts throng,
> Each tells his story, sings his song:
> And in the ruddy fire I trace
> The curves of each *Augustan* face.

Yet whatever they say, *all good and true book-lovers practise the pleasing and improving avocation of reading in bed.*[7]

So great is the inclination, which many account a bad habit, that some would have special books, imagined to be more suitable than others, set

---

[1] Buck, *Anecdotes*. i, 247.   [2] *Life of Osler*. Cushing. ii, 22.   [3] Died A.D. 521.
[4] Giles, *Chinese Biog. Dict.* 506.   [5] *The Trembling of the Veil.* 114.   [6] 'Oxford Nights', *Poetical Works.* 100.   [7] Eugene Field, *Love Affairs of a Bibliomaniac.* 31.

apart as bed-books; these they claim should be soothing, passive, meditative, wooing the imagination gently, sedative, calming the mind and so composing the body and spirit for sleep; and our late Regius Professor of Medicine at Oxford, Sir William Osler,[1] a stout bookfellow, reckons up another advantage of bed-reading, in a learned lecture of his not long since: *With half an hour's reading in bed every night as a steady practice*, he claims, *the busiest man can get a fair education before the plasma sets in the periganglionic spaces of his grey cortex.* But they miss the point. Your true bed-readers seek neither to cure insomnia nor to educate themselves: they read for reading's sake, and would make wakefulness a virtue, to be cultivated, not, within reason, denied: *Let sleep go. Let the morrow's duties go. Let health, prudence, and honour go. The bedside book for me is the book that will longest keep me awake.*[2] Reading against insomnia comes under the medicinal value of books, and I shall only say here that it is no more than an expedient and often a pain. Dr. Johnson *lamented much his inability to read during his last hours of restlessness; I used formerly,* he said, *when sleepless in bed, to read like a Turk.*[3] But his desire was to sleep, not to read.

The virtue of bed-reading is that it enables us *to extract the last drop of sweetness from this delightful hour,* and to do so *we must be conscious of our bed as well as of our book;*[4] such reading demands an acute consciousness, for it is an experience, none the less because we end as though *drowsed with the fume of poppies.* For reading as an opiate, then, seek elsewhere in this treatise; here are recorded only specimens of those whose bed-reading is for delight, as Charles Dickens when the other boys played *sat on his bed, reading for dear life;*[5] as Leigh Hunt read *Hudibras, at one desperate plunge,* when laid in bed with two scalded legs;[6] as Henry Bradshaw lay in bed so late to finish the first volume of *Alton Locke,* that he was *up only just in time for chapel;*[7] or as Herbert Spencer,[8] when a youth, would read in bed forbidden stories, the *Castle of Otranto, Mrs. Redcliffe* and the like, until the birds sang in the morning; and as in his old age he would gloat on the memory of how his mother crept into his room to see if the candle was out, and how he was not to be baulked of his *midnight gratification, for close to my bed was a fixed corner cupboard; and habitually, when I heard her steps on the stairs, I leapt out of bed, put the candle still burning into this cupboard, got into bed again and pretended to be asleep, until she, thinking all was as it should be, retired. Whereupon I brought out the candle and resumed my reading.* This boyish adventure is very much to the point of my argument, for fastidious bed-readers will read the books of their choice and for their own delecta-

---

[1] *Life.* Cushing. ii, 185.   [2] J. C. Squires, 'Reading in Bed', *Life at the Mermaid.* 119.   [3] *Life.* iv, 207.   [4] Hope Mirrlees, 'Bedside Books', *Life and Letters.* December 1928.   [5] *David Copperfield.*   [6] *Life.* Monkhouse. 35.   [7] *Memoir of Henry Bradshaw.* 39.   [8] *Autobiography.* i, 77–8.

tion, as Chaucer when he anticipated Herbert Spencer by choosing a Romance, although his aim was to entertain uninvited wakefulness:

> So when I saw I might not slepe,
> Til now late, this other night,
> Upon my bedde I sat upright,
> And bad oon reche me a boke,
> A romaunce, and he hit me took
> To rede and dryve the night away.[1]

There are, however, in spite of what I have said, certain books which by general consent and usage have come to be reckoned more appropriate bed-books than others; but any catalogue I could make would be prejudiced, exclusive of all taste but mine own, or, if more catholic, so inclusive as to be useless as a guide to those about to read in bed. Yet although it is plain that reading in bed is an inborn faculty and natural to most bookmen, the choice of book blending curiously with the mood, there are doubtless principles underlying the choice, and if, as I have said, consciousness of the pleasure is a *sine qua non*, that pleasure must not be so intense as to banish the desire to sleep irrecoverably. Bed-books must not disturb or rasp the nerves, and sleep being ultimately necessary, they should lull the mind into an exquisite slothfulness, fusing body and brain into a glow, with sleep waiting apart to be wooed willingly. The character of a bed-book must thus *approximate*, as all art in the opinion of Pater, *to the condition of music*, which I plainly prove from the words of Hope Mirrlees: *Let our book have some of the qualities of music. But they must be the qualities that music has for the unmusical, what we want are dreams, and sound without sense.*[2]

Of all books, then, I take that kind which we call rambling and discursive to be the best; and in this I find myself in agreement with Squire, who prescribes that they shall be neither *boring* nor too *exciting*; interesting on every *page but dramatic nowhere*, with *a stream of event but no definite break*,[3] in short, I say, works of culture or urbanity which may be opened and enjoyed at any page, as Boswell's *Johnson*, Burton's *Anatomy of Melancholy*, the *Reliquiae Wottonianae*, *The Doctor*, by Southey, Walpole's *Letters*, Pepys' *Diary*, Greville's *Journals*, *The Complete Angler*, Montaigne's *Essays*, Evelyn's *Diary*, the *Religio Medici*, the *Works* of Francis Rabelais, *Tristram Shandy*, *Don Quixote*, *Gil Blas*, the *Decameron*, the *Essays* of Charles Lamb, Plutarch's *Lives*; all manner of *analecta*: the *Deipnosophists* of Athenaeus and the *Attic Nights* of Aulus Gellius, Edward FitzGerald's *Polonius*, Frederick Locker's *Patchwork*, Southey's *Omniana* and *Commonplace Books*,

---

[1] *Book of the Duchess.* 44.   [2] 'Bedside Books', *Life and Letters.* December 1928.
[3] 'Reading in Bed', *Life at the Mermaid.* 118.

and the *Anecdotes* of William King, Joseph Spence, John Nichols and William Beloe; the *Table Talk* of Samuel Rogers, Leigh Hunt, Coleridge; *A Bookman's Budget*, by Austin Dobson; *Walpoliana*; and such mines of curious knowledge as the compendious entertainments of those early collectors and classifiers of knowledge who preceded our more exact observers and recorders, as, and I give only a few of my own favourites, the *Anthropometamorphosis* of John Bulwer and Lovell's *Panzoologicomineralogia*, the *Living Library* of Camerarius in John Molle's translation, and Hakewill's *Apologie*. I would include all genial and urbane epistles: Lady Mary Montague's, Charles Lamb's, Edward FitzGerald's, William Cowper's, and John Keats's; the *Epistolae Ho-Elianae*; *The Groombridge Diary* and *Pages from the Journals* of Mark Rutherford; Torr's *Small-Talk at Wreyland*, Doran's *Table Traits* (and his other chatterbooks), Captain Gronow's *Reminiscences*—but there is no end to them. And for poetry, what richer bed-books than the *Golden Treasury* or the *Oxford Book*, mines of purest English Song the sweetest in the World, our best product, our true soul's viaticum; with such books, in health or sickness, going to bed, or staying in bed perforce, becomes a holiday, upon which we may thank God for such a gift: *Deus nobis haec otia fecit.*[1]

Not without good reason, then, does Maurice Hewlett set down in *The Limits of the Readable*,[2] that if ever he took a book to bed, which he ingenuously confesses he never did, it would be of good-humoured *Essays*; not Hazlitt's—*Hazlitt is for youth, which can stand his ill-temper, perhaps be stimulated by it;* but rather *Lamb*, a volume of the *Tatler*, or Bagehot (*You can pick him up where you will find him good-humoured*); and Montaigne—*a perfect lucky-bag*, but neither he nor I need much labour to prove this, for well have the wise ones of all times known similar delights. Sir Kenelm Digby records in a letter to Edward, Earl of Dorset,[3] how, being *newly gotten into Bed* with the *Religio Medici*, he rejoiced that he *could easily persuade* that *good-natured creature* to be his *Bedfellow; to wake me*, he saith, *as long as I had any edge to entertaine myself with the delights I sucked from so noble a conversation. And truly, my lord*, he goes on, *I closed not my eyes till I had enricht myself with* (or at least exactly surveyed) *all the treasures that are lapped up in the folds of these few sheets;* and with what delight must that *very worthy, industrious, and curious*[4] Mr. Pepys have recorded how on December 12th, 1660, *home and to bed, reading myself to sleep, while the wench sat mending my breeches by my bedside*,[5] or again, cheery upon the thought of good business with T. Trice, he *lay reading 'Hobbs his Liberty and Necessity', a little but very shrewd piece, and so to sleep.*[6]

---

[1] 'God procured for us this leisure.' *Virgil. Ec.* i, 6.　　[2] *Extemporary Essays.* 120.
[3] *Observations upon Religio Medici.* (1644) 3–4.　　[4] Evelyn, *Diary.* 456.　　[5] Pepys, *Diary.* i, 307.　　[6] *Ib.* ii, 140.

Henry Crabb Robinson read *The Doctor* and *Crabbe's Life* in bed before six in the morning;[1] Voltaire was a confirmed lie-a-bed; when it was cold he passed most of the day in bed, arising only when the weather was fine, when he walked in his garden, or took an airing in his coach; his bed, says Dom Chandon,[2] *was always strewed with books*, and beside it an elegant table on which was water, *café-au-lait*, an inkstand and some slips of blank paper, to mark the pages he wished to read again or on which to make observations. He wrote in the margins of all his books, criticising, commenting, blaming, and praising, but he rarely read a work through, except when deeply interested. Diana of Poitiers rose at six, bathed in rain-water, rode a league or so and returned to bed, where she lay reading until midday.[3] Porson, Eugene Field gives out,[4] *was a veritable slave to the habit of reading in bed;* he would lie down with *books piled around him, light his pipe and start in upon some favourite volumes,* with *a jug of liquor at hand.*

Montaigne's *Essays* and Howell's *Letters* were Thackeray's bed-books: *if I wake at night I have one or the other of them,* he said, *to prattle me to sleep again;*[5] Wycherley never closed his eyes at night without dipping into the pages of *Montaigne, Rochefoucauld, Seneca* or *Gracian;*[6] Edward FitzGerald told Frederic Tennyson[7] that he had *read the sixth Book of Lucretius in bed;* he had not looked into it for more than a year, but *took it up by mistake fo one of Swift's dirty volumes; and, having got into bed with it, did not care to get out to change it;* and on another occasion he confesses to Bernard Barton that *this morning* (8. iv. 1848) *I read some of my old friend Sir Charles Grandison in bed;*[8] Sir Walter Raleigh lay in bed of a morning reading *Trollope;*[9] Francis Jenkinson, the Cambridge University Librarian, read Mark Pattison's *Memoirs* until 12.30 a.m. and became so absorbed that he continued reading them in bed until two o'clock.[10] *I invariably read in bed of a night,* Arnold Bennett records, *unless,* he adds, *paying in my temples the price of excess;* he once took *Montaigne* with him for a bed-book, whilst on a holiday, but, instead of the essayist, he found himself reading *a verbatim account of a poisoning trial in the Paris 'Journal'.*[11]

But there is as much diversity of taste here as elsewhere, and even Squire, who, as I have shown, prescribes those long still books which are the true bed-books, is himself a heretic, for he *shamelessly* confesses that however tired he might be, and *the whole contents of the British Museum at call* from his bed, he would *ask for a shocker.*[12] And here I consider, in conclusion,

---

[1] *Diary.* (1872) 212.   [2] *Memoirs of Voltaire.* 1786.   [3] Bushnell, *Trans. Bib. Soc.* December 1926. 286.   [4] *Love Affairs of a Bibliomaniac.* 35.   [5] Qt. Jerrold, *Autolycus of the Bookstalls.* 158.   [6] J. Roger Rees, *Diversions of a Bookworm.* 23–4.   [7] *Letters and Literary Remains.* i, 206.   [8] *Some New Letters of Edward FitzGerald.* 158.   [9] *Letters.* i, 272.   [10] *Francis Jenkinson.* Stewart. 12.   [11] 'Holiday Reading', *Books and Persons.* 159.   [12] 'Reading in Bed', *Life at the Mermaid.* 119.

that there is no difference of opinion upon the pleasure of reading in bed, and that the true state of the question is only this, that the practice hath many inconveniences, mischances, calamities, such as injury to eyesight, destruction of the will to sleep, and danger of fire through mishap to candle or lamp. These be mere diversions, outworn toys of imagination, for I have yet to hear of any coming to hurt by reading in bed; but the opposition is as insignificant as the risks are negligible, and on that note I may end, *audita querela*, having investigated the objections.

Part XIII

THE INFLUENCE OF BOOKS

I. GENERAL INFLUENCES CONSIDERED

How far the power of books extends; whether they cause changes in the condition of all men and women who read them, or whether all books or only some have this faculty, is a curious problem, and worthy to be considered; so, for the better understanding of it, I will make a brief generalisation of the nature and character of the effects (the exaltations, perturbations of the spirit of men), wherein they manifest themselves, in what manner and to what end. That they have the faculty to move men I need not further argue, though more evidence will be adduced as this dissertation unfolds itself; suffice it that, as all know, they can seize the reader

> As tempests seize a ship, and bear him on
> With a wild joy,[1]

although, I am well aware, most men are immune from such direct influence, being moved only at second hand, or third, or more remotely still, by the slow absorption of bookish effect from age to age. Some, on the other hand, believe, as Mark Pattison,[2] that writers, *with a professional tendency to magnify their office, have always been given to exaggerate the effect of printed words*, and whilst admitting that *there are examples of thought having been influenced by books*, he holds that such books have been *scientific, not rhetorical*. That this species of argument may be extended, I have no doubt, and I could amplify it with observations delivered by others much to the same end; but in the main they are erroneous, not such as are eminently fair, as you may read apart in this section of *Influences*, although I hold it opportune to be considered that it was *gunpowder*, as he[3] argues, not *Don Quixote*, which destroyed the *age of chivalry*.

I am, of course, not ignorant of the fact that writers are prejudiced in favour of their trade: their predisposition in this business is notorious; they are favourably placed for its propagation, and 'tis not likely they should cry stinking fish. Yet their assessment is not unreasonable, for if words have not always the sudden precision of gunfire, they strike deeper,

[1] Alexander Smith, *A Life-Drama.*   [2] *Milton.* 67.   [3] Pattison, *Milton.* 190.

266

and their slow effect reveals permutations more durable than the percussions of physical force. It is an old saying that *a blow with a word strikes deeper than a blow with a sword:*[1] how much deeper a blow with a book. Let us argue, therefore, that books are not always a sole or even a direct influence, and that their effect upon crowds is by diffusion rather than by knocks. So gradual their insinuation among masses of men that, as Sir James Frazer advises,[2] although *two or three generations of literature may do more to change thought than two or three thousand years of traditional life,* this change is effected only among those who come under the direct influence of books, *the mass of people who do not read books remain unaffected by the mental revolution wrought by literature,* so that, he gives out, *in Europe at the present day the superstitious beliefs and practices which have been handed down by word of mouth are generally of a far more archaic type than the religion depicted in the most ancient literature of the Aryan race.*

Some few are so bold as to argue that although men are *qualified for their work by knowledge,* they are also *negatively qualified for it by their ignorance;*[3] and this same observer holds that *the last generation of English country aristocracy was particularly rich in characters whose unity and charm was dependent upon the limitations of their culture, which would have been entirely altered, perhaps not for the better, by simply knowing a science or a literature that was closed to them.*[4] Yet whole eras are changed by books, even the manners and behaviour of those who cannot read, for, as Mathias reasons it, and many others uphold, *literature, well or ill conducted, is the Great Engine by which all civilized states must ultimately be supported or overthrown.*[5] I shall not here impose more than one instance on a matter of such general acceptance, namely, that revolution in the spirit of man, the overthrowing of the Dark Ages, which was hastened by the rediscovery of the ancient writers, because the best minds of those times were moved with *a spirit of tremulous delight, of awe and ecstasy,* when they read *the recaptured, the resurgent classics of Greece and Rome.*[6]

Having thus cleared the way, I may now advance that books, in the main and proper operation of their influence, affect *dissimilar parts:* those which we call *spiritual* and *instrumental,* or *inward* and *outward.* The office of the first or *inward* part functions by nutrition, the substantial act spiritually conceived of an organical body by which it is nourished, augmented, fed as a body is fed, to beget, by continuous rejuvenation of the tissues, another like unto itself, but remaining itself, by an act of transubstantiation, for as Hamerton holds, although *a thousand times more difficult to observe,* there is *a sort of intellectual chemistry which is quite as marvellous as material*

---

[1] 'Leviter volant, graviter vulnerant.' Bernardus, Qt. *Anat. of Melan.* (1904) i, 391.
[2] Preface to First Ed. *Golden Bough.* (1911) xiii.   [3] Hamerton, *Intellectual Life.* 77.
[4] *Ib.* 76.   [5] *Pursuits of Literature.* 13th Ed. 162.   [6] Lionel Johnson, *Post Liminium.* 211.

chemistry which *affects the whole character of the mind.*[1] This *inward* part is variously named soul, spirit, life-force, vital energy, the unconscious, and the like, and is variously and incontinently dilated upon by all and sundry: doctors of divinity, philosophers, theologians, physicists, psychologists, biologists, evolutionists, evangelists, revivalists; Presbyters, Roman Catholics, Quakers, Muggletonians, Anglicans, New Connectionists, Salvationists, Plymouth Brethren, Shakers, Fundamentalists, Peculiar People, Second Adventists, Theosophists, Christian Scientists, and Spiritualists; Jews, Buddhists, Taoists, Zoroastrians, Mohammedans, Confucians, and so *ad infinitum*, or seeming so; the parties concerned are innumerable almost, and scattered over the face of the earth, far and near, and so have been in all precedent ages, from the beginning of the world to these times, of all sorts and conditions.

The *outward* part is the brain. It lies in the upper region, and is, as Robert Burton so well says,[2] *a soft, marrowish, and white substance, engendered of the purest part of seed and spirits, included by many skins, and seated within the skull or brain-pan;* and he claims, as many others do, both past and present, that it is *the most noble organ under heaven, the dwelling-house and seat of the soul, the habitation of wisdom, memory, judgement, reason, and in which man is most like unto God,* and for that reason nature hath covered it with a skull of hard bone, and two skins or membranes, for the better protection of so curious and ingenious an engine. Later writers would not all go so far with him in these precedent matters, whether the brain is the noblest organ under heaven, the seat of the soul, or even that point at which man is most like unto God. But no rule is so general which admits not some exception; and to this therefore which hath been hitherto said there are many contingent diversions and deflexions, even from his contention, so stiffly upheld by the orthodox, that it is the habitation of wisdom, memory, judgement, reason, and the like, these being the constituents of the understanding, by which, as Burton again (after Melancthon),[3] *we perceive, remember and judge as well singulars as universals, having certain innate notices or beginnings of acts, a reflecting action, by which it judgeth of his own doings, and examines them.*

Out of this definition, which he says is *the power of the soul* working through the cerebral organ, pragmatical inferences may be deduced more consistent with later notions. Some reckon, as D. H. Lawrence, that the brain is but the *terminal instrument of the dynamic consciousness, a dynamo and accumulator, accumulating mechanical force* which it subjects to *certain machine-principles called ideals or ideas;*[4] which supports Bergson, who holds that the intelligence, *considered in what seems to be its original feature,* is *the faculty of manufacturing artificial objects, especially tools to make tools, and of indefinitely*

---

[1] *Intellectual Life.* 74.   [2] *Anat. of Melan.* (1904) i, 176.   [3] *Ib.* i, 188.   [4] *Psychoanalysis.* 121–3.

varying the manufacture.[1] How far the process continues and is related to will, conscience, instinct, need not detain me, for there are diverse opinions upon it, and of all these I should more aptly expand, but my theme will not permit. One of such tools only I will point out, as more necessary to my following discourse. It is that agent or tool which is called the wit of man, acumen or subtlety, sharpness of invention, which he doth invent of himself without a teacher, or learns anew from books or teachers who are the transmitters of book knowledge, abstracting those intelligible species from the phantasy, or directing them from the experience to the understanding; phantasy, or imagination, being an inner sense which, Burton saith, *doth more fully examine the species perceived by common sense, of things present or absent, and keeps them longer, recalling them to mind again, or making them new of his own.*[2]

In poets and other writers it forcibly works, as appears by innumerable fictions, theories, anticks, images, as Ovid's House of Sleep;[3] *Psyche's Palace* in *Apuleius*;[4] Swift's *Lilliput* and *Brobdingnag*;[5] the *Palace of Art* in Tennyson; More's *Utopia*, Harrington's *Oceana*, Butler's *Erewhon*, and William Morris his *Nowhere*; and all those dreams, phantasies, reveries, imaginings, which go into books and govern the mind of man, or at least should do, but in brutes it hath no existence, *ratio brutorum* being all the reason they have. Poets, story-tellers, philosophers, teachers, conceivers and makers of books are the sensitive points of the brain carrying its imaginative concepts to other brains; they are, as Thoreau boldly claims, an *irresistible aristocracy* exerting a greater *influence on mankind* than kings or emperors.[6]

They are the lines of communication between the insubstantial pageant of the world and that other world of dreams, that *Promised Land, City of the Sun, Utopia,* which is our immemorial ligation of sense and spirit; *for it is a fact of Nature that the soul is raised by true sublimity, it gains a proud step upwards, it is filled with joy and exultation, as though itself had produced what it hears:*[7]

What were our wanderings if without your goals?
As air and light, the glory ye dispense
Becomes our being—who of us can tell
What he had been, had Cadmus never taught
The art that fixes into form the thought—
Had Plato never spoken from his cell,
Or his high harp blind Homer never strung?
Kinder all earth hath grown since genial Shakespeare sung![8]

[1] *Creative Evolution.* 146.   [2] *Anat. of Melan.* (1904) i, 182.   [3] *Metam.* xi, 592 *seq.*
[4] *Metam.* Bk. v.   [5] *Gulliver.* Pts. i. and ii.   [6] *Walden.* Scott Lib. 101.   [7] Longinus, *The Sublime.* Trans. Prickard. 11–12.   [8] Bulwer-Lytton, 'The Souls of Books'.

I go into my library, and all history rolls before me. I breathe the morning air of the world while the scent of Eden's roses yet lingered in it, while it vibrated only to the world's first brood of nightingales, and to the laugh of Eve. I see the pyramids building; I hear the shoutings of the armies of Alexander; I feel the ground shake beneath the march of Cambyses. I sit as in a theatre—the stage is time, the play is the play of the world.[1] Or again, the people we meet in books are more real than our own acquaintances, and they command more of our allegiance. *The man in the street,* says Chesterton, *has more memories of Dickens, whom he has not read, than of Marie Corelli, whom he has,* and in those days when the novels of Dickens were coming out in monthly parts, *people talked as if real life were itself the interlude between one issue of 'Pickwick' and another;*[2] his *dear Sévigné* was much more to Edward FitzGerald than *most friends,*[3] and he heard Hamlet, Macbeth, and Shylock talking in his room, *all alive about* him;[4] so also Mary Coleridge, when reading *Plato,* found it difficult to believe that Socrates was *not in the next room.*[5] *I love more,* said Sterne, *the peerless knight of La Mancha, and would actually have gone farther to have paid a visit to him than to the greatest hero of antiquity.*[6]

Thus books, and the writers of them and the brain which first perceives what should be in them, are most truly tools, instruments, agents of imagination for moulding the wit of man or rousing his spirit. *The art of the pen,* as George Meredith well observes, *is to rouse the inward vision,* to *spring imagination with a word or phrase.*[7] Instances and examples to evince the truth of this aphorism are common amongst those treatises which so many have writ and in the numerous memoirs and memoranda of bookfolk, for all that civilized men are to-day is enshrined in books, and the words which are their constituents are the quintessence of our ideas, dreams, actions, desires, greater in this essence than in the diffused life out of which it is made: *no woman gives us the radiant dream that lurks beneath the word Woman; no wine realizes the intoxication imagined by the word Wine; no gold, pale gold or dusky gold, gives out the fulguration of the word Gold; there is no perfume that our deceived nostrils find equal to the word Perfume; no blue, no red that figures the tints with which our imaginations are coloured; all is too little for the word All.*[8] Well may Sir William Temple feel no wonder that the famous Dr. Harvey, when reading *Virgil, should sometimes throw him down upon the table, and say he had a devil*; or that Meric Casaubon *should find such charming pleasures and emotions as he describes* in *Lucretius;* or that *so many should cry, and with downright tears, at some tragedies of Shakespeare,* and that others should feel *turns and curdling of their blood* upon reading

[1] Alexander Smith, 'Books and Gardens', *Dreamthorp.* 248.   [2] *Charles Dickens.* 100.
[3] *Letters to Fanny Kemble.* 106.   [4] *Ib.* 68.   [5] *Gathered Leaves.* 11.   [6] *Tristram Shandy.* i, x.   [7] *Diana of the Crossways.* 137.   [8] Emile Hannequin, *Pastels in Prose.* Trans. Merrill. 203.

certain poems, as Octavia swooned at the recital of the sixth *Aeneid*.[1] *If,* says Leigh Hunt, *a passage in 'King Lear' brings the tears into our eyes, it is real as the touch of a sorrowful hand. If the flow of a song of Anacreon's intoxicates us, it is as true to a pulse within us as the wine he drank.*[2]

Books have made us what we are. *The use of letters,* says Gibbon,[3] *is the principal circumstance that distinguishes a civilized people from a herd of savages incapable of knowledge and reflection;* Caliban confesses as much when he says:

> Remember
> First to possess his books; for without them
> He's but a sot, as I am.[4]

Without the aid of books memory is soon dissipated, and the ideas entrusted to her charge corrupted. No longer supplied with models or materials, the mind forgets its powers, the judgement becomes feeble and lethargic, the imagination languid and irregular. Gibbon goes on to calculate the immense distance between the man of learning and the *illiterate* peasant: *The former, by reading and reflection, multiplies his own experience, and lives in distant ages and remote countries; whilst the latter, rooted to a single spot, and confined to a few years of existence, surpasses but very little his fellow-labourer the ox in the exercise of his mental faculties.* He notes like differences between nations, and concludes that without some *species of writing no people has ever preserved the faith ul annals of history, ever made any considerable progress in the abstract sciences, or ever possessed, in any tolerable degree of perfection, the useful and agreeable arts of life.* Samuel Butler would take us yet farther, for he holds that without literature *the development of civilization would have been impossible.*[5] Books thus may well be the elixir of civilization, for without them we are as the beasts that perish; their power includes and transcends all our most admirable faculties; in support of which I shall now parade some instances.

II. THE MIGHT OF WORDS

In this place we must consider first by what power books build and destroy, for they can build castles in the air, and put the foundations of them deep in the earth; and they can knock down what they have built; they can represent palaces, temples, armies, heroes, prodigies, and other admirable or strange objects to men's eyes; create visions, savours, tastes, deceive all the senses, and produce miraculous alterations, as all know. *Consider*

[1] Sir W. Temple, 'Of Poetry'.   [2] *The Indicator*. i, 64.   [3] *Decline and Fall*. ix.
[4] *The Tempest*. iii, 2.   [5] *Note Books*. 96,

whether any Rune in the wildest imagination of Mythologist ever did such wonders as, on the actual firm earth, some books have done! Who built St. Paul's Cathedral? demands Carlyle,[1] and he answers, *it was that divine Hebrew Book, the word partly of the man Moses, an outlaw tending his Midianitish herds, four thousand years ago, in the wilderness of Sinai!* Whitman's *Leaves of Grass* tumbled the world down for Robert Louis Stevenson.[2] When Petrarch gave a copy of St. Augustine's *Confessions* to a friend he claimed that *this book, which would enflame a heart of ice, must set your ardent soul on fire.*[3] That books are inflammable and give out heat is further attested by several reliable witnesses. Edward FitzGerald does not like to *live with* Carlyle's *Heroes and Hero-Worship* about the house, because *it smoulders;*[4] Dorothy Wordsworth's *Journals* set Dr. John Brown *on fire: I am nearly burnt out*, he tells Ruskin;[5] whilst Edith Sichel reports that *Paracelsus, Dramatic Lyrics*, and *Men and Women, warmed* Mary Coleridge *with their fire.*[6]

Small wonder that they move men, nations, mountains almost, for the best of them are concentrations of faith. *All Africa, to the limits of Ethiopia and Nigritia, obeys the book of the Koran, after bowing to the book of the Gospel. China is ruled by the moral book of Confucius, and a great part of India by the Veda. Persia was governed for ages by the books of one of the Zoroasters.*[7] *No greater moral change ever passed over a nation,* saith Green,[8] *than passed over England during the years which parted the middle of the reign of Elizabeth from the meeting of the Long Parliament;* the cause was the translation of the *Bible* into our common language: *England became the people of a book, and that book was the Bible. It was the one English book which was familiar to every Englishman;* it was read in churches and at home, and *everywhere its words kindled a startling enthusiasm;* it fathered our prose literature, but far greater than its effect on literature, saith mine author, was its effect on *the character of the people at large: the whole moral effect which is produced now-a-days by the religious newspaper, the tract, the essay, the lecture, the missionary report, the sermon, was then produced by the Bible alone.* It changed *the whole temper of the nation,* gave *a new conception of life and man,* and inspired *a new moral impulse* in every class. Yet, argues William Cory, *the political enthusiasm of Puritans and Cavaliers, the nobleness of the first race of modern English gentlemen, must be ascribed not to sacred or classical books only, but also to the imagination which flashed from the stage of Shakespeare,* as the Britons of a later time *were made more sweet of heart by 'the author of Waverley'.*[9] Thomas Carlyle affirms that the Church itself has been changed, reduced in power, by the introduction

[1] *Heroes and Hero Worship.* (1841) 259.   [2] *Art of Writing.* 80.   [3] Qt. Elton, *The Great Book-Collectors.* 51.   [4] *Letters and Literary Remains.* i, 71.   [5] Brown, *Letters.* 380.   [6] 'Memoir', *Gathered Leaves.* Mary Coleridge. 14.   [7] Voltaire, *Philosophical Dict.* 'Books'.   [8] *Short History of the English People.* Everyman Ed. ii, 431-3.   [9] *Guide to Modern English History.* i, 134-5.

of Books: *He that can write a true Book, to persuade England, is not he the Bishop and Archbishop, the Primate of England and of all England? Books are the real working effective Church of a modern country.* Nay, he concludes, *not only our preaching, but even our worship,* is accomplished by the means of printed books.[1]

Particular discontents and grievances have been stirred or allayed by them: so *A Book,* argues Benjamin Disraeli,[2] *may be as great a thing as a Battle, and there are systems of Philosophy that have produced as great Revolutions as any that have disturbed the social and political existence of our centuries: Magna Charta* and the *Declaration of Independence;* the *Contrat Social* of Rousseau and Tom Paine's *Rights of Man* and Karl Marx his *Das Kapital. The disclosure of the stores of Greek literature wrought the revolution of the Renaissance; the disclosure of the older mass of Hebrew literature wrought the revolution of the Reformation.*[3] Nor need we set our eyes so far back; the miracle of the book is not ended. Writers are our ancestors. *Rousseau,* in a notable dithyramb of Amiel, *is an ancestor in all things. He founded travelling on foot before Töpffer, reverie before René, literary botany before George Sand, the worship of nature before St. Pierre, the democratic theory before the Revolution of* 1789, *political discussion and theological discussion before Mirabeau and Renan, the science of teaching before Pestalozzi, and Alpine description before De Saussure;* further, he made music fashionable, public confessions popular, and formed a new French prose style: *the close, chastened, passionate, interwoven style we know so well.* No one had more influence upon the French Revolution; no one had more influence upon the nineteenth century, *for Byron, Châteaubriand, Madame de Staël and George Sand* are all descended from him.[4] *It is, however,* as Voltaire explained, *with books as with men: a very small number play a great part,*[5] and even then, as I said just now, the influence is by reflex action rather than by direct contact. *The world is fundamentally hostile to literature, in great part because the world is gregarious, and literature is a solitary pursuit.*[6] People are content to be influenced at second hand: *You are acquainted with neither Hippocrates, nor Boerhaave, nor Sydenham, but you place your body in the hands of those who can read them. You leave your soul entirely to the care of those who are paid for reading the Bible.*[7] The thought of the world has been changed by Harvey's *Exercitatio Anatomica de Motu Cordis et Sanguinis in Animalibus,* Bacon's *Novum Organum,* Newton's *Principia,* and Darwin's *Origin of Species,* yet few have read those works. So great has been the influence of the world's principal books that, says Emerson, *perhaps the human mind would be a*

---

[1] *Heroes and Hero Worship.* (1841) 263.   [2] 'Introduction' to *Memoir of Isaac D'Israeli.*   [3] Green, *Short History of the English People.* Everyman's Ed. ii, 432, [4] *Amiel's Journal.* Trans. Ward. 111.   [5] *Phil. Dict.* 'Books'.   [6] Andrew Lang. Intro. *Pleasures of Bookland.* Shaylor. xx.   [7] Voltaire, *op. cit.*

gainer if all the secondary writers were lost—say, in England, but all Shakespeare, Milton and Bacon—through the profounder study so drawn to those wonderful minds.[1] Yet great also is the influence of even lesser books. Viscount Morley[2] gives instance of *Areopagitica: the majestic classic of spiritual and intellectual freedom, with its height and spaciousness, its outbursts of shattering vituperation, its inflammatory scorn, its boundless power and overflow of speech in all the keys of passion;* and of John Stuart Mill *On Liberty:* no short book *ever instantly produced so wide and so important an effect;* and Huxley *On the Physical Basis of Life* (1867) made a *profound sensation* on his generation comparable only with the effects in a political epoch of such works as Swift's *Conduct of the Allies* and Burke's *French Revolution.* But this power of books needs no further exposition, it is well known, and the sum of it is in the popular saying: *The Pen is mightier than the Sword,*[3] and no wonder, for *what holy cities are to nomadic tribes—a symbol of race and a bond of union—great books are to the wandering souls of men; they are the Meccas of the mind. Homer was to Greece another Delphi.*[4] No knowing where this power works, or when it may peep out, or hit out; it is potential in all books; in the good, so called, and the bad, so called; the great and the small, the approved, and the disapproved. *The Godlike does ever, in very truth, endure there: now in this dialect, now in that, with various degrees of clearness; but if in Byron and Voltaire, how much more in the sphere-harmony of a Shakespeare, or a Goethe; the cathedral-music of a Milton; the humble genuine lark notes of a Burns.*[5] Many experts of renown have sought to fathom the mystery of this power of words and left naught but mystery in the end. Nor can I do better, or at best do more than guess, or try out a new theorem; for, as he[6] says, *certainly the Art of Writing is the most miraculous of all things man has devised;* not only in its ultimate condition of the completed book, but in each of its constituent words. *Each word,* says a modern lord of languages, *may be not a precious stone only, but one that has shone on Solomon's temple or in Cleopatra's hair. Out of these illustrious atoms all the freakish pinnacles and cupolas of the world's wit were made, all the glow and intensity of its eloquence and the sweet poignancy of song.*[7] How and in what way these miraculous elements of a miraculous craft have moved, changed and affected men, I shall now, in my blunt way, proceed to show.

III. LIBERATING THE SOUL OF MAN

That they cast spells and enslave the spirit of man, with a slavery which releases, by a curious paradox, the soul to newer freedoms, may be inferred

[1] *Society and Solitude:* 'Books'.   [2] *Recollections.* i, 60–62.   [3] Bulwer-Lytton, *Richelieu.* ii, 2.   [4] G. E. Woodberry, *Torch.* 176.   [5] Carlyle, *Heroes and Hero Worship.* (1841) 264.   [6] *Ib.* 258.   [7] C. E. Montague, *A Writer's Notes on his Trade.* 4.

from the precedent examples. There are many who could add to them
from their own knowledge, and some have done so, rejoicing in their
revelations of magical experiences and transformations. Robert Louis
Stevenson was *haunted* by *Love in the Valley*, he remembered waking *the
echoes of the hills about Hyerès*[1] with the lines:

> When her mother tends her before the laughing mirror,
>   Tying up her laces, looping up her hair,
> Often she thinks, were this wild thing wedded,
>   More love should I have, and much less care.
> When her mother tends her before the lighted mirror,
>   Loosening her laces, combing down her curls,
> Often she thinks, were this wild thing wedded,
>   I should miss but one for the many boys and girls.[2]

Later he fell in *slavery* to the *Lake of Innisfree*,[3] and earlier still Swinburne's
Poems and Ballads had *cast a spell* over him. Knowing so well this power to
stir the imagination, he makes a copy of *Virgil* open up for Robert Herrick
in *The Ebb-Tide*[4] visions of his youth in far-away England and all the
sweetness of the English countryside, as Wordsworth was calmed and
soothed and enabled to conquer uncomfortable entrancements by holding
in his hand some treasured volume,

> Poor earthly casket of immortal verse,
> Shakespeare, or Milton, labourers divine![5]

Nor is the effect at all time immediate. Books sow their influences as
seeds are sown, to grow and bloom anon. *What were the words in which
Meredith told me of that sunrise on the Adriatic, or Stevenson of the starry night
in the Cevennes?* asks Vernon Lee. *Not one of those words has remained in my
mind. But there is the shape into which they have moulded my thoughts and
emotions, unchangeable, enduring.*[6] Well may Dr. Johnson[7] confess that books
have *a secret influence on the understanding;* we cannot obliterate the ideas
they insidiously inculcate; *he that reads books of science, though without any
fixed idea of improvement, will grow more knowing; he that entertains himself
with moral or religious treatises will imperceptibly advance in goodness; the ideas
which are often offered to the mind will at last find a lucky moment when it is
disposed to receive them.*

That which they can do is unlimited, they are masters of destiny, rulers
of life and death: the forcible power of Plato's discourse of the Immortality
of the Soul *provoked divers Schollers unto death*, saith Montaigne,[8] *that so*

---

[1] *Letters.* ii, 324.   [2] George Meredith, 'Love in the Valley'.   [3] By W. B. Yeats.
[4] p. 3.   [5] *Prelude.* 164–5.   [6] *Handling of Words.* 83.   [7] *Adventurer.* 137.
[8] 'Apologie of Raymond Sebond', *Essays.* Ed. Seccombe. ii, 161.

they might more speedily enjoy the hopes he told them of. Likewise it cannot be denied, as will appear many times in this treatise, that they are reliable spiritual restoratives, returning men into the safe-keeping of themselves. A notable illustration of this power is recorded of Petrarch. He and his brother had climbed a hill overlooking the Rhone valley and commanding a distant view of the Bay of Marseilles, when fancy prompted him to open the volume of St. *Augustine* which he often carried with him, and by chance he lit upon this passage: *and men go abroad to wonder at the heights of the mountains, and the lofty billows of the sea; the long courses of rivers, the vast compass of the ocean and the circular motion of the stars, and yet pass themselves by,*[1] which so moved him that he gazed no more upon the scenery of hills and the sea, but descended the mountain in silence, his eyes turned inwardly upon himself and the inner riches of his own soul.[2] *Shelley* not only gave George Moore his *first soul,* but *led all its first flights.*[3] Well may William Cory wish that Charlotte Brontë *would come back to us, and count up the myriads to whom she has given new souls;*[4] but whether they liberate the soul or enslave it, rejuvenate or destroy it, assuage desires or inflame them, arouse the imagination, stimulate the intellect, or exalt the emotions, it is all one, books move men as no other devices, and are a Paradise, a Heaven on earth, if they be used aright, good for the body, and better for the soul.

IV. HOW THEY TEACH THE ART OF LIVING

To these divers uses must be added those more proper to the contents of books, what their authors are at when they write, and what their readers expect from them; for the reader, diverse as he is in kind, will have a purpose in his books even though most time they are no more than toys:

> Books should to one of these four ends conduce:
> For wisdom, piety, delight and use.[5]

What should they teach but *the art of living?* asks Dr. Johnson,[6] and he is answered by the poet,[7] that they give

> New views to life, and teach us how to live;

if they do that they accomplish all that we need of wisdom; and that they can do it, though we are not always willing to obey, few would deny. Most acclaim them for this very quality, for, saith Emerson,[8] *the theory of books is noble,* coming as it does from the brooding of the scholar of the

---

[1] *Confessions.* x, 8.   [2] Tatham, *Petrarca.* i, 323.   [3] *Confessions of a Young Man.* 1904. 11.   [4] *Letters and Journals.* 188.   [5] Dominico Mancini. Trans. by Sir John Denham.   [6] *Johnsonian Miscellanies.* i, 324.   [7] Crabbe, *The Library.*   [8] *The American Scholar.*

first age, who gave his thought new arrangement and uttered it into life, when it became truth: *it came to him, short-lived actions; it went out from him immortal thoughts. It came to him, business; it went from him, poetry. It was dead fact; now, it is quick thought. It can stand, and it can go. It now endures, it now flies, it now inspires:*

> 'Tis thine, the great, the golden chain to trace,
> Which runs through all connecting race with race.[1]

The true mirror of our reading is the course of our lives, for if, as Garrod holds, *it is life that shakes and rocks us*, it is *literature which stabilizes and confirms.*[2]

Zeuxidamus answered one that demanded of him why the Lacedemonians did not draw into a book the ordinances of prowess, that so their young might read them: *it is*, he said, *because they would rather accustome them to deeds and actions, than to bookes and writings*,[3] as Dr. Johnson sang in his *Vanity of Human Wishes*,

> Deign on the passing world to turn thine eyes,
> And pause awhile from letters to be wise;

yet many have been *desirous of considering sound learning and virtuous manners as convertible terms* and of believing that *the civilization of our barbarous manners would be essentially promoted by the promotion of useful letters.*[4] Mark Pattison argues, *they are not things to be learned in* themselves, but rather *so many different object-glasses, through which we can look at things;* which Maurice de Guérin[5] supports, where he claims that the *Etudes de la Nature* clears and enlightens a sense in us which is *veiled, vague, inactive:* the sense which *gathers in physical beauties and conveys them to the soul*, where they are in turn *spiritualized, harmonized*, and *combined with ideal beauties, and thus enlarges its sphere of love and adoration;* they *let us into the minds of men*, enjoins another,[6] and *lay open to us the secrets of our own.* They are *indispensable*, says Marie Valyère, *not so much for what they teach us as for what they suggest;* they both teach and suggest, as all know, and all can use them whatever their trade: *Homer is the poet for the warrior, Milton for the religionist, Tasso for women, Robert Southey for the patriot.*[7] There is a book for each one of us, and each convinces by its presence, suggestively and instructively. It was, I dare presume, for this reason that Sir Ferdinando Lapith built the privies at Crome at the top of three several towers, furnishing each with bookshelves containing *all the ripest products of human wisdom, such as the Proverbs*

---

[1] Crabbe, *The Library.*   [2] *Profession of Poetry.* 257.   [3] 'Of the Institution and Education of Children.' Montaigne, *Essays.* Ed. Seccombe. i, 205–6.   [4] Gilbert Wakefield, *Correspondence with C. J. Fox.* 124.   [5] *Journal.* Trans. Trebutien. 72.   [6] William Hazlitt.   [7] S. T. Coleridge, *Letters.* Ed. E. H. Coleridge. i, 178.

of Solomon, Boëthius's 'Consolations of Philosophy', the apophthegms of Epictetus and Marcus Aurelius, the 'Enchiridion' of Erasmus, and all other works, ancient and modern, which testify to the nobility of the human soul. He made his reasons clear in a tract, published in 1573, which he called *Certaine Priuy Counsels One of Her Maiestie's Most Honourable Priuy Counsel, F. L. Knight*, where he argued *the necessities of nature are so base and brutish that in obeying them we are apt to forget that we are the noblest creatures of the universe.* Books, he believed, would counteract these *degrading effects*: read more of this curious enterprise in *Crome Yellow.*[1]

Thus in this matter of wisdom it is not surprising to read Voltaire[2] asserting that all the known world, save only savage nations, *is governed by books*, and, in our own day, H. G. Wells arguing that nations cannot live under modern conditions unless *aerated with books*; for, as Frederick Denison Maurice observes,[3] *if they do not assist to make us better and more substantial men, they are only providing fuel for a fire larger, and more utterly destructive, than that which consumed the Library of the Ptolemies;* but *well managed*, as Jeremy Collier concedes, *they afford direction and discovery, strengthen the organ, enlarge the prospect of life.* Sir William Temple[4] gives out that modern scholars have recourse to the University *in quest of books, rather than men for their guides*, which Thomas Carlyle had in mind when he made that oracular declaration: *Once invent Printing, you metamorphosed all Universities or superseded them!*[5] for, as Bacon holds out, *books will speak plain, when Counsellors blanch*;[6]

> Ah! when will both in friendly beams unite,
> And pour on erring man resistless light?[7]

But dead counsellors are safest, Dr. Johnson[8] quotes out of Alphonsus of Aragon, and adds, *the grave puts an end to flattery and artifice, and the information that we receive from books is pure from interest, fear, or ambition.*

How much better, as Richard Baxter[9] counsels, to read a good book than listen to a mean preacher: *preachers, even, may be silenced or banished, when good books may be at hand; books may be kept at a smaller charge than preachers.* Good, therefore, to learn from Paul Bourget that *the crowd wants to use the book that it reads*, and if the time comes, which, if we are to believe Anatole France, it always does, when *books that were useful cease to be useful*, it matters little, since they have served their purpose and we need not *regret that they were written.* Let this not be the occasion of concern, for all things perish in time, some before, some after fruition: we have as yet no power to adjust this ordering of nature, even if we would; and in this

---

[1] Aldous Huxley. Chap. xi.   [2] *Dict. Phil.* 'Books'.   [3] *On Books.*   [4] *Ancient and Modern Learning.*   [5] *Heroes and Hero-Worship.* (1841) 261.   [6] *Essays.* 'Of Counsel.'   [7] Crabbe, *The Library.*   [8] *Rambler.* 87.   [9] *Christian Directory.*

general process of change books, being mortal, are mutable also, they come and go, blossom and fade, having sown their seeds. That they live longer than most of the works of man, is well known and sufficiently shown in this treatise, and Sir Thomas Browne holds[1] that our *Holy Bible* is the one work of man which is *too hard for the teeth of time, and cannot perish but in the general Flames, when all things shall confess their Ashes.*

Nor need they be what at all times are considered good books (Arsène Houssaye insists that it is only bad books that are good for anything); for books are like morals in Rudyard Kipling's expostulation:

. The wildest dreams of Kew are the facts of Khatmandhu,
And the crimes of Clapham chaste in Martaban.[2]

Good men down the ages have damned, burnt, expurgated, condemned and forbidden books, believing and making bad what others believed good. The most complete catalogue of the world's best books may thus be the *Index Expurgatorius* at the Vatican. How these Canutes and Partingtons have expostulated against the ocean of books or tried to sweep it up is well known and a common joke, to which I shall come anon.

V. WHERE BOOKS HAVE FAILED

Before I proceed farther, however, I must rescue myself from any suspicion of faith in the omnipotence of books which the precedent chapters may have occasioned. I support no such opinion. There was an odd observation made long ago by Joseph Glanvill, which puts my case. *'Tis no disparagement to Philosophy, that it cannot Deifie us, or make good the impossible promise of the Primitive Deceiver, yet those raised contemplations of God and Nature, wherewith Philosophy doth acquaint us, enlarge and ennoble the spirit, and infinitely advance it above an ordinary level;*[3] and although the diffusion of books through the whole community has worked greater effect than *artillery, machinery, and legislation,*[4] so that *mankind are the creatures of books,*[5] there is no news that these bookfed multitudes are all angels of culture. We are too often reminded that they are not by wars, cruelties, thefts, deceits, graspings, scandals, and all manner of uncharitable acts and unkindliness, which have forced some good and great men to despair, and to curse, as Beethoven did, the *miserable rabble* called humanity. Books increase and readers of them multiply; millionaires, as Andrew Carnegie, municipalities, states, endow and build libraries, but the *profanum vulgus,*

---

[1] *Religio Medici.* Pt. i, Sect. 23.   [2] 'In the Neolithic Age', *Seven Seas.* 127.
[3] 'Apology for Philosophy', *Scepsis Scientifica.* (1665) 175–6.   [4] Channing, *Address* at Boston. 1838.   [5] Leigh Hunt, *A Book for a Corner.*

the rabble, endureth for ever; the poor in spirit are always with us, and man is still as much *a burlesque of what he should be,*[1] as he was when Montaigne summed him up as a *many-headed, divers-armed, and furiously-raging monster; wretched, weake and miserable; whom if you consider well, what is he, but a crawling, and ever-moving Ants'-neast?*[2] and Dean Swift castigated him in *Gulliver;* and so he remains for Dean Inge to reprove in innumerable tracts and treatises in these present times. George Moore is therefore buttressed with logic when he asserts that *if good books did good, the world would have been converted long ago;* instead of that, recent events read more like a fulfilment of Leonardo da Vinci's prophecy that *creatures shall be upon the earth who will always be fighting one with another with very great losses with frequent deaths on either side. These shall set no bounds to their malice; by their fierce limbs a great number of the trees in the immense forests of the world shall be laid level with the ground; and when they have crammed themselves with food it shall gratify their desire to deal out death, affliction, labours, terrors and banishment to every living thing. And by reason of their boundless pride they shall wish to rise towards heaven, but the excessive weight of their limbs shall hold them down. There shall be nothing remaining on the earth or under the earth or in the waters that shall not be pursued and molested and destroyed, and that which is in one country taken away to another; and their own bodies shall be made the tomb and the means of transit of all the living bodies which they have slain. O Earth! what delays thee to open and hurl them headlong into the deep fissures of thy huge abysses and caverns, and no longer to display in the sight of heaven so savage and ruthless a monster?*[3]

That man had been neither destroyed nor arrested in his destructive progress Jeremy Taylor testified[4] in his day in a sermon preached at the funeral of that Worthy Knight, Sir George Dalstone, in the year 1657, where he besought his hearers to observe how many *righteous causes are oppressed, how many good men are reproached, how Religion is persecuted, upon what strange principles the greatest Princes of the World transact their greatest affairs, how easily they make Wars, and how suddenly they break Leagues, and at what expense and vast pensions they corrupt each other's Officers, and how the greatest part of mankind watches to devour one another, and they that are devoured are commonly the best, the poor, and the harmless, the gentle and uncrafty, the simple and religious,* and since *all good men are exposed to danger* he affirms that this world is *a place of Wasps and Insects, of Vipers and Dragons, of Tigers and Bears,* their victims *Sheep* who are *eaten by men, or devoured by Wolves and Foxes, or die of the rot,* and when they do not *they redeem their lives by giving their Fleece and their Milk* only to die when *their death will pay their*

---

[1] Schopenhauer, *Studies in Pessimism.* Trans. Saunders. 24.   [2] 'Apologie of Raymond Sebond', *Essays.* Ed. Seccombe. ii, 207.   [3] *Note-Books of Leonardo da Vinci.* McCurdy. 289.   [4] *The Worthy Communicant.* (1683) 398–9.

charges of the Knife; following upon which, we are prepared to learn from Schopenhauer, that although *man's range of vision embraces the whole of his life, and extends far into the past and the future*, in one respect, at least, the beasts are his superiors, in *their quiet, placid enjoyment of the present moment.*[1]

> And since he cannot spend and use aright
> The little time here given him in trust,
> But wasteth it in weary undelight
> Of foolish toil and trouble, strife and lust,
> He naturally claimeth to inherit
> The everlasting Future, that his merit
> May have full scope; as surely is most just.[2]

For more to this end, corroborative evidence of this *continuum* of folly, read it in *Jeremiah* and *Ecclesiastes*, *Erasmus*, *Voltaire* and *Swift*, *Schopenhauer*, *Nietzsche*, *Bernard Shaw*, *H. G. Wells*, *Spengler*, *ad infinitum et passim*, and arrest my digression, for excluding *the passionate few*,[3] *the acute but honourable minority*,[4] the world hath but two classes—those who take no notice of what it does and those who run with it for company.

VI. A BRIEF CATALOGUE OF ADVANTAGES

Of the diverse advantages which books have bestowed upon men, that of upholding in moments of depression, *amara temperare*,[5] is not least but most necessary, and especially conducing to the good of mankind: he who has once known their satisfaction, Emerson claims, *is provided with a resource against calamity*.[6] What *Virgil* has done others have done also: *Homer*, *Horace*, *Dante*, *Shakespeare*, among poets of the Western world; and in the Orient, *Confucius* in his *Discourses* and *Analects*; Lao-Tsze in his *Tao*; the *Mahabharata* with the Lord Buddha's Song, *Bhagavat Gita*, and the *Upanishads* of Hindustan; *Al Koran* of Mahomet; the *Zend-Avesta* of the Parsees who follow the word of Zarathustra; the *Talmud* of the Hebrews; and all the poets and story-tellers: *Hafiz* and *Omar Khayyam*, the *Arabian Nights* and the *Jataka*—the list has no end nor has their influence. *They support us in solitude, and keep us from becoming a burden to ourselves. They help us to forget the coarseness of men and things, compose our cares and our passions, and lay our disappointments to sleep;*[7] they are

> The noblest road to happiness below;[8]

[1] *Studies in Pessimism*. Trans. Saunders. 20.   [2] James Thomson (B.V.), *City of Dreadful Night*. xiii.   [3] Stendhal.   [4] George Meredith.   [5] Horace, 'To sweeten the bitters'.   [6] *Letters and Social Aims*. (1898) 129.   [7] Comtesse de Gaulis, *Memoirs*.   [8] George Crabbe, *The Library*.

they are links in the chain of consciousness, binding together the different scattered divisions of our personal identity; landmarks, guides in our journey through life; pegs and loops on which to hang up or from which to take down at pleasure *the wardrobe of moral imagination*; they are *for thoughts and for remembrance; they*

> Inform the head and rectify the heart;[1]

like Fortunatus's Wishing-Cap, they give us the best riches, those of Fancy, transporting us not (solely) over half the globe, but which is better, over half our lives—at a word's notice (read more in Hazlitt his *Plain Speaker*, ii. 66 *passim*); they are *the calmers as well as the instructors of the mind*, says Mrs. Inchbald; and purifiers of the body as well, for, if we are to believe a modern authority, to read the works of George Borrow *is to wash soul and body in the open air, to be purified from the stains of civilization, to meet and greet the Mighty Mother.*[2]

Charles Lamb cannot *sit and think: books think for me*, he said;[3] they *interpret what we see and experience*;[4] they add to our emotions, make the present live and the past survive; *Modern Painters* opened up *a new and glorious universe* for F. J. Furnivall;[5] by reading, a man *does as it were antedate his life*, making himself contemporary with ages past;[6] Zeno recommended as a prime means towards happiness resorting to the dead and holding familiar converse with them by means of books, for thus we should have *such good instructors as have been observed in our predecessors:*[7]

> The pen records tyme past and present both:
> Skill brings forth bookes, and bookes is nurse to troth.[8]

They are the legacies that genius leaves to mankind, *delivered down from generation to generation*, presents to the posterity of those yet unborn;[9] nothing so pleasant, so delightful, as Letters (saith Cicero), *by whose means the infinite of things, the incomprehensible greatness of nature, the heavens, the earth, and all the Seas of this vast universe, are made known to us.*[10] Further, they have taught us, he relates, *religion, moderation, stowtnesse, courage; redeemed our souls out of darknesse, to make her see* all things, high and low, first and last, and those between both. They store and supply us with all such things as *may make us live happily and well, and instruct us how to pass our time without sorrow or offense.* They are the keys which admit us to *the whole*

---

[1] *Ib.*   [2] Lionel Johnson, *Post Liminium.* 201.   [3] 'Detached Thoughts on Books and Reading.'   [4] W. E. Channing.   [5] Qt. John Monro, *F. J. Furnivall.* xxii. [6] Jeremy Collier, 'Of the Entertainment of Books', *Essays.*   [7] Preface. *Montaigne.* First Eng. Trans. (1620)   [8] Churchyard, *Worthiness of Wales.* (1776) 18. [9] Addison, *Spectator.* 166.   [10] 'Quibus infinitatem rerum atque naturae, et in hoc ipso mundo coelum, terras, maria cognoscimus.' *Tusc.* v, 36. Qt. Montaigne, *Essays.* Ed. Seccombe. ii, 228.

world of thought and fancy and imagination; to the company of saint and sage, of the wisest and the wittiest at their wisest and wittiest moments.[1] They are additional senses: they help us *to hear with the finest ears, and listen to the sweetest voices of all time,* and *to see with the keenest eyes;*[2] they are the eyes through which we look at the world of thought and things: *Virgil* and *Cicero* were to Petrarch additional eyes through which he looked into a new world, they are *the two eyes of our language,* he said, *gli occhi de la lingua nostra;*[3] and, since *Victor Hugo* carried Amiel *from world to world,* they are vehicles which transport us beyond ourselves.[4] And finally they are also the mirrors in which we look at ourselves:

> These to his memory—since he held them dear,
> Perchance as finding there unconsciously
> Some image of himself. . . .[5]

VII. LACHRYMAE MUSARUM

The power of books to cheer us out of our sad or sullen moods may not always follow the direct and merry path: it may reach its destination deviously by a tearful ellipse, or deflexion through the vale of tears; for if *The Innocents Abroad* and *Three Men in a Boat* have made whole nations laugh, others, as *East Lynne, The Old Curiosity Shop,* and *Clarissa,* have made them weep. Scaliger *never read Socrates' death in Plato's 'Phaedo' but he wept; Austin shed tears when he read the destruction of Troy;*[6] when Sara Fielding read *Clarissa,* she told Richardson, her heart glowed, she was overwhelmed, her only *vent* was tears;[7] an old Scotch doctor, a Jacobin and a freethinker, who, Sir George Trevelyan records,[8] could only be got to attend church by the positive orders of the Governor-General of the province in India where he was stationed, cried over the last volume of *Clarissa,* until *he was too ill to appear at dinner.*

Tears flowed in 1850 when Macaulay *cried his eyes out* over the last volume of that book,[9] and he gave Thackeray a vivid account of the effect of *Clarissa* on the English colony in India. He was passing the hot season in the Hills, with the Governor-General, and the Secretary of the Government, and the Commander-in-Chief, and their wives. He had *Clarissa* with him and when they began to read it *the whole station* bubbled over in

---

[1] J. R. Lowell, 'Books and Libraries', *Democracy and Other Addresses.* [2] *Ib.* [3] Qt. Tatham, *Francesco Petrarca.* 28. [4] *Amiel's Journal.* Trans. Ward. 85. [5] Tennyson, Dedication, *Idylls of the King.* The dedication is to Queen Victoria and the reference to Prince Albert. [6] Burton, *Anat. of Melan.* (1904) ii, 3, v. [7] *Correspondence of Richardson.* Barbauld. ii, 60. [8] *Macaulay.* i, 334. [9] *Ib.* ii, 237.

a passion of excitement about Miss Harlowe and *her scoundrelly Lovelace; the governor's wife seized the book; the secretary waited for it; the Chief Justice could not read it for tears.* Thackeray recounts that as Macaulay told this tale of woe to him in the Athenæum Club, *he acted the whole scene*, pacing up and down the club library. To complete my catalogue of the lachrymosities of our most bookish peer I give that instance of his reading aloud the story of Lefevre from *Tristram Shandy* to a party of friends visiting Lichfield on a Sunday in April 1849: *I read the story with many tears*, he confesses,[1] *and it was heard with tears, even by Trevelyan himself, who is not easily moved to that degree by fiction.*

Tears started to Dr. Johnson's eyes when, at Oban, he recited a passage from Goldsmith's *Traveller*, as Boswell helped him on with his greatcoat,[2] and *when he would try to repeat the celebrated 'Prosa Ecclesiastica pro Mortuis', as it is called, beginning 'Dies irae, Dies illa', he could never pass the stanza ending thus, 'Tantus labor non sit cassus', without bursting into a flood of tears.*[3] Charles Lamb *would read noble passages* from Milton, *actually weeping as he read*;[4] Heine, when a youth, *wept in his little room* over the death of the *most blessed heroes of freedom: King Aegis of Sparta, Caius and Tiberius Gracchus of Rome, Jesus of Jerusalem, and Robespierre of Paris;*[5] and earlier in his life he would steal into the Palace Garden at Düsseldorf to read *Don Quixote*, pronouncing the words aloud because of his lack of skill in reading, and thus were the birds and streams able to hear, and, being innocent, like children and like the boy himself, *knowing nothing of the irony of the world*, wept over the sorrows of the unhappy knight: *a veteran oak sobbed, and the waterfall* wagged his white beard the more and seemed to cry out upon the wickedness of the world.[6]

After hearing Panaef read *Poushkin* to him Tolstoy *sat down on a sofa and wept causeless but blissful tears*;[7] Francis Hindes Groome tells[8] that his grandfather, Rector of Monk Soham in Suffolk, was so *tender-hearted* that he was *moved to tears by the Waverley novels;* one night in 1881, during his residence on the Island of Madeira, William Cory was reading Lanfrey's *History*, when his wife, who was writing at the other end of the table, looked up, and observed that he was weeping: *Yes*, he said, *I am weeping as I wept fifty years ago over the death of Nelson.* He was wrought up with the news of *the disgraceful flight of our men from Majuba*, and *Lanfrey* induced tears which purged him of despair;[9] twice in his life, *twelve years apart*, he was thus *melted, prostrated and yet comforted* by *Les Misérables.*[10] Books filled Alexander Smith with awe as though he stood

[1] *Journal*. Qt. *The Times*. 7.xii.1928. [2] *Tour*. Hill. vi, 344. [3] Piozzi, *Anecdotes of Dr. Johnson*. Ed. S. C. Roberts 130. [4] *Lamb*. P. Fitzgerald. 169. [5] *Heinrich Heine's Memoirs*. Ed. Karpeles. i, 61. [6] *Ib*. i, 59. [7] *Life*. Maude. i, 161. [8] *Suffolk Friends*. 13. [9] Cory, *Letters and Journals*. 469. [10] *Ib*. 391.

In presence of a king. They give me tears;
Such glorious tears as Eve's fair daughters shed,
When first they clasped a Son of God, all bright
With burning plumes and splendours of the sky.[1]

Gray told Horace Walpole that the *Castle of Otranto* made the undergraduates at Cambridge *cry a little and all in general afraid to go to bed
o'nights*;[2] and the last scenes of *Henry V* made Edward FitzGerald *blubber*.[3]

But such examples are too frequent, so I shall end this chapter with an
anti-climax which is more in key with our Shavian era. Professor Garrod
confesses[4] that one day he was reading *East Lynne*, that lachrymatory
bomb which Mrs. Henry Wood threw so effectively at the Victorian age.
As he read he wept. *The manner in which the tears ran down* his cheeks made
him *an object of general attention*. An *elderly and benevolent clergyman*, moved
by this pathetic sight, *expressed the hope that* the weeping man was *not in
any trouble*, and was perplexed when he learnt *with perfect truth* that the
Professor *was only crying because this book was so bad a book. God forbid that
I should cry over 'Lear' or 'Othello'*, he says, *I should know that there was
something the matter either with Shakespeare or with myself*. The best books
strike too deep for tears.

VIII. CONSOLERS AND REFUGES

Leigh Hunt *entrenched* himself in his books equally against sorrow and the
weather;[5] they eased Montaigne of the *burden of weary-some sloth*;[6] Edward
FitzGerald *shut out the accursed 'Eastern Question'* by reading the stories of
Boccaccio;[7] Benjamin Robert Haydon worked with more *abstracted devotion* at his craft of painting when his books were near him, and after he
had *stuck at it all day* he would walk in the evening among his books *in
ecstasy*, reading nothing, but dwelling on what he had read with great
content, his imagination *crowded* with Milton's Satan and *all his revel host*,
and with Shakespeare's immortal crew: Hamlet, Lear, Falstaff, Cordelia,
Imogen, Macbeth, and Puck.[8] So necessary the companionship of books
to Isaac D'Israeli, that without a *command of his library* he was *nothing*.[9]

I may not here omit that use to which so many who are accounted wise
have put them, as means of retreat from the world itself and the noisome
weariness of mortal customs, which is well supported by Cicero, whose
ardency for books increased with his disgust of everything else: *summum*

---

[1] *A Life-Drama.*   [2] Gray, *Poems and Letters.* (1820) 433-4.   [3] *More Letters.* 150.
[4] *Profession of Poetry.* 257.   [5] *Essays,* 'My Books'. Camelot Ed. 287.   [6] 'Of Three
Commerces or Societies', *Essays.* Ed. Seccombe. iii, 52.   [7] *Letters and Literary
Remains.* i, 389.   [8] *Autobiography.* iii, 110.   [9] *The Croker Papers.* ii, 42.

me eorum studium tenet sicut odium iam ceterarum rerum;[1] and *not only scholars,* Walter Pater allows,[2] *but all disinterested lovers of books* will ever look to literature, as to all other fine art, *for a refuge, a sort of cloistral refuge, from a certain vulgarity in the actual world*; and he holds that a perfect poem like *Lycidas,* a perfect fiction like *Esmond,* the perfect handling of a theory like Newman's *Idea of a University,* has for them the same quality as a religious *retreat.*

Lionel Johnson, who read all night, slept all day, breakfasting when others dined, found his library his cloister, and when asked by Yeats whether such habits did not *separate him from men and women,* replied: *In my library I have all the knowledge of the world that I need.*[3] Books are thus a substitute for society. *Everywhere have.I sought peace and found it only in a corner with a book.*[4] *I too have found repose where he did,* said Robert Southey, *in books and retirement, but it was there alone I sought it: to these my nature, under the direction of a merciful Providence, led me betimes, and the world can offer nothing which should tempt me from them.*[5] By his *Imitation of Christ,* Thomas à Kempis hath medicined more sick souls than any other Christian writer outside of the Holy Scriptures; Eugénie de Guérin[6] speaks of *passages in it suited to all situations of the soul, remedies for every passion, a divine gentleness; anyone may read it with profit,* and she would *recommend it alike to the sick, to the world's unhappy ones, to persons given up to the darkest despair*; *had Judas read it,* she adds, *he would never have been able to hang himself.*

Such testimonies are innumerable, infinite in time and variety; for books are, and none but the profane would contest it, the chiefest consolers of man on this his earthly pilgrimage, *they are the soul's viaticum,* as Richard Whitlock owns in his *Zootomia,* which I have cited at length in my first chapter. They are a form of life within life, more real than reveries, more satisfying than dreams:

> Dream, who love dreams! forget all grief;
> Find in sleep's nothingness relief;
> Better my dreams! Dear, human books,
> With kindly voices, winning looks!
> Enchant me with your spells of art,
> And draw me homeward to your heart.[7]

And if, as it may happen, such consolations are not for all who read, nor at all times for all who love looks, they add to our riches, for *the world may be kind or unkind, it may seem to us to be hastening on the wings of enlight-*

[1] 'I have the greatest longing for books along with hatred of everything else.' *Ad Atticum.* i, 11.   [2] 'Style'. *Appreciations.* 14.   [3] Yeats, *The Trembling of the Veil.* 181.   [4] Thomas à Kempis.   [5] *Colloquies.* xiv.   [6] *Letters.* 141.   [7] Lionel Johnson, 'Oxford Nights', *Poetical Works.* 99.

enment and progress to an imminent millennium, or it may weigh us down with the sense of insoluble difficulty and irremediable wrong; but whatever else it be, so long as we have good health and a good library, it can hardly be dull.[1] For that reason, as Isaac D'Israeli follows it,[2] those tyrants and usurpers who possessed *sense as well as courage*, have proved the *most ardent patrons of literature*, knowing it to their interest *to turn aside the public mind from political speculations, and to afford their subjects the inexhaustible occupations of curiosity, and the consoling pleasures* of the *imagination*.

But I risk being over-tedious in these testimonies, which, howsoever in some men's too severe censures they may be held absurd and ridiculous, I am the bolder to insert, as not borrowed from circumforanean rogues and vagabonds, but out of the writings of worthy philosophers and poets, yet living some of them, and learned professors, in famous Universities, who are able to establish that which they have said, and vindicate themselves from all cavillers and ignorant persons.

---

[1] Balfour, 'The Pleasures of Reading', *Essays and Addresses*. 37.   [2] *Cur. of Lit.* i, 2–3.

Part XIV

BOOKS PHARMACEUTICALLY DISPOSED

I. THEIR MEDICINAL PROPERTIES GENERALLY CONSIDERED

The medical properties of books are well known to the learned and a *favourite theme with philosophers and students.*[1] They are *medicinal, stringent;*[2] *useful drugs and materials wherewith to temper and compose effective and strong medicines;*[3] as the poet Henry Vaughan well sang:

> By sucking you the wise, like bees, do grow
> Healing and rich.

No cause for wonder here, if we refer all this to *the narrow suture of the spirit and the body, inter-communicating their fortunes one unto another;*[4] as in all times physicians have noted the close connection and ready intercourse between the minds and bodies of men, and the histories are full of evidence of defects responding to mental, spiritual, emotional and other non-medicinal treatments which in some ages have been accounted miraculous.

The curative properties of the arts are well known, medicine itself being as much an art as a science, if not more. *Inventum est medicina meum*, said Apollo,[5] and if we are to believe Varro, Pliny, and Columella, most of the best medicines of the Greeks were derived from his Oracles, as many in all ages have derived prophylactics from colours, sounds, forms, and words, æsthetically disposed. Melody has many notable records in this respect, as Saul was helped by David's harp;

> Such sweet compulsion doth in music lie.[6]

In olden times wounds were cured by song, as Apuleius contends, out of *Homer*, that the blood of Ulysses was thus stayed as it gushed from the wound, by a chanted ditty;[7] and Aulus Gellius[8] gives an instance, out of

---

[1] 'Books as Doctors', *Attitudes and Avowals*. Richard Le Gallienne. 108. [2] Emerson, 'Books', *Society and Solitude*. 158.   [3] Milton, *Areopagitica*. Ed. Holt White. 74.
[4] Montaigne, 'Of the Force of Imagination', *Essays*. Ed. Seccombe. i, 108.
[5] 'Medicine is my invention.' Ovid. Met. i, 521.   [6] Milton, 'Arcades'. 68.
[7] *Apologia*. Trans. Butler. 74.   [8] *Attic Nights*. iv, 13.

288

Theophrastus, of people being cured of gouty pains by the soothing measures of a flute-player, which is supported by Democritus, who holds that flute-music is a remedy for *snake-bites* and many other maladies. Eloquence, which is words and feelings harmoniously arranged, is no less efficacious, whether applied to the ills of particular persons, or to the *body politic*, as when Demosthenes, *by the medicine of his words of praise*, healed the distemper of the Athenians, so that they were *brought to pride themselves no less on the battle against Philip than on the triumphs won at Marathon and Salamis.*[1]

Aches and pains often, as we know, trouble many without just physical cause, and there can be little doubt that it is these which yield most readily to a prescription of books. Cardan doubtless had this in mind when he called a library *the physic of the soul*, where *divine authors fortify the mind, make men bold and constant*; for (as Hyperius adds) *godly conference will not permit the mind to be tortured with absurd cogitations.*[2] Many memorable cures are examples of the efficacy of psychotherapy. A curious instance is cited out of his own experience by Samuel Butler.[3] A young man came to him *in a flood of tears over the loss of his grandmother, of whose death at the age of ninety-three he had just heard.* Butler tried all the *panaceas* without effect, and was on the point of giving him up in despair, when he thought of *crossing* the sorrow-stricken man with the ancient ballad of *Wednesday Cocking*, with the result that he *brightened up instantly* and *departed in as cheerful a state as he had been before in a desponding one.* Such methods are well known, and are much in favour for lulling the sorrows of children, for whom all manner of crude and primitive verses are reliable soothing-syrups; and I shall presently show how the most physical of maladies respond to a treatment of books; but before coming to the cures I must take my generalization yet a step further.

So to follow this equality or correspondence between books and medicine yet a little, I may mention how many have discerned a chemical relationship both in their appearance and condition, as Plato when he compares Socrates to the Apothecary's gallipot, that had owls, apes and satyrs on the outsides, but precious drugs within;[4] or Amiel, when he asserts that *Victor Hugo draws in sulphuric acid*;[5] and Byron means no less when, in a request to John Murray, he does not scruple to mix *soda-powders, Acton's corn-rubbers, and Scott's Romances.* A library pharmaceutically disposed, says one,[6] would have the appearance of a *dispensatory*, and might

[1] Longinus, *The Sublime.* Trans. Prickard. 39.   [2] Qt. Burton, *Anat. of Melan.* (1904) ii, 107, 108. According to *Diodorus Siculus.* i, 49, 3, this was the inscription over the door of the Library at Thebes.   [3] *Alps and Sanctuaries.* 55.   [4] Bacon, *Apophthegms.* Bohn Ed. 181.   [5] *Journal.* Trans. Ward. 91.   [6] Crabbe, *Works.* (1847) Cumberland. IV, ii, 32.

K

properly enough be so called. He is supported by no less an authority than Dr. Oliver Wendell Holmes, who looks upon a library as *a mental chemist shop filled with the crystals of all forms and hues* which come from the union of thought with *local circumstances and universal principle;*[1] for he supposes that *a man's mind does in time form a neutral salt with the elements in the universe for which it has special elective affinities;* which the Countess of Blessington also discovers in her diagnosis of poets as *the chemists of sentiment.*[2] The same doctrine is taught by Richard Le Gallienne, who stoutly maintains that the library will ultimately *take the place of the dispensary,* and, *instead of giving us prescriptions of nauseous drugs, the physician will write down the titles of delightful books—books tonic or narcotic, stimulating or sedative, as our need may be.*[3] After all this it is no wonder to find that a library is a hospital, as George Crabbe describes it in a verse of his:

> Where mental wealth the poor in thought may find,
> And mental physic the diseased in mind.[4]

In a collection of books he sees remedies for many ills, but mostly that *Balm of Gilead* which alleviates sick souls:

> See here the balms that passion's wounds assuage;
> See coolers here that damp the fire of rage;
> Here alteratives by slow degrees control
> The chronic habits of the sickly soul;
> And round the heart and o'er the aching head,
> Mild opiates here their sober influence spread.[5]

When we recall how many of our older book-collectors have been doctors, we cannot resist the notion that such benefactors of literature as Radcliffe, Mead, Sloane, Hunter, etc., had this advantage in mind when founding their libraries. And now let us examine the particular evidences of the medicinal properties and their pharmacopœial status.

II. PRESERVATIVES AND PROPHYLACTICS

Among the numerous evidences of the medicinal disposition of books I find several allied instances of fertilization and preservation, as when Lady Constance, in *Tancred, guanoed her mind by reading French novels,* and Matthew Arnold *read about a hundred lines of the 'Odyssey'* to keep himself from *putrefaction* during the drudgery of his inspectorship of schools.[6] The

---

[1] *Professor at the Breakfast Table.* (1902) 23–4.   [2] *Desultory Thoughts.* 48.   [3] Richard Le Gallienne, 'Books as Doctors', *Attitudes and Avowals.* 110–11.   [4] *The Library.* [5] *Ib.*   [6] *Letters.* i, 75.

preservative character of books had before his day been observed by Payne Fisher, who caused to be printed on the title-page of his *Elogia Sepulchralia* the words: *Miramur periisse Homines?* *Monumenta fatiscunt* (Anson), and *Nescia Musarum sed monumenta mori* (Ovid), which is thus Englished by a wit of that age:

> Men timely die, and Princes day by day
> Moulder to dust: but Books will live for aye,
> And re-embalm us in the coldest day![1]

So it is no news to learn that books are the great preservatives of history:

> Here all that live no more; preserved they lie,
> In tombs that open to the curious eye;[2]

and that, as the poet Vaughan sings:

> Cæsar had perished from the world of men,
> Had not his sword been rescued by his pen.[3]

Some, as Dr. Rosenbach,[4] argue that book-collecting acts as an elixir of life, keeping men young, *a new type of life insurance*; the *wonderful library* of Mr. W. A. White of New York *would take away the load of years from a Methusalah*, even *to read over the partial list of his treasures* would cause rejuvenation; and he asserts that his own Uncle Moses, a notable book-seller and booklover of Philadelphia, *grew younger and younger as he sat year after year surrounded by books*. That the reading of them may well be as efficacious in the opposite effect of giving ripeness to youth, is proved by Fuller, who says: *history maketh a young man to be old without either wrinkles or grey hair, privileging him with the experience of age without either the infirmities or the inconveniences thereof.*[5]

Finally in this class of their properties they are prophylactics against several diseases. Pliny the Younger *strengthened* his *digestion*, and thus prevented many ills, by reading aloud Greek or Latin orations;[6] and Dibdin records how the Nestor of bibliographers of his day ended a tirade against an epidemic of bibliophobia with a challenge to typhus, scarlatina, and even to the then prevailing cholera, feeling proof against those evils so long as he possessed his beloved books, and if Fate held the worst for him (he was then an octogenarian), he would die content, *hugging his Homer*.[7] For another bibliomaniac, Dibdin advocates *Russia leather* as a *charm and protection against epidemic miasmata of every description*; give him, he says,

---

[1] Dibdin, *Bibliophobia.* 78.   [2] George Crabbe, *The Library.*   [3] 'On Sir Thomas Bodley's Library'.   [4] *Books and Bidders.* 33.   [5] Qt. Lubbock, *Pleasures of Life.* i, 59.   [6] *Letters.* Melmoth. Loeb Ed. ix, 36.   [7] *Bibliophobia.* 65.

the treble-rowed entrenchment of his library and he will snap his fingers alike at *the arrows of fate and the canker of care,*[1] both of which predispose us to other ills.

Horace Walpole longed for a catalogue of *lounging books,* that one might take up *in the gout, low-spirits, ennui:* gay poetry, odd whimsical authors, as Rabelais, etc. *Even a catalogue raisonné of such might be in itself a good lounging book.*[2] Sterne commends his own *Tristram Shandy* as such a book, medicinal to that end: *'Tis wrote,* he saith, *against the spleen! in order, by a more frequent and a more convulsive elevation and depression of the diaphragm, and the succussations of the intercostal and abdominal muscles in laughter, to drive the gall and other bitter juices from the gall-bladder, liver, and sweetbread of his Majesty's subjects, with all the inimicitious passions which belong to them, down to their duodenums;*[3] and at the end of the fourth volume he once again dilates upon the curative properties of his novel. *True Shandeism,* he says, *opens the heart and lungs;* and, *like all those affections which partake of its nature, it forces the blood and other vital fluids of the body to run freely through their channels, and makes the wheel of life run long and cheerfully round;*[4] and there is even some little evidence, worth further exploration by the medical profession, which suggests that even paper and ink may be taken with beneficial results in some distempers. Samuel Butler cites an instance[5] of a man who was cured of a dangerous illness by swallowing the doctor's prescription, which he understood to be the medicine itself.

Bulwer-Lytton[6] would promote this faith to a practical account by forming a *curative* library whose compartments should no longer bear such labels as Philology, Natural Science, Poetry, but *according to the diseases for which they are severally good, bodily and mental: up from a dire calamity, or the pangs of the gout, down to a fit of spleen or a slight catarrh.* In such a bibliotorium treatment would be prescribed for all diseases. He advises light reading with a whey-posset and barley-water for a cold; biography, preferably of good men, when *some one sorrow, that is yet reparable, gets hold of your mind like a monomania;* and when, Heaven having denied you this or that, you feel that life is blank and empty, he prescribes the *Book of Books . . . the lignum vitae, the cardinal medicine for all.* But *books, taken indiscriminately,* he expostulates, *are no cure to the diseases and afflictions of the mind.* Scientific application is essential. No use flying to a novel or the last light book of fashion in a great sorrow: *one might as well take a rose-draught for the plague.*

Goethe, he says, was a physician who knew how to heal himself, for, when he lost his son, he found solace in a science that was new to him; so

---

[1] *Ib.* 50–51.   [2] *Walpoliana.* (1800) 166–7.   [3] *Tristram Shandy.* iv. 22.   [4] *Ib.* iv,32.
[5] *Note-Books.* 311.   [6] *The Caxtons.*

Bulwer hastens to prescribe *a course of science and hard reasoning* for all irremediable sorrows. *Bring the brain to act upon the heart!* he orders as a counter-irritant. If science be too much against the grain, take a strange language: Greek, Arabic, Scandinavian, Chinese, Welsh. For loss of fortune he advises *something elegant and cordial*, since here the head rather than the heart is affected, and thus he finds *the higher class of poets a valuable remedy*. For hypochondria what better than *a brisk course of travels— especially the early, out-of-the-way, marvellous, and legendary*. For that *vice of the mind* which he calls *sectarianism*, not religious, but little, narrow prejudices, gossiping, prying, backbiting, *a large and generous, mildly aperient course of history* he finds better than that hellebore with which the old leeches of the Middle Ages purged the cerebellum. He cured a disconsolate widower, who *obstinately refused every other medicament*, with *a strict course of geology*; and he brags of a not less notable cure of a young Cambridge student who had caught *a cold fit of freethinking, with great shiverings, from wading out of his depth in Spinoza*. He omits to name the remedy, although it was certainly efficacious, since his patient's *theological constitution* became so robust that he ate up *two livings and a deanery*.

III. THE CLAIM THAT THEY ARE CURE-ALLS DISCUSSED

Montesquieu *had never known a pain or a distress that he could not soothe by half an hour of a good book*;[1] but to guarantee so much is *vendere fumos*, such promises end in smoke, and those enthusiasts who promise that books will cure all ills go too far. Better stop with Pliny, who ventured no further than to say that there is no pain which literature cannot *alleviate*, for books are no cure-alls; only the quacks and charlatans of the market-place would say otherwise. To overstate the power of books is to do them harm and to harm those who seek restoration of health by them. *The longer I live*, said Sydney Smith, *the more I am convinced that the apothecary is of more importance than Seneca*.[2] I am not, however, unmindful of the fact that some few writers, by reason of the universality of their genius, may approximate to a universal remedy, like *Shakespeare*, who is a pharmacopœia in himself. Some would allow as much for others, as Richard Le Gallienne[3] for *Alexandre Dumas, who comes nearest of all writers to being a literary cure-all*; he is *incomparably the most useful of all writers* in *nervous diseases*, but *there is no form of sickness to which he may not be applied*, and a set of *Dumas*, he advises, is as *indispensable in a sick-room as a nurse or pure air*; for this reason,

---

[1] Qt. *Book-Lovers' Anth.* 386. [2] *Memoir.* Holland. i, 126. [3] 'Books as Doctors', *Attitudes and Avowals.* 114–15

in all cases likely to be prolonged, the doctor should immediately pre-scribe *Dumas* whatever subsequent treatment may be necessary.

I have brought enough evidence to prove their efficacy in cases of *ennui*, megrims, melancholy, and the like, and am therefore the more em-boldened to announce that even here they are not infallible. Books can do no more than open the door of consolation, but if the ingredients of consolation are not within us, how shall we be consoled? The inconsolable are beyond their reach:

> Not poppy, nor mandragora,
> Nor all the drowsy syrups of the world,
> Shall ever medicine thee to that sweet sleep
> Which thou owedst yesterday.[1]

Take, as a type, the case of Des Esseintes, who sought to ease the morbid irritations of his ingrowing consciousness by associating with all manner of strange and beautiful objects, among them, as I show in its place, unique copies of fantastic books, fearfully and wonderfully caparisoned. He pondered over his treasures as an amateur or novice adventuring among the mysteries of an apothecary's hoard. But to no satisfying end, for content was always farther from him than it is from most of us. To change the current of his tabid emotions, and *cool his brain*, he once tried *a course of emollient reading*, and reckoning the novels of Charles Dickens among the *solanaceæ*, he resorted to them. Books of this kind, he argued, being appropriate to the delicate condition of the convalescent whom sensational stories or other works *richer in phosphates* might only fatigue, would be appropriate also to his condition. But his theory collapsed in practice. Dickens produced just the opposite effect. His lovers were too chaste, too modestly draped, too *Protestant*; their *seraphic passions*, never going beyond a *coy dropping of the eyes, a blush, a tear of happiness, a squeez-ing of hands, exasperated him*. This *exaggerated virtue* drove him to the other extreme. He rushed into contrary excesses of thought: set himself to imagine passionate, full-bodied loves; frailties; ardent embraces, etc. So throwing Dickens aside he banished from his thoughts the *mock-modesty of Albion*, and dreamed of licentious practices and *salacious little sins* con-demned by the Church.[2]

At another time[3] he sought distraction from his tortured spirit in a Bodega wine shop within the arcades of the Rue de Rivoli, where over a glass of sherry, the *nerve-soothing stories, the gentle lenitives* of Dickens were scattered, and their place was taken by the *harsh repulsives*, the *cruel irritants of* Edgar Allan Poe; *the chill nightmare of the 'Cask of Amontillado'*, that haunting tale of the man walled-up in an underground chamber,

---

[1] *Othello.* iii, 3.   [2] Huysmans, *A Rebours.* Eng. trans. Paris. 137-8.   [3] *Ib.* 181.

seized upon his fancy, until even *the kindly and commonplace faces of the English and American customers who filled the hall seemed to reflect uncontrollable and abominable cravings, odious and instinctive plans of wickedness.* But perchance Des Esseintes was not in search of health, for Huysmans gives out that he was genuinely interested only in *sickly books*, those whose *health was undermined and exasperated by fever.*[1]

So, as in the pharmacopœia of doctors, what will cure one may kill another. But if any further proof of these medicinal qualities be demanded, let it be taken from the records of some inverse activities, for it has been advocated by many authorities, Doctors of Literature among them, that phylacteries have opposing or negative characters, as poisons are efficacious in some distempers, deadly in others. This danger is noted by Montaigne when acquiring *Sciences: We cannot suddenly put them into any other vessel, than our minde,* he says; *we swallow them in buying them, and goe from the market, either already affected or amended. There are some, which insteade of nourishing, doe but hinder and surcharge us; and other some, which under cover of curing, empoison us.*[2] Bulwer-Lytton was physically distressed by Buckle's *History of Civilization;*[3] Carlyle's *French Revolution,* when *a new book much in fashion,* so affected Edward FitzGerald as to impede his recovery from *influenza;*[4] Lockhart's *Scott* made Stevenson ill;[5] and Samuel Butler reports a still more serious case of a man who lined his hatbox with some sheets of Benbowe's poetry, which so strangely affected his hat that the first time he wore it afterwards he felt *a singing in his head, which within two days turned into a vertigo.* Well may Le Gallienne warn us of the risk of *prescribing the wrong author in a dangerous case*: half-hourly doses of *Keats* and *Shelley* in an attack of gout might so *accelerate the action of the heart* as to induce apoplexy.[6] But he is careful to note that patients crave for what is bad for them. Consumptives, for instance, yearn for *Maeterlinck* when they obviously need *Fielding, Dickens* and *Balzac,* so he warns book-doctors who have a craze for *Meredith, Pater,* or *Henry James,* against those potions when the patient should be given *doses of Marie Corelli.*[7]

Many authorities find religious treatises a sure remedy in several distempers, the physician *should by no means overlook the somewhat curious efficacy of sermons.*[8] But I have heard some complain of *Sermons* and other books of the kind (good otherwise) because they are too serious, too much dejecting men, aggravating offences. Great care and choice, much discretion are required in their application. I need do no more than mention the faith of men in the healing powers of the Holy Scriptures. If comfort

[1] *Ib.* 213.   [2] 'Of Physiognomy', *Essays.* Ed. Seccombe. iii, 362.   [3] *Mr. Hayward's Letters.* ii, 56.   [4] *Letters and Literary Remains.* i, 42.   [5] Stevenson, *Letters.* i, 301.   [6] 'Books as Doctors', *Attitudes and Avowals.* 112–13.   [7] *Ib.* 118.   [8] *Ib.* 117.

may be got from Philosophy, asks Burton,[1] what shall be had from Divinity? What shall *Austin, Cyprian, Gregory, Bernard's divine meditations afford us?* Nay, *what shall the Scripture itself, which is like an Apothecary's Shop, wherein are all remedies for all infirmities of mind, purgatives, cordials, alteratives, corroboratives, lenitives, etc.* Every disease, saith Austin, *hath a peculiar medicine in the Scripture*; which is supported by Donne, who advises that *the whole booke of Psalmes is Oleum effusion, an Oyntment poured out upon all sorts of sores, a Sear-cloth that souples all bruises, a Balme that searches all wounds*;[2] which Amiel also supports when he confesses (in his *Journal* for July 17th, 1859) that he had *just read seven chapters of the Gospel*, and *nothing calms* him so much. Le Gallienne reminds us that *a text suspended round the neck has seemed more than equal to a bottle of medicine*, and he would not consider it *fantastic to ascribe the vigorous health of our forefathers to their constant reading of the Bible.*[3] Yet even here the remedy is not always effective. When Coleridge was very ill Scott's *Novels* were *almost the only books* he could take. *I cannot at such times read the Bible*, he confessed, *my mind reflects on it, but I can't bear the open page.*[4]

Notwithstanding all that might be advanced to these effects both *pro* and *con*, there are many records of cures in times present which I cannot ignore, although they are none of them of my experience, but borrowed from printed testimonies, and for defence I must refer to the consciences of those I take them from. How many modern books of a religious kind have this power of healing I cannot tell, but by common report the most efficacious of them is *Science and Health*, by Mrs. Baker Eddy, and to this only I shall refer. In the appendix of that work it is claimed in precise words that *thousands* of people *have been reformed and healed through the perusal or study of this book*; and eighty-five testimonies are given from those who have benefited by this medicine. The maladies cured comprise the chief causes of human suffering: consumption, rheumatism, cancer, epilepsy, cataract, neurasthenia, deafness, Bright's disease, etc., some hereditary, others acquired. All the particular circumstances are set out and in many instances cures are alleged to have been made by a simple, yet devout, reading of a borrowed copy of the book.[5] I will say no more, but will let this epitome suffice, having broached it in keeping with my purpose, for I commonly make use of that which is rare and memorable, and every man may add his example or explanation. For my part, I neither deny nor affirm. I am interested in everything, surprised at nothing, and I am as ready as most men to snatch at some more accurate remedy than those chemical nostrums which are the broken reed of medicine. And I

---

[1] *Anat. of Melan.* (1904) ii, 108–9.   [2] 'Sermons', *Selected Passages*. L. P. Smith. 23.
[3] *Op. cit.* 109.   [4] *Table Talk*. 298.   [5] Science and Health. Mary Baker Eddy. (1918) 600–700.

firmly believe with Oliver Wendell Holmes, himself a medical man, *that if the whole 'materia medica' could be sunk to the bottom of the sea, it would be all the better for mankind and all the worse for the fishes*, of which, because many observers have written whole books, I will say nothing.

It is clear then that since no physical condition is static, or, indeed, similar to any other, no specific can be universal. Le Gallienne[1] is wise in this respect and he even contests the traditional belief in laughter as a universal specific, giving as an example that of *Mark Twain*, who must be prescribed with care in cases of *bronchitis* and *other pulmonary* diseases because laughter is *apt to provoke dangerous fits of coughing*. But further data are unnecessary, a wrongly prescribed book, or an overdose of literature being as dangerous as any other physic wrongly administered.

IV. RANGE OF THEIR MEDICINAL PROPERTIES

How far the medicinal character of books doth extend, it is hard to determine:

> But ask not, to what doctors I apply.
> Sworn to no master, of no sect am I.
> As drives the storm, at any door I knock,
> And house with Montaigne now, and now
> with Locke.[2]

Yet what a variety of bookmen hold of their effects, forces and operations, I will briefly show. Dibdin reports that Haslewood swooned away at Sotheby's when a copy of his *beloved Juliana Berners was knocked down* to a rival *at the freezing price of thirty-five shillings*. He was carried out of the sale-room *speechless*, and the *fainting-fit* was succeeded by *a solid, roaring fit of gout*. He was restored to his normal health by a mixture of nine grains of *Ritson's tartar* with three tablespoonfuls of *Braithwait's emollient*.[3] Whenever Jules Janin was overcome by the ridicule of his *confrères* after he had made *a more than usually egregious blunder* in his weekly article (such as calling the lobster the *Cardinal of the Seas or describing Smyrna as one of the Greek Islands*), he would soothe his distraught feelings by *fondling his first editions bound in crushed levant by Capé or Bauzonnet*. The treatment never failed.[4]

In the opposite defect they are equally efficacious, for as *the imagination moved and tossed by some vehemence, doth cast some darts, that may offend a strange object*,[5] it is well known that an opportune shock is recommended

[1] *Op. cit.* 116.   [2] Pope, *Epistles of Horace.* I, i, 23.   [3] *Bibliophobia.* 40.   [4] Gosse, *The Library of Edmund Gosse.* xxi.   [5] Montaigne, 'Of the Force of the Imagination', *Essays.* Ed. Seccombe. i, 108.

in diverse affections both of the mind and body. For that reason physicians prescribe counter-irritants. In modern times they have taken to electricity, showing great faith in its repercussions as an alterative. Some books are capable of giving such tempestuous shocks to the intelligence, the emotions, or to both, that they disturb the bloodstream and thus induce an action which breaks up obnoxious or obstructive matter, as, in surgery, tumours and calculi are dispersed by *electrolysis*. They galvanize atrophied or awaken dormant energies, and thus release new and generous life-forces, which have been known to restore sight to the blind and to make the mute vocal. Such phenomena are familiar also to sociologists, who have made many records of the revolution of individual and even national behaviour by book-shock. The French have a phrase, *épater les bourgeois*, which defines the process in one of its applications. It was said of Baudelaire that he slept under the bed instead of on it, to shock the middle classes, and Bernard Shaw's explosive wit was *avowedly designed to shock, prod and irritate the social consciousness of the bourgeoisie into practical moral zeal.*[1] But read more of this in my section of the *Fear of Books*.

There are as many varieties of these effects as there are emotional states, as fear, joy, sorrow, etc. Two remarkable instances are given by Aulus Gellius[2] out of *Herodotus*.[3] The first tells of the dumb son of King Crœsus, who, seeing his father in danger of death, was so shocked as to make a great effort to cry out to the enemy, and by doing so created in himself the power of speech and thus saved the King's life; the second tells of an athlete of Samos, by name Echeklous, who was speechless from birth and came to speak through an effort to expose cheating in the casting of lots between the Samians and their opponents. Erasmus laughed so violently on reading the *Epistolae Obscurorum Virorum*, a work written by Hottenius to expose the literary and moral errors and absurdities of the monks, and condemned to the flames by Leo X, *that he broke an imposthume, for which he was to have undergone an operation.*[4] Many such instances must lie buried in the histories of famous bibliophiles, but none more to my point than that of Peiresc, who, being *smitten with paralysis*, was restored by hearing a newly-arrived song in which a troubadour poet had celebrated the loves of the Lily and the Rose. He had lost all power of speech, but he was so greatly moved to express his liking for the song that words came to him, and *he forthwith uttered them, and at that very moment his limbs were all freed from the palsie.*[5] Of a like kind, being allied with the same causes, are those instances of transmutation by imaginative force which are familiar in our histories. Two of these I give for a taste, out of the authority of *Montaigne*.

[1] 'Shocking as a Fine Art', *The Eighteen-Nineties*, Holbrook Jackson. 5th ed. 131.   [2] v, 9. (Loeb Ed. i, 403–5)   [3] i, 85.   [4] Beloe, *Anecdotes*, i, 93–4.   [5] Qt. Dobson, *De Libris*. 247.

The first tells of a young girl, born near Pisa, who was *all shagd and hairy over and over*, by reason of the impression made upon her mother by *an image of Saint John Baptist, that was so painted, and hung over her bed.* The second he gives out of his own domestic experience: *There was lately seene a cat about my owne house, so earnestly eyeing a bird, sitting upon a tree, that he seeing the cat, they both so wistly fixed their looks one upon another, so long, that at last, the bird fell downe as dead in the Cat's pawes, either drunken by his owne strong imagination, or drawne by some attractive power of the Cat.*[1] But I must end these citations, and get back to books.

V. A DIVERSITY OF CURES

I may now give some particulars of their beneficent dispensations among invalids, making peace and pleasure counteract pain, as when Bulwer-Lytton found relief from influenza by reading the *Autobiography of Mrs. Piozzi*, which Mr. Hayward, Q.C., its editor, had sent him.[2] Miss Berry, during an illness at Little Strawberry, found comfort in such diverse works as *Wraxall* and *Montaigne*.[3] William Hazlitt[4] recommends *Tom Jones* as an excellent good physic against *indigestion*; and, more recently, that scrupulous annalist, Arnold Bennett, reports[5] that some plays of Labiche, which he had bought cheap, *certainly did something* to cure a stubborn attack of *neuralgia* from which he was suffering. Robert Louis Stevenson found the *Adventures of Sherlock Holmes* soothing when he suffered from the toothache, and on another occasion it relieved a pleurisy: *it will interest you as a medical man to know*, he told Dr. Conan Doyle, *that the cure was for the moment effectual.*[6] Richard Le Gallienne knows of a long-standing case of *asthma* cured by Tolstoy's *War and Peace*, and he has found Victor Hugo's works efficacious in the same disease;[7] whilst he advises *a course of Shakespeare* for gout, having great faith in the curative properties of *the crystalline air that blows about the peaks of the masterpieces*; and in all doubtful cases he prescribes *Alexandre Dumas*;[8] another witness finds like benefits from *Ben Jonson* or *Robert Burton*, whenever *a cold or other cause stays* him *in bed*.[9]

Dr. O'Rell, as Eugene Field records, included books in his dispensary and prescribed them confidently. A favourite was the *Noctes Ambrosianae*, and once when Eugene Field was stricken with melancholia through the loss of a coveted *Elzevir* at auction, O'Rell administered doses of Father

---

[1] 'Of the Force of the Imagination', *Essays*. Ed. Seccombe. i, 109.   [2] *M. Hayward's Letters*. ii, 56.   [3] *Letters*. Lewis. ii, 74.   [4] 'The Sick Chamber', *New Monthly Magazine*. August 1830.   [5] *Diary*.   [6] *Letters*. ii, 286-7.   [7] 'Books as Doctors', *Attitudes and Avowals*. 116.   [8] *Ib*. 114.   [9] Malcolm Macmillan, *Letters*. 141.

Prout's *Rogueries of Tom Moore* and Kit North's debate with the Ettrick Shepherd, with such good effect that the patient was effectively cured and within forty-eight hours he was hunting again and picked up on a book-stall, *for a mere song,* a first edition of *Special Providences in New England.*[1]

But even when a book can make no direct cure its power to soothe mind and body after or during pain is recognized by all the authorities. Thornton Wilder brings some evidence in support of this in the case of the Archbishop of Lima. This good man had exchanged the *Fathers* and *Councils,* in whom he had been deeply versed, for *the libertine masterpieces of Italy and France,* which he *re-read annually.* These works proved of great value as restoratives, for *even in the torments of the stone (happily dissolved by drinking the water from the springs of Santa Maria de Cluxambugua) he could find nothing more nourishing than the anecdotes of Brantôme and the divine Aretino.*[2] Aubrey Beardsley, during the consumption which killed him, was relieved of much distress by reading *Diderot* and Stendhal's *Le Rouge et le Noir,* and the *Works* of Friedrich Nietzsche made him feel *quite gay.*[3] An old doctor once came to Oliver Wendell Holmes with a *contrivance for people with broken knee-pans,* and recognizing that a mind agreeably employed disposes the body towards health, *he mentioned, in his written account of his contrivance, various works* which might serve that purpose, among them *Don Quixote, Tom Jones,* and *Watts on the Mind.*[4] We can well believe that when Mark Rutherford *lay dangerously ill of pneumonia,* his recovery was aided and abetted because he *lay quite still* whilst his nurse read *Jane Austen* to him,[5] *for in cases of lingering convalescence* books are *invaluable.*[6]

When an Arab is bitten by a poisonous snake, his friends resort to the *Koran,* reading certain passages over him; if these are the correct passages, the sufferer lives; if not, he dies.[7] So have ills been cured in our land and time by the silent recital of inspired passages from poet or philosopher. Ruskin attributes his resilience in the face of repeated attacks of brain fever to *Virgil.* Through all such troubles, which irritated his later years, he was enabled to hold out and recover by *having always murmured in my ears, at every new trial, one Latin line,*[8]

Tu ne cede malis, sed contra audentior ito.[9]
Yield not to any ills, but go all the bolder to face them.

Richard de Bury will have that even obsolete books, when their *rank*

---

[1] Field, *Love Affairs of a Bibliomaniac.* 179.   [2] *Bridge of San Luis Rey.* 102.   [3] *Last Letters.* 21–2.   [4] *The Autocrat of the Breakfast-Table.* (1902) 151.   [5] *The Groom-bridge Diary.* 78.   [6] 'Book-Love', *Fraser's Magazine.* 1847.   [7] *With Lawrence in Arabia.* Lowell Thomas. 196.   [8] Sir Edward Cook, *More Literary Recreations.* 77–8.   [9] *Aen.* vi, 95.

barbarism is *digested*, may *heal the pectoral arteries with the gift of eloquence.*[1]
Nor need we wonder at him, for a book is no dead thing:

> The thing's restorative
> I' the touch and sight.[2]

Experience teaches us that reading is not always necessary. Books may
affect one as much by sight as by reading. They cure by their presence,
composing or stimulating the mind or the emotions of those who do no
more than gaze upon them. *To cast mine eye upon good Authors*, said John
Donne, *kindles and refreshes* the mind, provoking agreeable meditations.[3]
Montaigne did not pretend to read all his books: it was sufficient to have
them near him. *In effect*, he says,[4] *I make no other use of them, than those
who know them not. I enjoy them, as a miser doth his gold; to know, that I may
enjoy them when I list; my minde is setled and satisfied by the right of possession.*
He never travelled without them in peace or war, yet passed many days
and months without using them. *It shall be anon, say I, or to-morrow, or
when I please; in the meane while the time runnes away, and passeth without
hurting me. For it is wonderful, what repose I take, and how I continue in this
consideration, that they are at my elbow to delight me when time shall serve.* . . .
This is the best munition I have found in this humane peregrination. Dr. Folliott,
in T. L. Peacock's *Crotchet Castle*,[5] supports Montaigne: *nothing more fit to
be looked at than the outside of a book; it is a resource against ennui, if ennui
should come upon you,* and, he goes on, *even if the medicine is unnecessary,
to have the resource and not to feel the ennui, to enjoy your bottle in the present,
and your book in the indefinite future, is a delightful condition of human existence;* which John Skelton has sung:

> It would have made a man whole that had been right sickly
> To behold how it was garnished and bound.[6]

This argument finds some support also in Dibdin,[7] where he tells how,
when Dr. Gossen lay on a bed of sickness, the first *Complutensian Polyglot
Bible* of Cardinal Ximenes, *in its original binding*, was brought to him *to
work a cure*; though whether it was efficacious to that end or not, he omits
to say.

VI. THE CURE OF MEGRIMS, MELANCHOLY AND LIKE DISTEMPERS

Nothing is more established in the pharmacopœia of books than their
power to relieve and even cure melancholy. A great volume could be

[1] *Philobiblon.* viii.   [2] Browning, *Ring and the Book.* i, 89–90.   [3] Letter to A. V.
Merced. 1609.   [4] 'Of Three Commerces or Societies', *Essays.* Ed. Seccombe. iii, 53.
[5] Chap. vii.   [6] *Replycacion against Scolers.*   [7] *Reminiscences.* i, 206.

filled with instances, of which I shall recite a few. When Madame de Sévigné was beleaguered in her country house by *rain interrupted only by storms*, she was *devoured by melancholy*, and kept alive only by reading.[1] *If I were in the country, and were distressed with that malady*, said Dr. Johnson, *I would force myself to take a book; and every time I did it I should find it the easier. Melancholy*, he adds, *should be diverted by every means but drinking*.[2] Montaigne[3] and many others have asserted the value of books for the relief of ill-humours, megrims, *tedium vitae*, blue devils, dumps, etc. *To divert me from any importunate imagination or insinuating conceit*, he declares, *there is no better way than to have recourse unto bookes: with ease they allure mee to them, and with facilitie they remove them all*. For him that is *overrun with solitariness*, or *carried away* with *pleasing melancholy* and *vain conceits*, or who knows not how to *spend his time*, or is *crucified with worldly care*, Robert Burton prescribes *study*[4] (provided always that the malady proceed not from overmuch of it), for he well knew, out of his own experience, when he spent so many happy and solitary hours in Bodley's Library compiling his great treatise on *Melancholy*, that, as a later poet hath it, books

> Are not companions—they are solitudes;
> We lose ourselves in them and all our cares.[5]

Let him take heed he do not overstretch his wits, and make a *skeleton* of himself. He warns also such *Inamoratos* as read nothing but playbooks, idle poems, jests, *Amadis of Gaul, the Knights of the Sun, the Seven Champions, Palmerin de Oliva, Huon of Bordeaux*, for such folk many times in the end prove as mad as *Don Quixote*.

Study Burton prescribes only for those who are idle, troubled in mind, or carried headlong with vain thoughts, *to distract their cogitations*. Nothing in such cases better than *the healing influence of studious pursuits to soothe and abstract*.[6] *Semper aliquid memoriter ediscant*, saith Piso, let them learn something without book, transcribe, translate, read the Scriptures, which Hyperius[7] holds sufficient of itself: *animus levatur inde a curis multa quiete et tranquillitate fruens*, the mind is erected thereby from all worldly cares, and has much quiet and tranquillity. *Reading is to the mind what exercise is to the body;*[8] 'tis the best nepenthe, surest cordial, sweetest alterative, presentest diverter. Rhasis enjoins continual conference to such melancholy men, perpetual discourse of some history, tale, poem, or news, *alternos sermones edere ac bibere, aeque jocundum quam cibus sive potus*,[9] which feedeth the

---

[1] *Letters*. i, 168–9.   [2] *Life*. Ed. Hill. iii, 5.   [3] 'Of Commerces', etc., *Essays*. Seccombe. iii, 52.   [4] *Anat. of Melan*. (1904) ii, 107.   [5] P. J. Bailey, *Festus*. [6] Lamb, 'Poor Relations', *Last Essays of Elia*.   [7] *De quotid. Script. lec. f. 77.* [8] Steele, *Tatler*. 147.   [9] *Ser. 38. ad Fratres Erem*.

mind as meat and drink the body, and pleaseth as much. We gather *virtue* from a *fable* or an *allegory*, says Steele,[1] *as health* by *hunting*; they rectify by *an agreeable pursuit that draws us on with pleasure*, making us insensible of fatigues. They bear us up, when we would sink in the sea of melancholy help us

To swim with bladders of philosophy.[2]

Ferdinand and Alphonso, Kings of Aragon and Sicily, were both cured by reading the Histories, one of *Curtius*, the other of *Livy*, which no prescribed physic could replace.[3] Camerarius relates as much of Lorenzo de Medici. Heathen philosophers are so full of divine precepts that, as some think, they are able alone to settle a distressed mind *Sunt verba et voces, quibus dolorem etc.*,[4] such are in *Epictetus, Plutarch*, and *Seneca. Qiualis ille, quae tela*, saith Lipsius, *adversus omnes animi casus administrat, & ipsam mortem, quomodo vitia eripit, infert virtutes!*[5] When I read *Seneca, methinks I am beyond all human fortunes, on the top of an hill above mortality.*[6] Plutarch said as much of *Homer*, for which cause Niceratus, in *Xenophon*,[7] was made by his parents to con Homer's *Iliad* and *Odyssey* without book, *ut in virum bonum evaderet*, as well to make him good and honest as to avoid idleness. Luther's *Commentary* healed the spiritual wounds, comforted the afflicted consciences, and relieved the tormented minds, of Bunyan and his friends.[8] Francis Bacon[9] gives out that *it were too long to go over the particular remedies which learning* (and he means book-learning) *doth minister to all the diseases of the mind; sometimes*, he goes on, *purging the ill humours, sometimes opening the obstructions, sometimes helping digestion, sometimes increasing appetite, sometimes healing the wounds and exulcerations thereof, and the like*. Weighed down with years and the spectacle of human folly, Thomas Carlyle found a prophylactic in *Plutarch*, who composed the *ruffled hair* of his *back in a sensible degree*, smoothing down *the loud inanity of many fools and idiots.*[10]

Hesiod held, and Macaulay after him marked the passage with three lines in his own copy of the poet,[11] that *if to one whose grief is fresh, as he sits silent with sorrow-stricken heart, a minstrel, the henchman of the Muses, celebrates the men of old and the Gods who possess Olympus, straightway he forgets*

---

[1] *Op. cit.* 147.   [2] Rochester, *A Satire Against Mankind*.   [3] Bodin, *Praefat. ad meth. hist.*   [4] 'There are words and sounds with which this grief may be assuaged.' Horace. I *Ep.* i, 34.   [5] 'What a man is he, what weapons doth he furnish against all affections of the mind, and against death itself, how he removes vices and implants virtues!'   [6] Lipsus, *Symposium*. iii, 5.   [7] *Symposium*. iii, 5.   [8] Mark Rutherford, *Bunyan*. 106.   [9] *Advancement of Learning*.   [10] *New Letters*. ii, 322.   [11] *Life and Letters*. Trevelyan. ii, 378.

his Melancholy, and remembers not at all his grief, beguiled by the blessed gift of the goddesses of song:[1]

εἰ γάρ τις καὶ πένθος ἔχων νεοκηδέι θυμῷ
ἄζηται κραδίην ἀκαχήμενος, αὐτὰρ ἀοιδὸς
Μουσάων θεράπων κλεῖα προτέρων ἀνθρώπων
ὑμνήσῃ, μάκαράς τε θεοὺς οἳ Ὄλυμπον ἔχουσι,
αἶψ᾽ ὅ γε δυσφρονέων ἐπιλήθεται, οὐδέ τι κηδεών
μέμνηται, ταχέως δὲ παρέτραπε δῶρα θεάων

Pliny the Younger would fly to his books, which were the *sovereign composers* of his grief;[2] and it was to books that the modern philosopher, Benedetto Croce,[3] turned when weighed down by the weakening of his faith. *As a sick man searches for medicine* he went to books on *apologetics,* but since these left him *cold,* he turned to *the words of truly religious minds,* and so *found comfort.* Charles James Fox called poetry *the great refreshment of the human mind,* and after *ruining himself at cards, he could sit down and derive an instant solace from Theocritus;*[4] and Lord Rosebery gives Mr. Gladstone as an example of a happy man, *one of the main sources of whose happiness was his bookishness.*[5] When Sir Humphrey Davy needed consolation from the tedium of a journey he flew not to inn or posting-house, but to his books,[6] thus supporting Jeremy Collier, that books *help us to forget the crossness of men and things.*[7]

Macaulay read himself out of the profound melancholy of a great bereavement. *Even now, I dare not, in the intervals of business, remain alone for a minute without a book in my hand.*[8] Well may he have argued at another time that *an interesting book acted as an anodyne;*[9] in which he has Sir Walter Scott's[10] support, where he says, *muddling among old books has the quality of a sedative, and saves the tear and wear of an overwrought brain.* James Payn goes so far as to call books *the blessed chloroform of the mind,*[11] and Richard Le Gallienne *can imagine painful operations being performed with no other anæsthetic than a chapter or two from the lives of D'Artagnan or Bussy D'Amboise.*[12] But if he and some other sceptics will not grant them power to act as anodynes in physical distress, they will not deny them power to heal broken hearts, to weld them as few other specifics could. They can *emolliently affect the nervous system,*[13] and are prime tests of sanity. William Cory took up Sidgwick's *Ethics* now and then to test whether his brain

[1] *Theog.* 98–103.   [2] 'Studia unicum doloris levamentum.' *Letters.* Melmoth. Loeb Ed. viii, 19.   [3] *An Autobiography.* Trans. R. G. Collingwood. 35.   [4] Rosebery, *Appreciations and Addresses.* 159.   [5] *Ib.* 169.   [6] Tom Hood, *Letter to the Manchester Athenæum.*   [7] *Essays upon several moral subjects.*   [8] *Life and Letters.* i, 387. [9] *Ib.* ii, 401.   [10] *Journal.* ii, 259.   [11] *Chambers's Journal.* 1864.   [12] 'Books as Doctors', *Attitudes and Avowals.* 115.   [13] Locker, *My Confidences.* 216.

was *softening*.[1] They can help keep *the head from crazing and the heart from breaking*;[2] for evidence of which read the story of how Henri IV of France fled for consolation to his books when abandoned by Gabrielle d'Estrèes,[3] and that of Macaulay, whose *life and reason* were saved by *literature* when they were endangered by the death of his beloved sister.[4]

VII. SPECIFIC FOR TEDIUM VITAE

Tom Hood found his *burden* in life lightened by a *load of books*. How this came about he expounds by the parable of the Kilkenny cats, which fought until they devoured one another. *It is not so generally known*, he adds, *that they left behind them an orphan kitten which, true to the breed, began to eat itself up, till it was diverted from the operation by a mouse.* He goes on to compare the human mind, under vexation, to that kitten. The mind is apt to prey upon itself, *unless drawn off by a new object; and none better for the purpose than a book; for example, one of Defoe's; for who, in reading his thrilling 'History of the Great Plague', would not be reconciled to a few little ones?*[5] Viscount Morley of Blackburn found literature a great restorative in many ill-humours, and he claims for *Wordsworth* that *he repairs the daily wear and tear, puts back what the fret of the day has rubbed thin or rubbed off, sending us forth in the morning whole.*[6] General Garfield would agree, for, when President of the United States, he refreshed himself by learning all the Congressional Library could tell him about *Horace* and the various editions and translations of his poems.[7]

It is this quality which ensures that curative consolation which books above all things made by men bring to the sick-room. How they have soothed pain, relieved tedium, engaged the mind and cheered the heart of the invalid is well known. No extension of what is already known and what has already been said is necessary. Books bring relief to anguish by opposing thought to pain, and, by thus releasing the healing forces of Nature herself, permit her to do her good work. They are infallible distractors, and therefore as good as a doctor. *Pain and sickness are charmed away by them.*[8] They are certain prophylactics against that *ennui* which reduces the vitality and exposes us to the attacks of disease, for they create interest in life, which in itself is now a recognized tonic both for individuals and nations, who may be thus saved from being bored to death. *Interest in*

---

[1] *Letters and Journals.* 445.   [2] Hood, *Letter to the Manchester Athenæum.* 1843.
[3] *The Great Book-Collectors.* Elton. 108.   [4] *Life and Letters.* i, 387.   [5] Hood, *Letter to the Manchester Athenæum.* 1843.   [6] *Recollections* i. 387.   [7] *Book-Lore.* i, 44.
[8] John Aikin, *Letters from a Father to his Son.*

life, says Rivers, *is the primary factor in the welfare of a people.*[1] That which banishes boredom promotes health and prolongs life. One holds that *the companionship of books is unquestionably one of the greatest antidotes to the ravages of time, and study is better than all medical formulas for the prolongation of life;*[2] which is no more than the belief of Richard Whitlock that *the Book-worme is of all Creatures the longest lived, the last in every Age living all the former, to whose Age Methuselahs was but Nonage.*[3] If thou art sick of soul, thy heart heavy, thy mind distressed, thou mayest happily recover by a regimen of books; no better spiritual pick-me-ups:

> If hipped my G. or languid you should feel,
> There are worse things than a course of Steele.[4]

Books enabled that moodiest of essayists, Hazlitt, to get through the year *without ever knowing what it* was *to feel ennui.*[5] He and others have found them tonics in convalescence, and at such times as the spirit is in reduced circumstances. This quality is well authenticated of some particular books. *Plato, like mountain air, sharpens our organs, and gives us an appetite for wholesome food;*[6] whilst *Epictetus,* says Dowden,[7] proved both *tonic* and *styptic* to Southey, when other writers had discommoded his *nervous sensibility.* Many have resorted to the poets with like success: *Homer rolling along the hexameter or trumpeted by Pope, will give one a hot glow of pleasure and raise a finer throb in the pulse.*[8]

VIII. BOOKS AS SOPORIFICS

As soporifics, promoters of *sleep that knits up the ravell'd sleave of care,*[9] they are of proved value. *Sometimes,* says a reliable witness,[10] *we read for a while and then feel as though we could peacefully go to sleep. Sometimes we struggle desperately to gum our failing attention to the acute analysis and deductions of our author. Our eyes squint and swim. Our head dizzies. We feel drunk, and, dropping the book from loose hands, just manage to get the light out before falling back into a dense and miry slumber.* Those neat lines of Alexander Pope tell us the same:

---

[1] 'The Psychological Factor', *Depopulation of Melanesia.* W. H. R. Rivers. 96.
[2] Roberts, *Book-Hunter in London.* xxii.   [3] *Zootomia.* 244.   [4] Inscribed by Austin Dobson in a copy of his *Selections from Steele,* presented to Sir Edmund Gosse. *The Library of Edmund Gosse.* 93.   [5] *Letters on the Dramatic Literature of the Age of Elizabeth.*   [6] Joubert, *Selected Thoughts.* Trans. Lyttleton. 181.   [7] *Southey.* 28.
[8] Harrison, *Choice of Books.* 29.   [9] *Macbeth.* ii, 2.   [10] Squire, 'Reading in Bed', *Life at the Mermaid.* 119-20.

Soft creeping, words on words, the sense compose,
At ev'ry line they stretch, they yawn, they doze.
As to soft gales top-heavy pines bow low
Their heads, and lift them as they cease to blow:
Thus oft they rear, and oft the head decline,
As breathe, or pause, by fits, the airs divine.
And now to this side, now to that they nod,
As verse, or prose, infuse the drowzy God.[1]

They contain *many a powerful opiate to soothe us into a sweet and temporary forgetfulness.*[2] *The greater part of bibliographical works,* Dibdin advises,[3] out of Lambinet (*Recherches, etc.* Intro. X), are *dry and soporific.* Coleridge finds Southey's *blank verse odes* so soporific that he will have *they are to poetry what dumb-bells are to music; they can be read only for exercise, or to make a man tired that he may be sleepy.*[4] And as the mere presence of books is a remedy in some ailments, so also the mere sound of them induces sleep. Gautier gives out[5] that *le bruit des feuilles tombant l'une sur l'autre invite immanquablement au sommeil,* the fall of the leaves one upon the other invites slumber, and sleep is, *après la mort, la meilleure chose de la vie.* Nothing so comforting as reading oneself to sleep. The better the book the better the effect. There are many instances.

Once upon a time, Taine and Renan spent a holiday together beside a lake in Savoy. On one occasion Renan had no desire to walk, so Taine *settled him comfortably under a tree,* with a volume of Balzac for company. Taine then took a walk. *When he returned Renan had fallen asleep, and Balzac had fallen into the water.* How Dorothy Wordsworth read her brother William to sleep when the bard was overwrought with meditation or the composition of poetry is common knowledge. All manner of books were used by her for this purpose and nearly always with success. She read to him *The Lover's Complaint* when he was in bed and *left him composed;*[6] she read him to sleep in the morning when he was *worn out* with *a bad night's rest,* but she does not name the book, although she records having composed herself afterwards with *the first book of 'Paradise Lost'.*[7] The remedy, however, was not always reliable, for at another time she sat by his bedside and read to him in *The Pleasures of Hope,* and *he could not fall asleep.*[8]

It is often rumoured that Wordsworth's works themselves have soporific qualities. A. E. Newton has a story of a man who took *The Excursion* as a sleeping-draught with great success. He kept a volume at his bedside, took

[1] *Dunciad.* ii, 389–96.   [2] 'Book-Lore', *Fraser's Magazine.* 1847.   [3] *Bibliomania.* Ed. 1811. 30.   [4] *Letters.* Ed. E. H. Coleridge. i, 108.   [5] Pref. *Les Jeunes-France.* [6] *Journals of Dorothy Wordsworth.* i, 118.   [7] *Ib.* i, 83.   [8] *Ib.* 86.

it up in wakeful moments, and was *soon in a profound slumber.*[1] But all are not of his opinion. John Stuart Mill valued Wordsworth's *Poems* for their tonic qualities; they proved for him a *medicine* which reacted upon both the *mind* and *feelings, because of their power of expressing not mere outward beauty, but states of feeling, and of thought coloured by feeling, under the excitement of beauty.*[2] But when all is said, the best soporifics are long draughts of erudition weighted with pedantry, as Amiel testifies after *three hours* with Lotze's *big volume, 'Geschichte der Aesthetik in Deutschland'*, which begins attractively, but soon falls into a monotony, producing *yawning, because, as he owns, the noise of a mill-wheel sends one to sleep, and these pages without paragraphs, these interminable chapters, and this incessant dialectical clatter, affect me as though I were listening to a word-mill.*[3]

[1] *A Magnificent Farce.* 144.　　[2] *Autobiography.* 148.　　[3] *Amiel's Journal.* Trans. Ward. 139.

Part XV

THE ORIGIN OF A SPECIES

I. TRANSMUTATION

We need not marvel that books change and translate, as well as uplift, their readers; we are transfigured by them, their wisdom, music, passion, mingle with our blood and quicken it, giving us like moments of magnificence,

> And let the multitudinous music of Greek
> Pass into me, till I am musical.[1]

How many transmutations books have brought about in the soul of man I cannot reckon; it would need great volumes to record the influence of holy books alone, and I shall not attempt it, as their power in this kind has so many historians. Secular or profane letters have as many victories, but they do not get the same advertisement. This chapter has several instances. But in order to reveal still more the variety of their operations I may relate how the tales of Gautier converted George Moore to Paganism. *I am what they made me*, he confesses.[2] Shelley had given him belief in humanity, pity for the poor, hatred of injustice, love, faith. *Gautier destroyed these illusions*, teaching him that *our boasted progress is but a pitfall into which the race is falling*, and that *the correction of form is the highest ideal*. He accepted *the simple conscience of the pagan world*, and would have held down his thumbs in the Coliseum *that a hundred gladiators might die* and *wash* him *free* of his *Christian soul with their blood*.

When he read *Thomson*, William Godwin believed that he became Thomson; when he read *Milton* he became Milton;[3] Sara Fielding read *Clarissa* and became *like the Harlowe's servant*, speechless;[4]

> With Egypt's Queen once more we sail the Nile
> And learn how worlds are bartered for a smile.[5]

The lover of reading, says Leigh Hunt, *will derive agreeable terror from* '*Sir Bertram*' *and the* '*Haunted Chamber*'; *will assent with delighted reason to*

---

[1] Digby Mackworth Dolben, *Poems*. 23.   [2] *Confessions of a Young Man*. (1904) 70.
[3] *The Inquirer*.   [4] *Correspondence of Richardson*. Barbauld. ii, 60.   [5] Bulwer-Lytton, 'The Souls of Books'.

*every sentence in Mrs: Barbauld's 'Essay'; will feel himself wandering into soli-
tudes with 'Gray'; shake hands with honest 'Sir Roger de Coverley'; be ready
to embrace 'Parson Adams', and to chuck 'Pounce' out of the window instead of
the hat; will travel with 'Marco Polo' and 'Mungo Park'; stay at home with
'Thomson'; retire with 'Cowley'; be industrious with 'Hutton'; sympathizing
with 'Gay and Mrs. Inchbald'; laughing with (and at) 'Buncle'; melancholy, and
forlorn, and self-restored, with the shipwrecked mariner of 'De Foe'.*[1] *I lift Homer,*
brags Alexander Smith, in his *Dreamthorp, and I shout with Achilles in the
trenches.* Spenser's *Faerie Queene makes us feel that without stepping a yard
from our native English ground, or deserting any of our common occupations, we
may be, ay and must be, engaged in a great fight with invisible enemies, and that
we have invisible champions on our side.*[2] So also Dr. Arnott,[3] who upheld
his books as the *miracle of all his possessions, more wonderful than the wishing-
cap of the Arabian tales,* for they transported him on an instant *not only to
all places, but to all times.* When William Hazlitt[4] re-read *Peregrine Pickle*
or *Tom Jones twenty years were struck off the list*; he became *a child again: Oh!
what a privilege to let this hump, like Christian's burthen, drop from off one's
back, and transport oneself, by the help of a little musty duodecimo, to the time
when 'ignorance was bliss';* for as Sir Thomas Overbury sings:

> Books are a part of man's prerogative,
> In formal ink they thoughts and voices hold,
> That we to them our solitude may give,
> And make time present travel that of old.
> Our life, Fame pieceth longer at the end.
> And Books it farther backward do extend.

Their grace to this end is well known and sufficient, and they concern
and help every man in like case, provided that he own an innate if hitherto
unapprehended graciousness which may answer to theirs, and the good
fortune to apply the *right book at the right moment*; for though *Peregrine
Pickle* or *Tom Jones* make so gentle a metamorphosis in the cosmogony of
a Hazlitt, they might have a reverse effect in one differently constituted,
as I have discoursed in its place. But this much I will supererogate, namely,
that the good bookman will seek out that food which is best suited to his
capacity, and he will be guided by an inborn sense or instinct of self-
preservation; for if, as Ben Jonson[5] well taxeth, *there be some men are born
only to suck out the poison of books,* so there are others who suck out only
good, and who have ever found in books those essences most fitting for

---

[1] Intro. *A Book for a Corner.*   [2] Maurice, *Friendship of Books.* 17.   [3] *Elements
of Physics.*   [4] 'On Reading Old Books', *The Plain Speaker.* 67–68.   [5] 'Timber,
or Discoveries.' *Works.* Cunningham. iii, 403.

their needs. Time and circumstances will invite the book. It matters little whether they turn to *The Compleat Angler*, which Charles Lamb states[1] it would *sweeten a man's temper at any time* to read, or the irascible *Carlyle*, to whom the cobbler of Condalkin in Ireland always turned when he was *wild* with his *neighbours*;[2] but whether it made him wilder or less wild is not told. In the meantime I may say that the wildest authors have often restored insurrectionary spirits to a gentle calm by giving them revolt by proxy, as Uncle Toby and Corporal Trim appeased their own martial perturbations by means of military books and the fortifications and dispositions of imaginary troops which those essays suggested; but apart from all this power to calm and soothe, books glorify and enhance by their presence. *Gentlemen*, Dibdin claims, *look more like gentlemen* when fine books *are spread out in rich magnificence before them*.[3]

No end to the power of the written word. Han Yu, the Chinese poet and statesman, is said to have driven away a great crocodile which was ravaging the water-courses of the province of Kwangtung, by composing a *denunciatory ultimatum* (still revered as a model of Chinese composition) which he threw into the river, together with a pig and a goat.[4] Dibdin speaks of a large party kept in perfect good humour, when dinner was *full twenty-seven minutes* late, by turning over an extra-illustrated copy of Ormerod's *Cheshire*; but no ordinary work could serve in such a crisis. You may try a *Chronicle* printed by *Verard*, or Gratian's *Decretals* by Eggesteyn, but they won't do; the ladies throw a freezing glance; the elderly gentlemen yawn; only *embellished* volumes will serve, *missals, radiant with burnished gold*, or topography illustrated like *Ormerod*.[5] Well did Queen Elizabeth ordain that in all churches there should be a desk with a copy of *The Paraphrase* of Erasmus placed in a convenient position for the people to read while waiting for the service.[6]

II. HOW BOOKS HAVE MADE AND CHANGED CHARACTER

How reasonable it is to affirm or conceive that books have powers beyond that of all other things created by man, even of man himself, I leave to the authors and patrons of that fancy to imagine; for my part I hold that books are no more than men and no less, whatever may be said for or against them; and if, as we read in *Oliver Wendell Holmes*,[7] *society is a strong solution of books*, man, being the social unit, can be no less, although what

---

[1] Letter to Coleridge. 28.x.1796.   [2] W. B. Yeats, *The Trembling of the Veil*. 98.
[3] *Bibliophobia*. 32.   [4] *Chinese Biog. Dict.* Giles. 255.   [5] *Bibliophobia*. 43.   [6] Janin. *Le Livre*. xxii.   [7] *The Autocrat of the Breakfast Table*. (1902) 57.

he puts in a book is rarely the whole of him; a book contains no more than what its author chooses to confess even though he is out to confess everything. Yet books are humanity in print, and cannot be less human for their humanity, which is ever prone to prefer illusion to reality. Books have all the faults and virtues of men, they are higher than the apish, lower than the angelic; they rise with man to Heaven and sink with him to Hell, and all the circles of exaltation and depravity are recorded and revealed in a Testament compact of *Dante* and *Milton, Montaigne* and *Shakespeare, Aretino* and *Macchiavelli, Thomas à Kempis* and *Job, Rabelais* and the *Marquis de Sade.* No further go, all of man and everyman are there, the rest embroidery for your delight, information for your instruction, particularities for peculiar and special gustation. What they will do to you, what effect they will have, what influence, none can say until they have done their work, for we are all the same and all different; let us judge by results; we shall know them when we see them.

Books move the heart, as all know; they stir the blood: *here is a book,* said R. L. Stevenson[1] of *The Egoist, to send the blood into men's faces;* they affect and cure; exalt, uplift, distress, deprave, depress, according to circumstance of time, place, or person; that is the upshot of the business; they are not sovereign prophylactics for all symptoms and conditions; sometimes they are positive, sometimes negative; mood, state, atmosphere, place, etc. playing their part: leave it at that, *quantum sufficit.* Nonsense has been written about them *ad nauseam,* to no good end, almost as much about them as in them: *to listen to some people, you might almost fancy it was within their power to build a barricade of books, and sit behind it mocking the slings and arrows of outrageous fortune;* all of which, or nearly all, he concludes, is but a vain pretence.[2] None the less, their power to persuade men and move nations is obvious to all.

If it be true that books can change the character of nations, and that, as Fontenelle holds,[3] a continuous course of reading Greek books would in the end make us as Greek as a succession of marriages with Greek women, they can no less affect individuals. *How many a man,* exclaims Thoreau,[4] *has dated a new era in his life from the reading of a book.* Such a record would fill a volume and encompass all history, for *in every man's memory, with the hours when life culminated are usually associated certain books which met his views.*[5] Some books, such as *Richard Feverel* and *Resurrection,* Mary Coleridge proclaims, are like experiences, *you are not quite the same after you have read* them *as you were before.*[6] A book, like a person, says Walter Pater,[7]

---

[1] *Art of Writing.* 86. [2] Augustine Birrell, Pref. to *Book-Hunter in Paris.* Uzanne. Intro. vii. [3] *Œuvres.* (1790) v, 280–3. Cited, Allier, *Mind of the Savage.* 2. [4] *Walden.* Scott Lib. 106. [5] Emerson, *Letters and Social Aims.* 129. [6] *Gathered Leaves.* 255. [7] *Marius the Epicurean.* i, 69.

has its fortunes with one; is lucky or unlucky in its falling in our way, and often by some happy accident counts with us for something more than its independent value; which is no wonder, for from particular books *come subtle influences which give stability to character and help to give a man a sane outlook on the complex problems of life.*[1]

Men of action as well as men of letters and men of affairs have at some time in their lives been influenced by a book, by a mere phrase in a book, to become new men or to enter into a new phase, era, call it what you will, nearer their heart's desire, nearer the true course of their destiny: *many times the reading of a book has made the fortune of a man, has decided his way of life.*[2] No more perspicuous examples could I cite than those of Don Quixote of La Mancha, who turned Knight-errant and went out into the world in quest of adventures under the influence of those romantic tales which he continually read, and Robert of Anjou, King of Naples and Jerusalem, who was of a *dull and sluggish* temper until *a spark was kindled in his mind by the fables of Aesop,* and from that moment he became a student of the *Schoolmen* and a collector of books.[3]

Sir William Macnaghten, the hero and victim of *the darkest episode in our Indian history,* declared that reading *Clarissa,* under Macaulay's influence, was *nothing less than an epoch in his life.*[4] *No time in life when books do not influence men.*[5] St. Augustine in his *Confessions*[6] tells how, in his nineteenth year, he fell upon a book of *Cicero—et usitato iam discendi ordine perveneram in librum cuiusdam Ciceronis—*called *Hortensius*; which with its exhortation to philosophy, *mutavit affectum meum, et te ipsum, domine, mutavit preces meas, et vota ac desideria mea fecit alia,* altered his affection, *turned my prayers to thee, O Lord,* gave him clean aims and desires. It inflamed him, made him to thirst after the immortality of wisdom with an incredible heat of spirit: *et immortalitatem sapientiae concupiscebam aestu cordis incredibili, et surgere coeperam, ut ad te redirem,* the Apostolic Scriptures being scarce known to him at that time.

Bunyan's *Pilgrim's Progress* has moved some men as profoundly as the *Bible,* or any other scripture, and John Bunyan himself is stirred as profoundly by Martin Luther's *Commentary on the Epistle to the Galatians.* The *God in whose hands are all our days and ways,* he says, *did cast into my hand, one day, a book of Martin Luther; it was his comment on the Galatians—it also was so old,* he records, *that it was ready to fall piece from piece if I did but turn it over.* He is much pleased that so old a book has fallen into his hands, and he has but a little way perused it, when he finds his own condition in Luther's experience, *so largely and profoundly handled, as if this book had been*

---

[1] Sir William Osler, *Life.* Cushing. ii, 23.   [2] Emerson, Address at Concord. 1873.
[3] Tatham, *Francesco Petrarca.* ii, 105.   [4] Trevelyan, *Life of Macaulay.* i, 335.   [5] Sir
Walter Besant.   [6] *S. Augustini Confessionum. Lib.* iii, 4. Loeb. i, 109–11.

written, he saith, *out of my heart*; and he desires to *let fall before all men* that he came to prefer this book of Martin Luther before all books (except the *Holy Bible*) that ever he had seen, as *most fit for a wounded conscience*; it healed his tortured spirit so that *he crouched no longer in terror with the burden on his back under that Hill which flashed fire on Christian, and he was enabled to walk in freedom by faith; it was the contagion of Luther's strength which was most serviceable to him.*[1] Mark Rutherford himself passed through a momentous spiritual experience after his first reading of the *Lyrical Ballads*. It was in his third year at college that he happened to find a copy *in paper boards* amongst a parcel of old books. He read one of the poems and then the rest. The book *conveyed* to him *no new doctrine*, yet he could only compare the change it wrought in him with that said to have been *wrought on Paul himself* by the Divine apparition on the road to Damascus.[2]

Many more such examples could be quoted from ancient works, but more than enough is too much, so to my modern instances. Take for one of them Tom Hood's confession[3] that a natural turn for reading and intellectual pursuits probably *preserved him from moral shipwreck* when young and deprived of *paternal pilotage; at the very least* his books keep him *aloof from the Ring, the Dog-pit, the Tavern, and the Saloon, with their degrading orgies; the reading animal*, he adds, *will not be content with the brutish wallowings that satisfy the unlearned pigs of the world*; and for another how Robert Louis Stevenson falls upon William Penn, his *Fruits of Solitude*, in a bookshop in San Francisco, at a time when he was *sick unto death*; he reads in it at all times and places and its peaceful and sweet companionship consoles and uplifts him;[4] it came *with what seemed a direct message from heaven;*[5] and for a third, the story of Lady Lugard, the journalist and traveller, told by W. T. Stead: she had been *reared in an atmosphere of almost Jacobite loyalty*, but one day she took with her into the branches of an apple-tree, at that time her favourite reading-place, a copy of Carlyle's *French Revolution*, and though she went *up the tree a Royalist and a Tory*, she came down *a passionate Democrat*,[6] a condition not desired by all, for Edward Dowden, at the other extreme, brags that he could always *cure* himself of *Radicalism by some sentence of Burke's*.[7] John Stuart Mill was *charmed out of juvenile despondency by Wordsworth*, and drawn *from hide-bound Benthamism by Coleridge*;[8] when William Morris first met with the chapter 'On the Nature of Gothic', in *The Stones of Venice*,[9] whilst he was still at Oxford, *it set fire to his enthusiasm, and kindled the beliefs of his whole life*,[10] and was

[1] Mark Rutherford, *John Bunyan*. 118.   [2] *Autobiography*. Coll. Ed. 18.   [3] *Letter to the Manchester Athenæum*. 1843.   [4] *The Letters of Robert Louis Stevenson*. i, 199–200.   [5] W. Penn, *Some Fruits of Solitude*. Preface. Gosse. x.   [6] *The Times*. 28.i.1929.   [7] *Fragments from Old Letters*. 193.   [8] Cory, *Letters and Journals*. 356. [9] By John Ruskin.   [10] Mackail, *William Morris*. ii, 275.

thus the first cause of the Arts and Crafts Movement which affected the decorative taste of Europe and America; Bernard Shaw was made a Land Reformer by the *Progress and Poverty* of Henry George, and a Socialist by Karl Marx's *Das Kapital*;[1] Darwin read, in his early schooldays, a copy of the *Wonders of the World*, and this book gave him the wish to travel in remote lands, *which, he says, was ultimately fulfilled by the voyage of the 'Beagle'*;[2] *Middlemarch* and *Adam Bede, The Rise and Influence of Rationalism* and *The History of Civilization*, were *momentous events* in the life of George Moore, and *Shelley* saves him from *intellectual savagery*.[3]

So I could go on until ink and paper give out. Past and present, it is all the same, books are necromancers, they exercise an influence more varied, more lasting, than any magic known to men. Histories, memoirs, biographies are alight with their doings, *sic itur ad astra*;[4] yet I have gathered a fardel more from these authorities not solely to buttress my contention, although *a good report maketh the bones fat*,[5] but because such citations are both good news and proper to my theme; and as I have hitherto dilated at random, in more general terms, I will now particularly insist, and prove with more special and evident illustrations.

George Eliot gives out[6] that *Rousseau's genius* sends an *electric thrill* through her *intellectual and moral frame*, awakening *new perceptions*, and making *man and nature a world of freer thought and feeling*; not by his teaching, but by *the rushing, mighty wind of his inspiration*. It was Rousseau also who kindled the genius of Tolstoy, who read the whole of him at college, including his *Dictionary of Music*; he *was more than enthusiastic about him, he worshipped him*.[7] At the age of fifteen he wears a *medallion* portrait of him next his skin instead of the *Orthodox cross*, and many of Rousseau's pages are so kin to him that it seems he must have written them himself. Cowley reads Spenser's *Faerie Queene* before he is twelve years old, and is made a poet thereby *as irremediably as a child is made an Eunuch*;[8] Shakespeare does as much for Scott,[9] and Samuel Rogers's muse is first inspired by Beattie's *Minstrel* at the age of ten.[10] Southey gets his first glimpse of *the mighty movement of the stream of human affairs* from *Gibbon*;[11] from the day that Lafcadio Hearn reads the *First Principles* of Herbert Spencer *a totally new intellectual life* is *opened* for him, so that he hopes *during the next two years to devour the rest of* that *oceanic philosophy*,[12] and Hazlitt's paper *On the Spirit of Obligations* is a *turning-point* in R. L. Stevenson's life.[13]

[1] Holbrook Jackson, *Bernard Shaw*. 55.   [2] *Life and Letters of Charles Darwin*. F. Darwin. i, 33.   [3] *Confessions of a Young Man*. 14, 4.   [4] Virgil, *Aeneid*. ix, 641. 'This is the starward way.'   [5] *Proverbs* xv, 30.   [6] Qt. Lord Morley, *Recollections*. i, 98–99.   [7] *Life*. Maude. i, 46.   [8] 'Of Myself', *Essays*.   [9] *Life*. Lockhart. i, 49   [10] Clayden, *Early Life of Samuel Rogers*. 58.   [11] *Southey*. Dowden. 20.   [12] *Life and Letters of Lafcadio Hearn*. Bisland. i, 374–5.   [13] 'The Influence of Books', *Art of Writing*. 87.

Dr. Johnson's mind was given its religious turn, when at Oxford, he he took up Law's '*Serious Call to a Holy Life*', *expecting to find it a dull book* (*as such books generally are*), *and perhaps to laugh at it*, he confesses; and Boswell adds, *from this time forward religion was the predominant object of his thoughts*.[2] The same work, which has *a strange and moving spiritual pedigree*, had a similar powerful effect upon John Wesley and George Whitefield; and the *celebrated* Thomas Scott, of Aston Sandford, to whom Newman (so he confesses in his *Apologia*), *humanly speaking*, almost owed his *soul*, dates *the beginning of his spiritual life* from the hour when he carelessly took up Law's *Serious Call*, a book he had *hitherto treated with contempt*.[3] The study of the *Phaedo* of Plato, at the age of sixteen, *effected on* Frederick Myers *a kind of conversion*, and *Sappho* and *Pindar* created *epochs* in his life;[4] the reading of Dumont's *Traité de Législation* marks *an epoch* in the life of John Stuart Mill, *one of the turning-points of his mental history*;[5] and later, in a deep dejection, when he vainly sought relief from his favourite books, and *became persuaded* that his *love of mankind, and of excellence for its own sake, had worn itself out*, he was restored to happy interest in life by an accidental reading of *Marmontel's Mémoires*; he changed when he came to the passage which relates the death of the author's father: *the distressed position of the family, and the sudden inspiration by which he, then a mere boy, felt and made them feel that he would be everything to them;* from that moment his *burden grew lighter*, hope returned, and although he had relapses, he *never again was as miserable* as he had been.

The great Duke of Marlborough, as a schoolboy, *imbibed* his passion for the military life from *Vegetius*; Harriet Martineau fixes her *mental destiny* for seven years by reading *Paradise Lost* at the age of seven;[6] Dr. John Brown reads Wordsworth's *Excursion* when he is eighteen and is *a different man from that time*;[7] Frederick James Furnivall is made a lifelong student of our early literature by Tennyson's *English Idylls*;[1] the *sense of romance* comes to Edmund Gosse after reading '*The Cameronian's Dream*', *by a certain James Hyslop, a schoolmaster on a man-of war*;[8] Dr. Delany tells Samuel Richardson that his mind is raised above *this poor terrestrial citadel of men* by reading Young's *Night Thoughts*;[9] William Cobbett dates the birth of his intellect from the reading of Swift's *Tale of a Tub*, which he bought for threepence in place of his supper, at the age of eleven;[10] his modern likeness, John Burns, when a boy, bought a copy of More's *Utopia* for sixpence, then a large sum of money for him: *This book has*

---

[1] *Life*. Boswell. Ed. Hill. i, 68–9.   [2] Birrell, 'Edward Gibbon', *Coll. Essays*. i, 231–2.   [3] *Fragments of Prose and Poetry*. 17–18.   [4] *Autobiography*. 64, 134–5, 40–1. [5] *Autobiography*. i, 42.   [6] *Letters of Dr. John Brown*. 286.   [7] Monro. *F. J. Furnivall*. xliii.   [8] *Father and Son*. (1909) 61.   [9] *Corr. of Richardson*. Barbauld. iv, 48.   [10] Qt. *Book-Lovers' Anth*. 184.

made me what I am, he told Edward Newton, *for me it is the greatest book in the world; the first book I ever bought: the corner-stone of my library, the foundation on which I have built my life.*[1] Samuel Butler met a man in New Zealand who imagined he was being *converted to Christianity* by reading Burton's *Anatomy of Melancholy*, got by mistake for Butler's *Analogy*, which a friend had advised him to read;[2] much as an old dame, *a very devout Methodist*, having *moved from Colchester to a house in the neighbourhood of the City Road*, mistook *the Hall of Science for a chapel, and sat at the feet of Charles Bradlaugh for many years, entranced by his eloquence, without questioning his orthodoxy or moulting a feather of her faith.*[3] Many more instances might I give, but find more of them in that section which treats of books as they are medicinally disposed, for they have much value in that kind and there are several authentic cases in which they have served as alteratives by their mere presence. But here I am expounding their effect on healthy readers, and, hope I have assembled sufficient evidence to incline you to go on with the argument.

III. THE POWER OF THE POET

A poet, *soaring in the high reason of his fancies, with his garland and singing-robes about him*,[4] is a force, moving mountains (what so stubborn, immobile, as a man, as the soul of man!), engines, powers, as some have well said, and I have cited in my preliminary discourse; upon the strength of those words and some other collateral assistances, I have run together, *con amore*, and to augment this tale of influences, a garland of opinions and experiences of the power of poetry, the sum of the following discourse being nothing but the sense of these words of Shelley: *Poets are the hierophants of an unapprehended inspiration; the mirrors of the gigantic shadows which futurity casts upon the present; the words which express what they understand not; the trumpets which sing to battle and feel not what they inspire; the influence which is moved not, but moves.*[5] Homer, Virgil, Dante, Shakespeare, their names are eras, epochs, histories, movements: *the birth of a poet is the principal event in chronology;*[6] they spell mankind and almost prove him, as so many claim on more slender evidence, cousin-german to the Gods themselves, nay, *nearness to Sappho made a man the equal of the gods*,[7] for poetry *is not the result of reason nor of intellect. It is the flower of magic, not logic.*[8] Well may Rogers proclaim[9] that poetry is *the language of the Gods*, for as the

---

[1] *A Magnificent Farce.* 253.   [2] *Note-Books of Samuel Butler.* 311.   [3] Bernard Shaw, Epist. Dedicatory, *Man and Superman.* xxxiv.   [4] Milton, *Reason of Church Government.* Intro. ii.   [5] 'A Defence of Poetry', *Prose Works.* ii, 38.   [6] Emerson, 'The Poet', *Essays.* 314.   [7] F. W. H. Myers, *Fragments of Prose and Poetry.* 19.   [8] Edith Sitwell, *Tradition and Experiment in Present-day Literature.* 97.   [9] *Italy.*

poets have made manifest the Gods to us, given them *a local habitation and a name*, so have they aggrandized all power soever, for good or ill; they buttress, uphold, exalt; there is *some awe mixed with the joy of our surprise*, Emerson asserts,[1] when a poet who lived hundreds of years ago says that which lies closest to our own soul which we also *had well-nigh thought and said*. They are Truth and Beauty, *all we know on earth, and all we need to know;*[2]

> And beauty making beautiful old rhyme
> In praise of ladies dead and lovely knights.[3]

They are notable teachers: the *general end* of Poetry, Dryden maintains, is to *instruct delightfully*; in *Limbo*, Dante saluted Homer, Horace, Ovid and Lucan, as *the eternal educators of mankind;*[4] Petrarch, *in an age rude and uncultivated, by his tuneful homage to his Laura, refined the manners of the lettered world, and filled Europe with love;*[5] our sage and serious Poet Spenser, Milton pronounced *a better teacher than Scotus or Aquinas;*[6] there is magic in their words, *like the language of the Gods,*

> Such as, of old, wise Bards employ'd, to make
> Unpolished men their wild retreats forsake:
> Law-giving Heroes, fam'd for taming brutes,
> And raising cities with their charming lutes,
> For rudest minds with harmony were caught,
> And civil life was by the Muses taught.[7]

For *truly*, as Montaigne advises, *Philosophy is nothing else but a sophisticated poesie: whence have these ancient Authors all their authorities, but from Poets? And the first were Poets themselves, and in their Art treated the same. Plato is but a loose Poet. All high and more than humane sciences are decked and enrolled with a Poetical stile.*[8] They are greater than scientists: *of all scientists is our poet the Monarch;*[9] *five hundred Sir Isaac Newtons go to the making up of a Shakespeare or a Milton;*[10] and there is no wonder, for the poet doth not only show the way, *but giveth so sweet a prospect into the way, as will entice any man to enter it; nay, he doth, as if your journey should lie through a fair vineyard, at the first give you a cluster of grapes, that, full of that taste, you may long to pass further;* and in his passion for the *winning of the mind from wickedness to virtue*, he will savour his admonishments with sweetness; *even as the child is*

---

[1] *The American Scholar.*   [2] Keats, *Ode on a Grecian Urn.*   [3] Shakespeare, *Sonnets,* cvi. [4] *Inferno.* iv, 88–90.   [5] Qt. Tatham. *Francesco Petrarca.* ii, 21.   [6] Milton, *Areopagitica.* Ed. Holt White. 65–6.   [7] Edmund Waller, 'Upon the Earl of Roscommon's Translation of Horace, De Arte Poetica', etc.   [8] 'Apologie of Raymond Sebond,' *Essays.* Ed. Seccombe. ii, 301.   [9] Sir Philip Sidney, *Apologie for Poetrie.*   [10] S. T. Coleridge. *Letters.* i, 352.

often brought to take wholesome things by hiding them in such other as have a pleasant taste; he comes with a tale *which holdeth children from play, and old men from the chimney corner;* so is it that men, he concludes,[1] will be glad to hear the tales of *Hercules, Achilles, Cyrus,* and *Aeneas;* and, *hearing them, must needs hear the right description of wisdom, valour, and justice; which, if they had been barely, that is to say philosophically, set out, they would swear they be brought to school again.* They are an improvement upon Nature herself, if we are to believe him, where he asserts that *nature never set forth the earth in so rich tapestry as divers poets have done, neither with pleasant rivers, fruitful trees, sweet-smelling flowers, nor whatsoever else may make the too much loved earth more lovely. Her world is brazen, the poets only deliver a golden;* yet it is not the nature of poetry to be merely a part, *nor yet a copy, of the real world* (*as we commonly understand that phrase*), *but to be a world by itself, independent, complete, autonomous.* They reproduce the mystery and wonder of life and death. *Have I not seene this divine saying in Plato,* saith Montaigne, that Nature is *nothing but an ænigmatical poesie?*[2] *Through the dim purple air of Dante fly those who have stained the world with the beauty of their sin.*[3] Well may Gibbon exhort[4] the Spensers whose nobility had been *illustrated and enriched by the trophies of Marlborough* to *consider the 'Faerie Queene' as the most precious jewel of their coronet.*

Poets are *the unacknowledged legislators of the world,* proclaims Shelley,[5] which is well known and many instances are recorded: *If a man were permitted to make all the ballads, he need not care who should make the laws of a nation,*[6] saith one, knowing the power of song; and in this spirit Lycurgus, the Lawgiver of Lacedaemon, *sent the Poet Thales from Crete to prepare and mollifie the Spartan surlinesse with his smooth songs and odes, the better to plant among them law and civility;* for they were *muselesse and unbookish,* he saith,[7] *minding nought but warre.* Well may Wordsworth hail them as *Powers:*

> For ever to be hallowed; only less,
> For what we are and what we may become,
> Than Nature's self, which is the breath of God,
> Or His pure Word by miracle revealed,[8]

for, as a modern poet complains,[9] *he would be a liar full of impudence who should dare to say that he felt wholly at ease with the awful Milton or Dante, with the dread death-march over death of dread Lucretius;* our reverence to these great ones being a *religion;* genius, like *love and beauty,* a *pledge of divinity and the everlasting,* and *a light perfected lyric lures us heavenward.*

---

[1] Sir Philip Sidney, *Apologie for Poetrie.* [2] 'Apologie of Raymond Sebond', *Essays.* Ed. Seccombe. ii, 301. [3] Oscar Wilde, *The Critic as Artist.* [4] *Memoirs.* Ed. Hill. 41. [5] 'Defence of Poetry', *Prose Works.* ii, 38. [6] Andrew Fletcher of Saltoun, 'Letter to the Marquis of Montrose'. [7] *Areopagitica.* Ed. Holt White, 25–6. [8] *Prelude.* v, 218–22. [9] Lionel Johnson, *Post Liminium.* 217.

No poet, says Frederick Myers,[1] *has lain so close to so many hearts* as (so Bacon called him) *the chastest poet and royalest, Virgilius Maro, that to the memory of man is known. No words so often as his have sprung to men's lips in moments of excitement and self-revelation, from the one fiery line retained and chanted by the untameable boy* (Claudius Albinus) *who was to be Emperor of Rome,*

> Arma a mens capio; nec sat rationis in armis[2]

to the impassioned prophecy of the great English statesman (Pitt) *as he pleaded till morning's light for freedom of a continent of slaves,*

> Nosque ubi primus equis Oriens adflavit anhelis,
> Illis sera rubens accendit lumina Vesper.[3]

And he cites[4] the *varied memories* which are stirred as we read *one line after another,* from Virgil's own lifetime down to the political debates of to-day. *On this line,*

> Hoc solum nomen quoniam de conjuge restat,[5]

the poet's own voice faltered as he read. At this,

> Tu Marcellus eris, etc.[6]

Augustus and Octavia melted into passionate weeping. Here the verse,

> Infelix simulacrum atque ipsius umbra Creusae,[7]

which Augustine quotes as typical in its majestic rhythm of all the pathos and the glory of pagan art, from which the Christian was bound to flee; then the couplet,

> Aude, hospes, contemnere opes, et te quoque dignum
> Finge deo, rebusque veni non asper egenis,[8]

which Fénelon could never read without admiring tears; now the line,

> Exoriare aliquis nostris ex ossibus ultor.[9]

Filippo Strozzi scrawled on his prison-wall, when he slew himself to avoid worse ill; then the words,

> Heu! fuge crudelis terras, fuge litus avarum,[10]

[1] Myers, 'Virgil', *Classical Essays.* 117–18.   [2] 'Arms I seize, distraught; though there is little sense in taking arms.' *Aen.* ii, 314.   [3] 'What time the sun at dawn breathes upon us with panting steeds, for them the ruddy glow of eve illumes the sky.' *Geo.* i, 250.   [4] *Op. cit.* 116–17.   [5] 'Since this name (guest) alone is left from that of husband.' *Aen.* iv, 324.   [6] 'Thou shalt be Marcellus', etc. *Aen.* vi, 883.   [7] 'The unhappy image and shade of Creusa herself.' *Aen.* ii, 771.   [8] 'Dare, stranger, to despise wealth and make thyself also worthy of the god, nor look roughly on our humble state.' *Aen.* viii, 364.   [9] 'May some avenger arise from my bones.' *Aen.* iv, 625.   [10] 'Ah, flee the cruel land, the greedy shore.' *Aen.* iii, 44.

which, *like a trumpet-call, roused Savonarola to seek the things that are above.*
This line

Manibus date lilia plenis[1]

*Dante heard on the lips of the Church Triumphant, at the opening of the Paradise
of God,* and last, though not exhausting the material for such a citation, he
recalls *the long roll of prophecies sought tremblingly in the monk's secret cell, or
echoing in the ears of emperors* (Claudius, Hadrian, Severus, etc.) *from Apollo's
shrine, which have answered the appeal made by so many an eager heart to the
Virgilian lots*—that *strange invocation* which *has been addressed,* he believes,
to *Homer, Virgil,* and the *Bible* alone; *the offspring of men's passionate desire
to bring to bear on their own lives the wisdom and the beauty which they revered
in the past, to make their prophets, in such wise as they might,*

Speak from those lips of immemorial speech,
If but one word for each.[2]

A like testimony Sir Theodore Martin gives of friendly *Horace,*[3] who
has been *a manual with men the most diverse in their natures, culture, and
pursuits.* Dante ranks him next after Homer; Montaigne knows him by
heart; Fénelon and Bossuet never weary of quoting him; La Fontaine
polishes his own exquisite style upon his model; Voltaire calls him *the best
of preachers;* Hooker escapes with him to the fields to seek oblivion of a
hard life, made harder by a shrewish spouse; Lord Chesterfield confessed
that *when he talked best he quoted Horace;* to Boileau and Wordsworth he is
equally dear; Condorcet dies in his dungeon with *Horace* by his side; when
Gibbon served in the militia, *on every march,* he says, *in every journey, Horace
was always in my pocket, and often in my hand;* and, Martin concludes, *as it
has been, so it is. In many a pocket, where this might be least expected, lies a well-
thumbed Horace; and in many a devout Christian heart the maxims of the gentle,
genial pagan find a place near the higher teachings of a greater master.*

Homer hath consoled others in many ages; and Dante places him first
among bards:

Di quel signor de l' altissimo canto
Che sovra li altri com' aquila vola;[4]

Of him the monarch of sublimest song,
That o'er the others like an eagle soars;[5]

Pope advised, believing as he did that *Nature and Homer were the same,*[6]

Be Homer's works your study and delight,
Read them by day, and meditate by night.[7]

[1] 'Fill my hands with lilies.' *Aen.* vi, 884.   [2] Qt. Myers. 'Virgil', *Classical Essays.*
117.   [3] *Horace.* Martin. viii.   [4] *Inferno.* iv, 95–6.   [5] Cary's translation.   [6] Pope,
Essay on Criticism. 135.   [7] *Ib.* 124–5.

Carteret[1] on his deathbed repeated with *sonorous emphasis* those six inspiring lines from the twelfth book of the *Iliad* (322–28), for he *worshipped and cherished Homer: 'Ah, friend,'* he said in the words of Sarpedon,[2] *'if once escaped from this battle we were ever to be ageless and immortal: neither would I fight myself in the foremost ranks, nor would I send thee into the war that giveth men renown; but now—for assuredly ten thousand fates of death do every way beset us, and these no mortal may escape nor avoid—now let us go forward.'*

The histories and memoirs are full of such accounts, praises and explanations, as all know, and I make this brief garland neither to augment nor to settle or conclude them, but because it would have been less appropriate not to do so, poetry being so high a peak in the range of bookish achievements. More may be added, if any man hath a mind to it, so to sum up all I shall conclude with these words which Montaigne writ of Poetry: *Whosoever discerneth her beautie with a constant, quicke-seeing, and settled looke, he can no more see and comprehend the same than the splendor of a lightning flash. It hath no communitie with our judgement; but ransaketh and ravisheth the same. The furie which prickes and moves him that can penetrate her, doth also stricke and wound a third man, if he heare it either handled or recited, as the Adamant stone drawes, not only a needle, but infuseth some of her beautie in the same, to draw others.*[3]

IV. LIFE IMITATES LETTERS

William Cory[4] asks what *apostolical succession* more interesting than *the tradition of thought and sentiment?* He sees whole generations of men, mighty movements and destinies, determined and moulded by books: *the gentlemanly behaviour of* our squires in the Civil War, brought about by the *translation of Tasso by Squire Fairfax; the interpretation given by Henry Wotton to woman-worship, in his poem to Elizabeth of Bohemia, telling on Eton lads such as Robert Boyle;* John Evelyn in his *Diary* showing how his character was formed by books; Sunderland (husband of Saccharissa), Lovelace, and Wogan, all *warmed by Philip Sidney; the charm and spell* of Vandyke's portraits *being both effect of Spenser-Sidney-Raleigh literature, and cause of Cavalier and Roundhead nobleness;* he traces the fact that our men were more chivalrous in the three wars with France between George I and the Revolution, than their forefathers of the Crécy-Agincourt days, and the behaviour of Frenchmen towards Britons, and vice versa, more courteous,

[1] Qt. Rosebery. Appreciations and Addresses. 161.   [2] Translation. Andrew Lang.
[3] 'Of Cato the Younger', *Essays.* Ed. Seccombe. i, 251.   [4] *Letters and Journals.*
416–17.

to literature, not to religion. Lord Chatham (apud Green) comes out as a sort of Joshua. Was he not moved by Books? Rachel Russell, a *sort of she-apostle to the governing families*; Lucy Hutchinson and Margaret Newcastle *helped towards lady-worship*, and the fruit of this growth in Fanny Burney's life. Every character described by literature, in fact, *the germ of characters and fragments of characters*, the stuff of creation, protoplasm, making or marring men, women, lives, eras, even nature itself is modified by books; Darwin makes us see the evolutionary processes which he saw, and if Mary Coleridge is a reliable guide, *Wordsworthian animals abound* in our Lake District, the *cows and sheep* looking *as if they knew the 'Ode to Immortality' by heart.*[1]

Oscar Wilde would have that *Literature always anticipates life. It does not copy it, but moulds it to its purpose.*[2] Hamlet invents modern thought: *The world has become sad because a puppet was once melancholy.* He cites stories of boys who *pillage the stalls of unfortunate applewomen, break into sweet-shops at night, and alarm old gentlemen who are returning home from the city by leaping out on them in suburban lanes, with black masks and unloaded revolvers*, after reading the adventures of *Jack Sheppard* and *Dick Turpin*; which many of our magistrates have supported when passing judgment on naughty boys made criminal by *Penny Dreadfuls.*

The mature are in like manner affected, if we are to believe Sir Henry Wotton, who will have that Felton became an assassin through the incentive of Eglesham's book against the Duke of Buckingham.[3] Wilde tells also of a governess who, soon after the appearance of *Vanity Fair*, becomes a veritable Becky Sharp, running away with the nephew of her employer and *making a great splash in society* in the manner of Mrs. Rawdon Crawley; *of a noble gentleman* who a few months after *The Newcomes* has reached *a fourth edition* dies with '*Adsum*' *on his lips*; of a certain Mr. Hyde, who, *shortly after Mr. Stevenson published his curious psychological story of transformation*, tramples upon a child by accident and takes refuge from the angry mob in a surgery, the door of which happens to be open. These strange incidents are accidental, unconscious, to those who act in them, but books rule their destiny, they know not why or how. It is another instance of Nature imitating Art, for, as he argues, *Life is Art's best, Art's only pupil.* He further holds that the Nihilist was *invented* by Yourguénieff and *completed* by Dostoieffsky, that the nineteenth century, *as we know it*, was *largely an invention* of Balzac, our Luciens de Rubempré, our Rastignacs, and De Marsays making their *first appearance on the stage of the 'Comédie Humaine'*; *young men*, he adds, *have committed suicide because Rolla did so, have died by their own hand because by his own hand Werther died. Think*, he asks, *what

[1] *Gathered Leaves.* 250.   [2] *Intentions.* 'The Decay of Lying.'   [3] Walpole, *Letters.* Cunningham. iv, 201. Note.

we owe to the imitation of Christ, of what we owe to the imitation of Caesar.
Thus do books have their way with men, making them or unmaking them, as when that *first glowing impression* of the *Metamorphoses* of Apuleius gives Marius a new revelation of life and never loses its power over him,[1] or when Dorian Gray opens the *yellow book*[2] Lord Henry Wotton had sent him and finds it *the strangest book he had ever read,* for it makes him feel that *in exquisite raiment, and to the delicate sound of flutes, the sins of the world were passing in dumb show before him.* He cannot free himself from its influence, it takes control of his life. It seems to him *to contain the story of his own life . . . before he had lived it;*[3] beneath its sway he becomes *more and more enamoured of his own beauty, more and more interested in the corruption of his own soul.*[4] In this strange book he reads Huysmans's careful record of that curious degenerate, Floressas des Esseintes, how he intoxicates himself with exotic books, Latins of the decadence, morbid romantics and over-sensitive moderns, *symbolists, Parnassians,* as Edgar Allan Poe, Charles Baudelaire, and Barbey d'Aurévilly; Stéphane Mallarmé, Arthur Rimbaud and Paul Verlaine; thus exhibiting the spiritual disturbance which afflicts so many in these times, and which forces him ever to be seeking some new and strange sensation, which he finds ultimately to his taste in Barbey d'Aurévilly: *those gamey flavours, those strains of disease and decay, that cankered surface, that taste of rotten-ripeness which he so loved to savour among the decadent writers, Latin and Monastic, of the early ages.*[5] He also finds in the *contorted epithets and beauties* of Verlaine a like *over-ripe flavour;*[6] the *Plaintes d'Automne et Frisson d'Hiver* of Mallarmé have a diction so *magnificently ordered* that it *lulled the senses, like some mournful incantation, some intoxicating melody, with thoughts of an irresistible seductiveness, stirring the soul of the sensitive reader whose quivering nerves vibrate with an acuteness that rises to ravishment, to pain itself.* It is books thus conceived that please him, books which appeal only to an *ideal reader,* by a *mental collaboration of consent* between *half a score of persons of superior intellect scattered up and down the world, a delectable feast of epicures,* appreciable by them only. Only the decadence of a literature moves him, as being *attacked by incurable organic disease, enfeebled by the decay of ideas, exhausted by the excess of grammatical subtlety, sensitive only to the whims of curiosity that torment a fever patient, and yet eager in its expiring hours to express every thought and fancy, frantic to make good all the omissions of the past, tortured on its deathbed by the craving to leave a record of the most subtle pangs of suffering,* which was incarnate in Mallarmé in *the most consummate expression.*[7]

These distinct effects are as much due to the reader as to the writer, for,

---

[1] Walter Pater, *Marius the Epicurean.* i, 69.   [2] The *A Rebours* of J. K. Huysmans.
[3] Oscar Wilde, *Dorian Grey.* 175-7.   [4] *Ib.* 179.   [5] *A Rebours.* xii, 220.   [6] *Ib.* xiv, 254.
[7] *Ib.* xiv, 268-70.

as I have erewhile hinted, reading is a partnership, and, as Vernon Lee holds, *the writer's intention is limited by the tempers and experience of the reader.*[1] Sometimes, and there is good evidence in support of the claim, the reader is more stout-hearted than the writer, going farther than he would go, believing more than he believed, taking more risks than he would have taken. I find a good instance in Lanson's account of Rousseau, whom he advertises as *a poor dreamy creature* approaching action *only with alarm and with every manner of precaution,* and *who understands the applications of his boldest doctrines in a way to reassure conservatives and satisfy opportunists.* Thus, *in the end, the work detaches itself from the author, lives its independent life, and, heavily charged with revolutionary explosives which neutralize the moderate and conciliatory elements Rousseau has put into it for his own satisfaction, it exasperates and inspires revolt and fires enthusiasms and irritates hatreds; it is the mother of violence, the source of all that is uncompromising, it launches the simple souls who give themselves up to its strange virtue upon the desperate quest of the absolute, an absolute to be realized now by anarchy and now by social despotism.*[2] Thus does the disciple outrace the master and overshoot his target; but the reader goes further even than that: he may not only exaggerate or otherwise distort the writer's idea, but he may, and does involuntarily, alter it to meet his own idea of that idea; even putting in things that are not there: *He who had thought he had understood something in my work,* Nietzsche complains, *had as a rule adjusted something in it to his own image—not infrequently the very opposite of myself.*[3] And finally, all the other influences of time and place, mood, health, weather, and so forth, contribute to the process of distortion, that *halo of vague something else,* which in addition to *the succession of images determined by the words of the writer,* induces in the reader *a simultaneous continuum in which it all takes place;* and *the reader's own experience, moving beneath the pressure of the word, brings into consciousness how many sights, how many feelings of which the author of that word can have no notion.*[4] In the end it often happens that the Darwinians are more Darwinian than Darwin, or so deflected from the path of the master's idea that they fill him with fear and even abhorrence, and are often repudiated by him; and yet in these deflexions the power of books is both checked and established, for the way to the inmost sanctuary of a book is through the spirit of the reader. The best disciple goes beyond the master. *Now I bid you lose me and find yourselves; and only when ye have all denied me will I come back unto you.*[5]

---

[1] *Handling of Words.* 80.   [2] *Annales de la Société Jean-Jacques Rousseau.* viii, 30–1.
Qt. Irving Babbitt. *Rousseau and Romanticism.* Intro. xvii–xviii.   [3] *Ecce Homo.*
Trans. Ludovici. 57.   [4] Vernon Lee, *Handling of Words.* 79–80.   [5] Nietzsche,
Thus Spake Zarathustra. Trans. Common. xxii, 3.

V. MEN WHO BECOME BOOKS: BIBLIANTHROPUS
DEFINED

If, as I have shown, *pro captu lectoris habent sua fata libelli*,[1] books, as I have also shown, make the fate of their readers; it is a *quid pro quo*, give and take. A true bookman, I have sufficiently argued, is congenitally disposed towards books (*all books as books interest me*),[2] and they to him; he attracts books as the magnet steel. Books, says Harold Child,[3] and I can support him out of mine own experience, *began to collect round me, to stick to me, to heap* themselves upon me. There is only a difference in degree between the big and the little collector, between the hoarder and the reader. If costly libraries grew about Heber in several of the capitals of Europe, smaller and less valuable collections marked the numerous migrations of Shelley. But no matter how buried or besieged, they know how to find the book they need: even the confusion of Magliabecchi's library at Florence *did not hinder him finding any book he wanted*,[4] and Thomas Watts, the first superintendent of the British Museum Reading Room, never forgot *a single book that passed through his hands* and *always remembered its exact place*.[5]

Everyone acquainted with bookmen can bring supporting evidence, without delving into past times or other lands, and I am obliged to Professor Prothero for discovering to me the clairvoyance of Henry Bradshaw in all such matters. In almost every page of his *Memoir* he shows that not only had the Cambridge librarian an infallible instinct for the contents and the character of a book, but that he could find any book he required either in his own library or elsewhere, at home or abroad, with the exact instinct for locality of a homing pigeon or migratory bird. His *insight* was so *exceptional*, says Blades,[6] that his *predictions seem to bring their own fulfilment*; like the owl with its prey he could find books in the dark;[7] like *the loadstone-fingered hero of the fairy tale*[8] he could draw out the 'lost' fragments of ancient manuscripts from their hiding places in the covers of other volumes or in neglected corners of old libraries or the muniment rooms of churches. He astonished librarians by discovering for them books in their own collections which they were convinced were not there, as when in 1864 he visited Bruges to examine a particular book in the library. The librarian *declared that the book had been removed by the French at the beginning of the century*. Bradshaw was not convinced, he persisted that the book had not been moved and at last *blurted out the letter, shelf, and number under which the*

---

[1] Terentius Maurus. 'The reader's fancy makes the fate of books.'   [2] *Francis Jenkinson*. Stewart. 38.   [3] 'Ego et libri mei', *Bibliophile's Almanack*. (1927) 15.
[4] D'Israeli, *Cur. of Lit.* ii, 177.   [5] G. F. Barwick, *Reading Room of the British Museum*. 111.   [6] Qt. *Memoir of Henry Bradshaw*. 225.   [7] *Ib*. 269.   [8] *Ib*. 138.

book would be found—and there it was; he had no note, *the class-mark was in his memory, along with all other particulars about the book.*[1] For more stories to this end read him. I have said enough to enable me now to suggest that bookmen belong to a special class of *homo sapiens*, since they are not primarily reasoners but possessors of instincts provoked and developed by a passionate attachment. This bookman, *biblianthropus*, is bookish by predisposition and bookish by habit, the one adding to the other until, by cumulative effect, a distinct type of man is produced.

The persistent memorizing of the results of intensive book-culture would be sufficient in itself to bring about this differentiation, for if instinct, as some maintain, be inherited memory, repetition of memorable experiences in a single lifetime, especially if they are pleasurable, produces the same effects in that life as it would produce in a succession of lives, if repeated over many generations, for in this reference *life is memory; the life of a creature is the memory of a creature*, and our variations but the materialized remembrance of experiences: *if*, saith mine author,[2] *we did not remember different things we should be absolutely like each other.* Bookmen are like each other in ratio to their unlikeness to other men. So great the influence of bookish experiences that constant and resolute bookmen may, some of them, take upon themselves the character and in some degree the appearance of books, as *things take the signature of thought.*[3] Some authorities go so far as to say that they become books, or, as those old-fashioned librarians recorded by Gerald Stanley Lee,[4] so *identified* with their books, so *wrought in* with them that they could not be *unmixed*; a conclusion confirmed by Eugene Field, who observed that old booksellers from long and close association *come to resemble their wares* not only in their looks but in their talk.[5]

I could enlarge upon this theme by bringing evidence in support from the general behaviour of civilized peoples who are all more or less, as I have hinted before, book-fed, or in the wider sense, newspaper-fed, reflections of the printed word, the modern world being, not always admirably, something of a bibliocracy, whose classes are Peripatetics, Platonists, Nietzscheans, Shavians, Darwinians, Wesleyans, Muggletonians, Freudians, Swedenborgians, Bergsonians, Mendelians, Johnsonians, etc., set severally in a democratic archipelago suffused by the propaganda of the periodical press. This, however, is beyond the frontiers of my theme, which is *biblianthropus* in his more concentrate form.

It may be reasonably argued that other processes of nature operate in bringing about these phenomena, as transfiguration or metempsychosis, the translation of one into the other, book into man, man into book, but this

[1] *Ib.* 113.   [2] Samuel Butler, *Life and Habit.* 300.   [3] Coleridge, *Aids to Reflection.* xxix.   [4] *Lost Art of Reading.* 73.   [5] *Love Affairs of a Bibliomaniac.* 122.

is not clear. At the same time, some are of opinion that it is so, as Jacob, who argues[1] that if the transmigration of souls is not a chimera, *inventée pour la consolation des âmes tendres* (invented for the consolation of pious souls), the soul of an old *bouquiniste* of his acquaintance would certainly pass after death into one of his books, if only to give life to *le ver rongeur*, the gnawing worm which digs its own grave *dans les feuilles solitaires d'un saint-Thomas ou d'un Cujas* (in the solitary pages of a Saint Thomas or a Cujas). That the souls of men pass into their books during life is more generally admitted: Le Long's *whole soul was in his library*;[2] show me a man's books and you show me the man himself, etc.

Yet if we have no clear testimony of metempsychosis, the case for change, both of body and mind, as a result of contact with books, is perceptibly ruled by that same law of *metamorphosis* which *holds throughout all the divisions of our world, astronomic, geologic, biologic, psychologic, sociologic, and the rest. We know that while a physically-cohering aggregate like the human body is getting larger and taking on its general shape, each of its organs is doing the same; that while each organ is growing and becoming unlike others, there is going on a differentiation and integration of its component tissues and vessels; and that even the components of these components are severally increasing and passing into more definitely heterogeneous structures.*[3] Such changes are observable within the limits of a single life by reason of what we do, see, think, eat, etc., and by its effect on the things which surround us and the people we meet. It may therefore be fairly reasoned that a particular change of personality may proceed from tender and continuous association with such potent companions as books, for, as Erasmus held,[4] *he that's violently in Love lives not in his own body, but in the thing he loves.*

If either of these theories be rejected as insufficient in itself, it may be supported by that process of transmutation by digestion which has various well-known manifestations in the colouring and size of men and animals and the customs of primitive peoples; nor is it unreasonable to suppose that as the inhabitants of the South Sea Islands and the wilds of Africa are able by projection of ideas to give a mysterious vitality to inanimate objects, so a biblio-animism may be at work making books men, men books; and if, on the other hand, as Milton believed,[5] the writer of a poem must himself *be a true poem*, or, as Victor Hugo held, the book is its writer,[6] I perceive no reason to suppose that a bookman may not himself become a book, seeing that we become what we absorb, *for*, Samuel Butler says,[7] *matter which has once been assimilated by any identity or personality, becomes for all*

---

[1] *Ma République.* 20.   [2] Dibdin, *Bibliomania.* (1811) 63.   [3] Herbert Spencer, *First Principles.* Popular Ed. 438–9.   [4] *Praise of Folly.* Trans. Wilson. (Oxford Ed. 1913) 184.   [5] *Apology for Smectymnuus. Prose Works.* (1697) 335.   [6] Qt. Richardson, *Choice of Books.* 107.   [7] *Life and Habit.* 140.

practical purposes part of the assimilating personality. Thus, as another authority affirms, *each reader, while receiving from the writer, is in reality, reabsorbing into his life, where it refreshes or poisons him, a residue of his own living; but melted into absorbable suppleness, combined and stirred into a new kind of efficacy by the choice of the writer.*[1] Which, if I follow mine author aright, is a particular interpretation of an idea *widely distributed* among primitive peoples, who, Lubbock gives out,[2] believe that *a persom imbibes the characteristics of an animal which he eats,* and he brings in support many curious instances. Here are a few for a taste, which I have taken from his work and other sources: the Mahouts in India give their elephants tiger's liver to make them courageous, and the eyes of a brown horned owl to make them see well at night;[3] the Malays of Singapore go further, for they are convinced that the man who eats tiger *acquires the sagacity as well as the courage of that animal;*[4] so also the natives of the Ivory Coast of Africa drink elephant's blood, which is supposed to endow them with the strength and courage required in hunting those animals;[5] on the other hand the Dyaks of Borneo allow their women and children to eat venison, but to the men it is forbidden lest they become as *faint-hearted* as deer.[6] In ancient times it was believed that women became fertile by eating frogs *because that animal lays so many eggs;*[7] the Caribs eat neither pig nor tortoise lest their eyes become as small as theirs;[8] the Dacotahs eat dog to induce canine sagacity and courage;[9] the Arabs attribute the passionate and revengeful character of their race to the eating of camel flesh;[10] Siberians eat bear's flesh because it gives a zest for the chase and makes them fearless;[11] and the Kaffirs have a universal faith in all such meats, for they make a powder of the dried flesh of various wild beasts which they administer with the object of imparting to the men *the qualities of several animals.*[12]

Human flesh has its *gourmets* in several ages and places, and some of these anthropophagi take it as an alterative or augmentative, as those Maoris who eat their most formidable enemies to become strong and indefatigable,[13] and that Chinese servant of an English merchant at the time of the Taiping rebellion who ate the heart of a rebel in order to become brave.[14] In times past this belief still persisted even in Europe, and in a recent instance of cannibalism among Gipsies in Czechoslovakia, one of them gave out that it was preferable to serve *the brain to children, so that they might*

[1] Vernon Lee, *Handling of Words.* 79.   [2] *Origin of Civilization.* 19.   [3] Forsyth, *Highlands of Central India.* 452.   [4] Keppel, *Visit to the Indian Archipelago.* 13.   [5] M. L. Morel. Qt. Allier, *Mind of the Savage.* 278.   [6] Keppel, *Exped. to Borneo.* i, 231.   [7] Inman, *Ancient Faiths in Ancient Names.* 383.   [8] Müller, *Geschichte der americanischen Urreligionen.* 221.   [9] Schoolcraft, *Indian Tribes.* ii, 80.   [10] Astley, *Coll. of Voyages.* ii, 143.   [11] Atkinson, *Upper and Lower Amoor.* 462.   [12] Callaway, *Religious System of the Amazulu.* iv, 438.   [13] Lubbock, *Origin of Civilization.* 20.   [14] Tylor, *Early Hist. of Man.* 131.

become more intelligent, and another disclosed that *woman's flesh was preferred by young men, who considered that it had a more delicate flavour and imagined that they thereby acquired enhanced powers of seduction.*[1] But apart from such effects, human flesh-eaters believe that this practice gives continuity to their kind, as it is plainly set forth in the words of a prisoner cannibal among cannibals, cited by Montaigne. *I have a song made by a prisoner,* he saith, *wherein is this clause, Let them boldly come altogether, and flocke in multitudes, to feed on him; for with him they shall feed upon their fathers, and grandfathers, and heretofore have served his body for food and nourishment: These muscles* (saith he), *this flesh, and these veines, are your owne; fond men as you are, you know not that the substance of your forefathers limbes is yet tied unto ours? Taste them well, for in them shall you finde the relish of your own flesh.*[2] Some people, saith mine author again, anciently kept the custom even of devouring their own fathers, holding this action, not only *for a testimonie of pietie and good affection,* but *in some sort reviving and regenerating them by the transmutation made in their quick flesh, by digestion and nourishment.*[3]

Nor is this belief in transformation confined to flesh-eating. New Zealanders encourage their children to swallow pebbles to make them hard and incapable of pity.[4] *Many remedies were selected on this principle,* says Lubbock, *until recent times; it is,* he continues, *from the same kind of idea that 'eyebright', because the flowers somewhat resemble an eye, was supposed to be good for ocular complaints.*[5]

Absorption is not the only process of transubstantiation; change by contact with environment is so well established, not only in character and function but in form, feature and expression, that I need not dilate upon it (read more in Lamarck, Darwin, Huxley, Spencer, Butler, etc.). *Every portion of our bodies,* says Sir W. Arbuthnot Lane (Chirurgeon to *Ye Sette of Odd Volumes*), *alters very definitely with any mechanical variation in our surroundings,* by concentration upon one pose which is *telescoped into a portion of the lifetime of the individual,*[6] and he illustrates this remark from the effects of certain poses of brewers' draymen, coal porters and shoemakers; from which I may infer by the same process that constant association with books, reading, turning over pages, holding, moving them from one place to another, as a daily habit over many years, may dispose the form and features of the bookman to a definite complexion or character, an approximation to a book or a library, blending in the end naturally with them; which is supported by William Godwin, who confesses that he himself is *a sort of intellectual chameleon, assuming the colour of the substances on which I*

---

[1] *Le Temps.* 11.iii.1927. Qt. Allier, *Mind of the Savage.* 203.   [2] 'Of the Caniballes,, *Essays.* Ed. Seccombe. i, 268.   [3] 'Apologie of Raymond Sebond.' *Ib.* ii, 369. [4] Yates, *New Zealand.* 82.   [5] *Op. cit.* 20.   [6] *The Influence which our Surroundings Exert upon Us.* 10–11.

rest.[1] It is thus something more than whimsy that made Father Angelo Finardi discover in the letters of Magliabecchi's name when Latinized— *Antonius Magliabechius*—the nearly perfect anagram—*Is unus bibliotheca magna—he is in himself a great library;*[2] and also made J. J. Jusserand see in Dr. E. J. Furnivall a *living and talking library* more *delightful and cheerful* than the British Museum.[3]

Leigh Hunt[4] finds it pleasant to reflect that all those great lovers of books in times past have themselves become books. *What better metamorphosis, he asks, could Pythagoras have desired? How Ovid and Horace exulted in anticipation of theirs! To the shape of a book so small yet so comprehensive, so slight yet so lasting, so insignificant yet so venerable,* turns *the mighty activity of Homer; the placid sage of Academus; the grandeur of Milton; the exuberance of Spenser, the pungent elegance of Pope, and the volatility of Prior;* and if life is memory, and human life conscious memory, a book, more than any other work of man, is an epitome of remembrance:

> When to the sessions of sweet silent thought
> I summon up remembrance of things past.[5]

A book thus considered becomes the one who wrote it, a living entity, as Milton knew, and therefore capable, as all living things, of reproducing itself. Samuel Butler went so far as to argue that the production of a book was involuntary, for just as the generation of a body is not the result of a parental desire for reproduction, but *the discontent of the germs with their surroundings inside those parents, and a desire on their part to have a separate maintenance,*[6] so literary creation is the desire of the book-germ within the author for a separate existence. Of his own books, he says: *I never make them: they grow; they come to me and insist on being written, and on being such and such.* He did not want to write *Erewhon;* he wanted to paint pictures; but *Erewhon* insisted on being written with so great a force that he could not resist.[7] So he would conclude that, just as *a hen is only an egg's way of making another egg,*[8] an author is no more than a book's way of producing another book. A book is thus alive, it gives out force, it has the mysterious power of effecting mutations, and if it be objected that these changes are not corporeal, few will deny that an unseen current moves powerfully through a real book and that this current is the man who wrote it, or, which is more to my purpose, the juice or essence of him. In this contention I find support in a writer[9] of our own day who gives out that the *De Rerum Natura* is charged with Lucretius, and *we are frequently brought into so sharp*

[1] *The Inquirer.* [2] Anderson, *Fragrance among Old Volumes.* 4. [3] F. J. Furnivall, *a Personal Record Book.* Monro. 91. [4] 'My Books', *Essays.* Camelot Ed. 301–2. [5] Shakespeare, *Sonnets.* xxx. [6] *Note-Books.* 16. [7] *Ib.* 106. [8] *Life and Habit.* 134. [9] Hope Mirrlees, *Life and Letters.* 563. Dec. 1928.

a contact with him that it resembles an electric shock, to which effect I have said some things already, and I now add this comment from Anatole France for another return to the main, which will augment with evidence this hypothesis; masterpieces are *books of life*, he says, and when we read them *we make them pass into ourselves*.[1] George Moore brings the evidence of his own experience to bear favourably upon this idea, for, he frankly confesses, a book is nothing to him unless it contribute to the *exact diet* his mind requires at that time. He receives, digests, and casts it away. *I discarded my books when I had assimilated as much of them as my system required;* but forever afterwards something of them is *incarnate* within him.[2]

Charles Lamb argues that *with long poring, George Dyer is grown almost into a book*. He saw him in the library at Oriel College, Oxford, *busy as a moth over some rotten archive*, standing beside the old shelves as passive as a book, and *longed to new-coat him in Russia, and assign him his place*, where *he might have mustered for a tall 'Scapula'*;[3] and Sydney Smith, as we know, saw Macaulay as *a book in breeches*.[4] Even women sometimes are subject to a like metamorphosis, as the heroine of Wright's *The Female Virtuosos* (1693), who was dubbed by Sir Maurice Meanwell *a walking University, a Library of Flesh*.

Books to bookmen are both food and cover; they live by the proxy of them, become books in mind if not in body, as that one, recorded by Hazlitt,[5] who believed implicitly in genius, truth, virtue, liberty, because he found the names of these things in books. *The legend of good women was to him no fiction*; life was like an *illumined missal*, and *all the people but so many figures in a 'camera obscura'*. He reads the world, *like a favourite volume, only to find beauties in it, or like an edition of some old work which he is preparing for the press, only to make emendations in it, and correct the errors that have inadvertently slipt in*. Their influence, power of suggestion, hath been widely noted; in fear of it Montaigne abstained from books when writing *Essays*. *When I write*, he confessed,[6] *I can well omit the company, and spare the remembrance of books; for feare they interrupt my forme; good authors deject me too-too much*, they *quaile* his *courage*; he strove, therefore, to imitate the painter who, having *bungler-like* drawn some cocks, forbade his boys to suffer any live cocks to come into his shop. To give himself some lustre or grace he had *rather neede of some Antinonydes the Musician's invention*; but in the end books won, for he could hardly be without *Plutarch*. In him he found, as so many have, before and since, a master of insinuation, of bookpower to turn men his ways: *he is so universall and so full, that upon all*

<hr/>

[1] *On Life and Letters*. Pref. Trans. Evans. xii.   [2] *Confessions of a Young Man.* (1909) 34–5.   [3] 'Oxford in the Vacation', *Essays of Elia*.   [4] *Memoir of Sydney Smith*. i, 363.   [5] 'On the Conversation of Authors.'   [6] 'Upon some Verses of Virgil', *Essays*. Ed. Seccombe. iii, 122–3.

occasions, and whatsoever extravagant subject you have undertaken, he intrudeth himselfe into your work, and gently reacheth you a helpe-affording hand, fraught with rare embellishments, and inexhaustible of precious riches. It *spights* him to note how much this excellent authority is so much exposed to the pillage of those which haunt him, but he himself is no better, no more immune, for no sooner does he so much as glance upon him but he pulls *some legge or wing from* him. The sum of all this being that, Montaigne knowing himself *of an Apish and imitating condition,* feared to be made into the books of others, for it was his wish, as he confessed, that *all the world may know me by my booke, and my booke by me.* His wish was fulfilled, for who knows his *Essays* knows him, who touches them touches him.

The bookman is a tree, another authority[1] gives out, *on which have been grafted Homer, Virgil, Milton, Dante, Petrarch; hence singular flowers which are not natural any more than they are artificial. With Homer, he has looked at the plain of Troy, and there lingers in his brain something of the light of the sky of Greece; he has taken something of the pensive beauty of Virgil as he wanders on the Aventine slopes; he sees the world like Milton through the grey mists of England, like Dante through the limpid burning sky of Italy.* And out of it all he makes for himself, as though he peered through multicoloured glasses, a new colour that is unique: *from all these glasses through which his life passes to reach the real world there is formed a particular tint,* which determines his imagination.

On that note I close this volume and affirm that bookmen, *men of letters,* students, and all manner of passionate readers are a species apart finding their sustenance in the printed word as plants imbibe air and fishes animalculæ; they do not look upon life with their own eyes, but through the eyes of books as through an optical glass, magnifying, intensifying, distorting or glorifying, according as they fancy it; or sometimes they eschew all common affairs and use books as kaleidoscopes to make for their own delight fantastic patterns which they use as substitutes for life. They become natives of a world of books, creatures of the printed word, and in the end cease to be men, as, by a gradual metastasis, they are resolved into bookmen: twice-born, first of woman (as every man) and then of books, and, by reason of this, unique and distinct from the rest.

[1] Doudan, *Lettres et Mélanges.*

Part XVI

LIBRARIES AND THE CARE OF BOOKS

I. THE PRAISE OF LIBRARIES

L ibraries are the best consolations, retreats, harbours, refuges of
the soul of man:

> Where never flippant tongue profane
> Shall entrance find,
> And whence the coarse unlettered multitude
> Shall babble far remote.[1]

But libraries need no defence, no applause, no excuse. *In a true verdict,*
Richard Whitlock claims,[2] *no such Treasure as a Library, and (if all be true)
the Hill Amara in Aethiopia, out-vieth either Indies with their Diamonds or Gold,
the Library of which place, some assure us, is so famous, as to have in it writings
of Enoch, Job, Abraham, Solomon, Titus Livius whole.* Nothing more precious
than a great library, nothing more noble. *Salute Trinity Library in my
name!*[3] Charles Lamb's request of Dorothy Wordsworth at Cambridge
epitomizes the veneration of all bookmen for these sanctuaries of the
written word. A city without a library is a desert and undesirable place.
The British Museum Library, said Jusserand, *is enough to make a city lovable.*[4]
Libraries are *not a luxury but one of the necessities of life;*[5] so to suppress them,
says Joseph Hall, would be *injurious to mankind, whose minds, like so many
candles, should be kindled by each other.*[6] They are *concert halls of the finest voices
gathered from all times and places;*[7] they are *the wardrobes of literature, whence
men, properly informed, might bring forth something for ornament, much for
curiosity, and more for use;*[8] they are the sanctuary of wisdom; the harbour
of imagination and vision; the resting-place of valuable authors: *the cedar
doors of a royal library fly open to receive them: aye, there they will be safe;*[9] they
are the manufactories of literature: *step into the Reading-room of the British
Museum; there is the greatest manufactory out of which we turn the books of the
season.*[10]

[1] Milton, *Ode to Rouse.* Trans. Cowper.   [2] *Zootomia.* (1654) 238–9.   [3] Lamb,
Letters. Ed. Lucas. i, 546.   [4] F. J. Furnivall, *a Personal Record.* Monro. 90.   [5] Henry
Ward Beecher, *Sermons.*   [6] *Occasional Meditations.*   [7] J. P. Richter, *Hesperus.*
[8] George Dyer. Qt. Southey, *Colloquies.* xiv.   [9] Walter Savage Landor, *Pericles
and Aspasia.*   [10] Mark Pattison, 'Books and Writers', *Fortnightly Review.*

They are the happy hunting-grounds not only of the student but of the plagiarist, the thief of ideas and phrases, whom Pope trounced in his satire on Colley Cibber:[1]

> Next o'er his books his eyes began to roll,
> In pleasing memory of all he stole,
> How here he sipped, how there he plundered snug,
> And sucked all o'er, like an industrious bug.

They are the mines where all may dig, the coverts which all may beat, the rivers in which all may angle:

> There towers Stagira's all-embracing sage,
> The Aldine anchor on his opening page;
> There sleeps the births of Plato's heavenly mind,
> In yon dark tomb by jealous clasps confined.

> *   *   *   *

> In those square sheets the songs of Maro fill
> The silvery types of smooth-leaved Baskerville;
> High over all, in close, compact array,
> Their classic wealth the Elzevirs display.[2]

They are a state in which all are equal according to capacity:

> Lo! all in silence, all in order stand,
> And mighty folios first, a lordly band;
> Then quartos their well-ordered ranks maintain,
> And light octavos fill a spacious plain.
> See yonder, ranged in more frequented rows,
> A humbler band of duodecimos;
> While undistinguished trifles swell the scene,
> The last new play and frittered magazine.

> Thus 'tis in life, where first the proud, the great,
> In leagued assembly keep their cumbrous state;
> Heavy and huge, they fill the world with dread,
> Are much admired, and are but little read:
> The commons next, a middle rank, are found;
> Professions fruitful pour their offspring round:
> Reasoners and wits are next their place allowed,
> And last, of vulgar tribes a countless crowd.[3]

[1] *The Dunciad.* i, 127–30.   [2] O. W. Holmes, 'The Study'.   [3] Crabbe, *The Library.*

They are a land flowing with milk and honey where all are fed according to their taste, and where luxuries and necessities are equally accessible and common to all:

> Unlike the hard, the selfish, and the proud,
> They fly not sullen from the suppliant crowd:
> Nor tell to various people various things,
> But show to subjects what they show to kings.[1]

Can the world afford a better sight, sweeter content, a fairer object, a more gracious aspect?

Libraries are given by Lord Bacon[2] the first place among the works of acts of merit towards learning. They *are as the shrines where all the relics of the ancient saints, full of true virtue, and that without delusion or imposture, are preserved:*

> Where still the shapes of parted souls abide
> Embalmed in verse![3]

They are the glory of modern cities and universities, as they were the lanterns of the dark ages before the Renaissance of Learning. De Thou's library was called the *Parnassus of the Muses*, and it was alleged that *those who had not seen the library of Thuanus, had not seen Paris.*[4] *The pride and glory of a monastery,* said Merryweather,[5] *was a well-stored library,* and much as he disliked the *monastic system, the cold, heartless, gloomy, ascetic atmosphere of the cloister,* he confessed that it would be difficult to convince him, with all those fine relics of their deeds before him, *those beauteous fanes dedicated to piety and God, those libraries so crowded with their vellum tomes, so gorgeously adorned, and the abundant evidence which history bears to their known charity and hospitable love, that these monks and their system were a scheme of dismal barbarism;* they were *the encouragers of literature,* the *preservers of books* and the *promulgators of civilization;*[6] and Dibdin advises[7] us to *look upon old abbeys and convents as the sacred depositories of the literature of past ages:*

> Here, duly placed on consecrated ground,
> The studious works of many an age are found.[8]

I might go on with this praise *ad infinitum,* but, lest I weary you, I shall conclude my recital with W. E. Channing's admonition that every man should *gather some good books under his roof, or obtain access for himself and family to some library.* Wise men through all the ages have acted thus, either by forming collections for themselves, or by founding and helping to

---

[1] *Ib.*   [2] *Of the Advancement of Learning.*   [3] Cowley, 'Pindaric Ode'.   [4] Collinson, *Life of Thuanus,* 237.   [5] *Bibliomania in the Middle Ages.* 9.   [6] *Bibliomania in the Middle Ages.* 18.   [7] *Bibliomania.* (1811) 201.   [8] *Alcuin.* Trans. McNicol.

maintain scholastic or public libraries. The first great systematic library is attributed to Aristotle; the first national library founded in Egypt was so esteemed that it was placed under the protection of the gods; and so hungry was one of the Ptolemys for books that he refused to give the famishing Athenians wheat until they handed over to him the original manuscripts of *Aeschylus, Sophocles* and *Euripides*.[1] Pisistratus projected the first Greek library, and he is believed to have been the collector of the scattered works of Homer; Sulla founded the first Roman library with books which he took from the Temple of Apollo, at Athens; Nicholas Niccoli founded the first University Library at Oxford before the days of Bodley, and Dick Whittington *richly endowed* the library of the Grey Friars in School Street, London.[2] Italy was enriched by the libraries founded and supported by the Medicis. There were *brick-libraries* in Nineveh, and libraries of *rolls* in Egypt and the East. *Every desert seems to have held a library, where the pillars of some temple lie in the sands.*[3] The traveller may still see the site of the bookroom of Rameses that was called *the Hospital of the Soul*. There was a library at the breast of the Sphinx, another where Cairo stands; there was one at Alexandria, and another at the House of Serapis; there were books at Ephesus and Antioch and Pergamus, where they made parchment as smooth as ivory; at Athens and Samos and Rome, and so on to our modern cities, Florence and Venice, Paris and Berlin, Moscow, Brussels, Madrid, Copenhagen, New York, Oxford, Cambridge, and London, which every town or village, large or small, would emulate according to its ability.

How much, Burton asks,[4] are all bound that are scholars, to those munificent Ptolemys, bountiful Maecenases, heroical patrons, divine spirits,

> — qui nobis haec otia fecit,
> Namque erit ille mihi semper Deus.[5]

> Who gave me all this comfort, in my eyes
> Will ever be a God!

that have provided for us so many well-furnished Libraries as well in our public Academies in most Cities, as in our private Colleges! *Look no further than our own Country*, Richard Whitlock commends,[6] *it more Arresteth the wondring Eye of an understanding Traveller, with Bodley's Library at Oxford, than all the stately buildings to the Humility of Devotions or Pride of Men, Temples, or Noble-men's Houses, and in a just esteem is England's rich Warehouse, though the covetous mole see no such worth in all Paul's Church Yard, as in one Lombard Street glittering shop*; Robert Burton singles out for praise Sir Thomas Bodley, founder of *our Public Library in Oxon*, Otho

[1] D'Israeli, *Cur. of Lit.* i, 2.   [2] Elton, *Great Book-Collectors*. 31.   [3] *Ib.* 2–3.
[4] *Anat. of Melan.* (1904) ii, 106.   [5] Virg. Eclog. i, 6–7.   [6] *Zootomia.* (1654) 239.

Nicholson (ours in Christ Church, Oxon), and the Right Reverend John Williams, Lord Bishop of Lincoln (with many other pious acts), who besides that at St. John's College in Cambridge, that in Westminster, was then likewise in fieri [engaged] with a Library at Lincoln (a noble precedent for all corporate Towns and Cities to imitate!). O quam te memorem (Vir illustrissime!) O how can I sufficiently eulogise you, most illustrious man? he exclaims.[1] Others would support his generous wish, as James I, who exclaimed in the Bodleian before the bust of its founder: *He should be called Sir Thomas Godley!*[2]

> Most noble Bodley! we are bound to thee
> For no small part of our eternity.[3]

His Library is a heaven of books, as Cowley sings in his *Pindaric Ode*:

> Which now all wonders printed plainly see
> That have been, are, or are to be,
> In the mysterious Library,
> The Beatific Bodley of the Dead!

To Charles Lamb *it seems as though all the souls of all the writers, that have bequeathed their labours to these Bodleians, were reposing there, as in some dormitory or middle state. I do not want to handle, to profane the leaves, their winding sheets,* he says, *and could as soon dislodge a shade.*[4] If my testimony were aught worth, I could say as much myself. No man ever took more delight in those Groves and Gardens of Books. But

> Tantalus a labris sitiens fugientia captat
> Flumina,[5]

thirsty Tantalus snatches at water which flees from his lips, and so Bodley's *foliage* falls from me, or I from it; *velle licet, potiri non licet.*[6] But it is all one, and I salute the Father of English libraries, with Henry Vaughan,

> Thou hast made us all thine heirs; whatever we
> Hereafter write, 'tis thy posterity,

for

> Of thy deeds, Bodley, from thine own pure spring
> A thousand Homers and sweet Lucans sing.[7]

What, asks William Drummond, *what oweth Oxford, nay this Isle, to the most worthy Bodley, whose Library, perhaps, containeth more excellent books*

---

[1] *Anat. of Melan.* (1904) ii, 106.   [2] Macray, *Annals of the Bodleian.* 31.   [3] Henry Vaughan, 'On Sir Thomas Bodley's Library'.   [4] 'Oxford in the Vacation', *Essays of Elia.*   [5] Horace, I. *Sat.* i, 68.   [6] Apuleius, 'I may wish, I may not have'.   [7] Peter Prideaux (Exeter Coll. 1613).

THEIR SIZE AND EXTENT

than the ancients by all their curious search could find?[1] And for answer read what John Henry, the old Oxford bookbinder, sang in his poem on *Oxford the Seat of the Muses*:

> A Publick Library, that all must own
> The like at present in the world's not known;
> In goodly piles and great variety
> Records and books promiscuous here do lye.[2]

II. THEIR SIZE AND EXTENT

What their size should be, how many books, invites many opinions. Some are for small collections, others for great. The first rise, as I have shown, from the men of one book, a library in itself (say they), to one hundred or one thousand books, more or less; the second have no limit save time to gather and space to hold them. For the one, *enough's as good as a feast*; as Melancthon, who would have only four authors in his library: *Pliny, Plutarch, Plato*, and *Ptolemy* the geographer.[3] For the other, no feast but a banquet, as Heber, who had five libraries; books everywhere, forests of them, jungles to wander in, feel about them, alleys, avenues, groves, lanes of books, no content or satisfaction else. Mark Pattison would have that no man could *respect himself* unless he possessed at least 1,000 volumes; and Rosenbach protests[4] *eternal amazement* that there exist collectors who are satisfied with *a limited number of exquisite books;* but such prescriptions are of small value. You may advise and give good precepts, as who cannot? How shall they be put in practice? Many men have sucked knowledge and joy out of one book, and in olden days a man of twenty books was a Crœsus. Philippe le Bon with his 3,200 MSS. was a millionaire in books for his day. Quantity is not everything. In the question of numbers even the method is confused, for (as a late writer[5] observes) it depends on what edition; one edition of Voltaire has ninety-four volumes, another but three. Goethe's works are only half the length, but they fill fifty-five volumes. But this is a quibble. The true strength of a library is the number and quality of its works, not the population of its volumes.

Thomas Carlyle valued his acquaintances by the extent of their libraries, *such an one*, he would argue, *is a valuable man, a man of 3,000 volumes*.[6] Thus we may say that certain men were worth so many books: Montaigne, 1,000;[7] Frederick Locker, 1,247;[8] Robert Burton, 1,700; Samuel Pepys,

[1] *Of Libraries.*   [2] Macray, *Annals of the Bodleian*. 219.   [3] D'Israeli, *Cur. of Lit*. i, 15.   [4] *Books and Bidders*. 57.   [5] Cecil Torr, *Small Talk at Wrayland*. 104–6.
[6] *New Letters*. (1904) i, 162.   [7] Edith Sichel, *Montaigne*. 54.   [8] This is the number of rare books recorded in the Locker Library *Catalogue* (1886) and *Appendix* (1900).

2,474; John Wilson Croker, 4,000; Thomas de Quincey, 5,000;[1] Gibbon, 7,000;[2] Southey, 14,000; John Forster, 18,000; Topham Beauclerk, 30,000;[3] Colbert, and Matthias Corvinus, King of Hungary, 50,000;[4] and George III, 60,000.[5]

In all times opulent men have built for their own delight and that of their friends libraries as great in extent as some of those national collections which are the glory of civilization. Duke Federigo made such a collection of books, at Urbino, *as had not been seen for a thousand years*, it was a *palace of delight* in which he hoped *to set a copy of every book in the world*. His catalogue is still preserved in the Vatican, and it shows the names of all the Classics, the Fathers, and the Schoolmen, many works upon Art, and almost all the Greek and Hebrew works that were known to exist.[6] The Fuggers of Augsburg formed noble libraries. Raimond Fugger had a great collection before the end of the fifteenth century, and his successor, Ulrić, is said to have *possessed as many books as there were stars in heaven*.[7] The books of Louis de Bruges were called *the bibliographical marvel of the age*.[8] The Dukes of Burgundy were of *the book-loving race of the Valois*, the brothers Charles le Sage, Jean Duc de Berry, and Philippe le Hardi of Burgundy, all founded celebrated libraries.[9] Dibdin hailed Lord Spencer's library at Althorp as the *finest private library in Europe*.[10] How many kings and queens of past times were lovers and protectors of books I need not recall: their names span history from the Ptolemys to the Plantagenets, Tudors, and Stuarts, whilst George III, according to Dibdin,[11] *has the glorious distinction of having collected the finest and largest library of any monarch in Europe*.

Fuller was against great collections, he would have that *books that stand thin on the shelves, yet so as the owner of them can bring forth every one of them into use, are better than far greater libraries*; which Bronson Alcott upholds,[12] for *good books, like good friends, are few and chosen; the more select the more enjoyable*. A dunce void of learning but full of books flouted a libraryless scholar with these words: *salve doctor sine libris*. But next day, the scholar coming into the jeerer's study, crowded with books: *Salvete libri*, saith he, *sine doctore*. Yet inveighing against multiplicity of books as Fuller does, he trespasses in that way himself and quotes in self-defence a learned man's compliment as his confession and conclusion: *Multi mei similes hoc morbo laborant, ut cum scribere nesciant tamen a scribendo temperare non possint:*[13] Many like myself suffer from this malady, of being unable to abstain from writing though they cannot write. There are those who believe the day of the great private library is over: *from the vast hall that it was, the library*

---

[1] *Opium-Eater*. ii.   [2] *Memoirs*. Ed. Hill. 234.   [3] Dibdin, *Bibliomania*. (1811) 524. [4] Elton, *Great Book-Collectors*. 82.   [5] Dibdin, *Reminiscences*. i, 347.   [6] Elton, *op. cit*. 80.   [7] *Ib*. 90–1.   [8] *Ib*. 93.   [9] *Ib*. 94.   [10] *Reminiscences*. ii, 560. [11] *Reminiscences*. 347.   [12] *Concord Days*.   [13] Qt. Fuller, *The Holy State and the Profane*.

of the amateur has shrunk to a closet, to a mere bookcase. The book has become a jewel and is kept in a kind of jewel-case.[1] Doubtless he is thinking of the collector of rare volumes, and to that extent he is correct. But there is a distinction between a collection of books and a library; and if that distinction exists only in the mind or attitude of the bookman, it is not less real. To the collector, books are treasures to be protected, to the bibliophile books are friends to be enjoyed. A collector's library will differ from that of a bibliophile, although the two are sometimes united, just as the method of one will differ from that of the other. What, in the last resort, is desirable for the collector is what is rare or curious; what in the last resort is desirable for the bibliophile is what is readable. It is the difference between a book as a curiosity and a book as a book. Each seeks what he desires, and finds not only what he seeks, but what he brings with him. Bookmen, therefore, are not rich according to the numerical strength of their libraries, but according to the quality of their books and their enjoyment of them.

III. BOOKMEN AND THEIR LITTLE LIBRARIES

Great readers and lovers of books depend not always upon libraries: *some of the most indefatigable devourers of literature have very few books,*[2] and the libraries of writers are as like as not the tools of their craft, *the books about books, the books about books about books, and so 'ad infinitum'.*[3] Shelley held that a good library consists of the *Greek Plays, Plato,* Lord Bacon's *Works, Shakespeare,* the Old Dramatists, *Milton, Goethe, Schiller, Dante, Petrarch, Boccaccio, Machiavelli, Guicciardini, Calderon,* and, *last, yet first,* the *Bible.* Extent of books is no mark of the love of what is in them. All the world is in one great book, for it reflects a man, within whom is everything, all the stars and all the heavens and *vast Hell* itself, which none knew better than Shelley, and many would support his choice in the past as in our time. Rich or poor, it matters not, wealth is in books, not in that which buys them:

I wonder often what the Vintners buy
One half so precious as the stuff they sell.[4]

All the books in the world (that are really books), claimed Richard Jefferies, *can be bought for* £10; man's whole thought for the price of *a watch* or a *good dog!*[5]

The library of the Emperor Severus consisted of *Horace* and *Virgil, Plato*

[1] Jacob. Qt. Lang, *Library.* 32.   [2] O. W. Holmes, *The Poet at the Breakfast-Table.*
[3] Harold Child, 'Ego et libri mei', *Bibliophile's Almanack.* (1927) 15.   [4] *Omar Khayyam.* 4th ed. xcv.   [5] 'The Pigeons at the British Museum', in *The Life of the Fields.*

and *Cicero*;[1] Richard of London, an abbot of Peterborough in the thirteenth century, had a *private library* of ten books;[2] when Boswell visited Pascal Paoli, he *was diverted with* the Corsican patriot's *English library*, which consisted of *some broken volumes* of the *Spectator* and *Tatler*, Pope's *Essay on Man*, *Gulliver's Travels*, *A History of France in Old English*, and Barclay's *Apology for the Quakers*;[3] John Bunyan's library consisteu of *The Bible* and *a parcell of books*, chiefly *Pilgrim's Progress* and others written by himself;[4] Ben Jonson had few books, but, *as was said of himself*, they were *like great Spanish Galleons*, bulky folios with *Sum Ben Jonson*, boldly inscribed in them.[5] Hazlitt, said Leigh Hunt,[6] *has no books, except mine, but he has Shakespeare and Rousseau by heart*; and although William Cowper had *never been able to live without books* since he first knew his letters, he told Lady Hesketh that he had *no books of his own* and welcomed Throckmorton's generosity in giving him *possession of his library; an acquisition of great value to me*, he adds.[7] Shakespeare, Voltaire, Humboldt, Comte, Goethe, *although ardent booklovers, had no collection of books to which the term library could fairly be applied*, and Lord Burleigh, Grotius, and Bonaparte *are said to have carried their libraries in their pockets*.[8]

Leigh Hunt disliked *a grand library*, one of those *immense apartments, with books all in Museum order, especially wire-safed*. He had nothing against *the Museum itself or public libraries*, holding them to be *capital places to go to, but not to sit in*. He hated to read in public or among strangers, and resented *the jealous silence; the dissatisfied looks of the messengers; the inability to help yourself; the not knowing whether you really ought to trouble the messengers, much less the Gentleman in black, or brown, who is, perhaps, half a trustee*.[9] A great library made Swift *melancholy*, and he valued in his own *little library the compilements of Graevius and Gronovius*, which made *thirty-one volumes in folio (given me by my Lord Bolingbroke), more than all books besides*, because *whoever comes into my closet casts his eyes immediately upon them, and will not vouchsafe to look upon Plato and Xenophon*.[10]

I might here insert many more opinions, but they all tend to one conclusion: *books are not entirely valued or intimately loved unless they are ranged about us as we sit at home*; and he[11] quotes out of a French authority: *studying at a public library is like staying at an inn*, a convenience, not a preference. These are the general notions of bookmen, especially those that are true bibliophiles; and they will support Macaulay[12] in his surprise at the *low*

---

[1] Janin, *Le Livre*. 75.   [2] Roberts, *Book-Hunter in London*. 4.   [3] *A Tour to Corsica*. Ed. S. C. Roberts. 34.   [4] *Reliquae Hearneanae*.   [5] Elton, *The Great Book-Collectors*. 114.   [6] 'My Books', *Essays*. Camelot Ed. 289.   [7] Letter. 30.viii.1787. [8] Roberts, *Book-Hunter in London*. xv.   [9] 'My Books', *Essays*. Camelot Ed. 289. [10] *Letter to Pope*. 5.iv.1729.   [11] Edmund Gosse, *Library of Edmund Gosse*. xvi. [12] *Life and Letters*. ii, 34.

visibility of books, if I may use a meteorological phrase, at the Vatican Library when he visited it, in 1838. *I had not the faintest notion I was in it*, he writes, *no books, no shelves, were visible. All was light and brilliant; nothing but white and red and gold; blazing arabesques, and paintings on ceiling and wall.* He was surprised, because he had imagined the *Vatican* as *a far sterner and darker Bodleian*; and when he realized that the books and MSS. were in wooden cases ranged round the walls, and saw the cases *painted in light colours* to harmonize with *the gay aspect of everything around them*, he said, *they might be musical instruments, masquerade dresses, or china for the dances and suppers* for which the apartments seemed to be meant. They bore, however, inscriptions more suited to his *notions of the place.* But he would have been less surprised and better pleased with the sight of books, as what bookman would not.

Benjamin Robert Haydon possessed a room of many books, but he read in comfort only in his *painting-room smelling of paint as it does*, where he brought down and placed on the top of his desk *about half a dozen favourites: Milton, Shakespeare, Dante, Tasso, Homer, Vasari, and above all, the Bible and Testament always to refer to, and Wordsworth;*[1] Charles Lamb had few books for so great a reader; he loved his *ragged veterans* and, says Crabb Robinson,[2] *throws away all modern books but retains even the trash he liked when a boy*; his collection, Leigh Hunt records,[3] *looks like what it is, a selection made at precious intervals from the book-stalls; now a Chaucer at nine and twopence; now a Montaigne or a Sir Thomas Browne at two shillings; now a Jeremy Taylor; a Spinoza; an old English Dramatist, Prior, and Sir Philip Sidney. There Mr. Southey takes his place again with an old Radical friend: there Jeremy Collier is at peace with Dryden: there the lion, Martin Luther, lies down with the Quaker lamb, Sewell: there Guzman d'Alfarache thinks himself fit company for Sir Charles Grandison, and has his claims admitted.* The *two or three hundred volumes* which were all Wordsworth's store, occupied, Thomas de Quincey[4] records, *a little homely painted bookcase, fixed into one of two shallow recesses* beside the chimney in his little sitting-room at Grasmere. The books were *ill-bound, or not bound at all—in boards, sometimes in tatters; many were imperfect as to the number of volumes, mutilated as to the number of pages: sometimes, where it seemed worth while, the defects being supplied by manuscript; sometimes not.* Sir Walter Scott, on the other hand, gathered about him a noble library *rich in the works of poets and magicians, of alchemists and anecdotists.*[5] For many years Sydney Smith's books *occupied only the end of his little dining-room*, but as soon as more prosperous times came they *boldly spread themselves over three sides of a pretty odd room, dignified by the name of library—about twenty-eight feet long and eight feet high*

[1] *Autobiography*. iii, 111.   [2] *Diary*. ii, 67.   [3] *Life and Letters*. ii, 34.   [4] 'The Lake Poets.' *Coll. Writings*. Ed. Masson. ii, 335.   [5] Lang, *Library*. 2.

—ending in a bay-window supported by pillars, looking into the garden, which he had obtained by throwing a pantry, a passage, and a shoe-hole together. In this pretty, gay room, records his daughter, *we breakfasted, he sat, and when alone we spent the evening with him.*[1] De Maistre confessed that his library was composed of novels and *a few poets* enshrined among the bric-à-brac in his curious and romantic room.[2] The library of the poet Gray was *very curious, as it contained a complete collection of Mr. Gray's books from his earliest age: from the school-books, and the book in which the first rude essays and drawings were made, to his latest and favourite studies in the ' Systema Naturale' of Linnaeus.*[3] More curious still was the library of Edward FitzGerald, who would bind up only those pages of an author which gave him pleasure. Among the books thus whimsically truncated, Crabbe's *Poems* was a favourite piece, and, for a further example, Carlyle's *Past and Present,* from which he divorced the chapter on 'The Ancient Monk' because he liked it best, and bound it in half-morocco, with the title *Carlyle's Monk.*[4]

Richard de Bury *had more books than all the other Bishops in England.*[5] He set up permanent libraries at his manor-houses and at his palace at Auckland. The floor of his hall was so strewn with manuscripts that it was hard to reach his presence, and his bedroom so full that it was not easy to get in or out or even to stand still without treading on them. So also lived that great scholar Sir Thomas More, besieged by books. *It is incredible,* wrote Erasmus, *what a thick ᶜrop of old books spread out on every side: there is so much erudition, not of any ordinary kind, but recondite and accurate and antique, both in Greek and Latin, that you need not go to Italy except for the pleasure of travelling.*[6]

Montaigne's library was situated on the third story of the tower of his château, above the main entrance, from whence he could see his garden. Thus was he in the way of achieving Cicero's idea of happiness, a library in a garden: *si hortum cum bibliotheca habes, nihil deerit (Ad Famil.* lib ix, epist. 4). The form of it was round, with no flat side, save for his desk and chair, from which, he says, *at one looke it offreth me the full sight of all my bookes, set round upon shelves or desks, five rancks one upon another.* There he spent his summer days, writing his essays, dreaming, or browsing upon his books *without order, without method, and by peece-meales,* turning over and *ransacking, now one book and now another.*[7] Dr. Johnson's book-room was up *four pairs of stairs* in an attic of his house in Gough Square. His window overlooked no garden, but it opened up a noble view of St. Paul's Cathedral, which gave him more joy than any more natural prospect.[8]

---

[1] *Memoir,* Holland. i, 241.   [2] *Journey Round my Room.* 95.   [3] *Gentleman's Magazine.* (1846) i, 29–33.   [4] Arnold, *Ventures in Book-Collecting.* 40.   [5] Elton, *Great Book-Collectors.* 38.   [6] *Ib.* 98.   [7] *Essays.* Seccombe. iii, 53–4.   [8] *Letters of Boswell to Temple.* 30–1.

The books were dusty and in great confusion, the floor strewn with manuscripts, which Boswell *beheld with a degree of veneration,* as well he might, *supposing they perhaps might contain portions of ' The Rambler' or of ' Rasselas'.* [1] On 3rd April 1776, he found Johnson busy *putting his books in order, and as they were generally very old ones, clouds of dust were flying around him. He had on a pair of gloves such as hedgers use,* and this spectacle put him in mind of his uncle Dr. Boswell's description of him: *A robust genius, born to grapple with whole libraries.* [2]

Petrarch, like Heber, collected libraries about himself wherever he went: one at Vaucluse, near Avignon, whither he went in 1337, and another at Parma which he called his *Second Parnassus.* [3] Gibbon called his library *a fine cabinet de particulier. Not content with filling up my double shelves,* he tells Deyverdun, [4] *the best room chosen for it, it has overflowed into the one over the street, into your old bedroom, into mine, into my nook in the Bentinck St. abode, and even into a cottage which I presented myself with at Hampton Court:*

> The thousand courtiers round me in a ring,
> My refuge is my palace, there I reign as king.

The *groundwork* of his collection consisted of *the pick of the Greek, Latin, Italian, French and English company,* and those *authors best esteemed by men of taste,* and *the ecclesiastics, the Byzantines, Orientals, all necessary to the historian of the ' decadence'.* Isaac D'Israeli's collection was so vast, says Croker, [5] that when it was removed it filled seventy cases. Well may Benjamin Disraeli have held that he was *born in a library.*

For the most part bookmen are particular and curious, especially those of the writing sort. If they can read anywhere for pastime and dalliance, as I have dilated, they can study or compose themselves for the work of writing, for the most part, only in special places or surroundings. Leigh Hunt disliked a *fine large study;* he liked space to breathe and walk about when he wanted to breathe and walk about, and for these exercises *a great library* next his study suited him best, but for the study itself, *give me,* he asks, *a small snug place, almost entirely walled with books,* and *one window, looking upon trees.* [6] Some prefer a place with no books: nothing but a chair or a table, as Epictetus. Coventry Patmore, although a *great reader,* was never fond of having more books in his study than those in use at the time. [7] Hazlitt would argue that these were philosophers, not *lovers of books,* did he not recall that Montaigne was both. Leigh Hunt, on the other hand, never forgot his books: even when writing he had them in *a sort of sidelong mind's-eye; like a second thought, which is none; like a waterfall or a*

---

[1] *Life.* Hill. i, 435–6. [2] *Ib.* iii, 7. [3] Elton, *Great Book-Collectors.* 48–9. [4] *Autobiography and Letters.* (1869) 287–8. [5] *Croker Papers.* ii, 42. [6] 'My Books', *Essays.* 288. [7] *Memoirs.* Champneys. i, 101.

whispering wind. He liked to be near a bookcase *affectionately open,* and thus *kindly enclosed* with his books and green leaves he could write.

Thomas Carlyle worked in a *little upper room* in Cheyne Row, Chelsea, projecting off from his bedroom, seven feet by eight feet, with a window looking out upon gardens, trees and houses at a distance, but no furniture save his desk and chair and a shelf of books. Here he sat *lifted above the noise of the world, peremptory to let no mortal enter upon his privacy.*[1] The greater part of his library was kept in a larger living-room, on a lower story of the house. Mark Rutherford visited the philosopher in the year 1868, and found him at breakfast in this room. *Everything,* he reports,[2] *was in exact order; no dust or confusion, and the books on the shelves were arranged with perfect evenness.* He noticed that when Carlyle replaced a book *he took pains to get it level with the others.* John Wilson Croker had *a book-drawing-room* full of *angles and irregularities,* which held 3,000 volumes, was *warm and comfortable* and had none of *the sombre formality of a library;* but he worked in *a little den of* 1,000 volumes.[3] Gibbon worked at the *Decline and Fall* in a little arbour overlooking the Lake at Lausanne, taking with him from his library the books he needed for the day's work. Coleridge's study at Keswick, Charles Lamb records in a letter to Thomas Manning,[4] was *a large, antique, ill-shaped room, with an old-fashioned organ never play'd upon, big enough for a church, shelves of scattered folios, an Aeolian harp, and an old sofa, half bed, etc. And all looking out upon the last fading view of Skiddaw, and his broad-breasted brethren.*

Among our modern poets, Lionel Johnson was a notable bookman. He had a *considerable library,* says W. B. Yeats,[5] far larger than that of any young man of his acquaintance, *so large that he wondered if it might not be possible to find some way of hanging new shelves from the ceiling like chandeliers. That room* (it was in Charlotte Street) was ever a pleasure to Yeats, *with its curtains of grey corduroy over door and window and bookcase, and its walls covered with brown paper. There was a portrait of Cardinal Newman, looking a little like Johnson himself, some religious pictures by Simeon Solomon, and works upon theology in Greek and Latin and a general air of neatness and severity; and talking there by candle-light it never seemed very difficult to murmur Villiers de Lisle Adam's proud words, 'As for living—our servants will do that for us'.*

Some have their libraries in the common sitting-room, which Leigh Hunt thought *hospitable.* Thus when Charles Lamb left Covent Garden for Colebrook Row, Islington, for his white cottage overlooking the New River and a spacious garden *with vines (I assure you), pears, strawberries, parsnips, leeks, carrots, cabbages, to delight the heart of old Alcinous,* he entered without passage into *a cheerful dining-room, all studded over and rough*

[1] *New Letters.* i, 301–2.   [2] *Pages from a Journal.* 2.   [3] *The Croker Papers.* ii, 195.
[4] 24.ix.1802.   [5] *The Trembling of the Veil.* 181–2.

with old books.[1] Wordsworth's few tattered books were on a shelf in the sitting-room at Dove Cottage, but there was a *library* at Rydal. A visitor asked to see the poet's study. The servant, he told Crabb Robinson, took him to the library, and said: *This is master's library, but he studies in the fields.*[2] Sir Walter Scott worked in his library at Abbotsford, where he loved to dally among his books for recreation, tasting this or that volume or arranging or cataloguing. *Before breakfast I employed myself in airing my old bibliomaniacal hobby, entering all the books lately acquired into a temporary catalogue, so as to have them shelved and marked.*[3] Many bibliophiles take a special delight in thus pottering among their books, changing them from one shelf to another, rearranging, grouping and regrouping, for convenience or appearance, or just for the pleasure of handling them.

Some have elaborate systems of classification in which much discretion must be used. Rimsky Korsakof, a Sergeant of the Guards who succeeded Loritz in the affections of Catherine the Second, Empress of Russia, gave the following order to his bookseller (saith William Davis[4]): *Fit me up a handsome library, little books above and great ones below.* 'Tis a method adopted in all times, as he records the instruction of a later bibliophile: *Range me,* he said, the *grenadiers* (folios) at bottom, battalions (*octavos*) in the middle, and light-bobs (*duodecimos*) at top. There are others who try diverse methods, but they are usually forced back to the simple tenet of arrangement by sizes. *I have tried to arrange my books by subjects, or alphabetically by authors' names,* saith one such,[5] *but it always ends in my arranging them by sizes;* and he sets out as a prime reason that a book placed alongside one that is higher and wider causes bulging where the taller book is not fully held, and the slightest bulge admits dust. But I find no golden rule. Each to his taste.

IV. ON CHOOSING A LIBRARY FOR A DESERT ISLAND

Many have speculated upon which are the best books, and it is no easy matter to come to a conclusion where there are so many claimants; especially is it difficult to decide upon what books, or book, were we confined to one, we would choose for an imprisonment, or if marooned on a desert island. Since this is a matter of familiar curiosity, what some of them have said upon it I shall briefly recount. The most fortunate of readers who may be forced to bring their libraries down to an irreducible minimum are these one-book-men whom I have discussed in an earlier chapter, for they have made a choice for all occasions. To make an en-

---

[1] *Letters.* (Everyman Ed.) ii, 65.   [2] Crabb Robinson, *Diary.* ii, 270.   [3] *Journal.* ii, 1.
[4] *Olio.* 107–8.   [5] Torr, *Small Talk at Wrayland.* 104–6.

forced choice has innumerable problems not readily to be solved. Yet some have adventured, in theory at all events, to that end. Schopenhauer declared that if the Almighty had to stint him to a single book he would choose *Helvetius*.[1] Mr. Justice McKinnon *has put it on record*, says Lewis Hind, *that, if he were cast on a desert island, he would find it difficult to decide between 'Pickwick' and 'Pride and Prejudice'*.[2] *Compelled to limit himself to the reading of one book*, Walter Jerrold *would unhesitatingly decide* upon Southey's *Select Works of the British Poets*, which he well calls *a library in a single volume*.[3] Leigh Hunt is divided, among poets, between Shakespeare and Spenser:

> But which take with me, could I take but one?
> Shakespeare—as long as I was unoppressed
> With the world's weight, making sad thoughts intenser;
> But did I wish, out of the common sun
> To lay a wounded heart in leafy rest,
> And dream of things far off and healing—Spenser.

Were I to sell my library, Diderot wrote,[4] *I would keep back Homer, Moses, and Richardson*. Those two great Cambridge scholars, Henry Jackson and Henry Sidgwick, if limited to three books would have *Shakespeare, Plato*, and *Aristotle*.[5]

Some, as I have shown in my dissertation on *Readers of Books*, have practised what they preached or preferred, and read one book over and over; but most claim a variety, even though it be within prescribed limits, as Robert Southey, whose hypothetical library of twelve English authors contained *Shakespeare, Chaucer, Spenser*, and *Milton; Lord Claren-don; Jackson, Jeremy Taylor*, and *South; Izaak Walton*, Sidney's *Arcadia*, Fuller's *Church History*, and *Sir Thomas Browne*, his *Hydriotaphia*. Such a collection, he claims, would prove *an inexhaustible reservoir*, a *Bank of England*, to its possessor.[6] John Ruskin[7] stoutly claimed that every reader who would keep out of *the salt swamps of literature* in these days of *book deluge* must seek to live on *a little rocky island* of his own, *with a spring and a lake in it, pure and good*. Whatever other books would compose that pure and good lake, *Homer, Plato, Aeschylus, Herodotus, Dante, Shakespeare*, and *Spenser* would be there. *If all the books in the world were in a blaze, the first twelve* Archdeacon Farrar would *snatch out of the flames* are, the *Bible*, the *Imitatio Christi, Homer, Aeschylus, Thucydides, Tacitus, Virgil, Marcus Aurelius, Dante, Shakespeare, Milton*, and *Wordsworth*; of living authors he

[1] Samuel Butler, *Memoir*, Festing Jones. ii, 374.   [2] 100 *Best Books*. xiv-xv.   [3] Walter Jerrold, *Autolycus of the Bookstalls*. 9.   [4] Qt. Roberts, *Book-Hunter in London*. xvi.   [5] *Henry Jackson, O.M., A Memoir*. Parry. 143.   [6] Letter to Grosvenor C. Bedford. Nov. 28, 1828.   [7] *The Elements of Drawing*.

would have rescued first *Tennyson, Browning,* and *Ruskin.*[1] Edward Fitz-Gerald claims that in a library *there should be only what is enduring and original,*[2] for, as Washington Irving puts out in his *Sketch Book, when all that is worldly turns to dross around us, these only retain their steady value.* Arnold Bennett[3] would not include more than one novel in a list of twenty books for a Desert Island, it would be either *The Brothers Karamazov, The Charterhouse of Parma,* or *The Woodlanders*; but, he says, André Gide, who as a youth made out such a list every quarter, would include no novels. At the banquet given to celebrate the completion of the *Oxford Dictionary,* Mr. Stanley Baldwin, then Prime Minister, told Professor Craigie that he chose that great work for his desert island reading: *I could live with your Dictionary,* he said; and he recalled that Lord Oxford not long since had said that *if he were cast on a desert island, and could only have one work, he would have the forty volumes of Balzac.*[4]

V. LIBRARIES THE IMAGE OF ONESELF

Emerson, Comte, Sir John Lubbock, Frederic Harrison, and others (read their long essays on this subject), have sought to act as guides through the labyrinths of books, to blaze a trail through the forests of literature, by teaching us how to select, for *there is always a selection in writers, and then a selection from the selection.*[5] They have framed catalogues of the best books, and set out to epitomize the genius of all the world, for some hold that every clime, every country and, more than that, every veracious writer, has proper remedies for the eradication of ignorance and the opening of the doors of the Temples of Wisdom. But, as the high priest[6] of the *Hundred Best Books* well knew, *it is one thing to own a library; another to use it wisely.* Of this noble subject how many panegyrics are worthily written!

Yet with all their framing of catalogues and proportioning of literature a man in the last resort must choose his own books. His library must be the expression of himself, rather than he of it, for a book, or any number of books, can do no more than bring out what is in him, richer perchance by this aid than it would have been. This studious art decoys us from the pursuit of things of whose obtaining we despair by bringing us home to ourselves, for *we carry with us the wonders we seek without us: There is all Africa and her prodigies in us; we are that bold and adventurous piece of nature which he that studies wisely learns in a compendium what others labour at in a*

---

[1] *Pall Mall Gazette.* 1886.   [2] *More Letters.* 104.   [3] *Evening Standard.* 6.xii.7.
[4] Speech at Goldsmiths' Hall. 6.vi.1928.   [5] Emerson, 'Books', *Society and Solitude.*
162.   [6] Lubbock, *On the Pleasure of Reading.*

divided piece and endless volume.[1] And just as the mind, as some suppose, harmonically composed, is roused up at the tones of music, so do books rouse up our slumbering souls, personalities, distinctions, making us at best what we truly are, but, without them, might not be. No guide save oneself to so great a mystery. A library is like life, and I say of books, as Thoreau of living, *we must gnaw our own bone.* For the rest, as Gosse advises,[2] *it takes a lifetime to form a library,* his own even remaining *pitifully unfinished after more than half a century of collecting;* but, he asks, *is not life unfinished too?*

> Ainsi font, font font
> Les petites marionettes,—
> Ainsi font, font font
> Trois p'tits tours, et puis s'en vont.

The marionettes in one box, and the books in the other; while a new set starts a new dance.

In this business of the choice of books I am with the Earl of Balfour when he confesses that at times he is tempted somewhat to vary the prayer of the poet, and to ask whether Heaven has not reserved in pity to this *much educating generation, some peaceful desert of literature as yet unclaimed by the crammer or the coach; where it might be possible for the student to wander, even perhaps to stray, at his own pleasure; without finding every beauty labelled, every difficulty engineered, every nook surveyed, and a professional cicerone standing at every corner to guide each succeeding traveller along the same well-worn round.*[3] I will not quarrel with those who think otherwise. They can do no harm, and catalogues of what one ought to read are an entertainment and a warning. Every reader worth his salt will choose his own hundred best books. A library, whether small or large, is a sea which we must chart for ourselves and explore for ourselves, our own intelligence for compass, and with a fair wind behind us or full steam ahead, we need not fear to reach the Islands of the Blest.

[1] Sir Thomas Browne, *Religio Medici.* xv.   [2] *Library of Edmund Gosse.* xiv.
[3] *Essays and Addresses.* 34–5.

Part XVII

BORROWERS, BIBLIOKLEPTS AND BESTOWERS

———————————————(⟨❖⟩)———————————————

I. THE BOOK-BORROWER

Many and sundry are the means by which people will come by books other than by purchase: some borrow naturally, not desiring to hoard them either in small or large quantities, and for such Lending Libraries have been founded; they may be genuine readers, but more often their reading is merely extensive, idle, killtime, having small connection with bookishness; they are not *pukka* book-folk, bibliophiles; and they are rarely stricken by bibliomania. Others are students, and there are those also who believe that, since books must be returned to their owners, borrowing enhances study by enforcing rapid and diligent perusal. James Howell[1] supports this idea, for when a student he borrowed *some sort of books* and was ever careful to restore them on the day assigned, *and in the interim to swallow of them as much as made for* his *turn.* This obliged him to read with haste, whereas otherwise, possessing the books, he would have not been so diligent in perusing them. The Bishop of Rochester returned books lent to him by Alexander Pope for another economical reason: to impress the poet by his punctuality so that he might borrow more. George Borrow had no such scruples, for he borrowed from Edward FitzGerald one of the three volumes of the *Shah Nama,* which he never returned.[2]

Charles Lamb was an honest borrower, returning the volumes as soon as he had read them. On one occasion he had borrowed from H. F. Carey a copy of Phillips's *Theatrum Poetarum* which he temporarily mislaid, and as he *went out to fetch it while the tripe was frying,* he believed that if it were lost he would *never like tripe again.*[3] Leigh Hunt borrowed books with as much facility as he lent them, and admitted that he could not contemplate a work that interested him on another's shelf without wishing to carry it off, but was always scrupulous in returning books thus acquired, a matter in which he believed himself more sinned against than sinning. Sometimes he borrowed books from miserly owners out of revenge: *I sometimes make*

[1] *Epistolae Ho-Elianae.* 10th Ed. 331.   [2] Edward FitzGerald, *Letters to Bernard Quaritch.* 7.   [3] *Letters.* Ed. Lucas. ii, 942.

extremes meet in a very sinful manner, and do it out of a refined revenge. It is like eating a miser's beef at him; and he contends on another occasion that the splendour of the binding of a borrowed book *dazzled* him into the *ostentatious piece of propriety* of returning it with undue haste, as if he had diminished the owner's fortunes by taking it away.[1] Shelley was not so scrupulous, but it must be said in extenuation that his defects in this matter were the result of absentmindedness rather than greed. *To lend Bysshe a book,* says Hogg, *was to bid it a long farewell, to take leave of it forever; but the pain of parting was often spared, for he bore away silently, reading it as he went, any work that caught his attention.* Hogg readily forgave him, his one regret being that the poet might presently lose the volume.[2]

Charles Lamb[3] advised Bernard Barton to *borrow rather* than buy so excellent a book as Hazlitt's *Spirit of the Age,* but he was suspicious of borrowers in general and threatened to frustrate them by chaining his books, *more Bodleiano,* for, he told Wordsworth, *of those who borrow some read slow; some mean to read and don't read; and some neither read nor mean to read, but borrow to leave you an opinion of their sagacity;* thus differing from his money-borrowing friends, for *when they borrow my money they never fail to make use of it.*[4] But he was only a conditional supporter of lending;[5] *to one like Elia,* he confesses, *whose treasures are rather cased in leather covers than closed in iron coffers, there is a class of alienators more formidable than those* who borrow money. He means, as he says, *those mutilators of collections, spoilers of the symmetry of shelves, and creators of odd volumes;* and gives as an example out of his own experience that of Comberbatch,[6] who is *matchless in his depredations.* The *foul gap in the bottom of a shelf,* in his little back study in Bloomsbury, *like a great eye-tooth knocked out,* once held the tallest of his folios, *Opera Bonaventurae,* a piece of *choice and massy* divinity; it was abstracted by Comberbatch upon a theory *more easy* for Lamb *to suffer by than to refute,* namely, that *the title to property in a book (my 'Bonaventura', for instance) is in exact ratio to the claimant's powers of understanding and appreciating the same.* A reasonable but dismal theory, for, as Lamb argues, *should he go on acting upon it, which of our shelves is safe?* He then proceeds to catalogue the depredations: *the slight vacuum in the left-hand case was whilom the commodious resting-place of Browne on Urn Burial. C. will hardly allege,* he interpolates, *that he knows more about that treatise than I do, who introduced it to him, and was indeed the first (of the moderns) to discover its beauties—but so have I known a foolish lover to praise his mistress in the presence of a rival more qualified to carry her off than himself.* He continues: *Here stood the 'Anatomy of Melancholy', in sober state.—There loitered the 'Compleat*

[1] *My Books.* Camelot Ed. 290–2.   [2] Hogg, *Shelley.* Lond. Lib. Ed. 361.   [3] *Letters.* (Everyman) ii, 109.   [4] *Ib.* i, 351.   [5] 'The Two Races of Men', *Essays of Elia.* [6] i.e. S. T. Coleridge.

Angler'; quiet as in life, by some stream side.—In yonder nook 'John Buncle', a widower-volume, with 'eyes closed', mourns his ravished mate. But his friend has two advantages over your common book-borrowers; when he returns volumes they are, as like as not, *enriched with annotations, tripling their value,* as I have told in its place; and if *sometimes, like the sea, he sweeps away a treasure, at another time he throws up as rich an equivalent to match it.* Lamb had a small *under-collection of this nature,* which his friend had *picked up* at forgotten *odd places, and deposited with as little memory at mine. I take in these orphans, the twice-deserted. These proselytes of the gate are welcome as the true Hebrews. There they stand in conjunction; natives, and naturalized.* He will charge no warehouse-room for these *deodands,* nor ever put himself to the trouble of selling them to pay expenses. *Reader,* he advises, *if haply thou art blessed with a moderate collection, be shy of showing it; or, if thy heart over-floweth to lend them, lend thy books; but let it be to such a one as S. T. C.*

The good bookman at his best will prefer, except in an emergency, to possess rather than borrow books, for a book is not fully known unless it is owned as well as read. Respect for the books of others is an indication of bibliophily. *I cannot comfortably read a book belonging to another person,* says Lafcadio Hearn, *because I feel all the time afraid of spoiling it.*[1] Edward Newton will have the support of all his compeers when he remonstrates against book-borrowing *per se;* if there is anything he likes less than borrowing a book it is lending one, and he places those who insist upon lending you a book you do not intend to read among bibliophilic bores.[2] Peter Daniel Huet was not averse from lending books, but his generosity was shaken after he lent books upon which he set the *highest value* to *two ladies of rank* with whom he was *familiary acquainted,* and of whose fidelity in keeping their promise to return them he had no doubt, *but,* he says, *I found myself mistaken in my opinion of their veracity, for they took away my books and never returned them.*[3] Guibert de Pixérécourt, whose device was *un livre et un ami qui ne change jamais,* inscribed above the lintel of his library door:

> Tel est le triste sort de tout livre prêté,
> Souvent il est perdu, toujours il est gâté;[4]

protected himself against such depredations by steadfastly refusing to lend his books. Paul Lacroix believed that Guibert would not have lent one to his own daughter. Once Lacroix asked him for the loan of a work of little value. Pixérécourt pointed to the verse above his lintel. *Yes,* said Lacroix, *but I thought that verse applied to everyone but me.* Pixérécourt thereupon made him a present of the book.[5] Bookfolk are not all of this mind. Some,

[1] *Life and Letters of Lafcadio Hearn.* Bisland. ii, 432.   [2] *A Magnificent Farce.* 79.
[3] Huet, *Memoirs.* Trans. Aikin. i, 257.   [4] 'Such is the sad lot of every lent book; it is often lost and always spoilt.'   [5] Lang, *The Library.* 44-5.

as Grolier, lend with a good heart; and it was said of that other French bibliophile, Pieresc, that he lent *a world of books* even though they were never returned.[1] Such philanthropists are few and not to be commended; but more of them under *Lenders*. Many will applaud the attitude of Lady Dorothy Nevill, who, so Sir Edmund Gosse[2] tells, *preserved her library* by pasting in each volume the legend: *This book has been stolen from Lady Dorothy Nevill*. This, he says sympathetically, was *drastic but practical*. For the rest we may be warned by John Hill Burton's[3] division of the learned world into those who return the books borrowed by them, and those who do not; excuse the latter as you may, and be warned by Leigh Hunt, who confesses in his essay *My Books*, that *on a moderate calculation*, he has lost in his time (he was then thirty-eight) *half-a-dozen decent-sized libraries*. I find such a warning established very pithily in a parable given by a correspondent to *The Times*:[4] *The owner of a country house was showing some visitors over a superb library. 'Do you ever lend books?' he was asked. 'No,' he replied promptly, 'only fools lend books.' Then, waving his hand to a many-shelved section filled with handsomely bound volumes, he added, 'All those books once belonged to fools'.* A fool and his books are soon parted.

For these and for other reasons which I shall unfold, borrowing books is not to be applauded, honoured, or encouraged except, as I have said, in emergencies or when confined within those limits prescribed in the public libraries. But thus much may I say of both lenders and borrowers, that generally, and no matter to what extent they cause knowledge and the art of letters to be disseminated among men, they discourage more than enough the ancient and honourable custom of forming a personal library, and endanger the integrity of those already formed, *for a book-collector whose books belonged also to his friends, even indirectly, even in a purely sentimental fashion, could not be a book-collector for a longer time than a week.*[5]

II. OF LENDERS OF BOOKS

Among the aphorisms of Polonius, *neither a borrower nor a lender be* is a precept with which all bibliophiles concur, even when their acts do not accord with its wisdom. 'Tis the general humour of many book-lovers to seclude their books, introducing them to a favoured few, but rarely permitting another even to touch them; they are not to be made common by any familiarity except that of their owner. There is a particular excuse for such parsimony in our own time, for those who have no inclination to

[1] *Great Book-Collectors*. Elton. 181.   [2] *The Library of Edmund Gosse*. xxi.   [3] *Book Hunter*. 43.   [4] Frank Hird. 7.iii.1928.   [5] H. P. du Bois, *Four Private Libraries of New York*. 45.

possess their own books have many chances of borrowing them from those institutions specially set up for that purpose; or, should they wish to possess them, the bookseller is accessible and books are cheap. For the rest, and in justice to these jealous ones, a book becomes a part of its owner; it is not for profane eyes or hands, and if it be a rare volume the perils of lending are greater.

In past times, however, even famous and devoted bibliophiles have taken delight in sharing their books with their friends. Notable among them Peiresc, who *sought books not for himself alone, but for any that stood in need of them;* and as he lent freely so he borrowed freely, *but such books as he borrowed, being neglected by their owners and ill-bound, he delivered to his binder to be rectified and beautified, so that having received them ill-bound and ill-favoured he returned them trim and handsome.*[1] But most notable among them is Grolier, that king of bookmen, who had inscribed on his volumes in letters of gold: *Io. Grolierii et amicorum*; and Horne quotes,[2] out of Le Roux de Lincy's *Recherches sur Jean Grolier*, that he went even farther by procuring several copies of certain books so that he could lend to more than one friend at a time, as, for instance, his five copies of *Virgil*, printed at the Aldine Press, 1527, all beautifully bound. We need no further proof of a munificence which was not content with sharing books but must share ungrudgingly the magnificence of its own tastes.[3]

With all bookmen who are neither churls nor niggards, I honour the name of Grolier, as I am bound to honour and revere all who serve the cause of books; but even before Grolier there were bibliophiles who delighted in sharing their happiness with their friends. In this distinction some believe that he was preceded by Thomas Maioli, and that the phrase which adds the charm of friendship to his elegant volumes may have been borrowed from Maioli, or from a celebrated Flemish collector named Marcus Laurinus, with whom he corresponded. But in those times the custom was not unusual. Rabelais had *a few valuable books* which he stamped with a like phrase in Greek, and the Latin form *occurs in many other libraries.*[4] Horne[5] records out of *Brunet* a copy of the *Quaestiones Naturales* of Alexander Aphrodisius (Venice, 1541), on the upper board of which is: *Io. Chevignardi et Amicorum*, and the British Museum has a copy of the *Castigationes* of Hermoland Barbarus (Basle, 1534), with the legend: *Renati Thevenyn et Amicorum*. In Germany, Pirckheimer was a lender, and

[1] Gassendi, *Peiresc*. Trans. Rand. Qt. Dobson, *De Libris*. 229–30.   [2] *The Binding of Books*. 72.   [3] Du Bois looks upon Grolier's generosity as a legend and inconsistent with the integrity of libraries. 'Grolier did not lend his books. His device was not inspired by the book; there was an art of book-covers, and the device meant that it was an art of France.' H. P. du Bois, *Four Private Libraries of New York*. 45.   [4] Elton, *Great Book-Collectors*. 141–2.   [5] *Op. cit.* 71–2.

356 BORROWERS, BIBLIOKLEPTS AND BESTOWERS

took for the device on the book-plate designed for him by Albrecht Dürer the words: *Sibi et Amicis;*[1] and in our land Sir Thomas Wotton (1521–87), called *the English Grolier,*[2] and Edmond Malone[3](1741–1812) used the same generous words. The authors of the *Great Book-Collectors* refer the origin of this amiable custom to a letter written by Philelpho, in 1427, wherein he quotes the Greek proverb[4] which affirms that *all things are common among friends;*[5] but Christian Charles de Savigny *leaves all the rest behind, exclaiming 'non mihi sed aliis'.*[6] Among the medieval Jews, Judah ben Samuel advises fathers to bequeath their books to sons who are most disposed to lend them, and Judah Ibn Tibbon also tolerates lending, with the caution that all books so lent should be called in at *every Passover and Tabernacles.*[7]

Many of our most distinguished bookmen have found rich delight in admitting friends, students, bibliographers, etc., to their libraries. Thomas J. Wise *is always willing to show, and often willing to lend, his possessions.*[8] Such generosity, says Dibdin,[9] is the *pars melior* of every book-collector, and he gives out that it was *the better part* with Heber: *the learned and curious. whether rich or poor,* had ever access to his library:

> His volumes, open as his heart,
> Delight, amusement, science, art,
> To every ear and eye impart.

His books were not *stagnant reservoirs of unprofitable water,* but *like a thousand rills, which run down from the lake on Snowdon's summit after a plentiful rain,* they served *to fertilize and adorn everything* to which they extended. I would add the name of Thomas de Quincey to my garland, although he was a student and bibliophile rather than a collector. In those days of the early nineteenth century when the hub of our literary world was the Lake District because of the foregathering there of Wordsworth, Coleridge, Southey, and De Quincey, the last-named of these writers dwelt about a mile distant from Wordsworth, near Grasmere; at that time Coleridge *lived as a visitor* with Wordsworth, and De Quincey gave him *a general licence* to use his own *considerable library.* Coleridge carried the books he needed over to Allan Bank, the Wordsworth cottage, and *he was in the habit of accumulating them so largely, that sometimes as many as five hundred were absent at once;* but they were all returned in time. *His very scrupulous honour in what regarded the rights of ownership* caused him to inscribe De

---

[1] Lang, *The Library.* 42.   [2] G. D. Hobson, *Thirty Bindings.* 32.   [3] Leicester Warren, *Study of Book-Plates.*   [4] κοινὰ τὰ τῶν φίλων.   [5] *Great Book-Collectors.* 142.   [6] Dibdin, *Bibliomania.* (1811) 175–6.   [7] Abrahams, *Jewish Life in the Middle Ages.* 352–3.   [8] R. Curle, *Ashley Library Catalogue.* Intro. i, ix.   [9] *Bibliomania.* (1811) 175–6.

Quincey's name on the fly-leaf of each volume, in order that they might *mix without danger* with his own and Wordsworth's books; this probity caused the owner some anxiety and trouble, for Coleridge had chosen to *dub* him *Esquire*, so that, many years after, it cost himself and a female friend *some weeks of labour to hunt out these multitudinous memorials and to erase this heraldic addition*, lest some might think he had conferred it on himself. De Quincey, however, is glad to record Coleridge's book-honesty because, in his experience, literary people are not always *so strict in respecting property of this description*; and he knows of more than one celebrated man who *professes as a maxim that he holds it no duty of honour to restore a borrowed book*, and several others *less celebrated*, who, *sans phrase*, exhibit an equally *lax morality*.[1]

How many books belonging to these generous bookmen have been lost or damaged is not recorded; but that Grolier lost many is well known, and Peiresc *lent his own books without any expectation of seeing them again*,[2] I say nothing of the rest, but few in these present times are forced to borrow or to lend, and the others would share the fears of the poet[3] rather than the generosity of Grolier:

> If borrowed books but home returned again!
> Or did they from their wandering escape
> In pristine grace, with no deflow'ring stain,
> No dog's-eared leaf, no binding all agape!
> Against my wish my action thus I shape:
> Like all true hearts, to share my treasures fain,
> I'd gladly lend—but parting's sad sweet pain.
> Ah, Grolier! Would thy motto I might ape.

And William Roberts[4] supports him when he doubts that the motto which Grolier adopted and acted upon *might have been a very safe principle in the sixteenth century*, but would fail *in the nineteenth when one's dearest friends are the most unmitigated book-thieves*, as Francis Jenkinson discovered, for when he came to catalogue the Acton Collection, which John Morley had given to Cambridge, he found many sets defective owing to *Lord Acton's habit of translating into practice Grolier's motto*.[5]

An instance parallel to this, and more notable because more disastrous, is that of Petrarch, who, in an age when books were precious possessions because of their scarcity, was in the habit of lending them to Convenevole, his old schoolmaster, then *oppressed at once by two taskmasters, poverty and old age*; one day the old scholar took away two volumes of *Cicero*, pretend-

[1] 'Literary Reminiscences', *Works*. ii, 191.   [2] C. T. Hagberg Wright, *Peiresc*. x.
[3] Halkett Lord, in *Book-Song*. 83.   [4] *The Book-Hunter in London*. xviii.   [5] *Francis Jenkinson*. Stewart. 36.

ing that he needed them for some work of his own; but as he delayed returning them Petrarch made inquiries, only to learn that Convenevole had sought to relieve his poverty by pawning them. Petrarch begged to know the name of the pawnbroker so that he might redeem the books. The schoolmaster, *full of shame and tears,* protested that it would be disgraceful to let another relieve him of a duty, and if given time he would redeem them himself. *I offered him for the purpose,* says Petrarch, *as much money as he wished, but he refused it, begging me not to brand this infamy upon him.* Though the poet put no faith in the promise, he held his peace, from unwillingness to distress one whom he loved. Shortly afterwards the *pressure of poverty* forced Convenevole to leave Avignon for his native Tuscany, where he died. Petrarch never recovered his *Ciceros,* thus losing *books and master together.*[1] Leigh Hunt[2] inveighs against those who take advantage of such generosity as well as those who proffer it, *a friend thinks no more of borrowing a book now-a-days, than a Roman did of borrowing a man's wife; and what is worse,* he says, *we are so far gone in our immoral notions on this subject, that we even lend it as easily as Cato did his spouse,* and he rightly claims that if we are to be wedded to our books, we should be allowed *the usual exclusive privileges of marriage,* which I stoutly maintain.

III. THE BOOK THIEF

Cousin german to borrowing is theft, or rather a sister, and continual companion, an assistant and a principal agent in procuring this mischief, as well they know who have custody of public libraries, and who have for this reason to exercise so great a care of their charges, for, as Isaac D'Israeli observes,[3] great collections of books are subject to other accidents besides *damp, worms and rats,* namely, *borrowers, not to say a word of the purloiners.* No protection to rely upon their consciences or nice feelings: this has been tried many times and, as Richard de Bury relates,[4] *it has ever been difficult so to restrain men by the laws of rectitude, that the astuteness of successors might not strive to transgress the bounds of their predecessors, and to infringe established rules in insolence and licence;* which many could support out of history, for book-thieves are neither to be restrained by law, punishment, nor even *Sus. per Coll.—Let him hang by the neck.* I know of no story closer to this point than that of John Leycestre and his wife, Cecilia, who were hanged for stealing a book from Stafford Church.[5]

But mistake me not, you that are worthy bookfolk, gentlemen, I honour

---

[1] Tatham, *Francesco Petrarca.* i, 168.   [2] 'Wedded to Books.' Qt. *Book-Lovers' Anth.* 278.   [3] *Curiosities of Literature.* i, 17–18.   [4] *Philobiblon.* Trans. Thomas. 114.   [5] *Book Lore.* iv, 163–4.

your names and persons, and with all submissiveness prostrate myself to your censure and service. There are amongst you, I do ingenuously confess, many well-deserving patrons and true bibliophiles, to my knowledge, besides many hundreds which I never saw, no doubt, or heard of, pillars of our commonwealth of literature and learning, whose worth, bounty, learning, forwardness, true zeal in bookfellowship and good esteem of all scholars and readers, ought to be consecrated to all posterity. But of your rank, there are a debauched, corrupt, covetous, greedy, acquisitive crew who will get books honestly if they can, but get books they will:

> Say, little book, what furtive hand
> Thee from thy fellow books conveyed?[1]

I know not what epithets to give them, for some few, if once tainted, find a particular thrill in theft like any shoplifter, pickpocket or other congenital or neurotic kleptomaniac. If they rise *to eminence* in their *disgusting profession, they will levy contributions in and out of season on a library or bookstall, or even on the house of a bosom friend,*[2] for, once they are off, this humour, so keen and hot, degenerates into madness. No phase of bookpassions cause greater anxiety or more vehement discontent among bibliophiles, yet, as you may easily perceive by observing your own or another's particular symptoms, there is something of the biblioklept in all who traffic among books; even, as Percy Fitzgerald persists, *borrowing is often akin to robbery.*[3] So that *there but for the grace of God go I*, might well be our private confession when we encounter a book thief, or when we are wrought up by thought of one who would purloin, divert, side-track, annex, and otherwise appropriate books not rightfully his own.

Knowing as we do something of the temptation to which bookmen are exposed when they see hoards of unapprehended treasures in the mansions of rich folk who have no faculty of enjoying such possessions, we may incline towards generosity in our opinion of them. I may cite in evidence the confessed case of Frederick Locker-Lampson, poet and bibliophile and father of warriors and statesmen. When he visited Babram, near Bosworth, the land of Robert Burton and George Eliot, he was bewitched both by the fair Lady Tadcaster and her library, and although he himself *unhesitatingly* placed *the fair lady first:*

> The power that she has o'er me lies,
> Not in her books but in her eyes,

he could not contemplate the library at Babram, with its many *desirable* volumes, without unlawful yearnings; and with some reason, for there

[1] W. Cowper, 'Ode to Rouse'. Trans. from Milton. [2] *Book Lore.* iv. 163.
[3] *Book-Fancier.* 84.

were quaint *Bibles*, patristic folios, choice old county histories, solemn Jest Books and Shakespeare quartos *of extraordinary rarity, rarissima! can you conceive it?* he gloats, *they have the four Shakespeare folios; the Sonnets* (1609); *Romeo and Juliet* (1599); *Richard II* (1598); *Richard III* (1597); *Midsummer Night's Dream* (Fisher, 1600); and the *Hamlet* (of 1604); *to say nothing of* Anthony Munday's *Banquet of Daintie Conceits* (1558) and Edmund Spenser's *Shepherd's Calendar*, first edition. Why has he not appropriated *a few of these little old books? Why? oh, why? They would never have been missed, and there would have been some chique in adding the 'Hamlet' of 1604 to one's starved little treasure-house at home—that is to say, if it had been stolen!*[1]

It must have been such an idea as this that was in the mind of Sir Henry Saville when he wrote that famous letter introducing Bodley to Sir Robert Cotton, wherein he said: *I give you faire warning that if you hold any booke so deare as that you would bee loath to have him out of your sight, set him aside beforehand.* Some would have it that this reference to those desirable books which now form the Cottonian Library at the British Museum charged Bodley with being a biblioklept. Gough upheld this opinion, and he brought a like charge against the Bishop of Ely, giving as evidence the apocryphal story of a gentleman who, calling on a friend, found him busily hiding his best books, and upon asking the reason, had for reply, *Don't you know, the Bishop of Ely dines with me to-day.* But it is a mere tale, and the good Bishop, *Father of Black-Letter Collectors*, was no more a biblioklept than Sir Thomas Bodley, and no less, for we who love books are all incipiently tainted, as I have said, and can prove:

> Prince, hear a hopeless Bard's appeal;
> Reverse the rules of Mine and Thine;
> Make it legitimate to steal
> The Books that never can be mine![2]

but read more of Saville and Cotton and Gough in *Hearne, Johannes Glastoniensis*.[3]

William Morris was another poet who could not resist the temptation to covet a fair volume in inaccessible possession of another owner; how he yearned for that copy of the *Apocalypse* from the Archbishop's library at Lambeth, *with the most amazing design and beauty in it*, and a *Psalter* belonging to the Duke of Rutland, even finer than Lord Aldenham's, which his lordship had bought for £1,000, both of which he saw at an Exhibition at Burlington House: *Such a book! my eyes! and I am beating my brains to see if I can find any thread of an intrigue to begin upon, so as to*

---

[1] *My Confidences*. Locker-Lampson. 229–30.   [2] Andrew Lang. *Books and Bookmen*. 134.   [3] See also *Book Lore*. iv, 161–4.

creep and crawl toward possession of it.[1] Leigh Hunt[2] confesses that he never had *a felonious intent upon a book but once,* and then under *circumstances so peculiar* that he could not look back upon the incident without believing *the conscience that induced* him to restore the book *sacrificed the spirit to the letter,* and for ever after he had *a grudge against it.* When Rosenbach was faced with the chance of being outbidden for the unique copy of Dr. Johnson's *Prologue,* which Garrick recited at the opening of Drury Lane Theatre in 1747, he *wished* that he might be *weak enough* to steal it.[3] Thus are they tempted, and though we commend them that resist, and condemn them that fall, otherwise (as I hold) there would be intolerable uncertainties for the safety of our books, yet in commiseration of their passion, whatever protections we may enforce, we must pity these dotards *who love not wisely but too well. Cuivis potest accidere, quod cuiquam potest.*[4] Who knows how he may be tempted? It is his fate to-day, it may be thine to-morrow. *Quae sua sors hodie est, cras fore vestra potest.*[5] We ought not to be so rash and rigorous in our censures as some are; charity will judge and hope the best; God be merciful unto us all!

IV. ALL MANNER OF BIBLIOKLEPTS

It is now necessary to examine this problem a little further, so, according to my methods, I shall catalogue some typical cases from the calendar of biblioklepts, for surely many of them were most heinous offenders. Merryweather[6] recounts how Peter of Blois, when on a visit to Paris, round about the year 1170, bought from *a public dealer in books* a *tempting collection on Jurisprudence;* having completed the bargain he departed, leaving the volume to be sent home after him; but no sooner had he gone than the Provost of Saxeburgh came in and, seeing the volume, conceived a great longing for it; hearing that it was no longer for sale he offered more money, without effect, and at the last was moved to take it away by force. Peter, displaying his great knowledge of civil law, maintained, and rightly, the illegality of the Provost's conduct, but law, honourable position, learning, even religion are no protection against this overweening desire, as my next example will prove.

It is storied how Cardinal Barberini, going one day to inspect the curious library of Montier, was attended, among other persons of quality, by Pamphilio, who later became Pope Innocent X. They were not long in the library when Pamphilio's bibliomania was so inflamed by what he saw that he could not resist the temptation to slip a small but rare volume

[1] *Life.* Mackail. ii, 329.   [2] 'My Books', *Essays.* Camelot Ed. 291.   [3] *Books and Bidders.* 14.   [4] 'What may happen to somebody may happen to anybody.' Seneca *De Tranq. An.* xi.   [5] Buchanan, *Eleg. lib.*   [6] *Bibliomania in the Middle Ages.* 30–1.

into his pocket. Cardinal Barberini had promised that he would answer for the honour of those with him, so when about to depart he said to Montier: '*While we are all here see to it that your books are intact, so that there may be no complaint hereafter.*' Montier ran his eyes over the shelves and announced the absence of the precious volume. Barberini shut the door and commanded him to search everyone present. All agreed except Pamphilio, which naturally brought suspicion upon him. Montier was resolute and he and Pamphilio came to blows, and during the scuffle the book fell out of the prelate's pocket and was joyously secured by its owner. Ever afterwards, it is said, Pamphilio nursed a hatred of the Barberini family, persecuting them on all possible occasions, and soon after his elevation to the Pontifical Chair he expelled the family from Rome.[1]

Janin relates that another Pope, when a Cardinal, stole a book from Menage; and 'tis well known that after the fall of La Rochelle Cardinal Richelieu carried off the library of that city, and that Cardinal Mazarin helped himself to the books of those French nobles whose feudal power had been broken in his day and by order of his policy. It was because holy men and others did not scruple to remove books from the library at Arundel that John Evelyn persuaded the Duke of Norfolk, who was negligent of his books, to present his library to the Royal Society; but not before he had suffered *priests and everybody to carry away and dispose of what they pleased; so that abundance of rare things was irrevocably gone.*[2] But in this business there is tit for tat, for as the priests have robbed so have they been robbed: André Tiraqueau, a native of Fontenay-le-Comte in Poitou, stole the *Letters* of Cicero from the monks of Prémontré, and when they threatened to hang him, Janin tells us[3]: *Oh! bien, dit-il, j'avais besoin du Cicéron; et puis, mes frères, on ne fait pas pendre un brave homme, qui a fait en douze ans douze enfants et douze tomes in-folio.*[4] Abbé Fléchier records how his reputation as a bibliophile was so spread abroad by a certain Père Raphael that all and sundry came to see his collection, among them two learned ladies *who carried off his Ovid;*[5] but the most cunning of all priestly biblioklepts was surely Don Vincente, of the Convent of Pobla, in Aragon, whom Andrew Lang calls *the great pattern of biblioklepts*, and well he may, for his *regrettable excesses* reach a daring ingenuity which place him among the most distinguished of criminals, as you shall learn.

Even royal persons have been biblioklepts. Jules Janin places Catherine de Medici *au premier rang des voleurs de livres:* in the first rank of book-thieves; according to Brantôme, after the death of the Marshal Strozzi,

---

[1] *Dict. of Anec.* (1809) i, 198–9.   [2] Evelyn, *Diary.* 29.viii.1678.   [3] *Le Livre.* 129.
[4] 'Really,' he said, 'I wanted the Cicero, and besides, my brethren, it is not right to hang a worthy man who in twelve years has produced twelve children and twelve volumes in folio.'   [5] *The Great Book-Collectors.* Elton. 150.

she seized the fine library of that great soldier and book-lover, promising some day to pay the value of it to his son, but never a penny did he get. Andrew Lang charges the Ptolemys[1] with being *thieves on a large scale;* a department of the Alexandrian Library was called *The Books from the Ships,* because it was filled with books stolen from passengers in vessels calling at that port. Sir Thomas Browne, in his *Musaeum Clausum,*[2] notes that the King of Spain took a ship of books and rarities from Siddy Hamet, King of Fez, whereof a great part was carried to the Escurial; and he tells of other manuscripts which were brought from the Libraries of Aethiopia by Zaga Zaba, and afterwards transported to Rome, to be scattered eventually by the soldiers of the Duke of Bourbon, when they barbarously sacked that city; and of how Julius Scaliger had some of his works stolen from him and sold in the Civil Wars under the Duke of Rohan.

Scholarly biblioklepts are innumerable, and one of them caused the dismissal of the curious and diligent Beloe from his Under-Librarianship at the British Museum. Beloe had admitted a man to the Reading Room, *with the sanction of the most respectable recommendation,* and, deceived by his excellent credentials, his frank and seemingly honest manner, *received him in the progress of many attendances with unsuspecting confidence.* Despite his *artful tale,* or perchance because of it, *ars est celare artem,* he was a biblioklept. He *proved to be dishonest* (Beloe tells), and *purloined valuable property which was in my custody,* for which accident *the good government of the institution required* Beloe's dismissal, which he accepted *without murmurs of resentment or querulous expostulation.*[3] John Evelyn's library at Wotton was despoiled of many rare volumes, at about the time of the publication of the *Diary,* by William Upcott, of the London Institution, who had been employed by Lady Evelyn to copy MSS. for that work, and was afterwards entrusted with the rearrangement of the library. Upcott *purloined books, letters, pictures, etc.,* so lavishly that Evelyn's library *became partially scattered,* and it was not until the *dispersion* of the biblioklept's books in 1846 that the extent of his depredations was revealed.[4] Evelyn himself suffered a like misfortune in his own lifetime, for he had book thieves among his most noble friends; as the Duke of Lauderdale, who came to Wotton *under pretence of a visit,* but really to borrow valuable MSS. which he never returned; Evelyn also lent to Burnet a quantity of precious MSS., as material for his *History of the Reformation,* but, *like other borrowed books,* says Roberts,[5] they *never came back.* There is no end to these accounts, so, as a final corollary to this dismal tale, take H. F. Stewart's admission that during the seventeenth and eighteenth centuries books were taken away from the Cambridge Library *in cartloads.*[6]

[1] *Library.* 53–4.   [2] *Works.* iii, 352–3.   [3] Beloe, *Anecdotes.* Preface. i, xvii.
[4] Horne, *Binding of Books.* 194.   [5] *Book-Hunter in London.* 28.   [6] *Francis Jenkinson.* 62.

Booksellers are sometimes biblioklepts; Janin gives an example of a Parisian member of *the trade* who was so greatly afflicted that he could not resist slipping any desirable book he saw into his pocket. Everyone came in time to know that weakness, and it was customary after an auction sale to ask him if by chance he had an Elzevir *Horace* or an Aldine *Ovid* in his pocket. After a search the bookseller would exclaim *Yes, yes, here it is; so much obliged to you; I am so absent minded!* and he would be allowed to pay for the volume.[1] Dibdin declares that David Garrick was a biblioklept and stole Alleyne's books from Dulwich. Libri, Inspector-General of Libraries under Louis Philippe, was the greatest and most cunning of French biblioklepts; he disguised his thefts from libraries by filling the gaps in the shelves with *sham volumes*, fashioned to pass for the originals; when he was caught and tried, in 1848, it was reckoned that the value of his book thefts amounted to £20,000. Several of the stolen books came into the British Museum Library, but, in 1883, our Government restored them to France;[2] some fragments of a *Pentateuch* were found in the Ashburnham Library, and as soon as it was discovered, eleven years after they had been bought, that they had been stolen by Libri from the Lyons Library, they were returned by Lord Ashburnham. *In the Bodleian*, another records,[3] *is a set of old tales and romances which Spenser lent Harvey, taking as a hostage, apparently, Harvey's copy of Lucian. Harvey had a poor opinion of such 'foolish' books, but he does not appear to have returned them to their rightful owner.*

Some cannot resist manuscripts, particularly rare or curious holographs and such-like documents. Horace Walpole told Malone of a Mr. West whose rage for *collecting was such that what he could not otherwise procure he stole*, and being executor to Lord Oxford (Harley), it was thought, *on very good grounds, that he secreted a great many curious letters and papers belonging* to that statesman.[4] Dr. Lockier, Dean of Peterborough, who was a notable *raconteur*, preserved in a large quarto volume every good story he had heard; the book used to lie in the parlour for the entertainment of his visitors, and it is a sign that its entertaining qualities were appreciated *because some-one or other thought it worth while to steal it.*[5]

To instance all such particulars were endless and tedious, so I shall conclude this part by summing them up in general, more especially those pirates who cruise about the bookstalls, and who are not always bookmad, but sometimes common thieves making a business of book-stealing as others make a business of picking locks or pockets. During the night the boxes of the Bouquiniers on the quays of *the gentle Seine* at Paris are forced

[1] Lang, *The Library*. 46–7.   [2] Madan, *Books in MSS*. 104.   [3] Roberts, *Book-Hunter in London*. 19.   [4] *Life of Malone*. Prior. 139–40.   [5] Bishop Newton's *Memoirs*. 48.

open and rifled by burglars, but, says Octave Uzanne,[1] *these Parisian pirates* would rifle any place, newspaper kiosks, cobblers' stalls, New Year's Day booths, costermongers' barrows, automatic machines, the receptacles in which scavengers keep their tools, even the Poor Boxes; but common thieves and professional pilferers shall have no place in this repast: I record the lapses of the bibliophile, the amateur biblioklept. Well-dressed, leisurely, buying even, now and then, he arrives with two or three books under his arm; he stops before a stall, places his own books down on top of a pile, handles volume after volume, decides upon none, picks up his bundle and departs, taking with him the *most interesting book in the box, which he was careful to slip among his own.* Another will haunt the stall, dipping into one volume and then another and slyly slipping one under his overcoat or cloak. Still another carries a newspaper carelessly in his left hand, picks up a book, *a duodecimo for choice,* reads a page or more and, as soon as the stallkeeper's back is turned, the book is shut and slipped between the folds of the newspaper, which he tucks under his arm *and strolls off peaceful and satisfied.* And as in Paris so in London: the bookshops of Charing Cross Road and the book-barrows of Farringdon Street are the covers which these amateurs beat to satisfy their inordinate passion.

V. ANTI-BIBLIOKLEPTIC MEASURES

I have no defence for such miscreants, though some would give them a measure of tolerance, realizing how sorely they are tempted and remembering how most of us can resist all things but temptation; others, as William Blades,[2] see no great ill in them, for if they injure the owners they do no more harm to the books than to transfer them from one set of bookshelves to another. Both Janin and Lang have a tenderness for those afflicted, the latter going so far as to analyse the moral position of the biblioklept in a short treatise after the manner of Aristotle, which you may read in *The Library,* 47–50, wherein he concludes that the biblioklept, although a *worse man,* is a better *citizen* than the Philistine in so far as he appreciates books. Merryweather[3] supports him in that he lauds such bookish covetousness as existed among the monks of medieval times as a stimulus towards book-collecting and the forming of libraries, as oftentimes a base fellow is the instrument of God's justice, as, forsooth, there is evidence therefor in two stories: one illustrating the peregrinations of a loan, the other of a theft. The first tells[4] of a unique manuscript of Castile which the Librarian of the Royal Library at Madrid lent to José Anthony Condé, who wished to edit it and forgot to return it. The volume ulti-

---

[1] *The Book-Hunter in Paris.* 147–58.   [2] *The Enemies of Books.* 117.   [3] *Bibliomania in the Middle Ages.* 30.   [4] *Annals of the Bodleian.* Macray. 118.

mately found its way into the Heber Library, and when that collection was broken up it changed its quarters to the Bibliothèque Nationale at Paris, and may yet find its way home to the Escurial. The second recounts how Thomas Allen, the astrologer, in the year 1601, presented the Bodleian with twenty MSS., among them an anonymous Greek treatise in Defence of the Use of Images. In 1600 this very MS. was entered in the Catalogue of New College Library as having been stolen from there the previous year. Macray may well think it strange that a book stolen from New College in 1599 should be given to the Bodleian in 1601, and holds that the donor and the thief were the same person.[1]

No end to such thefts: Sir Robert Cotton, Madan reports, once lent a celebrated eighth-century *Psalter* out of his own library, and never had it returned. The volume lived a wanderer's life, passing from hand to hand, until eventually it came to M. de Riddler, who, in 1718, gave it to the Utrecht Library, where it still rests and is known as the *Utrecht Psalter*. Henry Bradshaw recognized a valuable example of early printing, the *Sarum Breviary* of 1483, in the Bibliothèque Nationale at Paris, as the same copy which had been stolen from the Cambridge University Library in 1715.[2] But the list proceeds *ad infinitum*, no beginning, no end, and well may they make statutes, laws, conditions, rules, etc., to circumvent the rogues, however vain all such measures; and in addition devise locks, bolts, bars, and other engines of protection, as Robert Kilwardley, Archbishop of Canterbury (1273–9), directed that the books of the community at Merton College, Oxford, be kept *under three locks*, and William of Wykeham decreed that the books at New College be *secured by three locks, two large, and one small*, of the kind called a *clickett*;[3] the two former to be kept by the Senior Dean and the Bursar respectively; of the clickett each Fellow to have a separate key, and at night the door to be locked with all three keys.[4] To describe more particularly, to give further examples and instances, would require a considerable volume; I refer them, therefore, that expect a more ample satisfaction to those careful and elaborate treatises, devout and famous books of our learned historians (bibliomaniacs among the rest), that have abundance of evidence to prove there is ample reason at all times for such precautions as have been taken against biblioklepts, pilferers, embezzlers, borrowers tardy of redeeming their trust, and other bookish malefactors, rogues and depredators; and do at the least strive to confute their folly and madness, and to reduce them, *si fieri posset, ad sanam mentem*, to a better mind; though to small purpose many times.

---

[1] *Ib.* 24–5.   [2] *Books in Manuscript.* 104.   [3] *Care of Books.* Clark. 133.   [4] *Ib.* 137. Qt. out of *Commiss. Docts.* (Oxford) i, *Statutes of New Coll.* 97. 'De libris collegii conservandis et non alienandis.'

VI. BOOKS IN CHAINS

Well, therefore, may they formulate statutes for the safeguarding of these covetable treasures, for when the fortunate turn thieves (and who more fortunate than they that have access to a fair library?) it is time to lock, bolt and bar the treasury; and so they have done; and so they do even now, when books are no longer as precious stones, but multitudinous as the sands upon a sea beach. Every bibliophile is a miser, hoarding his treasures, doting upon them. He takes off his hat to Bodley and his Statutes. Necessary concomitants of affections such as his are these miserly promptings; they are the life of his passion, their privation its death. Thus will he contemplate protective measures with great content, even the chaining of books to their shelves, presses, lecterns, chests, tables, pulpits, desks, pews, etc., dreaming himself back into those days when most books were prisoners, barred as much against the vulgar herd as manacled against the biblioklept.

Thus enchained, books may still be seen in England, 1,500 of them in the Cathedral and 285 in All Saints' Church, at Hereford; 240 at Wimborne Abbey; and in lesser numbers or single copies in the churches of Abingdon, Bromsgrove, Chelsea, Cherbury, Cumnor, Frampton Cotterell, Grantham, Leyland, Malvern, Mancetter, Rochester, Southampton, Standon, Wiggenhall, Wootton, Worcester, York, at Merton College, Oxford, and some few others, but for the rest the books are gone, in spite of their chains, stolen, torn, broken up and otherwise dilapidated by long time, rough usage, fire, damp, etc., and the survivals locked in chests or behind glass, for the vandal is still abroad in the land. At the Parish Church of Tavistock, Jewel's *Works* (1560) and Erasmus his *Paraphrase of the New Testament done into English by Nicholas Udall* (1548) are so disposed, the former *locked up in a box*, the latter, *in a glass-covered case, also locked; we learn from Wood* that Foulis's *History of the Plots and conspiracies of our pretended saints the Presbyterians, has been so pleasing to the Royalists that they have chained it to desks in public places for the vulgar to read*; and the same authority records, out of Nicholas, *Test. Vetusta*, that Judge Littleton, who died in 1481, bequeathed to the Abbot and Convent of Hales Owen, in Shropshire, a book wherein is contained the *Constitutions Provincial, Gesta Romanorum* and other treatises therein, *which I will be laid and bounded with an yron chayne in some convenient parte within the saide church, at my costs, so that all priests and others may see and rede it whenne it pleaseth them.* Humphrey Oldfield left his Divinity books to the Church of the Sacred Trinity, Salford, where they were chained for two centuries, but became so dilapidated that many were cast out and a mere remnant of seventy-two deposited in the Free Library of the town.[1]

Books were enchained in most of the early libraries of Europe, as at the Sorbonne in Paris, where a library was first established in 1289, with books chained for the common convenience of the Fellows: *in communem sociorum utilitatem.*[2] The books in that noble Library at Cesena in Italy, founded by Domenico Malatesta Novello in 1452, are still attached to their desks by chains, and so also are those in the Medicean Library at Florence, which was designed by Michelangelo for Cardinal Giulio dei Medici and opened in 1571.[3] But why proceed? The custom is now abandoned, not, as I repeat, because the biblioklept is no more, but because other methods of circumventing him have been found. Towards the end of the eighteenth century the chaining of books was abandoned in England, but as late as 1815, John Fells, a mariner, gave £30 to found a theological library in the Church of St. Peter, Liverpool, and those books were fastened to open shelves in the vestry with rods and chains. In France chains were abandoned earlier. Gabriel Naudé, that generous bookman, keeper of the Mazarin Library, was able to rejoice that that great collection *was open to all the world without the exception of any living soul*; and readers were supplied with chairs, writing materials, and attendants to fetch and carry books, and to change them as often as required.[4]

VII. HOW THE ANCIENTS PROTECTED THEIR BOOKS

It is reported by Merryweather that the pride and glory of a monastery in the Middle Ages was a well stored library, which was committed to the care of the *armarian*, whose duty it was, according to the *Consuetudines canonicorum Regularium*,[5] to have all the books in his keeping catalogued for their safer preservation; and since, as he[6] says, *bibliomaniacs have not been remarkable for their memory or punctuality . . . and often forgetful to return the* [borrowed] *volume within the specified time*, the armarian was forbidden to lend books, even to neighbouring monasteries, without a bond against their return within a fixed time; or failing that, the security of a book of equal value was demanded. *Great and precious books* were not lent without the additional sanction of the Abbot, and at Durham this rule was not to be broken save on the authority of the Bishop. No lending, even to the monks themselves: books of martyrs, saintly lives, homilies, etc., *and other*

---

[1] Blades, *Books in Chains.*   [2] Delisle, *Cabinet des Manuscrits.* ii, 186. n. Qt. Clark, *Care of Books.* 164.   [3] *Ib.* vii.   [4] *The Great Book-Collectors.* Elton. 184.   [5] Cap. xxi. *Martene de Ant. Eccl. Ritibus.* iii, 262. Qt. Merryweather, 9.   [6] Merryweather, *Bibliomania in the Middle Ages.* 10–13.

large books the monks were allowed to take and study in private, but not the smaller ones or rare and choice volumes. Books so borrowed must not be lent. There was a *special dispensation* for sick brothers, but even then the books were to be returned to the armarian before dark.[1]

Hoping little *to restrain men by the laws of rectitude*, Richard de Bury[2] laid down rules for the use of the volumes granted by him to Oxford *as a perpetual gift for our soul and the souls of our parents, and also for the soul of the most illustrious King Edward the Third from the Conquest, and of the most pious Queen Philippa, his consort.* No book was to be lent unless a duplicate copy was in the library, and then only after the deposit of a security of greater value than the book borrowed. Both the keeper of the books and the borrowers had to swear to observe these rules. So also Roger de Insula, Dean of York (*circa* 1225), who gave several copies of the Bible to the University of Oxford, ordered that borrowers should give security of equal value of the books against their safe return.[3] Like precautions were taken in all centres of culture. Thus Lewis XI *borrowed a book from the Schools of Medicine* at Paris *upon a pledge of a silver vessel*,[4] but Cujacius was not so fortunate, for de Thou records that he saw in the Library at Cosmo *the famous original Pandect, taken at Constantinople, which Cujacius had in vain tried to borrow for a year, on a pledge of two thousand crowns.*[5]

Excommunication, curses and other pains and penalties were threatened or imposed upon tardy book-borrowers and embezzlers of books in those olden days. Pope Sixtus IV issued a Bull against *certain ecclesiastical and secular persons having:* as he well says, *no fear of God before their eyes*, who had taken *sundry volumes in theology and other faculties from the* Vatican *library, which volumes they still presume rashly and maliciously to hide and secretly to detain*, and, he adds, unless the books be returned within forty days, the offending persons are *ipso facto* excommunicated. If they are clerics they shall be held incapable of holding livings, and if laymen, of holding office;[6] and Bartolommeo Platina, Keeper of the Papal Books, heads his Register of Loans with the warning that those who fail to register their acknowledgement of books borrowed will incur the Pope's anger, *and his curse* unless they return them *uninjured within a very brief period.*[7]

The wrath of bookmen against those recreant borrowers, who are no less than thieves, is well known, and anathema has been favourably resorted to as a precaution and a preventive. Doubtless such warnings and imprecations have proved efficacious with the absent-minded borrower, but they can have little effect upon the shameless biblioklept; yet since in

[1] *Const. Canon. Reg. ap. Martene.* iii, 263. Qt. Merryweather, 13.   [2] *Philobiblon.* Trans. Thomas. 114–15.   [3] Wood, *Hist. Antiqu. Oxon.* ii, 48.   [4] Father Jacob, *On the First Libraries.* (1644) Qt. Collinson, *Life of Thuanus.* 240.   [5] Collinson, *op. cit.* 15.   [6] Clark, *Care of Books.* 209.   [7] *Ib.* 230.

all ages bookmen have resorted to such devices as special antidotes against pilferers, to mitigate and oppose them and to bring ease and quiet unto their own hearts, I will point out a few. Madame de Genlis *fenced the greater part of her library* with an incantation in verse:

> Inparibus meritis pendent tria corpora ramis;
> Dismas, et Gesmas, media est Divina Potestas;
> Alta petit Dismas, infelix infima Gesmas.
> Nos et res nostras conservet Summa Potestas!—
> Hos versus dicas, ne tu furto tua perdas.[1]

The same authority[2] gives another example which he thinks likely to restrain those who, though ignorant of classic lore, *may be credited with an aptitude for taking a quiet hint:*

> Si quisquis furetur
>   This little Libellum,
> Per Phoebum, per Jovem,
>   I'll kill him—I'll fell him.
> In ventrem illius,
>   I'll stick my scalpellum,
> And teach him to steal
>   My little Libellum.

In the Middle Ages, when books were scarce and precious because written by hand, anathemas were as terrible as they were numerous. This one is written in a Bible of the twelfth century: *Liber Sanctae Mariae Sanctique Nicolai in Arrinstein. Quem si quis abstulerit, morte moriatur, in sartagine coquatur, caducus morbus instet eum et febres, et rotetur, et suspendatur. Amen.*[3] Hearne recalls that in addition to those rebukes which the ancients placed at the end of their books for the special edification of such as should carp at their composition (as that in a Paraphrase of the Psalms in the Bodleian Library: *Quicunque alienaverit anathema sit. Qui culpat carmen sit maledictus. Amen.*) they added also anathemas against any that should steal or abuse them.[4]

---

[1] 'Three bodies, unequal in desert, hang upon the branches, Dismas and Gesmas, and the Divine Power between. Dismas looks aloft, unhappy Gesmas to the depths. May the Supreme Power protect us and ours. Recite these verses and you will not lose your belongings by theft.'   [2] *Book-Lore.* 164.   [3] Qt. W. Bradbrooke, *The Times,* 6.iii.1928. 'The book of St. Mary and St. Nicholas in Arrinstein. If anyone pilfers it, may he die the death, be boiled in a cauldron, may epilepsy and fever overtake him, may he be broken on the wheel and hanged. Amen.'   [4] 'If anyone steal it, let him be anathema! Whoever finds fault with it, let him be accursed. Amen.' *Diary.* 16.x.1709.

Macray records that only three out of all Duke Humphrey's MSS. are now in the Bodleian, one of them a *magnificent volume of Valerius Maximus* which had been made under the personal supervision of that good biblio-phile, Abbot Whethamstede, of St. Albans, who caused these words to be inscribed in it: *If any one steals this book may he come to the gallows or the rope of Judas.*[1] Of a like kind was that warning inscribed in the Rev. Richard Hooper's unique copy of the second edition of *The Art of Cookery made Plain and Easy* (1747):

> Steal not this Book my honest Friend
> For fear the Galows should be your hend,
> And when you die the Lord will say
> And wares the Book you stole away?

The threat of hanging is a favourite imprecation of the outraged biblio-phile, and there are many pleasant rhymes to that purpose:

> He that steals this booke
> Shall be hanged on a hooke.
> He that this book stelle wolde,
> Sone be his herte colde.
> That it may so be,
> Seith *Amen* for charite.[2]

But some think even hanging too good for such base fellows, and will stop at nothing in their wrath but the visitation of the curse of God upon the offender:

> Thys boke is one,
>   And God's curse is another;
> They that take the one
>   God geve them the other.[3]

Others seek some measure of protection for their treasures by stamping them with their armorial bearings or crest, inscribing them with their name, or attaching to their covers or end-papers a book-plate; but the sum of all such efforts is in the Library at Westminster, where there is a copy of Heylyn's *Help to English History* (1670) which contains this pithy admonition: *Exodus 20th c. 'Thou shalt not steal.'*[4] And, to end with Jean Crascot, *prendre un livre est un moins grand péché que de dire du mal de son prochain*, as well defame your neighbour as steal a book.[5]

---

[1] Qt. Elton, *Great Book-Collectors.* 58–9.   [2] Qt. H. S. Bennet, *England from Chaucer to Caxton.*   [3] Qt. H. S. Bennet, *op. cit.*   [4] *Romance of Book-Collecting.* 44.
[5] Qt. Janin, *Le Livre.* 129.

VIII. OF GIVING BOOKS

In order to the furtherance of *Bibliophily* (according to my poor measure), for which great and worthy purpose this treatise was first intended, I take this as a convenient place to set out a digression of gifts, to prove that I am not opposed to books having a place among donatives. I have sought to show by the evidence and approval of divers great and good men, that books are the noblest gifts of man to the ages which make up his world; that they are wholesome, companionable, desirable; an incomparable delight to us; and therefore precious, and so exposed to the attacks of greedy and covetous persons, as I have illustrated by many apt examples; and I have applauded the efforts of bibliophiles to protect their treasures from the ordinary rocks upon which such men would impinge and precipitate them: imprudent handling, perils of fire and water, neglect, dust, loss, theft, etc.; and thus set my face against borrowers, among the rest, who would divert books from the strait path of large and generous ownership. To say truth, suspicion of borrowers is a common humour of all bibliophiles. Many would rather give than lend, for in this way only can they purchase for themselves freedom from anxiety and trouble. I speak of sane bookmen, normal lovers of books, and say nothing of those prodigious bibliomaniacs who are mad on books as misers are mad on money. I have spoken of these at large in my section of *Bibliomania*; the precedent species are the subject of my present discourse, and I say again that they are averse from borrowers, for they know the dangers, oftentimes from experience, and, as the proverb advises, *once bitten, twice shy*. Oftentimes, also, to aggravate the rest, concur many other inconveniences, unthankful friends, decayed friends, bad neighbours, negligent servants, who are but once removed from those cunning, crafty ones, such as open doors sealed with subtle keys, and stealthily snatch and consume of dainty books; by which means they deplete on a sudden our bookish estates.

'Tis better to give than to lend, for *a gi̱ t is as a precious stone in the eyes of him that hath it*.[1] What more precious than books? they are the *pearls of great price*, incomparable jewels, kingly treasures, and as kings the great book-lovers have bestowed them; how regal those gifts of Bodley to Oxford; of Cotton to London; Rylands to Manchester; Petrarch to Venice; Salutati and Nicolo Niccoli to Florence. There is a great list of these benefactors. Peiresc did not only admit travellers studious in Art and Learning to visit his library, but at their departure he would give them *books, coins, and other things which seemed most suitable to their studies*, and we read in his *Life*, by Gassendi,[2] that as often as he was informed of books newly come forth, he would have some for himself and some to

[1] *Proverbs*. xvii, 8.   [2] English Ed. W. Rand, ii, 246.

distribute among his friends, according as he knew they would like the subject and matter thereof. Bradshaw presented his famous collection of Irish books to the University Library at Cambridge in return for *the liberal manner in which the University enabled him for more than seven years to pursue the studies which he had most at heart, and the confidence implied in the fact that no report of his work during that time was ever demanded of him;*[1] many could attest that such munificence is not dead, nor need I cite any more evidence than that of Richard Curle, who testifies that Thomas J. Wise in our own time *has enriched many a Public Library and many a private collector with his gifts.*[2]

Others have even printed books solely for their friends, as De Bure, who printed twelve copies of his *Musaeum Typographicum* (Paris 1755), giving every one away to book-loving friends, including his own copy;[3] and many have done as much in these present times, notably Frederick Locker, who took so keen a delight in bestowing his *London Lyrics* upon his friends that a collection of *ex dono* copies of the various editions and curious varieties of that delectable work inscribed by the author would make a brave show. It is the pleasant custom of several bibliophiles in times present to print, solely for presentation, private editions of their *rariora* in which they and their friends take a peculiar delight, following also the good example, in some instances, of those of other days, as Horace Walpole and Sir Egerton Brydges, and nearer our own time, the Rev. B. H. O. Daniel, of Oxford, who established their own private presses for that purpose.

There are some who give in self-defence, making the gift an insurance against borrowers, and such as these may well say *hoc habeo quodcunque dedi,*[4] what I have given I still possess. The tenet had a new meaning in a conspicuous achievement of John Evelyn when he rescued from Arundel Castle those precious volumes, including printed books of *the oldest impressions; most of the Fathers* printed at Basle, *before the Jesuits abused them with their expurgatory Indexes,* many of them given by Popes and Cardinals to the Earls of Arundel; and near one hundred MSS., *some in Greek of great concernment;* all of which he persuaded the Duke of Norfolk to give to the Royal Society.[5] When King James I presented that noble copy of his works, inscribed by his own hand and bound in crimson velvet, with the Royal Arms and other Heraldic devices stamped on blue *Turkey,* to Bodley's Library, the book was received at a special Convocation at St. Mary's Church, and carried from thence by Patrick Young, the chief of a special deputation which had brought the volume from London, to the

---

[1] *Memoir of Henry Bradshaw.* Prothero. 171, 173.   [2] *Ashley Lib. Cat.* Intro. i, ix.
[3] Dibdin, *Bibliomania.* (1811) 77.   [4] Seneca, *de Beneficiis.* vi, 3, 1.   [5] *Diary.* 29.viii.1678.

Library with *a great deal of solemnitie*.[1] The procession was accompanied by twenty-four Doctors in their scarlet robes, and the rest of *the bodie of the University*, and the book was received by Keeper Rouse, who made a *verie prettie speech*, and placed it *in archivis intuentibus nobis reliquis academicis* with *a great deale of respect*.

Books have been used as gifts in all ages and upon all occasions to express honour, power, friendship, love; and in some measure by great women also, as in the instance given out of *Hume*, on the authority of *Heylin*, by Dibdin,[2] *when Sir John Gage, Constable of the Tower, led* Lady Jane Grey *to execution, and desired some token of remembrance, 'she gave him her " Table-Book"*, *on which were written three sentences on seeing her husband's dead body: one in Greek, another in Latin, and a third in English.' A library*, saith D'Israeli,[3] *was a national gift, and the most honourable the Romans could bestow*; so that after the taking of Carthage the Senate rewarded the family of Regulus with the books found in that city; it was full reverence for such a custom that prompted Sir Thomas More to carry that *pretty fardel of books, in the small type of Aldus*, to the people of his *Utopia*.[4] When la Fontaine learnt that Peter Daniel Huet wished to see Tuscanella's Italian version of the *Institutes* of Quintillian, he not only brought that work to him as a present, but *adorned his gift with an elegant poem addressed to* Huet, *in which he satirized the sanity of those who place in competition, and even prefer, our own age to antiquity*.[5] James Boswell, moved by the smallness of the library of the Corsican leader, Paoli, augmented his collection with a gift of the works of *Harrington, of Sidney, of Addison, of Trenchard, of Gordon, and of other writers in favour of liberty*; as well as *some of our best books of morality and entertainment, in particular the Works of Mr. Samuel Johnson*; complete sets of the *Spectator, Tatler* and *Guardian*; and to the University of Corte he gave several of the Greek and Roman classics in the beautiful editions of Foulis of Glasgow.[6] Mark Antony gave to Cleopatra the library of Pergamus containing two hundred thousand volumes;[7] among them the tragedies of Aeschylus, Sophocles, and Euripides, which, saith Janin, con-convinced Cicero that Antony was incorrigible.[8]

But it is not my business to extend these instances, and I have said so much only to prove that parsimony is not innate among bibliophiles however vigilantly they ward their treasures from those losels who would misemploy them; for is it not a fond enterprise to love and protect books and to spread this regard in fertile places? These are the arts that speak a bookman truly noble, for who does not know that every good, the more

[1] Young, *Letter to his brother*. 8.vi.1620.   [2] *Bibliographical Decameron*. iii, 250. n. [3] 'Libraries', *Cur. of Lit*. 1, 3.   [4] More, *Utopia*.   [5] Huet, *Memoirs*. Trans. Aikin. ii, 189.   [6] *Tour in Corsica*. Ed. Roberts. 34.   [7] *Plutarch*. Ed. Clough. v, 212. [8] *Le Livre*. Janin. 104.

diffusive it is, by so much the better it is? Leigh Hunt was lucky in this respect, for he took a keen delight in spreading the news of his literary adventures by word and deed. At one time he was so enamoured of Cooke's editions of the poets that he could not rest until he had shared his love with his friends. He bought copies *over and over again and used to get up select sets which disappeared like buttered crumpets;* for he *could resist neither giving them away, nor possessing them.*[1] In surveying this state we can turn no way without meeting wonders of generosity, nor is it any paradox to say that, in spite of all these magnanimous ventures, it is no advantage to scatter books indiscriminately before the gullish commonalty, and may be, perhaps, a little saucy to call back the Muses from Helicon and to place them among strangers and where they are not welcome, for, so Dr. Johnson held, *people seldom read a book which is given to them;*[2] although the good Doctor did not mind taking the risk, as a familiar instance recorded by Boswell would suggest. John Wilkes once said to Boswell in tones loud enough for Dr. Johnson to hear, '*Dr. Johnson should make me a present of his "Lives of the Poets", as I am a poor patriot, who cannot afford to buy them.*' The Doctor *seemed to take no notice of this hint,* says Boswell; but presently he called to Mr. Dilly, his publisher, '*Pray, Sir, be so good as to send a set of my "Lives" to Mr. Wilkes, with my compliments.*' *This was accordingly done; and Mr. Wilkes paid Dr. Johnson a visit, was courteously received, and sat with him a long time.*[3]

So I would not discourage a discriminate benevolence in the bestowal of books. There are no more gracious gifts, properly disposed, none more convenient, none which more permanently evoke grateful thoughts of the giver, for to bestow a book appropriately is to share a friendship and to increase it; a good book in itself being a friend, and one, as I have shown, which can only alter for the better.

---

[1] Qt. *Leigh Hunt.* Blunden. 23. [2] *Life.* Ed. Hill. ii, 229–30. [3] *Ib.* iv, 107.

Part XVIII

THE CAPARISONING OF BOOKS

I. THE PRAISE OF GOOD BINDING

Amongst all these fair and enticing objects which procure book-love and bewitch the soul of the bibliophile, there is none so moving, so forcible, as a beautiful binding, *holding the whole in its strong grip and for very love becoming beautiful;*[1] and, best of all, when carrying a show of the quality and character of the book:

> Full goodly bounde in pleasaunt coverture
> Of damas, satyn, or els of velvet pure.[2]

Nothing so fair as a comely book, and its comeliness is first apparent and last recalled in its outer seeming, where it

> Nimbly and sweetly recommends itself
> Unto our gentle sense.[3]

A pleasant coverture pranked in rich leathers aglow with aureate fantasy: arabesques of gold, *aurum mosaicum*, golden powderings, *dentelles, dentelles à l'oiseau, fleurons*, cunningly devised and graciously conceived to guard, express and exalt the written word, looking, as Bonaventure d'Argonne said of Grolier's library, *as if the Muses had taken the outsides into their charge, as well as the contents*, so gay was the art and *esprit* of their delicate gilding.[4]

A well-bound book is a hymn of praise, a song of love. And when the bibliophile adorns his books thus he protects, honours and caresses them; adores and worships; *is entranced in admiration, roves in gazing ecstasy, from page to page, till here and there arrested by a choice vignette, or richly tinctured plate: at length, 'lassatus, necdum satiatus', with the beauties of the interior, he reverently closes the superbly plated leaves, turns to the sumptuous, silk-lined cover, and marvels at the verdant, red or purple pride of Russia, Turkey, or Morocco, glittering, in every part, with the mazy flourishes of golden decoration!—'Miror, immo etiam stupeo!' is the language of his heart*, saith Beresford, *if it cannot be of his tongue.*[5] So, as the poet sings:[6]

---

[1] *Ecce Mundus.* T. J. Cobden-Sanderson.   [2] Chaucer.   [3] *Macbeth.* i, 6.   [4] Qt. Elton, *The Great Book-Collectors.* 147–8.   [5] *Bibliosophia.* 10.   [6] Crabbe, *The Library.*

376

First, let us view the form, the size, the dress;
For these the manners, nay the mind express.

What theories they have propounded for the binding of books I shall now dilate, the varieties of materials and the manner of their decoration for the honour and glory of books and the conceit of their owners, for as Percy Fitzgerald[1] argues out of William Roscoe, a book is as proper an object for *elegant ornament* as the *head of a cane*, the *hilt of a sword*, or the *latchet of a shoe*. Ever since books have been books, and loved, their lovers have sought to express their passion by tricking them out in significant and eventful bindings. *Few men*, John Hill Burton claims,[2] are *entirely above this influence. The splendours of the private library began in the days of Lucullus.*[3] With the Jews of the Middle Ages the making of beautiful books was a religious act: ' *The wealthy must honour the Law,*' says the Talmud; 'tel them do this by paying for beautiful copies of the Scriptures';[4] and the monks of old sought to celebrate their love of holy books by calling to their aid goldsmiths and silversmiths, enamellers, embroiderers and carvers in wood and ivory, for the copying and caparisoning of their favourites. Their *snow-white vellum missals were emblazoned with gold, and sparkling with carmine and ultramarine blue.*[5] St. Boniface, when about to start on his mission through the German forest and the marches of Friesland, asked the Abbess Eadburga for a *Missal* on parchment gay with colours, to be as a glittering lamp and an illumination for the hearts of the Gentiles; he entreated her again to send him St. Peter's *Epistle* in *letters of gold*; and St. Wilfrid presented to his church at Ripon a *Book of the Gospels* on purple vellum, and a *Bible* with covers of pure gold, inlaid with precious stones.[6] So inordinate was the monks' love of fine books that they were reproved by St. Jerome, who expostulated: *Your books are covered with precious stones, and Christ died naked before the gate of his Temple.*[7]

All bibliophiles will be on the side of the monks, and methinks they would have the support of good Richard de Bury, who has written so nobly in defence of the love of books, in his *Philobiblon*, which is the true Breviary of all bibliophiles; for, as he says, *when truth shines forth in books, it commends itself to every impressionable sense;* to the sight when read; to the hearing when heard; and even *in a manner to the touch.*[8]

Nay doubly fair the Aldine pages seem,
Where, broadly gilt, illumin'd letters gleam.[9] ˙

[1] *The Book-Financier.* 99.   [2] *The Book-Hunter.* 29.   [3] Elton, *Great Book-Collectors.* 4.   [4] Profiat Duran, Abrahams, *Jewish Life in the Middle Ages.* 355. [5] Dibdin, *Bibliomania.* (1811) 199.   [6] Elton, *Great Book-Collectors.* 22.   [7] *Bookbinding.* Henry B. Wheatley. 1.   [8] *Philobiblon.* i, 10.   [9] Ferriar, *Bibliomania.*

But if some would go too far in the decorating of their treasures and others not far enough, let me prescribe a medium course, *in medio virtus*, seeking to avoid Scylla without falling into Charybdis, letting affection wait upon good taste. Nothing so good but it may be abused. Nothing better than affection (if opportunity used) for the preservation of books; but *a leather coat fashioned by Derome, or Le Gascon, or Duseuil, will win respect and careful handling for one specimen of an edition whereof all the others have perished;*[1] a faith which Peiresc, the great French bibliophile, held nearly two centuries and a half before him. *Good books*, he said, *were so badly used by the vulgar, that he would try to have them prized at least for their beauty*, and so save them from the tobacconist and the grocer.[2] This argument is not so pertinent to times present when books are so common that their extermination is unlikely, and a fine binding thus becomes an excuse for homage; it reveals our thanks and our love.

II. BEAUTY COMPOSED OF MANY QUALITIES

Beauty is a common object of all love, *ut paleam succinum, sic amorem forma trahit*, as amber draws a straw, so doth beauty love, and so also a beautiful book its lover, who is in turn drawn to embellish his books with the insignia of his passion, to bestow upon them all that his wealth may command: rich apparel and luxurious trappings, as those codices (*aureus* or *argentus*) of the time of Charles the Great, whose letters of gold or silver were written upon leaves of purple parchment bound in jewellery:

> Such charms thy beauty wears as might
> Desires in dying confest saints excite;[3]

or those books of the monks of Canterbury on pink vellum, with rubricated capitals, which Pope Gregory sent to Augustine;[4] or that *Psalter* of the ninth century written on purple vellum which rests in the Bodleian;[5] or St. Brigit of Kildare's decorated copy of the *Gospels* which to Gerard de Barri, who saw it in the year 1185, seemed a work *beyond the powers of mortal man, and worthy of an angel's skill*. Well may there have been a belief in those parts that the craftsman who made it received divine help,[6] for such a work is no less than that sung by the poet:

---

[1] Andrew Lang, *The Library*. 63.   [2] Elton, *The Great Book-Collectors*. 180
[3] Cowley.   [4] Elton, *Great Book-Collectors*. 19.   [5] *Ib.* 15.   [6] Macray, *Annals*. 472.

The margin was illumined all with golden rails
And bees, enpictured with grasshops and wasps,
With butterflies and fresh peacock tails,
Engloried with flowers and slimy snails;
Ennyield pictures well touched and quickly;
It would have made a man whole that had be right sickly
To behold how it was garnished and bound,
Encovered over with gold of tissue fine;
The clasps and bullions were worth a thousand pound;
With belassis and carbuncles the borders did shine;
With aurum mosaicum every other line
Was written.[1]

Every proper booklover has his dreams of the perfect book even though he may never possess it; and many would have their pets beautiful in every part, not only in their outer garments:

Morocco flames in scarlet, blue and green,
Impressed with burnished gold, or dazzling sheen,[2]

for *a book is a composite thing made up of many parts, and may be made beautiful by the beauty of each of its parts—its binding and decoration,*[3] or, as he says, *it may be made beautiful by the supreme beauty of one or more of its parts, all the other parts subordinating or even effacing themselves for the sake of this one or more, and each in turn being capable of playing this supreme part and each in its own peculiar and characteristic way*; and he would have that in its supreme beauty, in which all its several parts are confluent in excellence, there is *a symbol of the infinitely beautiful in which all things of beauty do ultimately merge.* It is an opinion which Platonists rather than bibliophiles would maintain at large, for the latter prefer to find comfort in the expedient of beauty as the decoration of love, the garment of affection, rather than seek to relate it with a universal symbol of subtle abstraction. The beloved book should be well and becomingly dressed, and that is enough, for book-love is in itself consistent and claims no justification beyond its own whim and content. A book, as I keep on saying, is intended in the main to be read, and to that end, as Edward FitzGerald demanded of a *Don Quixote* from Quaritch, it should be *well and handsomely bound—strong, well-opening, well-margined, and well-looking.*[4] Book-love is thus *a circle that doth ever move,* as Herrick sang of love itself,

In its own sweet eternity of love.

---

[1] John Skelton, *A Replycacion against Scolers.*   [2] Maccreery. Qt. *Book-Lovers' Anth.* 243.   [3] Cobden-Sanderson, 'The Book Beautiful', *Ecce Mundus.*   [4] *Letters to Bernard Quaritch.* 48.

None knew this better than Grolier, whose instructions to his printers have all the tenderness of love. One such injunction expounded his wishes for a new edition of Budaeus, *De Asse*, which he would have similar in form and characters to the Aldine *Politian* of 1498; *Addi volo decorem et elegantiam:* he wrote; *id praestabit delecta papyrus, litterarum concinnitas, et quae minime sint attritae, spaciosi margines; atque, ut planius dicam, volo eadem forma et notis describi quibus olim Politiani opera impressistis.*[1]

Books, like men, are subject to manners, behaviour; they are well or ill bred; well dressed or badly dressed. You can tell them for what they are at a glance. Oliver Wendell Holmes saw a noble quarto *Hedericus* lying in the midst of *an ignoble crowd of cheap books, and marked with a price* which he felt to be *an insult to scholarship, to the memory of Homer, and the awful shade of Aeschylus.* He loved it for its *looks and behaviour.* It had the grand manner and *a generous way of laying its treasures before you. No lifting of a rebellious leaf like an upstart servant that does not know his place and can never be taught manners, but tranquil, well-bred repose. A book,* he rightly holds, *may be a perfect gentleman in its aspect and demeanour*; and that book might have been *good company for personages like Roger Ascham and his pupils the Lady Elizabeth and the Lady Jane Grey.*[2] Identical arguments apply to the typography. A book, like a gentleman, should be *becomingly* composed, *appropriate to the dignity of the subject,* as Gissing found the first edition of Gibbon's *Decline and Fall,*[3] but guiltless of fuss or ostentation; no excuse for *a beautiful quarto page, where a neat rivulet of text shall meander through a meadow of margin.*[4] A fair page should be full and bright and clear with margins servants to the type. Fine printing, even when it is gay printing, is ever austere in form, because, although a craft in itself, it is not a thing in itself like a picture, but rather a bridge between creator and consumer, author and reader. It is primarily a means of communication between these two, and at its best it should do everything to induce and nothing to impede the traffic. Graciousness, friendliness, as well as dignity and austerity should be there, but always unobtrusively. Self-effacement is the etiquette of good printers.

A book is a piece of artifice or craftsmanship in all its several stages and parts, and in each it should be consistent with itself, its aims and purpose: clear to read, easy to hold, supple to open, strong to endure, dainty to touch, and fair to look upon, all these co-ordinate to one end, in an appropriate design, meet for its destiny, *mens sana in corpore sano,* stopping short only of mechanical exactitude, for tender human lapses

> Do more bewitch me than when art
> Is too precise in every part;[5]

[1] Qt. Horne, *Binding of Books.* 73–4.   [2] *The Poet at the Breakfast-Table.* (1902) 210–11.   [3] *Private Papers of Henry Ryecroft.* 36   [4] Sheridan, *School for Scandal.* i, 1.
[5] Robert Herrick, 'Delight in Disorder', *Hesperides.*

for as M. Aurelius Antoninus[1] well observes, *things which follow after the things which are produced according to nature contain something pleasing and attractive*, and he gives the pleasant instance of bread split in the baking *contrary to the baker's art*, which nevertheless is beautiful and appetizing. So with art.

That some books are upstarts, over-dressed, daws in borrowed feathers, is too well known to need any extended reference. But the fault is not theirs. They are at the mercy of unworthy owners, and defamed by vulgar and meretricious traders, who pander to showy tastes. The garish covers of the *table books* of the Victorian age, *Family Bible, School Prizes*, resemble real bindings as the images at a waxwork show resemble real people; and all that scum of *presentation booklets* tricked in *suede, degrained sheep*, and *yap* edges, are no more than *biblia-a-biblia*. The best way to destroy this species is to ignore them, as I shall do.

I hold it true that a strong, simple binding is best for normal reading; wisdom in this case being preferable to luxury. Yet, methinks, such lovely sights as a range of fair volumes,

Like gems that sparkle in the parent mine,[2]

do not only ravish and amaze, but please and entice,

Ut vidi, ut perii,[3]

I see and am undone, especially when this comeliness and beauty arise from the due proportion and character of the book; my desire is invoked, it will not be denied; I am enticed and ravished, as (let me take it for a parallel case) was Clitophon for Leucippe,[4] for, as he ingenuously confesses, no sooner had he come into her presence, but that he did *corde tremere, et oculis lascivis intueri*. In the reverse case, however, I have nothing but contempt for those inferior volumes which their owners, out of a vain conceit or false sense of value, trick out in unearned finery.

Was ever book containing such vile matter
So fairly bound? O, that deceit should dwell
In such a gorgeous palace![5]

Because, as Aristotle holds, no excellent mind is entirely exempt from some admixture of folly, it may follow that many a sound as well as silly fellow is taken in by such trash; but comeliness of binding is not therefore to be condemned, so 'tis fit to be inquired whether certain rules may be made of it for our guidance and judgment.

[1] *Thoughts of the Emperor Marcus Antoninus*. Long. iii, 107. [2] J. Maccreery, Qt. *Book-Lovers' Anth.* 243. [3] Virgil, *Eclogues*. viii, 41. [4] *Achilles Tatius*. i. [5] *Romeo and Juliet*. iii, 2.

A first rule which will not be contested is taken from the craft of building. A foundation stone must be *well and truly laid*, so also the foundations of a book, including its outer fabric, for as Frederick Locker-Lampson gives it, *a well-bound book mocks at time*.[1] Andrew Lang holds[2] that *the binding should unite solidity and elegance*, and he reminds us, as well he may, that the conditions of a well-bound book are not confined to a strong or appropriate cover, but extend to the opening and closing of the volume as well: *the book should open easily, and remain open at any page you please. It should never be necessary, in reading, to squeeze back the covers.* No book, however expensively bound, is well bound, unless it open with ease; and finally, for protection of the leaves as well as for the joy of anticipation, a cover should not open of a sudden upon the title-page or matter proper to the book: *no volume has a meaner appearance, than that which opens immediately upon the title*;[3] to counteract such deficiencies there are end-papers, plain or marbled, or patterned in many colours; and *doublures* of silk or vellum or leather, made to blend in the more luxurious books, by marquetery, mosaic, and other devices, with the tooling of the covers.

Such conditions presume good craftsmanship in each of the several operations of binding, from the *folding* and *sewing*, called *forwarding*, to the application of the final decorations, which is known as *finishing*. So much will be conceded by all; contention begins after all these excellences have been provided, but, if I leave out whim, idiosyncrasy, and the like (which is impossible, for they will do as they list), what I have formerly said of conditions I must now repeat in some measure of appearance. The conditions of appearance is finally, if not solely, aesthetical, a matter of taste, for taste when it is good regards the utilities, it seeks somewhat in the manner of the Platonist a fair union of the whole, the good and the true, as the ingredients of that beauty which he admires and values most when, as they say, it is *fit for its purpose*. The design of a binding must be architectonic, at one in purpose and expression with the book, its authorship, idea and construction, the same which Hartley Coleridge extols when he claims that *the binding of a book should always suit its complexion*,[4] which a later writer supports and extends in another aphorism: *a book should be bound in harmony with its character and value*;[5] as in times past de Thou was commended by Henry Stephens because his finely printed books were bound *in proportion to the cost of any copy*: the higher the cost *the more sumptuous the binding*.[6] The best bindings, those most assiduously regarded by bookmen of all degrees, possess such qualities as these principles of use and beauty would command, and will not be ignored, even when the

[1] *My Confidences*. ix.   [2] *Library*. 68–9.   [3] Horne, *Binding of Books*. 17.   [4] 'William Roscoe', *Biographia Borealis*.   [5] Andrew Lang, *The Library*. 64.   [6] Qt. Collinson, *Life of Thuanus*. 238.

bindings embody as well the whim of the bibliophile, if he be a man of taste.

III. VARIETY OF STYLE AND MATERIALS

What character the binding may have yields a diversity of opinions. Great books are written on this subject. But howsoever they be diverse, intricate, and hard to be confined, I will adventure yet, in this confusion, to bring them into some order; and so descend to particulars, remembering with Andrew Lang,[1] that the bibliophile, *if he could give rein to his passions*, would bind all his books in full coats of morocco, russia, or other fine materials. But every record affords examples that he will go further than full coating his treasures in luxurious leathers; he would add distinction to distinction by tooling, extra-gilding, inlaying, burnishing, bevelling, jewelling, etc., for his books are jewels; and the theory that *a jewel deserves a jewel case* is one which Sir Edmund Gosse supposes he shares with *every genuine lover of books*.[2]

Often in these days the passion for books is so nice that it sets certain favoured *rariora* above binding. What more *characteristic and harmonious* asks W. Carew Hazlitt,[3] than a *Caxton uncut in oaken boards, or even in a secondary vesture of vellum*, as the Holford copy of *Godfrey of Bouillon*? Or than a *Walton* in *primitive sheep* like the Huth copy? The purest first folio *Shakespeare* he ever saw was Miss Napier's copy in the *original calf*; and he knows of copies of Laneham's *Letter from Kenilworth*, 1575; Spenser's *Faery Queen*, 1590; Allot's *England's Parnassus*, 1600; and Davison's *Poetical Rhapsody*, 1611, in their *pristine vellum wrappers*. The Bodleian, he says, has a copy of Brathwaite's *most rare 'Good Wife'*, 1618, *just as it was received 280 years since from the stationer who issued it*. He gloats on them, and would rather have them in this simple and original state than in any grandeur of *habiliment* which the binder might give them.

Most bibliophiles in our time would support him, and go to great lengths to preserve the virginal state of their darlings, their *mint* loveliness, enshrining them for protection and honour in rich cases bearing the *counterjeit presentment* of books. Conquet, the French bookseller, who was known as *l'homme aux couvertures*, and whose shop, as *large as one's hand*, was on the Boulevard Bonne-Nouvelle, gave out that *a book of the Romanticists was imperfect if it lacked the paper covers wherein it originally appeared*.[4] How *lovingly*, saith a modern poet,[5] have some first editions been *preserved by their former owners*, who have enclosed them *in fragrant leathern cases*,

---

[1] *The Library.* 64.   [2] *Library of Edmund Gosse.* Intro. xxi.   [3] *Book-Collector.* 232–3.
[4] Henri Pène du Bois, *Four Private Libraries of New York.* 21.   [5] Thomas Moult.
Intro., *Forty Years in My Bookshop.* W. T. Spencer. xxviii.

cunningly fashioned so that they may stand on a library shelf and look like beauti-fully bound books instead of *the mere outer casing of a book.* I may give for example the *Missal* that Le Gascon bound in purple morocco, *doré à petits fers,* enclosed in *a case of violet sheep-skin,* and gave to the Guild of St. Jean.[1] Of old time in Ireland books were carefully protected in separate jewelled caskets called *theca* or *cumdach*; and upon the sides of these caskets, not upon the covers of books, were the richest decorations lavished;[2] just as in times past the bibliophiles of the monasteries, the same that St. Jerome reproved for too much book-worship, bedizened their favourites so resplendently in bindings of gold and silver, studded with precious stones, and inlaid panels of carved ivory or ingenious enamelling, that they resembled caskets for baubles rather than shrines of wisdom. Many such can be seen in our great libraries, the British Museum and the Bodleian, but in the Rylands Library is the finest collection in all England.[3]

Not that comeliness of adornment is to be condemned, still less those usual ornaments; but there is a decency and decorum in this as well as in other things; fit to be observed, becoming most books, and befitting their contents and estate. He is only fantastical that is not in fashion, bedecking his books in an old image of the Gothic Age, imitating the Past. Copying the antique, whether it is one century or another, is of no account: what is past is past, whether Grolier, Derome, Clovis Eve, Samuel Mearne, Roger Payne, it is all one: masterpieces cannot be repeated. There is nothing left but for our binders to express the spirit of the old masters in the language of our own day. Bindings in every age should follow the manner of attire generally received, changing forward, not backward, depending always upon good workmanship rather than ingenuity or novelty of effect. But when books are so new-fangled, so unstaid, so prodigious in their attires, beyond their means and fortunes, unbefitting their age, place, quality, condition, what should we think of them?

> A book? O rare one!
> Be not, as is our fangled world, a garment
> Nobler than that it covers: let thy effects
> So follow, to be most unlike our courtiers,
> As good as promise.[4]

Only pretenders to bibliophily would tolerate them or give them har-bourage. They who would turn the holy temples consecrated to wisdom, imagination, vision and great writing, into shops of impudence, parades for poseurs, *Beauty Parlours,* are no more of the true faith than those who

---

[1] Horne, *The Binding of Books.* 135.   [2] Madan, *Books in MS.* 49.   [3] *Ib.*
[4] *Cymbeline.* v, 4.

would trick them out in *Wardour Street* antiquities; for *sic transit gloria librorum*, thus passes the glory of books in a pose, a gaud, a vanity; they are degraded to baubles. Generally with such books, as with rich furred conies, their cases are far better than their bodies, and like the bark of a cinnamon tree, which is dearer than the whole bulk, their outward accoutrements are far more precious than their inward endowments. But I am over tedious, I confess, and whilst I stand gaping at gewgaws and inappropriate clothing I am delaying my relation of the allurements proper to bindings.

Books have been pampered, petted, and adorned in all periods with so many colours, fictitious flowers, gay devices, glittering heraldry, ornaments, curious needlework, eventful carvings, embossings, filigree, and with those inestimable riches of gold, silver, bronze and precious stones: pearls, rubies, diamonds, emeralds, carbuncles, garnets, with chrysoprase and turquoise, opal and amber. Thus have they made them opulent with patterned bosses and clasps and corner pieces of rare metals; enamel inlays and marquetry of precious woods, or inlaid miniature portraits or other ingenious devices and objects; fore-edges a-glitter with red and gold, or resplendent with pictures (as those of Samuel Mearne in the time of Charles II, and of Edwards of Halifax nearer our own day), or goffered quaintly or diapered with austere patterns. They have burnished panels that shine like mirrors; or are *grained* and *crushed* to produce cunning and delicious textures that entrance the touch. Some are covered with affluent decorations in *repoussé* and *intaglio*, or bedight with pictures or patterns in bright pigments; others are curiously marbled in rich colours, *clouded* or given *piebald* complexions; tricked out in diamond traceries, or radiations like the rings of tree-trunks. But most of all they have inspired subtle craftsmen to enchant their surfaces with patterns of gold. With *fillets* these artists have fashioned aureate borders of simple lines and woven them into scrolls and *arabesques*; with *petits fers* they have fabricated *au pointillé*, giving a lace-like caress, a silent *frou-frou* of elegance to covers and backs; or *à la fanfare*, to make them radiate in gold as rich sound spreads out from a flourish of trumpets; or *à semis*, translating their covertures into rich gowns powdered with stars and flowers:

> With the wreath'd trellis of a working brain,
>   With buds, and bells, and stars without a name,
> With all the gardener Fancy e'er could feign,
>   Who breeding flowers, will never breed the same.[1]

To achieve these allurements men have ranged the earth and trawled

[1] Keats, 'Ode to Psyche'.

the seas. Great trees, oak, sandal, mahogany, ebony, cedars of Lebanon
have rendered tribute:

> This old Decretal, won from Kloss's hoards,
> Thick-leaved, brass-cornered, ribbed with oaken boards,
> Stands the grey patriarch of the graver rows,
> Its fourth ripe century narrowing to its close;[1]

precious metals and stones from the bowels of the earth, as I have told;
pelts of beasts, birds, fishes, and even men (which last I discuss apart);
goats, antelopes, reindeer, horses, asses, sheep, oxen, pigs, does, seals,
kangaroos, lizards, snakes, sharks, dogfish, ostriches, etc., and dainty fabrics,
silks, damasks, velvets, brocades, tapestries, laces. Silk ribands and cords
for ties, and threads of silver and gold, and silk threads of many colours for
needlework. The materials of their glorious shows are further augmented
with ivory from the tusks of elephants, with the feathers of birds, with
shagreen and nacre, cloth of gold and silver tissue, spangles, tinsels and
whatsoever Africa, Asia, America, sea, land, or the art and industry of man
can offer. And more familiar and easy for every man's capacity, and the
common good, which is the chief end of binding, is that pedestrian cloth
invented by R. E. Lawson of Blackfriars, and first used by William
Pickering, in 1823, for his Diamond Classics,[2] and since then adopted by
publishers at large in an infinitude of textures, colourings, designs; in
linen, cotton: canvas, buckram, calico; repp, twill, etc., for all manner of
books; or those innumerable paper covers, plain or coloured; or the bright
metallic papers which come from China and make books look as though
they were bound in sheets of silver and gold, hammered and burnished.
But to spin off this thread, which is already grown too long, I must make
an end, for 'tis a catalogue which has no end because it is co-extensive
with human fancy, and the wherewithal to satisfy it.

Among the great variety of materials and methods proper to the caparisoning of books, predilection determines use and form. Some are for one
material, some for another; some like their books plain, others coloured;
some simple, others ornate; but de gustibus non est disputandum, and I will
not take upon me to decide which is best where so many are good, but
will describe a few famous examples of what has been done in that kind,
from those early times when old pious tracts and Bibles were bound in
wood, to the opulent age of morocco. Among bibliophiles of taste many
are for uniformity of binding, as Samuel Pepys,[3] and these have a favourite
leather; some, but chiefly in past times, will have nought but vellum:

---

[1] O.W. Holmes, 'The Study', Poems.   [2] Horne, Binding of Books. 44.   [3] Diary.
Wheatley. iv, 335.

Others in pride the virgin vellum wear
Beaded with gold—as breast of Venus fair;[1]

Dr. Gossel (an eighteenth-century bibliophile) had all his books bound in *milk-white vellum*;[2] but Hartley Coleridge would confine vellum to books of *glossy hot-pressed paper*, which look best in it. In our time William Morris and Cobden-Sanderson used vellum for the binding of many of the famous books issued by them from the *Kelmscott* and *Doves* presses. Sheep followed vellum in popular favour, but never greatly preferred among bibliophiles. Fuller's *honest fellows in leather jerkins* were doubtless of this kind. Then came calf, plain, marbled, mottled, sprinkled, etc., which ruled powerfully throughout the eighteenth century:

On some the tawny calf a coat bestows,
Where flowers and fillets beauteous forms compose;[3]

on many rather than some, in that age, did it bestow its honest favours, clothing so many gentlemen's libraries that it became a uniform for the patrician's collection, my lord having no other wish than to *case his volumes in congenial calf.*[4]

Morocco has now the place of honour, like an all-powerful king, and is not likely to be deposed, *without doubt, no coloured leather* is comparable to it, *either for beauty, or for use:*[5]

In red morocco drest he loves to boast
The bloody murder, or the yelling ghost.[6]

It was used by Grolier. King James I is credited with having introduced it into England, and it was the favourite leather of our renowned Roger Payne, and, nearer our day, Francis Bedford, the bookbinder, whom Locker-Lampson called the *emperor of morocco*.[7] Some go so far as to place it before all other leathers for utility and beauty: *the right leather to use for binding is morocco*.[8] Le Gascon held this opinion or he would not have bound so notable a book as the *Guirlande de Julie* in red morocco with a *doublure of the same*, enriched like the boards with a *semis* of the Letters I & L, in celebration of Julie Lucine, afterwards Madame de Montausier:[9] and the greater part of the books in the Medician Library, which were added to the Royal Library of France by Henri IV, were, says Father Jacob, *sumptuously bound in crimson morocco, the expense of which was defrayed from the rents of the expelled Jesuits.*[10]

---

[1] J. Maccreery, *Book-Lovers' Anth.* 243.　　[2] *The Pursuit of Literature.* 303.
[3] J. Maccreery, Qt. *op. cit.* 243.　　[4] Byron, *English Bards and Scotch Reviewers.* 720.
[5] Horne, *The Binding of Books.* 41.　　[6] Ferriar, *Bibliomania.* 62–3.　　[7] *My Confidences.* 197.　　[8] A. L. Humphreys, *The Private Library.* 53.　　[9] Horne, *Binding of Books.* 136.　　[10] Qt. Collinson, *Life of Thuanus.* 241.

Lang says that all bibliophiles prefer full morocco, or *if it did not age so fast*, russia, much loved also by Roger Payne.[1] Every lover of books loves russia for its fragrance alone, obtained from the bark of the birch tree with which it is dressed,

> Russia, exhaling from its scented pores
> Its saving power to these thrice-valued stores.[2]

It is the very bouquet of libraries. When Edward FitzGerald sent Professor Aldis Wright copies of his translation from the Persian, he had them *done up in Russia*, which, he wrote,[3] will help *to give your Library the fine Odour which all Libraries should breathe.* Hartley Coleridge holds that *sober brown Russia* rather than *military Morocco* is the proper binding for *pages venerably yellow*;[4] but Dibdin made the best of·both worlds by having his books clothed some in *Morocco*, others in *Russia*.[5]

IV. FITNESS FOR PURPOSE

In spite, however, of these diverse opinions and varied tastes, many good bookmen, especially in these days when we are much less given to ornamentation than our fathers were, hold that all regard for the clothing of volumes should begin and end at their protection, and their commendable attitude is summed up by John Henry, an Irish bookseller, practising in Oxford two centuries ago, who gave out that his trade was *clothing naked authors.*[6] *Have a care*, advises Peacham,[7] *of keeping your books handsome, and well bound, not casting away overmuch in their gilding or stringing for ostentation sake, like the prayer-books of girls and gallants, which are carried to church but for their outsides.* As we are endowed, enriched and delighted by books, our estate in them, our *bene esse*, ebbing and flowing with our commodity, so it behoves us to esteem them, for our wealth lasts no longer than their form; when that is gone, the object removed, farewell reading, learning, and the delightsome faculties which they engender. When King Alphonsus[8] was about to lay *the foundation of a castle at Naples*, he called for *Vitruvius his book of Architecture.* When he saw the book and found that it was *in very bad case, all dusty and without covers*, he said, *He that must cover us all, must not go uncovered himself*, and he commanded the book to be *fairly bound.* So, saith mine author: *Suffer them not to lie neglected, who must make you regarded; and go in torn coats, who must apparel your minds with the ornaments of knowledge, above the robes and riches of the most magnificent princes.*

[1] Horne, *Binding of Books*. 41.   [2] J. Maccreery, Qt. *Book-Lovers' Anth.* 243.
[3] *More Letters*. 104.   [4] 'William Roscoe', *Biographia Borealis*.   [5] *Bibliomania*.
(1811) 30.   [6] Macray, *Annals*. 219.   [7] *The Compleat Gentleman*.   [8] *The Compleat Gentleman*.

For this reason, which will not be opposed, the true bibliophile guards his books against neglect, wear and tear, seeking ever to maintain them in protective garb at the least; but even those whose humour is to be careless of their persons and estates, as the shepherd in Theocritus,[1] *et haec barba inculta est, squalidique capilli,* their beards flag, and they have no more care of adorning themselves, or of any business, caring not, as they say, which end goes forward; even such as these conceive and meditate upon pleasant and luxurious bindings sometimes, as Robert Burns, who was content with *the veriest ordinary copies* and *nice only in the appearance of his poets,*[2] and the *Bible,* which he would have dressed *with all the elegance* of the binder's craft.[3] No one loved a fine binding more ardently than Southey, and his books in *white and gold—vellum or parchment bound, with gilt lettering in the old English type which he loved—were arranged in effective positions pyramid-wise;* but one room, which he called the *Cottonian Library,* because it was filled with rows of *ragged veterans* reclad by domestic enterprise in brightly coloured cotton prints, *presenting a strange patchwork of colours.*[4] Charles Lamb,[5] most reliable epicurean of books, reduces such considerations to the principle that *to be strong-backed and neat-bound is the desideratum of a volume. Magnificence comes after,* but he puts in a caveat against lavishing it upon all kinds of books indiscriminately, which all bibliophiles this side of bibliomania will support. He would not, for instance, dress a set of magazines *in full suit,* and not without good cause, but I would make exception of those *Spectators, Ramblers, Tatlers, Idlers,* etc., which have conquered ephemerality by merit and won to an immortality of their own beside that of the Essayists themselves; and there are some few of like worth in these present times, but I need not reckon up this overmuch, as methinks I hear Charles Lamb's acquiescence *from his abode where the eternal are.*[6] Let me therefore conclude without let or hindrance the catalogue of whimsies which he wittily brings in support of his bibliopegist preferences. He would have his magazines in the *déshabille* of *half-Russia,* and for the rest he is guided by circumstances, whim, fancy, and those other indispensable ingredients of the incomparable Elian philosophy. In some respects, he claims, *the better a book is, the less it demands from the binding.* Fielding, Smollett, Sterne, and all that class of *self-reproductive* volumes we see perish with less regret because we know copies of them to be 'eterne'. But *where a book is at once both good and rare, the individual almost the species, and when* that *perishes,*

> We know not where is that Promethean torch
> That can its light relume——[7]

[1] *Idylls.* ii.   [2] *Letters.* (Scott Lib. Ed.) 240–42.   [3] *Ib.* 94.   [4] Dowden, *Southey.* 106.
[5] *Detached Thoughts on Books and Reading.*   [6] Shelley, *Adonais.*   [7] *Othello,* v, 2, as quoted by Lamb.

*no casket is rich enough, no casing sufficiently durable, to honour and keep safe
such a jewel.* He instances the *Life and Death of the Duke of Newcastle by his
Duchess,* and other delectable works *which seem hopeless ever to be reprinted;*
as *Sir Philip Sidney, Bishop Taylor,* Milton's *prose works, Fuller;* and all such
writers who have not *endenizened themselves* (*nor perhaps ever will*) *in the
national heart, so as to become stock books. It is good,* he sums up, *to possess
these in durable and costly covers.* On the other hand, he complains that it
would be *mere foppery to trick out in gay apparel* familiar authors like Shakespeare and Milton *unless the first editions;* and he thinks Thomson's *Seasons*
looks best *a little torn and dog's eared,* whilst *how beautiful,* he concludes, *to
a genuine lover of reading are the sullied leaves, and worn out appearance, nay,
the very odour* (*beyond Russia*) of old circulating library copies of *Tom
Jones* or *The Vicar of Wakefield.*[1]

Leigh Hunt[2] liked *a plain, good, old binding,* no matter how old provided
that it was durable, but his *Arabian Nights* he would have *bound in as fine
and flowery a style as possible.* Hartley Coleridge[3] supports Lamb in his
defence of fine dress for *rariora.* For the sole survivor, the member of a
family *that has escaped the trunk-makers and the pastry-cooks,* he would counsel *a little extravagance* in the binding; and he commends, as all good bookmen do, the man who *bestows on a tattered and shivering volume such decent
and comely apparel as may protect it from the insults of the vulgar, and the more
cutting slights of the fair.* Peiresc would have all his books finely bound,
even to fragments and *leaves half eaten,* for, he would say, *the best books when
they fall into unlearned men's hands were pitifully used.* He therefore endeavoured, *that they might be prized at least for the beauty of their binding, and
so escape the danger of the Tobacconist and Grocer,*[4] thus supporting Andrew
Lang's claim that fine binding not only adds grace to the library by
presenting to the eye the cheerful gilded rows of our volumes, but it is also *a
positive economy.*[5] Such examples of protective care and personal whim are
familiar and common and need not be enlarged, for I doubt not that all
bookmen will feel that Austin Dobson[6] has expressed them and their
fancies, when despite the luxurious toggery of his *First Editions* in their
Sheraton Shrine, he turns for real company, as Charles Lamb did, to his
familiars *en négligé*:

> Montaigne with his sheep-skin blistered,
> And Howell the worse for wear,
> And the worm-drilled Jesuit's Horace,
> And the little old cropped Molière—

---

[1] 'Detached Thoughts on Books and Reading.'   [2] 'My Books', *Essays.* (Camelot
Ed.) 292.   [3] 'William Roscoe', *Biographia Borealis.*   [4] *Life.* Gassendi. Trans.
Rand. ii, 255.   [5] *The Library.* 64.   [6] *Poetical Works,* 194.

And the Burton I bought for a florin,
And the Rabelais foxed and flea'd—
For the others I never have opened,
But those are the books I read.

But for those many times we find such great diversity among bindings, special treatment, costume, style, fashion, for particular books, there are as many more wherein the character of the collection hath a uniform plan. Sometimes this is inevitable, as in public libraries, where uniforms are as necessary as in an army. Thus at the British Museum all books are bound in *half morocco*, with cloth sides to match the colour of the leather, which varies for the different regiments: *red* for History, *blue* for Theology, *yellow* for Poetry, and *green* for Natural History. Their distinguishing marks or badges have an equal diversity for purposes of identification: *red* indicates that the book was *purchased*, *blue* that it was acquired under the *Copyright Act*, and *yellow* that it was a gift. At the Bodleian, Theology is dressed in *black*, Commerce in *maroon*, Medicine in *light brown*, Mathematics and Physics in *light green*, History in *dark red*, Poetry in *dark green*, Philology in *light red*, Classics in a *neutral tint*, and Miscellaneous in *dark blue*.[1] In institutional libraries of all kinds, Universities, Schools, Municipalities, Learned Societies, etc., some uniformity is necessary, and many are satisfied with any simple coverture embossed with the arms or name of the institution.

But apart from all such devices for use there is an *ensemble* of charm or dignity to express the innate temper of the collector. Thus Mary Queen of Scots bound all her books in *black morocco*[2] emblazoned with the Lion of Scotland; Louise of Lorraine had a *cabinet* of eighty volumes, at the castle of Chenonceau, bound (mostly by Nicholas Eve) in red, blue, and green morocco and *decorated with brilliant arabesques, or sprinkled with golden lilies;*[3] each of the three daughters of Louis XV had her own library specially and harmoniously bound: Madame Adelaide's in *red*, Madame Sophie's in *citron*, and Madame Victoire's in *green* morocco;[4] Madame de Chamillard, who *attached herself in all things to the Maintenon*, followed the *uncrowned Queen* into retirement, *retreat from vanity*, and gave up her taste for *gilt arabesques and crushed morocco*, and bound all her later acquisitions *à la Janséniste*: plain leather with the simplest line of *blind tooling*.[5] Peiresc had all his books bound in red morocco, his initials or cypher in gold;[6] Colbert's 50,000 printed books were all bound in a special morocco imported for him under a treaty with the Sultan;[7] de Thou favoured *morocco* decorated with rich tooling *à la fanfare*.[8]

[1] Fitzgerald, *The Book-Fancier*. 124. [2] Elton, *Great Book-Collectors*. 106. [3] *Ib*. 107.
[4] Fitzgerald, *op. cit.* 124. [5] Elton, *op. cit.* 195–6. [6] *Ib*. 180. [7] *Ib*. 188. [8] Horne, Binding of Books, 120.

Sir Thomas Wotton bound his books in three styles: one with *small round medallions of Mars and Lucrece*, another in *brown calf* with *black interlacings*, and the third with no decorations save his *armorial stamp with nine quarterings*;[1] Melancthon's books were *rough volumes in stamped pigskin*;[2] all the volumes in Lord Pembroke's library were *uniformly bound in dull red morocco, with a heavily gilt back and a very narrow dentelle round the sides, usually with small fleurons in the angles;*[3] the library of Odorico Pillone, of Casteldardo, in the Venetian State, comprised 170 volumes, for the most part fifteenth- and sixteenth-century *folios*, bound largely in dark *pig-skin, with brass bosses and clasps;* 140 had their edges painted, and 20 their covers *enriched by designs made by the pen, and washed in with Indian ink;*[4] Demetrio Canevari, physician to Pope Urban VIII, inherited a library of books in cameo-bindings;[5] Claude d'Urfé possessed 4,000 books all bound in *green velvet*;[6] Claude Gouffier, Duc de Rounnais, had his books *well clothed* in *painted bindings*;[7] Robert Harley, Earl of Oxford, had his library bound by Eliot and Chapman, at a cost of £18,000, each volume bearing *a rich centre-piece*, of lozenge form, surrounded by a broad, tooled border, a style now known as *Harleian*;[8] the leather was chiefly *red morocco*;[9] Hollis also preferred red morocco;[10] and the Duke of Roxburghe bound his collection of plays in half-morocco with marbled paper sides.[11] J. B. Inglis favoured olive-green morocco with *an Elizabethan gilt framework on the sides, showing an acorn in each angle, the edges of the bindings being flush with the edges of the leaves,*[12] but Samuel Ireland adopted *half-green morocco* so consistently that *contemporary book-collectors not infrequently refer to* his green livery.[13]

V. DEFENCE OF FINE BINDINGS

More opportune to my theme is that passion for fine, luxurious, distinguished bindings which has been formerly bestowed upon books to the admiration of these times, as may be seen in the honour we accord those great craftsmen of France and Germany, the Bozerains, Deseuilles, Deromes, Duvals, Eves, Lafertés, Lemonniers, Le Telliers, Padeloups, Rouettes, Staggmiers, and Walthers, the greatest of all past masters of this art; and those notable English binders Thomas Berthelet, in the sixteenth century, binder and printer to King Henry VIII, and *the first English binder to use gold tooling;*[14] Samuel Mearne, in the seventeenth, binder to King

[1] *Thirty Bindings*. G. D. Hobson. (1926) 32.   [2] Elton, *op. cit.* 90.   [3] Seymour de Ricci, *English Collectors of Books and Manuscripts*. 40.   [4] Horne, *The Binding of Books*. 34.   [5] *Ib.* 92.   [6] Elton, *The Great Book-Collectors*. 94.   [7] *Ib.* 103. [8] Horne, *op. cit.* 198.   [9] Wheatley, *Bookbinding*. 8.   [10] W. C. Hazlitt, *Book-Collector*. 249.   [11] *Ib.* 249.   [12] Seymour de Ricci, *English Collectors of Books and Manuscripts*. 97.   [13] *Ib.* 64.   [14] Davenport, *Byways among English Books*. 34.

Charles II, and inventor of the *Cottage* style of tooling;[1] Roger Payne, in
the eighteenth, and Faulkner, Hayday, Hering, Lewis, Bedford, Edwards
of Halifax, and Fazakerley of Liverpool, in the nineteenth; the masterpieces still created by Rivière, Zaehnsdorf, Roger de Coverley, Morell,
Douglas Cockerell, Sangorski & Sutcliffe, and such recent amateurs as
Sullivan and Cobden-Sanderson; well may he[2] say that *there are binders
who have immortalized themselves*. How that passion has been greater in
France than in England, how it has varied from age to age, in some
supreme, in others debased, and what tastes have prevailed among individuals and peoples I shall presently expatiate.

The coverings of books are commonly reduced into two inclinations,
utilitarian and *æsthetical*. The former I have discussed in a precedent part
of this discourse, and I need do no more than record *en passant* that I find
no mention in any authority of opposition to useful bindings or covers,
though, as I have also shown, some out of sentiment regard a tattered
volume with delight, doubtless looking upon such rags and tatters as the
scars of victory and of long and honourable service (poets *are apt to be
ragamuffins*[3]), and for that cause more graciously to be respected, more
fondly to be enjoyed. But on the other side there are various opinions.
Fine bindings are praised by some, discommended by others; but it is in
a diverse respect. Some would have no distinction of covering lest it
detract from the inside, or *sine qua non*, of a book. The quip (in *Crotchet
Castle*[4]) that *there is nothing more fit to be looked at than the outside of a book*
becomes a fear in the minds of others that books may come to be looked
at rather than read, as those books bound by Monnier which were more
a boudoir than a library;[5] and, as another observer ironically notes,[6] *an
Accidence in an old cover hath no grace in a Court library*. In some such
anxiety Lord Chesterfield advised his son that *due attention to the inside of
books, and due contempt for the outside*, was *the proper relation between a man
of sense and his books*. Of the same mind are several bibliophiles, but it is
no caveat against such particularity of dress as many others, in times past
and present, have thought fit and appropriate for their treasures, as the
French Romantics, whose works *wear ermine, purple, and laurel in an
Olympus of books*:[7]

> Embodied thought enjoys a splendid rest
> On guardian shelves, in emblem costume dressed;[8]

and although some bindings by the richness and rareness added to them

[1] *Ib.* 36.   [2] J. Hill Burton, *Book-Hunter*. 28.   [3] Hill Burton, *Book-Hunter*. 29.
[4] Thomas Love Peacock.   [5] Horne, *The Binding of Books*. 156.   [6] Nicholas
Breton, *Works*. Ed. Kentish-Wright. i, 64.   [7] H. P. du Bois, *Four Private Libraries
of New York*. 33   [8] J. Maccreery, Qt. *Book-Lovers' Anth*. 243.

by time and descent are too precious for general handling, fine bindings
can neither make fine books nor indispose true readers.

VI. CHARACTER AND SYMBOLISM

How far the clothing of a book should express the character of its subject,
author, or collector, hath been discussed at large by many authentic bookmen, as Octave Uzanne, Henri Pène de Bois, Andrew Lang, Hartley
Coleridge, Ambrose Firman, Didot, etc., and in general they conclude
that it is a matter of personal taste, and leave it at that;

> That book in many's eyes doth share the glory,
> That in gold clasps locks in the golden story.[1]

Some there are who disallow personal expression or any departure from
the normal, others argue that books are no more than *notes in the gamut of
plastic and decorative art*.[2] But argue and cavil as they will, whim will have
its say and way, with books as with other things, and, indeed, why should
any man be offended, or take exception at it? Variety is the salt of life:

> The world is so full of a number of things
> I'm sure we should all be as happy as Kings.[3]

I do not deny it, for out of Terrence I say: *homo sum et humani nihil a me
alienum puto*, I am a man and interested in everything human, a bookman
and interested in all bookishness. There is no great fault in this custom
and no such general extravagance, fantastic ambition, novelty for its own
sake, conceit, ostentation, as some suppose. *No one likes sheep's clothing for
his literature*,[4] but overweening pastures in binding are exceptional, and,
as one[5] answers, *some subtle relation there may be, and should be, between the
inside and the outside of a book, between its contents and ornamentation*. He
argues further that no man can produce a *right design* for a book without
knowing the book itself; but ornamentation, he rightly concludes, should
not *make itself too plainly felt in the design* and should not be *allegorical* or
emblematical.

Of attempts to express the character of a book in its binding are many
examples, many of them fantastical; a curious catalogue is given by Percy
Fitzgerald. *A Manual of Woodcarving*, he says, was bound in *wood*; *Tuber-
ville on Hunting in deerskin*; Fox's *Historical Works* in *doeskin*, and Bacon's

---

[1] *Romeo and Juliet*. i, 3.   [2] Henri Pène du Bois, *Four Private Libraries of New York*. 43.
[3] Robert Louis Stevenson, *A Child's Garden of Verses*.   [4] J. H. Burton, *The Book-
Hunter*. 29.   [5] Cobden-Sanderson. Qt. Horne, *The Binding of Books*. 211. 7.

Works in *hogskin*; Apuleius his *Golden Ass* in *ass's skin*. The Duke of Rox-burghe's library contained a collection of tracts respecting Mary Tofts (who pretended to be confined of rabbits) bound in *rabbit-skin*. The Hon. George Napier had a work relating to the celebrated dwarf, Jeffrey Hudson, *bound in a piece of Charles the First's silk waistcoat*; at Perry's sale a copy of the *New Year's Gift*, bound also in a piece of the same King's waistcoat, fetched eight guineas; and Macray (in his *Annals*, p. 67) records yet another instance in a *New Testament* said to be clothed in a like material from the same exalted wardrobe. Mordaunt Cracherode, father of the celebrated book-collector, wore buckskin breeches during a voyage round the world, and a book in his son's collection (now in the British Museum) is *bound in a part of these circumnavigating unmentionables;*[1] Davenport records that there are *plenty* of books *bound by amateur binders and covered with pieces of ladies' dresses,*[2] one in the British Museum, covered by the wife of Wordsworth, in *a piece of green material with white sprays upon it,* which was once a part of her own gown.[3] Horne[4] notes that there are books on Iceland bound in *seal-skin*; that there is a copy of Governor Phillips's *Voyage to Botany Bay* (1789), bound in the skin of the *kangaroo*, and he quotes out of Dibdin a reference to a copy of the *Historical Works* of Charles James Fox, which Jeffrey the bookseller had clothed in *foxskin*. It was to indicate their precious character that those two *Books of the Gospels* which Lanfranc lent to the Monks of St. Albans were *bound in silver and gold, and ornamented with precious stones,*[5] and for a like reason that Duke Federigo of Urbino caused his famous *Bible*, illuminated by a Florentine artist in 1478, to be bound in *gold brocade richly adorned with silver.*[6]

With some qualification such as the need for propriety, seemliness, and the like, I find that most bibliophiles have one and the same opinion in this adventure. It is the book-lover, not the bookbinder, who is the final arbiter: *The book-lover is the artist in bookbinding. He does not read, but he has read his books. He knows them perfectly. The covers that he composes for them shall prove this or prove that he is not a book-lover.*[7] The quality of book-binding is musical,[8] and a library should be composed, according to this authority, so that *every volume is unique in a novel sense: a volume of the printer and bookbinder made a volume of the artistic book-lover;*[9] a library thus formed is *a poem in the strict Greek sense, a composition* whose *expression is absolute, perfect, and definitive.*[10] But if expression in binding is sometimes a *rage which ostentation may have abused,* in the hands of the real *man of letters, the most fanciful bindings are often the emblems of his taste and feelings.*[11] The

[1] *The Book-Fancier.* 121–2.   [2] *Byways among English Books.* 76.   [3] *Ib.* 88.
[4] *The Binding of Books.* 40–1.   [5] Elton, *The Great Book-Collectors.* 27.   [6] *Ib.* 80.
[7] Henri Pène du Bois, *Four Private Libraries of New York.* 39.   [8] *Ib.* 40.   [9] *Ib.* 18.
[10] *Ib.* 19.   [11] D'Israeli, *Cur. of Lit.* i, 8.

books of Grolier, Dibdin quotes[1] out of Egnatio, *seemed to be the counter-part of himself, for neatness and splendour. Every judicious binder even,* Percy Fitzgerald[2] enjoins, *will have the decency to bind his volumes according to their degree and quality,* and so avoid, as another advises,[3] such a sight as he once saw of *a collection of old whitey-brown black-letter ballads, etc., so gorgeously tricked out,* that they reminded him of the *pious liberality* of those Catholics *who dress in silk and gold the images of saints, part of whose saintship consisted in wearing rags and hair-cloth;* of such shocks as that suffered by Charles Lamb when, setting out *to reach down a well-bound semblance of a volume,* in the hope of *a kind-hearted playbook,* he *came bolt upon a withering Population Essay.*[4]

So I shall not o'ershoot myself if I respect symbolical or expressionist binding for a most excellent and comely invention; and if it owns several lapses from the virtuous path of true excellence, such bindings are of some value if they do no more than reveal their inspirers; for *when all is done, whatsoever is not as we are, is not of any worth.*[5] But to convince all I cannot hope, to point alone at some few of the chief examples is that which I aim at.

Horne traces[6] the notion of symbolical bindings to medieval times, and he supports himself out of Dan John Lydgate, a monk of Bury, by the example of some verses which are addressed to the learned monk's translation of Boccaccio's *Falles of Princes* (1554):

> Blacke be thy bondes and thy wede also,
> Thou sorrowefull Booke of matter dysespeyred;
> In Token of thine inward mortall woe,
> Which is so bad it may not be impeyred.

He will have no *cloth of Tissue* or crimson velvet for so sad a chronicle, but it must go *weyle and wepe* like the *monke mowning under his hode.* In ancient Rome there is a like instance when Ovid would have that his *Tristia,* written in the early days of his banishment, was to go in *the guise that became an exile's book,* minus the ornaments which distinguish more fortunate volumes.[7] In such wise have they at all times decked their solemn tomes in sable. *Theology should be solemnly gorgeous,* says Hartley Coleridge;[8] *how absurd,* he exclaims, *to see the works of William Penn in flaming scarlet, and George Fox's 'Journal' in Bishop's purple!* He would have History *ornamented after the Gothic fashion,* Science, *as plain as is consistent with dignity,* and Poetry, *simplex munditiis.* Andrew Lang[9] would give our

---

[1] *Bibliomania.* (1811) 654.   [2] *The Book-Fancier.* 123–4.   [3] H. Coleridge, 'William Roscoe', *Biographia Borealis.*   [4] 'Detached Thoughts on Books and Reading.'
[5] Montaigne, 'Raymond Sebond', *Essays.* Ed. Seccombe. ii, 224.   [6] *Binding of Books.* 210–11.   [7] Ovid. Church. 114.   [8] 'William Roscoe', *Biographia Borealis.*
[9] *The Library.* 65.

old English books, as More's *Utopia*, covers of *stamped and blazoned calf*; Molière and Corneille, the *graceful contemporary style of Le Gascon*, where the pattern of gold recalls that *Point-de-Venise* lace *for which La Fontaine liked to ruin himself*. He would have a novelist of the eighteenth century in a cover *à la fanfare*, after Thouvenin; a *folio* Shakespeare, panelled russia, and English works of the late eighteenth century should be clothed in *the sturdy fashion of Roger Payne*, himself a measured believer in bibliopegic expressionism.

Cobden-Sanderson confessed that Tennyson's line, *grassy barrows of the happier dead*, suggested the bands of daisies with which he decorated a copy of *In Memoriam*, and he tells how he bound *Atalanta in Calydon* after being haunted by the passage in Swinburne's poem recounting Althæa's dream:

> I dreamed that out of this my womb had sprung
> Fire and a fire-brand. . . .
> And I with gathered raiment from the bed
> Sprang, and drew forth the brand, and cast on it
> Water, and trod the flame bare-foot, and crushed
> With naked hand spark beaten out of spark,
> And blew against and quenched it . . .
>   . . . again
> I dreamt, and saw the black brand burst on fire
> As a branch bursts in flower. . . .[1]

These lines, he confesses, *haunted me when I thought of the pattern of the cover, and came out, as will be seen, in the decoration. For the flame I used a seed-pod, and for the leaves a quivering heart, and I blent them together in the form of a brand that bursts on fire, and I set them torch-wise around the margins of the green cover, green for the young life burning away.*[2] In such an effort he comes near to the quality of expression demanded by the romanticists who fought against the traditional formality of the eighteenth century. The art of bookbinding, says one of them,[3] *is to create impressions and evoke images*, by a *more complicated and mysterious* method than *mere representation in conventional or realistic figures. It is not*, he well says, *by the colour of the leather or by a line copied at the music shop that a book of poems may be made expressive in its covers*, any more than *by copying all the leaves of a tree the idea of a tree may be communicated to anybody*. The covers of a well-bound book must be *decorated in conformity* with its *subject, the tone adopted, the effect desired, richly or gracefully, gaily or with tragic severity. Formerly*, he says, *a book was well bound* if it appeared in *Levant morocco of a Grolieresque or Le Gasconesque pattern;* but this was as absurd *as if an edict decreed that if*

---

[1] *Atalanta in Calydon.* (1868) 14–17.   [2] Qt. Horne, *The Binding of Books.* 212–13.
[3] Henri Pène du Bois, *Four Private Libraries of New York.* 40–1.

a woman wished to be dressed well she must wear *blue or green velvet;* on the contrary, *a woman may be well dressed in silk, velvet, damask stuffs, with pompadour flowers, or lily-white lawn, according to the scene wherein she appears, drawing-room, opera, park or library-room;* and so with books.

Octave Uzanne stiffly upholds, in *Les Caprices d'un Bibliophile* and *La Reliure Moderne*, the practice of symbolism. He would use scraps of old brocade, embroidery, Venice velvet, or what not, to achieve his aim; and another of my authorities[1] argues that a covering of some *dead fair lady's train goes well with a romance of Crébillon, and engravings by Marillier. Voici,* says Uzanne,[2] *un cartonnage Pompadour de notre invention.* His *facetiæ* he would bind in the skin of the *boa-constrictor;* fantastic books, as *Gaspard de la Nuit, The Confessions of an English Opium Eater,* the *Poems* of Poe or Gérard de Nerval, in the leathers of China and Japan, with *their strange tints and gilded devices.* Lang saw a new field of taste for the adventurous bibliophile in such imaginings, but Horne[3] feared that the notion had been *carried to an extreme by some designers,* who, *affecting the fashion of the Decadents,* appeared *to work in a spirit akin to that of Arthur Rimbaud's sonnet,* which found *in colours the definite sensations of language.* Didot is more restrained, and, as H. Coleridge will have, with him colours mainly express the character of the book; as the *Iliad* in red, and the *Odyssey* in blue morocco, because the old Greek rhapsodists wore scarlet when they recited the Wrath of Achilles, and blue when they chanted the Return of Odysseus; the writings of great Church dignitaries he would array in violet, those of Cardinals in scarlet, philosophers in black, and poets in *couleur-de-rose.* Such a collector, says Lang, might, were it possible, have dressed Goldsmith's *Poems* in a *coat of Tyrian bloom, satin grain.*

Many bibliophiles take pains to indicate on their bindings descent, status, as Kings, Princes, Noblemen, with emblazonings of heraldry, arms, cyphers, etc. Corporations, schools, clubs, and other institutions, give their books a stamp or symbol of character or ownership; others add mottoes to the same end, as Henry VIII, *Dieu et mon droit* and *Rex in aeternum vive,* and Henri III of France, *spes mea deus.* Grolier added to the elegance of his bindings diverse mottoes as: *Portio mea domine sit in terra viventium,*[4] *O remember my life is wind;* and a third out of *Virgil (Aen.* vi, 743), *Quisque suos patimur manes;*[5] on a copy of the *Vulgate* (1588), he had *Aeque difficulter,* which Horne would render, *the Golden mean is hard.*[6] On the lower boards of Maioli's copy of *Symbolicae Quaestiones,* Achilles Bocchius, Bologna, 1555, he has caused to be stamped the *enigmatical legend, inimici mei mea mihi non me mihi,* which Horne[7] interprets as *possunt inimici mei mea*

---

[1] Andrew Lang, *The Library.* 67.   [2] *Les Caprices d'un Bibliophile.*   [3] *The Binding of Books.* 211–12.   [4] 'Let my portion, O Lord, be in the land of the living.' [5] 'Each of us suffers his own doom.'   [6] *The Binding of Books.* 76–8.   [7] *Ib.* 85.

mihi eripere, non me mihi, my enemies are able to take mine from me, not me from myself. There are those who say what they would sometimes wish unsaid in their mottoes, as Diane de Poitiers, who was thus *hoist with her own Petard.* She was married early to Louis de Brezé, Comte de Maulevrier, and when she became a widow, in 1531, she took for her device an arrow, surrounded by laurels, rising from a tomb, and the inscription, *Sola vivit in illo.*[1] When later the Duc d'Orleans, afterwards Henri II, fell in love with her, this motto became an embarrassment; but, saith one,[2] Diane being of a high spirit found the means *to improve her royal amour* without seeming to abandon the regard *vowed for the memory of her husband.* So she withdrew the tomb and changed the gender of the pronoun in the inscription, *Sola vivit in illa.* Thus without compromising her, the arrow and laurels device remained on her books. On another volume of hers the words, *Consequitur quodcunque petit,*[3] are but an excuse for the elaborate compliment to the King, which follows on the lower board: *Nihil amplius optat.*[4] The books of Marguerite de Valois, Queen to Henry IV, had on their lower cover the legend: *Expectata non eludet.*[5] So whether the covers of books should behave frankly as covers or boldly as both covers and instruments for the expression of their contents I shall not further argue, for here again good taste is sole arbiter, and I can put up no reason why a book that is well and truly bound should not serve both useful purpose and curious expression.

VII. BIBLIOPEGIC DANDYISM

Binding commands most interest when it so expresses a particular personality, temperament or whim, as to be somewhat abnormal, much as a dandy is abnormal among men of fashion; for *the general characteristic of Dandyism is always to produce the unexpected, that which could not logically be anticipated by those accustomed to the yoke of rules.*[6] Octave Uzanne[7] argues, there is a *bibliophilic dandyism,* and Adam Smith, undandified in other things, confessed himself *a beau in his books.*[8] Many examples come from England, but more from France. Henri III of France became a dandy of gloom after the death of the Princess Condé, to whom he was affianced. He sought consolation among his books, and gave them strange covertures, sometimes binding them himself. He was extravagant and an idler, but passed laws against extravagance in his subjects; he forbade furs and

[1] 'She lives alone in that.'   [2] Bauchart, *Les Femmes Bibliophiles de France.* Qt. Horne. *Ib.* 108–9.   [3] 'She obtains whatever she seeks.'   [4] 'She desires nothing more.'   [5] 'If expected she will not play false.' Horne, *op. cit.* 123.   [6] J. A. Barbey D'Aurevilly, *Of Dandyism.* Trans. Ainslie. 22–3.   [7] *The Book-Hunter in Paris.* xxii.
[8] Percy Fitzgerald, *The Book-Fancier.* 99.

heavy chains on garments, but allowed *gilt edges and arabesques* on books. *His taste combined the gloomy and the grotesque, his clothes and his bindings alike being covered with skulls and cross-bones, and spangles to represent tears, with other conventional emblems of sorrow.*[1] It was to compensate bibliophiles for this period of mourning that, as some believe, either Nicholas or Clovis Eve invented the radiancy of binding *à la fanfare*, which, says Slater,[2] *resolved itself finally into a profusion of small flourished ornaments, so closely worked together* that they looked like *ethereal sprays, scrolls, and showers of golden rain.*

Huysmans make Des Esseintes, in *A Rebours*,[3] a beau of books. He would have his volumes in exotic bindings, for his relentless egoism, which was ever seeking new sensations and fantastic experiences, craved only what was unique among books, and what at all times expressed his own variable and restless moods. One of his books was *bound in wild ass's skin, first glazed under a hydraulic press, dappled in water-colour with silver clouds and provided with end-papers of old China silk, the pattern of which, now rather dim with age, had that grace of faded splendour that Mallarmé celebrated in a singularly delightful poem;* and when he set out to bedeck that poet's *L'Après-midi d'un Faune*, he gave it a covering of Japanese felt, *as white as curdled milk*, fastened with two cords, one pink, the other black, which met behind the binding and gave a hint of subtle colouring, suggesting, he would argue, love and abandonment, *the discreet intimation of the Faun's regrets, a vague foreshadowing of the melancholy that succeeds the transports of passion and the appeasement of the senses excited to frenzy by desire;*[4] but find more about him under *Bibliomania*. Oscar Wilde took up this idea in making Dorian Gray *procure from Paris no less than nine large-paper copies of the first edition of A Rebours*, which he had bound in *different colours, so that they might suit his different moods and the changing fancies of a nature over which he seemed, at times, to have entirely lost control.*[5]

Lucian de Rosny had books in his collection bound in *the skins of cat, garnet-coloured and buff, crocodile, mole, seal, fur of the Canadian black wolf, royal tiger, otter, white bear, sole, and rattlesnake.*[6] Henry VIII had his favourite volumes *plated with gold and silver and curiously embossed;*[7] Melissenda, Countess of Anjou, in the twelfth century, had a *Psalter* made for her, and the sides were of *carved ivory set with turquoises;*[8] Catherine de Medici's books were bound in white calf, powdered with golden flowers.[9] Diane de Poitiers, when Henri II became her lover, caused her copy of the Dialogues of Bartholomæus Camerarius, *De Praedestinatione*, Paris, 1556,

[1] Elton, *The Great Book-Collectors*. 107.   [2] *Romance of Book-Collecting*. 154.
[3] English Ed. Paris (1926) 263.   [4] *Ib.* 267   [5] *Dorian Gray*. (1910) 177.   [6] Fitzgerald, *Book-Fancier*. 123.   [7] Collier, *Eccl. Hist*. ii, 307.   [8] Madan, *Books in MS.* 49.
[9] Slater, *Romance of Book-Collecting*. 152.

to be covered with *white morocco*, with her bows and arrows and cipher of two D's interlaced with an H, tooled in black, and other books of hers were caparisoned in this pleasant foppery.[1] Marguerite de Valois was also a *belle* of books; her volumes, clothed in the manner of Clovis Eve and, some argue, bound by him, are decorated with a series of ovals, in the centre of which are flowers, or sprigs of oak or pomegranate, surrounded with palm-branches, the central oval of the upper cover having a shield charged with three *fleurs-de-lys* on a bend, and the lower cover bearing her motto, as I have shown in its place.

What more dandified than the library of King John of France at the *Louvre*,[2] with its Life of *Saint Louis* in a *chemise blanche*, and another in *cloth of gold; St. Gregory* and *Sir John Mandeville* in *indigo velvet, John of Salisbury* in a *silk coat and long girdle*, and most of the *Arabians* in *tawny silk ornamented with white roses and wreaths of foliage;* or that of Cardinal Wolsey, who had *numerous copies of the choicest books, bound in velvet of all colours, embossed with gold or silver, and studded with precious stones.*[3] Queen Elizabeth loved beautiful bindings all her days, and she would go so far as to make covers for her favourite books with her own hands. Several examples are preserved in the Bodleian: one such is her own translation from the French of *The Miroir or Glasse of the synnefull Soule*, which she bound when but eleven years of age in rich cloth with ornamental borders of gold and silver thread, her own initials in the centre on a ground of blue silk.[4] The books in *her gallery at Whitehall made a gallant show of MSS. and classics in red velvet, with clasps and jewelled sides, the French and Italian books standing by in morocco and gold;*[5] but her chief affection was for *embroidered and velvet bindings*, as Paul Hentzner[6] records in his *Itinerarium*, which he wrote after his visit to Whitehall in 1598: velvet in different colours, red dominant, with clasps of gold and silver, jewelled with pearls and precious stones. Her *Psalter* written by Esther Inglis, the famous calligrapher, was bound in crimson velvet set with pearls;[7] and her copy of the *Meditationum ac precationum Christianarum libellos*, Lyons, 1570, says Horne, had angle-pieces enamelled in colours, with a crowned rose, the initials E. R. and other ornaments, so exquisite in workmanship as to make the volume worthy to be placed beside the miniatures of Peter Oliver, and some jewellers of the time. It was belike as a compliment to the Queen's taste that Archbishop Parker, when sending her his book, *De Antiquitate Britannicae Ecclesiae*, was prompted to have the copy bound in green velvet, upon the sides of which were representations of *a paled deer-park*, with a rose-bush, snakes and various flowers, elaborately embroidered in gold and silver

---

[1] Horne, *The Binding of Books.* 109.   [2] Elton, *The Great Book-Collectors.* 60–1.
[3] Dibdin, *Bibliomania.* (1811) 299–300.   [4] Macray, *Annals.* 66.   [5] Elton, *op. cit.* 113.   [6] Qt. *Ib.* 174–5.   [7] Macray, *Annals of the Bodleian.* 62.

thread and silks of diverse colours.[1] Georges de la Motthe, a French
refugee, gave her, in 1586, a French *Panegyrical Poem* bound in a rich cover,
on either side of which are *brilliant bosses* protected by glass. For years it
was believed that these decorations were wrought of the feathers of the
humming bird, but they are now known to be of enamel.[2] This same
principle of dandyism is inculcated by Dean Swift in his *Battle of the Books*
when he ordains that the *Book of Fate*, which Mercury lays before Jupiter,
shall have covers of *celestial Turkey leather, clasps of silver double gilt*, and
such paper as *here on earth might pass for vellum*. In every age since the invention of books it has had its representatives, until times present when the
love of finery is expressed in handsome printing rather than magnificence
of coverture.

VIII. BOOKS BOUND IN HUMAN SKIN

Many bibliopegic dandies are so perverse that they are well pleased with
nothing but what is ordinarily inaccessible to others. If *calf* or *morocco* is
the fashion they are all out for *seal* or *shark*; they set the skins of *pythons*
and *cobras* against the popularity of *sheep* and *pig*; and the ivory loveliness
of vellum is translated out of its simplicity by strange dyes. Some few
amongst them seek to have at least one book bound in *human skin*, which
they immoderately extol above all others. This taste is nought for queasy
stomachs, but it gives a strange, and as some would have, an unholy
delight to those who find satisfaction in unusual ideas and quaint and
exotic experiences. Recent students of psychology class this taste among
aberrations of the mind, and some, as Bloch, refer it to sexual fetichism.
The female breast, for instance, is *a natural physiological fetich for the male
sex*, but apart from this normal attraction *there exists a remarkable variety of
breast fetichists, who employ the breast separated from the body for the binding
of books;*[3] and he quotes out of Witkowski's book that there are *certain
bibliomaniacs and erotomaniacs who have books bound with women's skin taken
from the region of the breast, so that the nipple forms a characteristic swelling on
the cover.*[4] There are some who doubt the existence of such bindings,
brushing aside the stories of them as they would the anecdotes of anglers,
sailors' yarns or old wives' tales. 'Tis something, I confess, to believe such
tales, yet the existence of books bound in the skin of men is well attested
by many reliable observers. But before I set out my facts let me deal with
what is legendary, lest it obscure what is true.

    In all periods of intense excitement, such as wars, revolutions, famines

---

[1] Elton, *op. cit.* 178.   [2] Macray, *op. cit.* 464.   [3] Iwan Bloch, *Sexual Life of our
Time.* (1909) 620.   [4] *Tétoniana.* (Paris, 1898) 35.

and pestilences, rumour plays a leading part in the distribution of news, as well we know who lived through the perils and anxieties of the Great War. Many there were in those days who believed that in the tragic autumn of 1914 great armies of Russians were transported from Archangel to the north of Scotland and thence by rail to the south of England to be shipped to France for the relief of our hard-pressed forces then falling back before the Germans in what looked like an irrecoverable retreat. Later it was recorded that our troops before Mons were under the special protection of hosts of Angels which had been seen by many of our soldiers; and still later, which is more to our purpose, it was reported in our newspapers that because of the shortage of fats and oils the Germans had organized a great factory where they transmuted the bodies of their own and their enemies' dead into those essential materials of life. Such tales are current in times of tribulation, and they are so neatly woven into the fabric of all the records that it is impossible to say where history begins and legend ends. Well may some reliable authorities announce that there is little difference between one and the other.

That human skin has been tanned in modern and remote times is now well authenticated. It is as amenable to the processes of tannery as the hide of any other animal, but there are marked differences in quality between skin and skin, some being crude and harsh to the touch, others soft and glossy; and few of my observant readers will be surprised to learn that the hides vary in thickness between a sixth and a seventieth of an inch.[1] Tanning increases the thickness and turns a tough skin into a *fine-grained* and soft leather. In appearance, Davenport[2] gives out, it resembles *calf*, but *it is difficult to get entirely rid of the hair;* another authority claims that it is more like *sheep* with a firm and close texture, soft to the touch, and susceptible of a fine polish; still another says it is porous like the hide of a pig. I can support this opinion out of my own observation of a piece of human leather from a hide tanned in London about thirty years ago, and now in the possession of Zaehnsdorf. This specimen resembles a soft pigskin. It is nearly an eighth of an inch thick, but Mr. Edwin Zaehnsdorf contends that the grain resembles morocco rather than pig. To make a usable leather manskin must be *saturated for several days in a strong solution of alum, Roman vitriol, and common salt, dried in the shade, and dressed in ordinary fashion.*[3]

The earliest reference I can find to the tanning of a human skin is in the legend of Marsyas, who imprudently challenged Apollo to a musical contest, and, failing, paid the agreed penalty of suffering himself to be flayed alive. Some say his skin was preserved in the form of a bladder or football, or, as others believe, a bottle: *they may skin me alive*, said Ctesippus, *if only*

[1] Villon, *The Leather Industry.*   [2] *The Book.* 180.   [3] *The Footwear Organiser,* June 1925.

my skin is made at last, not like that of Marsyas, into a leathern bottle, but into a piece of virtue.[1] An industrious legend of the days of the French Revolution tells how the bodies of aristocrats were sent to a tannery at Meudon, where their skins were turned into leather, and used for the binding of books as well as for other purposes. One of the most memorable of these tales·is that recorded of a pair of breeches made for a Frenchman whose servant girl had been executed for theft. This ingenious moralist never tired of denouncing the girl, and after each tirade he would slap his buttocks with great content, babbling: 'But here she is, the rogue: here she is!'

In 1684 Sir Robert Viner, Bart., that loyal Alderman of London, gave to Bodley's Library *a tanned human skin, together with a human skeleton and the dried body of a negro boy.*[2] William Harvey presented the College of Physicians with a tanned human skin, and there are specimens also at the University of Basle and the Physiological Museum of the Lycée at Versailles. At the American Centennial Exhibition a pack of playing cards made of human skin was exhibited. Villon, in his work on *The Leather Industry*, says that, in the eighteenth century, skins of paupers were used for children's shoes in Tewkesbury, Massachusetts, but that the custom was stopped by a legislative act which made the sale of human skins punishable by five years' imprisonment. But the most romantic story of the kind is that of General John Ziska of Bohemia, who *would have a drum made of his skin when he was dead, because he thought the noise of it would put his enemies to flight,*[3] as the noise of his fame did whilst he was alive.

Having thus established that human hides have been tanned, and that the hides are usable, it requires no ingenuity to extend its use to other purposes, and, having regard, as the lawyers say, to the close relationship between books and men, their humane behaviour, etc., I find the application of this sort of leather to books a logical if *macabre* enterprise. The development of this practice was encouraged in France by economic as well as temperamental circumstances. The art of bookbinding *disappeared during the revolutionary tempest*, saith one,[4] *and books were bound in human skin;* another authority[5] records that *one offspring of the horrors of the French Revolution was this grim humour of binding books with the skin of human beings;* and everyone remembers Carlyle's remark quoted in *Dr. Claudius,* that *the French nobles laughed at Rousseau's theories, but that their skins went to bind the second edition of his book.*[6] I could catalogue many more statements of the kind, but *sufficit,* for they cannot be supported by evidence,

[1] Plato, *Euthydemus.* Jowett. i, 210.   [2] Macray, *Annals.* 154.   [3] Burton, *Anat. of Mel.* Bohn Ed. i, 38. See also Carlyle, *Frederick the Great.* ix, 4.   [4] Philomneste Junior, *Bibliomania in the Present Day.* (1880) 16.   [5] Percy Fitzgerald, *Book-Fancier.* 122.   [6] Qt. *Book-Lore.* i, 125.

and many reliable authorities, including Sanson, the State Executioner, in his *Diary*, have disproved them. So if the tale endures we may conclude that it is because most people prefer legend to history: they believe best what they like best to believe.

Of books bound in human skin there are many examples in both public and private collections. In the Carnavalet Museum, Paris, Cyril Davenport[1] saw a copy of the *Constitution* of 1793 bound in the skin of a revolutionary; Dibdin notes a specimen from the library of the famous collector Dr. Askew, but he forgets to name the book; another historian says that at Marlborough House there is a book bound in the skin of Mary Putnam, a Yorkshire witch.[2] Percy Fitzgerald has several examples: that of the report of the trial and execution of Corder, who murdered Maria Martin at the Red Barn, bound in the skin of the murderer, which was tanned for the purpose by a surgeon of Bury St. Edmunds. He also records the sonnets of a Russian poet bound in the skin of his own leg, which had been amputated after a hunting accident, for *presentation to the lady of his heart;* and, finally, he reports how a collector was shown several volumes by a bookseller on St. Michael's Hill, Bristol, which had been sent for repair from the Bristol Law Library. *They were all bound in human skin, specially tanned for the purpose,* the leather having been obtained from *local culprits, flayed after execution.*[3] The *Journals* of the brothers de Goncourt have a reference to *an English virtuoso who had his books bound in human skin.*[4]

But our own people are not alone in this taste. The French astronomical writer, Camille Flammarion, once complimented a handsome countess who possessed beautiful shoulders on the charm of her skin. When she died she made arrangements for the skin on her back and shoulders to be tanned and sent to Flammarion in memory of his admiration for its recent wearer. The astronomer used a portion of it to bind one of his most famous books, *Ciel et Terre.* Another account states that some years ago an official of the School of Medicine at Paris had the skin of Campi, an assassin who was executed, tanned and used to bind the documents relating to his *post-mortem* examination.[5] André Leroy secured some small portions of the skin of the poet, Delille, with which he inlaid the sumptuous binding of a copy of the *Georgics.* Other French authors, including Alfred de Musset, have shown a preference for this kind of leather, and I doubt not that in many countries the taste for manskin bindings could be traced; but as I am not writing a treatise on this subject I shall end with the most recent instance I have been able to discover. In the year 1891 a doctor instructed Zaehnsdorf to bind a copy of Holbein's *Dance of Death* in the skin of a woman. The skin, which I have described above, was tanned by

[1] *The Book.* 180.   [2] Charles Gerring, *Notes on Bookbinding.* 19.   [3] *Book-Fancier.* 122–3.   [4] Qt. Saintsbury, *French Novel.* ii, 461   [5] *Book-Lore.* i, 125.

Sweeting of Shaftesbury Avenue, and the craftsmen who *covered* and *lettered* the volume are still living.[1] Human hair was appropriately used for the *headbands* in place of silk. It is not known where this book now rests, but it is believed to be in America.

[1] 1928.

Part XIX

THE MISFORTUNES OF BOOKS

I. TRIALS AND TRIBULATIONS

The trials and tribulations of books are equalled only by the trials and tribulations of mankind; their sufferings are identical with those of their creators, and if they live longer they are not immune from decay and death. They have been beaten and burnt, drowned, tortured, imprisoned, suppressed, executed, censored, exiled, reviled, condemned, buried; they are overworked and underworked, misused and maltreated in every manner known to fate and chance and the most ingenious of miscreants and misguided zealots. Jovian set fire to the Library at Antioch, as *part of his revenge against the Apostate;* and in many a war, the Eltons quote out of an *ancient bibliophile,* books have been dispersed abroad, *dismembered, stabbed, and mutilated; buried in the earth or drowned in the sea, and slain by all kinds of slaughter: how much of their blood the warlike Scipio shed: how many on the banishment of Boethius were scattered like sheep without a shepherd.*[1] The library of Matthias Corvinus, King of Hungary, containing 50,000 volumes, was destroyed by the Turks when they took Buda. *The janissaries tore off the metal coverings from the rarer MSS., and tossed others aside;* thus it came about that the only known copy of *Heliodorus,* from which all our editions of *Charicles* come, was found in an *open gutter.* Some books were burned, others hacked, maimed and trodden under foot.[2] The Archbishop Juvenal des Ursins, who died in the fifteenth century, had a fine library, but only one volume survived to our times. It was a noble *missal* on vellum, full of choice miniatures, and it came into the possession of Prince Soltikoff, and later was bought for 36,000 francs by Firmin-Didot, who gave it to the City of Paris in the year 1861, and it finally perished in the fires of the Commune.[3]

It is an ordinary thing for books to be lost, to fade away as though they had never been,

[1] Elton, *Great Book-Collectors.* 7.   [2] *Ib.* 82–4.   [3] Elton, *Great Book-Collectors.* 101

You and I will never read that volume.
Guido Reni, like his own eye's apple
Guarded long the treasure-book and loved it.
Guido Reni dying, all Bologna
Cried, and the world cried too, 'Ours the treasure!'
Suddenly, as rare things will, it vanished;[1]

but more often they have been so misused and neglected that they become
lost, *not always imprisoned in libraries, but rotting in oblivion*,[2] hidden, buried
in forgotten lumber rooms, unused attics, dark cellars of abbeys, monasteries, old churches, muniment chambers; and in lonely manor houses,
lofts, barns, old chests. There are innumerable instances, but I shall do no
more here than recall those 40,000 fragments of *Jewish 'superseded' literature*,
including fragments of the Hebrew *Ecclesiasticus*, discovered among some
pestiferous wrack in Egypt, by Dr. Solomon Schechter, and carried by him
to the University of Cambridge Library.[3] Books lie buried in great
libraries, as so many of our bibliographers have discovered, and even in
graves, many good men and even good bookmen desiring to have a
favourite volume buried with them; St. Columba thus brought his *Gospels
of the Church* to Derry, from Tours, where it had lain on the breast of St.
Martin a hundred years.[4] Nothing so familiar as these records of rare finds,
and you will hear more of them in the section of Book-Hunting. Here
I point at some of the stranger adventures of books, their hairbreadth
escapes from destruction; for how they have played hide-and-seek with
time, been lost and found, centuries intervening, is miraculous. It was a
miracle, Janin[5] claims, that the works of Aristotle were rescued from a
dark cellar where they had lain forgotten for years. But even then their
adventures were not ended, for they were bought by Appelicon, whose
library was seized by Sylla, and carried from Athens to Rome.

A like story I find in *Spence*,[6] how a lost manuscript of *Livy* was found
and lost again. During the great fire in the Seraglio at Constantinople,
some pieces of furniture, and, amongst the rest, several books, were flung
into the street. The Secretary of the French Embassy came there to witness
the conflagration, and as he threaded his way through the crowd, he saw
a man with a large volume, which he held open but obviously could not
read. The Secretary peeped over the page, saw at once that it was a MS.
of *Livy*, and upon peeping further, found that it had the *Second Decade*, as
well as the *first*, and might perchance have had all the lost books. He
offered the man a handsome reward if he would hide the book beneath
his robe, and follow him with it to his lodgings. The man agreed, but they

[1] Browning, 'One Word More', *Men and Women*.   [2] D'Israeli, *Cur. of Lit*. i, 32.
[3] Stewart, *Francis Jenkinson*. 85.   [4] Elton, *op. cit*. 16.   [5] *Le Livre*. xxiii.
[6] *Anecdotes*. 62.

were separated in the confusion and the Secretary lost forever the chance of recovering a great literary treasure.

Sometimes whole libraries have been mislaid, as that of Sir Kenelm Digby. When the troubles of the Rebellion drove him into exile he carried his books with him; but upon his return to England he could not fetch them back and they were confiscated by the French King, who sold them for 10,000 crowns. Only two of these volumes are now known to exist: they are *Verses in Praise of Col. John Digby* and *Peregrinations of Sidnam Poynes*, and both rest in the National Library at Paris.[1] It has sometimes happened that manuscripts have been discovered *in the last agonies of existence*, D'Israeli[2] records, and he tells again how Papirius Masson found, in ' house of a bookbinder of Lyons, the works of *Agobart*, on the point of being worked into the bindings of newer books, a common destiny of many old manuscripts and incunabula. Another man of letters was less fortunate, for he had reported to him a page of the *Second Decade of Livy* in the drum of a *battledore*, and hastening to the maker of battledores, he arrived only to find that *the man had finished the last page of Livy—a week before!* But the adventures of *Livy* would fill a volume.

Our historians are full of such stories, but among them all there is none more memorable than that of Tischendorf's recovery of the oldest manuscript of the *New Testament*, now called the *Codex Sinaiticus*. It is like one of those poetical fictions in which men believed to be dead, killed in the wars or lost at sea, return to their homes with great riches to live happy ever afterwards; or of sublunary spirits that can change the laws of nature, *sistere aquam fluviis, et vertere sidera retro*, etc.[3] But that this story is not false is clearly set forth both in *Madan*[4] and *Prothero*,[5] and in other trustworthy places.

In the middle part of last century Constantine Tischendorf was in the first rank of Biblical exegetists. For the good of his work on the *Greek Testament* he journeyed to the lands of the Holy Scriptures in order to confirm and augment his researches. In April 1844 he started out on his first *mission littéraire*, and in a while arrived at the Convent of St. Catherine, which reposes at the foot of Mount Sinai. *There, in the middle of the hall, as he crossed it, he saw a basket full of old parchment leaves on their way to the burning, and was told that two baskets had already gone! Looking at the leaves more closely, he perceived that they were parts of the Old Testament in Greek* of a very ancient character. The like was never seen before.

Tischendorf could scarce moderate his excitement, for he would not only arrest the burning but possess the manuscript, and he could not well

[1] Macray, *Annals*. 79–80. [2] *Cur. of Lit*. i, 34. [3] *Aeneid*. iv, 489.' Stop rivers, and turn the stars backwards in their course.' [4] *Books in Manuscript*. 111–13. [5] *Memoir of Henry Bradshaw*. 92–9.

do either without raising the suspicion of the monks as to the value of the rest, and their hope of some private gain. With dissembled zeal he induced them to reprieve this manuscript from dissolution by fire, but when he desired to take it away for further examination they obstinately refused to let him have more than *forty-three leaves*. He could get no more out of them, and his arguments could neither keep them in Cimmerian darkness nor yet open their eyes, so he returned to Germany with his forty-three precious leaves, which he edited under the title of the *Codex Frederico-Augustanus*, in compliment to the Saxon King, and then deposited them in the Library of Leipzig. The provenance of the manuscript he kept to himself, for he was in good hope of recovering the whole of it, and without these cautions he might have aroused the hunting instinct of others and thus been forestalled. In 1853 he again journeyed to Sinai, but he could find no trace of the *codex* save a few pages of *Genesis*, so returned disconsolate. A few years later he retraced his steps eastwards, under the patronage of the Czar, who was then *popular in the East as the protector of the Oriental Churches*. He arrived again at Sinai in February 1859.

Once more it seemed that he was to be disappointed, and he decided to depart, ordering his Bedouin servants to make ready, whilst he took a farewell walk with the steward of the House. This done the steward then invited him into a room, where the talk turned upon MSS., in the course of which he remarked: *I, too, have read a Septuagint*, and thereupon produced out of a wrapping of red cloth the MS. which Tischendorf had sought for so many years. Tischendorf begged permission to carry it to Cairo, where he could transcribe it. The steward raised no objection, provided that the permission of the Prior could be obtained. But the Prior had himself just left for Cairo on his way to Constantinople. A messenger was sent after him and in nine days returned with the necessary permission. Tischendorf made his transcription. But he was loth to part with the MS., and eventually conceived the idea of begging the volume as a gift to the Emperor of Russia. This last ruse succeeded and he carried the precious work away with him and deposited it in the Library at St. Petersburg. But the adventures of the *Codex Sinaiticus* were not yet ended, for, in 1862, one Simonides, a *Graeculus esuriens*, who had been convicted by Tischendorf of dealing in forged MSS., gave out that the *Codex Sinaiticus* was a forgery made by himself when a young man living at Mount Athos. A great argument followed in which some took one side and some the other. All was confusion, until Henry Bradshaw, our own great bibliographer of the University of Cambridge, came forward and established the originality of the *Codex* by proving, from internal evidence, that if Simonides had written such a book as he pretended, that book could not be identical with the *Codex Sinaiticus*.

Of hairbreadth escapes from total loss I find so many examples that it would take a great volume to relate them. I can therefore make but a selection which you may, if you love books (and I would have none else as my reader), take hold of for your peace. Read *Macray* for much comfortable news to this end, as that story of the almost complete restoration of the missing pages of the Bodleian copy of Fust and Schoeffer's *Vulgate Bible*, of 1642, which had been purchased in 1750. The copy was imperfect, many pages were missing and several restored in MS. In that condition the book remained until the year 1818, when the library received the Canonici Collection from Venice. Among some fragments found in one of the boxes were fourteen leaves of a *Bible*, which were at once recognized as part of the missing leaves from their own copy, which they were thus enabled to complete with the exception of four leaves.[1] So be not discouraged (O well-deserving bibliophiles), the perils to which your beloved books are subjected do not always end in disaster: fate may be often against them, yet it is sometimes in their favour. So to your further content, I'll tell you a story.[2]

Upon Midsummer's Eve, 1626, a cod-fish was brought to Cambridge Market and cut up for sale. In the cutting up of it there was found in the maw of the fish a thing which was hard, and proved to be a book in twelves, bound in parchment. It was drawn out of the belly of the fish with the garbage. The leaves were congealed with a jelly, and, upon being taken out, the mass gave off *an ancient and fish-like smell*, but, after a washing, it was seen to be a book, and those standing about looked upon it with wonder and admiration. Benjamin Prime, the Bachelor's Beadle, who was present at the opening of the fish, carried the book to Dr. Samuel Ward, Master of Sidney Sussex College, who took special notice of it, afterwards describing the discovery of this literary Jonah in a letter to Archbishop Usher. The leaves were carefully opened, and it was found to contain three Treatises entitled: *A Preparation for Death; the Treasure of Knowledge; A mirror, or Looking Glass to know thyself by, a Brief Instruction to teach one willing to die not to fear Death*. Dr. Ward had parts read to him and he *very well liked* what he heard, thinking it probably *a special admonition to us at Cambridge*. He thought the book must have been made in King Henry the Eighth's time *when the six articles were a-foot;* but Anthony Wood, in his *Athenae Oxonienses*, asserts that the author was Richard Tracy, a zealous Protestant, and that it was published in 1540, and dedicated to Thomas, Lord Cromwell. The book was eventually reprinted, under the title of *Vox Piscis, or the Book of the Fish, containing Three Treatises which were found in the belly of a Cod-fish, in Cambridge market, on Midsummer Eve last,*

[1] Macray, *Annals.* 233. [2] From Davis, *Olio.* 11–12, and *Dict. of Anec.* (1809) i, 189–90.

1626. In this reprint the editors erroneously ascribe the authorship to John Frith. Commenting on this strange present from the sea, Fuller saith: *The Wits of the University made themselves merry thereat; one (Thomas Randolph) making a long copy of verses thereon, whereof of this distich I remember:*

> If fishes thus do bring us books, then we
> May hope to equal Bodley's library.[1]

If we may believe the many fabulous tales which abound in our religious histories, books have had even stranger adventures than that recorded of the *Fish Book*. To this purpose there is the story of the *Gospels of St. Cuthbert*. The book was written in the year 688, and for close upon two centuries the monks of Lindisfarne reckoned it their most precious possession. When the Danes invaded that coast and burned down the Abbey, the monks of St. Cuthbert, who had hidden the Gospels in the holy man's tomb, went forth to seek a new habitation, carrying with them the Saint's body in an ark and the book in a chest. They sought to cross over to Ireland, where they hoped to re-establish their brotherhood in safety, but they were held up by a great storm. Their ship was driven back on the English coast and the book in its chest was washed overboard. Some time after, whilst sailing up the Solway Firth, they espied the lost work *shining in its golden cover* on the sandy beach. It was rescued and received back into their company with joy and thanksgiving, and for the next hundred years and more it accompanied the members of their order in all their wanderings, for during all that time they had no settled home. In 995 it found a resting place on the coffin of St. Cuthbert in the then newly built church at Durham, and remained there until early in the twelfth century, when on the restoration of the Abbey of Lindisfarne it was taken back to its first home, where it rested in peace until the outbreak of vandalism which sullied the dissolution of the monasteries, when it suffered the common experience of so many fine volumes and other precious objects. It was ravished of its golden covers, but by good fortune it escaped entire destruction, and finally came into the possession of that good bibliophile and protector of fair books, Sir Robert Cotton, later finding apotheosis among its peers, in the great and safe harbourage of the British Museum.[2]

---

[1] *Worthies of England.* That fishes are neither averse from swallowing printed matter nor capable of digesting it is corroborated by Admiral T. T. Jeans in his *Reminiscences*, where he tells how a lieutenant of H.M.S. *Volage*, then cruising with other men-of-war in the West Indies, was informed of his promotion two days in advance of the mail, by the discovery of a copy of *The Times* in the belly of a shark caught and hauled aboard her sister ship *Ruby*. The explanation suggested by the Admiral was that the mailboat had recently passed that way and some passenger had thrown overboard the paper, which one of the sharks which usually follow ships in those seas had swallowed.   [2] Elton, *Great Book-Collectors.* 18.

Having in these preliminaries shown you how adventurous are the lives of books in general, I may now proceed to particularize.

II. BOOKS LOST AND FOUND

To such extremities, risks, dangers, were our ancient classics put that, Isaac D'Israeli declares,[1] they *had a very narrow escape from total annihilation.* It is a marvel that any survive, and as it is, many have perished, and many we possess are but fragments. He has a lamentable narration of how *the most elegant compositions of classic Rome were converted into the psalms of a breviary, or the prayers of a missal;* because vellum was rare, *ignorance and barbarism* seized on those previous works and *industriously defaced pages once imagined to be immortal. Livy* and *Tacitus* thus suffered *to preserve the legend of a saint, and immortal truths were converted into clumsy fictions.* The bigger the book the quicker its destruction. Large pages more *profitably repaid their destroying industry,* furnishing as they did ampler scope for superscription. Thus a *Livy* or a *Diodorus* was preferred to the smaller books of *Cicero* or *Horace;* and some allow that *Juvenal, Persius,* and *Martial* have come down to us entire, rather than more sedate works, because these pious destroyers had a taste for *classical obscenities;* and *not long ago, at Rome,* he concludes, *a part of a book of Livy was found, between the lines of a parchment but half effaced, on which they had substituted a book of the Bible,* and in like circumstances came the more recent discovery of Cicero's *De Republica.* Poggio Bracciolini, a mighty rescuer of fair volumes, found copies of *Quintilian, Asconius* and *Flaccus* neglected in the monastery of St. Gall.[2] *The books,* he said, *were by no means housed as they deserved, but were all in a dark and noisome place at the foot of a tower, into which one would not cast a criminal condemned to death.*[3]

Among the instances of the recovery of manuscripts given by Isaac D'Israeli I take these for further evidence. We owe *Tacitus* to a copy found in a monastery in Westphalia; the original MS. of Justinian's *Code* was found accidentally by the Pisans when they took a city in Calabria, *that vast code of laws had been unknown from the time of that Emperor;* Montaigne's *Journal* of his travels in Italy was discovered by a Prebendary of Périgord at the Château de Montaigne, hidden away in *an old worm-eaten coffer,* which had long *held papers untouched by the incurious generations of Montaigne;* D'Israeli himself found *a considerable portion* of Lady Mary Wortley Montague's letters *in the hands of an attorney.*

But you have not yet heard the worst, or the best, for it is his relation,

---

[1] *Cur. of Lit.* i, 28–9.   [2] Merryweather, *Bibliomania in the Middle Ages.* 39–40
[3] Elton, *Great Book-Collectors.* 65.

out of *Colomiès*, of the rescue of the original *Magna Charta* from imminent destruction.[1] Sir Robert Cotton was one day at his tailor's, where he saw an ancient document which the thrifty tradesman was about to cut up for use as tape-measures. Upon examination the MS. proved to be the original *Magna Charta* which King John had signed, with all its appendages of seals and signatures. Sir Robert bought the *singular curiosity* for a trifle, thus restoring that which was *given over for lost*, and which, but for his quick wit, would in a few moments have been lost beyond all restoring. Whether this be a tale or not, the original *Magna Charta* was preserved in the Cottonian Library. *It exhibits marks of dilapidation*, but whether from the *invisible scythe of time, or the humble scissors of the tailor*, he leaves to *archaeological inquiry*.

Sir Thomas Browne, in his *Musaeum Clausum* or *Bibliotheca Abscondita*,[2] has a record of the *Life and Death of Avicenna*, confirming the account of his death by *taking nine clysters together in a fit of Colick; and not as Marius the Italian Poet delivereth, by being broken on the Wheel*. The book was left by Benjamin of Tudela, as he travelled from Saragossa to Jerusalem, in the hands of Abraham Jarchi, a famous Rabbi, of Lunet near Montpelier, and found in a vault when the walls of that city were demolished by Louis XIII. When the library of Corvinus was destroyed by the Turks at the sacking of Buda, some of the books were carried into neighbouring villages and about four hundred were piled up in a deserted tower, and there protected by the seal of the Grand Vizier. For many years attempts were made by various scholars to recover what remained of the Corvinian Library. Dr. Sambucus went about rescuing stray copies for the Emperor Rudolph. He was *a strange Quixotic figure, always riding alone, with swinging saddlebags, and a great mastiff running on either side*. Busbec, the traveller, was allowed to see but not to touch the heaped and decaying books in the tower; and it was not until the year 1686 that *about forty of the maltreated volumes were rescued by force of arms and set in a place of safety among the Emperor's books at Vienna*. For many years hunting the books of Corvinus was a favourite sport of bookmen, and volumes were discovered in divers places. Several now rest in the Vatican, others at Ferrara, and some in Florence. Mary of Austria gave two of the Corvinian books to the Librarie de Bourgogne at Brussels: the *Missal*, on which the sovereigns of Brabant were sworn, and the *Golden Gospels, long the pride of the Escorial*.[3]

Macray recounts, in an almost *incredible story* out of Warton's edition of Milton's *Poems*, how two of the Bodleian's early *Miltons*, both inscribed by the poet, were saved. About the year 1720 the two volumes, *Poems*

---

[1] 'Recovery of Manuscripts', *Cur. of Lit.* i.   [2] *Works*. Ed. Sayle. iii, 350.   [3] Elton, *Great Book-Collectors*. 84.

English and Latin and a collection of *political and polemical tracts*, were *thrown into a heap of duplicates*, and Nathaniel Crynes was allowed to *pick out* from among them *what he pleased for himself*, but being *a good Royalist he would not touch a book written by such a man as Milton*. The copies thus remained in the Library among the *throwouts*; but in any event they would have gone back to their real home, for the Crynes Collection was afterwards bequeathed to the Bodleian.[1]

How many great books have existed unknown and therefore buried in our public and private libraries is a long story. Madan[2] has a notable tale of the recovery of the *Gospel Book* of St. Margaret, Queen of Scotland, which had been lost for centuries and was found by accident, in the year 1887, on the shelves of *a small parish library* in Suffolk. Money was required by the good parishioners for the purchase of new books, and a number of books which the countryfolk could not read were done up in a fardel and sent to Sotheby's. Among them was the *Gospel Book* which had belonged to a Queen and a saint, and been saved by Christ from destruction by water. It was described at the Auction Sale as Latin Gospels, fourteenth century, and *passed into the Bodleian Library* for £6, where it was catalogued as *an ordinary accession*. Later an inscription of verses on the fly-leaf recounting its rescue from drowning aroused the interest of a lady to whom it was shown. She drew the attention to a similar story in Forbes-Leith's *Life of St. Margaret* and thus established the identity of the historic volume.

When Henry Bradshaw, father of English Bibliography, became Librarian at the Cambridge University Library, he found shelves of books which had *in all probability not been dusted for centuries*. No one knew what treasures lay there neglected, and ignorance was made more complete by the misnaming of volumes. A MS. of *Chaucer* was labelled *Piers Plowman*; a York *Manual*, *Ritule* (sic) *vetustum*; the Winchester *Pontifical* had *Missalia* on the back. In the year 1857, Bradshaw made his famous discovery of the *Book of Deer*, one of the most ancient of Celtic MSS., comprising the *Vulgate* version of the four Gospels *written by a scribe whose vernacular language was Gaelic*, which has since contributed to the elucidation of early Celtic history and philology;[3] and four years later he had the satisfaction of informing the British Museum authorities that their copy of the first *English Psalter* (1530:16mo) was the copy stolen from Cambridge some years before.[4] His notable successor in the same Library *was constantly discovering fresh treasures on the shelves.*[5] Such another tale as that of Bradshaw's discovery is the account of how Dr. Williamson[6] found the

---

[1] Macray, *Annals*. 56–7.   [2] *Books in Manuscript*. 122–5.   [3] Prothero, *Memoir of Bradshaw*. 66–71.   [4] *Ib*. 75.   [5] *Francis Jenkinson*. Stewart. 38.   [6] G. C. Williamson, *Behind My Library Door*. 68–9.

only copy of the famous *Service Book*, of 1612. This elegant piece of typo-graphy in *elephant folio* had been lost for twenty years and was last seen in 1876, when the modern edition was printed from it. The curious and learned doctor would not believe it had been destroyed, and determined to find it. He tracked it down to a monastery and found it lying among a lot of printer's rubbish in a room which had not been opened for twenty years, and carried it in triumph to the Prior, who was ignorant of the fact that his monastery possessed *a magnificent piece of printing* and a book which *constituted a landmark in the history of his order*. Didot was similarly fortunate when he was able to rescue *from a rubbish heap in an English cellar* a copy of the decorated Aldine *Homer* which had belonged to Francis I.[1]

Shakespeare's works have many adventures recorded of them, but none more exciting than that of a copy of the *Venus and Adonis* of 1596, which was sold at the disposal of Dr. Bernard's books in 1698 for one shilling and threepence. It was bound up with several other *rariora: Diana or the Son-nets of H. C.* [Henry Constable], 1592 or 1594; Daniel's *Sonnets*, with the *Complaint of Rosamond*, and the *Tragedie of Cleopatra*, 1594; Barnefield's *Sonnets*, with the *Legend of Cassandra*, 1595; *Fidessa*, by B. Giffin, 1596; *Diella*, by R. L., with the *Poem of Dom. Diego and Genevra*, 1596; *The Poem of Poems, or Sion's Muse*, by G. M. [Gervase Markham], 1596. This precious volume had strayed among various hands and was ultimately rescued from *among a parcel of old iron and other lumber*, in the hoard of a broker at Salisbury, for the sum of sixpence, by that elegant and ingenious writer, Dr. Joseph Warton, who presented it to Edmund Malone, who in turn bequeathed it with his other books to the Bodleian, where it still safely rests.[2] Even *first folios* have had their periods of neglect and tempor-ary loss. Maurice Hewlett was once staying at a country house, when in the ante-room of the library, where books had overflowed among *cart-ridges, garden-gloves and baskets, directories, Bradshaws, and things of that kind*, he *took down at random an old book, bare-backed, with faded green sides*, and found it to be a First Folio *Shakespeare* which the owners did not know they owned.[3]

At the sale of Dr. Askew's MSS., in 1775, a document which proved to be in the handwriting of Edward I was bought by a Mr. Jackson, *a Quaker, and a dealer in wines and spirits, with whom book-collecting was a passion*, and at the sale of his books it went to the British Museum; another example is that of the copy of *Flores Historiarum per Mathaeum Westmonasteriensem*, 1570, in the British Museum: this is the copy presented by Archbishop Parker to Queen Elizabeth. It *came into the hands* of Francis, Earl of Bed-ford, who bequeathed it to his secretary; and it was subsequently in Ritson's library. In Eton College Library there is a copy of the *Missale*

[1] Lang, *The Library*. 96.   [2] Prior, *Malone*. 178-9.   [3] *Extemporary Essays*. 121-2.

Romanum, Paris, 1530, which belonged to Mary Queen of Scots, and it has a sentence in her handwriting; it eventually came into the possession of Mary of Este, Queen to James II, then into the hands of a London bookseller, from whom it was bought by Bishop Fleetwood, and presented to the College Library.[1] But if I told of all those manuscripts and books which have been lost and found, or lamented all which have been irretrievably lost, there would be no end to my tale. 'Tis time that I should relieve you from the tedious length of this account. You have doubtless better and more profitable employment; yet in extenuation I may claim in some sort the right thus to test your patience, for, as Isaac Taylor well says, *the credit of ancient literature, the certainty of history, and the truth of religion, are all involved in the secure transmission of ancient books to modern times;*[2] for more in this kind, with many curious facts and incidents, read him.

III. NEGLECT AND MISUSAGE

Next to persecutors, if I may distinguish them, are those neglectors, irreverent or careless handlers, bullies of books, who are not far behind them as destroyers. Swift compared libraries to cemeteries, and as some authorities affirm that a spirit hovers over the monuments of the dead till the bodies are corrupted and turned to dust, so he believed a like restless spirit haunted every book, till dust or worms seized upon it. *Alas!* exclaims Janin,[3] *'tis no wonder that these miracles of the printers are priceless*, for before reaching us they have escaped so many dangers, confronted so many obstacles: unhealthy homes, damp cellars, either too hot or too cold; fire and water. When Leland visited Oxford after the suppression of the monasteries, he found few books, only *moths and beetles swarming over the empty shelves.*[4] It was no better at Cambridge, even in more recent times. *Nothing*, says Bradshaw, *could be more disgraceful than the way in which the manuscripts* of Bishop Moore's library, presented to the University by George I, *were literally shovelled into their places;* and for the thirty-five years that followed the presentation *the pillage was so unlimited that the only wonder is that we have any valuable books left.*[5] Every library, especially those that are old and large, or small and neglected, breeds its own inimical *flora* and *fauna*, mould, bookworms, moths, *anthrene, vorilette*, bugs, mice, rats, the story of whose devastations would fill many volumes. In addition Janin enumerates such enemies as dust, children, kittens, hot greasy hands,

[1] Roberts, *Book-Hunter in London*. 17.   [2] *Transmission of Ancient Books*. i.
[3] *Le Livre*. 109–10.   [4] Elton, *Great Book-Collectors*. 34.   [5] *Memoir of Bradshaw*, Prothero. 164.

o

les sales mains d'Hermogènes, and finally *les imbéciles et les brigands qui si tiennent autour des trônes, en chantant la chanson:*

> Eteignons les lumières,
> Et rallumons le feu. . . .
>
> Let's put out the lights,
> And stoke up the fire. . . .[1]

Many authorities support him, extending his catalogue, as William Blades, who would add[2] gas, bookbinders, houseflies, bugs, black-beetles, and servants; upon all of which he dilates at large. Rats and mice have doubtless browsed on books, growing fat if not wise. But sometimes their gnawings have been frustrated, as in that example, recorded by Bernard Shaw,[3] of the MS. of his own first novel, *Immaturity,* which, rejected by publishers, lay neglected until part of it *was devoured by mice, though even they had not been able to finish it;* but tough or tender, mice have no respect for either genius or masterpiece:

> Ho, ho! Master Mouse! safe at last in my cage
> You're caught, and there's nothing shall save you from dying:
> For, caitiff! you nibbled and tore Shakespeare's page,
> When close by your nose Tupper's nonsense was lying.[4]

Because these enemies of books are so malign in themselves, and so hard to be removed, *prevention is better than cure;* and the best averter of such rebellious carriers of destruction is wise and constant use. When Sir Thomas Bodley was told by his Librarian James that some of his books were infested with worms, he replied:[5] *I hope those little worms about the covers of your books come by reason of their newness, and that hereafter they will away.* For more to this end, see my Digression of Bookworms.[6]

Most of these misfortunes come by neglect, which is in itself a negative ill-usage. All those misaffections which I have named are as weeds in the garden of books; dust, mould, maggots, bugs, moths, beetles, and the like. are the zymotic diseases of books, and as devastating as the perils of direct attack and abuse. Petrarch gave a collection of books to the city of Venice, but many years afterwards they were found rotting away in a cellar: some had become mere dust, others were agglutinated by the damp into form-less masses, but a few survived and are still preserved in the Ducal palace.[7] The Library of Monte Cassino survived the desecrations of Lombard and Saracen only to risk destruction from neglect. When Boccaccio visited the

---

[1] *Le Livre.*   [2] *Enemies of Books. passim.*   [3] *Cashel Byron's Profession.* Preface, x.
[4] Anon. after Guichard, *Epigrams.* Leonard. 35.   [5] *Letters.* 43.   [6] xx, pp.
125–42, *post.*   [7] Elton, *Great Book-Collectors.* 52.

monastery he found noble manuscripts scattered and disordered in a door-less loft reached by a ladder. The books were white with dust and whole sheets had been ripped out and margins cut away. Boccaccio wept at the sight and demanded of a monk how such precious volumes had been so ill-used. He was told that the brethren needed money and would cut out enough leaves from a Bible to make a little Psalter, which they would sell, and they raised more revenue by disposing of the blank margins for use as 'briefs'.[1]

Yet dust, according to some authorities, is not in itself so damaging to books as the act of dusting them by unskilful or irreverent performers. Both Blades and Birrel stiffly maintain that *you should never dust books; let the dust lie until the rare hour arrives when you want to read a particular volume; then warily*, Birrell advises, *approach it with a snow-white napkin, take it down from its shelf, and, withdrawing to some back apartment, proceed to cleanse the tome*.[2] Blades has a terror of careless servants and rampant housewives conducting a Spring offensive, and if he admits that *books must now and then be taken out of their shelves, they should be tended lovingly and with judg-ment*, and he agrees with Birrell that *if dusting can be done just outside the room so much the better*.[3] I am with these reliable authorities in both their strictures and advices, but neither they nor I are ignorant of the fact that it is not only frenzied domesticity which desecrates our temples in pursuit of dust; bookmen themselves are often perverse offenders, and not least among them our learned Dr. Johnson, as I have shown,[4] but I will again recount the story for a caution, this time out of *Birrell*.[5] When about to dust his books the Doctor *drew on huge gloves, such as those once worn by hedgers and ditchers, and then, clutching his folios and octavos, he banged and buffeted them together until he was enveloped in a cloud of dust. This violent exercise over, the good doctor restored the volumes, all battered and bruised, to their places, where, of course, the dust resettled itself as speedily as possible*. It is the good fortune of books that such methods have been superseded by the invention of that ingenious engine called the vacuum cleaner, although I must not omit to mention that cleanliness does not satisfy all bookmen,

<hr/>

[1] *Ib*. 64. There are some who doubt this charge against the monks of Monte Cas-sino, the most recent being Cardinal Gasquet, who goes so far as to charge Boccac-cio with being something more than 'an excellent story-teller', for 'he did not hesitate to repay the hospitality of the monks of Monte Cassino by carrying off some of the treasures of their library'. The MS. of *Tacitus* at Florence, once Boc-caccio's, was 'abstracted from the Library of Cassino'. The Cardinal rightly defends the monks for preserving the important works of Varro, of Tacitus, of Apuleius, St. Hilary, and St. Jerome, and the celebrated Peregrinatio Aetheriae and other works 'the copies of which are the best we have'. Letter to *The Times*, 1.iv. 1929. [2] 'The Johnsonian Legend', *Collected Essays*. i, 143. [3] *Enemies of Books*. 126. [4] 'Bookmen and their Little Libraries.' ii, 10, *ante*. [5] *Op. cit*. i, 143-4.

for there are some who regard dust on books as a mark of age, and there-fore of distinction, much as connoisseurs will preserve with tender care the grimy encrustations on a bottle of an ancient and honourable wine; such enthusiasts as these consider the dust of the library, together with that of the crematorium and of the churchyard, *as in a measure sacred.*[1]

But abuse more direct and deliberate has been as common in most times, from their use as packing or tinder to the indignity of sanitary necessity, for although Gargantua discommends paper, and books as such are not named in his famous *torcheculatif,*[2] their use in this wise is histori-cally established and has become a byword in French *coprology. Avisez-y, doctes: parce que souvent d'espice, ou des mouchoirs de cul.*[3] There are those also, as that old English aphorist,[4] who go so far as to class the writer of *abund-ance of Books* with the begetter of *abundance of Children,* as a *Benefactor of the Publick,* because he furnishes it with *Bumfodder and Soldiers.* I must per-force be indefinite in such a record, so shall only add one instance in which Carew Hazlitt tells us that not so long since a copy of Caxton's *Recuyell of the Hystoryes of Troye* was found *hanging up in a water-closet at Harrogate;* part of it had already been consumed, but the remainder was rescued and *sold to a dealer in Manchester for thirty pounds.*[5] Many times rashly and un-advisedly are good books destined to an indignity which might be deemed infamous and ridiculous for even a newspaper, and if I were disposed to enlarge this theme, here might easily be recalled many unsavoury tales from our own early literature, and I would go on with it, but as Gran-gousier advised Gargantua, it is a *dull theme,* so to wander on would be no joke, the curious in such business may look for more in Thomas Dekker, his *Gul's Horn-Booke,* Dryden's *Mac Flecknoe,* Swift, etc.

As *martyrs of pies*[6] and victims of economy books have a long and tragi-cal history. To recount how many have been so destroyed would make a long list. They have suffered I know not what in this wise; but I can give no more than a taste, as the example which Macray gives out of the notes of Rawlinson how that collector came by many rare documents which had been disposed of as rubbish. *I lately rescued from the grocers, chandlers, etc.,* he records, in 1755, *a parcel of papers once the property of Compton and Robinson, successively Bishops of London;* amongst them *remarkable intelli-gences relating to Burnet and the Orange Court in Holland in those extraordinary times before* 1688; and letters from Bolingbroke, Oxford, Ormonde, Strafford, Prior, and the Elector and Electress of Hanover. At another time, from a shop whither they had been sentenced to serve for supporting *pyes, currents, sugar, etc.,* he redeemed *as many as came to* 12s. *at* 6d. *per*

---

[1] Cuthbertson, *Thirty-three Years' Adventures in Bookland.* 182.   [2] *Rabelais.* I, xiii.
[3] Beroalde de Verville, *Le Moyen de Parvenir.* xvi.   [4] *Laconics, or New Maxims.*
(1701) 118.   [5] *Book-Collecting.* (1904) 124.   [6] Dryden, *Mac Flecknoe.* 101.

pound. These included a collection of *ecclesiastical causes,* and the causes of Bishop Watson and the Duchess of Cleveland.[1]

The history of books teems with such accounts, not only from past ages but from nearer our own times. The letters which James Boswell addressed to his friend the Rev. William Temple were discovered, about the middle of last century, by a clergyman, in the shop of a Madame Noel, at Boulogne. He observed that the article he had bought was wrapped in a piece of paper bearing English writing. His interest was aroused, and upon examination the paper proved to be part of a letter written by the biographer of Dr. Johnson. He made further inquiries and discovered a goodly parcel of letters by the same hand which Madame Noel had purchased from a hawker, who passed through that seaport twice a year supplying the tradesfolk with wrapping paper. The clergyman immediately secured the whole parcel, and the letters are now among the treasures of our epistolary literature.[2] Another such rescue from the paw of the shopkeeper had a curious issue, if the tale D'Israeli[3] tells of Barbosa, Bishop of Ugento, be true. In the year 1649, that ecclesiastic printed among his works a treatise, called *de Officio Episcopi,* which he obtained by having perceived one of his domestics bring in a fish rolled in a piece of paper, which his curiosity led him to examine. His interest was immediately provoked and he ran out and searched the fish market until he found and secured the MS. from which the sheet had been torn.

Now and again in other circumstances of time and place whole libraries have been left to the risk of adventitious events, and some have suffered no further damage than dispersal, as the library formed by Edward Gibbon at Lausanne for the writing of his history of the *Decline and Fall of the Roman Empire.* Mary Berry tells how she saw this library when she visited that city, in 1803,[4] where it still remained, although, as I have shown in its place,[5] it had been bought by Beckford seven years earlier. *It is,* she says, *of all libraries I ever saw, that of which I should most covet the possession; that which seems exactly everything that any gentleman or gentlewoman fond of letters could wish.* The books were under the care of a Mr. Scholl, a physician of that place, and were all clean and in good condition. Several years before Beckford had packed up 2,500 out of 10,000 volumes, intending to send them to England, but they still remained there in their cases. In 1818 they were seen by another traveller, Henry Matthews,[6] *locked up in an uninhabited house.* In 1825, Birkbeck Hill records,[7] half of them were sold by Dr. Scholl (to whom Beckford eventually gave them) to Mr. Halliday, an Englishman, *who lived in a tower near Orbe.* The

[1] Macray, *Annals.* 239–40.   [2] *Letters of Boswell.* (1857) Preface, v.   [3] *Cur. of Lit.* i, 36.   [4] *Letters.* Ed. Lewis. ii, 260–1.   [5] 'Reading on a Journey.' i, 320, *ante.*
[6] *Diary of an Invalid.* (1820) 316.   [7] *Memoirs of Gibbon.* 339, n.

remainder were dispersed, some going to America, but many volumes were still in the possession of a resident of Geneva as lately as the year 1876, though I can find no record of them after that date.

Richard de Bury fulminates in a whole chapter[1] of his *Philobiblon* against the careless abusers of books in his time: as a youthful student lounging over his studies, *when the winter's frost is sharp, his nose running from the nipping cold* and dripping down and unwiped until *he has bedewed the book before him with ugly moisture;* another marks passages with the *fetid black filth of his nails,* and *distributing straws* between the pages so that *the halm may remind him of what his memory cannot retain,* thus distending the book from its *wonted closing.* Such abusers, he says, do not fear to eat fruit or cheese over the open pages, or to carry a cup to their mouths over them, dropping into the book crumbs and spots of liquid. They wet the pages with *spluttering showers* from their lips as they dispute with their companions, and when they pause in their studies to take a nap they fold their arms and sleep upon the book, crumpling the leaves, and then seek to mend them, to their further damage, by folding them back. When the rain is over and gone, and the flowers appear on the earth, they will sally forth and stuff their volumes *with violets, and primroses, with roses and quatrefoil.* They will use wet and perspiring hands to turn over pages; thumb white vellum with gloves covered with dirt: *with finger clad in long-used leather will hunt line by line through the pages;* throw them aside unclosed so that they get full of dust; make notes and other inky exercises in their margins.

In those times also there was a *class of thieves* who shamefully mutilated books by cutting away the margins and endpapers to use the materials for letters, *a kind of sacrilege,* he well says, *which should be prohibited by the threat of anathema.* As a preventive of some of these evils he puts out that no student should go to his books after meals without washing his hands. No grease-stained fingers should unfasten the clasps, or turn the leaves of a book; no crying child should be let admire the capital letters lest he soil the parchment, *for a child instantly touches what he sees.* And, finally, *let the clerk,* he advises, *take care also that the smutty scullion reeking from his stewpots does not touch the lily leaves of books, all unwashed.*

Many bookmen might I reckon up who have used books scurvily, tearing their leaves open with a finger or blunt instrument instead of using a paperknife of ivory or bone. James Thomson, the poet of *The Seasons,* did not scruple to attempt this delicate operation with his *candle-snuffers.*[2] *To introduce Wordsworth into one's library,* Southey tells De Quincey, *is like letting a bear into a tulip garden;* he had no mercy on his own or other

---

[1] xvii, 'Of showing due Propriety in the Custody of Books.'   [2] Burton, *The Book-Hunter.* 29.   [3] *Shelley.* London Lib. Ed. 62.

people's books, and once at tea-time De Quincey observed him take up a butter-knife to open the pages of a volume of Burke: *he tore his way into the heart of the volume with this knife, that left its greasy honours behind it on every page.*[1] De Quincey was not shocked at this proceeding, he was surprised only that Wordsworth should have been so precipitate in his vandalism, as a more appropriate book-knife could easily have been discovered; he was even inclined to extenuate the act because the book was a common one. *Had the book been an old black-letter book, having a value from its rarity,* he would *have been disturbed in an indescribable degree; but simply,* he is quick to add, lest perchance he be convicted of bibliophily, *with reference to the utter impossibility of reproducing that mode of value.* As for the *Burke,* he himself *had bought the book, with many others, at the sale of Sir Cecil Wray's library, for about two-thirds of the selling price.* He only mentions *the case to illustrate the excess of Wordsworth's outrages on books, which made him, in Southey's eyes, a mere monster; for Southey's library was his estate; and this difference of habits would alone have sufficed to alienate him from Wordsworth.*[2]

Others, as Richard de Bury observes, use books as receptacles for papers and other objects, thus straining their covers beyond bearing point. A clumsy offender was Selden, who would *buy his spectacles by the gross,* using them to mark the place in a book where he happened to leave off reading. *It was quite a common thing, soon after his library came to the Bodleian, for spectacles to drop out of the books as they were taken incautiously from the shelves.*[3] *It has been my custom,* Medwell, the American Grangeriser, ingenuously confesses, *for over forty years to insert articles, from magazines and newspapers, pertinent to the subjects, in my books; many of them are so full as nearly to burst their covers, and some I have been obliged to have rebound to save them;*[4] and like damage is done by botanists, who look upon a book as nothing more than a press for plants and flowers: a vestibule to the herbarium.

When Dr. Johnson was engaged upon his edition of *Shakespeare,* David Garrick refused to lend him copies of the old plays in his collection, *knowing that he treated books with a roughness ill-suited to their constitution,* and he thought that he had gone quite far enough *by asking Johnson to come to his library.* The great man took his revenge by saying nothing of Garrick in his Preface.[5] That Dr. Johnson was rough on books I have sufficiently noticed, but I cannot ignore another piece of evidence from his Life of Young,[6] where after commending the keenness bestowed by the poet upon

[1] De Quincey, 'Literary Reminiscences', *Collected Writings.* ii, 312–14.   [2] De Quincey, 'Literary Reminiscences', *Collected Writings.* Ed. Masson. ii, 312–14.
[3] Gordon Duff, *The Printers etc. of London.* 88.   [4] *Privately Illustrated Books.* 33.
[5] Leslie Stephen, *Johnson.* 66.   [6] *Lives of the Poets.* iv, 423.

the perusal of books, he proceeds to describe Young's crude method of marking pages, with evident approval: *When any passage pleased him, he appears to have folded down the leaf,* so that many of the books, which the Doctor had seen, *are by these notes of approbation so swelled beyond their real bulk, that they will not shut.*

Several learned men have not scrupled to treat books as though they were newspapers by tearing or cutting out extracts to save themselves the trouble of copying them. I have already noticed Edward FitzGerald's habit of pollarding literature by cutting out of his books the sections which gave him no pleasure and binding up only those which were to his taste, and, in order to show that such habits are not unusual among scholarly men, I shall cite a few further instances. Charles Darwin had no respect for books, *but merely considered them as tools to be worked with;* when they fell to pieces with rough use he held them together with metal clips; *he would cut a heavy book in half to make it more convenient to hold,* and he *would tear out, for the sake of saving room,* all the pages of pamphlets *except the one that interested him.*[1] Dr. Hughlings Jackson, founder of the science of neurology, had the same bad habit: *he had no compunction about tearing out any portion which interested him, and would frequently send to a friend a few leaves torn out of a book dealing with any subject in which he knew the friend to be interested.* His library was thus a collection of mutilated volumes. On purchasing a novel at a railway bookstall, which he often did, his first act was to rip off the covers, then to *tear the book in two, putting one half in one pocket and the other in the other.* One one such occasion the clerk at the stall stared at the performance of this sacrilegious act with such obvious amazement that Jackson, observing him, remarked: *You think I am mad, my boy, but it's the people who don't do this who are really mad.*[2] But no more fantastic desecration is recorded than that of Shelley, who had a passion for making and sailing paper boats. He could not resist the temptation to pursue these nautical adventures whenever he came to a pond, and any paper which came to his hand was requisitioned for this miniature shipbuilding. If he had stopped at letters and newspapers, or even those banknotes which are said to have augmented his curious purpose, he would not have figured in my black-list, but when all other raw material of the craft failed, he did not shrink from turning to one of *the portable volumes which were the companions of his rambles.* He applied their fly-leaves *as our ancestor Noah applied Gopher wood; but,* Hogg explains, *learning was so sacred in his eyes that he never trespassed farther upon the integrity of the copy.*[3]

Scholars do not hesitate to mix books with eating apparatus. *I have sometimes heard of an Iliad in a nutshell,* says Swift, *but it has been my fortune*

[1] *Life and Letters.* Francis Darwin. i, 150–1.   [2] James Taylor, 'Memoir', in *Neurological Fragments.* Jackson. 20–1.   [3] *Shelley.* London Lib. Ed. 62.

to have much oftener seen a nutshell in an Iliad.[1] Madan recalls[2] Dean Burgon's study table in Oriel with *forgotten tea-cups at various elevations, on jutting promontories of the alpine 'massif' of books.* George Gissing[3] makes shame-faced confession that the comeliest of his books, once *stately and fragrant,* show the results of unfair usage, and that in his various movings from one place to another *more than one has been foully injured by a great nail driven into a packing-case.* In such misfortunes he felt no regret, for so long as a volume held together he was not troubled by its outward show.

How readers of the commoner kind will wet their fingers to expedite the turning of pages is well known. But this naughty habit is not confined to rude fellows of the baser sort, for not so long ago *a learned vandal* was observed in the University Library at Cambridge in the act of *wetting his forefinger* for this same purpose. He was nicely rebuked by Jenkinson, the librarian, who *silently caught his hand and laid it on the table.*[4] Well may Madan disapprove of giving scholars permission to rove freely round the shelves of Bodley's Library. *The great men of literature,* he says, *are often the very persons* who could be least trusted in those rich store-rooms; and he goes on to recount their depredations, as pulling books out by the top of their backs, fingering them, turning leaves by *the application of moisture,* and holding them open on a table by *putting other volumes on them;* finally, *they seldom know how or where to put a volume back,* as he well remembers upon a sight of the Douce Room MSS. after a visit from Robinson Ellis or the Malone Room after Swinburne had been allowed to *sample it.*[5] *We have societies for the prevention of cruelty to children and other animals,* observes Walter Jerrold,[6] *why have we no society for the prevention of cruelty to books?* A favourable answer might have been more necessary in olden times, but even in our day there are not wanting those ingrates who misuse books and intreat them with neglect, for I find so experienced a witness as Dr. Hagberg Wright holding up the ancients as examples to some readers of our time. In bygone times readers, he says, *were counted by tens, but they loved the books they read, and handled them with reverence and care.* Nowadays readers have *deteriorated;* they do not love their books as their ancestors loved them. *Too often,* he says, *they handle them as bricks and buy them as furniture; they even mutilate them,* and if, as he believes, *book-lovers always remain lovers of books though some of them have degenerated into biblio-maniacs,*[7] many of them are rough wooers, if we may judge by the treatment of books in our lending libraries. One such library mentioned by Alexander Smith was no better than a *Greenwich Hospital for disabled novels*

[1] *Tale of a Tub.*   [2] *Ideal Bodleian.* 24.   [3] *Private Papers of Henry Ryecroft.* 30.
[4] Stewart, *Francis Jenkinson.* 118.   [5] *Ideal Bodleian.* 24.   [6] *Autolycus of the Book-stalls.* 40.   [7] 'Readers a Hundred Years Ago', *Nineteenth Century.* Aug. 1911.

and romances; each book had *been in the wars,* and *the tears of three generations* had *fallen upon their dusty pages.*[1]

In conclusion I must set out a few words on the perils of bookbinding, for although these dangers may be avoided by careful attention, the binder is still often a biblioclast by accident, stupidity or ignorance. In my chapter of first editions I have said something about 'condition', and how modern collectors demand their specimens in 'mint state', so here will do no more than commend a fashion which is both scientific and protective. Had it always prevailed, mutilated copies of rare books would not have been so common. Even so recently as the year 1881 Andrew Lang was not a fully convinced opponent of cut margins, for although he knew that *once the binder begins to clip he is unable to resist the seductive joy, and cuts the paper to the quick, even into the printed matter,* he was only *almost tempted to say that margins should always be left untouched.*[2] There is now no doubt. Margins should never be cut. All books should appear *intonsis capillis, with locks unshorn, as Motteley the old dealer used to say, an Elzevir in its paper wrapper may be worth more than the same tome in morocco, stamped with Longepierre's fleece of gold.*[3] No collector of our time would commit such an error as to rebind a fair copy, still less allow his binder to cut the margins of any book. The biblioclastic bookbinder is, however, still a menace, and Blades is so incensed against him that he is encouraged by memories of how Dante in his *Inferno deals out to the lost souls tortures suited with dramatic fitness to the past crimes of the victims,* to imagine that had he *to execute judgment on the criminal binders of certain precious volumes* he has seen, *where the untouched maiden sheets entrusted to their care have, by barbarous treatment, lost dignity, beauty and value,* he *would collect the paper shavings so ruthlessly shorn off, and roast the perpetrator of the outrage over their slow combustion.* He justifies this drastic punishment on the ground that, however much the plea of ignorance may have been justified in the past, there is no such excuse in these times, *when the historical and antiquarian value of old books is freely acknowledged.* Quarter therefore should not be given.[4]

IV. PERILS OF FIRE AND WATER

Now last of all to those external and accidental impediments, calamitous events and happenings, which we hear and see many times in the histories and in our own age, as burnings and drownings by carelessness or chance, as distinct from those deliberate tortures, persecutions, *autos-da-fé,* and other such horrible and execrable deeds, which evil effects frequently im-

[1] *Dreamthorp.* 16.   [2] *The Library.* 69.   [3] *Ib.* 69–70.   [4] Blades, *Enemies of Books.* 98.

peril books when victimized by religious and moral frenzy, fear, and excess of zeal. Experience teaches that though many books have died a violent death at the hands of fanatics, those good men in a hurry who have added so greatly to the pains and sorrows of human life, perchance as many have perished from careless handling, neglect, or the ordinary accidents which happen to all mortal things; among them fire has been a first enemy. So greatly and necessarily is this enemy feared that extraordinary precautions are taken by book-lovers for the protection of their treasures, witness Locker, who kept his rare editions in a room lined with steel.

Among the ancients there is the famous story of the *Sibylline Books*, which suffered mishaps from beginning to end; but I shall cite only the adventures of those of the *Cumæan Sibyl*, whom Aeneas consulted before his descent into the *Inferno*;[1] for the rest read more in *Diels, Maass, Schultess, Bouché-Leclerq, Fowler and Conway, Postgate, etc.* It was this Sibyl who was said to have offered Tarquin the Proud those nine magical volumes which contained the key to the future of Roman history. He was, I have no doubt, a bibliophobe, for he refused her offer. She then burned three, and offered him the remaining six for the same price. He again refused, so she burned three more. Tarquin then relented and bought the last three.[2] The precious books were protected with extraordinary care. At first they were guarded by two patricians, of Tarquin's appointing. In 367 B.C. the custodians were increased to ten, five patrician and five plebeian; and about the time of Sulla the number was further augmented by five, making fifteen in all. The *Books* were enshrined in the Temple of Jupiter on the Capitoline, where they perished when the Temple was destroyed by fire, in 83 B.C. The Senate set to work to restore the books by sending out ambassadors to collect the oracles anew in Erythraea, Ilium, Samos, Sicily, and Africa. They collected over one thousand verses, so many that some must have been spurious, and in order to establish a true canon, Augustus (in 12 B.C.) ordained a critical revision and burned a vast quantity of them as unauthentic; the remainder were placed by him in the Temple of Apollo Patrous on the Palatine. They survived there for four hundred years, when they were finally burned by Stilicho.

There is a memorable example of this sort of peril in the fire which blazed at Ashburnham House, Little Dean's Yard, in the City of Westminster, in 1731, ravaging with great havoc the Library of Sir John Cotton. Some there are who attribute this fire to *Dr. Bentley's villainy.* But they cannot prove it, and I for one would like to give Cotton's librarian *the benefit of the doubt,* especially as it is recorded by Dean Stanley that the Headmaster of Westminster, speeding to the rescue, saw a figure issue from the burning house *in his dressing-gown, a flowing wig on his head,*

[1] *Aeneid.* vi, 10.   [2] Dion. Halic., iv, 62.

428 THE MISFORTUNES OF BOOKS

and a huge volume under his arm: it was Bentley saving the *Alexandrine MS.* of the *New Testament.* Many others gave their help, notably Mr. Speaker Onslow and some of the trustees of the Library, who entered the burning house, worked at the pumping, broke open presses and rescued hundreds of volumes by throwing them out of the windows.[1]

More particular cases be these which follow. Stupidity and carelessness first, by which books and manuscripts have been cremated by the thoughtlessness or ignorance of their owners or their servants, as John Earle's translation of *Hooker*, which was *to make the learned of all nations happy,* but which perished to *light the fires* and help cook the bread and pies of his servants.[2] A like fate befell scores of Warburton's books at the stove of his cook Betty Barnes. One whole volume of the MS. of Carlyle's *French Revolution* was ignorantly burned by J. S. Mill's maidservant, and, as no duplicate existed, he was forced to rewrite it. When Tennyson asked him how he felt after this calamity, Carlyle said: *I just felt like a man swimming without water.*[3] The MS. of Conrad's *End of the Tether* was also accidentally destroyed by fire and had to be rewritten.[4] We know with what fortitude some of these authors met their misfortune, and how heroically they got down to the tedious job of reconstruction; but we can scarcely imagine their immediate anguish at so great a loss. Even the loss of so trivial a piece as a letter is annoying enough to most of us, as Horace Walpole well knew. *Nothing was ever so vexatious,* he confessed to Sir Horace Mann, as the burning of one of his letters upon which a hot coal had fallen as it lay in the hearth to dry while *he stepped into the next room for sealing wax. I have not time to write half of it again,* he complained.[5] Had it been a whole book vexation might have given place to despair. But I rove again.

Next to these adventures I must name those circumstances in which books have been condemned to death by otherwise reasonable bookmen temporarily afflicted with an enthusiasm which demands some ceremonial expression of destruction or, as they would call it, sacrifice, as when Prospero abjured his *rough magic* he broke his staff and buried it,

And deeper than did ever plummet sound[6]

he drowned his book. A like outbreak affected Leigh Hunt, when into the flame of the poet's funeral pyre he *threw the 'Lamia', found in Shelley's bosom,*[7] the self-same copy which he had given to his friend, asking him to keep it until he gave it back with his own hands, and Shelley *had probably been*

---

[1] Qt. Elton, *Great Book-Collectors.* 118–19. [2] *Microcosmographie.* Qt. n., Irwin. 341.
[3] *Tennyson, a Memoir.* Hallam, Lord Tennyson. i, 267. [4] Conrad, *Letters.* [5] *Letters,* Cunningham. v, 48. [6] *The Tempest.* v, 1. [7] *Leigh Hunt.* Blunden. 176.

reading it when surprised by the storm.[1] Such destructive impulses are not uncommon, and although their motive is generous enough, they are to be resisted, for they might arise as well from hatred so far as the result is concerned.

Damage by water is also a common misfortune, and many good books have been lost or damaged at sea or on our inland waterways, as on that occasion when Thomas Tanner, Bishop of St. Asaph, was carrying his books from Norwich to Oxford by water, they fell into the river, and, although rescued, they bear marks of their misadventure to this day, as anyone may prove by inspecting them at the Bodleian Library, to which they were ultimately bequeathed.[2] Dennis Daly, who with Edmond Malone was among the earliest collectors of first editions of Shakespeare and of our Elizabethan writers, was on a voyage when his ship foundered off Beachy Head, and all his first editions were lost.[3] Such misfortunes continue and will continue until there is no more sea, for men must go upon voyages and sail in ships, and books will ever be transported from one land to another. After the Huth Sale in 1912 that zealous young American collector, Harry Elkins Widener, slipped a volume of the second edition of Bacon's *Essays*, which he had just secured, into his pocket, saying, *I think I'll take that little Bacon with me in my pocket, and if I am shipwrecked it will go down with me. A few days later*, says Rosenbach, *he was one of the victims of the Titanic disaster.*[4] But I will shorten this discourse, which haply would draw me further than I would willingly follow, or need follow, for I have said enough to move the hearts of bibliophiles, and perchance, to encourage the kindlier instincts of the rest.

[1] *Autobiography of Leigh Hunt.* World's Classics Ed. 390.   [2] Macray, *Annals.* 211–12.
[3] Prior, *Malone.* 63.   [4] Rosenbach, *Books and Bidders.* 46.

Part XX

A DIGRESSION OF BOOKWORMS

I. A COMMON ENEMY IN EVERY AGE

Great inconvenience comes to books in all ages from the depredations of bookworms, which burrow through leaves and covers, feeding upon the paper, the leather and the boards so voraciously that, if not arrested, they will honeycomb the stoutest volumes into ruin. The bookworm is shy and small; he is more widely known by his ravages than by his aspect, and if there have been difficulties in giving him accurate definition, he has been recognized for what he is from early times. His importance is celebrated in the learned essays of Blades in England and O'Conor in America, and he has a paragraph to himself in Aristotle's *History of Animals*, which O'Conor quotes.[1] The Father of Philosophy gives out that this sapper of books is the smallest of all creatures and like a scorpion without a tail.

As he is a destroyer of books, nature's own biblioclast, he cannot be defended or tolerated, but he excites less indignation than his human prototype, because though he *does irreparable damage*, he is not to be *found every day*,[2] and is, by breeding and predilection, a feeder only upon neglected and forlorn books, departing from their pages as soon as they are caressed by human hands. *Quiet neglect is necessary to his existence;*[3] *dirty books, damp books, dusty books, and books that the owner never opens, are most exposed to the enemy;*[4] he becomes an *acknowledged tenant* of the library where he is often heard of but *seldom seen*,[5] therefore, as the poet[6] sings,

> Why should sons of science
> These puny rankling reptiles dread?
> 'Tis but to let their books be read,
> And bid the worms defiance,

O'Conor goes further when he confesses to a fellow-feeling for this minute lover of books: *I had ever been fond of books, but never of bugs; but*

[1] *Facts about Bookworms.* 24. [2] Arthur L. Humphreys, *Private Library.* 23.
[3] Blades, *Enemies of Books.* 84. [4] Lang, *Library.* 40. [5] Blades, *op. cit.* 63.
[6] J. Doraston, Qt. Blades, *Enemies of Books.* 61.

here was a bug that was fond of books, and for the sake of books I could be a friend to the bug by making his pedigree known to the world of letters. [1]

But of dispraise there has been plenty in prose and verse. Poets have appealed to him, and his devastations have many times served the purpose of satire, as in the Scottish bard,

> Through and through the inspired leaves,
> Ye maggots make your windings;
> But, Oh! respect his Lordship's taste,
> And spare his golden bindings. [2]

Anathemas have been hurled at him *in nearly every European language, old and new.* Classical scholars of other times have *thrown their spondees* and *dactyls* at him. [3] Euenus, the grammarian, in ancient Byzantium, condemned him in an epigram, [4] which Andrew Lang has made English: [5]

> Pest of the Muses, devourer of pages, in crannies that lurkest,
> Fruits of the Muses to taint, labour of learning to spoil;
> Wherefore, oh black-fleshed worm! wert thou born for the
>   evil thou workest?
> Wherefore thine own foul form shap'st thou with envious
>   toil?

Dibdin [6] records a *pretty poem* by Theodore Beza, which has been rendered into English verse by Thomas Parnell. The bard thus scolds a bookworm for playing *old gooseberry* with his *Catullus:*

> Insatiate brute, whose teeth abuse
> The sweetest servants of the Muse—
> Nay, never offer to deny,
> I took thee in the act to fly.
>
> His roses nipped in every page,
> My poor Anacreon mourns thy rage;
> By thee my Ovid wounded lies;
> By thee my Lesbia's Sparrow dies;
> Thy rabid teeth have half destroyed
> The work of love in Biddy Floyd;
> They rent Belinda's locks away,
> And spoiled the Blouzelind of Gay. [7]

---

[1] *Facts about Bookworms.* 19.   [2] Robert Burns.   [3] Blades, *Enemies of Books.* 63–4.
[4] *Anthol. Pal.* ix, 251.   [5] *Library.* 39.   [6] *Bibliographical Decameron.* ii, 447.
[7] Parnell's translation, *Book-Lovers' Anthology.* 250.

Pierre Petit, in 1683, says Blades,[1] dispraised him in Latin verses; he was *evidently moved by strong personal feelings against the 'invisum pecus'*, for he *addresses him as Bestia audax*, and *Pestis chartarum*, for

> Pene tu mihi passerem Catulli,
> Pene tu mihi Lesbiam abstulisti.[2]

and then:

> Quid dicam innumeros bene eruditos
> Quorum tu monumenta, tu labores
> Isto pessimo ventre devorasti?[3]

But what he is like and what harm he does is more perpendicular to my theme, so I proceed.

II. THE LEGENDARY BOOKWORM

Because of his diminutiveness, observers in times past, before the age of microscopes, have made of him a stranger beast than he is, as Aristotle with his tailless scorpion; and some have attributed powers to him which have not been supported by the evidence of time and experience, as Mentzelius, who records that he had heard the bookworm *crow like a cock unto his mate. I knew not*, he relates, *whether some local fowl was clamouring or whether there was but a beating in mine ears*. Yet even at that moment of uncertainty, he perceives on the writing-paper before him *a little insect that ceased not to carol like a very chanticleer, until, taking a magnifying glass, I assiduously observed him*. He was *about the bigness of a mite*, and he carried *a grey crest* and bowed his head low *over the bosom*. The *crowing noise* came from the *clashing of his wings against each other with an incessant din.*[4]

As recently as the year 1898 Father O'Conor was so bold as to say that *neither bookmen nor bookmakers have been able to tell us much more about the bookworm than Aristotle told twenty-three centuries ago.*[5] But in this respect he underestimates, for William Blades has contributed much to our knowledge of this devourer of books in a famous essay,[6] though I admit we have still much to learn. In the year 1744, the Royal Society of Science at Göttingen offered a prize, O'Conor gives out of *Petzholdt*,[7] for answers to the following questions: How many kinds of insects are there inimical to libraries and archives? What kind of material do these insects like best? and, What are the means of defence against them? Ninety-eight years later,

---

[1] *Enemies of Books*. 64.   [2] 'Almost hast thou robbed me of Catullus's sparrow and of Lesbia.'   [3] 'What shall I say of the innumerable scholars whose monuments and labours thou hast devoured with thy evil stomach?'   [4] Qt. Lang, *Library*. 39.   [5] *Facts about Bookworms*. 27–8.   [6] 'The Bookworm', *Enemies of Books*. ch. vi.   [7] *Facts about Bookworms*. 28.

in 1842, the Society of Bibliophiles of Mons offered a prize for a solution
of the same problems. But no notable addition to our knowledge resulted
from these offers, or I have not seen any record of them. *Even in our times*,
says *Lang*,[1] *the learned Mr. Blades, having a desire to exhibit bookworms to the
Caxtonians at the Caxton celebrations, could find few who had seen a bookworm,
much less heard him utter his native wood-notes wild*. So, following my usual
method, I shall give what facts are known from earliest times to the present
day, and by so doing help towards a clearer comprehension of this small
yet powerful pest.

III. THE BOOKWORM AND HIS
SEVERAL VARIETIES

Hooke, in his *Micrographia* (1667), was the first to record him in an English-
treatise; he sees him as *a small glistering pearl-coloured moth* with highly
developed powers of locomotion. Upon being disturbed, he is *observed
very nimbly to scud, and back away to some lurking cranny*, the better to
protect himself from any appearing danger. He owns *a conical body,
divided into fourteen several partitions*, like *so many several shells or shields*,
every one of which is *tiled over with a multitude of thin transparent scales*,
which from the *multiplicity of their reflecting surfaces* give him his pearly
colour. His head is big and blunt and his form tapers to the tail, *smaller and
smaller*, like a carrot. He is furnished with two clusters of eyes, each cluster
beset with a row of small bristles, much like the *cilia* or eyelashes, and perchance serving a like purpose. Two long horns, straight and tapering
towards the top, but *curiously ringed or knobbed*, project outwards from the
head, and they are *bristled like the marsh-weed, called horse-tail, or cat's tail*,
having each a knot or *fringed girdle of small hairs* with several bigger bristles
here and there dispersed among them. Besides these he has two shorter
horns or feelers, knotted and fringed, but wanting bristles and blunt at the
ends. Finally, he has three tails, *in every particular resembling the two longer
horns that grow out of the head*, and his legs are scaled and haired like the rest
of him.

Blades boldly affirms that this description and the picture which accom-
panies it in the *Micrographia* were evolved out of Hooke's *inner consciousness*, but better informed friends advised him that Hooke had mistaken
the *Lepisma*, which is often found in warm, damp corners of old houses,
for the bookworm.[2] This is opposed by Dr. Rees, in his *Cyclopaedia*
(v.E.2),[3] where he declares that Hooke describes the *larva* of the *tinus* or
tinea; and he is supported in our own day by O'Conor, who argues[4] that

---

[1] *The Library.* 39–40.   [2] *Enemies of Books.* 69.   [3] Qt. Dibdin, *Bibliographical
Decameron.* 444.   [4] *Facts about Bookworms.* 31.

Hooke gave a true description of *Lepisma saccharina*, of which he himself has found no less than three living specimens, and he presents a drawing of one of his own discoveries together with that of Hooke's in order to illustrate the resemblance.

Sylvester, in his *Laws of Verse*, notes Blades,[1] describes the bookworm as *a microscopic creature wriggling on the learned pages, which, when discovered, stiffens out into the resemblance of a streak of dirt.* The Rev. F. T. Havergal, *who had much trouble with bookworms in the Cathedral Library of Hereford,* says they are a kind of *death-watch*, with a hard outer skin, dark brown in colour, white body, and brown spots on their heads.[2] Blades[3] hunted bookworms in the British Museum and the Bodleian, and he sought information about the species from friends likely to have had experience of them. Dr. Garnett, our then Keeper of Books, gave him two specimens which had been caught in an old Hebrew *Commentary* recently arrived from Athens. One died early, the other lived in captivity for eighteen months. *He was longer, thinner, and more delicate looking than any of his English congeners; transparent like thin ivory, and a dark line ran through his body,* which Blades took to be the *intestinal canal.*

In 1879, Birdsall, the Northampton bookbinder, sent him *a fat little worm,* which Waterhouse, of the Entomological Department of the British Museum, identified as *Oecophora pseudospretella.*[4] During his first visit to Bodley's library in 1858 he stalked successfully *a fat glossy fellow,* about a third of an inch long, grazing upon a *Caxton.* This species had *a hard, shiny, white head,* which Blades believed to be usual, but Dr. Bandinel, Bodley's then librarian, assured him, as he killed the specimen, that *they have black heads sometimes.*[5] Lang says that *the black sort prevailed* in Byzantium.[6] Neither could they agree, in those days, about the size of the pest. Because it is of furtive habit and invisible for the most part, many authorities believed him to be diminutive and even microscopic. Blades[7] took the other extreme and maintained that both the *Oecophora* and the *Anobium* were half an inch in length; but O'Conor expostulates that *a bookworm half an inch long would be a monster.*[8] He has never seen one that exceeded one-eighth of an inch in length, and most of those examined by him were even shorter. The shortest, a specimen of *Ptinus fur*, was less than one-twenty-fifth of an inch long.[9]

Out of this confusion we come to realize that there is not one bookworm, but several, each with his own peculiar tastes and habits, and each warring against different parts of a book. Rees has an instance in *eruditus: which directs its attacks to those parts which are sewed together or glued down.* This authority discovers *another mischievous creature* in the *larva* of the small

[1] *Enemies of Books.* 65.   [2] *Enemies of Books.* 70–1.   [3] *Ib.* 75–6.   [4] *Ib.* 75.   [5] *Ib.* 82.
[6] *Library.* 38.   [7] *Op. cit.* 74.   [8] *Facts about Bookworms.* 32.   [9] *Ib.* 35.

moth of the *tinea* kind, which is *insinuated in the egg-state into the paper*, and when the *larva* is hatched, he *gnaws cylindrical cavities* through the leaves before spinning the web in which to rest during the *pupa* state; and he becomes a moth only to fly away and repeat the process in some other unfortunate book. Rees also affirms that the *larvae* of several species of the *Dermestes* prey upon the covers as well as upon the leaves of books. D'Alembert will have that a bookworm is a *little beetle* like a *cheese-mite which devours books merely because it is compelled to gnaw its way out into the air*.[1] He thinks also that it is predisposed to enjoy the paste used by bookbinders.

Kirby,[2] the entomologist, supports the theory of the paste-eating mite, which Rees calls *carus eruditus*, after Schrunk; and he adds a new species in the *larva* of *crambus pinguinalis*, which feeds upon bindings, burrowing into the leather, where it spins a robe for itself, covering it with *its own excrement*, and doing *no little injury*. He has also observed *the caterpillar of another little moth*, without discovering the species, which *takes its station in damp old books*, preferably *Black Letter*, many of which, worth their *weight in gold*, have in this way been *snatched by these destroyers from the hands of book-collectors*. In the year 1819 a contributor to the *Gentleman's Magazine*[3] espied a bookworm *taking a nap* in a half-bound copy of Wall's *Ceremonies of the University* (1798). He captured his *literary foe* and enclosed him in a beechen box, feeding him upon choice scraps of old paper and, for his Sunday dinner, pieces of an old Greek book which bore evidence of the labours of belligerents who had not only penetrated through *Pythagoras* but had even attacked *Demosthenes*.

In this book he found another of the same species, and beside him a dead fly or moth, *which probably was his parent*. This witness then gives a description of the grub under microscopic observation, which confirms that of Hooke. The worm resembles a *filbert-maggot*, and is of a *pearly-white* colour. The body is formed of *scaly rings*, capable of being contracted or extended at will. It is round in appearance, flat beneath, and covered with *white downy hairs*. Further, its form is thicker towards the head, which juts out from the body, and is of a *darker hue, approaching drab*. The mouth and eyes are of a *mahogany cast. It appears*, he says, *to be furnished with two tusks, of a saw-like form, with which it pierces the wood, leather, and paper, which form its food*. He was led to this last conclusion because when he found the specimen it was embedded in dust, which under the microscope clearly resembled *saw-dust*. In movement it was slow, and when touched curled into a ball like an armadillo or a hedgehog. His two specimens were nearly alike except that one was smaller and appeared to be younger than the other. They were both in the same box but divided by a partition; and

[1] Qt. Lang, *The Library*. 40. [2] *Introduction to Entomology*. (1816) i, 238. [3] ii, 135–6.

as the little one seemed anxious to get to the other, he put them together. *The younger approached his senior and saluted him with great affection, as if claiming some relationship. This the elder would not brook, and seemingly conscious of the superiority which a residence at the University had conferred upon him, he coolly avoided the Grecian tyro, and behaved to him much in the same way as a Senior Soph would to a young and uninitiated freshman.*

Dibdin made some researches into the natural history of this enemy of books, chiefly among bookbinders.[1] Payne and Foss had seen two specimens, *one was like a small maggot, the other had something of the head and horns of a bug.* Mr. Baber had seen only the *slough of one.* His friends Heber and Lang had caught one *in the very act of book-murder,* in the sale-room of Mr. King. At length he was enabled to examine a specimen for himself, for two were sent to him by Ogle & Co., who had imported them from Holland. One was alive and the other dead, but unfortunately the live one escaped, so that Dibdin had opportunity only of examining the dead one. It was *slightly curled up* and was *precisely similar* to a *filbert-maggot,* with *a mahogany-coloured head,* and when stretched out extended no more than a quarter of an inch in length. I could repeat many such particulars, but to no useful purpose, since they are all so diverse in detail that they establish nothing but the existence of bookworms; how many varieties and what they are is not sufficiently observed.

IV. NOMENCLATURE AND CLASSIFICATION

There is the same confusion when we come to the name of this elusive devastator of books. Blades has several guesses.[2] Hannett, in his work on *Bookbinding,* gives *Anglossa penguinalis* as the real name; Mrs. Gatty, in her *Parables, Hypothenemus eruditus;* Mr. Holmes (*Notes & Queries,* 1870), *Anobium paniceum;* and still others, *Acarus eruditus,* and *Anobium pertinax,* a specimen of the latter having been found in the British Museum, under Mr. Rye's keepership: it was one of two or three, but they were *weakly creatures.*[3] Blades himself examined a copy of Caxton's *Lyf of Oure Ladye,* which was so curiously *channelled* at the bottom of the pages, that he thought the destroyer to have been no true bookworm, but the larva of *Dermestes vulpinus,* a very voracious garden beetle, which *eats any kind of dry ligneous rubbish.*[4]

The ancient scorpion theory continued, in some measure, down to our own time, for I find it upheld by no less an authority than the *Encyclopaedia Britannica.*[5] Here the minute devastator is classed with the *Pseudoscorpiones* of the class *Arachnida,* the common British forms of which,

---

[1] *Bibliographical Decameron.* ii, 445–6.   [2] *Enemies of Books.* 70–1.   [3] *Ib.* 77.
[4] *Ib.* 83.   [5] 11th Ed. under 'Book-Scorpion'. iv, 233.

Chelifer cancroides and *Chiridium museorum*, are found in old furniture as well as in old books. O'Conor believes Aristotle's *tailless scorpion* to correspond with *Acarus cheyletus*, of the order *Acaridae*.[1] But he finally concludes[2] that the sum of our information from writers on the subject of bookworms, beginning with Aristotle and ending with our living authorities, is solely this: *that there is a bookworm, or that there are bookworms, with learned names—insects of some sort, which are suspected of eating books, though the charge is not proved against any particular one*. Yet he comes forward boldly, after much research, first-hand experience and *positive knowledge*, and says that the bookworm is a reality, that it is not rare, that it is still *doing decided mischief*, and finally that it has a name as well as a local habitation.

Blades, many years before O'Conor, was equally convinced that the bookworm was a reality. He believes, however, that the enemy is not one but several, and that he might be either a *caterpillar or a grub*. If the former, he is the *larva* of a *moth*, if the latter, of a *beetle*. And he thinks that as the holes made by them resemble closely those made by insects in *filberts* or *wood*, it may reasonably be supposed that bookworms are immigrants from among outdoor insects. Many old librarians hold to this opinion and object to opening their library windows. Blades finally divides his worms into two classes: (1) The Beetle, *Anobium*, which has varieties, as *A. pertinax*, *A. eruditus*, and *A. paniceum*. (2) The Moth, *Aecophora*, the species which attacks books being *Aecophora pseudospretella*.[3]

Into this confusion of opinion O'Conor throws the light of laborious and exact research. He approaches the dark problem with the technique of the man of science, accepting no opinion unless it can be supported out of his own experience, and by patient investigation substituting fact for hearsay and myth. He examined seventy-two specimens of various kinds of insects found in books, and legitimately to be classed as bookworms. He caught a *great many* whilst *alive and at work eating good books*. He also observed them in various other stages of their development. But he believes they do the greatest harm in the *larva state*.[4] *The bookworm is not a worm, in the scientific sense*, he says, but *the larva of certain insects belonging to the order of 'Coleoptera', or sheath-winged beetles;* and of these he has found seven different varieties either as *larvae* or as *imagos*. There are three of the former: *Sitodrepa panicea*, *Attagenus pellio*, and *Anthrenus varius*; and four of the latter: *Sitodrepa panicea*, *Lepisma saccharina*, *Ptinus fur*, and *Dermestes lardarius*.

In character and appearance they have many differences. *Sitodrepa panicea* is the most voracious. In the *larva* he is soft, white, six-legged, and

[1] *Facts about Bookworms*. 24. [2] *Ib*. 43. [3] *Enemies of Books*. 71-3. [4] *Facts about Bookworms*. 52.

bristled. *Attagenus pellio* is long, slender, salmon–coloured, and tailed with delicate hair; his form is that of a *miniature whale*, and in movement he is *most graceful*. *Sitodrepa panicea* is a small, *brown beetle*. *Lepisma Saccharina* is shaped like a cone with three thick tails; his motion is rapid, *like a flash of light*. *Ptinus fur* is a black–headed worm, and *seems willing to eat anything*. *Dermestes lardarius* is very common and resembles a microscopic hedge-hog; he also *will devour anything from a live insect to hard sole leather*. *Anthrenus varius* in the *larva* state is something between the almost round *Dermestes* and the elongated *Attagenus pellio*.[1]

These descriptions are original, the result of his own observations, and mark the turn in the story of the bookworm from myth to history. He does not say that the creatures described by earlier authors are not book-worms, but only that he *has met with none of them;* and he concludes that writers of the past have probably copied one from another, adopting names which have been *sanctioned by time*, without troubling to verify them. All of which is doubtless true.

V. HOW THE BOOKWORM DISCOVERED AMERICA

The first bookworms to discover America were of Italian origin. They reached Cornell University in a copy of the *Divine Comedy*. *From the appearance of the volume*, says Arnold,[2] *it is surmised that these bookworms were born and bred in the 'Inferno'; that during the voyage most of them were in 'Purgatory', and that on arrival at New York they all found themselves in 'Paradise'*. Whether this be true or not they took up residence at Cornell and *are credited with having given* to that University *a certain distinction which as a mere seat of learning it would not possess*. Despite this evidence most Americans, Blades declares,[3] believe that their rare books are not attacked by this bane, probably because they have *cost many dollars* and are *therefore well looked after*, which is as like as not. He quotes the *American Encyclo-paedia of Printing* (1871) in support of the argument that there are so few bookworms in that land that a worm-eaten book in a private library in Philadelphia is looked upon as a curiosity. Whether America passed through a bookwormless period is not clear, but by 1898 that period, if Humphreys is correct, was over, for he records[4] that there was then greater trouble from these boring insects in America than in England. Among the varieties observed by him were '*fish bugs*', '*silver fish*', *and* '*bustle tails*', scientifically known as '*Lepisma Saccharina*'; another, known as

[1] *Facts about Bookworms*. 57–64.   [2] *Ventures in Book-Collecting*. 8–9.   [3] *Enemeis of Books*. 85–7.   [4] *The Private Library*. 23.

'*buffalo bug*', or '*carpet bug*', which is the *Anthrenus varius*; and *Blatta Australasia, a species of cockroach.*

The legend of America's immunity from bookworms is for ever refuted by Father O'Conor's discovery of a specimen in the *venerable Georgetown Library,* in an old folio. He was a little brown fellow *covered with bristles* and looking *for all the world like a tiny hedgehog, curling himself in his spikes to insure protection.* After a little search another of the same kind was tracked down in the same volume.[1] The creatures were recognized as *Dermestes lardarii,* or *larvae* of the brown beetle. The capture aroused great interest. The specimens were passed from one savant to another. At the suggestion of the President of the University they were sent to Mr. Spofford, of the Library of Congress. He handed them to Professor Baird, of the Smithsonian Institute, and he, in turn, passed them on to the Chief of the Entomological Commission. Father O'Conor was so stirred by his discovery that he continued his researches, which he has recorded in the first separate work on this pest. During his investigations he also discovered bookworms in the libraries of Boston College; St. Joseph's College, Philadelphia; and St. Francis Xavier's College, New York. He had specimens reported from other libraries in various parts of the United States, and he has little doubt that *examination will prove the disastrous presence of many more.*[2]

VI. TASTES AND HABITS

Whether bookworms feed indiscriminately upon leather, wood, and paper, or whether each material supports its particular species is not clear. Yet there is no doubt that they are omnivorous when it comes to the subject of the volume:

> Him frantic hunger wildly drives
> Against a thousand authors' lives:
> Through all the fields of wit he flies.[3]

But my most learned authority[4] will have it that *a library of novels is quite safe: no true bookworm,* he says *would deign to feed on a popular novel.* Yet most claim that their ravages are indiscriminate and, according to Dibdin,[5] in the respect of bindings as well as the other, both inward and outward parts of a book. *Through boards and through leathers, amidst margin and printed text,* he says, *now breakfasting upon a syllogism of Duns Scotus, then*

---

[1] *Facts about Bookworms.* 15–16.   [2] *Ib.* 43–5.   [3] Theodore Beza, Trans. Parnell, *Book-Lovers' Anthology.* 250.   [4] O'Conor, *Facts about Bookworms.* 76.   [5] *Bibliographical Decameron.* ii, 447.

*dining upon a devotional sentiment of Lactantius, and afterwards supping upon
a bit of Vincent de Beauvais' legends, this diminutive but desperate pioneer urges
his 'forceful way'!* Nothing comes amiss to these creatures, their digestive powers
being wonderful. *They will nibble at Hebrew, eat largely of Greek, riot upon
Latin, and satiate themselves with Italian!* Blades thinks that they have so
nice a palate that they prefer *Black Letter*, and, for choice, a *Caxton*. Such
a fastidious taste would place them among the gourmets, for the bookworm fed on *Caxtons feasts more sumptuously than Cleopatra dreamed of
when she drank her dissolved pearl.*[1]

But such evidence as I can find does not uphold the Caxtonian hypothesis. Blades himself attempted to refresh a captured specimen with
fragments of a Caxton *Boëthius* served on the leaf of a seventeenth-century
book, but with little encouragement, for the captive turns from *Caxton*
to devour *a piece of the leaf,* and in three weeks he is dead *either from too
much fresh air, unaccustomed liberty, or change of food.*[2] This famous bookman
ventures upon the theory that the difficulty of keeping bookworms in
captivity is *due to their formation.* Their habit is to gnaw their way through
a book by means of their *horny jaws* and the contraction and expansion of
their bodies. Being legless, the burrow thus made is their chief support,
and once it is removed, all *leverage* is gone, they lose balance and *cannot eat
although surrounded by food.*[3]

Blades announces that bookworms dislike parchment, and that the
MSS. of the Middle Ages were therefore immune from attack, and he is
doubtful whether they attacked the papyrus of the Egyptians.[4] But since
the enemy was known to Aristotle it must have attacked the books of
Ancient Greece. *All through the Golden Age of Pericles,* says O'Conor,[5] *the
worm has been carrying on its work of destruction, and many a copy of Aristotle
has he eaten full of holes.* The Arabic MSS. brought from Cairo by Burck-
hardt, and now in the University Library at Cambridge, have been *con-
siderably injured* by bookworms.[6] From which it is clear that no kind of
book was immune in olden times, and no kind of old book escapes even
to-day if it is unused and neglected.

Books of our own time are protected from attack because they are not
so palatable as those of the past. There is a *scarcity of edible books* from the
bookworm's point of view. The cause given is the *adulteration of modern
paper.* His instinct, Blades argues,[7] *forbids him to eat china clay, the bleacher,
the plaster of Paris, the sulphate of barytes, the scores of adulterants now used to
mix with the fibre,* and therefore *the wise pages of the old literature are, in the
race against Time with modern rubbish, heavily handicapped.* This opinion is
contested by O'Conor, who saw enough evidence in the libraries of

[1] O'Conor, *op. cit.* 72.   [2] *Enemies of Books.* 75.   [3] *Ib.* 77.   [4] *Ib.* 62.   [5] *Op. cit.* 27.
[6] Holme, *Notes & Queries.* 1870.   [7] *Op. cit.* 83–4.

America to prove that new as well as old books are attacked, and that they consume *much modern paper every year.*[1]

I am with those who believe that although bookworms have an especial love for our older books, they are all kin to that black-headed species well known to O'Conor, which would feed on *any kind of book he could find.*[2] They will also eat any kind of binding, although Dibdin holds that *hog-skin* was *most favourable to them.*[3]

In some fair old book compact of sound paper unalloyed with chemicals they roam at will, turning the wisdom of the ages into a warren of burrows, until at length disintegration is complete, and what was once a book becomes a mere husk of dilapidated paper, a remnant, a ruin. Few, says Percy Fitzgerald,[4] *have an idea of the ravages* they cause: *their performances excite amazement.* In a little while they can sap the portliest folio to destruction, as in the pitiful story of an attack upon a *folio* printed by Schoeffer of Mentz, in 1477. The copy was of *very good unbleached paper, as thick as stout cartridge;* it had suffered a mass attack of worms on each flank. On the first leaf were 212 distinct holes running in lines more or less at right angles with the covers. The volume has 250 pages and the holes continue, though in decreasing numbers, through as many as 90 of them. The attack on the rear was conducted by a breed *not so ravenous,* for there are but 81 holes on the last page and they go no further inwards than the sixty-ninth. Fitzgerald gives this as a typical instance. Many worms eat a longer path. He has seen a tunnel running through two thick volumes, cover and all (in this he is supported by O'Conor, who saw a book eaten through *from cover to cover*[5]); and he once saw some *Caxton* leaves which had been *furrowed* rather than *tunnelled,* to so great an extent that it was difficult to raise one of them without its falling to pieces.

Father O'Conor adds many deplorable examples[6] to this catalogue of destruction. With a slight pull he has been able to detach all the binding from books attacked by these ravenous little creatures; he has five volumes of Hany's *Mineralogy* (Paris, 1801) with scarcely a page intact; in a leather-bound folio *Plutarch* he found *a hole piercing through cover and pages, and in another hole, embedded in the cover, the cocoon of an insect which had not pierced entirely through the cover.* In another *folio,* page after page is drilled, but half-way through the book the tunnel of the bookworm stops. No further trace of his work and no reason for the stoppage was forthcoming. Did he die beneath the thumb of some vigorous Dr. Bandinel? Did he reach a new stage of development, return to the tunnel he had so *cleverly constructed* and *walk out a full-grown beetle?* Or did some greedy *Dermestes* steal into his demesne and make a meal off him, *preferring his tender body to the tough*

[1] *Facts about Bookworms.* 74. [2] *Facts about Bookworms.* 39. [3] *Bibliographical Decameron.* ii, 447. [4] *Book-Fancier.* 252. [5] *Op. cit.* 69. [6] *Op. cit.* 69–71.

vegetable fibre of paper? It is a mystery. O'Conor cannot solve it; nor can I. The tallest of all such yarns is that of Peignot, who avows that he found twenty-seven volumes pierced in a straight line by one worm. But many, including Blades, think this is a tale.[1]

VII. PROPER MEASURES CONDUCIVE TO HIS DEFEAT

That the bookworm is still busy among our books there can be no doubt. He may be invisible, but he is there: *the fact that a librarian has never seen a bookworm does not prove that there are no 'worms' fattening in the very choicest morsels in his library.*[2] How to protect out books from them is therefore a question of some moment. But we need not go far afield for a remedy. To sum up all in brief: prevention is the best cure and use the best preventive. Bookworms love books but abhor readers. Bibliophiles are their worst enemies, for they will be handling books, stroking, caressing them, dipping into their depths, and thus disturbing that dusty peace which is the bookworm's heaven. Active usage is a sovereign remedy, even for books which by accident, misfortune, or other circumstance have been exposed to attack. Yet forasmuch as all cannot embrace or apply this good counsel it is proper that we should consider the medicaments which have been advised.

The earliest remedy that I find recorded is that of Prediger, in his *Instructions to German Bookbinders* (Leipsig, 1741), whom Dibdin quotes,[3] out of Rees's *Cyclopaedia*, and Rees from *Mélanges d'Hist. Nat.* vol v. Believing that the mischief begins with the binding, he would have *starch* (which they dislike) used instead of *flour* for the making of the paste; and in addition he prescribes a slight dusting of the *sheets* and the *shelves* with *powdered alum and pepper.* In the months of March, July, and September, he would further have the books themselves *rubbed with a piece of woollen cloth, steeped in powdered alum.* Sir John Thorold, *one of our first-rate bibliomaniacs during the time of the Pinelli sale,* used to be particular, so Payne informed Dibdin, in his directions to the binder to have *a due proportion of alum* in the paste. O'Connor approves of Prediger's treatment, on the ground that it is not the alum but the rubbing which is efficacious.[4]

It was supposed at one time, Pinkerton records,[5] that *a binding of Russia leather secured books against insects*; but this supposal was exploded when volumes bound thus were found in Paris *pierced in every direction.* Bozerian, *the first bookbinder in Paris,* told him that the sole remedy was *to steep the*

---

[1] *Enemies of Books.* 78–85.   [2] *Facts about Bookworms.* 76.   [3] *Bibliographical Decameron.* ii, 446.   [4] *Op. cit.* 78.   [5] *Recollections of Paris.*

blank leaves in muriatic acid. Some advise fumigation by tobacco, or disinfecting with camphor and other preparations. Yet even if these devices drive the enemy from the outworks they cannot scare him from the heart of the closed books, where he may continue his evil work in safety. Prof. Riley, of the U.S. Entomological Commission, following Prediger, would begin at the *paste*, but with *corrosive sublimate*, not *alum*; and, for further precaution, he prescribes the subjecting of the infected volumes to *a considerable heat in the baking oven*, taking care, he is careful to add, *not to burn the leather brittle*, in which precaution all bibliophiles will concur. *It would be even better*, says my ingenious professor, *to place them in a watertight box and then sink them into hot water*; and, he concludes, *though it has not yet been tried, I have faith that pure' Pyrethrum' powder scattered among books in a closed vessel would also effectually free them*;[1] which is like a faith cure, and perchance as dangerous as the method of Frederick Locker's elderly clergyman who sought to purify a *Pynson* which was *infected with worms— alive with them*, by burying the volume in his garden.[2]

I myself, on the other hand, would advise in place of all such nostrums nothing save cleanliness, fresh air and reading; and since, as O'Conor affirms, the eggs of the bookworm are laid in the dust which is on or about books, the first step is to remove the dust. So, to sum up all, if the bookworm has already penetrated the volume, you can best drive him out by becoming a bookworm yourself. Nothing will more greatly expedite his evacuation of your bibliographical territory.

[1] Qt. *Facts about Bookworms.* 87.   [2] Locker-Lampson, *My Confidences.* 198–9.

Part XXI

OF BOOK-HUNTING

---◦===◦❖◦===◦---

I. A REVIEW OF THE CHASE

Book-Hunting is a great Sport, and many books are written of it; one[1] would have it a *royal sport as old as literature—as literature, that is, inscribed upon any material more portable than that of the Rosetta stone; no hobby so old, so enduring, or respectable,* says Percy Fitzgerald,[2] *almost from the first days of writing it declared itself,* and still flourishes, *the very literature of the subject is enormous, would fill a small library.* It is a wonder to hear what is related of illustrious collectors in this behalf, how many rich men are employed about it, how many booksellers, auctioneers, itinerant vendors, agents of all sorts, how much revenue consumed on this disport, how much time is spent upon it every year in London, New York, and Paris alone.

Many other sports and recreations there be, much in use, as athletics, card playing, dancing, shooting, sailing, motoring, flying, which many commend in just volumes, but none more consuming, none arousing greater devotion or keener delight. It is *mainly a personal affair, which begins and ends with a life:*[3] *once a collector, always a collector;*[4] book-hunting, like Rumour in *Virgil,* grows as it goes, *vires acquirit eundo;*[5] but it requires as much study and perspicacity as the rest, and is to be preferred before many of them; athletics and hunting are very laborious, and many dangers accompany them; but this is still and quiet. And if so be the book-hunter catch no book, yet he hath a wholesome walk to the bookshops, pleasant talk belike with booksellers, often entertaining characters and well-informed withal; he hath the good company of books, converse with them, dipping here and there, tasting title-pages, pleasing his touch with the feel of a smooth binding or his eyes by the sight of a well-proportioned page, or having his pulse quickened by the sight of some rarity, as Haslewood, Dibdin's friend, when he first saw Juliana Berners' *Boke of Hawkyng, Huntyng, etc.*[6]

---

[1] G. H. Powell, *Excursions in Libraria.* 3.   [2] *The Book-Fancier.*   [3] W. Carew Hazlitt, *The Book-Collector.* 25.   [4] Andrew Lang, *Books and Bookmen.* 131.   [5] *Aeneid.* iv, 175.   [6] *Bibliomania.* (1811) 118.

He hears the prattle of the book-market, which he thinks better than the noise of hounds, or the blast of horns, and all the sport that they can make, for of all *these impassioned pursuits, there is none more disturbing, more distressing in deception and hope, more intellectually absorbing, more obstinate in ill-success, more insatiable in triumph, more abundant in joys, noble, healthy and pure, than book-hunting;*[1] it is not easy; there are difficulties of acquisition, saith Powell,[2] necessities of research, and many snares and pitfalls beset those who go forth to the chase unequipped with the necessary knowledge, and, if they stalk the big game of the book world, with the necessary money. No use hunting *Caxtons* or *First Folio Shakespeares* with a pop-gun; at the same time I would not set up the most expensive books as the best hunting, even though so experienced an authority as Rosenbach will have that tracking down Bibles in manuscript is the *greatest sport of all* because *it takes a king's ransom to secure a really fine one.*[3] It is a varied sport and there is good hunting for all. *My sport is book-hunting*, says Newton,[4] *I look upon it as a game, a game requiring skill, some money, and luck*; and if there is more in a book than in any other hunted thing once you have caught it, the game's the thing when the hunt is on. According to Mr. Gladstone a book-collector ought to possess these six qualities: *Appetite, leisure, wealth, knowledge, discrimination, and perseverance*; a formidable list, but be not daunted, for he himself had, by his own confession, but two of these qualities, the first and the last, and even so continued to collect some 35,000 volumes.[5]

If the ordinary sports which are used abroad, as fishing, shooting, hawking, chasing of foxes, hares, rabbits, deer, boars and the like, be, as Camden in his *Staffordshire* relates, *hilares venandi labores*, because they recreate body and mind, what shall I say of book-hunting? Xenophon (in *De Venatione*, cap. i) graces ordinary hunting with a great name, *Deorum munus*, the gift of the Gods, a princely sport, which men have ever used, saith Langius, *epist.* 59, *lib.* 2, as well for health as for pleasure, and do to this day, here and elsewhere all over the world, for *there is nothing in which all mankind, civilized or savage, have more agreed, than in making some sort of chase part of their business or amusement.*[6] 'Tis true that book-hunting can claim no such extent of devotion among noblemen, but that it hath devotees among all classes and in all civilized realms cannot be denied; and some so dote upon it that as Bohemus (*de mor. gent. lib.* 3. *cap.* 12) saith of ordinary hunting, *communiter venantur, quod sibi solis licere contendunt*,[7] 'tis all their study, their exercise, ordinary business, all their talk; which proves

---

[1] Octave Uzanne, *The Book-Hunter in Paris.* 110.   [2] *Excursions in Libraria.* 35.
[3] *Books and Bidders.* 221.   [4] *Amenities of Book-Collecting.* 123.   [5] Letter to Bernard Quaritch. 9.ix.1896.   [6] Charles James Fox, *Correspondence with Wakefield.* 80.
[7] 'They hunt ordinarily, and maintain that they alone are permitted to do this.'

that they are proper hunters and, as such, like to the rest, and in some kind all men are hunters, as Octave Uzanne[1] declares: *Lovers are but hunters after women; actors hunters after success; misers hunters after gold, policemen hunters after men; and are we not,* he asks, *all in chase of excitement?*

Many can witness to the excitement of book-hunting, and some, as I shall show, dwell too much upon it: they can do nothing else, discourse of nought else, so that they could in some sort be taxed, as Paulus Jovius (in his *Descr. Brit.*) taxed our English Nobility *for living in the country so much, and too frequent use of it, as if they had no other means but Hawking and Hunting to approve themselves gentlemen with.* A like reproach may be made against some book-hunters, as those rich men who, saith John Hill Burton,[2] *purchase fine and dear books by deputy,* for vanity, as the *nouveaux riches* buy yachts, deer forests, stables of race-horses, etc., for show, conceit, empty pride. Such idle and wealthy amateurs, even though they enjoy their books somewhat, are like to sensualists who employ *souteneurs,* they hunt by *procuration* and very properly are despised by their procurers, says Charles Asselineau,[3] who despise them *comme le garde-chasse et le braconnier mépriseront toujours le maître lâche et maladroit qui triomphe par leur addresse,* as gamekeepers and poachers despise clumsy and incompetent sportsmen. Or those *dilettanti* who become slaves of the fashion for what is merely rare, amassing belike *volumes of forgotten verse which have no merit but their rarity,* whom Chapman[4] places as lower than philatelists: *the collector of postage-stamps is a humanist by comparison.* Even, he saith, *those whose wealth enables them to fly at higher game, have no better title to respect if mere rarity be their lure,* theirs, *a petty ambition,* themselves, *unworthy custodians, swine among their pearls.* In this matter most opinions will concur with those words of Charles Monselet where he protests that *mere purchasing does not constitute collecting,* for *anyone with money can buy*; rather is it *he who seeks, uncovers, and wrests from obscurity that which is worth preservation whom we may safely call an amateur.*[5]

The book-hunter must be moved by the love of the *chasse à livres,* or of the books themselves, or both. Some claim that the desire for books is enough in itself, although our mighty hunter Heber combined a country life of farming and hunting with a town life of book-collecting and study.[6] But I confess the chase of books is a passion which lasts throughout life and may, this side of dotage, legitimately outrace all other passions; as in Richard Smith, who *lived to a very great age and spent a good part of it almost entirely in the search of books,*[7] and the Emperor Julian, who confessed, and his words afterwards were carved over the door of his library at Antioch:

[1] *Book-Hunter in Paris.* 109–10.   [2] *Book-Hunter.* 163.   [3] *L'Enfer du Bibliophile.* 7. [4] 'Old Books and Modern Reprints', *The Portrait of a Scholar.* 48.   [5] Qt. Tredwell, *Privately Illustrated Books.* 23.   [6] Dibdin, *Bibliomania.* (1811) 173.   [7] *Ib.* 399.

some love horses, or hawks, or hounds, but I from my boyhood have pined with a desire for books.[1] But it is not probable that the Emperor hunted his own books, pursued them himself, tasting *the unquestionable delight in buying an odd volume and haunting the stalls in a search for its companion;*[2] he more likely resembled Henry Huth, who never searched for books himself but sat in wait for them to be brought to him; he was not a hunter of books but the builder of a library, or, as W. C. Hazlitt asserts,[3] one who had his library *made for him.* At his best the book-hunter loves both the chase and the quarry, as true hunters at all times have delighted in the pursuit and capture of what they need, *because it affords a kind of sportive excitement.*[4]

The book-hunter must be keen, earnest, skilful; *he must not be—and the great collector never has been—a dilettante: least of all to-day, when collection is almost an exact science.*[5] T. J. Wise, in our own time, is a notable example of the complete hunter of books. He combines the maximum of skill in pursuit with the maximum of bibliographical interest in possession: *the chief characteristic which will keep his name alive in the history of books is that he was the first to insist on specializing the system of entries and to give it a scientific uniformity and accuracy.*[6] As a favourable example of the good book-hunter in past times, I would point to Peiresc, a mighty hunter before the Lord, if ever there was one; he hunted books personally in all places, adorned them in *gold, purple, and all manner of neat and curious workmanship,* by the hands of the most excellent craftsmen, who were part of his household; he diligently read his books, and his next care was to travel over Europe seeking more treasures for his library; but his own efforts did not satisfy his hunger, so he sent others from his own house, into all the islands of the Ægean Sea, to the mountain Athos, to Constantinople, to Alexandria, to Memphis and to Carthage, who for him and with his money sought to procure the most ancient books in the Greek, Hebrew, Arabic, Persian, Coptic, and Æthiopian languages.[7]

But as in the labours, exercises and recreations of hunting animals or birds or fishes, some properly belong to the body, some to the mind, so among book-hunters some are material, seeking only to satisfy acquisitive desires, others intellectual, seeking more opportunely to exalt and nourish a taste for books and what is in them. Octave Uzanne[8] gives, out of *Quentin-Bauchart,* that there are two clear-cut classes of book-collectors, one looking upon a book as *un objet de mode et de luxe,* or as a sort of *valeur de Bourse,* stock exchange quotation, whose fluctuations they follow with

---

[1] Qt. Elton, *The Great Book-Collectors.* 7.   [2] Jerrold, *Autolycus of the Bookstalls.* 10.
[3] *Book-Collector.* 44–5.   [4] Andrew Lang, *The Library.* Second Ed. 17.   [5] Sawyer & Darton, *English Books: 1475–1900.* i, 29–30.   [6] Sir Edmund Gosse, *Sunday Times.* 15.i.1928.   [7] *Life.* Gassendi. Trans. Rand. Qt. Horne, *Binding of Books.* 129–30.   [8] *Les Zigzags d'un Curieux.* 43.

a gamester's interest; the other seeking books for their contents, *pour sa rareté et sa belle condition matérielle de texte et de reliure*; these last, he well says, are *les purs, la phalange d'élite des bibliophiles*. The former, those who hunt for profit, and it is incredible how much they can do in such case, are no more than tradesmen, or speculators; *the collector of English first editions*, Aldous Huxley states,[1] *is wholly a speculator*, never knowing *what time may have in store*; he might use any other quarry for his purpose: merchandise, stocks and shares, and the like; the market-place or the stock exchange, not the study or the library, his proper place, and an analysis of his operations more opportune to a discourse on commerce. Others are not much better than those products of *consols at* 100 who, in the satiric opinion of Disraeli, *considered books a luxury, almost as elegant and necessary as ottomans, bonbons, and pier-glasses.*[2] Yet I have no fear for the general behaviour of bookmen, for, as Mr. Gladstone concludes, *book-collecting may have its quirks and eccentricities, but, on the whole, it is a vitalizing element in a society honeycombed by several sources of corruption.*[3]

In America book-collecting with some is already commercialized, as Rosenbach confesses:[4] *some of the most discerning men in Wall Street purchase rare books as an investment*; they keep them in strong rooms with stocks and shares and bonds, believing that *such treasures will always sell at a premium, even when the market is tumbling and Wall Street is in a panic.* But, I repeat with Lang,[5] *book-collecting ought not to be a mere trade, or a mere fad; its object is to secure the comforts of a home for examples really rare or beautiful, or interesting as relics.* John Hill Burton[6] has an axiom that *the mercenary spirit must not be admitted to a share in the enjoyments of the book-hunter*; he will not allow that a thought should be given to the value of the books, even after the bookman *has taken his last survey of his treasures, and spent his last hour in that quiet library*; he must not allow *money-making—even for those he is to leave behind—to be combined with his pursuit*, for if he do so *it loses its fresh relish, its exhilarating influence, and becomes the source of wretched cares and paltry anxieties*; nor will he regret in the end that *the hobby which was his enjoyment has been in any wise the more costly to him*, if he has not made it a means of mercenary money-getting.

Many will agree with Lang[7] when he argues that although there is much reason in this, *there is room for difference of opinion*, for it is one thing for the collector to be able to reflect that the money he has spent on books is not lost, and that his family may be richer for his taste, and another to buy books as a speculator buys shares, meaning to sell again when he has a profit; and I see no harm in the former finding consolation in moments

[1] 'Bibliophiles', *On the Margin.* 64.   [2] *Vivian Grey.*   [3] Letter to Bernard Quaritch, 9.ix.1896.   [4] *Books and Bidders.* 79–80.   [5] *The Library.* Second Ed. xiv.   [6] *Book-Hunter.* 106–8.   [7] *Library.* 7.

of pecuniary panic, for *rare books are a safe investment; the stock can never go down.*[1] Hill Burton,[2] on the other hand, would have no collector sell his books without *urgent and necessary* reason; he disallows barter of any kind; but, perhaps, he would exonerate one who, knowing the value of his books, sold them during his lifetime, as Milton did, because *he thought he could dispose of them to greater advantage than his wife would be able to do;*[3] let the collector, he enjoins,[4] confine his attention to *purchasing* only. *No good ever comes of gentlemen amateurs buying and selling;* they will either become *systematic losers* or *acquire shabby habits.* As for those who hunt for possession, hoarding and accumulating greedily and inordinately, I shall speak of them when I come to bibliomania.

The postulates I would advance for the true book-hunter are few and simple: 1. He must hunt the books himself and not by proxy, *must actually undergo the anxiety, the fatigue, and, so far as purse is concerned, the risks of the chase.*[5] 2. He must love his quarry, as the fox-hunter declares he loves the fox, but without his desire to destroy it. 3. He must keep his books for useful studies, delightful reading, or the companionship of their presence: *own all the books you can, use all the books you own, and as many more as you can get.*[6] 4. He must hunt the books he himself likes and not those approved by fashion, custom, etc. Never hunt the book you ought to hunt, only those you want. *We should try to purchase the books which disenchant us least.*[7] *The one best and sufficient reason for a man to buy a book is because he thinks he will be happier with it than without it.*[8] He that is animated by such motives is almost ravished with the pleasure of the game. Book-hunting will be his chief delight and he will judge all places by their capacity to provide him with the means of gratifying his taste.

II. COLLECTIONS REFLECT THE COLLECTOR

In the last resort a collection of books should interpret a subject or express the character of the collector. It ought to be possible to judge a man by his books, his library should be his portrait. *The very essence of a collection of books is that it should have individuality,* and he[9] sees no virtue in collecting *the same set of first editions as are collected by numbers of other persons.* Henry Yates Thompson loved illuminated manuscripts and set out to collect

[1] Rosenbach, *Books and Bidders.* 33. [2] *Op. cit.* 106. [3] Mark Pattison, *Milton.* 143. [4] *Op. cit.* 106. [5] Burton, *Book-Hunter.* 163. [6] An American, qt. by William Roberts, *The Book-Hunter in London.* xxii. [7] Andrew Lang, *The Library.* Preface. xv. [8] A. E. Newton, *Amenities of Book-Collecting.* 119. [9] Williams, *Elements of Book-Collecting.* 123.

one hundred illustrating the best the world had to show;[1] but if few biblio-philes are purse-competent to follow him, many can follow a less golden gleam, as Lord de Tabley, who *valued his first edition for the text's sake, not for the bare fact of rarity*;[2] this is no very far remove from collecting to read and enjoy, which I account most wise. *Book-collectors*, Birrell holds,[3] *should be voracious but not omnivorous*, and he gives out, as I myself would, that the library of our greatest contemporary book-hunter, T. J. Wise, is *wonderful* for the particular reason that he made *it to please himself*; he collected books that were *spiritually precious*[4] to him. Wise by name and wise by nature, he has believed in his own thought, followed his gleam, and proved once again Emerson's dictum[5] that *what is true for you in your private heart is true for all men*, and *genius*, he says, is no more than that. In book-collecting as in other things, the sum of all is that *what interests you is what concerns you*.[6] Now to this end and purpose alone I also hold the Ashley Library to be wonderful, but it has an added wonder in that it reveals so exquisite a discrimination and so great a reverence for our masterpieces of literature; he has watched *that gleam of light which flashes across his mind from within* and so caught *the lustre of the firmament of bards and sages*.[7] He was fully resolved to do as much from the start, and the great catalogue of his life's work and love, which *is in effect a history of English literature during the last* 300 *years*,[8] may well appear as a blazing star, or an Angel, to his sight. So I may conclude this chapter with a pet admonition that you should follow your star, hoping it will be ever in the ascendant; *to thine own self be true*, in books as in all things, and thy collection will escape that sameness which is nonentity, even though thy treasures were all stars of the auction room, for as the poet sings: *Inveniet quod quisque velit: non omnibus unum est quod placet: hic spinas colligit, ille rosas*,[9] every man shall find his own desire; no one thing pleases all; one gathers thorns, another roses; go then, good hunters all, and

Gather ye rosebuds while ye may.[10]

III. THE JOY OF BOOK-HUNTING

It is a sweet game which few bookmen can resist, even when they feel that they are too much engaged in it. Andrew Lang confesses how he had repented, sinned, struggled, and fallen: *thrown catalogues, unopened, into*

[1] Seymour de Ricci, *English Collectors of Books and Manuscripts*. 169.   [2] Gossel 'Lord de Tabley', *Critical Kit-Kats*. 190.   [3] *Ashley Library Catalogue*. Intro. ii, viii, [4] Richard Curle, *Ib*. i, x.   [5] *Essays*. First Series. 37.   [6] Hamerton, *Intellectua. Life*. 125.   [7] Emerson, *op. cit*.   [8] David Nichol Smith. *Ashley Lib. Cat*. Intro. viii, x.   [9] Petronius.   [10] Herrick, 'To the Virgins, to make much of Time'.

the waste-paper basket; withheld his feet *from the paths that lead to Sotheby's and to Puttick's; crossed the street to avoid a book-stall:* to no avail: *the fatal moment of temptation arrived* and he *succumbed to the soft seductions of Eisen, or Cochin, or an old book on Angling.* Probably, he imagines, Grolier *was thinking of such weaknesses when he chose his devices 'Tanquam Ventus' and 'quisque suos patimur Manes'.*[1] Newton was thus tempted by Skelton's *Pithy, Pleasant and Profitable Works* (1568), and when he had fallen and was later appalled at the great price he had paid for it he sought to liquidate the expense by smoking *several cheap cigars on the night of its arrival.*[2]

No sport so seductive, so rich in temptations, falls, repentances, so fraught with achievements and disappointments. What joy to return home after a day's sport with your pockets bulging books! Charles Nodier was greedy of such happiness, for he had capacious pockets in his *wide great-coat* for this purpose.[3] Lord de Tabley was *cheered up by buying a copy of* Henry Lawes's *Ayres for the Theorbo; or, Bas Viol,* 1653, *with some Herrick and Lovelace pieces set.*[4] *Transport lit up the countenance of Lisardo* when told that he had succeeded in a desperate struggle with George Baker for De Bure's *Bibliographie Instructive,* Gaignat's *Catalogue,* and two copies of the *Duc de la Vallière;* but he evinced *heavy affliction on being told that he had failed in his attack upon the best editions* of Le Long's *Bibliotheca Sacra,* Fresnoy's *Méthode pour étudier,* and Baillet's *Jugemens des Savans,* which had been *carried off at the point of the bayonet by an irresistible onset from Atticus*[5] [Heber]; and when Charles Asselineau[6] composes himself for sleep on the thought of a day's book-hunting to-morrow, *Eh, bien, je bouquinerai demain!* he falls into the comforting reverie of *les quais éclairés d'une lumière douce et gaie, et les parapets émaillés de volumes de toutes couleurs:* the quays in a soft light and the parapets enamelled with books of many colours. Anatole France knows of *no sweeter, gentler pleasure than to go a-book-hunting along the Quais of Paris,* and like a true bookman he thinks not only of the carcass of the book but of its ghostly associations: *As you stir up the dust of the penny box you wake from their slumbers countless ghosts of tragic or alluring aspect.*[7]

To produce the true *elements of enjoyment, the book-hunter's treasures must not be his mere property, they must be his achievements—each one of them recalling the excitement of the chase and the happiness of success;*[8] as T. J. Wise enjoys the *romance of the patient waiting, and the swift pounce on the wanted book at last unexpectedly appearing.*[9] Southey makes a bag of *seventy-five goodly folios, and about as many more volumes of smaller calibre,* on an expedition to

[1] 'A Bookman's Purgatory', *Books and Bookmen.* 131–2.   [2] *A Magnificent Farce.* 62.
[3] Lang, *The Library.* 3.   [4] Qt. Gosse, 'Lord de Tabley', *Critical Kit-Kats.* 191–2
[5] Dibdin, *Bibliomania.* (1811) 183.   [6] *L'Enfer du Bibliophile.* 22.   [7] Pierre Nozière.
Trans. J. Lewis May. 70.   [8] Burton, *Book-Hunter.* 166.   [9] Curle, *Ashley Lib. Cat.* i, xi.

Utrecht; he is in delicious fear that they may not reach home safely. *Heaven send them a safe delivery at Keswick*, he prays, adding, *it does me good to think of them, to anticipate the joy I shall have in receiving and arranging, and profit in using them.*[1] But if joy is greater in achievement, it is more permanent in the chase, as in all good hunting: *the ordinary book-hunter has a store of joys and delight*, even in anticipation of fruition,[2] as in the achievements of Wise, who formed the Ashley Library *without the assistance of agents or advisers.*[3] No book-joy greater than this; 'tis far beyond all that prestige and opulence can give. But I do not doubt the passionate delight of those great book-lovers of the past (and of the present) who have hunted by proxy; as Richard de Bury, who rejoiced in all catches, whether of his own taking or that of his agents or scouts. The best of them, he tells us, were the wandering Friars, who would compass land and sea to meet his desires: *With such eager huntsmen what leveret could lie hid?* he asks; *with such fishermen, what single little fish could escape the net, the hook, and the trawl?*

With what ecstasy they follow the scent of rare volumes, like hounds hunting up hill and down dale, hath many records. Snuffy Davy, in *The Antiquary*, is a notable example and type of many, *a very prince of scouts for searching blind alleys, cellars, and stalls*; with *the scent of a slow-hound* and *snap of a bull-dog*, he would *detect you an old black-letter ballad among the leaves of a law-paper, and find an 'editio princeps' under the mask of a school Corderius.* Like all good hunters they have an instinct for their quarry; *a quick sensibility* as that of Lord Clive for *Aldines;*[4] *nothing would seem to have escaped the lynx-like vision* of Narcissus Luttrell.[5] They are guided by a super-sense, an unerring clairvoyance; the bibliophile *has a natural affinity for paper and print, he is attracted to a book like a needle to a magnet; he makes straight for it, hovers about it, and finally takes it up, and gloats over it.*[6]

Pre-eminent among them was Henry Bradshaw, whose particular quarry was manuscripts and incunabula; there was none like him, for he tracked down mighty tomes with the infallibility of a Red Indian hunter; he followed the scent of a lurking specimen of palæotypography with the persistence of a bloodhound: *unlike most other hunters, he rarely, if ever, returned empty-handed*, for he added knowledge, observation and inference, to instinct, marking *down his game before he started on the chase.* A gloss-hunt was the joy of his life, relaxation, recreation; he brought to bear upon his sport *the zest and keenness of a boy, combined with the cunning of an experienced hunter.*[7] Nor was it solely the sport which fascinated him: book-hunting with Bradshaw was research, he is the biologist of books, the Darwin of

---

[1] *Letters*. Milford. 400.   [2] Fitzgerald, *Book-Fancier*. 4.   [3] D. N. Smith, *Ashley Lib. Cat.* Intro. viii.   [4] Dibdin, *Reminiscences.* i, 401.   [5] Dibdin, *Bibliomania.* (1811) 427.   [6] M.A.C. 'Vagaries of Book-Buyers', *Book-Lore.* iv, 137.   [7] Prothero, *Henry Bradshaw.* 237.

bibliography, revealing fundamental truths by a close observation and co-ordination of hitherto unapprehended facts, and for that reason his captures became discoveries, his achievements restorations: *he never forgot a specimen of type which he had once examined; a single page, or even a tiny fragment of a page, would often enable him to name the book to which it belonged, its printer, and its date*; and even that was not his sole method, for to *the acute observation of varieties in type* he added a recognition of the artistry of the fathers of printing: *he regarded the printers of the fifteenth century as artists, and printing as an art, almost in the same sense as that in which painting and engraving are arts*,[1] as distinct as the art of Dürer or Botticelli.

IV. THE TECHNIQUE OF THE CHASE

There are many ways of hunting books. In ancient times they were among the legitimate spoils of war, and several ancient libraries could trace their descent from Bellona. *The Romans learned to be book-collectors in gathering the spoils of war*; and[2] in later times also rare and beautiful books have been thus honoured and ravished; but those methods are foreign to the present discourse, coming more appropriately in my section of the Adventures of Books. Some would have that the best way to form a library is to buy it complete; which may be so, but 'tis not hunting. Naudé bought up the whole stock of a bookseller for Cardinal Mazarin, and when he passed through a town he left it *as bare of printed paper as if a tornado had passed, and blown the leaves away;*[3] Bagford[4] records that the Earl of Sunderland bought Mr. Hadrian Beverland's entire collection of *valuable authors in polite learning*, and he gives as his opinion that this is *the best and most expeditious way to procure a good library*; or even better still is the method of the *Earl of Anglesea, who bought several libraries entire, as Oldenburgh's, etc.*;[5] or that further example, given by Dibdin,[6] of the Duke of Devonshire, who bought for *a sum little short of £10,000* the library of Dr. Dampier, Bishop of Ely; or of King George III, who bought that of Consul Smith of Vienna. William Oldys[7] speaks of dealing in books by weight: *sent a letter to Ames about the twenty hundredweight of waste books, at 25s. per cwt.*

Yet I can hardly approve of this course, it smells too much of *Bibliomania*, or shop-keeping, and trade is a kill-sport, as all know. Private libraries are best enjoyed when they are *built up bit by bit*;[8] from *small beginnings* such great libraries as those of Henry Huth and Christie-Miller

---

[1] Prothero, *Henry Bradshaw*. 359-60.　[2] Elton, *Great Book-Collectors*. 3-4.　[3] Lang, *The Library*. 31.　[4] *Gentleman's Magazine*. (1916) ii, 395-7.　[5] Afterwards in Lord Spencer's Library at Althorp, and now in the Rylands Library, Manchester.
[6] *Reminiscences*. i, 362, 363,　[7] *Diary*. 11-12.　[8] Lang, *The Library*.

have grown.[1] The best motto of the book-hunter is *festina lente*; there is plenty of time, for the world of books is an eternity in its own right; *go slowly*, says one,[2] *begin by filling in the background with the commoner and cheaper books*, passing on later to the *rarities*, and if the process is long it is enjoyable, *the mere leisureliness of it adds depth to knowledge*, so *what need is there of haste? Why should he long to bring his pleasures to an end?* Book-hunting is of the character of what Horace Walpole called *serendipity*, which, saith Andrew Lang,[3] *is the luck of falling on just the literary document which one wants at the moment*; he would have that it is a kind of *angling*.[4] To Petrarch it was both *angling* and *hawking: you are aware*, he writes, *in what lakes I am wont to fish and in what woods I go a hawking*;[5] George Moore, on the other hand, is translated by this sport into a prime quarry of all anglers, for as a young man he *pursued the works of Les Jeunes-France along the quays and through every 'passage' in Paris like a pike after minnows*.

Dibdin calls himself a *book-fisherman*;[6] T. J. Wise is so meticulous in the pursuit of his favourite quarry that Gosse compares him with the angler *who caught a salmon by accident and threw it in again, because when he was out to fish for perch he wished to catch perch*;[7] Dr. Bethune, an American collector, fished for books in the winter and for fishes in the summer, and all his books celebrated his summer sport of angling, so that he pursued it by their proxy when the streams were frozen over. He fished out of the deeps of catalogues and the quiet reaches of the bookshops in the endless stream of books which flows from owner to owner, all books which celebrated angling, more particularly those which had for centre the masterwork of Izaak Walton, the *Compleat Angler*, in all its forms, any work mentioned by Walton, or tending to illustrate our most notable angler's rambles by Lea or Dove, and all commentaries, praises, estimates, etc., of him, examples of his manuscript, autographs, portraits, flanked and buttressed by a miscellaneous assortment of essays in *ichthyology*, and treatises of angling by other hands both ancient and modern.[8]

A collector walks in the London or Paris streets, as he does by Tweed or Spey, says Lang,[9] *the shining stores of M. Damascène Morgand, in the Passage des Panoramas*, are streams rich with rare fishes; here he always felt like Brassicanus in the King of Hungary's Library, *non in Bibliotheca, sed in gremio Jovis*, not in a library, but in Paradise; but it is *not given to everyone to cast angle in those preserves*; they are for *dukes and millionaires*, like the Duke of Roxburghe, who also *revelled in book-collecting and angling*. But there are streams to suit all anglers, good sport for all fishers of books, rich or poor:

[1] Davenport, *Byways among English Books*. 6.   [2] Iolo A. Williams, *Elements of Book-Collecting*. 115–16.   [3] *The Library*. 2.   [4] *Ib*. 8–9.   [5] Tatham, *Francesco Petrarca*. ii, 37.   [6] *Bibliomania*. (1811)   [7] 'The Ashley Library', *Sunday Times*. 15.i.1928.   [8] Burton, *Book-Hunter*. 87–8.   [9] *The Library*. 8–9.

little tributary streets, with lowlier stalls, shy pools, where the humbler fisher may hope *to raise an Elzevir, or an old French play, a first edition of Shelley, or a Restoration comedy.*

They are hunting at all seasons and at all hours. Richard Smith,[1] a determined hunter of the time of Charles II, *was known every day to walk his rounds* of the book-haunts of London, hunting through the shops of Little Britain and St. Paul's Churchyard, *where his great skill and experience enabled him to make choice of what was not obvious to every man's eye.* Some take a particular pleasure to go a-hunting at early morning, others late at night. Lord de Tabley thought nothing of *hanging about a book-shop at six o'clock in the morning, waiting for the shutters to be taken down;*[2] Islington Cattle Market was, saith Roberts,[3] *a happy hunting-ground,* but it was always the *early prowler* who caught the rarity—the hunter who got there at eight or nine o'clock in the morning: very little but rubbish left for the *post-prandial* visitor. The best time in Paris is early morning, the '*take is on'*, advised Lang,[4] *from half-past seven to half-past nine a.m.* Mr. Oldbuck's *little Elzevirs* were the *trophies of many a walk by night and morning through the Cowgate, the Canongate, the Bow, and Saint Mary's Wynd—wherever, in fine, there were to be found brokers and traders, those miscellaneous dealers in things rare and curious.*[5]

V. THE OPULENT HUNTER

If the greatest prizes fall to him that hath the best weapon, which in these days of financial valuation is the deepest moneybag, still rare captures are often the reward of skill, intelligence and patience, ever the most reliable equipment of the complete bibliophile. He that hath a pot of money and can procure any book by writing out a cheque can never taste the particular delights of book-hunting as they are known to them that gape after desirable copies and hunt beyond their means; who buy books with their food and clothing; with their homes; who stake their comfort on a dice-throw for a first edition; who sacrifice their peace of mind for an *Elzevir,* in anticipation of the peace that passeth understanding which is the *ignis fatuus* of all gamblers. Many such inconveniences, lets and hindrances there are, which cross their projects, and crucify poor bookmen, which sometimes may be put off, and sometimes again cannot be so easily removed. But put case the hunt is on, the game afoot, whether he fishes a ten-pound treasure out of the twopenny box or buys a book for the pound he can ill

[1] Roberts, *Book-Hunter in London.* 33.   [2] Gosse, 'Lord de Tabley', *Critical Kit-Kats.* 191.   [3] *The Book-Hunter in London.* 163.   [4] *The Library.* 11.   [5] Scott, *The Antiquary.*

afford to spend, he enjoys an ecstasy which no millionaire who bids a fortune for a volume can ever experience.

Whether the rich or the poor collector is happier is hard to settle; some say the enjoyment is equal. Henri Pène du Bois maintains that *a fortune may be a positive force against the formation of a library;*[1] another authority[2] warns us against being too positive whether it is to the rich or the poor collector that *the romantic element chiefly or more powerfully attaches itself;* and Gosse, commenting on the notable fact that Wise does not offer any explanation on the absence of Shakespeare *quartos* and *folios* from his library, concludes, and I am with him, that the hunting of such books having *become the sport of millionaires, it can no longer offer any attractions to scholarly modesty;*[3] so I say with Publilius, *feras, non culpes, quod vitari non potest,*[4] what can't be cured must be endured, and if because of the great expense of Lais

Οὐ παντὸς ἀνδρὸς ἐς Κόρινθον ἔσθ ὁ πλοῦς,[5]

Not every man may go to Corinth town,

I do boldly claim that the collector who can buy everything that takes his fancy without regard for the outlay, who has all the best *finds* offered to him by the bookseller, whose agents attend every important auction sale, and who knows for certain that he has only to sit and wait for all the good books to fall into his lap, can never taste the ecstasies of such men as Charles Lamb and Samuel Taylor Coleridge, *who had to pause before they laid out a few shillings* on books they most ardently desired; or that bibliophile recorded by Lord Lytton in *Zanoni* who after years of hunting succeeded in forming an almost perfect library of works in occult philosophy, but so poor was he that he had to open a bookshop and trade, *as it were, in his own flesh and blood:*[6] if a customer entered, his countenance fell; *but let him depart empty-handed, and he would smile gaily, oblivious for a time of bare cupboard and inward cravings.*

To go without a meal rather than a book is a common experience. A poet known to Banville *lunched when he could, and formed a library of all the masterpieces of all the literatures by judicious and repeated acquisitions from the humble penny box.*[7] The process is long and not without difficulties, but altogether more delightsome than any successes known to such men as ˙are damned to riches, for a poor man takes more pleasure in an ordinary meal's meat, which he hath but seldom, than they do with all their exotic dainties and continual viands: *voluptates commendat rarior usus,*[8] 'tis the rarity and necessity that makes a thing acceptable and pleasant; and the

[1] *Four Private Libraries of New York.* 118.   [2] W. C. Hazlitt, *Book-Collector.* 14–15.
[3] 'The Ashley Library', *Sunday Times.* 15.1.1928.   [4] *Mimes.* Meyer. v, 176.
[5] Qt. Aulus Gellius, *Attic Nights.* I, 8.   [6] Roberts, *Book-Hunter in London.* xx.
[7] Uzanne, *Book-Hunter in Paris.* 112.   [8] *Juvenal.* xi, 208.

sweetest victories are those achieved *per abrupta*. Edmund Gosse was once defeated at an auction by Lord Roseberry, and in his distress he *dropped a tear on the shoulder* of a friendly bookseller. *He gets everything*, Gosse grumbled, *he was born to get everything*. *No*, said the bibliopole, not everything. *He has not, and never will have, the exquisite pleasure of buying what he knows he cannot afford*.[1]

In several authors have I found many stories to confirm what I have said: as that notable among the rest, of George Gissing and the First Edition of *Gibbon*.[2] It was in the days of his nonage when he lived in poverty that he lost his head before a copy of that noble work displayed in the window of the little bookshop in Euston Road near to Portland Road Station; the price asked was but one shilling a volume, a great sum for his poor pocket, but he was fascinated beyond material resources, beyond himself; the volumes ravished his heart; *to possess those clean-paged quartos*, he said, *I would have sold my coat*. But there was no cause for this, for he had the money at home, and having spoken with the book-seller, he *walked home, took the cash* (as he tells the story himself), *walked back again, and—carried the tomes from the west end of Euston Road to a street in Islington far beyond the 'Angel'. I did it in two journeys—twice—three times, reckoning the walk for the money—did I descend Euston Road, and climb Pentonville*. Consciousness of time, fatigue, expense, was driven away: his joy in the purchase drove out every other thought, and the end of the last journey *saw him upon a chair, perspiring, flaccid, aching—exultant!* Now go and brag of your riches, your power of purse; to enlarge or illustrate this potency of money is to set a candle to the sun; and yet I have no wish to dogmatize, although I am, perforce, disposed to exalt the joys of them that hunt on a limited exchequer, for they are all I know out of my own experience. But self do, self have, as the saying is, whether rich or poor; so let every opinionative fellow maintain his own paradox, be it what it will; and whether a Huntington, who hunts by proxy of an agent with an unlimited commission, rejoices as greatly in his bag as a bibliophile who has hooked one fish with his dinner as bait, I shall not attempt to decide. They may contend and rail, *pro* and *con, et adhuc sub judice lis est*; so let them agree as they will, I proceed.

Some have added to these joys the delight of dazzling the eyes of wealthier and emulous rivals by showing them a treasure captured for a few pence, and revelling in their *surprise and envy; these*, he claims,[3] *are the white moments of life, that repay the toil and pains and sedulous attention* necessary for the chase. Those book-hunters *to middle fortune born*, who are *obliged to wait and watch an opportunity*, must learn, Lang advises, in a

[1] *Library of Edmund Gosse*. Pref. xxii.   [2] *Private Papers of Henry Ryecroft*. 34–5.
[3] Mr. Oldbuck, in *The Antiquary*.

'*Letter to a Young American Book-Hunter*',[1] that the Stoics *endure and abstain.* They must abstain from *rushing at every volume which seems to be a bargain*; it is *probably not even a bargain*, and can seldom be cheap if it is not needed. *Low prices*, Carew Hazlitt says,[2] *do not alone establish cheapness: cheap books are those which are obtained by accident under the current value;* and he gives as an example how in the time of the later Stuart kings, Narcissus Luttrell *found from one penny to sixpence* enough to pay *for some of the most precious volumes in our language*, a shilling commanding a Caxton; the Huths of those days were hunting *ancient typography in the form of the classics, large paper copies of contemporary historians, or the publications of Hearne.* You must also turn your back, Lang suggests,[3] on books which are the *latest fashion*, for which *wild prices are given by competitive millionaires*, unless, he wisely adds, *you meet them for fourpence on a bookstall*: an unlikely happening, for *real bargains are so rare that you may hunt for a lifetime and never meet one.* The best plan, *for a man who has to see that his collection is worth what it cost him*, is to specialize, to confine himself to a *single line*; and finally, *never (or 'hardly ever') buy an imperfect book*, '*tis a constant source of regret, an eyesore*; for the rest there is always *the pleasure of Hope and the consolation of books, quietem inveniendam in abditis recessibus et libellulis.*[4] To sum up all of this, I say with Jeremy Collier, *he that would relish success to purpose, should keep his Passion cool, and his Expectation low; and then 'tis possible his Fortune might exceed his Fancy.*[5]

VI THE HAPPY HUNTER

When they have tracked down their quarry, the hunt is not ended: the catch is not consummated until the book is safely landed or netted. Book-hunting is not only the art of spotting rarities, it is the art of making bargains, as the hunter well knows. When he *drops on a 'find'* his demeanour changes: he does not betray his luck by the *slightest facial movement* as he handles the *precious volume*. Should he think the dealer is watching him, he will, provided that no other bibliophile is hovering about, *put down the book and turn to something else*; and in a little while he will *take it up again with a nonchalant air*, and giving it a look of contempt as though to indicate its worthlessness, he will inquire the price; hesitate; haggle; until he finally secures for twopence, grudgingly tendered, what may be worth many pounds.[6] *How often*, Mr. Oldbuck confesses,[7] *have I stood haggling on a halfpenny, lest, by a too ready acquiescence in the dealer's first price, he should be led*

[1] *Letters on Literature.* 113–22.   [2] *Book-Collector.* 21.   [3] *Letters on Literature.* 113. [4] 'that rest may be found in secluded corners and books.'   [5] 'Eagerness of Desire', *Essays.* ii, 44.   [6] M. A. C., 'Vagaries of Book-Buyers', *Book-Lore.* iv, 137. [7] Scott, *Antiquary.*

to suspect the value I set upon the article! He trembled, lest some passing stranger should chop in between him and the prize, and looked upon every poor divinity student as a rival amateur or prowling bookseller in disguise; and he recalls the *sly satisfaction* as he pays and pockets the find, *affecting a cold indifference, while the hand trembles with pleasure.* He was a sly hunter, cunning, and a wheedler; *see this bundle of ballads, not one of them later than 1700,* he brags, *I wheedled an old woman out of these, who loved them better than her psalm-book.* Tobacco snuff, and the *Complete Syren,* were the equivalents. For a copy of the *Complaynt of Scotland* he *sat out the drinking of two dozen bottles of strong ale with the late learned proprietor,* who in gratitude bequeathed it to him by his last will.

And well may they fear competition, for every good book or MS. has many seekers after it. A painful instance is that of W. T. Spencer,[1] who had for sale the MS. of *The Cricket on the Hearth* at £2,000. He held this *desirable item* in his possession for some time without finding a buyer in England, when on a day two famous American booksellers arrived, each eager to capture the treasure. The one who reached the bookshop first offered £1,500 without success, and then raised his offer to £1,750. Whilst this haggling was going on Mr. Spencer's assistant asked him to speak to another customer who urgently wanted to see him. This man was Mr. Brooks, the bookseller, of Minneapolis, who made a definite offer of £2,000 for the MS. and threatened Mr. Spencer with no more business dealings unless he accepted the offer. He gripped him by the coat and pleaded with desperation until Spencer gave way on condition that Brooks explained the situation to his compatriot bookseller, which he agreed to do. Mr. Spencer pacified his irate and disappointed customer with a copy of *American Notes* inscribed by Dickens to Carlyle; and worth £250, and Mr. Brooks sold the MS. of *The Cricket on the Hearth* in America for £2,250. Thus, says Spencer, *ended an incident in which the most beautiful article I have had to sell during my forty years' experience was the cause of the most unpleasant transaction I have ever been concerned in.* This precious MS. is now in the Pierpont Morgan Library.

The sum of it all is that the happiest hunter is he who stalks and tracks down what he likes best and what he can read and enjoy, with such reservations as I have made for the satisfaction of luxurious tastes, sentiment, and legitimate pride in possession: *de meo ligurire libidost:*[2] my fancy to taste what I like best. For the rest he will aspire, as Cracherode and Thomas Grenville did,[3] always to possess fine copies; condition is everything; the best books in the best state; avoiding always the temptations of trade-inspired booms, when prices are deliberately sky-rocketed by cunning

[1] *Forty Years in My Bookshop.* 101–4.   [2] Catullus, *Fragmenta.* Loeb Ed. 182.
[3] Seymour de Ricci, *English Collectors of Books and Manuscripts.* 60, 114.

dealers, as snares for bibliomaniacs. In *every artificial furore the good, bad and indifferent are apt to rise and to fall together, while it is reserved only for the first to experience a revival,* 'tis ever, he saith,[1] the *Revival of the Fittest.* The accomplished book-hunter has an instinct for the fittest, and whilst he would not be surprised to find it anywhere, he has an instinct also for its most likely habitat; nor is wealth, as I have shown, always the final determinant,

> Something there is more needful than Expense,
> And something previous ev'n to Taste—'tis Sense.[2]

VII. FEARS AND TREPIDATIONS

Book-hunters have delicious fears that the game will die out, the streams run dry, rare books become so rare that none but the millionaire shall capture them. Thus Thomas Baker, the seventeenth-century collector, who left a portion of his library to St. John's College, Cambridge, complained to Humfrey Wanley that *the men of quality lay out so much for books, and give such high prices,* that there is nothing left for *poor scholars,* for when he *bid a fair price for an old book,* he was told that the *quality* would *give twice as much,* and it was as much as he could do *to pick up a few at tolerable prices, and despair of any more;*[3] so Carew Hazlitt[4] complains in our times that *the game is up, for the three-kingdoms have been well-nigh ransacked and exhausted,* and *the country town is as bare as a bird's tail of anything but commonplace stuff.* The provincial centres are *sterile enough,* but *the rural districts are dried up,* the West *has been threaded through,* and *the two ancient Universities* yield little, because the members of the colleges, who know good books when they see them, *hunt in these preserves* themselves; Dublin no longer yields its *proportion of finds,* and even *the capital of Scotland has lost its ancient prestige as a cover for this sort of sport. The Harvest,* saith another,[5] *has all been gathered long ago, and nothing is left but gleanings in fields already raked. Incunabula,* the *Elizabethans, Shakespeareana,* are now the quarry of the millionaire collector, and desirable seventeenth-century copies are going the same way; *not enough scarce books of this period to go round,* say Sawyer & Darton,[6] *and the shrinkage of supply has already begun to keep pace with the ferocity of demand.*

Assellineau[7] reckons up these inconveniences and recalls how there were

[1] W. Carew Hazlitt, *Book-Collecting.* 189. [2] Pope, *Moral Essays.* iv, 41–2. [3] Qt. Roberts, *Book-Hunter in London.* 34. [4] *The Book-Collector.* 11–12. [5] J. H. Slater, *The Romance of Book-Collecting.* 75. [6] *English Books:* 1475–1900. i, 175. [7] *L'Enfer du Bibliophile.* 15.

such fears in his day, when collectors for the previous twenty years complained that nothing was ever found on the Quais of Paris, but, he says, in ten years' time there may still be a single opportunity to be seized. *Nodier et Parison, par exemple,* find *sur les quais l'un le 'Marot' d' Etienne Dolet, l'autre le 'César' de Montaigne, payé à sa vente* fifteen hundred francs, and had cost him eighteen *sous.* Anatole France recalls[1] how he used to meet on the Quais of Paris *crabbed old bibliophiles* who would always be telling him long stories about their ill-luck, and they would fall to belauding the good old days when not a morning passed but someone happened upon an '*editio princeps*' *of some classic masterpiece between the Pont Neuf and the Pont Royal.* But there is still hope.

Newton[2] is not downhearted, though R. B. Adam, of Buffalo, inherits from his father all the best *Johnsoniana,* and William M. Elkins, of Philadelphia, has everything of Goldsmith. Foiled in those directions, he looks over the field of his favourites: *Byron: Mr. Morgan has them all, every one; Shelley is too voluminous, running into thousands before a fair start is had; when Mr. Thomas J. Wise shows you his Shelleys, you simply expire with envy; Lamb: Mr. Spoor's carriage blocks the way; it is a carriage only by courtesy, it being in fact a well-furnished van; Oscar Wilde: it is quite useless; John B. Stetson has everything. Tennyson: I have not forgotten that rare day I spent in Mr. W. H. Arnold's library, looking over his Tennyson material, progress in that direction is impossible; Keats: here I collide with Miss Amy Lowell, with the usual result*; and contemplating the catalogue of twenty-nine quarto *Shakespeares* with which Rosenbach inaugurated his New York shop, and millionaires scrambling for them, although the *values* ran *to something like thousands of dollars a page,* he realizes that the day of the mutability of Shakespeare's *Quartos* is nearly ended; *the scramble is almost over,* and *any further proceedings will partake of the nature of a triumphal procession;*[3] yet notwithstanding all this he has netted a delectable collection with certain Johnson, Lamb, Wilde, and Shakespeare catches, which even Pierpont Morgan would not despise.

So cheer up, I say, be not dismayed; *spes alit agricolas;*[4] *there is more day to dawn, the sun is but a morning star,*[5] and a lowering morning may turn to a fair afternoon. Good books, desirable copies, *rariora,* unique *items,* were always scarce, and always will be. Pope Sylvester II had, in the tenth century, *to borrow so simple a work as Caesar, in return for eight volumes of Boethius on Astrology, and three hundred years later Roger Bacon complained that he could not get even a minor work of Cicero for love or money.*[6] Classical *books grow scarcer every day,* Dibdin moaned, *and the love of literature, and of*

---

[1] *Pierre Nozière.* Trans. J. Lewis May. 71.   [2] *A Magnificent Farce.* 114.   [3] *A Magnificent Farce.* 126–7.   [4] *Tibullus.* ii, 6, 21. 'Hope cheers the farmer.'   [5] Thoreau, *Walden.* 331.   [6] Powell, *Excursions in Libraria.* 4.

possessing rare and interesting works, increases in an equal ratio.[1] Yet our collectors go on collecting; great libraries are still being formed, there are more small libraries than ever there were, although prices for choice copies and rare editions were never higher; and although great collections are bequeathed entire to nations, great collections are still being dispersed among booksellers, and the streams and coverts are thus replenished.

Patience in book-hunting is a most sovereign recipe, *patience, vigilance and personal activity;*[2] and there are still covers, territories, preserves, which have not yet been beaten by the millionaire, *the chance of finding a prize to-day has not diminished, but increased,*[3] and if it had not, the true book-hunter would *never allow himself to believe that the wonderful old volumes of hundreds of years ago had all been found*; to-day, to-morrow, next week, *he must surely unearth some unrecorded book.*[4] So I conclude with Octave Uzanne[5] where he states that a collection is never *complet*, and that the collector who declares a collection complete ceases to be a collector; and he gives Archimedes Poulet-Malassis as the true type of the eternal book-hunter, for he pasted in each of his captures an *eau forte* by Braquemont showing an open book illuminated by *ce grand cri de joie victorieuse: Je l'ai! Eureka!* and in this *triomphe de Don Juan* he reaches forward to the next and unending resolution: *A d'autres maintenant!* Thus he proves that the capture itself doth entice him to seize upon more, and this story of his will agree with those of Dibdin, Lang, Hill Burton, etc. *Sed abunde fabularum audivimus*, enough of tales: *ubi Romanus vicit ibi habitat.*[6] The passing of the quarry is not yet. *Quod absit!*

But even when all these fears have been reckoned up they are no more than the burden of old age, *molesta senectus*, if not of the collector then of collecting, aided and abetted by fashion and vain competition, stimulated by the wily bookseller, and, therefore, all fear is a fancy without ground, without sense, without wisdom. The way to combat it is to forestall this fashion-born wiliness and to stamp upon all aptness to self-deception by ceasing, as I have hinted many times, to play the *sedulous ape* and following your own whim. Make tracks into unexplored territories, blaze your own trail. *I sometimes wonder*, says A. J. A. Symons, *at the willingness of my collecting friends to keep to the track along which the booksellers march, ignoring the attractive by-ways that open at every turn.*[7] 'Tis only by such methods that fears and trepidations may be allayed and that natural or acquired sagacity developed by which collectors can contrive to hunt significantly and wittily.

---

[1] *Bibliomania.* (1811) 517.   [2] *Ib.* 109.   [3] Sawyer & Darton, *English Books:* 1475–1900. i, 30.   [4] Rosenbach *Books and Bidders.* 51.   [5] *Zigzags d'un Curieux.* 209.   [6] 'Where the Roman has conquered there he settles.'   [7] 'The Book-Collector's Apology', *The Book-Collector's Quarterly.* i, 54.

VIII. OF HUNTING GROUNDS

If the Heaven of the bibliophile, then, be penetrable, as the best authorities deliver, it were not amiss in this dissertation of hunting books to make a petty progress into those territories where game is most likely to abound; and if 'tis true that many good places are lost which our predecessors made use of, as some will inform you, many new fields are discovered to the book-hunter's good, so that no age ever saw the like, nor were the hunters ever more wily in pursuit of their quarry:

> The knowing Angler, in the winding brook,
> Knows what the Fish, and where to bait his Hook,
> The Fowler and the Hunts-man know by Name
> The certain Haunts and Harbour of their Game.
> So must the Rover beat the likeliest Grounds;
> Th' Assemblies where his quarry most abounds.[1]

Mighty hunters of books encompass the earth, tracking down their quarry in all places, sacred and profane, monasteries and churches, castles and palaces; manor houses and rectories; flats, villas, cottages; shops of many kinds; town or country, it is all one, and the earth is all one to them as they cross the sea in swift liners, cover the land by train or automobile, and cleave the air in flying machines. Nor does their hunting end at such personal contact as modern transport opens up to them: they hunt from wherever they are, throwing their nets over all lands by telephone, telegram, cable and radio, so that time and place and circumstances are annihilated in this sweet game, as in no other sport. All races, languages, nations, lands, that have books and such culture as only books can give, are territories, no place too exalted or too mean; but if good books may be found anywhere, good territories and plentiful seas for our trawling are limited.

The bookman appraises towns by the number of their bookshops: if they be few, the towns are dull, monotonous, ugly; to be shunned, disliked, or, at best, endured. He that should be admitted on a sudden to the sight of such places as Charing Cross Road or Farringdon Road in London, wherein all manner of books are displayed for sale in numerous shops and on many stalls, could not choose, though he were never so poor of purse, but be much recreated by the sight; or in Paris to *the long sweep of the Quais, where some eighty bouquinistes set their boxes on the walls of the embankment of the Seine.*[2] And book-hunting is the more delightsome and fortunate in this, that it is most favourable in pleasant, ripe old towns,

[1] Dryden, *Ovid's Art of Love*. i.   [2] Andrew Lang, *Library*. Second Ed. 10.

where men have thought out ideas, dreamed dreams and seen visions for ages, and by this portent are like the Fortunate Islands, *sponte sua per se dabat omnia tellus, where all things grew without plowing or sowing.*[1] *This is one of the advantages of living in an old country. The Colonies are not the home for the collector.*[2]

Game abounds in fair-built cities of age-long culture, in London and Paris and Rome. *No place like London for the lover of books*, says Dibdin.[3] *Oh God of Gods in Zion!* exclaims Richard de Bury,[4] *what a rushing river of joy gladdens my heart as often as I have a chance of going to Paris! There the days seem always short; there are the goodly collections on the delicate fragrant bookshelves.* In Oxford, *the Muses' Paradise:*[5] *beautiful city! so venerable, so lovely, so serene! steeped in sentiment as she is, spreading her gardens to the moonlight, and whispering from her towers the last enchantments of the Middle Age;*[6] Cambridge, Edinburgh, Bath, York; Florence and Venice and Naples; Heidelberg, Vienna, Dublin; wherever there are books to be hunted is heaven for the bibliophile and doubly heaven in that his territories are in themselves beautiful to be remembered many years after with singular delight. *For see the praise the ancients bestowed on them, the Elysian Fields could offer nothing to a dead philosopher that a live Parisian cannot enjoy on the Quais between the Pont Royal and the Pont Notre-Dame.*[7] What more pleasant recreation than that of Aretaeus (*cap.* 7), *deambulatio per amoena loca*, to make a petty progress, a merry journey now and then with some good companion, to hunt books, see cities, castles, libraries, treasuries of art, to bag rich quarry and first gloat upon it in such pleasant circumstances? If, as so many contend, it will *laxae animos*, refresh the souls of men, to see fair-built cities, streets, theatres, temples, monuments, fountains, etc., *to hunt in such delightful coverts*[8] hath in it a supereminent quality of more excellent worth. Go on, then, merrily to heaven!

IX. HUNTING BY CATALOGUE

In book-hunting, says one,[9] *the prime object is to have something to hunt for*, and the character of the hunted determines the quality of the hunter. The true book-hunter *considers himself a finder or discoverer rather than a purchaser, an industrious prowler in unlikely regions.*[10] He would, on second thoughts,

---

[1] Erasmus, *Praise of Folly.* Trans. Wilson. Oxford Ed. 15.   [2] Lang, *op. cit.* 10. [3] *Reminiscences.* ii, 897.   [4] *Philobiblon.*   [5] Cowley, 'Pindaric Ode'.   [6] Matthew Arnold, Preface, *Essays in Criticism.*   [7] Anatole France, *Pierre Nozière.* Trans. J. Lewis May. 70.   [8] Richard de Bury, *Philobiblon.* Qt. Elton, *Great Book-Collectors.* 38.   [9] J. Roger Rees, *The Pleasures of a Book-Worm.* 30.   [10] Burton, *The Book-Hunter.* 50–1.

divide them into two classes: the *private prowler* and the *auction-hunter*, the difference recalling the *stalker* and the *hunter proper*.[1] There is also that kind of armchair hunting by means of catalogues which many in these days commend. *More and more is it becoming the custom*, says Octave Uzanne,[2] *for the bibliophile to hunt at home, and there, by the fireside, run through the catalogues of the booksellers. Book catalogues, which reach the collector through the post, give him all the pleasures of the sport at home.*[3] *Good catalogues*, Fitzgerald advises,[4] are *always agreeable and piquant reading. No reading more easy, more fascinating, and more delightful than that of a catalogue*, says Sylvestre Bonnard;[5] he may well argue so, for the catalogue is a hunting territory in itself which over one hundred years past was recognized by that Attila among book-lovers, John Bagford,[6] as conducing *to improving the learned in the knowledge of scarce and valuable books, which before stood dusty in studies, shops, and warehouses.* Dr. Rosenbach,[7] himself a determined hunter by catalogue, looks upon this kind of hunting, in its more acute forms, as *a deadly malady* which may attack *all collectors at one stage or another*; he calls it *catalogitis*, and in aggravated cases, affected by *the most insidious germ of the disease*, they gloat on catalogues for themselves, seeing in them the symbol of possession even when they are not hunting. *By God!* declaimed Paterson, the bibliographer and auctioneer, *Croft's catalogue*[8] *is my chef d'oeuvre, out and out;*[9] *a bookstall had irresistible charms*, Dibdin confessed,[10] *but the catalogues of Payne, Faulder, White, and Egerton, exhibited so many stars upon which he loved to gaze with an indescribable satisfaction.*

But in spite of risks of dotage, 'tis a distinguished and profitable form of pursuit, as Rosenbach well knows, for though he registers himself as a victim of *catalogitis*, he attributes many catches to the sport, and I think there is method in the madness which inspired him to order (as Charles Nodier before him) overcoats with extra and unusually large pockets, so that he is become *a sort of literary marsupial*, carrying his young, in the form of old catalogues, in his pouch, *never sure into what they may develop*, as he bounds from sale to sale.[11] A. E. Newton[12] always has a few catalogues which he *marks industriously, one check means a book that I own, and I note with interest the prices; another, a book that I would like to have; while yet another indicates a book to which under no circumstances would I give a place on my shelves.*

I know many that are of this habit, and many more instances could I give out of good books that have been written on this theme, although

[1] *Ib.* 88. [2] *The Book-Hunter in Paris.* 124. [3] Andrew Lang, *The Library.* 17. [4] *Book-Fancier.* 12. [5] *The Crime of Sylvestre Bonnard.* Anatole France. [6] *Gentleman's Magazine.* (1816) ii, 510. [7] *Books and Bidders.* 170. [8] *Bibliotheca Croftsiana.* (1783) [9] Dibdin, *Bibliomania.* (1811) 526. [10] *Reminiscences.* i, 193. [11] *Books and Bidders.* 172. [12] *Amenities of Book-Collecting.* 65–6.

there be some who inveigh against catalogues, as Iolo A. Williams,[1] who will have that buying from them is *never very satisfactory*; but lest my discourse become too tedious long, I shall conclude with a confession of Leigh Hunt[2] that he opens a *new catalogue of old books with all the fervour and ivory folder of a first love*, often reading them at tea and dinner, and practising a fictitious book-hunt, *by putting crosses against dozens of volumes in the list, out of the pure imagination of buying them, the possibility being out of the question;* he was a poet, but not a few bibliophiles and book-hunters also have been tempted through circumstances or whim to similar flights of imagination; but 'tis a poor substitute for the book itself, and if it trouble the mind overmuch, produces certain kinds of madness or craziness; of which in their place; thus George Gissing, who knew the joy of going through catalogues, *ticking here and there a possible purchase*, in his poorer days, when he could *seldom spare money, kept catalogues as much as possible out of sight,*[3] for he knew, as Dibdin[4] before him, that they help *to inflame the passions* of book-lovers and *to fill the coffers of the booksellers.*

That they love thus to have their passions stirred is well known, 'tis a part of the game, as when Francis Jenkinson, acting upon the suggestion of Bradshaw that he should form a systematic collection of Cambridge books similar to that done for Oxford by Madan, *began an eager perusal of booksellers' catalogues and a feverish excitement over items caught or missed which only ceased with the exhaustion of the supply.*[5] And finally I may add some testimony that catalogues are in themselves inestimable instructors in the art of hunting, for the information they give of the rise and fall of prices; but when they record the contents of great collections bibliographically displayed they become *hunting-grounds* of a special sort in themselves; thus Mr. Wise's Catalogue of his Ashley Library, writes Alfred W. Pollard,[6] *is the best hunting-ground I know of for the possibilities which must be considered, because he has set himself more strenuously than any one before him to answer the questions with which bibliography is concerned.* In such works you hunt for information for the perfecting of your technique before you sally forth upon the bookward trail.

X. OF BOOKSTALLING

Best of hunting-grounds, say some authorities, are the bookstalls, where *the literature of all the ages* is represented in a diverting mixture, *from the immortal verse of Homer to the mortal prose of the railway novel;*[7] and book-

[1] *Elements of Book-Collecting.* 106.   [2] *Retrospective Review.*   [3] *Private Papers of Henry Ryecroft.* 44.   [4] *Bibliomania.* (1811) 397.   [5] *Francis Jenkinson.* Stewart. 23: [6] *Ashley Lib. Cat.* Intro. ix, xv.   [7] George Eliot, *Daniel Deronda.*

stalling is a prime faculty in the quest of literary treasure: *the custom is more than tinctured with the odour of respectability by the fact that Roxburghe's famous Duke, Lord Macaulay the historian, and Mr. Gladstone the omnivorous, have been inveterate grubbers among the bookstalls.*[1] Leigh Hunt, Charles Lamb, Bulwer-Lytton, were confessed frequenters of the bookstalls; and Southey had *a mania for them,* could not pass one without *just running his eye over for one minute, even if the coach which was to take him to see Coleridge at Hampstead was within the time of starting.*[2] In happier days, says Dowden, *the bookstalls of London knew the tall figure, the rapid stride, the quick-seeking eye, the eager fingers.*[3] Percy Fitzgerald[4] has many like instances: Dr. John North, who *delighted in the small editions of the classics by Seb. Gryphius,* would devote *many hours together* to the sport, regardless of time; the Rev. Richard Farmer, D.D., whose library was sold, in 1798, for £2,210, loved the bookstalls; the Rev. J. Brand, who had a still finer library of *unique, scarce, rare and curious works,* which fetched £6,000 at the beginning of last century, visited almost daily the bookstalls covering that wide territory between Piccadilly and Mile End; the Duke of Roxburghe *wandered industriously and zealously from bookshop to bookstall over the world;* and he gives an instance of a Queen falling under thrall to this fascinating branch of the sport. Madame d'Arblay is his authority for the story that Queen Charlotte generally sent a clever servant to do her bookstalling for her, but she herself with one of her ladies was *in the habit of paying visits to Holywell Street and Ludgate Hill where secondhand books were offered for sale.*

Most authorities give them praise: *your ardent Bibliophile, saith one,*[5] *cannot pass a secondhand bookstall; he will cross the street, or go down a pestilential-looking alley, and grope among rags and dirt and filth to gratify his all-consuming passion; the sport given by bookstalls is full of variety and charm.*[6] *Of the numerous ways and means of acquiring books open to the book-hunter in London, there is none more pleasant or popular than Bookstalling;*[7] it is equally *fascinating,* saith mine author, *to the man of small means or of no means at all,* and there is plenty of good hunting-ground, east, west, north, south, at all seasons. Among those who take a contrary view, one[8] announces that usually *an hour spent among the stalls has proved nothing but an hour pleasurably wasted,* the reason being that *the bookstalls are regularly searched by eagle-eyed individuals who earn a scanty living by picking up from the stalls anything that might be attractive in a bookshop;* and Percy Fitzgerald[9] holds out small hope for rich or rare finds in these days of *perfected and methodized* bookselling; *the finding of an old Shakespeare quarto bound up with a lot of tracts is a dream;*

[1] Roberts, *Book-Hunter in London.* 149. [2] Qt. *Book-Hunter in London.* 150.
[3] Southey. 104. [4] *Book-Fancier.* 4–5. [5] *Book-Lore.* iv, 137. [6] Lang, *The Library.* 9.
[7] Roberts, *Book-Hunter in London.* 149. [8] Iolo A. Williams, *Elements of Book-Collecting.* 104. [9] *Book-Fancier.* 11.

still *men of taste and judgment* may make their rounds and *find pleasure in redeeming many a pretty and useful volume*, worth more than the shilling or two paid for them. But he misses the point when he presumes so stiffly that the pleasure of book-hunting depends upon such big game as the early Shakespeariana. Little fishes are also sweet, as all good epicures know; and *the bookstall keeper of to-day*, says Octave Uzanne,[1] *has thousands of rarities which are still in the chrysalis stage of their evolution to curiosity*, which may suddenly emerge into the perfect *imago* by *the dawning history of the time or the sudden eccentricity of events;* his stall, or boxes on the Quais of Paris (and the argument is good for London, too), *though drained by every literary bloodhound of luxury and fashion*, still contain treasures in the making which may be missed by the *actual bibliophile*, but which are caught by the *savant* and enlightened bookman, who *infallibly pounces* upon some previous volume of which he alone knows the value.

XI. OF BOOKSHOPPING

Next to the bookstall on the upward track is the bookshop, which must remain the chief and most fertile preserve of the bibliophile, it is the Heaven of Bookmen, sung by the bard:

> Friend, do not Heber and de Thou,
> And Scott, and Southey, kind and wise,
> *La chasse au bouquin* still pursue
> Within the Book-man's Paradise?[2]

No collector has been able to resist the temptations and chances of these rich territories. Bookshops fill their dreams. They are their El Dorado, their Utopia, their City of the Sun, Land of Heart's Desire. In them the journeys of all bookmen end in a galaxy of golden books. *If you want delicious copies in lovely binding, of works of a sumptuous character, go and drink coffee with Mr. Miller, of Albemarle Street—under the warm light of an Argand lamp—amidst a blaze of morocco and russia coating, which brings to your recollection the view of the Temple of the Sun in the play of Pizarro;*[3] or if you are content with humbler quarry you may *search hopefully in those delightful shops where all is chaos (save sometimes in the mind of the proprietor) and books lie in great heaps upon the floor;* here you may rout out your *treasures amid clouds of dust and the scuttlings of disturbed blackbeetles.*[4] Every hunter loves to prowl in such a jungle as that described by Moult,[5] which

[1] *Book-Hunter in Paris*. 4–5.   [2] Andrew Lang, *Rhymes à la Mode*. 75.   [3] Dibdin, *Bibliomania*. (1811) 406.   [4] Iolo A. Williams, *Elements of Book-Collecting*.   [5] Pref., *Forty Years in My Bookshop*. Spencer. xxiv–v.

is typical of the rest of its kind, where it is difficult to move without bringing down a stack of books about your head. The floor *a fairy gold mine*, where you stumble over *folios and portfolios of such rarity that one would think their guardian shockingly careless.* How they love these coverts I need not tell, it is too well known: no forest so romantic as a forest of bookshelves, no groves so enchanting as groves of books, no mountain so impressive as a range of them. Stacked and stored in order, or disorder, they enchant the eye of the hunter. Bookshops are the first and foremost of fine sights in all the fair cities of the world, and the surest retreats of delectable temptation.

Lord Spencer went to Rome for a whole year hunting for a copy of the *Martial* of Sweynheym and Pannartz (1473), and when he had tracked it down he hastened back to England with it, not stopping on the way, and without visiting either the Coliseum or the Vatican. Southey hunted in bookshops as keenly as on the stalls: *Lisbon, Paris, Milan, Amsterdam, contributed to the rich confusion that, from time to time, burdened the floors of library and bed-rooms and passages in Greta Hall;* but *above all he was remembered at Brussels by that best of bookmen, Verbeyst,*[1] who had 300,000 volumes to choose from and loved them all. Lord Macaulay had a passion for bookshops: there was scarcely a dusty old specimen in any court or out-of-the-way corner in London which had escaped his attention: *no one so ready to mount a ladder and scour the top shelf for quarto pamphlets, or curious literary relics of a bygone age, and come down after an hour's examination covered with dust and cobwebs, sending for a bun to take the place of his usual luncheon;*[2] and *the book fancier,* he records, often came on Mr. Gladstone's track, *and has seen a little parcel set aside to be sent home to Downing Street;* sometimes when he has been *cheapening a book in a more public place than Holywell Street,* he has been forced to make retreat under the gaze of vulgar gapers who assembled to watch the *eminent virtuoso.*[3]

In general, the keepers of these rich preserves are friendly and intelligent men; though at some periods this opinion would have been challenged. When the future Bishop of Avranches is spending more in the purchase of books than his fortune allows, he is warned by Gabriel Naudé *to be on his guard against the craft of booksellers;*[4] just as at a later date another asserts that *booksellers in the gross are taken for no better than a pack of knaves and atheists,* but, he adds, *only by prejudic'd men,* for *among them there is a retail of men who are no strangers to religion and honesty.*[5] But since, in those times, bookseller and publisher were one and the same, it is as like as not that the former has borne much of a traditional opprobrium intended for the latter, especially when it was inspired by professional men of letters, and

[1] Dowden, *Southey.* 104.   [2] Fitzgerald, *Book-Fancier.* 6.   [3] *Ib.* 8.   [4] Huet, *Memoirs.* Trans. Aikin. i, 61.   [5] *Religio Bibliopolae.* (1728) 1.

of them the less fortunate, for rich and successful writers have little ill-feeling towards publishers. Jacob[1] divides booksellers into three classes: *Bouquinistes à la mode, bouquinistes de la vielle roche,* and *bouquinistes avares,* and I doubt not that there is some wisdom in his classification, for booksellers are various, good and bad, sly and frank, straight and crooked, wise, wayward, mean, generous, greedy, open-handed, proud, humble, quiet, noisy, well read and ill read, as other tradesmen are; but there is, I find, a numerous company of the best of them.

XII. OF AUCTIONS

The auction room *calls forth courage, promptness, and the spirit of adventure; of all branches of the sport,* says Rosenbach,[2] *that of attending book auctions is the greatest, the most stirring;* a patient mathematician may know the number of facets of the *Koh-i-nur* diamond, but no one will ever be able to count *the emotional reflections which take place during a book auction in the hearts and minds of men and women who are enamoured of books.* The lust of books is here seen at its height: *faces that are usually marvellous poker portraits, become sharply distorted; eyes which ordinarily indulge an almost studied innocence shoot sudden darts of fire.*[3] At the sale of the library of Paris de Meyzieux, in 1790, *you might have seen the most notorious bibliomaniacs, with blood inflamed and fancies intoxicated, rushing to examine the matchless volumes.*[4] 'Tis a great adventure. Other adventures may pall, *lose their glamour,* but this *brings a delightful thrill never to be duplicated.* Andrew Lang[5] asserts that it is near to gambling: *the chamber has the look of a dingy gambling room,* and the crowd like that at Monte Carlo.

Though some have condemned, none has been able to set a term to the folly and extravagance which have so often been characteristic of the book-auction, ever since it was introduced into England in 1678: *the fury of book-maniacs,* saith Dibdin,[6] *will sometimes, from the hot and hasty passions which are stirred up by the poisonous miasmata floating in the auction room, give a sum twice or thrice beyond the real value of the books bidden for!* and he has been frequently amused to note *the vehemence and rapture with which a dirty little volume is contended for and embraced*—*while a respectable bookseller, like Portius, coolly observes across the table*—'*I have a better copy on sale at one third of the price*'; but, he concludes,[7] *if you pay dearly for favourite volumes, you have them,* which *is comfort enough.*

If the rewards are greater, for a book is more than money, the chances,

---

[1] *Ma République.* 13.   [2] *Books and Bidders.* 75.   [3] *Ib.* 38–9.   [4] Dibdin, *Bibliomania.* (1811) 544–5.   [5] *The Library.* 19.   [6] *Bibliomania.* (1811) 405.   [7] *Ib.* 406.

the fears and the thrills are the same, even if you bid by proxy, as Horace Walpole well knew, when he instructed Graham to buy Winstanley's *Views of Audley Inn* at the sale of Meade's Library, concluding that the *thin dirty folio* was worth about fifteen shillings. Graham bid up to *nine-and-forty guineas*, when, fearing that the price had gone high enough, he asked for an adjournment of the sale so that he might consult his principal; Walpole *started in a fright*, but he was relieved when he learnt that another bookseller who *had luckily had an unlimited commission* was prepared to bid fifty. *I think*, said Walpole, I *shall never give an unbounded commission again, even for Views of 'Les Rochers'!*[1] Unlimited commission is often given to booksellers by rival millionaires in our day, for the rich amateur rarely experiences the thrills of the auction room in person. *In London*, saith one,[2] *nine out of every ten bidders are professional dealers;* the private bidder is, he believes, at a disadvantage, his presence is often resented by the *trade*, and they will bid against him out of jealousy.

There are those who would speculate on the curious twist which gives speculation, even in books, such a fascination. Roberts[3] regrets that Adam Smith did not devote a section of the *Wealth of Nations* to this subject, for, *in a general way*, he says, *books are subject, like other merchandise, to the laws of supply and demand;* but unlike many kinds of goods the *demand fluctuates according to fashion* rather than *any real, tangible want;* it is in the auction room that these fluctuations are to be observed in process, in the making, at passion heat; there treasures are *scattered, like the Sibylline leaves, by the winds of fate;*[4] for *most of the great books of the world have found their way to the auction room at one time or another*, and *nearly every collector enters* this field *to enjoy its seductive pleasures some time during the period of his fever;*[5] *the auction room is the great leveller of all manner of unmerited fame, and it may be taken, as a general rule, to be an infallible guide.*[6] But that is a sweeping statement which few will support in these times when all book-values have risen at auction, and many new values have been created which have small relationship with merit; they are very often the *wild prices* given by *competitive millionaires*[7] or speculative booksellers. But *the great historic sales have more than a financial value: they give books a pedigree, which is a romance in itself.*[8]

What more concerns me here is the keen spirit which the auction room excites among all book-hunters; they *follow* price movements with the same ardour with which racing men follow *form*, or cricket, football and

[1] Letter to Richard Bentley. 13.xii.1754. [2] Iolo A. Williams, *Elements of Book-Collecting*. 109–10. [3] *Book-Hunter in London*. 98. [4] Dibdin, *Bibliomania*. (1811) 405. [5] Rosenbach, *Books and Bidders*. 56. [6] *Book-Hunter in London*. 118. [7] Lang, *Letters on Literature*. 117. [8] Sawyer & Darton, *English Books: 1475–1900*. i, 25.

baseball *fans* follow the achievements of their athletic heroes, but with more sportsmanship than most of the others, since, even in these days of living by proxy, they play the game, partake of its activities, as well as take a delight in being observers of it. Horace Walpole showed his preference for the game, even over that of politics, by quitting the House of Commons during a debate to attend a *sale of books*.[1] But in all these adventures, I may safely conclude that, although the chase is relished, the quarry itself is the aim, and most keenly enjoyed.

XIII. A DIGRESSION OF BUYING BOOKS

To this disquisition of methods I may well annex a list of those peculiarities which beset even the bibliophile when buying books, for despite the great expenditure of money in which many will indulge, more of them seek books for a little or no money, begging, borrowing, bargaining, beating down the dealer, and even stealing (and not only perforce, for, so great the temptation to get books for nothing, they will steal rather than buy, even when well able to pay), upon which I have said enough already.

Mark Pattison complains that the bookseller's bill in an ordinary middle-class family is *shamefully small*, and he thinks it *monstrous* that *a man earning £1,000 a year should spend less than £1 a week on books*. But Lord Morley argues that a shilling in the pound spent on books by a clerk earning £200 a year, or by a workman earning a quarter of that sum, is more than can be reasonably expected. This may be true, but few indulge even so limited an extravagance; indeed, Arnold Bennett not long ago announced that he had *scarcely ever met a soul, who* could *be said to make a habit of buying new books*.[2] Most people look upon money spent on books as money wasted: *the public hates to spend money on books*,[3] although they do not hesitate to spend lavishly on such ephemera as newspapers, magazines, popular novels, etc. But these are beneath our argument: they enter not within the precincts of those who know that the return from the investment of a good book is immeasurable and not comparable with other profits, since books bear an unseen dividend which only the bookman can realize. A material profit also goes with some books which, although it does not affect the disinterested bibliophile, is often used by him in extenuation of his extravagance. Thus Sylvestre de Sacy, contemplating a costly volume, argued that such expenditure was a form of saving: *Vous voyez bien qu'il avait raison d'acheter des livres! C'était sa manière de faire des économies;*[4] the American bibliophile, Hagen, well knew this, for when a

[1] *Letters*. Cunningham. iv, 201.   [2] *Books and Persons*. (1919) 26.   [3] Lang, Intro., *Pleasures of Bookland*. Shaylor. xxi.   [4] Qt. Gustave Mouravit, *Le Livre et la Petite Bibliothèque d'Amateur*. 47–8.

friend, alarmed at his increasing expenditure on books, advised him to buy bonds, he replied: *No, my books are worth more than your bonds.*[1] Mouravit supports this claim with an opinion that well-chosen books double their value in ten years, and with an appeal to housewives *qui avez le bonheur de posséder un mari bibliophile,* to rejoice instead of frowning when new books invade all parts of the house, for in these inconveniences she should see the fortune of her children increasing.[2]

Many have thought as much in all times: there have been ages, says Isaac D'Israeli,[3] when for the possession of a manuscript *a man would transfer an estate; or leave in pawn for its loan hundreds of golden crowns; and when even the sale or loan of a manuscript was considered of such importance as to have been solemnly registered by public acts;* which Thomas Carlyle supports in his *Heroes and Hero-Worship*: in past times, he says, *a man for a single book had to give an estate of land.* Lest you think all this is but opinion, I must cite some evidence, which is not difficult. Don Quixote's eagerness and infatuation reached such a pitch, that *he sold many an acre of tillage-land to buy books of chivalry;*[4] and it is recorded that a Countess of Anjou, in the thirteenth century, offered for a collection of *homilies* three hogsheads of wheat, rye and millet, and two hundred sable skins;[5] Heinsius gave a hundred gold pieces for the copy of Ulric von Hutten's *Pasquinades* which Count Hohendorf afterwards placed among the Imperial rarities of Vienna;[6] Pope Nicholas V engaged Phillepho to copy the *Iliad* and the *Odyssey,* and gave him for his work a retaining fee, a palace, and a farm in the Campagna, and he made a deposit of ten thousand pieces of gold to be paid on the completion of the contract.[7] Richard de Bury bought thirty volumes from the Abbey of St. Albans for *fifty pounds weight of silver,* but the monks *continually protested* that the books should not have been sold, so after the death ·of Richard they were returned, some by gift, others by purchase from his executors.[8] It is reported in his treatise of the *Recovery of Manuscripts,*[9] that in those times, and earlier, *usurers themselves* reckoned books among precious objects and security for money: a student of Pavia, who was reduced by his debaucheries, raised a new fortune on a *Law* MS., and a grammarian, ruined by fire, rebuilt his house with two small volumes of Cicero. But I digress too far, having made my point, so will now return to the main theme of this chapter.

Lord Chesterfield was gratified to learn that his son spent his *pin money not in gewgaws and baubles, but in buying good and useful books;* this he thought an *excellent symptom* which gave him very good hopes.[10] But whether they

---

[1] Newton, *Magnificent Farce.* 60.   [2] *Op. cit.* 66.   [3] 'Recovery of MS.', *Cur. of Lit.* i, 30.   [4] *Don Quixote.* i.   [5] Janin, *Le Livre.* xi.   [6] Elton, *Great Book-Collectors.* 89.   [7] Elton, *Great Book-Collectors.* 70–1.   [8] D'Israeli, *Cur. of Lit.* i, 7.   [9] *Ib.* i, 30.   [10] *Letters to his Son.* 23.viii.1748.

be large or small buyers they all rejoice in a bargain: some from shortness of cash, as Charles Lamb when he *hit upon Fairfax's 'Godfrey of Bullen', for half-a-crown*, and commanded Coleridge to rejoice with him,[1] or when he *picked up a copy of Quarles for ninepence! ! ! O tempora! O lectores!*[2] which he offers to Southey. Others from natural love of a bargain. And all like good value, and resent paying for an unsatisfactory book, as Edward FitzGerald when he bought Macaulay's *'Memoirs', in a hurry to read; and found that he might just as well have waited for Mudie, and saved his money too.*[3] Macaulay himself was a free but careful spender. When he was making a collection for his voyage to India he bought largely, but no *trashy books* which would bear only one reading for him, only *good books for a library*, books that would keep, wear well, cut-and-come-again books, and in this wise he practised economy, getting more and better books for his money. *I have my eye on all the book-stalls* (he writes to his sister, Hannah, 4:i:1834), *and I shall no longer suffer you, when we walk together in London, to drag me past them as you used to do.*[4]

Mr. Pepys was even more careful, and would resist the temptation to buy books by dipping into volumes at the bookseller's: *I thank God*, he wrote on one such occasion, *I can read and never buy a book, though I have a great mind to it;*[5] but he so loved to acquire bookish treasures that a little windfall in the way of commission would encourage him to add to his collection, as when on December 10th, 1663, he had gained *in the office by a stationer's bill to the King about 40s. or £3,* he went to St. Paul's Church-yard to lay it out in books: *found myself at a great loss where to choose, and do see how my nature would gladly return to the laying out my money in this trade. Could not tell whether to lay out my money for books of pleasure, as plays, which my nature was most earnest in; but, at last after seeing Chaucer, Dugdale's History of Paul's, Stow's London, Gesner, History of Trent, besides Shakespeare, Jonson, and Beaumont's plays, I at last chose Dr. Fuller's Worthys, the Cabbala, or Collections of Letters of State, and a little book Delices de Hollande, with another little book or two, all of good use or serious pleasure; and Hudibras, both parts.*[6]

Oliver Wendell Holmes so reverenced books that when a good one came his way he looked upon the event as an intervention of Providence; he thinks no price within reason too high, and on one occasion he considers a bookseller *has insulted one or two gentlemanly books by selling them to him at very low-bred and shamefully insufficient prices.*[7] When Huet first visited Paris in his youthful days he flew immediately to the booksellers' shops, where he spent money accumulated by sparing himself from his

[1] *Letters.* (Everyman) i, 83.   [2] *Ib.* i, 99–100.   [3] *More Letters.* 183.   [4] *Life and Letters.* i, 314.   [5] *Diary.* Wheatley. ii, 392.   [6] *Ib.* ii, 370–1.   [7] *The Poet at the Breakfast-Table.* (1902) 214.

pleasures, so that his *purse was usually in a very exhausted state;* yet when he returned to Caen he was consoled by the knowledge that his *library was so much augmented that no other in* the *district equalled it either in number or choice of volumes.*[1] The good George Herbert[2] protested and vowed that although he studied *Thrift* and was still *scarce able with much ado to make one half year's allowance shake hands with the other,* yet if *a Book of four or five shillings come in my way, I buy it, though I fast for it;* yea, he adds, *sometimes of ten shillings.* But there is joy in such impecuniosities, for, as John Ruskin concludes, *no book is ever worth so much to its reader as one that has been coveted for a year, and bought out of saved half-pence.*

The chance of finding a book below its *market value* is the hope of all book-hunters, but there are those who argue that there is some unfairness in this: *the loyal heart would feel a twinge or scruple,* says Percy Fitzgerald,[3] *as he carries off from the humble and ignorant dealer, for a shilling or two, a volume that may be worth ten or twenty pounds. No sophistry, he concludes, will veil the sharpness of the transaction, in which profit is made of poverty and ignorance.* He gives as a pertinent example the story of a book-hunter named Wilson, who *picked up* a copy of Caxton's *Game of Chess* for two-pence. He sold it to Osborne, the bookseller, for £20, who sold it in turn to Dr. Askew for £65, on whose death it was purchased by the Windsor Library for £370. If the book had continued to change hands at this rate, he says, its value then would have risen to £2,000. But it is not obvious who was victimized after the initial transaction, or even before it, as the original bookseller may be presumed to have made a profit on the two-pence he got for the book. Wilson certainly had an advantage over him, as Osborne had over Wilson; but Askew's heirs had an advantage over both, the upshot being that it is difficult to say either which advantage was unfair, or whether each of them was due to chance rather than ignorance: the lucky chance being the growing fashion for *incunabula,* which has continued to our days.

In all such adventures, Lang believes that *a question of casuistry* arises; and he instances as illustrating the complexities of the problem the case of Paul Lacroix, who bought an original *Tartuffe,* with the King's Arms, for two francs. He gave it to a famous French collector, and on the same day the bookseller discovered his error, but the collector refused to return the book or to pay the proper price; this conduct Lang disapproves, and to support his contention and prove his case, he recalls that he himself bought from *a lady bookseller* the three original volumes of *Alfred de Musset* for a shilling a piece, *she declined to accept a higher ransom, alleging that it was well for customers to have a bargain now and then.*[4] Fitzgerald[5] argues that it ought

[1] Huet, *Memoirs.* Trans. Aikin. i, 51.   [2] *Remains.* 305.   [3] *Book-Fancier.* 8–9.
[4] *The Library.* xiii.   [5] *Book-Fancier.* 9.

not to be difficult to make *an equitable decision* in such cases: *the buyer*, for example, *as discoverer, being entitled to the larger share; the owner to the rest.*

There are instances of the kind within my own experience, but altogether I have found as he has, and many another book-hunter, that although some booksellers demand excessive prices out of greed, cupidity, or even ignorance of values, most are content with a normal profit. In our times, because of the sharpness of both bookseller and book-collector, a bargain is doubly appreciated and taken proudly as it occurs, but the occurrences are increasingly rare. The knowing specialist hopes to circumvent inflated or even market values by hunting those territories in which his speciality is disregarded. 'Tis only as a last resort that he seeks his game in the domains of those who are as expert as himself. The collector is more fortunate who is *ahead of his time*, and seeks *a kind of book which no one else wants*, for *he will be able to find not only his common books, but also his rarities, in the cheaper bookshops, and all at equally low prices; he will then know to the full the joys of the pioneer;*[1] like the collector of unconsidered trifles in *Asselineau*,[2] who bears the laughter of his friends with fortitude and the consolatory thought that *dans dix ans, dans vingt ans, tu viendras me les demander à genoux; tu ne les auras pas!*

So I conclude, having no better argument, with John Selden's discovery that the *giving of a bookseller his price for his books has this advantage, he that will do so shall have the refusal of whatsoever comes to his hand, and so by that means get many things, which otherwise he never would have seen. So 'tis in giving a bawd her price.*[3]

XIV. THE BOOK-HUNTER ANATOMIZED

What manner of men become book-hunters is a matter of some difference of opinion. They are the subject of whole essays, and shall (some of them) be more opportunely dilated elsewhere. In the meantime thus much may I say of them, that generally they are a gentle and inoffensive breed, *keeping themselves to themselves*, in the vulgar phrase, and pursuing their genial or learned quarry without arousing the envy or even the interest of the common herd, who could by no means understand them, if perchance they ever learnt of their existence. Yet never, so far as Anatole France knew, *did any of them deserve the scorn of the vulgar*, for not one of them but is *distinguished*, he assures us, *by refined taste, a cultured mind, and gentle ways.*[4] Another observer holds that they are men *of simple manners and tastes, whose holiday is a prowl among 'old bookshops', and whose triumph*

[1] Iolo A. Williams, *Elements of Book-Collecting*. 105.   [2] *L'Enfer du Bibliophile*. 17.
[3] *Table-Talk*. (1797) 40-1.   [4] *Pierre Nozière*. Trans. J. Lewis May. 73.

is to return home with some mouldy but precious little duodecimo.[1] They are often so absorbed in the chase and preservation of books that they have no time, even for reading. There are some who relate that book-collectors are not necessarily book-lovers: *the book-lover is active, creative, powerful, and his distant relative, the book-collector, passive, indifferent, flaccid*.[2] At the same time the best of them presumably must have some affection for books, for *if the mind of a man be not pure, exalted, enthusiastic; if his heart be not filled with the immense love for beauty and humanity that poets have, he may collect books, he shall not form a library:*[3] those who cannot follow this enthusiast so far will find greater content in the words of so experienced an authority as A. J. A. Symons, who has never permitted his books to forget their primary duty of being read, and who maintains that a collection of unread books is *still, spiritually, part of a bookseller's stock*.[4]

Some hold that book-hunters lack time, even for idle vices, and of all classes of men they cause least concern to the state. Augustine Birrell[5] puts it that they are immune from revolutionary doctrine, no habits *more alien to the doctrine of the Communist than those of the collector, and there is no collector, not even the basest of them all, the Belial of his tribe, the man who collects money, whose sense of the joys of ownership is keener than the book-collector's.* But there is a fallacy here, for in my own experience are Communists whose Communism breaks down at books, as well it may, and although I am with him and those others who acclaim book-collectors as for the most part quiet and unworldly men, I would put in a caveat against any broad generalization, for belike they are only sedentary and peaceful when they are among their books; for even if there be few Communist book-collectors, which I question, many revolutionaries have been both bibliophiles and bibliomanes. Take for a taste John O'Leary, the head of the Fenian Brotherhood, who was *discovered*, says W. B. Yeats,[6] by Stephens. the father of Fenianism, *searching the second-hand bookstalls for rare editions.* When Yeats came to know him years afterwards, and after the Fenian trouble in Ireland had given way to a new trouble, *he still searched the second-hand bookstalls* tranquilly on the Dublin Quays, and he had a *great number of books, especially of Irish history and literature.*

Others point out less agreeable differences, such as a pensive sadness, a melancholy which seems to imbue them and which they share with the whole of the collecting tribe. I find an example supporting this theory in Beloe,[7] where he gives out that a Quaker namesake of my own, a dealer

---

[1] Percy Fitzgerald, *Book-Fancier*. 2.   [2] Henri Pène du Bois, *Four Libraries of New York*. 93.   [3] *Ib*. 119.   [4] 'The Book-Collector's Apology', *Book-Collector's Quarterly*. i, 50–1. For more on this theme see 'Do Bibliomaniacs Read Their Books?' *Post*, 291–300.   [5] *Collected Essays*. iii, 243.   [6] *The Trembling of the Veil*. 95.   [7] *Anecdotes*. i, 33.

in wines and spirits in the city of London, who had *a great passion for books*, which he hunted at *all the most considerable sales, destroyed himself in a fit of melancholy*. But,· methinks, this is an exceptional case, and I can find no more evidence to support it. Rosenbach[1] believes that their *ruling passion is humour, that they see the joyous, fantastic and capricious, and are never sérieux* or *bowed down with the gravity of their calling;* which may be true in some cases, yet some reliable witnesses account it otherwise: *believe me,* says Locker-Lampson,[2] *there is exhilaration in collecting*, and he *would call it a perennial joy, if it were not so often pierced with despair.* One kind Locker recognizes as *tolerably tiresome, dullish fellows, but unmistakable;* but he could *pick out your genuine collector from a crowd of any number of non-collecting beings.* Anatole France[3] has observed this dolour, and sets it down to the wish of all collectors *to stuff the universe into a cupboard*, and, since the dream is unrealizable, *true collectors have, like lovers, an infinite sadness, even in their happiness. They know well that they can never put the world under lock and key in a glass case. Hence their profound melancholy.*

Perchance the book-hunter seeks not books, but some unattainable association with knowledge—the fruit of the Tree of Knowledge of Good and Evil. *He stalks his prey through noble shops, poor wheelbarrows, by scent, by the bait of a good catalogue, by mere chance. He emerges at last, into a place where pride and covetousness are no longer deadly sins, but the austere restrained virtues of the true lover of good books;*[4] and there is more chance of this *true love* in our own times when books have been made *the servants of thought and science rather than the tyrants of taste and dilettantism.*[5] I know some are of the opinion that a book-collector is a vain, grasping, avaricious fellow. Percy Fitzgerald reports[6] that *his greed, akin to that of the miser, would make him sacrifice all that is human to all that is of paper. He is likely enough to be morose, snarling, grasping, and would find the most exquisite pleasure in getting from some poor but ignorant dealer for a shilling what was worth guineas. This,* he concludes, *is the triumph of the 'chasse à livres'.* Sometimes he cannot sleep o' nights for thinking of a rare book he would like to own, and when the coveted volume is in the hands of another collector he falls to brooding upon the owner's expectation of life:

> With greedy haste he cons it o'er and o'er
> And every time he views it, thinks it more;

for *book-collectors* (Rosenbach will have no exceptions)[7] *are buzzards who stretch their wings in anticipation as they wait patiently for a colleague's demise;*

[1] *Books and Bidders.* 241.   [2] *My Confidences.* 188–9.   [3] 'Bibliophilia', *On Life and Letters.* Trans. A. W. Evans. Second Series. 66.   [4] Sawyer & Darton, *English Books:* 1475–1900. 20.   [5] G. L. Gomme, Preface, *Literary Curiosities.* Gentleman's Magazine Library.   [6] *Book-Fancier.* 7.   [7] *Books and Bidders.* 17–18.

*and then they swoop down and ghoulishly grab some long-coveted treasure from
the dear departed's trove.* But *personal vanity, the mainspring of collecting*,
Seymour de Ricci observes, *has continually given way to local and national
pride.* In England, he says, *to be a collector has nearly always meant—to be a
patriot*,[1] which I hope is true.

That the collector is fickle many rightly believe, and, being a lover, it is
not strange. Dibdin argues[2] that it is not dishonourable in them to change
or transfer their taste, or augment it, as when they have *formerly sworn to
purchase no old book but Machlinia's first edition of Littleton's 'Tenures'*, they
*cannot resist, now and then, the delicious impulse of becoming masters of a black-
letter chronicle or romance.* If, says William Roberts,[3] *he cannot obtain what
he wants just exactly when he wants it, he does not care about it;* and sometimes
this keen temper is checked by a diffidence which is probably morbid,
and more proper for consideration under *Bibliomania*, as when Huth,
having tracked down a *Mazarin Bible*, let Quaritch, who had given £2,625
for it and was willing to sell it for £25 profit, keep it for two years before
he had the courage to order it home; confessing to W. C. Hazlitt that he was
rather ashamed of himself.[4] Yet I hold that there is a sane side even to this
discrepancy: *what is the use of going right over the old track again? There is an
adder in the path which your own feet have worn. You must make tracks into the
Unknown*.[5] But they are no worse than other hunters, unless evilly disposed, which sometimes happens, and no better; and whether they are gay
or morose depends upon character; the chase is ever exhilarating, but *inter
delicias semper aliquid saevi nos strangulat:*

> Ay, in the very temple of Delight
> Veil'd Melancholy has her sovran shrine,[6]

and often the moment of conquest is heavy with regret as vague as victory
itself. Such moments are not unknown to the book-collector. Edmund
Gosse once dined alone with Lord de Tabley at Onslow Square, and he
noticed that his host was *strangely distraught.* Presently the post came, *and
Warren (as he then was) tore open the envelope wildly; he read the first words,
and sank back faint in his chair, hiding his eyes with his hands.* Gosse imagined some *terrible calamity had happened to him, but it was only that he had
secured a first edition of Shelley's 'Alastor' at a country auction, and—la joie
faisait peur!*[7]

---

[1] *English Collectors of Books and Manuscripts.* 193.   [2] *Bibliomania.* (1811) 176.
[3] *Book-Hunter in London.* xxx.   [4] *Book-Collector.* 44–5.   [5] Thoreau, *Letters*.
20.v.1860.   [6] Keats, 'Ode on Melancholy'.   [7] Gosse, 'Lord de Tabley', *Critical
Kit-Kats.* 190–1.

Part XXII

OF DESIRABLE BOOKS

————————◁◀◈▶▷————————

I. THE KINDS OF BOOKS THAT ARE HUNTED

The quarry varies with the hunter;[1] it varies even between one country and another, as between England and France. English collectors prefer specimens in their original condition, as near *issue* or *mint state* as possible, but French *goût* insists upon all manner of garniture: fine paper, elegant illustrations, dainty coverings, etc. Some French bookmen of the romantic period valued Voltaire's works solely for the vignettes; Edmond and Jules de Goncourt *picked them out of the fifteen-cent boxes of the parapets on the quays of Paris, as archæologists picked out of neglected graveyards figurines of Tanagra.*[2] A copy of a book, no matter how valuable intrinsically, makes no appeal to a French collector unless *it is in a particular vesture, with a particular 'ex libris', and of a particular measurement in millésimes.*[3] A French bibliophile, he says, has no love for original *vellum* or even *calf*, and where we would have a rarity in such homely clothing boxed for protection like a gem, he would have it rebound magnificently to glorify its quality, and so make it worthy of his *cabinet choisi; and in nine cases out of ten he will not buy a book born out of France.*[4] Our native collectors he groups mainly into two great classes which contain all concomitant varieties: one *Specialist, the other Miscellaneous;* the first I shall dilate anon, the second shall have his own explication at once.

Of the miscellaneous class are *graduated and varying types*, and of these Hazlitt discerns six varieties, which he grades as follows: 1. The *Omnivorous Accumulator, who does not insist on condition or binding*, and who *buys everything—whole libraries and catalogues at a swoop;* as Richard Heber and Sir Thomas Phillips. 2. *The Normal Promiscuous Buyer, to whom anything in the guise of a book is a sure bait*, as Thomas Jolley, Joseph Tasker, Edward Hailstone, and Edward Solly. 3. A nondescript group whose members *repudiate specialism as narrowing and troublesome, and who impose on themselves no restraint save perchance in the direction of theology, science, and 'arcana',*

[1] Lang, *The Library.* 19.　　[2] Henri Pène du Bois, *Four Private Libraries of New York.* 85.　　[3] W. C. Hazlitt, *Book-Collector.* 194.　　[4] *Ib.* 238.

480

and who *stop peremptorily at 'belles lettres'*, as Singer, Mitford, Bliss, Bandinel, Forster, Cosens, Ireland, Crossley, and Sir John Simeon. 4. Another nondescript group whose taste mine author makes no clearer than to say it hath *a stronger tendency to draw the line at character or condition*, and he names as representatives Capell, Malone, Douce, Bright, Chalmers, Collier, Ouvry, Bolton, Corney, David Laing, E. F. Rimbault, Halliwell-Phillips, Frederick Locker, W. H. Miller, Henry Cunliffe, R. S. Turner, and Henry Huth. 5. The *Fastidious Dilettanti*: these buy a book in *the same spirit as they might do a picture or a piece of majolica;* they make a small class, and *accepted types* are Sir Andrew Fountaine, Sir David Dundas, and Samuel Addington. 6. He gives no name to this group, but includes all those personal collectors, *the most interesting and intelligent type*, who, *after a certain amount of preparatory thought and training*, buy only books for which they have *a personal relish*.[1] Here we have clear evidence of the variety of the sport, but on further examination it is shown to be even more varied.[2]

The inclinations of persons are vastly different in their collecting, saith Bagford,[3] and he gives as evidence Lord Clarendon, who collected books *mainly about the affairs of Ireland and its government;* Mr. Wilde, *formerly living in Bloomsbury*, architecture and agriculture; *a gentleman that lives in the Inner Temple*, necromancy and magic; Mr. Thomas Britton, *the smallcoal man in Clerkenwell*, chemistry, also *Musick, prickt by his own hand;* Dr. Beaumont, who had *collected for some years past whatever he could relating to* mystical divinity, spirits, witchcraft, and such-like subjects; Captain Aston, voyages and travels (the *strength* of Roger Wilbraham's library, saith Dibdin,[4] also lay in his *Voyages and Travels*); Mr. Serjeant, a surgeon, in Hatton Garden, *the best editions and fairest impressions of classics;* Captain Hatton, English history; Mr. Topham, a complete collection of books in the Greek language relating to Greek learning; and Mr. Huckle, *on Tower Hill, hath been admirably curious in collecting the nicest books* in Latin, Spanish, Italian, and French; *some, of late*, he concludes, *have been curious to collect those of the Large Paper; not long since 'Mr. Bateman bought Dr. Stanley's study of books, wherein were the most of that kind that have been seen together for some years.* A short study of *Lowndes* and of Martin's *Privately Printed Books*, I may add out of Carew Hazlitt,[5] *will suffice to show that not only a library, but a tolerably extended one*, might be formed of Large Paper Copies, as is proved by the *voluminous inheritance of now rather neglected and undervalued curiosities of this kind*, made by Utterson, Halliwell, Laing, Maidment, Eyton, and Turnbull. *Almost as soon as book-collecting*

---

[1] W. C. Hazlitt, *Book-Collector*. 81–2.   [2] For more recent news of this theme, see Seymour de Ricci, *English Collectors of Books and Manuscripts* (1530–1930) *and their Marks of Ownership*. Cambridge. 1930.   [3] *Gentleman's Magazine*. (1816) ii, 395–7.   [4] *Reminiscences*. i, 497.   [5] *Book-Collector*. 189.

became at all general, Roberts asserts,[1] *the 'faddy' man came into existence;* among them he names Dr. John Webster, of Clitheroe, who died in June, 1682, aged seventy-two, and who had formed a library of *books of romance* and '*the black art*', but as he wrote a learned treatise on *witchcraft,* his collection was the raw material of his research, not a *fad,* as that of John Rennie, the engineer, who made *a speciality of mathematical books, of which he had a collection nearly complete in all languages;* Dr. Benjamin Moseley's library, sold in March, 1814, was composed for the most part of *astrology, magic,* and *facetiæ,* and the Rev. J. Stainforth, whose library was sold at Sotheby's in 1867, collected only *books relating to women*: he aimed to secure not only every book, *but every edition of such books.* He was a most determined book-hunter, saith mine author, and when Holywell Street was at its lowest moral ebb, this eccentric gentleman used to visit all the bookshops almost daily, his inquiry being: '*Have you any women for me to-day?*'

No accounting for their tastes, either in quantity or quality, which vary according to time and place: *Here were editions esteemed as being the first, and there stood others scarcely less regarded as being the last and best. Here was a book valued because it had the author's final improvements, and there another which (strange to tell!) was in request because it had them not. One was precious because it was a folio, another because it was a duodecimo; some because they were short; the merit of this lay in the title-page, of that in the arrangement of the letters in the word Finis.*[2] A hundred years ago they were all for fine texts of the *Classics* finely bound, and a while before that they hoarded and revelled in vast tomes of *Theology*; J. Hill Burton cites an opulent collector under the name of Magnus Lucullus, Esq., as a devotee of the former, who would only have *the best and most complete editions,* in *perfect condition;* he had all the *Classics* in their *old original morocco, without a scratch or abrasure, gilt-edged, vellum-jointed, their backs blazing in tooled gold.*[3] The birth of Printing created a demand for manuscripts, and at the Renaissance, says D'Israeli,[4] *every part of Europe and Greece was ransacked, and the glorious end considered,* which was the discovery of lost authors of antiquity, *manuscript hunting* became a prime sport, a fashion, a means of spending fortunes: *the glory of possessing a manuscript of Cicero seemed to approximate to that of being its author. People have been bitten with a taste for a library of lost authors,* and, he thinks,[5] *Chaucer may have led the way in this kind of work.* Anatole France[6] naïvely records that there are bibliophiles who collect *incunabula,* those *humble monuments of the Xylography* of the fifteenth century, and whom the *Biblia pauperum,* with *its crude illustrations,* charms more than all

---

[1] *Book-Hunter in London.* xxviii.   [2] Sir Walter Scott, *Antiquary.*   [3] *Book-Hunter.* 47.
[4] 'Recovery of MSS.', *Cur. of Lit.* i, 31–2.   [5] Bradshaw, *Memoir.* Prothero. 216.
[6] *Life and Letter.* Trans. A. W. Evans. Second Series. 66.

the seductions of nature joined to all the enchantments of art; he has known also those who collect Royal bindings made for Henri II, Diane de Poitiers, and Henri III, and toolings of the sixteenth and seventeenth centuries, as well as those who seek only *morocco binding with the arms of princes and queens,* and finally those who will have nothing but original editions of the *Classics.*

But if the nature of the quarry varies, as I have shown, with the collector, in the main the books hunted fall into three categories, Typography, Subject, Coverture. One seeks out *Incunabula,* as Bishop More, the *Father of Black Letter,*[1] who began this sport in the late seventh century; and Dibdin reports[2] that Haslewood had the same passion plus another for Izaak Walton; he was *a respectable and praiseworthy man, continually walking in a thick forest of black-letter,* who preferred *a printed book before the year* 1550 *to a turtle dressed according to the rules of Mr. Farley,* yet he could *ever and anon sally forth to enjoy a stroll along the river side with Izaak Walton in his hand;* another is for Bibles, another for Ballads: Humphrey Wanley *had the greatest collection of English Bibles, Psalters, etc., that ever any one man had,*[3] the result of twenty years' hunting; Bagford was never idle, and if he could not meet with better things *he would divert himself with looking over Ballads and was mightily pleased if he met with any that were old;* Anthony à Wood made a good collection of Ballads, but was *outdone by Mr. Bagford.*[4] So it goes on; some pursue Plays, others Play-bills; another will have nothing but Poetry, as Narcissus Luttrell: *Let the volume be great or small— or contain good, bad, or indifferent warblings of the muse—his insatiable craving had 'stomach for them all';*[5] some, called *Rubricists,* are possessed of a sacred rage for books having the contents and marginal reference printed in red ink, and others 'go at' *flowered capitals.*[6] Another kind wants *broad margins,* and some, *not unimportant for number and zeal,* have sought only books *marked by peculiar mistakes or errors of the press;*[7] still another will have nought but *Association Books,* hunting only for copies which belonged to illustrious collectors; or he may dote only on bindings, finding no interest in the contents, pictures or printing; for him *a quite valueless seventeenth-century book that has been bound by Samuel Mearne becomes, from that fact alone, an object of much esteem,* and *in the case of French bindings of the first rank it frequently happens at sales that books of no value from the literary point of view fetch many hundreds of pounds for the sake of the bindings alone.*[8]

I will open these mysteries no farther if I may have leave to sum up with an opinion that whatever bookmen have collected in times past, the proliferation of books in times present will force them to become specialists.

[1] Dibdin, *Bibliomania.* (1811) 421.   [2] *Reminiscences.* i, 416.   [3] Dibdin, *op. cit.* 459, [4] *Ib.* 435.   [5] *Ib.* 427–8.   [6] Burton, *Book-Hunter.* 63–4.   [7] *Ib.* 66.   [8] Davenport. *Byways among English Books.* 5.

The realm of books is so vast, illimitable, that *no man can be universal, even if he had the wealth of a dozen Rothschilds, or the mental vigour and versatility of a hundred Gladstones.*[1] This is very plain, even in the case of modern books. The choice is infinite, as varied as life itself; *as many as are the species of rare and beautiful books*, saith Lang, *so many are the species of collectors;* which opinion of his in his book of *The Library* he much labours to demonstrate and prove. *One man*, he says, *will go home hugging a volume of sermons, another with a bulky collection of catalogues; others are captivated by black-letter, others by the plays of such obscurities as Nabbes and Glapthorne;* but they are all agreed on one point: *the love of printed paper;* even, he concludes, *an Elzevir man* can sympathize with Charles Lamb's attachment to the famous *folio Beaumont and Fletcher* which he made the object of a memorable hunt in Covent Garden, as I have recorded in its place; and having that opinion he cannot hold with Lamb for not caring for a *first folio Shakespeare; a bibliophile*, he complains, *who could say this could say anything*, and most of them will support him. But in the main he speaks truly when he claims that they all have in common a love of books, which is proved in so many instances when they begin by hunting one kind, as *Elzevirs*, or *Aldines, First Editions*, or *Large Paper, Horae, Incunabula, Private Presses, Plays, Chapbooks, Emblems*, or what not, and end by becoming bookish Nimrods, hunting distinguished or curious books of all kinds, as Winston H. Hagen, who *formed a plan to secure a small but important collection which should consist of the monumental works of the leading authors from Chaucer to the present day: a First Folio Shakespeare*, 1623; *Paradise Lost*, 1667; Burton's *Anatomy*, 1621; Pope's *Dunciad*, 1728; Goldsmith's *Vicar of Wakefield*, 1766, etc., but it was not enough, once the hunt was on he could not contain his passion and he became *a collector of all English books;*[2] or, as Frederick Locker-Lampson, who sought to make a representative collection of favourites in our great literary periods, sixteenth, seventeenth, and eighteenth centuries, preferring *his books to be small, he had special loves to serve*, but *catholicity was not his boast;*[3] his object—and, says Seymour de Ricci,[4] *it is indeed strange that nobody should have had the idea before him—was to secure the masterpieces (and the masterpieces only) of English literature, from Chaucer to Swinburne.* Sir Edmund Gosse holds[5] *that it is in the nature of a famous author to undergo a sort of bibliographical expansion;* and thus, as I have shown, specialization ends in a synthesis of an author or a class of authors which in itself is a new generalization; as he saith, at first, the best book of an author *alone is wanted; then curiosity is awakened about the other and less striking*

---

[1] Roberts, *Book-Hunter in London*. Intro. xxx.   [2] Chew, *Essays and Verses about Books*. 103.   [3] E. V. Lucas, *Ashley Lib. Cat.* Intro. V, viii.   [4] *English Collectors of Books and Manuscripts*, 1530–1930. 174–5.   [5] 'The Ashley Library', *Sunday Times*. 15.i.1928.

works of the same writer; then to books about him or by his friends, and finally, *books issued in ridicule or abuse of him are swept into the great bibliographical net.*

I know many book-hunters are of opinion that our modern books are weak, imperfect, not so well concocted or of such force, as those of other days and places; not so fit to be *collected* and used as quarry, and will therefore fetch their books from afar off: Black-Letters out of Nuremberg and Basle, Aldines from Venice, Elzevirs from Holland, Plantins from Brussels, illustrated volumes from Paris, cuneiform tablets from Nineveh, papyri from Egypt, and ideographs on rice paper from far Cathay;

> And we have manuscripts in peacock styles
>   By Ali of Damascus;[1]

and if they come nearer home they will stop at Caxton, Pynson, and Wynkyn de Worde. Many times they are so over curious in this kind, that they think they do nothing unless they hunt the rich manuscripts of the Middle Ages, Runic arabesques from Ireland, or those gospels and venerated writings of the fathers designed in *liquid gold on parchment of richest purple with illuminations of exquisite workmanship,* which Merryweather[2] so much approves, and so of the rest. But such tastes, if persisted in too severely, become far-fetched; and although I am mindful of the saying that time makes poems better as it does wines, and that this same parallel may be continued with books, which ripen in the process of the same sun, yet without all question, if we have not these rare exotic books, I hold that, at home and in our own time, which is in virtue equivalent unto them, ours will serve as well as those past tomes, if they be taken in proportionable quantity, hunted and qualified aright, if not better, and more proper to our constitutions. So 'tis for the most part, as Pliny writes to Gallus,[3] *we are careless of that which is near us, and follow that which is afar off, to know which we will travel and sail beyond the seas, wholly neglecting that which is under our eyes;* this sort are no better than *the idiot* in the satiric poet[4]

> who praises with enthusiastic tone,
> All centuries but this, and every country but his own.

And even then foreign books or old books *per se* have no special charm for the book-hunter: he is selective or he is no sound hunter. Of all the *books printed before the beginning of the sixteenth century, not more than 300 are considered worth reprinting, and not more than 500 are sought after,* my authority[5] wrote in 1895; and although the increase of book-collectors and

---

[1] Flecker, *The Golden Journey to Samarkand.* 6.   [2] *Bibliomania in the Middle Ages.* 36.
[3] *Epistles.* Loeb Ed. viii, 20.   [4] Gilbert, *Songs of a Savoyard.* 44.   [5] Roberts, *Book-Hunter in London.* xxii.

booksellers has increased the number and variety of books deemed *desirable*, the moral is unaltered. But all book-hunters are agreed that whatsoever the kind of book hunted the quality must be good: *no qualification, nothing secondary, nothing dubious;*[1] condition is everything: *far wiser*, Lang advises,[2] *to buy seldom, and at a high price, than to run round the stalls collecting twopenny treasures*, a counsel he ever regretted not taking himself in his early days; books with pages in facsimile are *twopenny treasures*; the name of *short Elzevirs, incomplete Angling curiosities*, etc., is legion; they are examples to be avoided, together with *the habit of miscellaneous buying.*

What they will collect in future days is beyond all guessing, but as fashions and tastes have changed from time to time, and many of the books hunted to-day languished in neglect in past times, so what we hunt as prizes may pass out of favour and new favourites take their place. Walter Jerrold[3] prophesies that *Pirated Editions* may yet come so greatly into favour as to surpass the *craze* for Aldines and Elzevirs, or the *Limited Editions* of Strawberry Hill or Kelmscott; Iolo A. Williams advises[4] the collection of books which have been *studied by comparatively few people*, and there is much wisdom in this, both from the aspect of utility and economy, especially if a collection is seen in *a vision as a well-articulated thing: a group of lenses so focused as to reveal every aspect of some object in the storehouse of knowledge;* Dr. Rosenbach supports him in this and gives out that there are still hundreds of varieties of books *unnoticed in the auction room*, neglected on the bookseller's shelves, *disregarded by the conventional collector, waiting for the man of imagination to discover them.*[5]

II. OF RARE BOOKS

But of all varieties of books those that are most desirable and most affected by collectors are those which are rare naturally, books which have become rare *by the process of the suns. Clement was* Dibdin's *Hortus Adonidis*, his *seductive digressions* and *interminable notes upon notes*, his *rare, très rare, excessivement rare, introuvable*, etc., *delighted* and *distracted* him *by turns.*[6] But *scarcity* is not enough: rarity is relative; *absolute rarity—or uniqueness—exists only when it is definitely known that but one copy of a book was ever printed, or that but one contains a certain feature;* even uniqueness is not the *determining factor;*[7] *rarity by itself is of no interest to collectors;*[8] a rare

---

[1] W. C. Hazlitt, *Book-Collector*. 169.   [2] *The Library*. Preface to Second Ed. xii· [3] *The Autolycus of the Bookstalls*. 37.   [4] *Elements of Book-Collecting*. 95.   [5] *Books and Bidders*. 182.   [6] Dibdin, *Reminiscences*. i, 205.   [7] Sawyer & Darton, *English Books*, 1475–1900. i, 4–5.   [8] Pollard, *Fine Books*. 8.

book, to be desirable, must have some distinction beyond its rarity: it must be qualitatively as well as quantitatively rare, and *literary value* is *almost the sole final determinant of price*,[1] even if, as Lang claims,[2] *no rarity which adds to knowledge is really valueless.* More than 18,000 works are computed to have been printed before the end of the fifteenth century; *all of these,* Lang argues,[3] *cannot possibly be of interest,* many are *rare* merely because they are *uninteresting: they have not been preserved because they were thought not worth preserving;* but he warns us against hasty conclusions, as *because a book found no favour in its own age, therefore it has no claim on our attention,* and he gives for example the story of a bookseller who bought the remainder of Keats's *Endymion* for fourpence a copy. Yet again, the quality of a book may not be confined to its contents: the book itself may have value as a piece of craftsmanship, a work of art, a curiosity. *A book's first life, it is true,* says George Moore, *depends upon its contents, but two or three years after publication the pagination, the print, the paper, the cover, and the shape of the book begin to attract, and year by year they attract more and more until the book attains the glory of a Chinese vase in which there is nothing but a little dust.*[4]

Books which have thus become rare are, in our time, the axed stars of the bibliophile's adoration; books only that are threatened with extinction win to immortality in the temple of bibliographical fame; books that have escaped death; books that have been despised and rejected of critics and readers alike, and come after long years into their own; books that *fall asleep like the chrysalis, and awaken to glitter in the sun of popularity like the butterfly;*[5] as those First Editions of Thomas Hardy's novels, *Desperate Remedies, Under the Greenwood Tree,* and *A Pair of Blue Eyes,* of which Tinsley the publisher could sell no more than twenty copies of each out of the five hundred copies printed, so was forced to get rid of the *remainder* in sheets to a barrowman, who bound them roughly together in brown paper, three volumes in one, and *hawked* them *under a naphtha lamp at the corner of Jackson's Rd. and Holloway Rd. for 15d. a copy.*[6] Books that have been slain in their day by neglect and contumely to rise gloriously from the dead at the hour of recognition; books that have been lost and found; books born out of their due time; books that have been ugly ducklings and become swans; books that have defied time and fate; books that have distinguished themselves by contact with distinguished persons; books that have taken part in great adventures or great events; and those, still more fortunate, so beloved at birth that they have been almost caressed out of life; as those early English books which were so amusing that *they*

---

[1] Sawyer & Darton, *op. cit.* i, 10. [2] *The Library.* xv. [3] *Ib.* 97. [4] *Impressions and Opinions.* (1913) Pref. vi. [5] Sir Walter Scott, Letter to Lady Louisa Stuart. 21.ii.1825. [6] Spencer, *Forty Years in My Bookshop.* 240.

were used up, thumbed out of existence;[1] but *it would be difficult to name any great work, still read, still to be for ever read, which is not rare in its first edition.*[2]

'Tis the common practice of all good bookmen, I say, to desire such books; they have bestowed infinite value upon those which are extant at this day, some will have them even if their possession involves vast sums, great fortunes even. Bibliophiles of puny means can only gaze at such treasures from afar, yet Fate is with them now and then, for it is a *curious phenomenon in the old book trade* that rarities *do not always remain rare;* volumes multiply mysteriously, being drawn from their hiding places by *the rumour of scarcity, and value, and of a hunt after them,*[3] although they seldom multiply so greatly as to be other than rare. Books become rare not solely by neglect or ill-usage, or by such accidents as fires, floods, shipwrecks, wars, earthquakes, volcanic eruptions, all of which have devastated libraries in their time, but by the fluctuation of taste and the haphazard of fashion: *mill and fire have consumed the discarded favourites of bygone generations, just as at the present moment we pulp or burn from day to day cartloads of old science, and theology, and law, and fiction;*[4] during the Great War books of all kinds were *pulped* by the ton to meet the paper shortage of those lean years. Thus do books become rare by chance, accident, ill-usage, or erosion of the years; some other rarities are produced by none of these fortuitous or natural causes, but through the ingenious manipulation of cunning or covetous men; but more of these in my next section.

III. BOOKS ARTIFICIALLY RAREFIED

Some books are born rare, some achieve rarity, others have rarity thrust upon them. Of the first are those which are unique from birth because only one copy has been made for a particular purpose, such as *La Guirlande de Julie,* with which the Duc de Montausier sought to win Julia d'Angennes de Rambouillet from a vow of constant even if Platonic affection for Gustavus Adolphus,[5] and the *Garland of Rachel,* which the English scholar Daniel printed on his own press at Oxford, for his daughter, with contributions in poetry from his own poet friends, and to whom only he gave copies. But only one copy of the *Garland of Julia* was made. It took the form of an album of flowers painted by an artist who at that time was considered to be *the most excellent for painting flowers in the manner called miniature; and to each flower was subjoined its epigram or inscription, in verse, composed with great elegance and ingenuity, partly by* Montausier himself, *and*

---

[1] *Book-Hunter.* 218–19.   [2] Sawyer & Darton, *English Books,* 1475–1900. i, 19.
[3] Burton, *Book-Hunter.* 225.   [4] W. Carew Hazlitt, *Book-Collector.* 18.   [5] Isaac D'Israeli, *Cur. of Lit.* i, 433–6.

partly by the most refined poets of the age, inscribed by *a penman so eminent in his art, that all the relics of his hand are valued at a high price*, the whole being bound in *scented Spanish leather*, then an article of great luxury.[1]

Those that achieve rarity are more numerous and are discussed above. Those which have rarity thrust upon them are in a class apart. Their condition is not the result of any natural process, but cunningly devised by interested persons to inflame or feed desire. If a book is common, or rare but not unique, they will set out to make it so by devious means. One will seek to cajole a living author into inscribing a copy as though it had been a gift; another will foster rarity by securing to himself all the known copies of a book already scarce, destroying all save one, which he hugs to himself as a miser his gold. This method is proper to *Bibliomania*, which I dilate in its place, but I may insert here Dibdin's story[2] of his own attempt to rarify his *Bibliographical Decameron* by artificial attenuation.

The work was originally issued in a notable three-volume edition, from Bulmer's Shakespeare Press, in 1817. It was elegantly printed and most generously illustrated; and out of a desire to give his *subscribers* value for their money, Dibdin contrived to make a reprint impossible except at a forbidding price. To that end he invited his bibliographical friends and supporters to dine with him, ostensibly *to carry away with them their respective copies, in small or large paper, bound by Lewis, in morocco or russia*, but actually to take part in a bibliomaniacal orgy of incendiarism. Some twelve *guests obeyed the summons*, and *somewhat of an extraordinary surprise awaited them*. The surprise was unfolded in two acts. In the first the guests were presented with a tray of *the choicest wooden blocks*, which had been used in the illustrating of the *Decameron*, with the *urgent request* to each that he would *help himself* to one or more of the *woodcuts* as a *memento* of the occasion. They helped themselves *liberally*, as he wished them to do, and fell to discussing what they would do with these souvenirs. Some were for converting them into *snuff-boxes*, others into drinking cups, and still others advocated glazing and framing. At this point the host opened his second act. Like the first, its focus was a tray of wood blocks. But this time the guests were invited to take a block each and *throw it into the fire*. If the first act was a surprise this was *an astonishment*, and *a thrill of horror seemed to pervade every bosom*. There were remonstrances and entreaties, but *in vain*. Dibdin was not only firm but active in the cause, and, he confesses, *I led the way to this unparalleled act of Incendiarism, by throwing the ugly and frightful figure of Lucifer*[3] *into his natural element . . . the flames*. Thus encouraged, the party joined in the dance of death. Mr. Baron Bolland took the

[1] Huet, *Memoirs*. Trans. Aikin. ii, 272. [2] *Reminiscences*. ii, 625–30. [3] The block of the frontispiece to *Le Livre de la Diablerie*, by Elvy Damernal, which occupies page 218, vol. i, of the *Bibliographical Decameron*.

largest and most expensive block of the *Triumphs of the Emperor Maximilian*, and, with a slight, hesitant pause, sent it after *Lucifer;* then Mr. Hibbert followed the leader with the *full plumaged Knight*. Sir Francis Freeling *twice hesitated* before he cast the expressive physiognomy of *Baptista Porta* to the flames. Mr. Alexander Chalmers *groaned inwardly* as he advanced with the *Dancing Bear*, but Bruin none the less joined the conflagration of Devils, Knights and Emperors. Mr. Henry Drury seemed to move *oculis aversis* as he incinerated *St. Gregory performing High Mass*. Then followed Utterson, Boswell, Pontons, Markland, and Haslewood, each, in the war-time phrase, *doing his bit*, so that before they *descended to dinner*, the flames had devoured property which, says the chief conspirator, cost its owner upwards of £100 sterling.

After dinner the ceremony was continued. *Another and another trayful of Decameronic Blocks followed the destiny of their precursors*, but not without some effort to preserve them. *James Boswell orationized. Mr. Haslewood twice rose, and twice sat down, in vain*. The *secret orders had been peremptory* and the game proceeded until *the gathering of three years' anxious cost and careful selection were annihilated in less than five hours*. He then goes on to excuse the holocaust, not that there was any need, for as many copies were printed as have been needed down even to our own time. There is little doubt that he enjoyed the *ruthless act*, and gloated over the thought that in *barbarity of principle* it equalled *the firing of the Alexandrine Library by Omar*. But he faced this *small sacrifice* to effect *a great saving, for who henceforward could doubt the value of the Impressions?* There was no longer any risk that anyone could *rob and pawn*, and *be guilty of piracy*. The *Decameron* was secure among the *rariora*. The *whispers of scepticism*, and the slanderous insinuations, already current, that illegitimate use would be made of the blocks, passed away at this pentecost of destruction.

Another method of contraception is that practised by lovers of the unique who cause to be printed slender editions which they distribute among a few friends or deposit in a select number of public libraries, as the vellum copy of the *Vinegar Bible* which was deposited in the Bodleian by Baskett the printer, in 1719. Two other copies on vellum were struck off: one was placed in the King's library and the other in that of the Duke of Chandos. Some go still further by printing editions of a single copy which they keep to themselves.

The hero of *A Rebours*[1] was a morbid devotee of the unique, and he was rich enough to print his favourite books in editions of one copy. He had Poe's *Arthur Gordon Pym* thus specially printed for him on *pure linen-laid paper, hand picked, bearing a sea-gull for water-mark*, and bound in sea-green morocco; his copy of the *Diaboliques* of Barbey d'Aurévilly was specially

[1] Huysmans, *A Rebours*. 28.

printed for him on an *authentic vellum blessed by the Church*. He chose a type whose *outlandish serifs and flourishes, twisted into horns and hoofs*, affected a *Satanic contour*. The ink was Bishop's violet and the borders of Cardinal purple.[1] He would seek out printers distinguished for the peculiar quality of their typography all over France, and even in England. Sometimes he would have a book reproduced like an old tract, sometimes in Gothic characters, like a *Book of Hours*. His copy of *Baudelaire*[2] was in this format. It recalled a *Missal* but was printed on a light Japanese paper, *spongy in texture, as soft as elder-pith* and *faintly tinged with pink over its milky white*. This edition was confined to one copy and it was bound outside and in with a sow-skin, picked out of a thousand. It was flesh-coloured, freckled with bristle marks, and decorated with *dentelles* in black from designs by a great artist.

Des Esseintes was as fastidious about the paper he used; no ordinary paper would do, each book must be unique in format as well as number. Rare papers of every make and from many lands were brought to him: the silvery Chinese, the pearly gold of Japan, white Whatmans, brown Dutch, Turkey grains, and the rare papers from Seychal mills, which are tinted to resemble chamois leather. They were reviewed and most of them condemned for being too ordinary. He was disgusted with our modern machine-made papers, and commissioned laid papers to be specially made for him by the most ancient of processes. With a weary gesture of contempt he imported from London coarse papers made of flock and finished with a hard repped surface like a Victorian furnishing fabric, whilst *further to accentuate his scorn of the bibliophile*, he employed a tradesman of Lubeck to make him a glorified *candle-paper, bluish in tint, crackling and rather brittle, in the substance of which the straw-lines were replaced by gold spangles like those which glitter in Danzig brandy*. He thus secured a library which was in itself unique as well as in being composed of unique copies: unique in character, number, and shape, the sizes of the pages generally being unusual. He possessed treasures specially bound by Lortic, Trautz-Bauzonnet, Chambolle, Capé, in irreproachable covers of antique silk, stamped ox-leather and Cape goat. There were full leather bindings and bindings panelled and mosaic'd; there were bindings with watered silk linings instead of end-papers, and bindings adorned like Church service-books with clasps and metal corners, and others were ornamented by Gruel-Engelmann in oxidized silver and transparent enamel. But I must proceed.

Such artificial sterilization of bibliophily is not without defenders in an age which peacocks itself on its possessions and is ever seeking to acquire that which another lacks: the bibliomane desires quantity, the bibliophile, quality; so specialization hath its chance and the little library becomes rich

[1] Huysmans, *A Rebours*. 218.   [2] *Ib.* 190-2.

with coveted treasures, unique copies, first issues of first editions, dedication copies, association books, of which there are not enough to go round, and so the craving of the collector must be satisfied by other means: books are specially limited for him so that he may not starve or be thrown into a frenzy of unsatisfied desire.

This passion for rarity is so voracious, and often so uncritical, that it has not failed to attract the knowing publisher and bookseller, who see in it fair game for their merchandizing arts. Thus do they print *limited editions*, editions on *large paper*, hand-made, deckled and uncut and wide-margined; and editions still more *limited* on *japon vellum* and even *vellum* itself, as in days of old before paper was known: *the Edition de Luxe, Large, Larger and Largest Paper*, says Carew Hazlitt,[1] *on yellow paper, blue paper, writing paper, on papier de Hollande, de Chine, or d'Inde*. Copies are numbered and great show is made of the promise to distribute the type. Even the author is pressed into this quaint service of gratifying the bibliomaniac by cheating time, for he comes forth and signs his name on the uniquely created copies. Type even has been destroyed. Cobden-Sanderson cast the Doves Types into the River Thames, where they still rest. Among the French, one observes,[2] *bibliophily would seem to have become a kind of mania, and, what is more, a highly organized and thoroughly exploited mania*. He turns at once to the fly-leaf of a new French book, knowing that he will be pained by what he finds there, *for in what disgusts and irritates one there is always a certain odious fascination*. And what does he find? Elaborate notes on the varieties of paper and sizes in which the volume may be obtained. Thus in a recent offender he found printed in block capitals and occupying at least twenty lines: Il a été tiré de cet ouvrage, après impositions spéciales, 133 exemplaires in-4. Tellière sur papier-vergé pur-fil Lafume-Navarre, au filigrane de la *Nouvelle Revue Française*, dont 17 exemplaires hors commerce, marqués de A à R, 100 exemplaires réservés aux Bibliophiles de la *Nouvelle Revue Française*, numérotés de I à C, 15 exemplaires numérotés de CI à CXV; 1040 exemplaires sur papier vélin pur-fil Lafume-Navarre, dont dix exemplaires hors commerce marqués de a à j, 800 exemplaires réservés aux amis de l'Edition originale, numérotés de 1 à 800, 30 exemplaires d'auteur, hors commerce, numérotés de 801 à 830, et 200 exemplaires numérotés de 831 à 1030, ce tirage constituant proprement et authentiquement l'Edition originale.

So must bibliophiles choose, if choose they can, from the multitude of *limited editions* within *limited editions*. Limited libraries, *petites bibliothèques*, may be formed *sur chine* or *sur vergé de Rives, sur Papier de Japon*, or *sur vellum*. Nor need they go to France for such adventures in exclusiveness, in each land wherein civilization has reached the point of bibliomania the

---

[1] *Book-Collector*. 189.   [2] Aldous Huxley, 'Bibliophily', in *On the Margin*. 61.

passion may be served: in America, in Holland, Germany, Czechoslovakia, Italy, or in England, *limited editions* spawn widely in *Large Paper, ad personam*, on such classic and neo-classic papers as Whatman, Van Gelder, Arnold, Kelmscott, Foster, and so forth, for there is no end to them.

Some recognize the desire for limited editions to be a symptom of bibliomania, as Dibdin:[1] *Like a true Bibliomaniac*, the Translator of Arrian's *Book of Hunting* printed but a *limited* edition of his book; the argument is supported by the case of William Beckford, who was artificial and eccentric in all things; he wrote his famous tale *Vathek* in French (as Oscar Wilde his *Salomé*), and in excess of the ordinary edition printed twenty-five large paper copies, one of which he sent to his friend and colleague in dandyism, Benjamin Disraeli.[2] When such editions are sold in the open market, Edward FitzGerald holds that the high price asked for copies *simply announces that the Book is only worth its Price because of only so few Copies being printed: which is but a bad recommendation*;[3] but it may be such an unnecessary barrier against vulgarization as that erected by Thomas Taylor, who, at the instance of the old Duke of Norfolk, *printed fifty copies in quarto of a translation of the works of Plato and Aristotle*, refusing a larger edition *lest these authors should get into the hands of the vulgar*; a commendable but unnecessary precaution, for, as Hazlitt, my authority for this story, says: *there was no danger of a run in that way*.[4] Others, as W. Carew Hazlitt,[5] will have that the *Edition de Luxe is dilettantism 'in extremis'*; and that it should be limited to *nugae literariae* and such-like *bagatelles*, which *no mortal sought to read*, and which therefore might be *harmlessly printed on any material, of any latitude or longitude, in any type, etc.*, according to taste or fashion, but generally fashion. I am disposed favourably towards Edward Newton when he boldly gives out that only the *immature collector will deprive himself of the pleasure of 'collecting'* by buying such books; on the other hand he would encourage the rich man to buy those '*subscription*' books which are produced *especially for his benefit*, for by such cunning tactics he hopes the real books may escape into the possession of those men of poorer estate who know and love them.[6] And finally among these opinions comes that of Richard Le Gallienne announcing that *limited editions aim to set a limit* to the *careless procreation* of books: *they are*, he says, *literary Malthusians*.[7] To this I might add many things, but one thing I shall remark before I leave the subject, namely that what is deliberately made to be rare can never be of real value, and this argument holds for books as for many other desirable things.

---

[1] *Bibliophobia.* 100. The Edition comprised 250 copies.   [2] Beaconsfield, *Correspondence with his Sister.* 17-18.   [3] *Letters to Bernard Quaritch.* 47.   [4] 'On Reading New Books', *Monthly Magazine.* July 1827.   [5] *Book-Collector.* 191-2.   [6] *Amenities of Book-Collecting.* 55.   [7] 'Limited Editions', *Prose Fancies.* (1894) 121.

IV. OF FIRST EDITIONS

First among genuine or natural *rariora, selten, rarissima, très rares, introuvables*, and first in the range of bibliophilic desire, esteem, within the ambit of all those covetous, acquisitive, envious, etc., glances of the book–collector, are *editiones principes*; as he said: *a first edition has, for me, something about it which sets the imagination on fire.*[1] Some authorities have been so bold as to deny their charm and value: *the first edition has been a favourite theme for the scorn of those who love it not;*[2] especially do they condemn the collection of the first editions of our contemporary authors. Notable among these antagonists is Andrew Lang,[3] who marvels that the first editions of Robert Louis Stevenson should be *four or five times as valuable* as Sir Walter Scott's. It is a mystery, he gives out, which puzzles and diverts the modern author, and a grievous form of popularity arising from *the ignorance of collectors*. He is supported by Iolo Williams,[4] who expostulates that *this form of book-collecting is almost certainly the least productive of all*; the bibliophile, he advises, will *find his peculiar energies and talents far more usefully and pleasurably employed in the study of old books.* W. Carew Hazlitt,[5] a quarter of a century ago, carried his antipathy to the collecting of modern first editions so far as to infer from a temporary lapse of interest that the demand had definitely ceased. *It is extremely doubtful*, he ventured to prophesy, *whether the taste will ever assume again the same unhealthy proportions*; methinks he is more prejudiced than reasonable, but his reason, where he had one, was that the high prices *realized* for Byron, Shelley, Keats, Coleridge, Lamb, Dickens, Thackeray, Tennyson, etc., brought more and more copies from their hiding places, thus proving to his own satisfaction that such rarities existed in greater numbers than was supposed, and must, therefore, as they say, *come down in value.* What he did not foresee was the great increase in the number of collectors which our times have witnessed, and the consequent increased demand for books which, when all is said, must *in rerum natura* be limited in number.

But let them expostulate! First editions, those immortal fledgelings of authorship, first editions of first books, still warm from the creative nest; first-fruits with the bloom of the author's love still upon them; first flights with the adorable clumsiness of all young things; copies which reflect the author's first hot, flushed stare of rapture when he looked upon what he had made and saw that it was good; such books will ever entrance the bookman. The first edition is *the very imago that flattered its author's eye;*[6]

[1] Iolo A. Williams, *Elements of Book-Collecting.* 7.   [2] Richard Le Gallienne. Pref. *Compleat Angler.* (Reprint 1896) v.   [3] *The Library.* Preface. Second Ed. xiv. [4] *Elements of Book-Collecting.* 117.   [5] Book-Collector. 169.   [6] R. W. Chapman, *The Portrait of a Scholar.* 49.

what the writer himself saw when he first uttered his thought into the world;[1] *we love to read the great productions of the human mind as they were written,*[2] but they must be first editions of a classic, or at least the work of a reputable author. Their value, Iolo Williams computes,[3] has three factors: first, *the importance of the book itself*; second, *the number of people who wish to study it*; and, third, *the number of copies that exist. A genuine first edition is in its small way a monument of history;*[4] *in a court of law only first-hand evidence is accepted, and a first edition corresponds almost exactly to first-hand evidence.*[5] They are a *sine qua non*, indispensable to the proper study of books and their writers, for *each time a piece of writing is reproduced it is liable to two kinds of change—by deliberate correction and by the intrusion of fresh errors of printing or transcription.*[6] Isaac D'Israeli[7] warned students that in second editions *the author omits, as well as adds, or makes alterations from prudential reasons,* and *these displeasing truths which he 'corrects' as he might call them, are so many losses to truth itself.* To this opinion he reckons up the advantage of comparing first with subsequent editions for the satisfaction of tracing the *variations* of a work when a man of genius has revised it; for, as Rosenbach declares,[8] *a first edition is almost as much the original work of its author as the painting is of the artist.* An *editio princeps* in its highest form, that of the first printed books, needs no defence: well may Hill Burton[9] claim that it is *not a mere toy* and that it can be justified on grounds of antiquity alone: *if you look around you will see very few movables coeval with it, genuine articles of furniture so old as the 'editio princeps' are very rare.* The preservation of our modern first editions is a safeguard for posterity, for books endure through time more surely than most things. The sum of it all being that first editions are the proto-plasm of bibliography, indeed, as Gosse announces,[10] *bibliography, in its modern sense, did not begin until collectors began to prize the earliest issue of the books they loved.* And, finally, a first edition may have *aesthetic value* as well as *sentimental, historic,* or *legal; not everyone realizes how clearly the quality of fineness in first impression belongs, as a rule, to type*; and this quality is doubly evident in illustrated books.[11]

The collection of such editions, says Andrew Lang, *is the most respectable, the most useful, and, alas,* he adds, *the most expensive of the amateur's pursuits.* It is justified on scientific grounds: the collectors of *first editions* may *regard his taste as a kind of hand-maid of critical science,* for he preserves, for students of the future, books which show the earliest versions of literary creations. But Lang does not deny or undervalue its *sentimental side:* the amateur likes

[1] Sawyer & Darton, *English Books: 1475–1900.* i, 15.   [2] Macaulay, Essay on Boswell.   [3] *Elements of Book-Collecting.* 8.   [4] Powell, *Excursions in Libraria.* 39. [5] Iolo A. Williams, *Elements of Book-Collecting.* 5.   [6] *Ib.* 6.   [7] *Cur. of Lit.* i, 16–17. [8] *Books and Bidders.* 39.   [9] *Book-Hunter.* 167.   [10] *Sunday Times.* 15.i.1928. [11] Sawyer & Darton, *English Books,* 1475–1900. i, 15–16,

to see the book in its form *as the author knew it;* he takes pleasure in the *first edition* of *Les Précieuses Ridicules* (1660) because it is just as Molière saw it when he was *fresh in the business of authorship,* and wrote, *Mon Dieu, qu'un Auteur est neuf, la première fois qu'on l'imprime.* Thus volumes published during a great writer's life *seem to bring us closer to his spirit,*[1] as Lang himself sings of one such favourite:

> Fair first editions, duly prized,
>   Above them all, methinks I rate
> The tome where Walton's hand revised
>   His wonderful receipts for bait![2]

David Ancillon was the earliest to seek out first editions;[3] but between his time and ours the affection has passed through dark ages of disesteem and neglect. Even the Bodleian at one time cast away its first editions in favour of more recent and more complete copies. In the catalogue of 1635 a *First Folio Shakespeare* is recorded, but in that of 1674 a *Third Folio* only is named, an exchange for the later edition having been made. It was in 1821, when the Malone Collection was acquired, that Bodley's Library again possessed a *First Folio.*[4] Not until the Askew Sale in 1775 was there any stiff competition for first editions of the Greek and Latin classics,[5] and as late as Isaac D'Israeli's time the quest for such copies needed defence, and as I have shown, there are still in our own day some who inveigh against the passion for *editiones principes* of modern writers. Bayle approved Ancillon's plan of never waiting for second editions on the ground that a second may never appear, but though the authorities are full of contrary opinions, such precepts can do little good, for when they have said all, the first edition remains true to the author's pristine conception of his work, which he contemplated in the first flush of creation, as God His world, found it good, and so sent it forth in print to be approved or condemned. He may improve it in succeeding editions, as all would expect, but the first-fruit with the bloom upon it has no equal for the palate of the epicure. A first edition enshrines and immortalizes the glow and passion of youth before

> The first, faint, hesitant, elusive hint
> Of that invasion of the vandal years,[6]

which comes so often with the reprinting and tinkering of texts. All of this is confessed in the poet,

---

[1] *The Library.* 112, 22–3.   [2] 'To F. L.', *Books and Bookmen.* 39.   [3] Elton, *Great Book-Collectors.* 189.   [4] Macray, *Annals.* 52.   [5] Roberts, *Book-Hunter in London.* 128.   [6] Sir William Watson, *Poems.* ii, 22.

Books unto virgins I compare,
Who at the first but slender are,
But yet more uncorrupt by far
Than when they grow much bulkier.[1]

A first edition must be loved for itself, even though it has value as a literary tool to blaze a path to the author's primitive intentions, for as Isaac D'Israeli approves,[2] in a true thesis, though beyond explication: *There are also other secrets, well known to the intelligent curious, who are versed in affairs relating to books.* Therefore, he concludes, *let no lover of books be too hastily censured for his passion,* which, *if indulged with judgment, is useful,* and I say, with all those *in the secret.* it is a happy and beneficent passion, *la première édition d'un ouvrage m'eût été plus precieuse que les autres,*[3] and that those who are *unable to feel this sentiment can never taste the full pleasure of book-collecting.*[4] This it is, I doubt not, which makes Dr. Rosenbach scorn those *intelligent people—who would just as soon have an edition of Keats's 'Poems' well printed on good paper, in a handsome modern binding, as a first edition in original boards! I only hope,* he exclaims, *I shall never meet them.*[5] Some will dispute this last attitude of his in its literal aspect, but a grasp of its inward meaning makes it more carefully to be respected, for although this fancy for first editions may be under no obligation to reason, and rather to be adored than explicated, it is none the less real; so if the attempted reasons I have given in its defence were swept aside, the amateur of first editions would still labour to make good his desire, nor are any other editions likely to be preferred.

V. UNIQUE COPIES

The passion for unique copies must by most be gratified by the proxy of public libraries or the collections of rich men. I refer to such books which are unique in themselves, by virtue of the circumstances of their production, character, or survival, as distinct from *association* or *artificial rarefaction,* both of which I discuss apart. Among such first place must be given to the *Papyrus Prisse* at the Louvre, Paris, containing eighteen pages of the Hieratic writing of the Egyptians: it is ascribed to the year B.C. 2500, and is believed to be the oldest book in existence.[6] The oldest Greek MS. is a *Papyrus* of the *Persae,* a play by Timotheus, of the fourth century before our Lord, it is now in the Berlin Library;[7] and of this class I may name as

---

[1] John Ellis. (1740) Qt. Timperley, *Songs of the Press.* (1833) 89.   [2] *Cur. of Lit.* i, 16–17.   [3] Proust, *Le Temps Retrouvé.* 36.   [4] Iolo A. Williams, *Elements of Book-Collecting.* 6.   [5] *Books and Bidders.* 39.   [6] Madan, *Books in MS.* 107.   [7] *Ib.* 108.

tragic relics of what once were books, those four papyrus-rolls in the Bodleian which were recovered from the ruins of Herculaneum, *burnt to a crust.*[1] That great class of books which were written by hand before the age of printing I can but mention, for each copy has its own distinction, and an account of them would make a stout catalogue.

There have been those who claimed to own or to wot of the *rarest book in the world*, as Osborne, the bookseller, who made this claim for the only known copy on vellum of the *Breviarium secundum regulam beati Yoidori, dictum Mozarabes*, printed at Toledo in 1502, by command of Cardinal Ximenes,[2] but no one can support such claims, and they are of no real value, for what is merely unique is not necessarily desirable, else such curiosities as that copy of the *Koran written on one large sheet of calico, made up in a priest's vesture, or cope*, which *Mr. Barlow (since Bishop of Lincoln), bibliothecarius of the Bodleian Library*, showed to John Evelyn, when he visited the Library in 1654, were the most desirable.[3] Such things are curiosities rather than bibliographical treasures: they may appeal to romantics, collectors, showmen, curators of museums, not to bibliophiles. And among such curiosities I would place all those ingenious examples of *micrography* which indefatigable penmen have made for amazement, not for use. But first let me tell you a tale out of *Huet*.[4] When his Highness the Dauphin was one day confined to his bed by a slight illness, and those who stood around were endeavouring to entertain him with pleasant talk, mention was made of a man who boasted that he had written Homer's *Iliad* in characters so minute that the whole could be enclosed in a walnut-shell. The company was incredulous, but Huet contended not only that it could be done but that he could do it. They expressed astonishment, and in order to allay any impression that he was an idle braggart, Huet proceeded to prove the statement. He took *the fourth part of a common leaf of paper, and on its narrower side wrote a single line in so small a character that it contained twenty verses of the 'Iliad'*. He calculated that each page of the paper could hold 120 such lines, making 2,400 Homeric verses; and as the leaf so divided made eight pages it would afford room for 19,000 verses, whereas the whole number in the *Iliad* does not exceed 17,100. *Thus by a single line* he claimed to have *demonstrated* his *position*.

Peter Bales, in the year 1575, wrote the *Lord's Prayer*, the *Creed*, the *Ten Commandments*, two short Latin Prayers, his name, date, motto, etc., on a silver penny. This curious work was covered with *crystal*, mounted in a golden ring and presented to Queen Elizabeth, together with a *cunningly devised spectacle (or lens)*. Three centuries later, Alexander George Findlay wrote the *Lord's Prayer*, the *Ten Commandments*, *Psalm I* and the *Benedictus*

---

[1] Macray, *Annals of the Bodleian*. 466.   [2] *Ib.* 358.   [3] Evelyn, *Diary*. 11.vii.1654.
[4] *Memoirs*. Trans. Aikin. ii, 176–7.

on a threepenny piece; and D. W. Kettle, of the *Sette of Odde Volumes*, who records[1] these and many other *quaint* happenings of the kind, gives out that another micro-indefatigabalist wrote the *Lord's Prayer* with a diamond on the 316,000th part of an inch of glass, and he calculates that at that scale of concentration the whole of the 3,566,480 letters of the *Bible* could be confined within the space of one 16,000th of an inch! Nor does his queer record end at such efforts, for he tells the story of that diligent eighteenth-century dwarf, Matthew Buchinger, who possessed neither hands nor legs, yet he married four times, fathered eleven children, and became the most remarkable micrographist of his day, making many minute MSS., including a portrait of himself, the lines being composed of seven *Psalms* and the *Lord's Prayer*. Other *drawings* of the kind exist: there is a portrait of Charles I in St. John's College, Oxford, the lines of the face and hair being composed of *Psalms*; and in the British Museum are portraits of Queen Anne and Prince George of Denmark, written by George Dundas, in 1702, which are so finely done that they were regarded as engravings, until Sir F. Madden discovered by accident that they were the work of a micrographist. An extraordinary example, and unique in more than one way, is that copy of the *Book of Common Prayer*, 1717, engraved throughout on *silver*, by our deft calligraphist, John Sturt; each page has emblematic borders, and for frontispiece there is a portrait of King George I, composed of lines of minute lettering giving the *Lord's Prayer*, the *Creed*, the *Ten Commandments*, the Twenty-first *Psalm*, and *Prayers* for the *King and Royal Family*.[2]

But these are not to be classed among those works most sought after by bibliophiles: they are curiosities of literature and of interest only to those who are curious about what is quaint, eccentric, etc., rather than that which is valuable as well as peculiar, as the *Prompters' Surreptitious* '*Hamlet*', which is dated a year earlier than the ordinary First Edition, and in which the ghost is made to walk on in *nightgown and slippers*;[3] the unique copy of Udall's *Ralph Roister Doister* in the Eton College Library, or the only perfect *Aesop* in the Royal Collection at Windsor. There are degrees of unique as of ordinary rarity, and no trumped-up curiosity, whatever ingenuity has gone to its construction, can arouse the interest of the true bibliophile.

VI. OF PEDIGREE COPIES

'Tis the common humour of all bookmen to desire that which is curious or rare, and among such humours, one most opportunely to be com-

[1] *Pens, Ink and Paper.* 65–9. [2] Davenport, *Byways among English Books.* 21.
[3] Dibdin, *Bibliomania.* (1811) 813.

mended is the passion for books which are discriminated by the marks of precedent possessors, signatures, dedication, notes, memoranda, etc., or by recorded pedigrees showing a descent of distinguished ownership. *A book is the more valuable to me*, wrote Southey,[1] *when I know to whom it has belonged, and through what 'scenes and changes' it has past*; and he would like the history of such books *recorded in the fly-leaf, as carefully as the pedigree of a race-horse is preserved*; and a living authority gives out that *the bibliographer's ideal would be to compel each and every volume to tell its own history.*[2] These are reasonable demands, for a book takes up and retains something of the spirit of its past owners and becomes alive and memorable from its experiences, as the books of Gleeson White: *something personal clings to these pets of his, one cherishes a book he cherished as a relic of a friend, as well as a thing of beauty in itself.*[3] Great care is taken by astute collectors to give an additional character to their treasures by the inclusion of material personally associated with the author, a pleasant custom invented by French bibliophiles and practised most consistently by them. *The books of the library of the Romanticists*, says Henri Pène du Bois, *are all first editions, uncut with the original paper covers, bound by an artist, faultless, explained with notes, ornamented with scarce illustrations, illuminated with autograph letters and verses of the authors.*[4]

Among books proper to this section are those with a *provenance* or *pedigree*, tracing their ownership from library to library, collector to collector, or from collector to bookseller, and back again, according to the changes and chances of life, until they find safe harbourage in one of the great national collections, which is the end and destiny of all rare books; for every true bibliophile sees in the continuity of a great national library the final and most desirable immortality for precious books: *Fancy a library to which Petrarch left all his books: going on still, containing books written and annotated by his own hand and Boccaccio's. . . .*[5] The *Second Folio Shakespeare*, which Charles I, on the eve of his execution, gave to Sir Thomas Herbert, passed successively into the libraries of Dr. Mead, Dr. Askew, George Steevens, and finally back again into the Royal Library in the reign of George III.[6] *The Bedford Missal*, the most famous of all English MSS., is a *resplendent and costly tome*,[7] containing the Prayers and *Religious Exercises* of John, Duke of Bedford, Regent of France, and executed for him in the fifteenth century. It contains fifty-nine miniature paintings and over a thousand smaller miniatures, all displayed in *brilliant borders of golden foliage*

[1] *Sir Thomas More: Colloquies.* ii, 338.   [2] Seymour de Ricci, *English Collectors of Books and Manuscripts* (1530–1930). 3.   [3] York Powell, *Cat. Lib. of Gleeson White.* (1899.) x.   [4] *Four Private Libraries of New York.* 23.   [5] Henry Bradshaw, *Memoir.* Prothero. 127.   [6] Roberts, *Book-Hunter in London.* 141.   [7] Dibdin, *Bibliographical Decameron.* i, cxxxvi-ix, note.

and variegated flowers; and in addition to these it contains the only known portraits of the Duke and his Duchess, Anne of Burgundy. It was presented by the Duchess, *by order of her husband,* to Henry VI when he went to be crowned in France. At the siege of Rouen it is supposed to have fallen into the hands of Charles VI, and later it came into the possession of Henri II. Subsequently it belonged to both Diana of Poitiers and Catherine de Medici, whose arms it bears; when it passed from these famous owners, it came over to England, having been purchased in France for £100 by Lady Frances Finch, who bequeathed it to her daughter, the lady of Sir Robert Worseley of Appuldurcombe, in the Isle of Wight, Lady Worseley sold it to Edward Harley, the second Earl of Oxford, and it descended from him to his daughter, the Duchess of Portland. At her sale in 1786 it was bought for 203 guineas by James Edwards, the bookseller, with King George III as underbidder at 200 guineas. At the disposal of Edwards's library it went to the Marquis of Blandford, afterwards Duke of Marlborough for 650 guineas. The Duke *parted with it on consideration of a loan of three hundred guineas* to John Milner, who afterwards bought it outright for £800, and later sold it to John Broadly, F.S.A., at the sale of whose library in 1833 it was purchased for Sir John Tobin, an Alderman of Liverpool, for 1,000 guineas. In 1838 it became the property by gift of the Rev. John Tobin, M.A., incumbent of Liscard, Cheshire, who sold it, in 1853, to Boone, the bookseller of Bond Street. Boone offered it to the British Museum for £3,000,[1] but as all bibliophiles know, this treasure did not become the property of the nation until the year 1930, when it was rescued from expatriation by the generosity of Mr. Pierpont Morgan, who lent the great sum of £33,000, its purchase price, to the British Museum, provided that the amount were refunded to him within a year. The money was collected and the adventures of the *Bedford Horae* are now ended. For a full description of its parts and character read Gough's eighty-three pages and the *Catalogue of the Library of Mr. Edwards*, No. 830, 1815, and for the auction-battle at the Edwards Sale, Dibdin, *Bibl. Dec.* i, cxxxvii-viii.

W. C. Hazlitt had *a sensation of awe* when he took up such volumes: he felt that *they had passed through some holy ordeal, as if they had been canonised;*[2] *we give,* Lang truly says, *a certain piety and care to books once dear to Longepierre, or Harley, or d'Hoym, or Buckle, to Madame de Maintenon, or Walpole, to Grolier, or Askew, or de Thou, or Heber;* and he holds that such copies should be handed down from *worthy owners to owners not unworthy.*[3]

All ancient books are, in some measure, pedigree books, even though they bear no indication of precedent ownership or history of their adven-

---

[1] Qt. Fitzgerald, *Book-Fancier.* 103-4. From *Sanders MS.*   [2] *Book-Collector.* 236.
[3] *The Library.* 23.

tures among bibliophiles. Many a bookman has fallen into a reverie upon such a thought, inspired, as James Russell Lowell,[1] by some *foundling of the bookstall, bearing the engraved blazon of some extinct baronetcy within its cover, its leaves enshrining memorial-flowers of some passion smothered while the Stuarts were not yet unkinged, suggestive of the trail of lace ruffles, burnt here and there with ashes from the pipe of some dozing poet, its binding worn and weather-stained, that has felt the inquisitive finger, perhaps, of Malone, or thrilled to the touch of Lamb, doubtful between desire and the odd sixpence.* What more delightful than to follow the fortunes of a book—*an early copy of the English Bible, a First Folio Shakespeare, through its successive ownerships from the time of its issuing from the press to the early days of the twentieth century when it reposes among the most valued possessions of a rich bibliophile.*[2]

How much more to be cherished are those books which bear the personal inscriptions of their authors, *ex dono auctorum*, volumes *which the author gave in the pride of his heart to the poet who was his 'Master', to the critic whom he feared, to the friend with whom he was on terms of mutual admiration;*[3] or bearing but the signatures or arms of distinguished owners; *to experience the strange unforgettable thrill at a sight of the self-same page that was once looked upon, even by the master whose writing it bears.*[4] The excellent scholar and collector, Peiresc, doted on such books: *if*, said his biographer,[5] *he had received by gift, or had bought Books which had belonged to learned men, he esteemed them so much the more highly, by how much the fuller they were of such things as they had inserted with their own handwriting.* Peiresc was so moved by love of learning that he could not endure the thought *that the least invention or observation of any man should be lost.*

Southey[6] confessed that he had much of the feeling in which *the superstition concerning relics has originated*; he was sorry when he saw *the name of a former owner obliterated in a book, or the plate of his arms defaced. Poor memorials though they be,* he yet holds that *they are something saved for awhile from oblivion and he would be almost as unwilling to destroy them, as to efface the* Hic jacet *of a tombstone.* Jules Janin was with him in this *affection: Il n'y a rien de plus charmant,* he exclaims,[7] *que de retrouver dans le coin d'un beau livre, écrit avec soin, quelque sentence à l'usage des lecteurs à venir, par les honnêtes gens désireux de laisser un souvenir et d'en confier la garde à l'écrivain qui les avait charmés,* what more charming than to discover souvenirs written by great readers on the margins or fly-leaves: they are treasures added to those of the writers; and he joyously recites a catalogue of the names of books thus enriched, *signés par ces noms si magnifiques et si divers:* Luther, Tasso, de

[1] *Library of Old Authors.*   [2] Walter Jerrold, *The Autolycus of the Bookstalls.* 25
[3] Lang, *The Library.* 13.   [4] Moult. Intro. *Forty Years in My Bookshop.* Spencer xxii.   [5] Gassendi, *Life.* Trans. Laud. (1657) 199.   [6] *Sir Thomas More: Colloquies* ii, 339.   [7] *Le Livre.* 394.

Thou, Scaliger, Desportes, Saumaise, Bochart, Baluze, Balesdens, M. de
Sévigné, Bachet de Mériziac, Huet Burmann, Secousse, Grosley, Goujet
(*il fut perdu, le malheureaux, pour avoir perdu ses livres!*) l'abbé Mercier de
Saint Léger, l'abbé Rive, Morellet, Adry, Barthélémy, Caron, Alfieri,
Naigeon, Delambre, Bast, Chardon de la Rochette, Brunck, Malesherbes,
Voltaire, Wyttenbach, Villoison, Heber *l'insatiable bibliophile*, Eusèbe
Salverte, le Brun, Dulaure, P. L. Courier, Nodier, Letronne, Eloi Johan-
neau, Boissonade and Napoleon:

> Page after page the much-enduring men
> Explored the deeps and shallows of the pen,
> Till, every former note and comment known,
> They marked the spacious margin with their own.[1]

I know not how many great men have so annotated their books, but
I prize them above all other *association copies*. I might even put in a defence
of those books which have been annotated by unknown hands, but there
would be so many *provisos* that it would have small value; marginal notes
can so rarely stand on their quality as wise, witty, etc., that books of this
class must, in the main, justify their existence by the prestige of their
commentating owners; as Hill Burton says,[2] *what is often said of other crimes
may be said of this, that if the perpetrator be sufficiently illustrious, it becomes a
virtue*; if Milton had left *his autograph annotations on the first folio Shakespeare*, he would have been pardoned and applauded, and the copy would
have been treasured beyond any known copy, but the notes of an ordinary
person would be a defacement. It is therefore the quality of the owner
which augments such books: what would we not give for a copy from
Montaigne's library with some of those *marginalia* which ever delighted
mine essayist: *it hath often been my chance*, he confesses, *to light upon bookes,
which I supposed to be new, and never to have read, which I had not understanding
diligently read and run-over many yeares before, and all bescribbled with my notes.*[3]
In later years it was his custom to note opinions at the end of a book, to
set down censure or approval, so that at any time he could turn to the
opinion he had conceived of an author at the first reading.

Charles Lamb lent books to Coleridge, the most laborious annotator
of his time, and they were always returned *with usury; enriched with annotations tripling their values*; in matter *oftentimes, and almost in quantity, not
unfrequently, vying with the originals*; thus Lamb concludes, *in no very clerkly
hand*, Coleridge left his mark *in Daniel: in old Burton: in Sir Thomas
Browne; and abstruse cogitations in his Greville, now, alas!* he laments, *wandering in Pagan Lands.*[4] Arnold[5] records a shabby copy of Donne's *Poems*

[1] George Crabbe, *The Library.* [2] *Book-Hunter.* 185-6. [3] 'Of Bookes', *Essays.*
Ed. Seccombe. ii, 126. [4] 'The Two Races of Men', *Essays of Elia.* [5] *Ventures
in Book-Collecting.* 23-4.

with Coleridge's autograph notes bespreading the inside of the covers, the one remaining fly-leaf and the margins; at the bottom of the back cover Coleridge wrote: *I shall die soon, my dear Charles Lamb, and then you will not be sorry that I have bescribbled your book.*

Bookmen like nothing better than to recall and recite the names and decorations of treasures which have thus been made illustrious and increased in value by various owners. Southey[1] brags of his copies of the *Chronicle of King D. Manoel,* by Damian de Goes, and the *General History of Spain,* by Esteban de Garibay, each signed by its author, together with the copy of Casaubon's *Epistles* sent to him from Florence by Landor, which had once belonged to the Library at Milan, the possession of which he justifies by advertising that it had inspired, since leaving the Library, one of the *most pleasing* of the *Imaginary Conversations; this beautiful dialogue,* he believes, would never have been written had the book *remained there in its place upon the shelf, for the worms to finish the work which they had begun;* now he points at the *book with which Lauderdale amused himself, when Cromwell kept him prisoner in Windsor Castle,* and anon to a copy of the *Apophthegmata* collected by Conrad Lycosthenes, and published, after drastic expurgation, by the Jesuits, as a commonplace book, in which a Portuguese scholar has entered *a hearty vow* that he will not lend or part with the book: *Faço voto a Jesu Christo ne nao largar este livro da mao e emprestalhe a alguem. Anno Dni.* 1664. He never tired of reciting the names and associations of the pedigree books he had assembled at his home among the Cumberland mountains:[2] *Yonder 'Acta Sanctorum' belonged to the Capuchines, at Ghent. This book of St. Bridget's 'Revelations' came from the Carmelite Nunnery at Bruges. That copy of Alain Chartier, from the Jesuits' College at Louvain; that 'Imago Primi Saeculi Societatis', from their College at Ruremond. Here are books from Colbert's library; here others from the Lamoignon one. And here two volumes[3] of a work printed in a convent at Manila, and brought from thence when that city was taken by Sir William Draper.* Each treasure is upheld as a pearl beyond price, and every bibliophile is the same: all their geese are swans, which is as it should be; the essence and particular knowledge of these *rarae aves* I shall now enlarge.

VII. THE MOST DESIRABLE ASSOCIATION COPIES

Spencer,[4] the bookseller, claims that the copy of Keats's *Endymion,* inscribed *To Percy Bysshe Shelley, Esq., from his friend J. K.,* is *the most won-*

[1] *Sir Thomas More: Colloquies.* ii, 339–42.   [2] *Sir Thomas More: Colloquies.* ii, 337.
[3] *Chronicles of the Bare-footed Franciscans in the Philippines, etc.*   [4] *Forty Years in My Bookshop.* 182.

derful book in the world; but of this there may be more opinions than one; the truth of the matter is that all notable association books are the most wonderful books in the world. There would be no more wonderful book, if the authenticity be certain, than Shakespeare's copy of the *Metamorphoses*, printed by Aldus, in 1502, with its abbreviated signature of the poet, and the words: *This little Booke of Ovid was given to me by W. Hall who sayd it was once Will Shakespere's, T. B.* 1682.[1] But it is plain that by all the rules of bibliolatry that is best which is at once rare, fine and distinguished, and if to this be added, as I have said before, the competition of rich men for its possession, we have then a basis of financial value; generally all take this view. But with association copies these three rules fly apart or behave otherwise erratically. Rarity in itself is no more a privilege of these books than of others: this quality is accidental, all association books of authentic descent being unique. Nor can I find any surer guide in condition, which is so powerful a determinant of value in other classes. Here it is nothing: distinction is condition. The meanest, most draggle-tailed, foxed, flead, dog's-eared drab of a volume is conditioned not by appearance but by association. If its pedigree is distinguished it can afford to ignore appearances. In fine, we may say of them all that if they are distinguished all other defects are blotted out, for in such circumstances all faults are forgiven.

Distinction being all and liable to variation of time and place, the mysterious mutations of fashion and the whimsies of taste and opinion, it is beyond the power of any man to say whether one association book of distinction is superior to another. What is superior to-day may be inferior to-morrow. In the eighteenth century Shakespeare's *Ovid* would have taken second place to Pope's *Horace*; in the eighteen-thirties a *Proverbial Philosophy* inscribed by Tupper might have fetched a higher price than the dedication copy of *Prometheus Unbound*. But yesterday the name of Tupper stood against the world and now there's none so poor to do it reverence. But you must not jump at conclusions: what I have just said implies no law or rule in favour of distinguished works, it is distinction of association that counts, yet when that is combined with a distinguished and admirable book the counting is naturally higher. At the same time I doubt not that Lord Holland was happy enough when he *brought together all the various copies upon which he could lay hands of Fox's 'History of the Reign of James II' which had belonged to distinguished people*, and among those thus secured were copies from the libraries of Sir James Mackintosh, Sir Philip Francis, C. E. Jerningham, Samuel Rogers, and General Fitzpatrick.[2] I could cite many such instances, but what I have said is enough for guidance through these labyrinths; I will content myself, therefore, with

[1] Macray, *Annals of the Bodleian*. 379. This volume is in the Bodleian. [2] Roberts, *Book-Hunter in London*. 86.

general observations, remembering always that at this day there are many who would for a mercenary end swell a gnat to an elephant: *ex musca elephantem*. It is not my business to sift too narrowly where whim plays so great a part, affecting me as much as the rest, so let me take the evidence of bibliophily and recite a catalogue of volumes which have stood the test of time and the vagaries of taste.

It is evident that what is adorable at any moment is best for the bibliophile, and if his taste is true to himself (none other matters) it will remain

For ever warm and still to be enjoy'd.[1]

At the same time, and it is no reversal of my argument, some association copies stand out from the commonalty of books because of their association with persons who stand out not alone from common men but from distinguished men. This is inevitable, and desire is naturally affected by it. I may go no farther again for an example than Shakespeare, whose reputation has fluctuated in the past and, for all I know or you know or anyone else knows, may do so again. He has been challenged in present times by Bernard Shaw in England, Walt Whitman in America and Count Tolstoy in Russia, but these affronts have engendered no apprehensions, and he, not they, remains supreme.

A book read and handled by Shakespeare would in all men's estimates stand high among association copies, and if, further, it had been inscribed by him, and finally had passed through various other celebrated hands, its value would be still greater. Such a book exists. It is Shakespeare's inscribed copy of Florio's *Montaigne*; which once belonged to Pope, who gave it to Gay, is known to have been read and enjoyed by Dr. Johnson, was owned in our own era by Frederick Locker-Lampson, and now reposes on its honours in the British Museum.[2] I give this book as a type, an aristocrat, to be placed alongside other eligible pedigree copies, such as the *Sophocles* which was Shelley's companion when he was drowned in the Bay of Spezzia,[3] and that copy of the *Advancement of Learning* (now lost from the Bodleian) which Bacon gave to Bodley with a letter in which he truly said: *You, having built an ark to save learning from deluge, deserve propriety in any new instrument or engine whereby learning should be improved or advanced;*[4] and the *Venus and Adonis*, one of the only two existing copies of the first edition, bequeathed to Bodley's Library by Robert Burton; and, to name but one more, the copy of Bacon's *Essays* in the same collection presented by the author to the Duke of Buckingham.

In so diverse a company there are numerous tastes; some prefer books of pious association, as those two copies of the Gospels in Latin, one now

[1] Keats, 'Ode on a Grecian Urn'.   [2] *Book-Lovers' Anthology*. 374.   [3] In the Bodleian.   [4] Macray, *Annals*, 35.

in the Bodleian and the other at Cambridge, which St. Augustine is said to have brought to England, in A.D. 597, or the *Gospel of St. John*, taken from his tomb and now at Stonyhurst;[1] or Queen Margaret of Scotland's *Gospel Book* which in the eleventh century had been dropped by a priest into a stream and given up for lost, and would have been had not a soldier of the party plunged head first into the water and so retrieved it. The circumstances of this recovery are in themselves noteworthy, for when the book was found to be uninjured by its immersion, the onlookers believed that Christ had interposed to protect the sacred volume, and He was accordingly thanked in Latin hexameters, which are inscribed on one of its fly-leaves.[2] Among other desirable books of this kind I may cite in conclusion that complete *Bible* of the fifth century, known as the *Codex Alexandrinus*, which Cyril Lucar, Patriarch of Constantinople, secured in Alexandria, where it had lain for centuries, and presented to Charles I, in 1628; this book was inherited by King George II, who gave it to the British Museum;[3] and copies of the *Fathers* in the Bodleian which belonged to Henry VIII.[4]

There are bibliophiles who will place high in this intimate category those books which have aided the affections of famous men and women in love; for how such books have acted as charms, *philtres*, talismans, in this wise is well known. A collection of the books which have been links in the passions of great lovers might be of all collections the most fragrant. Among them would rest *La Guirlande de Julie*.[5] Not less desirable, to my mind, is the Marchesa Guiccioli's copy of *Corinne*,[6] which Lord Byron found on a seat in her garden at Bologna, and on a fly-leaf of which he declared his love for her: *I have read this book in your garden;—my love, you were absent, or else I could not have read it. It is a favourite book of yours, and the writer was a friend of mine. You will not understand these English words, and others will not understand them—which is the reason I have not scrawled them in Italian. But you will recognize the handwriting of him who passionately loved you, and you will divine that, over a book which was yours, he could only think of love. In that word, beautiful in all languages, but most so in yours—Amor mio —is comprised my existence here and hereafter,—to what purpose you will decide, my destiny rests with you, and you are a woman, eighteen years of age, and two out of a convent. I wish that you had stayed there, with all my heart—or, at least, that I had never met you in your married state. But all this is too late. I love you, and you love me,—at least you say so, and act as if you did so, which last is a great consolation in all events. But I more than love you, and cannot cease to love you. Think of me sometimes*, he concludes, *when the Alps and the ocean divide*

---

[1] Madan, *Books in MS.* 30, 49. [2] *Ib.* 122–5. [3] Madan, *Books in MS.* 82–3.
[4] Macray, *Annals.* 32. [5] See *ante*, p. 202. [6] Scoones, *Four Centuries of English Letters.* 489–90.

us,—but they never will, unless you wish it. The mere names of such adorable copies are *sweet symphonies,*[1] so that it is a joy to recite them, and for your fuller delight I shall bundle up a posy of them to hang upon this part in its concluding chapter.

VIII. A POSY OF FRAGRANT VOLUMES

A great catalogue will be compiled some day of all those famous association copies with a curious and sentimental history. It will be the most tantalizing and the most precious of catalogues, for it will represent that part of this studious passion which so doth amuse us in pursuit of books whose obtaining we despair. *What,* sighs Rosenbach, *would I not give to possess the charred remains of the Bible to which Savonarola clung when he died!*[2] In such an august list, as I imagine it, will be enrolled Charles Lamb's folio *Beaumont and Fletcher,* bought late one night in Covent Garden instead of a new suit of clothes which he badly needed; and the copy of Chapman's *Homer* which Leigh Hunt caught him kissing; the first edition of Cary's *Dante* carried by Keats on his Scottish tour,[3] and Gray's copy of Dryden's *Virgil* which belonged to Pope and carried his signature;[4] the copy of *Spenser,* 1679, at Trinity College Library, Cambridge, with notes in the hand of Dryden, certified by the hand of Jacob Tonson, and the first folio *Montaigne* and *certain Learned and Elegant Workes of the Right Honourable Fulke, Lord Brooke,* 1633, bearing Ben Jonson's signature;[5] the *Biblia Graeca Septuaginta,* Frankfort, 1594, with which Dr. Johnson felled Osborne, the bookseller, and the copy of Martin's *Western Isles,* in the Advocates' Library at Edinburgh, with Boswell's note that it *accompanied Mr. Samuel Johnson and me in our Tour to the Hebrides,* and the *Cocker's Arithmetic* Dr. Johnson gave to the *Highland nymph* on that tour; Johnson's copy of Burton's *Anatomy,* the only book which got him out of bed two hours earlier than was necessary; the *Dedication Copy* of Robert Louis Stevenson's *Child's Garden of Verses,* inscribed to the author's nurse, Alison Cunningham;[6] the *Golden Ass* which Marius and Flavian read together at White Nights;[7] the Spanish translation of the *English Prayer Book,* given to Wellington by the Ladies of Llangollen and carried by him throughout the Peninsular War, and after again given by him to Georgiana, Lady de Ros, in 1837;[8] the *Aesop,* in the Bodleian, given by Henry VIII to Anne Boleyn;[9] Petrarch's copy of the *Confessions of* St. Augustine which was his

[1] D. G. Rossetti, 'The Blessed Damozel'. [2] *Books and Bidders.* 229. [3] 'You say I must study Dante—well, the only books I have with me are those three little volumes.' Keats to Benjamin Bailey. Dated, Inverary, 18.vii.1818. [4] *Gent. Mag.* (1846) i, 29–33. [5] W. C. Hazlitt, *Book-Collector.* 200–1. [6] Spencer, *Forty Years in My Bookshop.* 168. [7] *Marius the Epicurean.* Pater. i, 40. [8] *Life of Lady de Ros.* Swinton. 148–52. [9] Macray, *Annals.* 32.

constant companion for forty years;[1] Matthew Arnold's copy of the *Vanity of Dogmatizing*, by Joseph Glanvill, in which he found the story of his *Scholar Gipsy* and which he gave to Robert Browning;[2] the *Bible* in John Evelyn's library at Wotton, which Charles I carried on the day he was beheaded; the *Prayer-Book* he found in the King's pocket after his execution, which later belonged to Francis Bedford, the bookbinder;[3] and the King's *Second Folio Shakespeare*, with the words *Dum Spiro, Spero, C. R.*, which he gave to Sir Thomas Herbert, the night before his execution, and in which Herbert had written: *Ex dono serenissimi Regis Car. servo suo Humiliss. T. Herbert*;[4] the *Ronsard* which Chateslard carried with him when going to his death on the scaffold; the Quarto *Greek Testament*, given to Dr. Johnson by Lady Spencer, which Benjamin Robert Haydon found Lord Melbourne reading, on 1st March 1835;[5] the *Pensées de Paschal* given by Dr. Johnson to Boswell, *that*, said Boswell, *I might not interrupt him during his devotional exercises*;[6] Petrarch's inscribed and annotated MS. of *Livy* in the *Bibliothèque Nationale*, which belonged successively to Cardinal Colonna and Raimondo Soranzo;[7] and his *Virgil*,[8] with its pathetic marginal reference, in Petrarch's handwriting, to the death of Laura, of the Black Death, in 1348; or M. Dubois' copy of Richelet's *Dictionnaire des rimes* bearing Boileau's *beau parafe*, and evidence that the illustrious author of *l'Art Poétique* had made good use of it all his life;[9] the *memorial* written on a bone of Buddha, and presented to the Chinese Emperor, Hsien Tsung, in A.D. 819;[10] St. Columba's copy of St. Fruinen's·*Psalter*, called the *Book of Battles*, which, if carried three times round an enemy in the course of the sun, brought certain victory;[11] the *Elegantissimum libellum diversa scripturae genera continentem*, etc., a MS. of the *Book of Proverbs*, dated 1599, in which every chapter, as well as the dedication to the Earl of Essex, is written in a different character, by the famous calligrapher Esther Inglis;[12] the Kelmscott *Chaucer* given by Bernard Shaw to Auguste Rodin, with the inscription:

> I have seen two masters at work, Morris who made this book,
> The other Rodin the Great, who fashioned my head in clay;
> I give the book to Rodin, scrawling my name in a nook
> Of the shrine their works shall hallow when mine are dust;[13]

[1] Tatham, *Francesco Petrarca*. i, 306.   [2] This book was lately in the possession of Elkin Mathews Ltd.   [3] Roberts, *Book-Hunter in London*. 87.   [4] *Ib*. 141.   [5] Haydon, *Autobiography and Journals*. iii, 12.   [6] 'I preserve the book with reverence', Boswell records. 'His presenting it to me is marked upon it with his own hand, and I have found in it a truly divine unction.' *Life of Johnson*. Ed. Hill. iii, 380.   [7] Tatham, *Francesco Petrarca*. i, 166–7.   [8] In the Milan Library.   [9] Janin *Le Livre*. 231.   [10] Giles, *Chinese Biog. Dict.* 255.   [11] Elton, *Great Book-Collectors*. 17.   [12] Macray, *Annals*. 62. Presented to the Bodleian by Sir Thomas Neville, K.B. 1620.   [13] *Table-Talk of G. B. S. Henderson*. 90–1.

Mr. Shandy's copy of Bruscambille's *Prologue on Noses*, for which he gave three half-crowns;[1] one of the nine copies of the *editio princeps* of *A Rebours*, which Dorian Gray had bound in different colours to soothe his various moods, and his copy of Gautier's *Émaux et Camées*, on Japanese paper, with the etching by Jacquemart, bound in citron-green leather, with a design of gilt trellis-work and dotted pomegranates;[2] Madame de Pompadour's copy of *Brantôme*;[3] Boffin's copy of *Gibbon*;[4] Gargantua's *huge pantoufled or thick covered breviary*, weighing *eleven hundred and six pounds*, which they carried before him to church *in a great basket*;[5] and finally, and more curious perchance than all the rest, the originals of those three books in Mendean characters, in the Huntingdon Collection, of which Smith saith, in his Life of Bernard (1704), p. 21, two were said to have been given by God to Adam, and the third to the Angels, 330,000 years before Adam.[6]

---

[1] Sterne, *Tristram Shandy*. iii, chap. 35. [2] Oscar Wilde, *Picture of Dorian Gray*. 176, 227. [3] Lang, *The Library*. 117. [4] Mr. Bown preferred 'fine bold reading, some splendid book in a gorging Lord Mayor's Show of wollumes'. Dickens, *Our Mutual Friend*. v. [5] Rabelais. Bohn Ed. i,170. [6] Macray, *Annals of the Bodleian*. 162.

Part XXIII

OF BIBLIOMANIA OR BOOK-MADNESS

───────────❦───────────

I. DEFINITION AND DIFFERENTIATION

Having thus generally anatomized the body and soul of books and the love of them, as a preparative to the rest, I may now proceed to treat of my intended object *ad unguem*,[1] to most bookmen's capacity, and after many ambages perspicuously define what this bibliomania is, show his name and differences, and how a man may become *l'étrange maniaque qu'on nomme bibliomane*.[2] The name is imposed from the matter; and the *disease called bibliomania*[3] denominated from the material cause. Some difference I find amongst writers about its nature, whether it is a disease or a fad, harmful or benign, and in what way it differs from normal book affections; but I should rather refer it to madness, as some of them do: the most illustrious of bibliophiles is not immune from insanity, not, in fact, always free from taint, for *we that are true lovers, run into strange capers*,[4] but *dans chaque manie on aperçoit aisément un grain de folie*,[5] the insanity is spiced with folly; yet it must be denominated a disease because it implies limitation of functional usefulness: *morbus est habitus cuiusque corporis contra naturam, qui usum eius facit deteriorem*,[6] disease is an unnatural condition of any body, which impairs its usefulness. Dibdin admits that it is insane, a *miasma* or *book plague*,[7] but *of all species of insanity the most rational and praiseworthy*.[8] It is a *darling passion*;[9] *amabilis insania*,[10] a fond delusion; a sweet madness; a soothing affliction.

But *of all species of afflictions* it has *the least moral turpitude attached to it*: if men have erred under its influence, *their aberrations have been marked with an excess of intellectual fervour* rather than *a desire of baser gratifications*;[11] which happens as often as some pleasing dotage not only clears the mind of its troublesome cares, but renders it more jocund, and to make every man more jocund and acceptable to himself is the chief point of felicity. So to many it is most pleasant, and some will have that it is *opprobriously*

---

[1] Lit., to the nail, i.e. exactly. [2] Eustace Mouravit, *Le Livre et la Petite Bibliothèque d'Amateur.* 4. [3] Dibdin, *Bibliomania.* (1811) 618. [4] *As You Like It.* ii, 4. [5] Jacob, *Ma République.* 56. [6] Labeo. Qt. Gellius, *Attic Nights.* (Loeb Ed.) iv, 2. [7] *Bibliomania.* (1811) 543. [8] *Ib.* 124. [9] *Ib.* 593. [10] Horace. [11] Augustine Birrell.

termed a disease of the mind and is *no madness at all unless* ' *Omnis amans amens*' be a truthful adage.[1] Austin Dobson has elegantly expressed this humour:

> Books, books again, and books once more!
> These are our theme, which some miscall
> Mere madness, setting little store
> On copies either short or tall.[2]

Some there are who rejoice to make bold with numbers of books, free from all morbid care or concern; while others are knowing, scientifical, classifying whilst hoarding, protecting whilst misering, as hereafter shall be declared; but for the most part they dote and illustrate in their manner the crazy symptoms of egomania: *il y a chez ces bibliomanes une passion concentrée purement égoïste et nourrie de son propre aliment,* a prey to the self-centred passion of the egoist, which feeds on itself, and which would be regarded as profane were not its object *un mystere au monde.*[3]

Despite contrary arguments, then, many are convinced that it is a mania, and, as such, according to some, it is to be avoided: *collecting rare books and forgotten authors is perhaps of all the collecting manias the most foolish,* and he[4] is so bold as to rate it lower than the collecting of *china,* which is *occasionally beautiful,* or beetles, which are *at least droll*; rare books, he wildly maintains, are *worthless books,* because their rarity usually consists in some *blunder in the text,* or because they *contain something exceptionally nasty or silly,* and, he sums it up, interest in them shows lack of respect for *the greatest productions of the greatest men in the world.* This last, no doubt, is true in general, but specifically applied it lacks substance and proportion, as I shall prove elsewhere. *Beware of the Bibliomanie,* Lord Chesterfield[5] warns his son, imagining the dangers of a young man acquiring a passion for *scarce* rather than *good* books, or, as he puts it, *understanding editions and title-pages too well.* Peignot condemns *la fureur de posséder des livres, non pas tant pour s'instruire, que pour les avoir et pour en repaître sa vue,*[6] the passion for possessing books, not for instruction or the pleasure of reading of them, but to gratify the eye by looking on them; and he is stoutly upheld by an earlier critic: *non enim cogitant quales ipsi sed qualibus induti vestibus sint, et quanta pompa fortunaque praefulgeant—sunt enim omnino ridiculi, qui in nuda librorum quantumvis selectissimorum multitudine gloriantur, et inde doctos sese atque admirandos esse sibi persuadent:*[7] no thought for the books themselves, but only of the pomp and circumstance with which they shine forth; those who glory in such possession, however select, fine, etc., persuading

---

[1] Tredwell, *Privately Illustrated Books.* 475, 53.   [2] *Poetical Works.* 391.   [3] Jacob, *Ma République.* 51.   [4] Frederic Harrison, *Choice of Books.* 87.   [5] *Letters.* ii, 315. [6] *Dictionnaire de Bibliologie.* i, 51.   [7] Draudius, *Bibliotheca Classica.* (1611) Qt. Dibdin, *Bibliomania.* (1811) 32–3.

themselves that they are learned, and so to be admired, are merely ridiculous.

The common sort define it to be a kind of dotage having for its ordinary companions acquisitiveness and miserliness: the passion to collect, hoard, without any apparent occasion; bibliomaniacs *buy whatever comes in their way: buy their books at so much a yard.*[1] D'Israeli argues[2] a craving only for possession to be a main symptom of the disease, and that *weak minds* are mostly susceptible to it; their *motley libraries* are *mad-houses of the human mind*; tombs of books when *the possessor will not communicate them*; out of *Bruyère*,[3] he recalls a visit to such a collector, where that philosopher was like to faint on the staircase from the strong smell of morocco leather; and out of Lucian, an invective against an ignorant bibliomane who, after turning over the pages of an old book, *admired the date.* Such a one is compared to a pilot with no knowledge of navigation; to a rider who cannot keep his seat; to a man with defective feet clothed in embroidered slippers in which he cannot stand; to Thersites wearing the armour of Achilles, tottering at every step, leering with little eyes out of an enormous helmet. Why do you buy so many books? You have no hair, yet purchase a comb; blind, and will have a mirror; deaf, and get you musical instruments. Source only of vexation such collections, and subjects for the *silent invasions* of worms and *the nibbling triumph of rats.* But I descend to particulars. The *summum genus*, whatever they say, is dotage if no worse, which in some cases, as I shall prove, it is; they dote on their books *standing in rows like regiments of Oriental guards, scintillating in the rays of the sun,*[4] and they know and are content that these regiments will never go into battle or even so much as strut or frolic in tattoo or jamboree.

There is another kind of inordinate bookman who hoards books only to treat them with contempt and indifference; or who out of a derangement of conceit does not scruple to clutter his abode with works which are beyond the reach of his intelligence:

> Style am I busy bokes assemblynge,
> For to have plenty it is a pleasant thynge
> In my conceyt, and to have them ay in my honde:
> But what they mene do I nat understounde;[5]

and Janin[6] cites an instance out of *Brantôme*, a saying of Louis XI of a prelate of his realm who had a fine library which he never looked at, *qu'il ressembloit à un bossu porteur d'une belle grosse bosse sur le dos et qui ne la voyoit pas*, like a hunchback who carried a load which he never saw; but

---

[1] George Augustus Sala, in *Book Lore.* iv. 27. [2] *Cur. of Lit.* i, 13-14. [3] 'The Enthusiastic Collector', *Characters.* [4] *Book Lore.* iv, 139. [5] Brandt, *Ship of Fools.* Qt. D'Israeli, *Cur. of Lit.* i, 93. [6] *Le Livre.* 378.

they are all alike in this respect; scarce a hair's breadth between neglect and idle adoration. Nodier[1] is more to the point when he maintains that the difference between a bibliophile and a bibliomane is that one chooses books, and the other amasses them; that one appreciates them, and the other measures and weighs them; and the delicious fever of the one is the delirium of the other. *Brandt* appoints the non-reading collector of books chief of his *Ship of Fools*:

> I am the first fool of all the whole navie,
> To keep the poop, the helm and eke the sail,
> For this is my mind, this one pleasure have I;
> Of books to have great plenty and aparayle.
> I take no wisdom by them, nor yet avail
> Nor them perceive not: and then I them despise.

Yet here again I find some variation of opinion, for W. T. Rogers[2] argues that a *bibliomane* is one who *buys at random or gives chase to the greatest rarities, with the sole object of possessing them*, and he is confronted by Falconer Madan,[3] who holds that, far from being obsessed by possession, *bibliomaniacs live only for the pleasures of the chase*, and they *despise common or inexpensive books*, as Dibdin, who doted on *the portly forms of Large Paper*, and the *princely garb of Red Morocco*.[4] If this be insanity, then the whole world is a madhouse, for love of luxury is a general craze; but such inordinate appetites are as cold to wit or wisdom as they are wallowish to appearance. 'Tis a common dotage rather than madness.

These humours have some analogy with the chief symptoms, but they are not in themselves sufficient evidence of mania. They are no more than partial or occasional symptoms, which have interest only as they contribute among the rest to the diagnosis of misaffected passion and distempered taste, but whether they are true diagnostics I will not now dispute, or of their differences, or how they are caused; these shall be more opportunely spoken of elsewhere, and are now only signified. 'Tis not the first time we have met, nor the last time we shall meet such confusions of evidence in this treatise; but, after all this rabble of opinions, they conclude that, at least in outward aspect, this distemperature includes as a main symptom an excessive regard for books, an obsession or inordinate passion for a great many books; but at this John Ruskin[5] takes exception and warmly maintains that a man who spends lavishly on his library, even though he ruin himself, is not on that account a *bibliomaniac: you call him*

---

[1] Qt. Derome, *Les Editions Originales des Romantiques.* i, 216.   [2] *Manual of Bibliography.* 32.   [3] *The Daniel Press.* 45.   [4] *Bibliophobia.* 72.   [5] *Sesame and Lilies.* (1924) 54.

mad, he expostulates, *but you never call one a horse-maniac, though men ruin themselves every day by their horses*; neither the risk of ruin for books nor desire for a great many are in themselves efficient symptoms. Merry-weather cannot imagine a *more useful or more essential person, in the fourteenth century, than the bibliomaniac, for that surely was the harvest day for the gathering in of that food on which the minds of future generations were to subsist.*[1] Lord Rosebery[2] acquits that persistent bookman, Mr. Gladstone, of any *suspicion of bibliomania*, because he loved books for their contents rather than their appearance: *to first editions or broad margins or vellum copies he was indifferent*; but even he might have been taken with the *noble disease*, had he been a *very wealthy man*; which methinks is a fallacy, for riches may aid the mania, they do not cause it; but there is a difference of opinion even here, for I find Nodier saying that it sometimes happens that a bibliophile becomes a bibliomaniac through weakness of spirit or increase of fortune.[3] Isaac D'Israeli comes nearer to a true diagnosis of this phase where he calls them bibliomaniacs that *collect an enormous heap of books without intelligent curiosity*.[4]

But they do not differ only *secundum majus et minus*, in quantity alone, the one being a degree to the other, and both proceeding from the same cause. They differ *intenso et remisso gradu*, as the humour is intended or remitted from its central cause, which is madness about books, whether few or many, cheap or costly, rare or common, fair, fine or foul; and the character of the enthusiasm is as diverse: intelligent or unintelligent, learned or ignorant. Dotage, fatuity, or folly, is a common denominator of all the species, and is apprehended under the name and *summum genus* of them all; even if it is no more than the defect of a good quality, *the logic of an accurate mind overtaxed*.[5] Most of our authorities write promiscuously of them all because of their affinity, but they are confounded in the end by obscurantist partiality of sentiment, thus failing to bring to a full age a definition distinguished from, on the one hand, those crazed curiosities and fantastical whims which come and go again, as fashions in drugs, religion, or apparel; or, on the other, from a true or sane love of books for what they are or for what they contain. They confound with all these that obsession of a book as an end in itself, *le livre pour le livre*,[6] which is its chief symptom, to which each and every other symptom is an appendix. *Le bibliophile possède des livres*, saith Mouravit, *le bibliomane en est possédé*;[7] but of bibliophiles I will speak apart.

[1] *Bibliomania in the Middle Ages*. 85.　　[2] *Appreciations and Addresses*. 150.　　[3] Qt. Derome, *Les Editions Originales des Romantiques*. i, 216.　　[4] *Cur. of Lit*. i, 13.
[5] O. W. Holmes, *Autocrat of the Breakfast-Table*. 38.　　[6] Gustave Mouravit, *Le Livre et la Petite Bibliothèque d'Amateur*. 4.　　[7] *Ib*. 103.

II. WHETHER IT IS ACQUIRED OR
HEREDITARY

Bibliomania, the subject of our present discourse, can be either in disposition or habit, inbred or acquired. In disposition is that chronic bibliomania which may begin early in youth and last through life, or lie dormant, as in so many instances, until middle age, when it bursts forth, dominating the life of the victim like a consumption devouring his time, means, etc. Bibliomania in this sense has the character of disease. It is no less a disease when, as in my second category, it is acquired, and may thus even be more acute, as frequently happens with those perturbations which are not chronic or inbred; as in the examples of Heber, *who is said to have caught the disease from Bindley*,[1] and the Duke of Marlborough, who is supposed to have been infected by Prince Eugene.[2] Francis Douce, the *Prospero* of Dibdin's *Bibliomania*, thinks the *Catalogue raisonné* of catalogues in that notable work *will certainly multiply the number of Maniacs*;[3] for as the Rev. John Sackville Bale, Rector of Whithyham, told Dibdin, *this kind of madness is very catching*.[4]

A trustworthy authority in our day supports him with the belief that, in his own case, a bookish disposition was imposed by the gift of books from one godmother and two godfathers at his christening: *it would seem*, he relates,[5] *as if there had been a conspiracy to make a bookish thing of me, when I was meant to be a gardener, a hunting man, a soldier, a whiskey-taster, or something wholesome like that*. The gifts included *Bishop Heber's Hymns* and Millais's *Parables*. He always liked the latter, '*Sunday book*' *though it was*, but never knew what a treasure he had got until one day at Brasenose his *fellow undergraduate and now old (be-knighted) friend*, C. J. Holmes, *went mad over it*. Yet the development of the craze is not always sudden, *sometimes, like the measles, it is slow and obstinate about 'coming out'*, and in such cases treatment should be rapid, or *serious results may ensue*.[6] But whether acute or chronic, acquired or inbred, an overweening passion for books hath the same symptoms, either general or particular, wherever or whenever it is found, whatever the manner of its expression; whether it be a mania for acquisition (*the pleasant mania of collecting*[7]), specialization, hoarding, reading, parsimoniousness, it is all one and the same, and different from other manias only in the material of its obsessions.

Whether it is hereditary I have no proof, but I doubt it, as most authentic instances of true dotage are solitary; yet I will not extend this argument

---

[1] William Roberts, *Book-Hunter in London*. 45.   [2] Dibdin, *Bibliomania*. (1811) 425.
[3] Dibdin, *Reminiscences*. i, 308.   [4] *Ib*. ii, 644.   [5] Harold Child, 'Ego at Libri Mei', *Bibliophile's Almanack*. (1927) 13.   [6] Eugene Field, *Love Affairs of a Bibliomaniac*. 50.
[7] Lang, *Library*. 33.

nor dogmatize upon it, since it is an open question; and I will not here stand to discuss whether it is endemic or epidemic, though most would approve by observation or experience that it is the former, general or habitual among the more civilized nations; yet there are times when it rages acutely among numbers of bookmen at one and the same time, with all the outward signs of *epidemic mania*, as those morbid religious *movements* or states of panic, which affect masses of people. *About the year* 1700, Seymour de Ricci reports,[1] *several members of the British nobility became simultaneously seized by a violent desire to collect incunabula*; the outbreak *seems to have lasted but a couple of decades*, and *in most cases the books were treated with more respect than real interest.* No further epidemic of *bibliomania in the peerage* until *the first years of the nineteenth century.* That outbreak is referred to by Dibdin:[2] *the Black-letter-omania, which raged so furiously in the course of the last spring at the sale of Dr. Wright's Books, has broken out with still greater violence at the present auction of Major Pearson's Library;* and he seems to think that there is a species of *auction-mania* peculiar to the *warm weather*, when collectors are susceptible to the *rabies (biblio-canina)*, which might *rage to such an extent* that *the poor madmen would not only be snarling and barking, but absolutely biting each other, and whomsoever they met,* whilst the *chagrin at their disappointments continued*; and he advises the auctioneer to keep *a tub of salt water* at hand as a preventative *wherein the bidders should be dipped on their departure.*[3] But most commonly, it is a solitary dotage, affecting quiet and sedentary men, and as the causes are diverse, so the signs are almost infinite.

III. OBSCURANTIST AUTHORITIES

Every age will yield examples; they are as familiar as they are numerous; you may run and read them; yet the record of them is so diverse and confused, that some are of opinion that the disease itself is diverse and confused. Many new and old writers have spoken confusedly of it, confounding *bibliomania* and *bibliophily*, bookish obsession with love of books, as Dibdin, Merryweather, John Hill Burton, Eugene Field; even Leigh Hunt commends[4] Petrarch as the *God of Bibliomaniacs* when *God of Bibliophiles* would better have described him; they will have any intense *bookishness* no other than *bibliomania* in kind, differing only in degree. What wonder that they should be confused about the persons so afflicted.

I have examined Dibdin's study of *Bibliomania*, believing that there I

---

[1] *English Collectors of Books and Manuscripts.* 33, 43.   [2] *Bibliomania.* (1811) 537.
[3] *Reminiscences.* i, 310.   [4] 'My Books', *Essays.* (Camelot Ed.) 295.

should discover clear reasons and expositions in this matter; yet I profess I met not with the least suggestion in all that farrago but what it had been ridiculous for me to have gone about to answer. Dibdin does little but tell odd tales, and repeat gossip. His reasonings are trifling, his inferences childish; and when he ventures to philosophize he is soon tangled up in his own garrulity; so that it is small wonder to me that most modern readers laugh at him, without taking trouble to do more than dip into his vast treatises, in which I confess they are mistaken, for there is instruction in them, and amusement, too, if obliquely savoured. It is true that he records many instances of true bibliomania, but he himself is so little capable of distinguishing, with any consistency, lunacy from sanity, that he treats book-madness and book-love as interchangeable conditions. He has a habit also of classing readers among bibliomaniacs, as in the case of the distinguished collector and student of the history of medicine, Dr. Francis Bernard, whose library was sold in the year 1698. *Neither beautiful binding, nor amplitude of margin, ever delighted his eye or rejoiced his heart: for he was a stiff, hard, and straightforward reader, and learned in Literary History beyond all his contemporaries*; and yet, after giving him this character of a true student and legitimate user of books, he exclaims, *let Bernard be numbered among the most learned and eminent bibliomaniacs.*[1] As a final proof of this muddleheadedness, I may cite his reference to Prosper Marchand, the bibliographer, who died in 1753, leaving his books and MSS., *in the true spirit of a bibliomaniac, to the University of Leyden.*[2] Dibdin is full of such toys, and it is clear that a confused enthusiasm has deprived him of understanding, even to the extent of citing *Bibliomania* as a thing in itself which can be loved apart; *his love of Bibliomania*, he saith to Heber,[3] was a *ruling passion strong in death.*

But Dibdin is not alone in his obscurantism; too many think as he does; it is the habit of most to echo him. In the past he has a notable supporter in Vogt: *Quis non amabilem eam laudabit insaniam: quae universae rei litterariae non obfuit, sed profuit; historiae litterariae doctrinam insigniter locupletavit; ingentemque exercitum voluminum, quibus alias aut in remotiora Bibliothecarum publicarum scrinia commidgradum erat, aut plane pereundum, a carceribus et interitu vindicavit, exoptatissimaeque luci et eruditorum usui multiplici feliciter restituit?*[4] Who will not praise that darling madness which has fostered rather than injured the world of letters; which has wonderfully enriched our knowledge of the history of literature; which has saved from imprisonment and death a great host of volumes that might have been buried in the shelves of public libraries or totally destroyed, and by so doing happily restored them to the welcome light of day and the manifold use of

---

[1] *Bibliomania.* (1811) 418–19.   [2] *Ib.* 74.   [3] *Reminiscences.* i, 432.   [4] Qt. Preface, *Bibliomania.* (1811) ix, from Catalogus Librorum Rariorum. (1793) Praef. ix.

scholars? The editor of the *Retrospective Review*, for some such reason, would make the very science of bibliography no better than a kind of madness. The knowledge of the *external qualities* of books, *and the adventitious circumstances attending their formation or history, has become a science,* he says, *professors devote their lives to it, with an enthusiasm not unworthy of a higher calling,* and have thus *earned the name of bibliomaniacs.*[1]

Another example of this sort of confusion I may cite out of a French writer, who will have that, of all creatures created by God, the bibliophile is *le plus égoïste et le plus féroce;*[2] a description which might have been more aptly applied to a bibliomane. Du Bois is so bold as to doubt the very existence of bibliophiles at certain times. *Books like those of Dibdin,* he complains, *were written for book-collectors of an epoch when there were no booklovers.*[3] So they go on until an anonymous pamphleteer declares that *to most persons, this amassing of literary treasures is simply a 'mania';*[4] and to bring these discrepancies down to times present I find a London bookseller advising the members of his trade that *the bibliomaniac is one who has a love of books, for their own sakes,* and is thus to be differentiated from the *bibliophile, who loves his books for the literature that is in them.*[5]

Again, they are divided whether it is a disease or merely an eccentricity; but for the most part they will have it both ways, a mania that is not mad, or a dotage that is harmless, and, instead of seeking to detect symptoms, causes, and the like, they make away with vague generalizations and unruly sentiments; *well would it have been,* Birrell[6] observes, *if the historians of book-hunting had caught but a little of the graceful simplicity of Izaak Walton and Gilbert White;* instead, and for the most part, they are *masses of affectation, boasters of bargains, retailers of prices, never touching the heart or refining the fancy. Gilbert White has made many naturalists, Izaak Walton many an angler; but sham raptures over rare volumes, and bombastic accounts of bygone auctions have never helped to swell the ranks of the noble army of book-hunters,* or (I say), which is more to our purpose, they have never helped us to distinguish between a bookman and a bookmaniac.

In such obscurity, such variety and confused mixtures of symptoms and sentiments do I find this section of my theme, that it is impossible without some further examination to make any certainty of distinction; the true symptoms can scarce be discerned by the most accurate observers. 'Tis hard, I confess, yet nevertheless I will adventure through the midst of these perplexities, and, led by the clue or thread of the best writers, extricate myself (or try to) out of this labyrinth of doubts and errors.

---

[1] Intro., *Retrospective Review*. vii.   [2] Edm. Texier. Qt. Gustave Mouravit, *Le Livre et la Petite Bibliothèque d'Amateur.* 129.   [3] *Four Private Libraries of New York.* 39.   [4] *Bibliomania.* (Edinburgh. 1867)   [5] J. G. Wilson, *The Business of Bookselling.* 30.   [6] Preface, Uzanne, *Book-Hunter in Paris.* vii.

IV. EARLY HISTORY OF THE MALADY

No age or class of persons has been immune from bibliomania. In ancient Rome there were *bibliomaniacs in profusion;* towards the end of the Republic it became the fashion to have a library as *part of the household furniture;* booksellers tempted them with catalogues nailed to the doorposts of their shops in the Argiletum and the Vicus Sandalarius, *as their prototypes in Holywell Street do now, and as Maunsell first did in London in* 1595. Seneca ridiculed the mania, inveighing against those who knew nothing about books but the *outsides.*[1] That it was true bibliomania cannot be denied, for, saith Uzanne,[2] they collected *enthusiastically,* manuscripts in rolls, *autographic when possible,* works on parchment, papyrus, linen and leather; books of wood or tablets, the waxed polyptychs of which Pliny speaks, and those *Libri elephantini* which, according to Turnebus, were written on plates of ivory, or, as Scaliger relates, on the intestines of elephants. Merryweather records how it was endemic in the monasteries of the Middle Ages in the days of the manuscript, when you could *find in some cowled monk a bibliomaniac as warm and enthusiastic in his way as the renowned 'Atticus',*[3] *or the noble Roxburghe, of more recent times,*[4] and how, after the invention of printing, it *took mighty strides, and many collectors, full of ardour in the pursuit, became renowned for the vast book stores they amassed together.*[5]

Kings and queens in those early days of the printed book did not escape the *prevalent though harmless malady. The vast resources of Henry VIII were employed in collecting a library of which a modern millionaire* collector *might well be proud; Queen Elizabeth and Lady Jane Grey were submissive victims of the bibliomania.*[6] But whether they were truly afflicted with the mania or but partially, or sometimes even not at all, is not clear, for the diagnosis is not easy, and a beneficent enthusiasm for books or study, or even the pleasure of reading, is often, as I have shown, confounded with bibliomania. Notwithstanding such errors in diagnosis, bibliomania was correctly observed in the year 1494, by Sebastian Brandt, and recorded in his *Narrenschiff*, or Ship of Fools.

Theodore of Tarsus, we are told, *introduced bibliomania* into Great Britain;[7] and Don Quixote de la Mancha, says Sir Walter Scott,[8] was *the most determined as well as earliest bibliomaniac upon record, as among other slight indications of an infirm understanding, he exchanged fields and farms for*

[1] 'The Book Trade in Ancient Rome', *Book Lore*. iii, 125.   [2] *The Book-Hunter in Paris*. 12–13.   [3] The pseudonym for Heber in Dibdin's *Bibliomania*.   [4] *Bibliomania in the Midle Ages*. 9.   [5] *Ib*. 204.   [6] Harper, *Book-Lovers, Bibliomaniacs and Book Clubs*. 11–12.   [7] Merryweather, *Bibliomania in the Middle Ages*. 42.·   [8] *The Antiquary*.

folios and quartos of chivalry; but Theodore was *the father of Anglo-Saxon Literature,* therefore a scholar and a writer rather than a bibliomane, and Don Quixote acquired books not for themselves but for the stories of chivalrous knights whose deeds were the inspiration of those strange adventures which Cervantes invented as a whip for romantic pretensions.

Bibliomania now encompasses the earth; wherever civilization exists there will you find it: from Europe to the Americas, from China to Australasia. It reaches its height in the great capitals where civilization is crystallized: London, Rome, Paris, New York, Berlin, Vienna, etc., but Jacob announces[1] (and many would agree with him) that Paris is its most notable area: *Paris est à coup sûr le paradis des fous et des bibliomanes,* the heaven of lunatics and bibliomaniacs. And if no period is immune from attack, some variation in its intensity is recorded, as in 1832, when Dibdin lamented[2] its temporary decline; the periods of its greatest intensity seem to have been those medieval times dilated by Merryweather,[3] the period of Italian Renaissance following the dawn of printing, the eighteenth century in France and England, the early nineteenth century in England, and in the United States of America to-day.

[1] *Ma République.* 56.   [2] *Bibliophobia. Remarks on the Present Languid and Depressed State of Literature and the Book Trade.* By Mercurius Rusticus. [Thomas Frognall Dibdin.] (1832)   [3] *Bibliomania in the Middle Ages.* (1849)

Part XXIV

THE SYMPTOMS OF BIBLIOMANIA

───────────── ❦ ─────────────

I. THE SYMPTOMS INTRODUCED

Let us now consider what is known of this malady, and find out true varieties, if it be possible, of such characters, symptoms, indications, as happen to those more definitely afflicted, so that we may the more readily discover whence proceed that variety of habits, the distinct character, or characters, of exemplary cases; for some are wise, subtle, witty; others dull, sad, and heavy; some intelligent, some ignorant; they are moody and miserly, vain and bragging; but all mad insofar as they are unduly obsessed, inordinate obsession to any purpose being *signum alienatae mentis;*[1] which is supported by Arnaud, who defines a morbid obsession as *an imperative idea associated with a state of anxiety,*although there need be *no marked disorder of consciousness or judgment.*[2] They are thus indicated rather by the manner of the obsession than the character of the books collected, which is against Dibdin, who will have[3] that the *symptoms of the disease,* as well as the *character of the bibliomaniac,* are discoverable in the very books themselves; but that books are anything more than provocatives cannot be maintained:

> They are like beauties, and may blessings prove,
> When we with caution study them, or love;
> But when to either we our souls devote,
> We grow unfitted for that world, and dote.[4]

Madness does not lie in a normal or contained desire for incunabula, first editions, manuscripts, private press books, bindings, nor yet for vellum, large paper, unique, presentation, or uncut copies, all of which are in themselves proper to normal desire, meet for the fulfilment of book-love. The difference lies in the intensity of the desire, its quality and practice, and to what extent the patient is conscious of it:

[1] A sign of insanity.   [2] *Sur la théorie de l'obsession.* Qt. Rosanoff, *Manual of Psychiatry.* 319.   [3] *Bibliomania.* (1811) 650.   [4] Crabbe, 'The Brothers' Meeting,' *Tales of the Hall.*

But some go mad on one side of the head,
And know that sense from this mad side has fled;
The wise side acts the part of a wise brother,
And checks the mad vagaries of the other.[1]

To be mad and know it is half way to sanity. *They are all mad in my family*, said Edward FitzGerald, *with all difference: I know I am*, and in this he advertised his sanity. Of this kind was Bedford, our notable English binder: *nothing*, saith Locker-Lampson,[2] *of the 'durus arator' about this emperor of morocco—he appreciated tall copies; he respected half-titles and fly-leaves, especially the fly-leaf A before the title; he venerated margins, but a cautious and furtive humour* kept him sane. Most bibliomaniacs have died protesting their sanity, and 'tis for this reason that certain observers misinterpret and warp the meaning of the word.

I may now attempt to define such symptoms as properly belong to bibliomania. Of these some are general, some particular to each class. General to all are an extraordinary love and affection shown towards all books and their writers. Bookmen are normal according to the extent and balance of this affection. The abnormal are consumed by an acute, restless passion for books, rather than by love of them. They take excessive care of them, as Van Hulthem, who so feared his books getting soiled by dust or smoke that he lit no fire, even in the depth of winter, and was often so cold in bed that he contrived to warm his feet by laying a folio on them as it were an extra blanket.[3] They seek the shadow and ignore the substance, as that *mad fellowe in Nicholas Breton*,[4] who in *a poeticall furie. imagining he had a Mistres, made love to his conceit;* for the substance of a book is its spirit or inward sense, its shadow its form or outward mould. They are all out for possession *per se*, becoming slaves of their collections.[5] They *amass books not for use but from the lust of possession*,[6] or, in the other extreme, for inordinate consumption. Both conditions are a distortion of legitimate and appropriate usage. They are *busied in a perversion of book-taste* or in *the short-lived pleasures of sensual gratification:*[7] *bonum est pauxillum amare sane, insane non bonum est*,[8] moderation in love is good; mad love is bad love, whatever the object. Bibliomania is perverted bibliophily. It *seizes hold of rational beings, and so perverts them that in the sufferer's mind the human race exists for the sake of the books, and not the books for the sake of the human race.*[9] These perverts cannot see books without coveting, yearning, craving for them. They can as little bear the thought of better collections

---

[1] *The Craniad.* 35. [2] *My Confidences.* 197. [3] Mouravit, *Le Livre de la Petite Bibliothèque d' Amateur.* 134. [4] *Works.* Ed. Kentish-Wright. i, 66. [5] A symptom wrongly attributed by Anatole France to Bibliophily. *Life and Letters.* 67. [6] Petrarch, *Francesco Petrarca.* Tatham. ii, 36. [7] Dibdin, *Bibliomania.* (1811) 177. [8] Plautus, *Curc.* 1, 3, 20. [9] Harrison, *Choice of Books.* 87.

than their own as they can that of profane hands touching their books. Edmund Texier had a friend who possessed a desire to burn his own library after visiting that of the duc d'Aumale.[1] Grapina, a wealthy collector, removed his books from Lisbon to the country because people kept using them, when he himself would not run the risk of spoiling his treasures by reading them;[2] and Nodier was seriously agitated when he endeavoured to decide whether it was better to preserve a book in all its virginity, or send it to be bound by Trautz-Bauzonnet.[3] Like the Prince de Soubise, they are afflicted with *a frenzy for books.*[4] They find not the satisfaction of enjoyment, but the unrest of frenzy. A confession in *Household Words* of March 26th, 1857, supports this conclusion. The sufferer was overcome with desire for *a unique and matchless impression* of the *Nuremberg Chronicle,* which he saw at Sotheby's. For days his thoughts were dominated by this desire. He *discoursed Nuremberg Chronicle; ate, drank, inhaled nothing but Nuremberg Chronicle;* dropped in at *stray hours to look after its safety, and glared savagely at other parties who were turning over its leaves.*

The bibliomaniac can never be said to enjoy his books; and I would doubt if he enjoys even the pursuit of them: he is too anxious, too passionately inclined to hunt. *How often,* an experienced bookseller observes,[5] *have I watched a customer turning over the leaves of a Dickens volume, as though hypnotized.* Mr. Gladstone, who was never completely overcome by the mania, could not resist books. He would go into a bookshop and buy everything in sight, and those rejected one day would perchance be secured the next, and sometimes at *advanced prices.* He would send his purchases by the cartload to Hawarden.[6] *When I want a book, it is as a tiger wants a sheep,* says another: *I must have it with one spring, and, if I miss it, go away defeated and hungry;*[7] and in his old age Southey became *completely dead to all but books.*[8] This sort of thing

Gets overnear to doting,[9]

for if, as Jeremy Collier insists, *nothing draws so finely as Affection,* yet there *must be some Colouring extraordinary to justify the Ardour and reconcile the Dotage to Sense;*[10] which is no more than Amiel intends when he prescribes passions to be the *diminutives of madness.*[11] How mad they are, how fantastic in small occasions, rash and inconsiderate in their proceedings, how they dote, every page almost of this section will witness.

[1] Qt. Mouravit, *Le Livre de la Petite Bibliothèque d'Amateur.* 129.   [2] *Ib.* 32.   [3] *Ib.* 33.
[4] Elton, *Great Book-Collectors.* 174.   [5] Spencer, *Forty Years in My Bookshop.* 92.
[6] Field, *Love Affairs of a Bibliomaniac.* 136–7.   [7] O. W. Holmes, *The Poet at the Breakfast-Table.* (1902) 210.   [8] Crabb Robinson, *Diary.* Third Ed. ii, 214.
[9] Cory, *Ionica.* 32.   [10] 'Eagerness of Desire', *Essays.* ii, 43–4.   [11] *Journal.* Trans. Ward. 154.

II. WHEREIN THE MADNESS LIES

That bibliomania overthrows the natural judgement, and perverts the good estate of body and mind, all honest observers will agree. *I have known men to hazard their fortunes,* says Rosenbach,[1] *go long journeys half-way about the world, forget friendship, even lie, cheat, and steal, all for the gain of a book;* and all our historians hold that it is as frequent in all places and times as it was in Italy during the Renaissance of Learning, when the hunt for manuscripts was at its height, and *a kind of mania possessed many who exhausted their fortunes in distant voyages and profuse prices.*[2] But even in those times the mania was so linked with the good and same purposes of learning that, as in the instance of the Medici, it must be classed as a parabibliomania rather than a true dotage or frenzy. Lorenzo the Magnificent made Politian and Mirandula his book-hunters-in-chief, and prayed they might find *such a store of good books* that he would have to *pawn his furniture to pay for them;* and it is said of Pope Nicholas V that to own books was *his pride, pleasure, passion, and avarice.*[3]

Oft-times they are stricken suddenly for a particular book which they have never previously wanted, or even heard of: now it becomes a consuming need, a fierce desire; how lovely, how tall, how comely the copy, till he sees another. Uzanne[4] cites an instance in the Comte de Toustain, for whom *every book purchased lost its charm,* and who spent his life in selling back to one bookseller that which he had bought from another; or in making complicated exchanges with which he was never contented. Covetousness, says Jacob,[5] is a prime symptom of envy: *Le bibliomane envieux désire tout ce qu'il ne possède pas,* and as soon as he gains possession his interest flags and fails, and he is off on some new trail. He has no peace of mind so long as another possess what he desires, *aussitôt sa quiétude est aux abois, il ne mange plus, il ne dort plus, il ne vit plus que pour la conquête du bienheureux livre qu'il convoite;* he neither eats nor sleeps, his sole object in life is to possess the adorable volume; active and unscrupulous in pursuit, he does not stay even at intrigue or seduction to obtain the books which excite his lust; their possessors are his enemies, and he longs for their death if he may not otherwise obtain their treasures, which makes him a potential murderer, and, but for the grace of God, a Don Vincente, the monk of Poblet in Aragon, who murdered several collectors and students in order to obtain their most precious books.[6] No sacrifice of time, energy, or even fortune, is too great for such lunatics; but in the end it is all the same,

[1] *Books and Bidders.* 37.   [2] D'Israeli, *Cur. of Lit.* i, 31.   [3] Elton, *Great Book-Collectors.* 67–9.   [4] *Book-Hunter in Paris.* 137.   [5] *Ma République.* 52–3.   [6] Janin, *Le Livre.*

possession merely stimulates desire, and the craving for more books continues; the morbid thirst is unassuaged. The bibliomane is unhappy, as all envious folk are, *et son malheur recommence à chaque nouveau désir*, his unhappiness is renewed with every fresh desire. He is the Lovelace of books, continuously infatuated with them and in eternal, relentless, and obstinate pursuit, until they are in his grasp, when they become worthless and he neglects them, *il cherche une autre victime.*[1]

Nor do they consider whether the desired volume has any more reality than their own hallucinations of need, for once stricken with the mania they will pursue a myth, an *ignis fatuus*, as that story in *Jacob*[2] *of un célèbre maniaque*, who, hearing someone speak *d'un livre imaginaire* made a pilgrimage in quest of it; he would have given anything for it, even *la pierre philosophale;* and when his quest failed he died of chagrin, thinking that a rival had found the treasure. *No such thing as the 'golden mediocrity' of Horace in book pursuits, they set their hearts on certain copies, and 'coûte qu'il coûte', they must secure them;*[3] and in some rare cases they are distressed by the presence of any books which are not within the realm of their particular madness. Burton[4] has an instance of one whose *strange nervous temperament* was so sensitive that *the existence within his dwelling-place of any book not of his own special kind, would impart to him the sort of feeling of uneasy horror which a bee is said to feel when an earwig comes into its cell;* or, and these be common symptoms, they refuse to recognize the worth of any books not in their own collections, or within the ambit of their own predilection, or any book knowledge but their own, as *Inchrule Brewer*, who replied, when a notable collector was named as one who knew something about books: *He know about books! Nothing—nothing at all, unless, perhaps, about their insides;*[5] being passionately attached to *size, he derived his nickname from the practice of keeping, as his inseparable pocket-companion,* a folding *inch-rule* with which he measured rare books and bought them by length and breadth; he was *guiltless of all intermeddling* with their contents.[6]

Fear is a concomitant of obsession, and in their frenzy for particular books they are tormented by delusions of conspiracies to deprive them of the ecstasy of possession. Even the plenitude of books causes *a miserable distraction of choice*, in which Thomas de Quincey[7] discovers *the germ of a madness* whose chief symptom is such *an enormous 'gluttonism' for books, that literature becomes much more a source of torment than pleasure.* Some will seek to prevent others from getting books: they cannot bear competition, and a confraternity of opulence fills them with rage. Dr. John North, brother of Lord Keeper North, was thus afflicted, and *entered into a conspiracy* with Robert Scott, a renowned bookseller of that age, *to deprive*

---

[1] *Ma République.* 54.   [2] *Op. cit.* 54.   [3] Dibdin, *Bibliomania.* (1811)   [4] *Book-Hunter.* 21.   [5] *Ib.* 32.   [6] *Book-Hunter.* 25.   [7] *Letters to a Young Man.*

all bibliomaniacs of a chance of procuring rare and curious volumes, by sweeping everything that came to market in the shape of a book into their own curiously-wrought and widely-spread nets.[1] Douce imagined that Lang's *large paper* copy of the *Bibliographical Decameron* might *possibly render his castle an object of some future siege, by an army of Bibliomaniacs;*[2]

> Nor did a Stanley's choice editions
> Cause less enfuriate competitions
> With Bibliomanians, lur'd at finding
> To paper large join'd splendid binding.[3]

They fret for them, rage, fight if needs be, as during the widespread interest which was aroused by the publication in English of *Le Diable Boiteux*, entitled *The Devil on Two Sticks*. The demand had been inordinate and the *first edition* was rapidly absorbed, when two *noblemen* entered a bookshop, each tuned to a high pitch of passion for the book. Only one copy remained and both of them laid claim to it; hotly disputing the ownership, they drew swords, and blood would have been shed had not the bookseller borrowed an extra copy of the *casus belli* and so restored peace.[4] I confess that it is the quintessence of infelicity to slip into so bellicose a temper; or to be filled with envies, resentments, jealousies, as so many of these dizzards are: as Guibert de Pixérécourt, who, being outbid at an auction, turned on the victor with vindictive hatred: *I will have the book when your collection is sold after your death.* And he kept his word.[5]

> What wild desires, what restless torments seize
> The hapless man, who feels the book-disease![6]

Not without good cause, therefore, is it called a *mania*, though Dr. Ferriar maintains[7] that it is no more than *a respectable foible*, which he tried to *touch with as much delicacy as possible* in his poem of the *Bibliomania*.

III. ITS MAIN CHARACTER AN OBSESSION

The character peculiar to bibliomania in all its parts and processes is, as I have shown, obsession; it is an inordinate, extravagant, excessive traffic or association with books, classes of books, or even parts of books; and, undoubtedly, it may be pronounced of all addicts, that they are very slaves, drudges for the time, madmen, fools, dizzards, beside themselves; bibliophiles grown *vertiginous* and fallen from *the battlements of Heaven*.[8] The

---

[1] Dibdin, *Bibliomania*. (1811) 409–10. [2] Dibdin, *Reminiscences*. ii, 637. [3] [Caulfield] *Chalcographimania*. 69. [4] *Dict. of Anecdotes*. (1809) i, 200. [5] Lang, *The Library*. 18. [6] Ferriar, *The Bibliomania*. 1–2. [7] Letter, 30.v.1811. Qt. Dibdin, *Reminiscences*. i, 3*nts* *of* eremy Taylor, *Holy Dying*.

very best of them, if once overtaken with this passion, the most staid, scholarly, grave, generous and wise, otherwise able to govern themselves, in this commit many absurdities, many enormities, unbefitting their gravity and persons. The aberration reveals itself even in what they say about books; in a tendency to the use of superlatives when discussing their passion. *If the Gods could read,* George Henry Freeling tells Dibdin, *they would never be without a copy of the Bibliographical Decameron in their side pocket.*[1] *No greater inspiration is necessary to an unsullied moral life than a full and absolute fellowship with an illustrated copy, full bound, by Matthews, in crushed levant, of Boswell's Johnson, or Walton's Compleat Angler.*[2] It is not a taste, but, as William Carew Hazlitt[3] said of Heber, *a voracious passion;* the taste, in itself, is a virtue, *people,* Lang will have,[4] *are happier* because of it, *so long,* he adds, *as they possess it, and it does not, like the demons of Scripture, possess them;* to that end it may begin simply, *acquiring almost insensibly an inclination to expand and diverge,* until one becomes, not *the owner of a taste,* but *the victim of an insatiable passion.*[5]

The bibliomane proper is known, then, for his intemperate attachment to books, which he will acquire at any cost and hoard in any quantity, for *avarice or some animal instinct,*[6] regardless of their use as instruments of learning or delight: they have *but one idea, but one love, but one passion: books.*[7] Lucian could not conceive what benefit such hoarders got out of books, for although they gloated on them, and embalmed them in rich covers, they themselves remained ignorant. When a man fails to benefit from books, *what else is he doing,* he asks, *but buying haunts for mice and lodgings for worms, and excuses to thrash his servants for negligence?*[8]

Next to him is the specialist. He also is morbidly acquisitive, but he seeks to hoard only books of one class, one author or printer or publisher, or one edition, or one kind of edition; extreme cases desire only unique copies: *we have at the present day,* saith Dibdin,[9] *absolute madmen in search after black-letter, large paper, and uncut copies.* In such cases there is a madness for rarity *per se;* the bibliomane will open his eyes *with an hideous stare at an old book, and after turning over the pages, chiefly admire the date of its publication;*[10] intrinsic value is of no account, authorship, art, intelligence, beauty, curiosity, none of these enter into his reckoning: books might as well be blocks or stones; *works deemed worthless by those who should know most about them, are toiled after by the ravening book-hunter,* his chief and only joy to add *rarity to rarity* that he may be *alone in the world.*[11] They will have

[1] Dibdin, *Reminiscences.* ii, 650.   [2] Tredwell, *Privately Illustrated Books.* 27.   [3] *Confessions of a Collector.* 23.   [4] *Library.* 6.   [5] W. C. Hazlitt, *Book-Collector.* 92.
[6] Elton, *Great Book-Collectors.* 193.   [7] Flaubert, *Bibliomania.* Trans. Koch. 9.
[8] 'Ignorant Book-Collector', *Lucian.* Loeb Ed. iii, 195.   [9] *Bibliomania.* (1811) 380.
[10] *Lucian.* Qt. *Ib.* 651.   [11] Powell, *Excursions in Libraria.* 15.

them at any cost; this form of *bibliomania is rampant*, he saith, at most times. August Beyer,[1] in the preface to his *Memoriae* (1734), is surprised at English, Dutch, French and German collectors in *a sort of tacit mutual conspiracy* to outbid each other for *certain little known booklets*, probably useless, and, he puts out, *I was unable to conjecture any motive, except the vanity of ostentation, why educated men should prefer rare books to good books.*

And finally, for I have already discussed those who are made from over-reading,[2] there is the bibliomaniac who specializes in parts of books, as pictures, title-pages, colophons, types, bindings, book-plates, etc., as Ames, Bagford, Wanley, Granger, Proeme, etc., who are typical addicts in this respect. Of these three primary classifications, all varieties are but members, as shall now be specified.

IV. OF HOARDING

Of those bibliomanes who hoard for the love of it, one will go methodically to work, laboriously adding to his store until it becomes *a veritable Frankenstein eating up elbow-room and bearing down like an avalanche on space.*[3] He unconsciously becomes its slave and will sacrifice all for his monster, as that French collector, Boulard, *the most thorough-going of bibliomaniacs* (Octave Uzanne calls him[4]) who bought books by the yard, by the rood, by the acre; retail and wholesale; by the basket, by the heap; filling drawing-room, vestibules, lumber-rooms, stairs, bedrooms, cupboards, with them until his house *bent under the weight*. Nodier records that Boulard accumulated some 600,000 volumes, which he stored in six houses, evicting the tenants as his hoard grew.[5] Like mad eroticists they are impelled by an unruly instinct which can never be appeased:

> Bent are our minds and all our thoughts on fire,
> Still striving in the pangs of hot desire;
> At once like misers wallowing in their store
> Of full possession, yet desiring more.[6]

All books were fish that came to the net of our own Heber; *a book is a book*, he said, and he bought *all that came in his way, by cart-loads and ship-loads, whole libraries*, in duplicate, quadruplicate, and multiplications of single editions, *ad infinitum*, on many of which he never cast his eyes; and for *'curiosity or dotage' none could beat Mr. Thomas Rawlinson;* whose *vast*

[1] Qt. *Ib.* 20–1.   [2] See Vol. I, Pts. vi and vii.   [3] Thomas Moult, Intro. to Spencer, *Forty Years in My Bookshop*. xxv.   [4] *The Book-Hunter in Paris*. 129–30.
[5] Qt. Derome, *Editions Originales des Romantiques*. i, 216–17.   [6] Rochester, *Poems on Affairs of State*. (1697) Addenda. 13.

collections were disposed in seventeen or eighteen auctions before the final sale in 1733;[1] he was the *Leviathan of book-collectors* satirized by Addison in the *Tatler* under the name of *Tom Folio*.[2] Books crowded him out of the house and home. His chambers in Gray's Inn were so completely filled with them that his bed had to be moved into the passage.[3] There are some who resist this temptation in time to save themselves from complete mania, as Lord Orrery, who denied himself more than a glimpse of Warburton's *Shakespeare* because his *house was to little too hold any more Shakespeares*.[4] A true book-addict or bibliomane would have fallen before these advances, even if he had to sleep in the lobby or build an annexe. But all bookmen are touched in this respect, the disposition to craziness is generally evident, if revealed only in their resistance to its advances or regret at its repulse, for they give way to its seductions and combat them alternately and each time with remorse. Henry Bradshaw lived *parsimoniously*, yet *bought more books than he could afford;*[5] and he is an example of many, as every bookseller could tell you. But wealth is not necessary to feed this inordinate craving. If the afflicted one is rich his riches will not be enough to satisfy his craving, if poor his poverty no final hindrance: he will get books honestly if he can, but get books he will. I have devoted space to several of these varieties, so here shall give only some few specimens of those who have appeased their passion at great cost, or by overcoming great difficulties.

Ælfride, *the proud King of Northumbria, so fondly coveted* a certain beautiful codex, owned by Benedict Biscop, *the most enthusiastic bibliomaniac of the age*, that he gave in exchange for it *a portion of eight hides of land near the River Fresca;*[6] Antonio Becatelli told Alfonso, King of Naples, that he had sold all his property to pay for a copy of *Livy* written in a fair hand,[7] but love of learning may have prompted the act; not so Ulric Fugger of Augsburg, Chamberlain to Pope Paul IV, who spent so much on books that his relations procured an action in law declaring him to be incapable of managing his estates, which, saith Thuanus, so affected him that he died of melancholy at Heidelberg, in 1584, bequeathing his library to the Elector Palatine.[8]

How they have impoverished themselves to gratify their passion hath many records; but *over-spending* on books is not in itself a true symptom: *a keen collector always spends a little more than he ought on his collection;*[9] here, as in those other symptoms, the determinant is excessive craze or morbid indifference to consequences. St. Jerome is said to have *exhausted his purse*

[1] Oldys, *Memoir, etc.* (1862) 101.   [2] Dibdin, *Bibliomania.* (1811) 455.   [3] Elton, *Great Book-Collectors.* 213–14.   [4] Orrery, *Letters.* i, 320.   [5] Prothero, *Henry Bradshaw.* 81.   [6] Merryweather, *Bibliomania in the Middle Ages.* 105, 107.   [7] Elton, *Great Book-Collectors.* 79.   [8] *Dict. of Anec.* (1809) i, 187–9.   [9] Williams, *Eléments of Book-Collecting.* 4.

in buying the works of Origen;[1] but however indiscreet this may have been (and even that is doubtful), it is no proof of mania. Canevari, who wrote five learned medical works, formed a library so vast in extent and so luxuriously bound that his fortune was absorbed and he passed for a miser.[2] Mouravit tells of a French enthusiast, named Gaullieur, who denied himself the necessities of life and wore the same suit for twenty years, so that he could buy books; he dined off a ha'p'orth of bread the day he paid ten louis for *un petit in-12 relié parchemin, chef-d'œuvre de Jean Tournes*.[3] Lauwers was another bookish anchorite who was content to live on a penny a day, and who died in poverty, but surrounded with books not one of which would he exchange for a bite of bread.[4] Pillet also, says Octave Uzanne,[5] *carried the rage for old books to such an excess that he deprived himself of food and clothing*, and spent all he had to buy more. So many books did he amass in this way that *his lodgings began to give way;* the number was *incalculable*, and it was necessary to load *many horse vehicles again and again*, when they were removed to the Jesuits at Chambéry, to whom he bequeathed them. Antoine Renouard, as a youth, devoted all his savings to acquiring books, *parties of pleasure and elegancies of toilet, everything was sacrificed to my beloved books*.[6] Hill Burton confirms[7] this by a notable example which happened in his own time. Archdeacon Meadow accumulated so many books that he was forced to sell a *considerable proportion of his collection*. As the auction of his books proceeded he could not contain himself. The gradual disappearance of his treasures moved him to passionate anguish, so that he left the room and returned in a while disguised as a *military gentleman* and began bidding for his own books. Such a morbid dependence upon books is obsessive, and, indeed, it is the pattern, image, epitome of all bibliomania.

Those who are bitten by this grasping passion will not be denied, and suffer all the agonies of jealousy and the tortures of covetousness when their inordinate needs are frustrated. Not content with their own, they neigh after other men's books like fed horses, *raptores virginum et viduarum*, as all know. Instance those savants of the time of the Stuart kings, who were like *octopi*, devastating whole districts, and daily growing fatter and more bloated at the expense of everything that moved within reach of their *spreading tendrils*;[8] or David Ancillon, the first collector of *First Editions*, a self-confessed victim: *I am troubled with the Bibliomania, or disease of buying books*.[9] The Rev. Richard Farmer, D.D., whose library was *dis-*

[1] Voltaire, 'Books', *Phil. Dict.* [2] H. P. du Bois, *Four Private Libraries of New York*. 43. [3] Gustave Mouravit, *Le Livre et la Petite Bibliothèque d'Amateur*. 26. [4] *Ib*. 135–6. [5] *The Book-Hunter in Paris*. 128. [6] Elton, *Great Book-Collectors*. 201. [7] *Book-Hunter*. 16–17. [8] Slater, *Romance of Book-Collecting*. 12. [9] Qt. Bayle. Eng. Ed. i, 672.

persed in 1798, had many symptoms of bibliomania: books were the beginning and the end of his existence; he lived for them and among them, they were scattered all over his house; he loved everything that was *rare or interesting in the literature of former ages,* saith Dibdin,[1] and *as he walked the streets of London, careless of his dress,* or *whether his wig was full-bottomed or narrow-bottomed, he would talk and 'mutter strange speeches' to himself, thinking all the time of some curious discovery he had recently made;* and when he was not hunting for books himself he had his *foragers, jackals and avant-couriers,* ever in full cry in his interest.

George Steevens, the Shakespearian scholar, had method in his madness, for he not only amassed an unrivalled library of Shakespeariana, but his collection was the basis of an admirable contribution to Shakespearian learning. He was of an eccentric disposition, living at Hampstead *embosomed in books, shrubs, and trees,* either *too coy* or *too unsociable to mingle with his neighbours;* his peculiar habits, Dibdin admits,[2] *sometimes betrayed the flights of a madman, and sometimes the asperities of a cynic.* He was fickle in his friendships, and once his animosity had been aroused, however capricious or unfounded the cause, he was never known to relent. His one other consistent attachment was to the drama. He would watch with rapt enthusiasm the performances of the strolling players who visited Hampstead, *towards whom his gallantry was something more substantial than mere admiration and applause; for he would make liberal presents of gloves, shoes, and stockings— especially to the female part of the company.*

But beyond all of them in these islands Richard Heber is supreme: *a bibliomaniac, if ever there was one.*[3] He had knowledge, learning, accomplishments and riches; books were his master-passion, his true and inveterate aim; he was *a bibliomaniac in the more unpleasant sense of the word; no confirmed drunkard, no incurable opium-eater,* had less *self-control;*[4] to see a book was to desire it, to desire it was to possess it; *the great and strong passion of his life was to amass such a library as no individual before him had ever amassed.*[5] He loved books from childhood, began to collect at Oxford for purposes of study, and was normal until he met with a copy of Henry Peacham's *Valley of Varietie,* 1638, which he showed to Bindley, who described it *as rather a curious book. Why this incident should have set Heber on his terrible career* is not known, but sure it is that, from that hour, *the love of books blinded him to everything else.* His collection was *omnigenous,* and he never ceased to accumulate books of all kinds, buying them *by all methods, in all places, at all times;* once by a single purchase he secured 30,000 volumes. He disliked large paper copies because they took up too

---

[1] Dibdin, *Bibliomania.* (1811) 565.   [2] *Ib.* 586.   [3] Seymour de Ricci, *English Collectors of Books and Manuscripts.* 102.   [4] Roberts, *Book-Hunter in London.* 45–7.
[5] *Literary Gazette.* Qt. Dibdin, *Reminiscences.* i, 440.

much room. In the end he accumulated 147,000[1] volumes, which he stored in eight houses, two in London, and one each in Hodnet, Paris, Brussels, Antwerp, Ghent, and Germany. Towards the end of his life he *shrunk into his privacy at Pimlico*, betaking himself to his *chronicles and romances, with an increased zest, as if there were nothing in life comparable with these treasures.*[2]

He died, as he would have wished, among his books in the, room in which he had been born. This was his den or lair, a place of safety and secrecy for himself and his books. Dibdin had long been frustrated in his desire to visit it, but *the mystic veil, which for twenty-five years had separated me from this chamber*, he records,[3] *was now effectually drawn aside by the iron hand of Death*, and he saw what no one was permitted to see during Heber's lifetime—the inner sanctuary, the *holy of holies* of a bibliomaniac—*I looked round me with amazement, I had never seen rooms, cupboards, passages, and corridors, so choked, so suffocated with books. Treble rows were here, double rows were there. Hundreds of slim quartos—several upon each other—were longitudinally placed over thin and stunted duodecimos, reaching from one extremity of a shelf to another. Up to the very ceiling the piles of volumes extended; while the floor was strewn with them, in loose and numerous heaps. When I looked on all this, and thought what might be at Hodnet, and upon the Continent, it were difficult to describe my emotions. 'Vox faucibus haesit!'* His ruling passion was strong to the last, saith Sir Egerton Bridges,[4] for the morning of his death he ordered more books from Thorpe. But with all this passion for books *en masse*, he was an authentic lover of reading and scholarship, and readily helped students: *scarcely a scholar or author of distinction, in his own country, but what readily applied to him, and as readily found his wants supplied:*[5]

> His volumes, open as his heart,
> Delight, instruction, science, art,
> To every ear and eye impart.[6]

V. BIBLIOTAPHS AND BOOK MISERS

That type which is more to be lamented among the book-mad is the bibliotaph, defined by Jean Joseph Rive, in his *Chasse Aux Bibliographes*, as one who *buries his books*, by keeping them under lock and key or framed in glass cases, cupboards, chests, drawers, etc. He is a miser, cousin german to the recluse who buries himself among his books, as Magliabecchi, Chen

[1] De Ricci says that Heber collected between two and three hundred thousand volumes. *Op. cit.* 102.   [2] *Atlas.* 25.i.1834. Qt. Dibdin, *op. cit.* i, 446.   [3] Dibdin, *op. cit.* i, 434–7.   [4] Qt. Fitzgerald, *Book-Fancier.* 230.   [5] Qt. from *The Atlas.* 25.i.1834. Dibdin, *op. cit.* i, 446.   [6] Sir Walter Scott.

Hsien–chang, and others. In some cases book-misering develops early, but in most who are thus afflicted it is a sign of senile dotage. *It is difficult to know at what moment one becomes a miser of books*, says Rosenbach,[1] and he gives the instance of his uncle, Moses Polock, a bookseller, who in old age kept *a fireproof vault in the rear of his office, where he secreted rarities no one ever saw; he feared showing the most precious lest he part with one in a moment of weakness.*

Our ancestors were great hiders of manuscripts, says Isaac D'Israeli;[2] Dr. Dee's singular MSS. were found in the secret drawer of a chest, which passed through many hands, but the MSS. remained undiscovered; and the vast collection of State-papers belonging to Thurloe, Secretary to Cromwell, which formed about seventy volumes, were found only when they accidentally fell out of the false ceiling of his chambers in Lincoln's Inn; but doubtless he was a purposeful bibliotaph, otherwise the documents might not have survived those revolutionary times.

Another deliberate bibliotaph is John Stewart, or *Walking Stewart*, as he was called because of his great travels through the countries of the world, mostly afoot, in search of the underlying principles of morality. He explicated his ideas for the moral rejuvenation of mankind by means of a *return to nature* in The Apocalypse of Nature, the Harp of Apollo, and the Sophiometer. These works he believed to contain a new evangel for the salvation of man, and he was convinced, not only that they were the product of *unparalleled energies of genius*, but that they were so revolutionary that the rulers of nations would conspire to destroy them: *hunt them out for extermination as keenly as Herod did the innocents of Bethlehem*. He sought to arrest this fate by recommending those of his readers who were impressed by his teaching to save his books for posterity by burying a copy or copies of each work, *properly secured from damp, etc., at a depth of seven or eight feet below the surface of the earth; and,* saith Thomas de Quincey, *on their death-beds to communicate the knowledge of this fact to some confidential friends, who in their turn were to send down the tradition to some discreet persons of the next generation;* the knowledge was thus to be *whispered down from generation to generation* until such a time as people were intelligent enough to adopt the Stewartian teaching. This curious author, though a bibliotaph, was not a bibliomaniac, for his aim was preservative, not possessive; and De Quincey so far humoured him as to promise that he would bury *The Harp of Apollo* in his own orchard at Grasmere, and *The Apocalypse of Nature* in one of the coves of Helvellyn.[3]

A more pertinent example of the morbid bibliotaph is recorded by Blades;[4] this was the late Sir Thomas Phillips, of Middle Hill, who

[1] *Books and Bidders.* 19.   [2] *Cur. of Lit.* i, 38.   [3] *Notes of a Late Opium-eater.*
[4] *The Enemies of Books.* 121–2.

acquired *bibliographical treasures simply to bury them.* He bought books by the library, crammed his mansion with them, and *never even saw what he had bought.* He possessed and lost among his own books the first book printed in the English language: *The Recuyell of the Histories of Troye;* and no wonder, saith mine author, *when cases of books bought twenty years before his death were never opened, and the only knowledge of their contents was the Sale Catalogue or the bookseller's invoice.* Burton[1] is still more to our purpose in his memorable account of an Irish absentee, or, more accurately, refugee, since he had made himself so odious on his ample estate that he could not live there, and was known by many hard names, as the Vampire, Dragon, etc. He was a shameless book miser, but how he set about collecting books *is one of the inscrutable mysteries which surround the diagnosis of this peculiar malady.* He neither read his books, nor indulged in *the fondling and complacent examination of their exterior and general condition; nor yet did he luxuriate in the collective pride—like that of David when he numbered his people —of beholding how his volumes increased in multitude, and ranged with one another like well-sized and properly dressed troops, along an ample area of book-shelves.* His hoard was heaped at large in garrets, cellars, and warerooms, not for his own delight, but to prevent others enjoying them, for, *ignorant as the monster was, he had an instinct for knowing what other people wanted, and was thus enabled to snatch rare and curious volumes from the grasp of systematic collectors.* He would attend auctions and bid spitefully against all who showed desire for a particular volume; but this was his undoing, for his victims learnt to trick him into buying worthless books at high prices by the simple process of encouraging him to bid against them, so that in the end *the devouring monster disappeared as mysteriously as he had come.*

Thomas Rawlinson had *a miserly craving after good books,* and he lived and died, says Oldys, *among his bundles, piles, and bulwarks of paper.*[2] But who can reckon up the oddity, parsimony, mean servitude, the foolish phantasms and vanities of such deranged book-lovers, their fears, torments, idle grasping? I could repeat centuries of such; and heap up more if I did reckon all those who hoard, hide, bury, etc., books for whatever purpose, good or bad, and the good purpose worse than the bad, as often happens with those afflicted with a mania for goodness: they are a crew who dote from stupidity. Tell me what greater dotage or blindness can there be than the tale of that *homo absurdus,* a Mr. Horneck, a clergyman, who, Locker records,[3] *must have been mature in dullness from his earliest years.* This man *picked up a wonderful bargain in the shape of a thin folio from the Pynson Press,* the imprint: *Lond: In vico vulgacetor Flete Streete,* 1510; it was quite perfect and of *curious rarity.* He recounted how he had secured this treasure after much manœuvring, for one sovereign, and how some little

[1] *The Book-Hunter.* 55–6.   [2] *Memoir and Diary.* 101.   [3] *My Confidences.* 198–9.

while afterwards he noted that the volume was *infested with worms*, and in order to prevent the rest of his books from being infested in like manner he interred the *Pynson* in his garden. *I took prompt and effectual measures to prevent that,* he said, *I buried the Pynson—I put him under ground, sir.* He reckoned garden mould a great purifier. Locker asked how long the book had been buried. *Oh,* said the bibliotaph, *he is still there!* When did he mean to dig it up? *Dig it up? I do not know that I shall ever dig it up!* and, turning to his wife, he said: *You remember, my dear, I buried it under the apple-tree opposite your boudoir window; you know it was the spring when the Persian cat kittened in my sermon-box. It's curious how time flies. It must be eight years since I buried Pynson.* Well may Locker comment: *Habent sua fata libelli.*

Book-misers and book-buriers for the most part are demented by fears of deprivation to which all those who dote upon books are liable. I must, however, oppose to this tenet the case of Augustine Birrell, who bears few traces of delusion in his book-love, but who became a temporary bibliotaph. In his early days he bought, for 8s. 6d. (because there was plenty for the money) the nineteen-volume edition of *Hannah More*, in full calf. He was never able to read very greatly in these works: *no one of her nineteen volumes ever haunted his pillow,* and time came when his shelves were full and, the stream of incoming volumes being constant, he was pressed for room; he had *to do something, and quickly too, for sorely needed was Miss More's shelf;* so he buried the volumes in the garden, and cheerfully stamped them down.[1] This story furnishes an example of ruthlessness, but it is no more than a precautionary or strategic act of bibliotaphism, and no true example of mania.

In a class apart are those who indulge in ceremonial burying, as the Jews, who treated both disused and forbidden books in this way. It was against their faith to destroy any religious book, or even any scrap of paper containing the name of God. These were first stored in a secret chamber, called Genizah, and periodically they were removed and buried underground with a ceremony followed by a feast; and in Egypt it was believed that such burials induced a downfall of rain.[2] A more intimate custom is common to several nations, for *from time immemorial humanity has craved the boon of carrying to the grave some book particularly loved in life,* Eugene Field records,[3] and he gave instructions that when he was *done with earth* certain of his books were to be buried with him. The Egyptians interred manuscripts with their dead, as most of our Egyptologists tell; *the mummies of distinguished persons,* saith Beloe,[4] *are said to be seldom without one of these rolls, and no mummy has been known to contain more than two. Their*

---

[1] 'Hannah More once More', *Collected Essays.* ii, 255.   [2] *Jewish Enc.* v, 612–13.
[3] *Love Affairs of a Bibliomaniac.* 168–70.   [4] *Anecdotes.* i, 57.

position is sometimes under the arms, sometimes between the thighs, and some-times even in the hand of the deceased, which hath been artificially made to enclose them. The custom survived in ancient Rome: Numa Pomphilius desired to have a number of his books buried with him, and five centuries later a curious story is told by Livy of two stone chests bearing inscriptions in Greek and Latin, which were found at the foot of the Janiculum, one pur-porting to contain the body of Numa, the other, his books; the first was found to be empty; the second contained fourteen books in philosophy and law, which were *publicly burned as tending to undermine the established religion.*[1] And, finally, books and newspapers are often buried under the foundation stones of modern buildings, or even interned within a piece of statuary, as, 'tis said, a copy of the *Henriade* of Voltaire was put inside the belly of the horse of the statue of Henri IV on the Pont Neuf.[2]

How many bookmen have wished a favourite book to go with them into oblivion I have no means of knowing, but that there are many I have no doubt: among them, certainly, is Sir Thomas Browne, who expressed such a wish in his will: *On my coffin when in the grave I desire may be deposited in its leather case or coffin my Elzevir's Horace, 'Comes Viae Vitaeque dulcis et utilis', worn out with and by me.*[3] Another aspect of this symbolical passion is provided by a grim event in the life of Dante Gabriel Rossetti. He was so overwhelmed with desolation at the death of his wife that he caused the manuscript of his love poems to be lowered into the grave with her body, an act, however, of which he repented, for some years after-wards he recovered the manuscript, and the poems were published in the year 1872. But more to my theme is the story of how Tennyson was buried with the volume of *Shakespeare* which he had held during his last moments: *We placed 'Cymbeline' with him, and a laurel wreath from Virgil's tomb, and wreaths of roses, the flower which he loved above all flowers, and some of his Alexandrian laurel, the poet's laurel;*[4] and Cushing tells how they left the body of the good bibliophile, Sir William Osler, in the Lady Chapel of Christ Church, Oxford, *beside the famous 'watching chamber' which overlooks the shrine of the Saint, and with the quaint effigy of his beloved Robert Burton near by—lying in the scarlet gown of Oxford, his bier covered with a plain velvet pall on which lay a single sheaf of lilies and his favourite copy of the 'Religio'.*[5]

These examples are enough to satisfy, more might cloy with sadness, for even a bookman cannot be eased for long in the thought of death by the knowledge that his treasures will be near him at the end. What is more sweet and precious than life? The life of the bookman, being sweetened by his books, must yet a little sweeter be in the belief that the warm com-

[1] *Encyc. Brit.* Eleventh Ed. xix, 847 (s.v. Numa Pompilius) [2] Derome, *Editions Originales des Romantiques.* i, 211, note. [3] Qt., *Life of Osler.* Cushing. ii, 681. [4] *Tennyson: a Memoir.* By his Son. ii, 429. [5] *Life of Osler.* ii, 686.

panionship of a favourite will continue after he is cold. But whether this be so or not, 'tis a consolation to his friends thus to celebrate his taste, for are they not most happy when they do these things?

VI. OF PLURALISTS

'Tis a common humour of some bibliomaniacs to fasten upon one book, desiring it passionately in all its editions, forms, variations; or *they conceive a passion for a particular author, and feed it in such abundance that it develops into an obsession' an exclusion, so that their whole lifetime is devoted to one author,*[1] all others are nought; in their dotage they make a God of a book; consecrate time, money, health, to a library which is devoid of variety and can never be other than a curiosity: *ici, Petrarch se multiplie en douze cents volumes; la, ce sera Voltaire en dix mille pièces réunies une à une;* or they will create a *cimetière de paperasses* out of play-books or pamphlets on the French Revolution.[2] John L. Lawson, of Buffalo, as Newton observes,[3] *might be said to collect nothing but Quarto Plays;* but since he accumulates other books as well, he is not truly of the demented type, and *as he shows them, and rightly too, as if they were Whistler etchings,* he has the malady, if at all, in a mild form, as Newton himself, whose *passion* for Boswell's *Johnson* can only be appeased by *four copies* of the first edition, in various states.[4] Only less mild is the case of Eugene Field, who had *thirty odd editions of Béranger,*[5] but this was excess of love of the poet rather than acute acquisitiveness. But such records are nothing to what is to come, for in some extreme cases they go on blindly multiplying copies of the same book *ad libitum,* as Francis Fry, of Bristol who collected 1,200 editions of the Bible,[6] and that Archdeacon Meadow, in *Burton,*[7] who carried home one day 372 rare Bibles; at another time, when defeated in an auction contest for a certain book, he resignedly said: *Well, so be it—but I daresay I have ten or twelve copies at home.*

A curious case is that of Charles, Earl of Sutherland, the greatest book-collector of his day. He bought the whole library of Hadrian Beverland and a great number of Pétau's books, and was such a hoarder of multiple copies that *no bookseller hath so many editions of the same book as he, for he hath all, especially of the classics.*[8] That Thomas Rawlinson was *a bibliomaniac there can be no question, for if he had a score of copies of one book, he would purchase another for the mere gratification of possessing it;*[9] the sight of a dif-

---

[1] Spencer, *Forty Years in My Bookshop.* 27.   [2] Jacob, *Ma République.* 55–6.   [3] *A Magnificent Farce.* 126.   [4] *Amenities of Book-Collecting.* 175.   [5] Field, *Love Affairs of a Bibliomaniac.* 102.   [6] *Book-Lore.* v, 118.   [7] *Book-Hunter.* 15.   [8] Qt. Elton, *Great Book-Collectors.* 209.   [9] Roberts, *Book-Hunter in London.* 39.

ferent edition, a fairer copy, a larger paper, moved him to *such a pitch of curiosity or dotage* that he must secure it even though he already owned *twenty of the same sort.*[1] Heber had a like passion: his *duplicates, triplicates— and even more of rare and costly volumes, had no end;* of the *first Aristotle and the first Plato alone, he had hardly fewer than five copies.* His system of *doubling, trebling, and even quadrupling,* had *neither definite object nor boundary.* Dibdin,[2] who is my authority, traces it to *a rapaciousness of hunger and thirst, such as the world never saw before, and is not likely to see again.* Another example is that of Edmund Waterton, son of Charles Waterton, the naturalist; he was moved by an unruly desire for the *Imitatio Christi,* and gathered about him 1,500 different editions, printed and in MS. He commissioned booksellers all over Europe to procure copies for him, and one of *the pleasures of his life was to see the foreign packets come by post. He kept an oblong volume like a washing-book, with all the editions he knew of, some thousands in all,* and his chief delight was *ticking one more off the lengthy desiderata,* like *a schoolboy marking off the 'days of the holidays'.*[3]

Heber was a shameless pluralist: he had *an ungovernable passion,* saith Dibdin,[4] *for more copies of a book than there were ever parties to a deed, or stamens to a plant;* his friends and fellow bibliomanes threatened *vengeance against* this *despotic spirit,* but without effect, for, like most of them, he could defend his eccentricity with nice logic. He claimed that no man could *comfortably do without three copies of a book*—one for a show copy to be kept at his country house, another for his own use, and a third to lend to his friends.[5] Edward Solly was a pluralist, possessing six or seven copies each of a large number of works. He justified himself on the plea that he liked *to have one to read, one to make notes in, another with notes by a previous owner, one in a choice binding, a 'tall' copy, a short ditto, etc.*[6] In order to subvert the menace of *pluralism* Dibdin advocated an Act of Parliament which would provide *that no gentleman shall purchase more than two copies of a work; one for his town, the other for his country residence.*[7] Sir Walter Scott advised Lady Louisa Stuart[8] *that there are many reasons for not parting with duplicates, for they may have a value in being tall, or a value in being short, or perhaps in having the leaves uncut, or some peculiar and interesting misprint, no end,* he concludes, to *the risque of selection;* an argument, I say, which has all the *stigmata* of mania, as he well knew; but he is no saner when he gives out as a *serious reason* for hoarding the existence of hidden characteristics of value, which may only be divulged by time: *banish to the top shelf,* he argues, *but not to the bookstall,* forgetting that the bookstall is the gateway to ultimate freedom, discovery, and preservation.

[1] Oldys, *Memoir and Diary.* 101.   [2] *Reminiscences.* ii, 940–1.   [3] Roberts, *op. cit.* 96.
[4] *Bibliomania.* (1811) 175.   [5] *Op. cit.* 46.   [6] *Ib.* 137.   [7] *Bibliomania.* (1811) 175.
[8] *Letters.* ii, 240.

Others, ignoring individual authors, will have books of one class, as angling. Americana, travel, emblems, juvenile, facetiæ, theology, etc. Wanley *made a great progress towards collecting books relating to the Service of the Church*, which included *the several versions and impressions of the Holy Bible in English and Latin, Psalters, Primers, and Common Prayer-Books.*[1] This mania for logical completeness is as common as it is varied: *if it seems expedient to possess an example or two of ancient typography*, a sufferer from this form of the disease will not be content until he has accumulated *every example in the market*; certain service-books of the Romish Church have archæological and literary value, so he *orders every copy he sees advertised*; he learns of *some curious volumes illustrative of ritualism and the various holy orders*, and *proceeds to drain the booksellers' shelves throughout the universe of every bit of sorry stuff* of the kind; a dozen or so books of emblems are supposed to throw light on passages in *Shakespeare, this is sufficient leverage for the concentration under the unfortunate gentleman's roof of a closely packed cart-load*,[2] which is a task to no purpose, and a sure symptom of mania.

VII. THE MANIA FOR RARITY

Natural rarity is a strong loadstone of itself, as you have heard, a great temptation: rare books, scarce or unique *copies*, pierce to the very heart of the bibliophile, and they are desired and coveted inordinately by the bibliomane, who dotes on scarcity before utility; there is no greater allurement; rarity makes desire, 'tis like sauce to their meat; if they but hear of a unique copy they are mad for it; they care not for beauty, truth, art, wisdom, charm. If the book be rare, then it is fair, fine, absolute, and perfect; then they burn like fire, they dote upon it, rave for it, and are ready to mope and fret themselves if they may not have it. Nothing so familiar in these days, and in past times, as for a bibliomane to sacrifice all for a piece of scarcity; and though it be a dunce's album, and have never a wise thought to its pages, neither good writing, nor good seeming, an empty piece, but only rarity, it will have twenty bidders in an instant. But rarity in some measure is desired of all, whether they love sanely or insanely, and knowing booksellers and publishers *seek out many inventions* to appease their hunger. 'Tis not amiss, in its place, though some speak bitterly against it, for, as Dr. Johnson held, *value is more frequently raised by scarcity than by use. That which lay neglected when it was common, rises in estimation as its quantity becomes less*, and *we seldom learn the true want of what we have till it is discovered that we can have no more.*[3] There is a mean in all things;

---

[1] Bagford, *Gentleman's Magazine.* (1816) ii, 509.   [2] W. C. Hazlitt, *Book-Collector.* 148.   [3] *Idler.* 103.

the pursuit of rarity is a pleasant recreation of the mind, if sober and generous (such as it is with those bibliophiles who seek to preserve specimens of ancient writing or printing, or to encourage new), but if tempestuously pursued out of mere covetousness, envy, greed, jealousy, it is crazy.

A curious case, recorded by Roberts,[1] is that of a visit paid by the Marquis d'Argenson to a renowned bibliomaniac who had but recently secured a scarce book at *a fabulous price*. Having been graciously permitted by its owner to inspect the treasure, the Marquis ventured innocently to remark that he had probably bought it with the philanthropic intention of having it reprinted. *'Heaven forbid!' he exclaimed in a horrified tone, 'how could you suppose me capable of such an act of folly! If I were, the book would be no longer scarce, and would have no value whatever. Besides,' he added, 'I doubt, between ourselves, if it be worth reprinting.' 'In that case,' said the Marquis, 'its rarity appears to be its only attraction.' 'Just so,' he complacently agreed, 'and that is quite enough for me.'* This is a clear instance of love of rarity for its own sake. Snuffy Davy, in *The Antiquary*, as I have shown,[2] had method in his madness. He doted on one book because it was a *first edition* and on another because it was the *last*; here was a book valued because it had its author's *final improvements*, and there another esteemed because it had them not; as fineness, fairness, tallness; original state (wrappers, boards, cloth) or sumptuously rebound; thick or thin, or large or small paper; opened or unopened; cut or uncut; association, inscribed, *ex dono* or *ex libris*; no peculiar distinction which might not add value to a volume provided that *the indispensable quality of scarcity, or rare occurrence, was attached to it.*

Sir Walter Scott himself was not immune from this perturbation, as he proved, *malgré lui*, in a letter to Lady Louisa Stuart, warning her against disposing of surplus books from the library at Ditton Park: *value*, he saith,[3] *depends on anything rather than sense and utility. Dread, my dear Lady Louisa, that in preferring some comely quarto to a shabby duodecimo your ladyship may be rejecting the 'editio princeps'. Consider*, he concludes, *that in banishing some antiquated piece of 'polissonerie', you may destroy the very work for which the author lost his ears two centuries since, and which has become almost priceless*; and well may he believe the ignorant disposal of bibliophilic surplusage to be *hazardous*, remembering so many tales of rare finds in such accumulations, one of which he gives as an instance and a warning. It is the well-known story of Dibdin going down to Lincoln Cathedral and offering to the library a selection of some of the *best and most readable modern authors* in exchange for some of their *antiquarian treasures*. They were *confounded with his liberality* when they received in exchange for the

[1] *Book-Hunter in London.* xviii.   [2] See p. 614, *ante*.   [3] *Letters.* ii, 240.

old tomes new ones worth £300; but, as the saying is, they reckoned without their host, for, as Scott claims, Dibdin, like *Tam o' Shanter*.

Kenn'd what was what fou brawly.

Yet when they heard that Dibdin had sold his *Lincoln Nosegay* for £1,800 they awoke to wisdom, and when he returned to *repeat his researches*, they *indignantly refused* him admission to the library. Sir Walter himself was ever on the edge of bibliomania without becoming seriously afflicted. He set a high value on rarity, as, when he visited Pickering's bookshop for the first time, he entered in his Journal[1] that he had seen some *dramatic reprints* which he *loved very much*, but although they were *dear* they had *not the dignity of scarcity*, therefore, *bibliomaniacs pass them by as if they were plated candlesticks*. Horace Walpole told George Montague[2] that *people are mad after* his Strawberry Hill Edition of Lord Herbert of Cherbury's *Life, because only 200 were printed*; and, later, he warns him against lending his copy: *Don't lend your Lord Herbert, it will grow as dirty as the street; and there are so few, and they have been so lent about, and so dirtied, the few clean ones will be very valuable*.

Most book-collectors are somewhat affected by this trouble, which in its simple stages is a harmless, mild fad, of no interest to pathologic research; but in its aggravated and acute stages it becomes a raging folly and a true symptom of bibliomania. I will cite a pertinent example from fiction, which may be paralleled in greater or lesser degree in real life. It is that of Des Esseintes, in *A Rebours*,[3] whose egomania had for one symptom so great a dislike of normal people that he was instantly repelled by a book which had acquired *diffusion of appreciation among the common herd*; any such approbation made him doubt his own judgment, and he sought to discover in the rashly admired volume some hitherto unperceived blemish. In order to avoid dilemmas of the kind, and at the same time to gratify his passion, he read only what was *caviare to the general*, and his mania for the unique was so imperative that he had special editions composed of a *single copy* of his favourite works printed and fantastically bound, as I have shown under Books Artificially Rarefied.

But lest you may conclude that all examples are thus clearly defined and specialized, I shall recite an instance of diffused dotage, the symptom whereof is as much an assured sign, an inseparable companion, as those other symptoms already named. My authority[4] records that *Fitzpatrick Smart Esq.* was neither *omnivorous* in his tastes, nor a *specialist* in the ordinary sense of that term; you could not classify his library *according to any of the accepted nomenclatures*: his dotage was not upon black-letter, tall

[1] 16.v.1828.   [2] *Letters*. Ed. Cunningham. iv, 302, 307.   [3] J. K. Huysmans. 137
[4] Burton, *Book-Hunter*. 19–20.

or uncut copies; neither was he *a rough-edge man, or an early-English-dramatist, or an Elzevirian, or a broadsider, or a pasquinader, or an old-brown-calf man, or a Grangerite, or a tawny-moroccoite, or a gilt-topper, a marbled-insider, or an 'editio princeps' man*; he had no regard for appearance and no purpose of research or study. His mania was peculiar to himself, and in this might have been sane, had it not taken that egoistic turn which can see nothing but itself. He sought out the literature of certain historical events, *chiefly of a tragic or a scandalous kind*; such books he tracked down with indefatigable diligence, *no anxiety and toil, no payable price* was grudged for their *acquisition, but if the book were an inch out of his line, it might be trampled in the mire for aught he cared, be it as rare or costly as it could be.*

Part XXV

THE CAUSES OF BIBLIOMANIA

———————— ⟨⟨◇⟩⟩ ————————

I. ITS CAUSES IN GENERAL

What bibliomania is I have sufficiently declared in my foregoing chapters. I will now only point at the causes which make men dote excessively upon books, how it comes about, by what manner they are so deranged, that we may the more adequately search out a cure. Of its origin at large the authorities are silent, insomuch that we might conclude it to be a natural impediment, as a red nose, a hare lip, squint eyes, crooked legs, or any such imperfection, or divergence from normality. But in our day the best physicians will accept no such short cut to knowledge. They will discover a cause for all things, as those who have sought out a first cause of Nature herself and all the mysteries of life, and 'tis fit it should be so, and therefore with good discretion I proceed.

'Tis more difficult. I admit, to diagnose the cause than its effects, whether it be a malady wholly inborn or acquired, for many men are bookish by nature, *a puero*; reading early, without obvious instruction, as I have shown in its place, devoted to books from youth. *The earliest word I was known to utter was 'book'*, says Sir Edmund Gosse,[1] *laying my hand upon a specimen to show what I meant.* Lord Rosebery, saith William Cory,[2] was looking forward to making the acquaintance of Henry Bradshaw, the bibliographer, *with the natural eagerness of a budding bibliomaniac*; he was then but a youth at Eton. Edward Gordon Duff *began collecting before he could read, and he used to trot with his 1d. weekly pocket-money to the bookseller's, say 'Book please', and go away hugging whatever scrapings of the press the shopman chose to bestow.*[3] J. O. Halliwell-Phillips *collected books and manuscripts, mainly relating to Shakespeare*, from his youth, and *as a boy of seventeen*, at Cambridge, *he made a collection of some* 130 *mathematical and astrological manuscripts.*[4]

Dr. Rosenbach was under the spell of the *haunting atmosphere* of his

---

[1] *The Library of Edmund Gosse.* xv.   [2] *Letters and Journals.* 75.   [3] H. F. Stewart, *Francis Jenkinson.* 30.   [4] Seymour de Ricci, *English Collectors of Books and Manuscripts.* 144.

Uncle Moses Polock's bookshop at nine years old; the old shop drew him as ships, wharves, etc., draw other boys, but *spellbound* as he was, he could *hardly realize* at that age *the full quality of mystery and intangible beauty which becomes a part of the atmosphere wherever fine books are brought together*; but it *entered* his *bones then, and has grown out of all proportion ever since.* He began collecting at eleven, when an illustrated edition of *Reynard the Fox* was knocked down to him for twenty-four dollars at Henkels' auction room *on Chestnut Street,* and he walked away feeling for the first time in his life *that swooning yet triumphant, that enervating* yet *heroic combination of emotions the born bibliomaniac enjoys so intensely with the purchase of each rare book.* Observing this phenomenon, Henkels the auctioneer said he had seen *bibliomania* start at an early age, and *run in families,* but this was *the first baby Bibliomaniac* to come his way. At the University, books *enthralled* Rosenbach *to a disastrous extent, he attended book sales at all hours of the day and night,* neglected his studies, bought books, *whether he could afford them or not,* forgot to eat or sleep; but, withal, he confesses that the early stages of the mania are not the *most virulent.*[1]

Antoine Renouard, at the age of seventeen, sacrificed his savings for a copy of *Epictetus* printed on vellum, which he bought at a sale, in the year 1785.[2] Cardinal de Lomenie de Brienne, in *almost early youth,* Dibdin records,[3] *pushed his love of book-collecting to an excess hardly equalled by any of his predecessors; when he was but a young ecclesiastic, books were his ruling passion, and his attachment to fellow bibliomaniacs was ardent and general.* Heber *was born a bibliomaniac,*[4] he had a collection of books and compiled a *catalogue* of them when he was eight years old, and when only ten he asked his father to buy a set of books at a sale, which he understood to be *the best editions of the classics.*[5] Dibdin, himself a parabibliomaniac, was drawn early to books, and at eight was already a reader of histories and works of *soldiery*; his first schoolmaster gave him the run of his private room, where there were many books; it was in this *sanctum sanctorum* of an *indulgent master* that for the *first time* he *caught, or fancied he caught, the electric spark of the Bibliomania*; it was in some measure a case of contagion, for his master *was now and then the purchaser of old books by the sack-full,* which he would tumble out upon floor, arm-chair, or table, as it might happen; but he attributes the direct cause of affection to a copy of Sandby's *Horace with cuts,* which was thus tumbled out, fixing his attention, although he could not read a word of the text.[6] But the ground was prepared, an unsound disposition already existing: *I can well remember, and will as fearlessly avow,* he confesses in another place,[7] *the book ardour of my own boyish and almost*

---

[1] *Books and Bidders.* 4, 11–13.   [2] Elton, *The Great Book-Collectors.* 201.   [3] *Bibliomania.* (1811) 113.   [4] *The Atlas.* 25.i.1834. Qt. Dibdin, *Reminiscences.* i, 446.   [5] *Literary Gazette.* Qt. *Ib.* i, 441.   [6] *Ib.* i, 50–1.   [7] *Bibliographical Decameron.* iii, 376.

childish days. At that time *gilt covers, with broad blotches of red, blue, and yellow, used to be the usual 'envelope' of books for children,* and on his arrival in England from Calcutta (where he was born) at the age of five, he was *quickly put in possession of a little library of this bibliopegistic description,* and thirty-five years later, he could still remember the *transport* with which he would carry copies to bed and hug them all night; but he admits of no *emotions of Bibliomania* until he saw *Sandby's Horace, but what would have been those 'emotions', he concludes, had it been Pine's edition of the same poet!*

I may therefore conclude from such evidence that bibliomania may be inborn (if not hereditary, of which I have no proof); if not the disease itself (which is unlikely), the disposition; and if more direct evidence be called for, *accedit eodem testis locuples,*[1] a trustworthy witness supports me, in Locker-Lampson; so take as a further instance his story of James Gibbs, a bookseller friend, who kept shop for several decades at 8 Great Newport Street. Gibbs was a collector from birth. *This lust,* saith mine author,[2] *asserted itself early; his mother told him that while he was yet a babe in arms, he would instinctively clutch at any print or drawing that came within his reach; indeed he may be said to have been doing this, and not much else, all his life.* Lest you say this is a tale, I will relate a modern instance in this very sort which proves beyond cavil that bibliomania may be inborn, and so eagerly bent at a tender age as to lead to despair and death. Charles Henry Watkins, a London boy of our own time, who had been nervous and reclusive from early days, so doted upon books that he removed himself entirely from his fellows: *he spent all his time reading; never wanted to play*; nor did he read books of adventure, fairy tales, detective stories, and such like writing proper to small boys, but *encyclopaedias* and other *big books, histories and heavy reading; too old for him,* his father thought, but there was no stopping him, no cure, and this prodigious book-lover ended by hanging himself, at the age of fourteen and a half years. To reckon up the inward workings of this tragedy of bibliomania is beyond our science, so I conclude this relation without comment, leaving the facts as I took them from the report of the Coroner's inquest,[3] at which the boy was pronounced to have been of unsound mind.

'Tis difficult even, Dr. Johnson admits,[4] *to enumerate* the several causes which procure to books *the honour of perusal,* and his catalogue of motives for reading—spite, vanity, curiosity, hope, fear, love, hatred, *every passion* he concludes, *which incites to any other action*—might equally serve for the causes of bibliomania; so if vain readers, as he shrewdly remarks, *read for other purposes than the attainment of practical knowledge,* so those inordinate vain collectors hoard and store books for other than intelligent purposes:

[1] Cicero.   [2] *My Confidences.* 390.   [3] *Evening Standard.* 5.viii.27.   [4] *The Adventurer.* 137.

it is a vanity to persuade the world one hath much learning, by getting a great library, Thomas Fuller declares,[1] as soon would he believe *everyone is valiant that hath a well-furnished armoury*. But, to do them justice, few bibliomaniacs make a virtue of their learning. Whether, then, this craze be for books or book-knowledge, it is all one, a mania, and therefore a malady; and if its causes are not particular, but several and different, they all spring from a like defect: a *germ*, as Dr. Rosenbach advises,[2] *heredity* or *contagion*, 'tis all one; and the predisposition being present, all that is required is, in the psychological phrase, a *trigger incident*, a sudden revelation, to give it *awareness*, being, activity, *a local habitation*: the name will follow. *Quod erat demonstrandum.*

II. GREED A CAUSE

I could cite an infinite variety of examples and opinions without arriving at any certain conclusion of the origin, or *first cause*, of the more immediate causes of dotage, for what is most apparent may be least important in the diagnosis of any defect; obsession being no more than a link in a chain of causes, determining, in so far as it determines anything, only the succeeding link, and being itself a helpless effect of some preceding force, action, circumstance, etc., and to that extent a symptom rather than a cause. Such are greed, or morbid acquisitiveness; covetousness, envy, and vanity, which, as I show, lead to craving for bulk, number, plurality, and such like bookish derangements. It would be tedious dull, and serve no useful purpose, if I sought to trace these causes or symptoms to their primitive ancestry in the infinitude of the past, for I confess I am not able to understand it, *finitum de infinito non potest statuere*,[3] we can sooner determine with Cicero[4] *quid non sint quam quid sint*;[5] our voluble authorities Ferriar, Dibdin, Beresford, Janin, John Hill Burton, Octave Uzanne, are weak,dry, obscure, defective in these mysteries, or our quickest wits, as an owl's eyes at the sun's light, wax dull and are not sufficient to apprehend them; yet, as in the rest, I will adventure to say something to this point.

Since, as philosophers concur, all phenomena are a modification or extension of some precedent cause, and not creative of themselves, it follows that greed of books is not spontaneous, but concomitant in a chain of events or circumstances. It may become a thing in itself with its own laws of taste, long after its first cause is forgotten or is continuate solely in the unconscious or subliminal self. The symptoms become causes in a circle revolving of its own independency, set up in business for itself. In

---

[1] *Marvellous Wisdom and Quaint Conceits of Thomas Fuller, D.D.* 105.   [2] *Books and Bidders*. 13.   [3] Austin, *De Trinit.* iii, 1. 'The finite cannot decide about the infinite.'   [4] *De Nat. Deorum.* i, 21.   [5] 'What they are not than what they are.'

this state it is a habit, and may be good or bad as it effects the weal or woe of a man's self or his fellows. These states have several names in several places: we commonly call them hobbies, games, or sports, when normal, and crazes, manias, etc., when abnormal. Fear is a prime instigator of some of them. Fear of starvation produces gluttony, but when the cause departs the effect remains in over-eating for its own sake. Fear of poverty produces hoarding, chiefly, in our age, of money, and, when security is established, money-making becomes a sole occupation, with no object but to make more. So with the aggrandisement of books. Students, scholars, bibliophiles, were forced to own them because there were no public libraries, and in past times, before the invention of printing, books were so costly that they were accessible to none but the rich and powerful. The poor scholar was at the mercy of rich men for even that reading which was necessary to his studies; and when books were assembled in monasteries and universities, only members were allowed to read them, and in most instances it was forbidden to remove the books from the libraries. Little wonder that book-hunger became acute, or that when men were able to possess their own books they hoarded more than they needed out of fear of short rations. These causes I will dilate, and treat of by themselves, in my next chapters, as a bastard-branch, or kind of book-hunger, insatiate but without nourishing qualities, of the character of diabetes.

III. SOME SECONDARY CAUSES

Having thus briefly opened up the primary causes, which are inbred in us, I shall now proceed, according to my proposed method, to the adventitious characteristics which are acquired after we are born. In this labyrinth of accidental causes, the farther I wander the more intricate I find the passage, *multae ambages*, etc., and new causes as so many by-paths offer themselves to be discussed. To search out all were an Herculean task, and fitter for Theseus; so I will follow my intended thread, and point only at some of the chiefest. And these are either evident and remote, or inward, antecedent, and near; contingent in either case, as some would say, upon an inbred tendency which offers bibliomania a natural purchase, as in the case of the Duke of Roxburghe, who became a collector of books and a partial bibliomane through *having been crossed in love*,[1] which is clearly a secondary, outward and adventitious cause, and harmless, unless he were apt to the disease.

First among such causes is acquisitiveness, they are *eaten up with a never-ending craze for acquisition, and undying desire of possession*,[2] like the thirst

[1] Burton, *Book-Hunter*. 90.   [2] *Book-Lore*. iv, 138.

of Tantalus. It is, Dr. Rosenbach advises,[1] an *expressive pride in ownership that verges on madness*. I name acquisitiveness, in the first place, as the root of these mischiefs, which, Hydra-like, hath many heads, compelling them to commit follies, and to make megalomaniacs compacts (and what not?) to their own ends, that bring a heavy visitation upon themselves and others, for allied with it, and arising out of it, is that covetousness which consumes and rages with so many of them. Sometimes the humour is of a sudden, springing spontaneously into being at the first temptation of a desirable book: the mere publication of a description of the *Bedford Missal*, Dibdin confesses,[2] was *sufficient to inflame the ardour, and sharpen the weapons of the most indifferent book-knight*, and to *animate the 'thorough-bred' with a degree of mettle approaching* to madness.

But most authorities believe it to be of slower growth, with several antecedent causes, as the protective instinct which moved Sir Thomas Phillips to collect manuscripts and John Ratcliffe to collect early English books;[3] or *love of beautiful things*, great ideas, etc., degenerating into *an unholy alliance* between *subtle knowledge and sheer covetousness and pride*;[4] *a species of mania founded on enthusiasm*, one holds, leading to *covetousness* only if *indulged to excess*, when the victims lose healthy control over their actions,[5] and cannot moderate themselves, as with Rawlinson: his *covetousness after those books he had not increased with the multiplication of those he had*.[6] How much covetousness and greed are allied with envy is not easy to discover, but that the relationship is close none will deny; Aldous Huxley[7] ingenuously confesses that he was moved to an intense *blast of moral indignation* at the spectacle of Mr. Smith of New York buying eighty thousand pounds worth of books at the Britwell Court sale. He diagnoses *moral indignation*, however, as a symptom of *some ignoble passion*, and the *basic cause* of his own indignation as envy. But this is health compared with that capricious state which covets, acquires, and instantly develops indifference to the possession, or an irritable discontent with it. For, as Jeremy Collier long ago made out, *Envy is of all others the most ungratifying and disconsolate Passion. There is Power for Ambition*, he says, *and Pleasure for Luxury, and Pelf even for Covetousness; but Envy can give nothing but Vexation*.[8]

All agree that bibliomania is a flame which feeds on itself and its effects. No marvel, Petrarch says,[9] *if books enkindle and inflame our minds, both openly by their own warmth and attractiveness, and secretly by furnishing the names of others contained in them*; which was no more than what Dr. John-

[1] *Books and Bidders*. 8.   [2] *Bibliographical Decameron*. i, cxxxvi-vii.   [3] Seymour de Ricci, *English Collectors of Books and Manuscripts*. 119, 52.   [4] Sawyer & Darton, *English Books*, 1475–1900. i, 19–20.   [5] *Book-Lore*. iv, 163.   [6] Oldys, *Memoir and Diary*. 101.   [7] 'Bibliophily', *On the Margin*. 65–6.   [8] 'Of Envy', *Essays*. ii, 115.   [9] Tatham, *Francesco Petrarca*. ii, 36.

son meant when he said that *in all collections, the desire of augmenting it grows stronger in proportion to the advance in acquisition; as motion is accelerated by the continuance of the impetus;*[1] which is supported by the evidence of Sir Thomas Phillips, *the greatest collector of* manuscripts *the world has ever known: As I advanced,* he confesses, *the ardour of the pursuit increased until at last I became a perfect vello-maniac, and I gave any price that was asked.*[2] And if this were not enough, extraneous and fortuitous circumstances, as difficulty of acquisition, are a potent cause, and one of them, *rarity,* and its concomitant *costliness,* a prime stimulant: Watson's *History of the Art of Printing happens to be rare, therefore,* saith Dibdin, *bibliomaniacs hunt after it.*[3] But Petrarch sees little harm in covetousness, and *frankly and truthfully* confesses,[4] *though,* he says, *I blush for it,* that *the coveting of books first by Pisistratus, afterwards by Ptolemy Philadelphus, is nobler than the avarice of Crassus, despite the fact that the latter has had many more imitators.* All success, saith mine author, excites cupidity, *yet with books there is something peculiar. Gold, silver, jewels, purple raiment, fine houses, broad acres, pantings, caparisoned steeds, afford a dumb and superficial pleasure; books delight us to the marrow*; adding to knowledge, making friends, etc.; and so he would forgive such covetous passion as they inspire. Yea, but methinks I hear some men except at these words that, though this be true which he has said of scholars, or true in some measure, for all things are relative, even our vices, there is a perspicuous difference between a covetous desire for mere possession and a covetous desire for extended use; those of the former category are like Indians, they have stone of gold but know not the worth of it, but those of the latter (as Petrarch himself) transmutes the gold into still more precious metal and thus give it greater worth.

IV. VANITY A CAUSE

Vanity is a concomitant of covetousness, for *a man either collects books for his own intellectual profit, which is sane, or out of pure ostentatious vanity;*[5] an opinion which was expressed also by the Critic in Petrarch's *Dialogue of Fortune,* but he added, *to gain glory by books you must not only possess them but know them; their lodgings must be in your brain and not on your book-shelf.*[6]

> Not in his authors' liveries alone
> Is Codrus' erudite ambition shown.
> Editions various, at high prices bought,
> Inform the world what Codrus would be thought.[7]

[1] *Boswell's Life.* Ed. Hill. iv, 105–6.   [2] Qt. Seymour de Ricci, *English Collectors of Books and Manuscripts.* 119.   [3] *Bibliomania.* (1811) 69.   [4] Tatham, *Francesco Petrarca.* l.c.   [5] Roberts, *The Book-Hunter in London.* xvii.   [6] Qt. Elton, *Great Book-Collectors.* 47.   [7] Edward Young, *The Love of Fame.*

'Tis a paranoia common to most ages, and, if the satirist is to be trusted in his tirade against Fulvio Orsini, that powerful figure of the Italian Renaissance, who was born a beggar and died a leader of learning, it is common also to the learned as well as the profane: *Here is a library like an arsenal, stored with all the requisites for any campaign. The owner buys all the books that come his way: it is true he will not read them; but he will have them magnificiently bound, and ranged on the shelves with a mighty show, and there he will salute them several times a day, and will bring his friends and servants to make their acquaintance.*[1] A still more curious example is given by Mouravit of a Mr. Servien, a pompous fellow who, when he lay a-dying, remembered that he was bookless, and was disturbed by the thought of what people would say of him when they found no library among his effects. Go, he ordered, *go and buy one for me.*[2] But this, as like as not, is a tale, so take it for a sign, as the poet[3] sings:

> The cheapest page of wit, or genuine sense,
> Outweighs the uncut copy's wild expense.
> What coxcomb would avow the absurd excess
> To choose his friends, not for their parts, but dress?

Few have a good word for vanity, yet it is not in itself bad, and may often lead to admirable achievement. Field is not disturbed to think that it enters into all phases of book-collecting, for just as a flirt may be ensnared in the love of his victim, so may vanity lead the bookish coxcomb to *veneration and the love of books.*[4]

A high price to one so afflicted is a temptation and peril; it enhoneys and allures, inflames him with renewed madness for possession. *Nothing tends to the preservation of anything so much as making it bear a high price.*[5] Oftentimes dotards will pay double the value for a modern First Edition from a second-hand bookseller which the publishers are still offering at its price of issue, and *there are collectors so foolish*, says Williams,[6] *that they will not buy a book at all unless they are asked a good stiff price for it*; he hopes *such lunacy is not common*, but I find many instances of it. Read what Sawyer and Darton have written lately of this defect in our present age, in their stout volumes on *English Books: 1475–1900*; what prodigious prices, what bookish *Apicii, Luculli, Heliogabali*, our times afford! They would all sup with Cleopatra, and drink no wine unless pearls had been dissolved in it.

. . . Magis illa juvant quae pluris emuntur,[7]

---

[1] Qt. Elton, *op. cit.* 159.   [2] *Le Livre et la Petite Bibliothèque d'Amateur.* 118–19.
[3] Ferriar, *Bibliomania.* [4] *Love Affairs of a Bibliomaniac.* 49.   [5] Sir Thomas Phillips. Qt. de Ricci, *English Collectors of Books and Manuscripts.* 120.   [6] *Elements of Book-Collecting.* 103.   [7] Juvenal. xi, 16.

the costliest dishes afford most gratification, the dearest cates are best: *in these Bibliomanian times the collector conceives that he has purchased a bargain if he procures a volume for one hundred guineas, the price which it brought at the Duke of Roxburghe's sale;*[1] and 'tis an ordinary thing to bestow fifty or a hundred pounds on a few leaves, or a thousand pounds on a first edition. Huntington gave £15,100 for one of the only two perfect copies of the first edition of *Venus and Adonis;* Dr. Rosenbach of New York gave £21,200 for a copy of the *Gutenberg Bible,* for which Mr. E. Goldston of London had paid the Benedictine monks of Melk in Austria £12,000 only a few weeks before. Such prices are toys in our time: bibliomania scorns all that is cheap, except to hope that it may become dear. They are like those reprehended by Seneca,[2] who loathed the very light because it was free, and who are offended with the sun's heat, and those cool blasts, because we buy them not. They gloat on prices, and nothing pleases them but what is expensive. If one appraises a shabby but rare little pamphlet of no intrinsic value at a high price, they will covet it for that reason alone: its value is *wholly a scarcity value;* but it is the same with books of nobler status, as those rare editions of classical works which no one heeds until someone bids high for them.

Take, for example, the story of the copy of the First Edition of *Il Decamerone di Boccaccio,* 1471, which was sold by auction at the dispersal of the Roxburgh Library, in 1812, for £2,260, which up to that time was the highest sum of money ever given for a book. The copy had long been coveted by bookmen, both sane and insane; it was *perhaps the most notorious volume in existence;*[3] and Nicol, in his *Preface* to the Sale Catalogue of the Library, described it as *one of the scarcest, if not the scarcest book in existence,* for it had preserved its *uniquity* for over three hundred years; it had been *a bone of contention* among collectors in the reign of the first two Georges: Lord Sunderland and Lord Oxford had both coveted it, but it became the property of the Duke of Roxburghe, *for the gallant price of* 100 *guineas;* which Marchand, in his *Histoire de L'Imprimerie* (1740) notes among the excessive prices up to then given for rare books. When the record price of 1812 was known among collectors, a craze for the book set in; bookmen were afflicted with a desire for copies as though they had been stricken by some infectious disease: every man pretending to some information about books *was set a-hunting* for it: *from the half-ruined mansion on the summit of the Vosges to the castellated heights along the Rhine,* a search was made; some supposed copies might lurk in Swiss chalets, and *Berne, Basle, and Zürich were examined with the sedulous pertinacity of an excise officer;* Italy was *ransacked;* all the cradle-towns of the art of printing were *explored; a*

---

[1] [Caulfield], *Chalcographimania.* (1814) 75.   [2] *Nat. Quaest.* cap. ult.   [3] Dibdin, *Bibliographical Decameron.* iii, 62.

copy might be still lurking in the Subiaco monastery; Perugia, Brescia, and Bologna, places then rarely visited by Englishmen, *were minutely examined, in vain*; and the only result of all this mighty hunting was a glimpse of the copies in the Magliabecchi at Florence and the Vaticano at Rome, which *were public property, and could not be removed.*[1]

That this craze was irrational cannot be denied; these hunters had no desire to read Boccaccio in the First Edition, or to study its bibliographical or typographical parts: they were moved by its high price, and such pleasure as they might have procured from the discovery of another copy would have been related to its *monetary* rather than its *literary* value. Aldous Huxley[2] argues, a picture may give *aesthetic pleasure*, and in buying a picture, *one buys the unique right to feel that pleasure*; with a book it is different; nobody, he says, can pretend that '*Venus and Adonis*' is more delightful when read in a fifteen thousand pound unique copy than in a volume costing one shilling; on the whole, the shilling edition is the better, so he concludes that *the purchaser of the fabulously expensive old book is satisfying only his possessive instinct*, and, doubtless, I would add, his vanity.

V. FASHION A CAUSE

Fashion is a prime cause of all collecting, not *desire for what is perfect, but for what is most run after, what is the fashion*;[3] so *the world of fashion comprehends books as well as bonnets and dresses;*[4] *the choice of books, like the toilet of gentility, is governed by fashion, whose laws admit of no appeal;*[5] *the passion for books, like other forms of desire, has its changes of fashion*, and *it is not always easy to justify the caprices of taste;*[6]

> Taste, tho' misled, may yet some purpose gain,
> But Fashion guides a book-compelling train;[7]

There can be no doubt that several famous libraries have derived their origin from the mere vanity of emulating a fashionable pursuit;[8] in the old days, saith Quentin-Bauchart,[9] and by the side of the *bibliophiles de race*, there were certain noble lords who possessed books because it was *de bon ton* to own

[1] Dibdin, *Reminiscences*. i, 360–1.   [2] 'Bibliophily', *On the Margin*. 65.   [3] La Bruyère, 'The Enthusiastic Collector', *Characters*. Trans. Lee. 68.   [4] W. C. Hazlitt, *Book-Collector*. 167.   [5] Philomneste Junior, *Bibliomania in the Present Day*. 8–9.   [6] Lang, 'Bibliomania in France', *Books and Bookmen*. 91.   [7] Ferriar, *Bibliomania*. 105–6.   [8] Roberts, *Book-Hunter in London*. 25.   [9] Qt. Uzanne, *Zigzags d'un Curieux*. 43.

them; but they neither cared for them nor opened them. Those who are thus afflicted need no explication, they are self-evident dizzards *ab imis unguibus usque ad verticem summum,* from top to toe; and Seymour de Ricci has come to their aid with a handbook[1] pointing at the *two or three thousand British and American books which fashion has decided are the most desirable for the up-to-date collector.* Yet because it is a common humour in our day, will not be left, and cannot be helped, i still must descend to the particulars, according to plan; but *nihil praeter rem loquar,* I shall say nothing beside the mark.

Many, saith Benjamin Franklin, *fear less the being in hell than out of the fashion.* Sometimes they are made for *Theology,* at others for *Incunabula,* at another time it is *First Editions* or *Association Copies, Bindings* or *Large Paper;* Elzevirs are plentiful or uncommon according to fashion; the taste for *Incunabula slumbered in the latter half of the sixteenth, and all the seventeenth century, and revived with the third jubilee of printing in* 1740;[2] Dibdin observed the passing of the fashion for fine editions of the classics;[3] *fine bindings again became the fashion* after the Roxburghe sale, in 1812, says de Ricci;[4] *fifty years ago,* notes Lang,[5] *Brunet expressed his contempt for the designs of Boucher; now they are at the top of the fashion,* and he gives many instances of changes in taste at the dictation of this tyrant, none of them having any regard for intrinsic value. *A hundred years hence,* he says, *the original editions of Thackeray, or of Miss Greenaway's Christmas books, or 'Modern Painters', may be the ruling passion, and Aldines and Elzevirs, black-letter and French vignettes may all be despised.*[6] W. C. Hazlitt complains[7] that he has seen *many cranks and fancies successively take possession of the public;* and he enumerates early typography; early poetry and romances; books of hours; books of emblems; Roman Catholic literature; liturgies; Bewick; Bartolozzi; the first edition (which was sometimes also the last); books on vellum, on india paper, or on yellow or some other bizarre colour or material, debarring perusal of the publication; copies with remarkable blunders or with some of the text inadvertently omitted; *all of these,* he says, *have had their day, but* some of them *drop out of season* for a period and *then reappear for a second or third brief term* of life or favour. Gosse[8] believes that *we have only to examine the libraries of our immediate ancestors to discover how totally they differed from ourselves in every department of bibliophily;* preferring editions of *the classics in pompous bindings, with a sprinkling of more sombre eighteenth-century theology, to any other species of furniture for their book-rooms;*

[1] *Book-Collector's Guide.*   [2] Lang, *The Library.* 98.   [3] *Bibliophobia, passim.*
[4] *English Collectors of Books and Manuscripts.* 71.   [5] *The Library.* 113.   [6] *The Library.* 114.   [7] *Book-Collector.* 136.   [8] *Sunday Times.* 15.i.1928.

And who can say, what books, matured by age,
May tempt, in future days, the reader's rage?
How flush'd with joy, the Bibliomane may show
His Carr's *uncut* and Cottle's *fair* in row;
May point with conscious pride, to envying throngs,
His Holcroft's dramas, and his Dimond's songs?

. . . . .

I leave to those whom headstrong fashion rules
Dame Julian Berners, and the *Ship of Fools*.[1]

Carew Hazlitt does not hesitate to hint[2] that these changes of fashion are not without *trade* stimulus: one fashion *usually prevails long enough to suit the purposes of the trade*, before it makes way for another; well may Symons condemn as absurd the restriction of *attention to the small number of selected (but not always select) authors whose works are offered for sale in every other bookseller's catalogue*.[3] But whether booksellers originate or merely promote this craze they admittedly benefit from it, for fashion increases demand and therefore price, and some collectors (or amateur traders) buy fashionable first editions in the hope of selling them at a profit, *and this stimulus*, saith a knowing bookseller, *which is always in operation, is a good thing for us*, meaning members of his own trade, *because it confirms our friend in his bookbuying habits*.[4]

Though they give reasons for their excitement, many of them pretty, it is all one, they dote at the command of fashion; whatever comes they will follow the fashion, and have a good opinion of themselves because of it; *there have been men*, Slater reports,[5] *who would buy any book, whether they wanted it or not, on the chance of someone else wanting it*, either then or in days to come, and he gives Rossi as an instance of one who was *so saturated with the suspicion that fashion would change at* any moment that the stalls by which he passed were *like towns through which Attila or the Tartars had swept, with ruin in their train*. The *enterprising individual*, saith Roberts,[6] who, on receiving a catalogue of medical books, wired to the bookseller: *What will you take for the lot?* and on a price being quoted, telegraphed: *Send them along*, was *clearly a person who wished to be fashionable*. And I may take it as a certificate of sanity, when Dibdin, protesting against the retreat of fashion from the old classics, exclaimed: *What care I for the capriciousness of public*

[1] Ferriar, *Bibliomania*. [2] *Book-Collector*. 167. [3] A. J. A. Symons, 'The Book-Collector's Apology', *The Book-Collector's Quarterly*. i, 55. [4] J. G. Wilson, *The Business of Bookselling*. 30. [5] *Romance of Book-Collecting*. 4. [6] *Book-Hunter in London*. xvii.

taste? Shall my first folio Aldine Demosthenes and Rhetores be less coveted, less embraced, than heretofore?

Dear as the ruddy drops that warm my heart

shall be, to me, my Elzevir and Olivet Ciceros! Nor let old Scapula and Facciolati droop their towering heads—and, shew me the man who shall dare to undervalue my larger paper Barnes's Euripides, West's Pindar, and Potter's Lycophron. Will any creature, short of a confirmed idiot, presume to write me down an ass, because I have over and over again tossed up my head at the pitiful offer of three score and ten sovereigns for my large paper Grenville's Homer?[1] We properly call that *dotage*, as Laurentius[2] interprets it, *when some one principal faculty of the mind, as imagination, or reason, is corrupted*, and if this be so, fashion needs no further support as a prime cause; its power to corrupt by deviation of the mind from its natural trend and judgment is obvious and well known, even among normal folks: *What signifies whether they read it or not?* Horace Walpole asks[3] of his edition of Lord Herbert of Cherbury's *Life. There will be a new fashion, or a new something or other, that will do just as well, before you can convey your copy to them; and if they do these things in a green tree, what shall be done in the dry?*[4]

---

[1] Dibdin, *Bibliophobia*. 64–5.   [2] Cap. de mal.   [3] *Letters*. Ed. Cunningham. iv, 307.
[4] Speech, First Edition Club Dinner, Savoy Hotel, Dec. 1928.

Part XXVI

DO BIBLIOMANIACS READ THEIR BOOKS?

<hr>

I. DOTING WITHOUT READING

It is rightly argued by some that to look *at* a book is not the same as to look *in* one, and they make the true sign of a bibliomaniac hoarding without reading. *The book-collector*, Shane Leslie gives out,[1] *is the hermaphrodite of literature: neither a reader nor a writer.* That

> Book-collectors read not what they buy[2]

is a common observation. Every age furnishes evidence of those who hoard books without reading them. One such is reproached by Lucian: *Nobody who knows you*, he complains, *would think you do it on account of their helpfulness, or use, any more than a bald man would buy a comb, a blind man a mirror, a deaf-mute a flute-player, an eunuch a concubine, a landsman an oar, or a seaman a plough.*[3] There are many who insist that this is a prime symptom; others stoutly contest the view: *some books are to be read, others are to be collected*;[4] and Ferguson[5] as boldy maintains that *the larger number of books are not for reading; their importance does not depend upon their contents, but upon themselves.* To read books *sacred to external inspection*, saith John Hill Burton,[6] would be *a scandal, such as it would be among a hunting set to hint that a man had killed a fox; books*, he avers,[7] *should be used decently and respectfully—reverently*; but he will not tolerate *the doctrine that there are volumes too splendid for use, too fine almost to be looked at, as Brummel said of some of his Dresden china.*

> To what is writ you blissfully are blind,
> You worship books—according to your lights.
> The tome's true worth your niggard sense above,
> You prize the body—'tis the soul I love.[8]

The Rev. James Beresford will not have such neglect of the true purpose of a book to be a symptom of bibliomania, but the result of *a high*

[1] Luke xxiii, 31. [2] Ferriar, *Bibliomania.* [3] *Lucian.* 'Ignorant Book-Collector.' Loeb Ed. iii, 197. [4] A. Edward Newton, *Amenities of Book-Collecting.* 8. [5] *Aspects of Bibliography.* 6–7. [6] *The Book-Hunter.* 18. [7] *Ib.* 165–6. [8] Halkett Lord, qt. *Book-Lore.* ii, 99.

and dignified passion, which he names *Bibliosophia,* and defines as *an appetite for collecting Books—carefully distinguished from, wholly unconnected with, nay absolutely repugnant to, all idea of reading them.*[1] Whether it be a sign of mania or not, it has been condemned and satirized in most ages as silly stupid, vain, foppish or conceited:

> His Study! with what Authors is it stor'd!
> In Books, not Authors, curious is my Lord;
> To all their dated backs he turns you round;
> Those Aldus printed, those Du Suëil has bound.
> Lo, some are Vellum, and the rest as good,
> For all his Lordship knows—but they are Wood.[2]

Pope defines it in a footnote[3] as *a false Taste in Books,* an example of *the vanity in collecting them, more frequent in men of fortune than the study to understand them;* there are many who delight chiefly in the elegance of print or binding, and *some have carried it so far as to cause the upper shelves to be filled with painted books of wood; others pique themselves so much upon books in a language they do not understand, as to exclude the most useful in one they do:*

> For Locke or Milton 'tis in vain to look,
> These shelves admit not any modern book.[4]

How many such divisions as Beresford's might be made I will not essay but, saving his reverence, I will adventure that instead of making clear what was hitherto obscure, he makes *confusion worse confounded,* by starting a new hare; but the more the experts contend, the more they are involved in a labyrinth of errors.

It is to avoid these paradoxes that I have set out a new hypothesis, not out of vanity or idle argument, but in a scientifical spirit with the purpose of determining the true tenets of the matter; and I am prepared to defend my first postulate, that bibliomaniacs are book-mad by nature, against all cavils, and that, as a concomitant, they coin uses for books foreign to their purpose, and behave towards them so inordinately as to convict themselves of aberration, obsession, and other symptoms of true *mania,* as Addison's *Tom Folio,* that *broker in learning* who had *a greater esteem for Aldus and Elzevir, than for Virgil and Horace;* who, when he gives an account of an author, treats not of what he wrote but of the name of the editor, the year the work was printed; *cries up the goodness of the paper and is transported by the beauty of the letter;* those who *talk of fineness of style, justness of thought or the brightness of any particular passage,* are looked upon by Tom as *men*

---

[1] *Bibliosophia.* 4.   [2] Pope, *Moral Essays.* iv, 133–8.   [3] *Works.* Ed. Warburton. iii, 308.   [4] Pope, *op. cit.* iv, 139–40.

of superficial learning and flashy parts; he admired Daniel Heinsius' edition of *Virgil* because *after the strictest and most malicious examination* he *could find but two faults in him*; one of them in the *Aeneid*, where are *two commas instead of a parenthesis*; and another in the third *Georgic*, where *you may find a semi-colon turned upside down*; well may Addison call him a *learned idiot*, and class him with those editors, commentators, interpreters, scholiasts, and critics, who possess *deep learning without common sense*. Nor was this the disposition only of Addison; others have said as much, and the sum is this: books are for use; they exist for bookish purposes, *are meant to be read, and reading, moreover, is good for them, it lets air and light in among their leaves*, thus preventing *the ravages of fustiness and damp*,[1] and other evils; and those who treat them otherwise are bent on ostentation rather than on any spiritual advantage, even if they escape dotage.

II. NON-READING NOT A SOLE SYMPTOM

I hold, then, that it is a primary symptom of bibliomania to dote on books without any desire to read them; to accumulate copies for the sake of hoarding them; to be concerned about external condition rather than internal quality:

> The Bibliomane exclaims, with haggard eye,
> 'No margin!' turns in haste, and scorns to buy.[2]

To regard books as *so much furniture* and to contemplate their *gorgeous exteriors* with a *knowing expression*,[3] whatever men advance in defence of it, is to meet dotage halfway, and whether they be crazy or not, I hold with Sir Walter Raleigh that *when readers turn by natural development into fanciers they become immune to books*.[4] Does a man that is cold desire to wear fine raiment? Does not a cloth suit become him as well, and keep him as warm, as all their silks, satins, damasks, taffetas and tissues? Is not home-spun cloth as great a preservative against cold as a coat of *Tartar* lamb's wool, dyed in grain, or a gown of Giants' beards?

Note, by the way, there is, in opposition to this argument, the example of Dibdin, who numbered amongst symptoms, to be *well read in old books* and, as he confessed of himself,[5] *I am an arrant Bibliomaniac, I love books dearly, the very sight, touch, and, more, the perusal*; but this is weak and insufficient, as he himself betrays in his last chapter, and I am no' way altered from my opinion, for as the Rev. Mr. Beresford[6] saw, and retorted in his

---

[1] Iolo A. Williams, *Elements of Book-Collecting*. 18–19.   [2] Ferriar, *Bibliomania*. 42–3.
[3] *Book-Lore*. iv, 139.   [4] *Letters*. ii, 465.   [5] *Bibliomania*. (1811) 4.   [6] *Bibliosophia*. 3.

satire: *Bibliomania, Mr. D!—and is this the softest title which you can afford to the noble passion for literary accumulation—that passion, to which, throughout the very book in which it is thus stigmatized, you almost avow that you are, yourself, a voluntary, if not an exulting Victim?* In the end, as he rightly allows, Dibdin leaves us in the dark. It is not clear which side he takes between *the two great parties of Book-hunters—those who collect and those who read*, so that, he concludes, the *censorious* might regard him as *a literary Trimmer*. But Dibdin has not even the cunning of a *Trimmer*, he is a word-spinner and a sentimentalist; very garrulous, too often trivial, and, like many of them, addicted to catachresis, and *inebriated with the exuberance of his own verbosity*.[1] The sum of it is that many bookmen are romantically in love with the word and must be saved from themselves, as R. M. Field would rescue his brother, Eugene, from *these self-accusations, bibliophily rather than bibliomania* being *the word to characterize his conscientious purpose*, which was to *own* books *to the full extent, inwardly as well as outwardly*;[2] and some other authorities have held that reading is the prime test of bibliophily, and that the love of books and the love of reading are identical: *aimer le livre, aimer la lecture, sont donc une seule et même chose pour tout esprit cultivé*; and that an immense gulf separates the bibliophile from the bibliomaniac.[3]

They all leave out of account that legitimate and sane type of bookman who has books for reading and books for sentiment, as Andrew Lang, who admits that it is not necessary for a collector to read all his books, and that he himself possessed an Aldine *Homer* and a *Caliergus his Theocritus*, but preferred to read those authors *in a cheap German edition; the old editions*, he explains, *we buy mainly for their beauty, the sentiment of their antiquity, and their associations*;[4] or the bookmen who combine hoarding with a gracious scholarship, as Montaigne, who enjoyed books *as a miser doth his gold*, but took equal joy in the thought that he could use them when he would by *right of possession*; and they thus became for him medicine for the soul and solace for the heart;[5] or in our own time that good bookman, Lord de Tabley, who read *every book he bought, and with critical gusto*.[6]

I could tell many a pleasant tale to this purpose, but at best they would do no more than illustrate marginal cases, and they are strange in respect to my main argument, which is to expound true mania. That we are all mad in some sort I have set out in a precedent section, but not wholly mad: *I scarce know any one in all mankind that is wise at all hours, or has nor some tang or other of madness*.[7] So true bookmen are all tainted with biblio-

---

[1] Mr. Disraeli, on Mr. Gladstone, *House of Commons*. (1878)   [2] Pref., *Love Affairs of a Bibliomaniac*. vii-viii.   [3] Gustave Mouravit, *Le Livre et la Petite Bibliothèque d'Amateur*. 4.   [4] 'Letter to a Young American Book-Hunter', *Letters on Literature*. 114.   [5] *Essays*. Ed. Seccombe. i, 53.   [6] Gosse, 'Lord de Tabley', *Critical Kit-Kats*. 190.   [7] Erasmus, *Praise of Folly*. Trans. Wilson. 77.

mania, but are not therefore bibliomaniacs; the least mad, as I have also shown, are those who perceive and acknowledge their own lunacy. I will not, therefore, insert here any further expository sentences; only this I will add, that if it be considered aright, bibliomania may be as complete in one as in many symptoms. 'Tis a common sign this; for when once the humours are stirred, and the imagination misaffected, it will express itself in divers forms; and many such absurd symptoms will accompany sanity itself. It is, therefore, a reasonable presumption that the book-hoarder who does not read is one type of bibliomane and that non-reading is not a basic symptom. Jacob supports[1] this argument when he attributes the symptom to *le bibliomane vaniteux* who collects *belles éditions* for show and not for use, *il ne lit pas et souvent il n'a jamais lu*, he does not read and often never has read; he collects books as another may collect shells, pictures, minerals, etc., his library is a museum, which he displays vainly to all comers, regardless of whether they know what a book is, still less a beautiful book; it satisfies his conceit *jacere margaritas ante porcos*, to cast pearls before swine.

III. INORDINATE READING A SYMPTOM

That they do not read their books is thus only partly true, even if their object for the most part is books, not reading. Nor is reading in itself a sign of book-sanity; some offend in one extreme, if too many in the other; there are mad readers as well as sane readers, as I have shown. Leo Allatius[2] calls an *insatiable passion of the mind for literature*, a *thirst* or *madness*; it continually inspired him to seek what was *new* in books; and there are those students, as I have again shown in its place, who sacrifice not only wealth and comfort to their passion, but health and beauty; they toil and moil, but what reap they? Continued *literary labour*, Apuleius confessed,[3] swept away such charm as his person ever possessed, reduced him to *a lean habit of body, sucked away all the freshness of life*, destroyed his complexion, impaired his vigour; he allowed his hair to become *tangled, twisted and unkempt like a lump of tow, shaggy and irregular in length*, and *so knotted and matted that the tangle is past the art of man to unravel*; he spurned all other pleasure and ceased not, night or day, from studying and writing, to the neglect and derangement of his bodily health. Every authority can cite examples of bibliomanes who were great readers, and obsessive reading is a symptom of bibliomania.

I shall do no more in this place than cite a few examples, as that in *Dibdin*[4] of the infatuated *bookworm*, Adrian Baillet, librarian to Lamoignous

[1] *Ma République.* 51–2.   [2] Qt. *In Praise of Books.* Swan. 3.   [3] *Apologia.* Trans. Butler. 4–5.   [4] *Bibliomania.* (1811) 57–8.

562 DO BIBLIOMANIACS READ THEIR BOOKS?

who lived and died for books, having no life apart from them; who treated his body as a recalcitrant and insolent enemy which required constant subjection; and would not suffer it to rest more than five hours a night, or take more than one meal a day; who drank no wine, never came near the fire, and walked out of doors but once a week. In this wise his intellect or, rather, his memory grew amain, but his body degenerated into physical wreckage; he became afflicted with ulcers, and an *erysipelatous affection* made him a hideous sight to all beholders. He died at the age of fifty-six, a librarian of *unparalleled diligence and sagacity*, the author of the bibliographical works *Jugemens des Savans* (1722) in eight volumes, quarto, and the *Catalogue des Matières* in thirty-five volumes, folio. For a further taste, take the Abbé Boisot, *who lived entirely for books*;[1] Carneades, who was so deeply plunged in an overweening desire for knowledge, so *besotted* with it, that he never had leisure to cut his hair, or pare his nails;[2] Isaac Read, who never departed from his books, his library serving as *parlour, kitchen, and hall*;[3] Huet, who so immoderately employed his eyes in continual reading that he *brought a fluxion upon them, which terminated in the disorder called by the ancient physicians Epiphora*;[4] and Ancillon, of whom they say[5] he never left his books, day or night, except when he went to preach to his humble congregation, fearing to miss the golden thoughts which he believed might lurk in the dullest volume. Out of *Leigh Hunt*[6] I take the case of Mrs. West, wife of Benjamin West the painter, who was so *fond of books* that she *ultimately became a martyr to them*, and *the physician declared that she lost the use of her limbs by sitting in-doors* reading; and Dibdin cites[7] T. de Ocheda as always to be found in Lord Spencer's library, at Althorp, *close to a lamp, with one of the 'Fathers' before him*. He had read *them all through twice. His reading was prodigious; he read walking, sitting, and standing*, but mine author does not *think his intellectual receiver digested the enormous quantity of food introduced into it.*

From disposition, reading in such cases proceeds to a habit, and habit becomes a monomania, an absorbing passion deleting all normal interests, to which purpose there is a tale of Budaeus, the philogolist. When a servant rushed into his study to warn him that the house was on fire, Budaeus replied: *Tell my wife that I never interfere with the household:*[8] and he went on reading. They are reading-mad: *book-struck* men, says A. B. Alcott,[9] *are of all readers the least wise;* none less so than Don Quixote,[10] who gave himself up to reading books of chivalry *with such ardour and avidity*, that he

[1] Elton, *Great Book-Collectors*. 192.   [2] Montaigne, *Essays*. Seccombe. i, 199.
[3] Dibdin, *Bibliomania*. (1811) 609.   [4] *Memoirs*. Aikin. i, 210.   [5] Elton, *op. cit*. 190.
[6] *Autobiography*. World's Classics. 25–6.   [7] *Reminiscences*. ii, 593.   [8] Elton, *Great Book-Collectors*. 100.   [9] 'Tablets', qt. *Book-Lovers' Anth*. 6.   [10] Cervantes, *Don Quixote*. i and v.

almost entirely neglected his field sports and even the management of his property; *it was often my uncle's way*, testifieth his niece, *to stay two days and nights poring over these unholy books of misadventures, after which he would fling the books away and snatch up his sword and fall to slashing the walls; and when he was tired out he would say he had killed four giants like four towers; and the sweat that flowed from him when he was weary he said was the blood of the wounds he had received in battle; and then he would drink a jug of cold water and become calm and quiet, saying that this water was a most precious potion which the sage Esquife, a great magician and friend of his, had brought him.* And to make an end of this recital of instances there are those who read sanely and hoard insanely, as Richard Heber, our most notable book-hoarder; it was a *saving grace*, as they say, in his dotage, that he read and discussed at length his reading with his cronies. He would *moot Greek metres* with Dr. Drury, *fight over derivatives and etymons* with Roger Wilbraham, *quote long passages of their father's biography of Dr. Johnson* with the Boswells, and *ring changes on 'Robin Hood Garlands'* with Dodd or Haslewood; and he was *much attached* to the *lower school of* the *old Latin Poets*: Lucan, Claudian, and Silius Italicus.[1]

But to leave tales and to sum it up, obsession is a general symptom, whether it be of reading, or *le livre pour le livre*, whether read or unread. This latter is a prime and continuate symptom, overwhelming the rest: an inseparable companion to acquisitiveness, greed, and an outrageous desire of possession:

'Tis strange, the Miser should his cares employy
To gain those riches he can ne'er enjoy:
Is it less strange, the Prodigal should waste
His wealth, to purchase what he ne'er can taste?[2]

Dibdin provides an illustration in his bibliomaniacal romance, *Philemon*, where he makes Mr. Joline say: *We do not gather books to read them, my Boeotian friend*, which Henry Harper[3] supports: the idea that they read their books is *a childish illusion. In early days* (he quotes out of Walter Bagehot) *there is an opinion that the obvious thing to do with a horse is to ride it; with a cake, to eat it; with a sixpence, to spend it. A few boyish persons*, he saith, *carry this further, and think that the natural thing to do with a book is to read it. The mere reading of a rare book is a puerility, an idiosyncrasy of adolescence.*

When Locker-Lampson complained to Bedford that a book which he had bound for him did not shut properly, Bedford exclaimed, *Why bless me, sir, you've been reading it!* The collector seldom *condescends*, he says, *to become a student.* He had not been reading the book, and told him so, but

---

[1] Dibdin, *Reminiscences.* i, 431–2.   [2] Pope, *Moral Essays.* iv, 1–4.   [3] *Book-lovers, Bibliomaniacs, and Book Clubs.* 62–3.

he *understood the reasonableness of his reproach*.[1] Ownership, they argue, is the true distinction. The numismatist does not collect coins to spend them, or the philatelist stamps to use them. As well ask a man to drink tea out of his priceless Crown Derby cup, or serve ginger out of his *sang de boeuf* jar of the Ming Dynasty, as expect a bibliomane to read, still less let his friends read, his first edition of *Endymion* or his first quarto *Hamlet*. But shall he not within reason possess such treasures; may he not glut his eyes on such delightful objects as a binding by Clovis Eve or Derome, Samuel Mearn or Roger Payne, or soberly disport himself with them for sheer joy? 'Tis a pretty defence which, however some may misconstrue, I, for my part, will interpret to the best, and I do therefore acknowledge that there are some books so high above the rest, that they are as so many glittering stars, for admiration not for use, too fair and frail for *human nature's daily food;* 'tis fit it should be so, and I see no harm in it, but I require a moderation, as well as a just reason; so although I admit there is no standard of moderation and that our judgment is bridled in all its parts, there is a common measure of sanity in the way of a man with a book, which is to love it for what he gets out of it and not solely for what it is. The defect of this leads to eccentricity or worse; what else did the poet insinuate?

> Like Poets, born, in vain Collectors strive
> To cross their Fate, and learn the art to thrive.
> Like Cacus, bent to tame their struggling will,
> The tyrant-passion drags them backward still:
> Even I, debarr'd of ease and studious hours,
> Confess, mid' anxious toil, its lurking powers.[2]

---

[1] *My Confidences.* 197. [2] Ferriar, *Bibliomania.* 131-6.

Part XXVII

VARIETIES OF BIBLIOMANIA

———————◆◇◆———————

I. IT IS COMMON TO ALL BOOKMEN

Symptoms are either universal or particular—peculiar to persons, species, or circumstances. Some signs are obscure, some manifest and obvious; some material, some mental; varying according to their inward or outward causes, habits, and conditions, or from humours variously mixed. As they are passionate or hot, determined, hesitate, whimsical, curious, selective, acquisitive or destructive, they are *bibliomania multiformis*. The book-mad are known by their characteristics; and as wine produceth diverse effects, and as that herb *Tortocella* in *Laurentius*[1] makes some laugh, some weep, some sleep, some dance, some sing, some howl, some drink, etc., so doth this our bibliomania work several signs in several parties.

But who can speak sufficiently of these varieties, or prescribe rules to comprehend them? They are irregular, obscure, various; as soon count the stars as catalogue the diversities of book-mania. As the symptoms are confounded (which I have shown), so are the varieties, sometimes with learning, as you may perceive by those several examples collected by Burton, D'Israeli, Wanley, etc.; sometimes with vanity, greed, envy (all of which I have expounded in the *Causes*); and for all I know they may be confused and intermixed with other diseases. 'Tis hard, I confess; yet I have disposed of them as I could. For hitherto I have expatiated in more general terms, speaking promiscuously of such ordinary signs which occur amongst them. For rarely are they all to be found in one man: that were to be a monster, not a man; but some in one, some in another, and that often successively or at several times; which I have been the more curious to express and report, not to upbraid any victim, or to deride (I rather pity them, and, if I may confess it, envy some of milder affliction), but the better to discern and, where necessary, suggest remedies unto them; and, not least, to show that the best and soundest of us all is in equal danger. Thus my examples may warn and thereby help us by inculcating discretion to moderate ourselves, to be more wary in the midst of these dangers.

[1] Qt. *Anat. Mel.* Bohn. i, 440.

II. THE PRINCIPAL VARIETIES NAMED

Of the varieties of bibliomania there are several opinions, for it hath *as many heads as the famed Briaraeus,*[1] and some authorities have set out classifications of symptoms by which the passion may be more exactly observed. The sum of these I will briefly epitomize (for I light my candle from their torches) and enlarge upon occasion, as shall seem best to me, and that after my own method. Jacob,[2] the French bibliophile, distinguishes five kinds: *les exclusifs, les fantasques, les envieux, les vaniteux et les thésauriseurs.* Field, in America, following his legendary friend, Dr. O'Rell, discovers but two, or rather one with two stages, *Primary* and *Secondary,* the first being *false,* or *chicken-bibliomania,* and the second, *true bibliomania.* He also claims that O'Rell has discovered the *bacillus librorum,* which is the suspected cause of the disease, for which he composed a lymph, a *milligram* of which injected into the *femoral artery* of a cat, caused the animal to eat the covers of Field's copy of *Rabelais.*[3] Dibdin denominated eight classes which most will agree are distinguished by no more than outward signs, according to optic principles, visible appearances. These are, saith mine author,[4] first, a passion for *Large Paper;* secondly, for *Uncut Copies;* thirdly, for *Extra-illustrated Copies;* fourthly, for *Unique Copies;* fifthly, for *Copies Printed Upon Vellum;* sixthly, for *First Editions;* seventhly, for *True Editions;* and eighthly, for *Books Printed in the Black-Letter* (Charles Lamb confessed that he was *not bibliomanist enough to like black-letter*),[5] and, he might have added, fine binding, fine printing, *suppressed books,* and *Private Presses.* Of these there are many subdivisions, divers degrees of madness and folly, some more than others, yet all miserably out, perplexed, doting and beside themselves for the sake of books; and we can add to and subtract from such a list at our pleasure, subdivide in the concrete or abstract, according to our desire for verisimilitude. But I am not ignorant in the meantime (notwithstanding this which I have said) that some extension of Dibdin's outward signs is to be commended, more especially if we acknowledge that his examples are not symptoms of disease *per se,* but may in their proper place and circumstance expound, not bibliomania but *bibliosanity* such as George Steeven's passion for *Shakesperiana,* Sir Edmund Gosse's for first editions of *Restoration Plays,* etc. I could recite a great catalogue of them.

We must not, therefore, even in *Dibdin,* hope to have all things answer our own expectation, for he, and some others, in their anxiety to uphold

[1] W. C. Hazlitt, *History of Book-Collecting.* 19.   [2] *Ma République.* 49.   [3] *Love Affairs of a Bibliomaniac.* 143–5.   [4] *Bibliomania.* (1811) 653.   [5] *Letters.* Everyman Ed. ii, 75.

their own passion, even when it was sane, as in most cases it was, accepted and defended a stigmatic title, as I have shown apart; who shall say which of those great collectors of the late days of the eighteenth and early days of the nineteenth century, catalogued by Bagford,[1] were mad, and which sane? The Earl of Carbery, who made *a noble collection, including all that relate to mystical divinity;* the Earl of Kent, who collected *English Historians, visitations, and pedigrees;* the Earl of Pembroke, who collected *books of medals, lives, effigies, of all great and learned men, kings, princes, dukes, and great generals; with abundance of others of pomp and state;* the Lord Somers, who made *an admirable collection of books relating to the laws of this land and other countries, in Latin, French, Italian, and Spanish?* Mr. Secretary Pepys collected books on various subjects, as English history, maritime affairs, the power and constitution of the Admiralty and Sea Laws; *copy-books* of all the masters of Europe, Italian, French, German, Flemish, Dutch, Spanish, and English, *all digested according to their time and country, pasted on large paper and bound up;* and mathematics, music, and several other subjects, *all excellent in their kinds.*

In the main, then, I may venture to repeat my belief that book-collecting is sane when its object is not ostentation of possession, but use:

> 'Tis use alone that sanctifies Expense,
> And Splendour borrows all her rays from Sense;[2]

but there be many differences here even, as the collector, imagined and condemned by Frederic Harrison,[3] who spent half a lifetime and half his fortune in amassing *a library of old plays, every one of them worthless in diction, in plot, in sentiment, and in purpose; a collection for more stupid and uninteresting than the burlesques and pantomimes* current in his time; what Hill Burton calls[4] that *painfully low and grovelling type of the malady,* which buys any book because it is *cheap,* with no discrimination of good from bad books, useful from useless, and mixing such *biblia-a-biblia* as old directories, registers of magistrates and voters, road-books, etc., with classics, and rejoicing only when he has made a *better bargain* than a fellow collector.

But I have no desire to be over-subtle lest I confound where I would expound, and my most severe critic will not deny that books are for use, however wide the terms of the usage, and I would make it wide enough to admit all who are sane enough to stop this side of obsession, as, on the one hand, Richard Smith, that strenuous hunter in the Restoration period, who was *infinitely curious and inquisitive after books,* and suffered nothing

---

[1] *Gentleman's Magazine.* (1816) ii, 395–7.   [2] Pope, *Moral Essays,* iv. 179–80.
[3] *Choice of Books.* 86.   [4] *Book-Hunter.* 162–3.

to escape him which *fell within the compass of his learning*, for *he had not the vanity of desiring to be master of more than he knew how to use;*[1] and on the other, Petrarch's friend, Raimondo Soranzo, an Advocate of Avignon, who was *a great collector of books of all kinds*, but, except *Law Books and Livy*, he collected more *for the pleasure of collecting than of reading them.*[2] In the first of these instances we have sanity, in the second, if not mania, at least dotage; or, for your better understanding, the two states are both revealed in the person of Raimondo, who approaches his *Law* and his *Livy* sanely, and is dotingly affected by the rest. Remembering, therefore, that all book-collecting is not mad but may become so, since *nihil est ab omni parte beatum*,[3]

> There's no perfection is so absolute,
> That some impurity doth not pollute;

and whatsoever is under the moon is subject to decay and perversion; so we may proceed.

III. A VARIETY OF COLLECTOMANIA

Bibliomania is (as I have said before) inordinate or corrupt book-love, and let them dissemble as they will, *the miserable mania of gathering editions and copies* and *of frantically hunting*[4] after rarities is no more than that, and no less. For the most part they are swung as in a vortex, by an inbred passion of acquired habit. Octave Uzanne[5] will have that victims of the mania undergo a curious crystallization of the brain as remarkable as the *transformisme des Hyménoptères*; 'tis a pathological state which begins normally with book-love and ends in *collectionomanie*. The bibliophile becomes a chrysalis in his library, and when he is thought to be a hermit in his *cocon maroquiné*, he of a sudden reveals himself winged and ardent for the *chasse au bibelot*; from a faithful adherence *au livre janséniste*, he is seduced by *la fanfare des dorures et le damasquinage des petits fers;* gradually he becomes sensitive to *Ex libris* and *Ex dono*, but when *l'estampe de premier tirage* inoculates him with its *virus terrible*, he is in the grip of *l'illustromanie*, a notorious symptom of the malady. He next craves for *unique* books, enriched with original drawings, autograph letters, inscriptions, marginal notes, etc.; or he will have none but books which have become *objets d'art*, curiosities, rare pieces for the cabinet rather than the book-shelf. *Ce bijou bibliographique*, he advises, *ce bibelot de la folie interfoliée a réclamé jalousement*

---

[1] Preface. Cat. of Richard Smith's Books. Qt. Dibdin, *Bibliomania*. (1811) 399.
[2] Tatham, *Francesco Petrarca*. i, 166.   [3] Horace, *Odes*. ii, 16.   [4] Percy Fitzgerald, *Charles Lamb*. 7.   [5] *Zigzags d'un Curieux*. 203–4.

un cadre, it must have a *milieu* of colours and *contrastes artistiques*, and alone
in its niche it calls for the companionship of *le missel à chasuble d'argent, le
drageoir et la miniature;* it insists upon being couched *sur une vieille étoffe aux
tons mourants et aux fleurs délicieusement animées*, and he says, it makes
all the unreasonable demands of a mistress and creates in the soul of
its possessor a *collectionomanie furieuse* before which he falls a helpless
victim.

The proper classification, therefore, is not so much into the kinds or
qualities of books doted on, as the quality or character of the dotage itself;
and in this wise Jean-Joseph Rive (*Chasse aux Bibliographes*) has given us
some true designations, which Peignot hath amplified, as *Bibliotaphe*, one
who buries books by keeping them under lock and key; *Bibliognoste*, one
who dotes on title-pages, dates, colophons, imprints, etc. To these Peignot
adds *Bibliolyte*, for one who destroys books completely, as distinct from
the *Biblioclast*, who is the simple book-tearer or breaker; he also offers up
the correction of *Bibliotaft*, a book-burier, for Rive's *Bibliotaphe*, which is,
more properly, a book-grave. To these classes I could add several names,
but will do no more than announce the biblioklept or book-thief, who is
often an imbecile; but if I do not make the list longer it is for sufficient
reasons, not least of which is a fear of slipping into that habit of our
modern physicians of refining so upon names as to risk the danger of in-
venting diseases to fit them; and if names are abused in number and invention there is an equal danger of obsessive regard for them, as the old
proverb hath it, *give a dog a bad name and hang him;* so these names which
I have enumerated and amplified out of *Rive* and Peignot are not all
denominations of madness in themselves, but may become so with increasing morbidity of what they define, whether it be a general madness
or an arrested symptom.

First, then, to those varieties of Dibdin I will add as recognizable symptoms an unruly passion for *Ex dono* or *Inscribed Copies, Association Copies,
Private Press Books, Printers' Type Books, Examples of Fine Printing*, and
Bindings. But, again, this method hath no end, and is too general for my
purpose, for bibliomania is as infinite and varied as books, and extends
from a general and overwhelming passion for books as such, to the most
fastidious and fantastically subtle selection and specialization; impossible,
saith W. C. Hazlitt,[1] to name any variety of book-collecting which hath
not been so classed: love of books regardless of bindings, or bindings
regardless of books; desire for *works with woodcuts* of certain printers,
places, or dates; limitation of size, *for a candidate for admittance to some
cabinets may not exceed so many inches in altitude*, etc., and Dibdin himself
hath it that *a passion for books illustrated, or adorned with numerous prints, is*

[1] *Hist. of Book-Collecting.* 19-20.

a very general and violent symptom of the Bibliomania; a willing victim of this phase being that Marquis of Blandford

whose bright glow
Spent thousands on Boccaccio,[1]

but who *has also a most incurable itch for books of emblems, which he will purchase at any price.*[2] Thus one is for *Angling* books, another for *Topography*, a third for *Bibliography*; another will confine *Angling* to *Izaak Walton*, *Topography* to *York* or *Bermondsey*, Bibliography to *Numismata* or *Incunabula*; and so they go on, subdividing, specializing, refining, *true clerks of the collection, they mix memoranda with ambition, and reducing Art to statistics, they 'file' the fifteenth century, and 'pigeon-hole' the antique.*[3]

They reduce Authors to a simple equation, and will have one book of one writer in all his varieties, as *Gulliver's Travels*, Boswell's *Johnson*, or the *Vicar of Wakefield*; the *Compleat Angler;* the *Pilgrim's Progress*, or the *Religio Medici*, of which Sir William Osler had fifty-five editions.[4] No end to such specialization; some are for *Keepsakes* and *Forget-me-nots*, *Prayer Books* or *Bibles*, as Archdeacon Meadow, as I have noted, who went to London to be examined by a Committee of the House of Commons, and suddenly disappeared, returning home penniless, *followed by a wagon containing* 372 *copies of rare editions of the 'Bible'.*[5] Some will have none but new books, modern editions; others, and they outnumber them, are for none but old books, while some will have only manuscripts; one of this last class condemns *printed books as a novelty of this later age; but a manuscript he pores on everlastingly, especially if the cover be all moth-eaten, and the dust make a parenthesis between every syllable.*[6] No end to their variety, and their whims are infinite; each has his own taste (apart from the semi-mad herd of imitators, fashion-mongers, who echo the taste of the originals); taste varies with class, condition, scholarship, etc., and even amongst the unlearned there are different palates. But a catalogue of them, I say, would be coextensive with books, ending only, if it could end, which I doubt, with the ultimate subdivision of books into infinitesimal variations and subtleties of typography, grammar, spelling, etc.

IV. OF BIBLIOCLASTS OR BOOK DESTROYERS

You have heard what bibliomania can do of itself to impel men to hoard and covet books with inordinate greed and passion, now you shall hear

[1] Satiricus Sculptor, Esq. *Chalcographimania.* (1814) 30.   [2] *Ib.* 31, n.   [3] Whistler, *Gentle Art of Making Enemies.* 149.   [4] *Life.* Cushing ii, 22.   [5] Burton, *The Book-Hunter.* 15.   [6] John Earle, 'An Antiquary', *Microcosmography.*

what it can perform, on the negative side, as an instigator of destruction, which is many times worse (if it be possible) than those precedent symptoms which I have dilated, because the satisfaction of their book-lust causes greater mischief. Few creatures more despicable than the book-destroyer. But they are not all mad: some are merely mischievous; the careless and their misaffections I reserve for another place. Some few there are who possess a whimsical sense of economy which moves them to destroy all those passages of a book which they dislike, and to retain only their favourite parts. Voltaire made such abridgements of celebrated authors, preserving only what he thought good, and frequently reducing several volumes to one;[1] Edward FitzGerald gutted his favourite books in a like manner and kept a library of rebound favourite pages at his home and on board his sailing boat *Scandal* at Lowestoft; another instance, recorded by Anatole France,[2] tells of a strange *bibliomaniac* in Paris who tore out so many offending pages that his library contained only one complete volume; the rest *were composed of fragments and remnants magnificently bound.*

I shall do no more than point at that other group of book-tearers who brag how they use unenjoyed books as *pipe-lighters.* I have an instance, in my own knowledge, of a poet who evoked a pittance by reviewing the works of his brother bards, and always left one of the reviewed copies on his hearth, from which he ripped up pages to light his pipe; and there is another case of a recent writer on books who ingenuously confessed that he kept a *condemned book handy* on his desk, *tearing leaves out when pipe-lighters or book-markers were in demand.*[3] There may be many such, but they are not our concern, being examples of vanity or cynicism rather than insanity, and I am of opinion that such inconveniences will be mitigated or most easily corrected if generally ignored. And with them I may leave those print and portrait collectors who look upon books as no more than hunting-grounds for pictures, or for extra-illustrating;[4] or those biblio-klepts who confine their thefts to pages of books rather than to whole volumes, some tricking the bookseller by buying a volume, reading it, removing a few pages, and then returning it as incomplete; many more, might I reckon up, who are a feral plague to books, as I have sufficiently declared; but read about them in Octave Uzanne, his *Book-Hunter in Paris.*

Closer to my theme and to madness more nearly allied are those cases of deliberate destruction to establish rarity. Dibdin, J. H. Burton recalls, *warmed his convivial guests at a comfortable fire, fed by woodcuts from which had been printed* the impression of his *Bibliographical Decameron.* It was *a quaint fancy,* he cracks, *deemed to be a pretty and appropriate form of hospitality, while*

[1] *Memoirs of Voltaire.* Chandon. 271. [2] *On Life and Letters.* 2nd Series. 65.
[3] W. G. Clifford, *Books in Bottles.* 12. [4] See 'Of Grangeritis', chap. xxviii, *post.*

it effectually assured the subscribers to his costly volumes that the vulgar world who buy cheap books was definitively cut off from participating in their privileges. [1] The great object of a collector, saith Grose, [2] *is to possess that not possessed by any other*, and he knew of one who paid *enormous prices* for scarce prints *in order to destroy them*, and by so doing make his own impressions more scarce and valuable. Of this kind also was Captain Douglas, the *Cruikshank* collector, who bought *several hundred copies* of *Points of Humour* at Dr. Truman's sale and made a *bonfire*, despite W. T. Spencer's protestations, of all save three copies. [3] Such a trick is common to many amateurs, even among growers of flowers, as those tulip specialists in Holland who are said to pay *their thousands of dollars for a duplicate tuber, that they may have the satisfaction of crushing it under the heel.* [4]

Among biblioclasts some act in groups, *cornering* copies of a rare book and making *a 'pool' of any volumes which are not immaculate;* from among these they *complete or perfect* as many copies as possible, and destroy the remainder; they will then *burn a work which is perfect*, provided that each member of the group has *a copy in better condition.* [5] Another would make an already rare book still more rare by acquiring all extant copies, as he also records. [6] They love to snatch them from the possession of normal collectors and to hug them to themselves. It was the great glory of one such grabber *to get hold of a unique book and shut it up. There were known to be just two copies of a spare quarto called 'Rout upon Rout, or the Rabblers Rabbled.' by Felix Nixon. He possessed one copy; the other, by indomitable perseverance, he also got hold of, and then his heart was glad within him; and he felt it glow with well-merited pride when an accomplished scholar, desiring to complete an epoch in literary history on which that book threw some light, besought the owner to allow him a sight of it, were it but for a few minutes, and the request was refused. 'I might as well ask him,' said the animal, who was rather proud of his firmness than ashamed of his churlishness, 'to make me a present of his brains and reputation.'*

But these are obvious tricks to gratify greed, get opinion or money, and for the most part they reveal morbid derangement, but it requires no especial argument to prove it; nor need we run so far for examples in worse kind, for we have a just volume published by William Blades to this purpose. In his *Enemies of Books*, he devotes a whole chapter to an account of book-tearers, destroyers, and the like, with several offenders' names together and a catalogue of their misdeeds. It was a chief caveat of his that *two-legged depredators, who ought to have known better, have perhaps*

---

[1] *The Book-Hunter.* 55. This incident is described under 'Books Artificially Rarefied'. xxii, *ante.*   [2] *Olio.* 57.   [3] Spencer, *Forty Years in My Bookshop.* 31.   [4] Burton, *Book-Hunter.* 54.   [5] Slater, *Romance of Book-Collecting.* 99–100.   [6] Burton, *op. cit.* 57.

done as much real damage in libraries as any other enemy;[1] Andrew Lang stoutly declares[2] such a *Book-Ghoul* to be *more hateful than the biblioklept,* because he combines larceny with destruction: *He is a collector of title-pages, frontispieces, illustrations, and book-plates. He prowls furtively among public and private libraries, inserting wetted threads, which slowly eat away the illustrations he covets; and he broods, like the obscene demon of Arabian superstitions, over the fragments of the mighty dead.* He divides this variety into three classes: *The antiquarian ghoul who steals title-pages and colophons. The æsthetic ghoul who cuts illuminated initials out of manuscripts;* and the *petty, trivial, and almost idiotic ghoul of our own days, who sponges the fly-leaves and boards of books for the purpose of cribbing the book-plates.*[3] This type is still regarded as a *Book-Ghoul,* even though his aim is *grangerization. Uncompromising book-collectors* branded James Gibbs, the grangerite-bookseller, as *a book-ghoul, a reptile who regards title-page and colophon as his natural prey.*[4] Distinguished among them was that *wicked old biblioclast,* John Bagford, a founder of the Society of Antiquaries, whose aberration was title-pages, imprints, colophons, etc., and *who went about the country, from library to library,* tearing them out of rare books of all sorts and sizes, pictures, title-pages, initials, colophons, etc., for the purpose of illustrating a *History of Printing,* which he contemplated writing, but proceeded no further with it than the pictures. Bagford was born in Fetter Lane, and died in the year 1816 at the age of sixty-five, of disappointment, it is said, because he lost hope of finding one of *Caxton's impossible title-pages,* for which he had searched all his life.[5]

In his younger days he had been a shoemaker, and later a bookseller, with a shop in the Great Turnstile. His professional life was spent collecting prints and books for Harley, Earl of Oxford, and John More, Bishop of Ely, whose libraries he greatly enriched, and his spare time in making his own collections[6] of title-pages, devices, emblems, cuts, prints, and tail-pieces, for his intended history, which, Dr. Richard Garnett in our day has maintained, he was not competent to write even if he had got all the materials.[7]

To make this great fardel, which filled forty-two folio volumes,[8] he travelled into Holland and other parts, and brought a vast number of scarce books and prints into England, the greater part of which were bought by the Earl of Oxford, whose *faithful book-jackall*[9] he was. Well may Dibdin[1] call him *the most hungry and rapacious of all book and print*

[1] *Enemies of Books.* 109.   [2] *The Library.* 56.   [3] *Ib.* 59.   [4] Locker-Lampson, *My Confidences.* 391.   [5] Humphrey Wanley catalogues them in a letter to Sir Hans Sloane. Nichols, *Anecdotes.* i, 530–6.   [6] Qt. Bulloch, *Art of Extra-Illustrating.* 15. [7] Now in the Harleian Coll., British Museum.   [8] Dibdin, *Bibliographical Decameron.* iii, 281, n.   [9] *Bibliomania.* (1811) 431, n.

collectors, for his ravages *spared neither the most delicate nor costly specimens;* and methinks·he says well when he asserts that *a modern collector and lover of perfect copies will witness, with shuddering, among Bagford's immense collection of title-pages in the Museum the frontispiece of the 'Complutensian Polyglot',* and Chauncy's *'History of Hertfordshire', torn out to illustrate an 'History of Printing';* this *scourge of the book-world* was responsible for the mutilation of 25,000 volumes, including such *priceless jewels* as the *Bible of Gutenberg* and the *Polyglot* of Cardinal Ximenes.[1]

But although his mania was noxious, there are those, as Hearne (in the preface to Guil. Roper, *Vita D. Thomae Mori*), who saw in him a useful protector of curious information and a guide to books which might else have been forgotten.[2] There is little doubt that Bagford had no sense of guilt in what he did; after the manner of all who are obsessed, mad, insane, crazy, he was convinced of his own rightness. He saw in his hoard of shreds and patches the raw material of knowledge, and not only did he rejoice in his own ghoulishness but in that of others also, as Wanley, who had collected *thousands of fragments of old writings, some near 1,000 years old,* including a *piece of Virgil, with figures not far beyond that in the Vatican.* His fragments were in *divers languages, Greek, Latin, Saxon, etc.,* and he gloats on the thought that in extent and variety *the like is not in Europe,* and that with proper encouragement, *as Mabillon had in France,* we might have had even *a greater variety of specimens from him.* In extenuation of this hoard of devastated documents Bagford claims that *no man could make better use of them,* that Wanley was probably the first that ever made the discovery that MSS. were used by the ancients as *Palimpsests: some years ago, in the Bodleian Library, he showed me a MS. in Greek that had been twice wrote on;* he is also *an excellent critick of the antiquity of all sorts of letters, Greek, Roman, Gothic, Saxon, etc., what century they were wrote in, the several sorts of ink in each country; the vellum, paper, parchment they were wrote on;* besides all of which, he saith, *he intends towards a Saxon Bible;* therefore *this collection of his deserves a very great encomium.*[3]

In our own time W. C. Hazlitt[4] has warned us to recall, before we *condemn these biblioclasts, that it is not so much that they have rendered books imperfect by the abstraction of leaves or title-pages, as that they have actually preserved the sole testimony for the existence of hundreds of tracts, broadsides, books, etc.* I do thankfully acknowledge it, but 'tis to no purpose to destroy your subject in order to make history, this smacks too much of those

[1] Elton, *Great Book-Collectors.* 121.   [2] De Ricci among moderns thinks that 'John Bagford has perhaps been maligned', for 'he seems to have gathered his materials, not so much by mutilating complete volumes, as by saving from destruction imperfect copies', etc. *English Collectors of Books and Manuscripts.* 34.   [3] *Gentleman's Magazine.* (1816) ii, 509–10.   [4] *Book-Collecting.* 124.

Chinamen who burned their houses down to procure roast pig;[1] he that does as much is an intemperate, a weak, a silly, and indiscreet man, and a mischievous biblioclast to boot. The like may be said of all biblioclasts, whatever their object: *such a pursuit is neither useful nor meritorious, even if you shut your eyes to the injury done,* and indulge your admiration for *the great beauty in some of the titles,* as William Blades would do with that collection made by a more recent idiot, Proeme, who had a *craze* for *title-pages,* which *he ruthlessly extracts, frequently leaving the decapitated carcase of the books, for which he cares not, behind him.* Unlike Bagford, he had no object, no excuse, but simply followed *a senseless kind of classification,* filling volume after volume, one with *engraved titles,* another with *coarse or quaint titles,* a third with *Printer's devices.*[2] He makes mention[3] of a *similar mania* for hoarding the *illuminated initials* taken from the pages of ancient MSS., which was common at the beginning of last century; he himself bought one such collection of beautiful fragments comprising *a large portion of nearly twenty different MSS., mostly Horae, showing twelve varieties of fifteenth-century handwriting in Latin, French, Dutch, and German.* But such collections are less easily come by in our own day, for the world has grown out of its biblioclasts, or weeded them out; and however much we tolerated the book-tearer in times past, he would receive short shrift from our modern bookmen; perchance past orgies of destruction have glutted and wearied our passion in that kind, for we must be besotted ere we become wise, and dazed before we can be led.

---

[1] Lamb, 'Dissertation on Roast Pig', *Essays of Elia.*   [2] Blades, *Enemies of Books.*
112–13.   [3] *Ib.* 117–18.

Part XXVIII

OF GRANGERITIS

—————————⟨⟩—————————

I. GRANGERITIS DIAGNOSED

Many men prefer pictures, engravings, etchings, lithographs, prints of all kinds, to books, and among them are those chalcographian[1] dizzards, mad on picture-books, who look upon the printed word solely as the raw material of graphic interpretation; they have no use for books but to extend them inordinately by a process called *Grangerizing*, or *extra-illustration*, which is defined as the insertion *of prints which do not belong to the book, but which are pertinent to the subject treated:*[2]

> Torn from their destined page (unworthy meed
> Of knightly counsel, and heroic deed),
> Not Faithorne's stroke, nor Field's own types can save
> The gallant Veres, and one-eyed Ogle brave.
> Indignant readers seek the image fled
> And curse the busy fool, who—*wants a head;*[3]

and although, as Tredwell, a notorious offender, will have, *no man ever became an illustrator who was not a lover of books,*[4] du Bois as emphatically gives out that it is a *singularly perverted idea, conceived at a time when there were no book-lovers.*[5]

Grangerizing is a vehement passion, a furious perturbation to be closely observed and radically treated wherever it appears, for it is a contagious and delirious mania endangering many books: finely illustrated volumes having least immunity from this mischievous form of collecting. *Nulla scabies*, as he said,[6] *superstitione scabiosor:* as he that is bitten with a mad dog bites others, and all in the end become mad; either out of affection of novelty, vanity, or blind zeal, the giddy-headed will embrace the *deep intricacies of Granger,*[7] and without farther examination approve them.

[1] This word was used by James Caulfield in his Hudibrastic 'poem', *Chalcographimania*, published pseudonymously in 1814, to expose the excesses of the print-collectors and print-sellers of that time.   [2] Tredwell, *Privately Illustrated Books.* 29.
[3] Ferriar, *Bibliomania.* 121–7.   [4] *Op. cit.* 55.   [5] *Four Private Libraries of New York.* 117.   [6] 'No scab festers worse than superstition.' Jovianus Pont. *Ant. Dial.*
[7] Satiricus Sculptor, Esq., *Chalcographimania.* (1814) 14.

One authority goes so far as to make it the extreme stage of bibliomania: it is *so far removed from the indicative stages* of the disease *as to render it entirely inappropriate as a proper single characteristic; it is,* he says, *the whole disease in its worst form.*[1] Dibdin goes even further when he frankly declares that *the Grangerite is madder than the Bibliomaniac.*[2] But these commentators exaggerate, for, miserable infatuation though it is, grangeritis is but a symptom, and it is often isolated from other morbid tendencies of bookishness. Field is more to be relied on when he regards it as only *one of the unfortunate stages of bibliomania.* He believes that its period of activity is five years, but he has heard of a case of ten years' duration which *still gives no symptom of abating in virulence.*[3] Another of my authorities believes that it has no *incipient stage of infection* in America, but bursts *out full grown and equipped like Pallas Athena from the brain of Jupiter.*[4] It has few defenders save those afflicted, for it is obnoxious and insensate unless confined within the bounds set by Dibdin[5] and Bulloch,[6] namely, the construction of commentaries out of such materials as newspapers, magazines, and other periodicals, or separate and specially made pictures, as photographs, etchings, engravings, etc. All other forms are morbid and biblioclastic, deserving the castigations which have been used against them, for although it is not the whole of bibliomania, it is *a very general and violent symptom;*[7] the patient is *a sort of literary Attila or Gengis Khan, who has spread terror and ruin around him;*[8] and he pursues his *obscene passion*[9] with a *fiendish fascination:*[10] *the moment* Irving Brown[11] *came into possession of a book, it was put under the rack to extort its capacity for illustration.*[12] *Of one hundred books extended by the insertion of prints which were not made for them, ninety-nine are ruined; the hundredth book is no longer a book: it is a museum, or at best, a crazy-quilt made of patches cut out of gowns of queens and scullions.*[13]

Its origin is unknown. Most authorities make the Rev. James Granger its first exponent, and they designate it after him; but, as Dibdin prescribes, whoever will be at the pains of reading the preface of the *Biographical History of England*, will see that Granger *sheltered himself under the authorities of Evelyn, Ashmole, and others, and that he alone is not to be considered as responsible for all the mischief which this passion for collecting prints has occasioned.*[14] The monks of Little Gidding were pre-Granger grangerizers, and so, if we are to believe Bulloch,[15] was that *infinitely Curious and Inquisitive* Richard Smith, whose books were sold at auction in Great Bartholo-

[1] Harper, *Book-Lovers, Bibliomaniacs and Book Clubs.* 32.   [2] *Bibliomania.* (1811) 680. Note.   [3] *Love Affairs of a Bibliomaniac.* 154.   [4] Tredwell, *Privately Illustrated Books.* 54.   [5] *Bibliomania.* (1811) 669.   [6] *Art of Extra-Illustrating. Passim.*   [7] Dibdin, *op. cit.* 666–7.   [8] Burton, *Book-Hunter.* 83.   [9] Locker-Lampson, *My Confidences.* 391.   [10] Bulloch, *op. cit.* 14.   [11] A lawyer of Troy, U.S.A.   [12] Tredwell, *op. cit.* 114–15.   [13] H. P. du Bois, *Four Private Libraries of New York.* 117.   [14] *Bibliomania.* (1809) 61.   [15] *Op. cit.* 10.

mew's Close on May 15th, 1682. But there is little doubt that it was at its height in Granger's day, when it swept through the realm of books *with undiminished force*[1] like an epidemic. Granger stimulated the *germ*, he did not invent it:

> by Granger school'd
> In Paper-books, superbly gilt and tool'd,
> He pastes, from injur'd volumes snipt away,
> His *English Heads*, in chronicled array.[2]

The diseased were first impelled to attack historical works, *Clarendon* being a favourite victim. It soon spread to assaults on the poets, the first to feel the blow being Shakespeare and Chatterton. Then the insensate taste for spoliation spread in all directions. Tredwell says that two classes of books have an *irresistible attractiveness* for grangerizers, sport and drama,[3] but he also knew an enthusiast who extended *The Book of Cats*, by Charles H. Ross, and another, for there is no limit to this taste, who grangerized bawdry. But when they are truly possessed with this odd zeal, and misled with ambition, grangerites find many other baits to inveigle and lure their passion, they go farther and yet farther afield, and under cover of the search for perfection they become crazy in their desire not to miss an illustratable point or find a suitable picture:

> Who, swearing not a line to miss,
> Doats on the leaf his fingers kiss,
> Thanking the *Words* for all his bliss.[4]

As the dotage spreads it awakens and links up with hitherto dormant business instincts, so that many booksellers, printsellers, etc., have seized the advantage and made a pot of money out of the disease, as Purcell, of Red Lion Passage, and Harvey, of St. James's Street, who were almost *as much printsellers as booksellers, making one book by destroying many others;*[5] and James Gibbs, of Great Newport Street, *who, in his time*, says Locker-Lampson,[6] *has illustrated a great number of books*, and *ruthlessly sacrificed, mutilated, and broken up many a rare but probably imperfect work*. His chief passion was the *Bible*, which he extended to *more than sixty volumes folio, each so thick that he could hardly lift it from the counter;* the number of *Bibles* he cut up in erecting this monument would (saith mine author) have *satisfied Mr. Tom Paine.*

Such symptoms are common to them all, whether they are amateurs or whether they make a trade of it. Not that these things (as I have said

[1] Dibdin, *op. cit.* 668.   [2] Ferriar, *Bibliomania.* 117–20.   [3] *Privately Illustrated Books.* 104.   [4] Beresford, *Bibliosophia.* v.   [5] Roberts, *Book-Hunter in London.* 165.
[6] *My Confidences.* 390–1.

of pluralism) are to be discommended of themselves, for they are helpful in some cases and good,and I therefore admit that proviso of Roberts', who still regards *the system as in many ways a pernicious one*, although *a vast amount of cant* has been *wasted* on it.

II. LEGITIMATE GRANGERIZING

It is, perchance, in this place, proper to distinguish between *grangerizing* and what I have named *grangeritis*: the first is normal, if it makes knowledge, information, or delight its object; as those curious collections of Gibbs of *Barbers* and Broadley of *Corpulence*, which I can imagine entertaining and instructive; or, again, if it adds interest to a volume by, as one advises,[1] reasonable augmentation rather than deliberate extension, I see no harm done. The second is a morbid state because of an inflamed ambition to push the illustration of a theme to its furthest conclusions in each and every one of its essential and inessential ramifications. In this way madness lies, not alone in hectic research and wild pursuit of materials, but in the character of the passion which seeks to substitute pictures for thoughts and the written word, in itself a notable relapse into barbarism, which is a general symptom of inferior minds, as they who promote picture-theatres and picture-papers well know. *No book was ever yet written*, one addict confesses, *which is so self-rendering that it may not be invested with new qualities or brightened with a new halo by illustration.*[2] Such lapses are to be avoided. The best means to avoid such inconveniences is to take away causes and occasions.

To this purpose J. M. Bulloch, in his treatise of *The Art of Extra-Illustration*, supposes that legitimate grangerizing concerns itself with the preservation and co-ordination of useful or prospectively useful information from our ephemeral periodical publications; and he gives as a special reason the fact that such popular journals, pamphlets, etc., have less chance of survival in private collections than more serious and permanent works, *what is common to-day almost invariably* becoming *rare to-morrow*; and, even in these days, searching the files of newspapers at the public libraries is discommended because of its inconvenience and toilsomeness. Who would proceed in this wise, and I commend his tenets, should consult him, for he reckons up many ingenious devices. And I would add that if grangerizing be thus opportunely and soberly used there is no argument against its further extension into those less purposeful realms of personal pleasure wherein whim, fancy, predilection, are sole inspirers and concomitants,

[1] H. P. du Bois, *Four Private Libraries of New York*. 118.   [2] Tredwell, *Privately Illustrated Books*. 436.

especially for those who are engaged most part in affairs. Such recreations are pleasant and medicinal, in support of which I commend Machiavelli's reply to a friend who reprehended him for dancing as beside his dignity: *qui sapit interdiu vix unquam noctu desipit,* he that is wise by day is seldom foolish at night.

I will, however, leave the choice of book or subject to those concerned, the whole world of letters being open to them, and there being no region without interest to the scientific or curious explorer. And if, I say again, good things may be abused, and that which was first invented to refresh men's weary spirits when they come from other labours and studies, to exhilarate the mind, to entertain time and company (tedious otherwise in long solitary winter nights), and keep them from worse matters; if so honest an exercise is contrarily perverted, yet I will take the chance with all good bookmen, warning them against those bad ones whom I condemn; and in this good hope proceed.

III. BOOK GHOULS

In the other extreme, or in the defect, march those impious biblioclasts, book-tearers, book-ghouls, collectomaniacs and dizzards, impenitent, unthankful ego-maniacs, that will acknowledge no standards of book-conduct outside their own, and in such matters have cauterized consciences,[1] behave in a reprobate sense towards books, and are thus unworthy of our mercy. Tredwell confesses[2] that the first book to be grangerized by him was Giraud's *Birds of Long Island,* for which he *dismembered the rare and splendid* quarto belonging to *The Natural History of the State of New York.* He never forgave himself for that *piece of vandalism,* yet he has *committed many and greater since,* and naively excuses himself on the ground that a man cannot be *an orthodox collector or a true bibliophile who had not at one time committed a great and foolish extravagance;* and he exonerates others of his kind, even those who have *pitchforked prints into folios badly mounted, and sometimes mutilated,* because they have saved prints from destruction.

Such fellows are no better than bookish impostors, well deserving the anathemas that have been heaped upon them by bibliophiles, as that stout imprecation of William P. Cutter[3] against those who have grangerized Dibdin: *May the spectre of Thomas Frognall Dibdin haunt the souls of these impious rascals, and torture them with never-ceasing visions of unobtainable and rare portraits, non-existent autographs, and elusive engravings;* and well may he thus execrate them in the name of Dibdin, for the *Bibliomania* and the

---

[1] 1 Timothy iv, 2.   [2] *Privately Illustrated Books.* 29–30, 37.   [3] Qt. Harper, *Book-Lovers, Bibliomaniacs and Book Clubs.* 33.

Decameron are favourite resorts for their orgies, as Dibdin knew: *Pamphilephus possesses a copy of Mr. Dibdin's 'Decameron' in 10 vols. ornamented to suffocation with embellishments; such a series, or congeries, of graphic illustrations —comprising everything remote and capricious—was surely never before concentrated or brought together;*[1] this, perchance, was the copy referred to by mine author in his *Reminiscences*[2] as belonging to George Henry Freeling, Esq., and now expanded by *two octavo supplements*, and another, *not quite completed, in folio;* each volume was bound in morocco by Charles Lewis, *with distinct title and woodcut;* there were *about fifteen hundred* extra illustrations in the original ten volumes, and they are *at once the most felicitous and stupendous triumph of book-ardour* with which he is acquainted. Again, he records[3] how William Turner, a *worthy wight* resident in Islington, extra-illustrated the *Bibliomania* with 211 prints; the *Decameron* with 400 prints; the *Tour* with 961 prints in large paper and 517 in small paper; the *Bibliotheca Spenceriana* and *Aedes Althorpianae* with 389 prints, and the *Library Companion* with 593 prints. *O rare William Turner!* he exclaims, abandoning his earlier condemnation of such practices, *to talk of seeing 'his like again' is mere, visionary prattle!*

Those afflicted by this derangement are the most flagrant of all book-defectives, for they soon expose themselves to a *reductio ad absurdum*, refining upon refinement, extending the limited by the illusion of size, deepening the shadows by reflections, pushing variety to the perdition of inane repetition, and translating the opportunity of a pictorial record of historical events into an impenitent hair-splitting, as John Hill Burton well shows in his satirical suggestions for grangerizing Isaac Watts, the lines,

> How doth the little busy bee
> Improve each shining hour,
> And gather honey all the day
> From every opening flower!

The verse prescribes for all the portraits of the author; pictures of houses in which he was born and lived; all the views of Southampton and its Gothic Gate and Wall, etc.; any *scraps* connected with the inauguration of the Watts statue; a picture of the poet being whipped at school for making verses instead of attending to his studies; all kinds of engravings of bees, bee-hives, with a portrait of Huber, and views of Mt. Hybla; picture of Samson and the Lion, illustrations of the Fable of the *Bear and the Bees*, or of the Roman story of the *Sic vos non vobis;* illustration of periodical called *The Bee*, and portrait of its editor, Dr. Anderson, and any prints illustrating his pursuits; portrait of the editor's grandfather, Sir James Outram, *the*

[1] *Bibliophobia.* 44.   [2] ii, 649–51.   [3] *Ib.* i, 325–6.

Bayard of the Indian Service, and illustrations of his career; engravings of the Life of Bayard, and of the Bourbons, who introduced bees into the insignia of royalty in France. *When the illustrator comes to the last line, which invites him to add to what he has already collected a representation of 'every opening flower'*, it is easy to see that he has indeed a rich garden of *delights before him*.[1] Many will recognize in this irony a true picture of the operations of the covetous wretch, *the monster that doth make the meat he feeds on*, and whose chief danger is his aptitude for such an overweening dotage that he will go on in ever widening circles of destruction, for books are but the raw material of his mania.

Such are the common effects of this intemperance, but lest you may conclude that he exaggerates, I will show to what an extent this infirmity can be carried by giving the famous example of the extra-illustrated *Clarendon* in the Bodleian. In the first rank of grangerizers I may well reckon Alexander Hendraw Sutherland, F.S.A., who *extended* the six folio volumes of Clarendon's *History of the Rebellion* and *Life*, and Burnet's *History of Our Own Times*, into sixty-one volumes in elephant folio, by inlaying and binding up 19,224 illustrations at a cost of £20,000. Sutherland began his task in 1795, and when he died, in 1820, it was continued and completed by his widow, who presented the stupendous collection to the Bodleian in 1837. *Every person and views of every place in any way mentioned in the text, or connected with its subject-matter*, saith Macray,[2] is illustrated: there are 743 portraits of Charles I; 552 of Charles II; 431 of William III; 373 of Cromwell; 276 of James II; 184 of James I; and 175 of Mary II; of topographical views there is the same extravagance, 309 of London, 166 of Westminster, etc. This is not the only example, nor is it yet alone in its obesity, for Davenport records[3] that *a Mr. Irwin of Oswep* extended the *Bible* to sixty volumes; Mouravit tells how de Saint-Mauris distended the *Works* of Voltaire with 12,800 portraits, those of notable personages being repeated as often as their names were mentioned in the text;[4] whole libraries could be made of such escapades; Tredwell *grangerized* sixty different works, and he had a library of three hundred *extended* books.[5] And if many are but toys to these, they are parts and main actions of grangeritis, which, with such exceptions as I have set apart for tolerance, are the capers of crazed imaginations, and sane bookmen will uphold Field when he says that *there is more joy over one Grangerite that repenteth than over ninety and nine just men that need no repentance*.[6]

---

[1] *Book-Hunter*. 83–6.   [2] *Annals*. 331–3.   [3] *Byways among English Books*. 17.
[4] *Le Livre et la Petite Bibliothèque d'Amateur*. 186.   [5] Tredwell, *Privately Illustrated Books*. 32.   [6] *Love Affairs of a Bibliomaniac*. 155.

Part *XXIX*

THE CURE OF BIBLIOMANIA

———————⟪◇⟫———————

I. WHETHER IT IS CURABLE OR NOT

Inveterate bibliomania, howsoever it may seem to be a continuate, inexorable disease (*that incurable mental infirmity*[1]), hard to be cured, accompanying them to their graves most part, as Thomas Rawlinson, who lived and died *in his bundles, piles, and bulwarks of paper, in dust and cobwebs;*[2] yet many times it may be helped, even that which is most violent, or at least, according to Ferriar,[3] it may be mitigated by reading:

> With deep concern the curious bid me tell,
> Why no Black-letter dignifies my cell?
> No Caxton? Pynson? In defence I plead
> One simple fact: I only buy to read.

Dibdin[4] believes that *Grangeritis*, a virulent and dangerous form of the disease, is *the least liable to mischief, if judiciously treated*, but in its advanced stages it is *almost incurable*; an opinion supported by Eugene Field.[5] It may, therefore, be hard to cure, but not impossible, for him even who is most grievously affected, if he be but willing to be helped. *Nil desperandum.* Having discovered the cause, to effect a cure will depend upon your power to remove it, and no mere argument can do that, for the truth is, as Glanvill long ago suspected, *this world is a very Bedlam, and he that would cure Madmen, must not attempt it by Reasoning, or indeavour to shew the absurdity of their Conceits; but such a course must be taken, as may restore the Mind to a right Crasis; and that (when it is effected) will reduce, and rectifie the extravagances of the distemper'd Brain, which Disputes and Oppositions will but inflame and make worse.* Thus he instances when *frantick persons are fond of Feathers, and mightily taken with the employment of picking straws*, no use to expound to them *the vanity of the Objects of their Delights;* and when, he adds, the Melancholist is afraid to sit down, *supposing himself of Glass*, little purpose to declare to him *the ridiculousness of his Fears;* the *disposition of the Head* must be altered before the *particular Phrensie* can be cured.[6]

---

[1] R. M. Field. Pref. E. Field, *Love Affairs of a Bibliomaniac.* v.   [2] Oldys, *Memoir and Diary.* 101.   [3] *Bibliomania.*   [4] *Bibliomania.* (1811) 668.   [5] *Op. cit.* 144.
[6] 'The Usefulness of Real Philosophy to Religion', *Essays.* (1676) 14-15.

Upon this good hope I will proceed, using the same method in the cure which I have formerly used in rehearsing of the causes: first general, then particular; and those according to their general species. *Does this madness*

> Grow with our growth, and strengthen with our strength?

Will not such volcanic fury burn out in time?[1] Many are of opinion that the blind and headstrong passion is a habit, *morbus sonticus* or *chronicus*, a chronic or continuate disease, a settled humour, not errant, but fixed; and as it was long increasing, so, now being (pleasant or painful) grown to a habit, it will hardly be removed; counsel can do no good: once a bibliomane, always a bibliomane:

> Quae enim res in se neque consilium neque modum
> Habet ullum, eam consilio regere non potes.[2]

> Which thing hath neither judgement nor an end,
> How should advice or counsel it amend?

If once he become a collector of books, *nothing will ever cure him; he may not have time to look at them after he has bought them; nor shelves on which to place them; nor, if some people may be believed, money to pay for them;* even, says my authority,[3] during the European war, when food was short, taxation crushing, funds low, there were many who thus continued undauntedly to collect books, which I can support out of mine own experience.

Others take the opposite side, and one good authority[4] asserts that certain manifestations of the disease carry with them their own cure. There are those who multiply editions of the same book *regardless of text; who possess more separate Bibles than there are chapters in Holy Writ; who pounce upon every volume in which the name of Shakespeare is mentioned;* such a deliberate and cold-blooded game might be played with balls or counters, the man who indulges in it has no stability, he says, and may at any moment *break away to the collecting of orchids or pen-wipers.* They change from one to another like the wolf, who, though never so hungry and ready to eat, yet if he see another prey, he forsakes his meat and follows after it. Such a wolf, Pliny holds,[5] in the heart is ambitious to covetousness: it makes no use of what it hath got, but greedily hunteth after more, even to the extent of Aesop's dog, who lost the bone in his mouth by snapping at its reflection in the water.

But cases of this kind, though common enough, are not to be reckoned more than having a likeness to true bibliomania. An Ohio physician

---

[1] Dibdin, *Bibliomania*. (1811) 583.   [2] Terence. *Eun.* I, i, 12–13.   [3] *The Author.*
April 1918.   [4] Gosse, *The Library of Edmund Gosse.* xiii.   [5] *Nat. Hist.* i, 22.

named Woodbury (Eugene Field recalls)[1] says *that bibliomania can be aborted*, but on the other hand *a very large majority of his profession are of the opinion that the actual malady must run a regular course*, and they maintain that *the cases quoted as cured by Woodbury were not genuine, but were bastard or false phases*, like *chickenpox* and the *German measles*. There is something in this argument, for many curable cases of so-called bibliomania are rather to be classed at large among those who are afflicted with that morbid acquisitiveness which is endemic in our civilization and as varied as it is widespread. They dote on any portable properties that take their fancy, how useless, how absurd, is no matter:

> Some gems collect; some medals prize,
> And view the rust with lovers' eyes.[2]

They pounce upon things which are useless save for their purpose, and it suffices if they can hoard them up. *Collecting*, saith La Bruyère, *is not a taste for what is good and beautiful, but for what is rare and unique, for things that other men do not possess*.[3] Thus they accumulate old china, jewels, precious stones, silver and gold wares, brass candlesticks, bellows, snuff-boxes, coins, medals, pictures; or those wonders of nature, butterflies, beetles, birds' eggs, etc., beautiful in their place, but petty tragedies in a show-case and as like nature as waxworks at a village fair are like men. But mark how they covet and hoard as much all manner of useless used things, second-hand, outworn: as crests, postage stamps, postmarks; some are mad for suits of armour, old swords, rifles, pistols, and other engines of war; daggers, stilettos, rapiers, cartridge cases, blunderbusses, or old shakos and helmets of soldiers and policemen, cudgels, batons, etc., no end to this mania, as all know full well: man is a *collecting animal, he makes collections of everything*.[4] *Vexat mentes insana cupido*, they are mad upon their sport, cranks, fanatics. *There has lately been an auction of stuffed birds*, Horace Walpole tells Mann, *and*, he says, *as natural history is in fashion, there are physicians and others who paid forty and fifty guineas for a single Chinese pheasant; you may buy a live one for five*.[5] Mr. *Robert Samber*, Oldys records,[6] collected *all the printed tobacco-papers he could anywhere light of;* Sir Walter Raleigh met an American who bragged that he was *the only scissors-fancier in the world*, and who claimed to have collected *three tons weight of scissors, including most that had belonged to the crowned heads of Europe;*[7] but these are toys in comparison with those *cat-tail maniacs* of the

---

[1] *Love Affairs of a Bibliomaniac*. 51.   [2] Gay, 'To a Lady on Her Passion for Old China'.   [3] 'The Enthusiastic Collector', *Selections*. Lee. 68.   [4] Tredwell, *Privately Illustrated Books*. 48.   [5] *Letters*. Cunningham. v, 236.   [6] *Memoir and Diary*. 98.   [7] *Letters*. i, 182–3.

United States of America, who, saith Henry Harper,[1] *amputated and preserved the tails of as many cats in the neighbourhood as they could.*

That they change readily from one fad to another at the command of
this fashion or that, as children hoard tram-tickets, cigarette-cards and the
like, cannot be denied, and it is not all folly, but rather to be commended
in moderation if they are saved thus from sillier prepossessions; nor would
I condemn all collecting spontaneously derived, knowing as I do that such
hobbies, even when unscientifically disposed, are valuable sedatives and
lenitives for distracted and aimless men. I would prefer, therefore, to stop
this argument with a generous opinion of Mark Rutherford that *men
should not be too curious in analysing and condemning any means which nature
devises to save them from themselves, whether it be coins, old books, curiosities,
butterflies, or fossils.*[2] Yet it is an erroneous opinion that these fopperies,
wherewith the world is so much affected, have (I say again) any profound
relationship with bibliomania or many germane symptoms. Hoarders of
this kind are collectors and nothing more; 'tis an accident, a mere chance,
what they collect, books or what not; and the things on which they dote
are of the moment, mere birds of passage, subjects of a caprice, a fickle
mood; they love and loathe all sorts according to whim:

> The Worldly Hope men set their Hearts upon
> Turns Ashes—or it prospers; and anon,
>   Like Snow upon the Desert's dusty Face
> Lighting a little Hour or two—is gone.[3]

With books it is the same, there is no personal attachment, and an *impersonal collector of books is a mere conduit pipe. he has never really owned a
book at all, he has simply become a channel between one owner and another, a
mere fiction of conveyance.*[4] But let no man think that these fickle ones are
free of all taint: they are mad while they dote, and may flit restlessly from
one lust of acquisition to another, as all know. D. H. Lawrence[5] hath an
instance in his story 'None of that', of a woman who was *mad on 'things'*,
but *only for a time*. She got tired of everything, *especially of her own enthusiasms*. But while the attack lasted it was a passionate craze. At one time
she hoarded old furniture and brocades: *she would go mad if she saw someone
get a piece of velvet brocade with the misty bloom of years on it, that she coveted.
She coveted such things with lust, and would go into a strange sensual trance,
looking at some old worm-eaten chair.*

'Tis in vain to set upon those that are thus busy: whilst the lust is on
them they are mad, whether it is for books, pictures, china, medals, or any

---

[1] *Book-Lovers, Bibliomaniacs and Book Clubs.* 15.   [2] *Autobiography.* Coll. Ed. 107.
[3] *Omar Khayyam.* Trans. FitzGerald. 1st Ed. 14.   [4] F. York Powell, Intro. *Cat.
Lib. of Gleeson White.* (1899) x-xi.   [5] *The Woman Who Rode Away.* 273.

other thing, but it is an *acute* madness and may pass with its immediate or remote cause. For the most part they are harmless to all save themselves, and they harm themselves mainly in the loss of the profound or subtle tastes and sensations which come with love and constancy. Marcel Proust[1] would imply that distinction between one form of collectomania and another is largely determined by the object of the pursuit: *certainly,* he concludes, *it is more reasonable to devote one's life to women than to postage stamps or old snuff-boxes, even to pictures or statues;* most women, at least, will approve this saying, although they will be less unanimous in his final warning against the perils of obsession; *make changes,* he advises, *have not one woman only, but several*: a policy which hath been carried to its logical conclusion among Mahommedans and several other peoples, but without overcoming Proust's difficulty that to live with a woman altogether is to cease *to see any of the things that made you love her,* for variety is not immune from the indifference, the blunted taste of undue familiarity and monotony. In all such cases depth of love is the remedy, and the argument equally applies to book-collecting. Those who hoard books regardless of their contents, who follow *the bare pleasure of collecting for the sake of collecting,* are reduced to *an ignoble delight in indulging acquisitiveness,* and if they are, Pollard observes,[2] *redeemed to some extent by the higher pleasure of overcoming difficulties and observing the rules of the game,* they are still like *rose-fanciers who cannot distinguish one odour from another.*

II. VARIOUS CURES CONSIDERED

The bibliomane may vary the theme of his craze from one kind of book to another, but not from books to lesser things, nor would I advise such an attempt, for bibliomania is developed, not by what it feeds on but by the manner of its feeding: *a passion for books is perfectly compatible with any situation, however active and arduous;*[3] but it must be a normal controllable and useful passion; and if, as one saith,[4] *a bibliomaniac might be called an insane or crazy bibliophile,* the remedy is to expel what is insane, crazy, morbid, as Guicciardini[5] quotes (out of *Crol. Chym.*) *praecipuum in medico, qui aegrotum curat, ut cor bene defendat,* the first work of physic in a diseased body is to repel the venomous humours from the heart; because a disease once seated in this metropolis is incurable: *though ye take from a covetous man all his treasure,* saith Milton,[6] *he hath yet one jewell left; ye cannot bereave*

---

[1] *The Guermantes' Way.* Trans. Scott-Moncrieff. ii, 58.   [2] Alfred W. Pollard, *Fine Books.* 7.   [3] Dibdin, *Bibliomania.* (1811) 423.   [4] Harper, *Book-Lovers, Bibliomaniacs and Book Clubs.* 13.   [5] *Aphorismes Civill and Militarie.* Trans. Dallington. (1629) 44.   [6] *Areopagitica.* Ed. Holt White. 89.

him of his covetousness; and since bibliomania is a perversion of booklove, it must be treated by causing books to be rightly understood and seasonably applied.

This remedy is prescribed upon many occasions, with the object of translating the derangement of passion into the sanity of affection, the desire for possession into the desire for use. *Desire to have many books, and never to use them, is like a child,* saith Peacham,[1] *that will have a candle burning by him, all the while he is sleeping;* the remedy implied is to use his books; let him read them. *Books were made for use, and not for ostentation,* saith another commentator,[2] *in vain do they boast of full libraries that are contented to live with empty heads.* But how to fill their heads they do not say, and the cure is not easy, for you have your horse at the water but you cannot make him drink. Yet I have no doubt that the canalization of an idle and morbid passion into a practical study of books as books, or of any science or art which they express, is the best of all prophylactics against madness, for, *in spite of folly, vulgarity and extravagance, the collecting of books is a pursuit for sane people. Its heart is sound, and its very blood is the record of man's achievement in the conquest of knowledge;* the collector must make his collection *a marshalling of the evidence which exists in some corner—however small and dark—of the hall of written knowledge,* he will then, says my authority,[3] find his pursuit profitable, useful, and pleasant; and, I will add, may thus escape dotage, as Eugene Field, whose *mania for books kept him continually buying,* but *the love of books supervened to make them a part of himself and his life.*[4]

The love of bibliomaniacs for first editions filled Tennyson with *horror,* for *first editions are in many cases the worst editions;*[5] he would have them read books at their best, and not hoard them for the foppery of chronological precedence. Most bibliophiles, though loving first editions for sufficient reasons, would support him. I could cite many opinions, as Sir Edmund Gosse, whose collection owned many most excellent books in numerous rare states: *I have been a bibliophile, but never in the least a bibliomaniac,*[6] he says; or Beverley Chew,[7] himself a bibliophile, when he says of his friends, those great American bookmen, Robert Hoe and Winston H. Hagen, that the one in the midst of his books ever impressed him with *the wide extent of his reading,* and that the other *became a collector because he was essentially a book-lover and student of literature.* Dr. Johnson supports such collecting, although he disapproved of collecting many editions of a book, *which were all the same, except as to the paper and print,* but *he would*

---

[1] *The Compleat Gentleman.*   [2] Sir W. Waller. *Divine Meditations.*   [3] Williams, *Elements of Book-Collecting.* 11.   [4] R. M. Field. Intro. *Love Affairs of a Bibliomaniac.*
[5] *Memoir.* By Hallam, Lord Tennyson. i, 118.   [6] *The Library of Edmund Gosse.* xiii.
[7] *Essays and Verses about Books.* 100-103.

have the original, and all the translations, and all the editions which had any variations in the text.[1] He commended the collection of editions of *Horace* made by the learned Dr. Douglas, who had a closet filled with them; and he concludes that *every man should try to collect one book in that manner, and present it to a publick library.*

> To prove me, Goddess! clear of all design,
> Bid me with Pollio sup, as well as dine:
> There all the learn'd shall at the labour stand,
> And Douglas lend his soft, obstetric hand.[2]

As much difference between a bibliophile and a bibliomaniac, saith Harper,[3] as between *a slight cold and the advanced stages of consumption*, and he prescribes *rational treatment* if we would bring the bibliomaniac back into *the congenial folds of bibliophilism*, but no response to this remedy if he has *passed beyond the curative stages into the vast and dreamy realms of extra-illustrating or 'grangerizing'*. No remedy but study for the mania of duplication, for, as Hill Burton[4] so well hath it, when the collector buys his first duplicate *it is like the first secret dram swallowed in the forenoon—the first pawning of the silver spoons—or any other first step downwards you may please to liken it to.* But study itself when it becomes an obsession is a symptom of bibliomania demanding special treatment; as in the case of the son of James Howell's friend, Master Serjeant D. *I fear*, saith Howell, *he hath too much mind for his body, and that superabounds with fancy, which brings him to these fits of distemper, proceeding from the black humour of melancholy; moreover, I have observ'd that he is too much given to his study and self-society, 'specially to converse with dead Men, I mean Books.* The remedy he prescribes is marriage: *I could wish he were well marry'd, it may wean him from that bookish and thoughtful humour. Women*, he decides, *were created for the comfort of men*, and he has known that some *have proved the best Helleborum.*[5] Yea, but this is very good counsel, and rightly applied to them that are young, and will use it, or that are able to work and get their living by the sweat of their brows, by their trade, profession, calling, etc., but what shall we do with them that are slaves to books by nature, impotent before the ravages of the book-disease?

Frederic Harrison prescribes[6] the study of *the doings of a great book-collector—who once lived in La Mancha.* Yes, but though Don Quixote trespassed in this kind, his dotage was not on books but on romantic tales, it was only when he ceased to be a bookman and became a man of action that he became also the dizzard who has enchanted bookfolk for three

---

[1] Boswell's *Life*. Ed. Hill. iv, 279.   [2] Pope, *Dunciad*. iv, 391–4.   [3] *Book-Lovers, Bibliomaniacs and Book Clubs*. 13–14.   [4] *The Book-Hunter*. 16.   [5] *Epistolae Ho-Elianae*. (1737) 357.   [6] *Choice of Books*. 87.

hundred years. Distraction may cure in some cases, as Howell hoped marriage would cure his friend's son; but if such remedies were efficacious there would be no married bibliomaniacs; and as this passion is most eminent in men, it is as common among married men as bachelors. I find, however, a relation by Gissing[1] which supports Howell's wife-cure. The particulars are these: Christopherson was a case of true bibliomania; he had all the symptoms of acquisitive dotage; he haunted the bookstalls; stacked books in his rooms, three deep against the walls; when he was reduced to poverty by a business failure, he still hunted and hoarded books, living on sixpence a day so that he could gratify his passion; his young wife (he was twenty years her elder) went out to work for him and joyfully allowed him to buy more books out of her earnings of thirty shillings a week; then her health failed and the country was prescribed as the only cure; a relative offered them a cottage free of rent, but would not allow the books to be taken there; Christopherson refused to go; his wife grew worse and was at the point of death, when his blind passion gave place to sanity; he sold most of his books, and they left for the country cottage (where his wife's health rallied), with only a small box of books, which he could conveniently read. He was thus cured by a tardy but true love of his wife.

Andrew Lang[2] says that *we can make* that dotage which is governed by what Sir William Watson calls

the futile decalogue of Mode,[3]

less useless by making it personal, not by following any fashion. And well he may, for fashion is a *fickle jade*, and those overcome by her are no more than fools, even when they are not mad. Fashion in the collecting of books is as capricious as in the reading of them; *it is not strange when as the greatest wonder lasteth but nine days*, says Lyly,[4] *that a new work should not endure but three months.* This is a puzzle which many have tried to answer without success; for fashion is as mysterious as it is powerful, nor is there a known remedy against it, we are all tainted: *every generation laughs at the old fashions, but follows religiously the new;*[5] but if, as he holds,[6] *it is the luxurious and dissipated who set the fashions which the herd so diligently follow*, the remedy is to break with the herd; and the way to begin is to collect only those books which you yourself prefer, which are necessary to you as a single separate person, and not one of the crowd. *Insist on yourself; never imitate.*[7] Fashion is meretriciously encouraged among collectors as, in Lyly's opinion, it was among publishers and tailors. *In my mind*, he argues,

[1] 'Christopherson', *The House of Cobwebs.* (1919) 47–67.   [2] *The Library.* xv.
[3] 'The Things that are more Excellent', *Poems.* i, 176.   [4] *Euphues.*   [5] Thoreau, *Walden.* (Scott Library) 24.   [6] *Ib.* 35.   [7] Emerson, *Essays.* 67.

Printers and Tailors are bound chiefly to pray for gentlemen, the one hath so many fantasies to print, the other such divers fashions to make, that the pressing-iron of the one is never out of the fire, nor the printing-press of the other any time lieth still, and there is little doubt they do much hurt upon minds that are impressive to such influences; but the only salvation is to resist them, within reason, for to be out of the fashion entirely is to suffer an eclipse from one's fellow-men.

III. BIBLIOPHILIA THE ONLY REMEDY

In his *Bibliomania*[1] Dibdin gives as an *acquisition* to the *Materia Medica,* of which even *first-rate physicians may not be aware,* a new remedy which reverses the pharmaceutical practice of our Homoeopathists. They claim to cure a disease by treatment with minute doses of the drug which in larger doses would cause or encourage it, in the vulgar phrase, *a hair off the tail of the dog that bit him.* Dibdin would increase the dose *ad nauseam,* until a cure is effected. I may take for example his remedy for grangeritis: any passage from any book may be taken, and the patient afflicted with that malady induced to *extra-*illustrate it *ad libitum.* He gives as a sample passage, suitable for the treatment, one, taken at random, from *Speed:*[2] *Henry le Spenser, the warlike Bishop of Norwich, being drawn on by Pope Urban to preach the Crusade, and to be general against Clement (whom sundry Cardinals and great Prelates had also elected Pope), having a fifteenth granted to him, for that purpose, by Parliament,* etc. Here are only four lines, and, *properly illustrated,* they should be treated thus: 1. Procure all portraits of *Henry le Spenser,* at all periods of his life. 2. Obtain every view, ancient and modern, of *Norwich,* and portraits of every *Bishop* of that See. 3. Every portrait of *Pope Urban,* as many prints or drawings as possible illustrating *the Crusade,* and etchings (if there be any) of *Peter the Hermit* and *Richard I.* 4. Every print of *Clement.* 5. As many fine prints of *Cardinals* and *Prelates* as will impress you with a proper idea of the *Conclave.* 6. Views of the *Houses of Parliament,* A.D. 1383. Lest any *fastidious or cynical* critic accuse him of *gross exaggeration or ignorance in this receipt,* he says that *a late distinguished and highly respectable female* collector, who began to *grangerize* the *Bible,* procured no fewer than seven hundred prints towards the illustration of the twentieth to twenty-fifth verses of the first chapter of Genesis.

For more general symptoms he prescribes five remedies, which he dilates at length in his conclusion.[3] *In the first place,* he says, *the Bibliomania is materially softened, or rendered mild,* by substituting *intrinsic excellence* for

---

[1] Ed. 1811. 665–6.   [2] *Hist. Gt. Brit.* (1632) 721.¹   [3] *Bibliomania.* (1811) 735–41.

exterior splendour, and the study of *useful* and *profitable* works; the second would seek to limit the *propagation of the disorder* by *reprinting scarce and intrinsically valuable works;* the third prescribes *the editing of our best ancient authors;* the fourth, *the erection of Public Institutions* for *the diffusing of a love of books;* and the fifth, *the Study of Bibliography.* For my part I think these suggestions of Dibdin much too general, conceiving it likely that there may be as great a variety of dangers in his remedies as in the disease itself. The cure of madness by the sublimation of the passion which inflames it, or its canalization for some useful purpose, is a common practice of our best physicians; but they must have foundations upon which to build their cures. *Intrinsic excellence* cannot be substituted for *exterior splendour* unless there exist an unawakened taste for the former; what are useful or profitable works is a matter of opinion, and they are as much a cause of doting as their opposites; reprinting *scarce and intrinsically valuable books* is a prime cause of bibliomania; editing ancient authors is like enough to become an obsession in itself, so that the cure may be as bad as the disease; the erection of *Public Institutions* to promote the *love of books* is a costly prescription which could only be taken by men who are so rich that they have no time to be mad about anything but money; the best of his remedies is the *study of Bibliography*, for, as Norman Douglas observes,[1] *around the bibliographer's table there lies a passionless calm, unruffled* even *by politics or sex-problems*, and it is by establishing a state of calm that the disease may best be corrected and counterpoised. Let him that dotes meditate on this; let him see the advent of success in others, and so hope for his own cure.

Other good rules and precepts are advised which, if not alone, yet, certainly, conjoined may do much; the first of which is, I say again, *obstare principiis*,[2] to withstand the beginnings, *Quisquis in primo obstitit, Pepulitque amorem tutus ac victor fuit,*[3] he that will but resist at first,

Yet love not books beyond their proper worth,[4]

may easily be a *conqueror at last*. 'Tis true, indeed, and all-sufficient this, I do confess, if they could resist, but they are obdurate, unwilling, they enjoy their state, revel in their alienation; and in spite of what I have said, I would not press my cures in all cases, for some, though doting, are no more injurious than any other absorbed playboys; and I say of all honest recreations, God hath indulged them to refresh, ease, solace, and comfort us. *If any one in his early youth,* as he said,[5] *has experienced some slight symptoms of the malady, which his constitution, through a tough struggle with the world, and a busy training in after life, has been enabled to throw off, he will yet look back with fond associations to the scenes of his dangerous indulgence;* will

[1] *Siren-Land*. Revised Ed. 68.   [2] Ovid, *Rem. Am.* 91.   [3] Seneca, Hipp. ll. 132-3.
[4] Crabbe, 'The Brothers' Meeting', *Tales of the Hall*.   [5] Burton, *Book-Hunter*. 59.

or nill, they must acknowledge it, for 'tis a pleasant disease, despite the strange effects which have been shown in the symptoms. Try, therefore, those former remedies as we may, he would be a pick-thank who failed to cherish some tenderness for dotards who, though they cause damage to themselves, their estates, and peace of mind, bestow the boon of preservation upon the cause of their mania. Let us not forget it and, remembering, forgive them their folly, for they are commendable in their good parts, and, sure, it is one of these that, in hoarding books privily or greedily, they have protected them from outrage and such-like accidents or occasions proceeding from ignorance, stupidity, or superstition. And if from the point of view of its ultimate purpose, which is to be read, *a book protected is a book dead*,[1] it has the chance of rising again, which in the other extreme would be impossible. It is for that reason that I have set forth and examined *without prejudice* as many opinions as I could discover; nor have I overlooked the danger of drawing inferences from opinions which have a tainted source, such, for instance, as might come from *a sort of people*, observed by Pliny, *who, though they are themselves slaves to every lust, shew a kind of jealous resentment against the vices of others; and are most severe upon those they most resemble.*[2]

I could give many instances, but be it as it is, the argument is most evident. To be moderate in all things is a good counsel, even to a bare sufficiency. Enough is too much. *The soul, like the body, goes lightly clad when in good health; weakness wraps itself up*, and 'tis *a sure sign of infirmity to have many wants;* we live, just as we swim, the better for being lightly burdened, for in *this stormy life, as on the stormy ocean*, heavy things sink us, light things buoy us up; and the gods surpass men, saith mine author,[3] in that they lack nothing, *wherefore he of mankind whose needs are smallest is most like unto the gods.* And if the book-mad have missed the point of authorship by an inordinate love of possession or a lust of undigested learning, they have missed also the delicacy and other good qualities saner affection is endowed with, for *quum captus sis, ad moderationem revocare animum prudentia singularis,*[4] when thou art once in love, to moderate thyself is a singular point of wisdom; and those who do not know how to taste these delights in the affair of books are more fitted for our pity than our scorn, and in that they have deferred and not denied to others the final enjoyment of their hoarded treasures, they have earned our indulgence. But this is as clear as the sun, and needs no other illustration.

[1] Sir Walter Raleigh, *Letters*. ii, 465.
[2] *Letters*. Melmoth. Loeb Ed. viii, 22.
[3] Apuleius, *Apologia*. 21. Trans. Butler.
[4] *Heliodorus*. iv. 10.

Part XXX

OF BIBLIOPHILY

─────────◄░►─────────

I. BOOK-LOVE A PROPER SUBJECT

There may not be wanting, I suppose, one or another that will discommend some part of this treatise of Book-love, and object that it is too light, too comical in such a subject to speak of love-symptoms, too fantastical; but they go too far and, by overniceness, mock at truth, for *behind all the paraphernalia of bibliography, behind the bookshops, auctions, exhibitions, catalogues, collations and research which define the collector's efforts, is the single fact of the love of books.*[1] Love is a proper subject in all its aspects for cheerful and even merry discourse, as I would let these cavillers and counterfeit *Catos*[2] know. It is by the naughtiness of men that, as Caussinus[3] observes, *castis auribus vox amoris suspecta sit, et invisa*, the very name of love is odious to chaste ears, and not for any harm in it, for we are *as prone to love, as the sun is to shine*, saith Thomas Traherne,[4] *it being the most delightful and natural employment of the Soul of Man; without which you are dark and miserable.* And he bids us therefore not to shun it, but rather to consider its vigour, its extent, its excellency, *objects without love being a delusion of life.* The wise do not deprecate this affection, nor do they vilify it in the manner of those moral pedants whose *goodness* makes them to fear love and to envy the love which others seek. It is an ungrateful, nay, superstitious scrupulousness, for, as that good Dr. Donne, Dean of St. Paul's, so well argued, *to desire without fruition is a rage, and to enjoy without desire is a stupidity; in the first alone we think of nothing, but that which we then would have; and in the second alone, we are not for that when we have it; in the first, we are without it; in the second, we were as good as we were, for we have no pleasure in it; nothing that can give us satisfaction, but when those two concur,* amare *and* frui, *to love and to enjoy.*[5] More ill follows the efforts of the killjoy than those of the love-joy or joy-lover, for love enters into all things, inspiring and exalting. It is greater than hope, and it is greater than faith, it is God himself: *God is love*—my authorities are well known. Those

---

[1] A. J. A. Symons, 'The Book-Collector's Apology', *Book-Collector's Quarterly.* i, 56. [2] Martial. xi, 2. [3] De Eloquent. Lib. 8, cap. 14. 'de affectibus'. [4] *Centuries of Meditation.* 124. [5] *Sermons: Selected Passages.* Ed. L. P. Smith. 26.

who would deny love, therefore, are atheists. But I stray from my theme. I presume I need no such apologies. I need not, as Socrates in *Plato*, cover my face when I speak of love, or blush and hide mine eyes, as Pallas did in her hood when she was consulted by Jupiter about Mercury's marriage, *quod super nuptiis virgo consulitur*, I bring no such lascivious, obscene, or wanton discourse. I shall not offend your chaster ears with anything that is here written. Condemn me not, then, good Reader, nor censure me hardly, if some part of this treatise to thy thinking as yet be too light, but consider it in its true relationship with what hath gone before and what cometh after. *Omnia munda mundis:*[1]

> There's nothing either good or bad
> But thinking makes it so,[2]

mala mens, malus animus,[3] 'tis as 'tis taken; *honi soit qui mal y pense*. There is the less fear of thy ill opinion in that I in nowise oppose that which is bad to that which is good, but relate only those phenomena of love of books (which of all the *philiae* is most innocent) that are necessary to my theme. At worst 'tis a comical subject, for, as few will deny, there are better subjects for love even than books. Give me leave, therefore, to refresh my Muse a little, and, my worthy Readers, to expatiate in this delightsome field, *hoc deliciarum campo*, as Fonseca terms it, to season a solemn discourse with a more pleasing aspersion of the love of books, the passion men have had for them, *passing the love of women*. 'Tis good to sweeten our life with some pleasing toys, as Matius invites us,

> Quapropter edulcare convenit vitam,[4]

since, as Pliny[5] tells us, *magna pars studiosorum amoenitates quaerimus*, most of our students love such pleasant subjects, and *what is the student but a lover courting a fickle mistress who ever eludes his grasp?*[6] If this is considered to be unreasonable, let us console ourselves with George Savile, Marquis of Halifax, where he saith: *Men generally state their wants by their Fancy, and not by their Reason;*[7] as the poet[8] sings:

> Then let wingèd Fancy wander
> Through the thought still spread beyond her;
> Open wide the mind's cage-door,
> She'll dart forth, and cloudward soar.

[1] 'Unto the pure all things are pure.' *Titus* i, 15.   [2] *Hamlet*. ii, 2.   [3] Terence, *Andr*. i, 137.   [4] Aulus Gellius, *Attic Nights*. xv, 25.   [5] *Nat. Hist*. Preface.   [6] Osler, *The Student Life*. (1928) 4.   [7] *Character of King Charles II*, etc. 162.   [8] Keats, 'Fancy'.

II. VARIETIES OF LOVE

Love, universally taken, is defined to be a *Desire*, as a word of more ample signification; and though Plato,[1] in that profound parable of the charioteer and the two horses of Socrates, which he made him recite to Phaedrus under a plane-tree by the banks of the Ilissus, makes a difference between wanton and spiritual desire, which many others have done, as Leon Hebraeus:[2] still, *amor est voluntarius affectus et desiderium re bona fruendi*, love is a voluntary affection, and desire to enjoy that which is good. Plotinus[3] thinks it worth the labour to consider well of love, whether it be a god or a devil, or passion of the mind, or partly god, partly devil, partly passion, and the conclusion arrived at is that in some measure love is compact of all three, and the greatest that which uses desire *to enslave the vicious and emancipate the virtuous elements. Human discipline or divine inspiration* (says Socrates) *can confer no greater blessing on man than this.*[4] Stendhal[5] dilates and modifies the common definition, and will have love to be a fourfold delectation of the heart *of which every sincere development has a character of beauty:* (1) *Passion Love*—that of the Portuguese nun, Marianna Alcaforado, for the Chevalier de Chamilly; Héloïse for Abelard; Captain de Vésel, and Sergeant de Cento. (2) *Gallant Love*—that which ruled Paris towards 1760, to be found in the *memoirs* and *novels* of the period, in Crébillon, Lauzun, Duclos, Marmontel, Chamfort, Mme. d'Epinay, etc. (3) *Physical Love*—the hunting kind, chasing prettiness for pleasure common to all, from sixteen onwards, *however parched and unhappy the character.* (4) *Vanity Love*—sub-physical, with *transports of feeling* on gratification of pride in distinguished associations, as of titled or prominent persons, men and women of genius; as when pretty women at the Court of King Lewis of Holland could not help finding any man charming who was a Duke or Prince. Some stricken by this sort of love can attain physical pleasure upon the *greatest possible exercise of pride*, in so far as they practise cruelties on the companions of their pleasures, as in *Alfieri*, as Nero, etc., hence the horrors of the *Justine ou les Malheurs de la Vertu*, of the Marquis de Sade; for more of this read Krafft-Ebing, Lombroso, Havelock Ellis, etc. Nor must I omit mention of those naturalists, as Remy de Gourmont, who support the theologians in their belief that the love act is *more bestiarum: Love is profoundly animal; therein is its beauty;*[6] nor, yet again, those who still uphold the taste of the days of Louis XV, when *the ideal of love was nothing more than desire, and love itself was voluptuousness.*[7]

[1] *Phaedrus.* 246 sqq.   [2] *Dialogi de Amore.*   [3] *Enneades.* iii, 5.   [4] *Phaedrus.* Trans. Jowett. ii, 133.   [5] *On Love.* Trans. P. S. and C. N. S. Woolf. 19–21.   [6] Remy de Gourmont, *Philosophy of Love.* Trans. Ezra Pound. 16.   [7] Edmond and Jules de Goncourt, *Love in the Eighteenth Century.* (English Ed. 1905) 7.

Otto Weininger[1] taxes these former definitions, and will not have love to be defined by desire or appetite, for *in love man is only loving himself,* not his empirical self, his meannesses, weaknesses, vulgarities, his failure and littleness, which he outwardly exhibits; but all that he wishes to be and ought to be: all that is true in him, profound, innate, real, free from *the fetters of necessity, the taint of earth,* which agrees in part with Plato. But whatever it is, this love varies as its object varies, and it would always make that object amiable, fair, gracious, and pleasant. *Beauty,* according to Havelock Ellis,[2] *is largely a name for sexual attractiveness.* If love is desirable then it is good, because *all things desire that which is good,* as we are taught, *omnia appetunt bonum,*[3] or at least that which seems to be good, for tastes differ, though we all mean the same thing and search for it, whatever the philosophers may say or whatever it may be, for we know not what we would have it be, but are continuously seeking it—

Call'd him soft names in many a musèd rhyme,—[4]

beauty, truth, life, joy, as though we would build an image, fane, temple, what not, to hold the mystery.

It is a deep-rooted longing, which we cannot root out, and would not if we could, and our brains, intellects, are ever on the alert to capture it, and as Bergson will have, *roads may fork or by-ways be opened along which dissociated elements may evolve in an independent manner, but nevertheless it is in virtue of the primitive impetus of the whole that the movement of the parts continues.*[5] In this eternal quest woman is only one counter, one symbol (as man may be for woman if they adventure in the same realms, which some doubt). *Love has, indeed, an ivy-like gift for clinging to any pretext:*[6] property, tasks, ambitions, conflicts, etc., are symbols, and art—pictures, poetry, music, sculptures; medals, stamps, curiosities, *bric-à-brac,* books, which men seek and cherish as the savage his *totem.* Sir Walter Raleigh frankly announces[7] that the parallel of book-affection with love is not *an analogy, but an identity. It is really,* he says, *a problem of generation.* Some, according to Benedetto Croce,[8] have tried to deduce the pleasure of art from that of the genitals, while others among the more recent æstheticians confidently find the origin of the æsthetical impulse in the pleasure of *conquering* and of *triumphing* over the female. They season their belief (says Croce) with much *anecdotal erudition,* with *heaven knows what degree of credibility,* from the customs of savage people. No need, however, for such assistance, *since in ordinary life we meet poets who adorn themselves with their poetry, like cocks raising their crests, or turkeys spreading out their tails;* and just

---

[1] *Sex and Character.* 243.   [2] *Psychology of Sex.* v, 21.   [3] Aristotle, *Nicom. Eth.* i, 1.
[4] Keats, *Ode to a Nightingale.* vi.   [5] *Creative Evolution.* 57.   [6] Plutarch, *Select Essays.* Tucker. i, 172.   [7] *Letters.* 352.   [8] *Aesthetic.* 83.

as he concludes that *anyone who does this, in so far as he does it, is not a poet, but a poor fool of a cock or a turkey, and the desire for the victorious conquest of women has nothing to do with the fact of art,* so bibliophilia[1] in some cases may have passed so far beyond the love of women as to have taken its place. Books are a fetich in the tribe of bibliophiles, possessing all the sanctity which *taboo* gives to primitive possessions and all the magic of the *totem. No love,* exclaims Anatole France,[2] *without fetichism, and let us do justice to the lovers of old blackened paper, that they are quite as mad as other lovers;* and since you heard how this tyrant love rageth among men and women, now let us consider what passions it causeth amongst men and books, for *it is because the passion for books is a sentimental passion that people who have not felt it always fail to understand it.*[3] Love proper to books is the subject of my following discourse.

III. SYMPTOMS OF BIBLIOPHILY

Many are the symptoms to discern book-lovers by—

—quis enim bene celet amorem?[4]

A great library easily begets affection, which may deepen into love, says Birrell.[5] Merryweather does not surprise us when he owns that his *very soul was on fire when in the midst of a library,*[6] for *can a man carry fire in his bosom,* and not burn?[7] In all their talk of books they use the language of amorists, as so many of my citations in this section will show.

When *expatiating* on his books, Richard de Bury unbosoms himself of all the *rapture of love;*[8] when Bradshaw showed a rare manuscript to a friend, he handled it passionately, *filled with an emotion as infectious as it was real;*[9] bibliography, Dibdin writes,[10] was the *darling delight* of Rosicrucius, *una voluptas et meditatio assidua (Vita Jacobi Le Long,* p. xx. *Bibliotheca Sacra.* 1778); Meerman, author of the *Origines Typographicae,* was *passionately addicted to rare and curious books;*[11] and Henri Pène du Bois records that there were no books in the library of the Comte de Fortas that were not *ardently loved;*[12] Peter Daniel Huet *had a warm and constant attachment to*

---

[1] This word is first found says Gustave Mouravit (*Le Livre et la Bibliothèque d'Amateur.* 403), in a work by Selden, the pseudonym of Christianus Liberius Germanus: *Bibliophilia, sive de scribendis, legendis et aestimandis libris exercitatio parvenetica.* Utrecht, 1681.   [2] 'Bibliophilia', *Life and Letters.* Second Series. 62–3. [3] Lang, 'Bibliomania in France', *Books and Bookmen.* 91.   [4] Ovid, *Heroides.* xii, 37. 'For who can conceal love?'   [5] 'In the Name of the Bodleian', *Coll. Essays.* iii, 187. [6] *Bibliomania in the Middle Ages.* iv.   [7] *Proverbs* v, 27.   [8] Merryweather, *op. cit.* 77.   [9] Prothero, *Henry Bradshaw.* 331.   [10] *Bibliomania.* (1811) 169–70. [11] *Ib.* 76–7.   [12] *Four Private Libraries of New York.* 104.

books;[1] and *what bibliophile*, asks Merryweather, *can look unmoved* upon the Venerable Bede's copy of *St. Cuthbert's Gospels, without indeed all the warmth of his book-love kindling forth into a very frenzy of rapture and veneration?*[2] Dibdin himself was as *passionately* affected by them. He *loved history* exceedingly, and took *a violent affection* for Rushworth's *Collections*; but *Burton* and *Gibbon* were the objects of his *steadiest attachment, Gibbon*, however, *commanding a more consecutive attention and a more frequent reflection.*[3] Hearne *was so warm a lover of everything in the shape of a Book* that he confessed to jumping *almost out of his skin for joy* on reading a MS. which Thomas Rawlinson had sent him: *vix credi potest qua voluptate, qua animi alacritate, perlegerim*, etc.[4] Before his time Archbishop Parker *was smitten with everything attached to a book.*[5] *My darling books!* cried Silvestre de Sacy, *I do love you all! It seems as if, by long and sweet companionship, you had become part of myself,*[6] which Augustine Birrell supports when he says, *the man who has a library of his own collection is able to contemplate himself objectively, and is justified in believing in his own existence*, and in the gloaming when he contemplates *his loved ones* he may exclaim, *they are mine and I am theirs.*[7]

Among the characteristics of book-lovers, not to be overpassed if once they fall in love, is the desire to turn their affection into rhymes, ballads and sonnets, and among the bookman's *erotopaegnia* are many pleasant songs, for as Plutarch holds, *they will be Witnesses and Trumpeters of their Paramours' good parts, bedecking them with verses and commendatory songs, as we do statues with gold, that they may be remembered and admired of all.* Young, and even ancient, men will dote in this kind, as Austin Dobson, Andrew Lang, Lord de Tabley, Richard le Gallienne, Eugene Field, and many more I could quote, but read them in that anthology of pleasant delights, *Book-Song*, made by Gleeson White, if you would know a nest of singing-birds and their amorous ditties about books. And as true lovers they will at all times and in all places be telling love-stories of favourites: how they yearned for this *association copy*, made a fair capture of that *Elzevir*; how they won this early *Donne* or lost that uncut *Keats*. They recall golden memories of passionate adventures in old libraries where

> Out of every shadowy nook
> Spirit faces seem to look,
> Some with smiling eyes, and some
> With a sad entreaty dumb;

---

[1] *Memoirs*. Trans. Aikin. i, 14.   [2] Merryweather, *op. cit.* 88.   [3] *Reminiscences*. i, 88, 90.   [4] Dibdin, *Bibliomania.* (1811) 443.   [5] *Ib.* 340.   [6] Qt. Fitzgerald, *Book-Fancier.* 1.   [7] *Coll. Essays.* iii, 80.

He who shepherded his sheep
On the wild Sicilian steep,
He above whose grave are set
Sprays of Roman violet;
Poets, sages,—all who wrought
In the crucible of thought.[1]

Such objects are their sole delight, their continual meditation:

The very paper haunts your dreams at night;[2]

and out of them an earnest longing comes, *pruriens corpus, pruriens animal,* amorous conceits, tickling thoughts, sweet and pleasant hopes; hence it is, they can think, or speak almost of no other subject:

If thou has not sat as I do now,
Wearying thy hearer in thy mistress' praise,
Thou hast not loved.[3]

When Dibdin visited the Marquis of Bute's library at Luton, his *fancy was inflamed: I went—I saw—and was enraptured;* and like a love-sick bard he must dedicate his forthcoming book, *Typographical Antiquities,* to the noble inspirer of those raptures.[4]

But these are toys in respect to the knowledge that lovers will hazard everything for their mistress' sake or to behold their sweetheart. As Phaedria trembled at the sight of Thais, Lord de Tabley grew *physically faint with joy at securing an 'Alastor' of 1816, and tears sprang to his eyes at the unexpected arrival of a Milton's 'Poems' of 1645.*[5] George Gissing is thrilled by *the first glimpse of a new binding when the inmost protective wrapper had been folded back;* and he opens a parcel new come from the bookseller with *throbbing heart* and *hand that trembled;* he takes up a volume whose title he has known for a lifetime, reverently embraces it, gently opens it, his eyes becoming *dim with excitement* as he *glances over the chapter-headings,* gloating on anticipated joys. No one more than he, so he brags, has taken so much to heart that sentence from the *Imitatio: In omnibus requiem quaesivi, et nusquam inveni nisi in angula cum libro.*[6] Leigh Hunt *purred* with *Quiet enjoyment* as he hung *over a book he loved;*[7] Edmund Waller was unable to read Chapman's *Homer* without *rapture;*[8] Sydney Smith was *passionately fond of books;*[9] Mark Rutherford could not tell what feelings *Virgil* gave him:

---

[1] Clinton Scollard, *Book-Song.* 107.   [2] Halkett Lord, *Book Lore.* ii, 99.   [3] *As You Like It.* ii, 4.   [4] Dibdin, *Reminiscences.* i, 275–6.   [5] Gosse, Intro. *Library of Edmund Gosse.* xviii-xix.   [6] *Private Papers of Henry Ryecroft.* 44–5.   [7] Percy Fitzgerald, *Charles Lamb.* 17.   [8] Johnson, *Lives of the Poets.* (1781) i, 400.   [9] *Memoir.* Lady Holland. i, 181.

no relationship so tender, so intimate;[1] C. E. Montague is *an amorist of words;*[2] and *for some of his little, rare seventeenth-century volumes,* Lord de Tabley *had an almost petulant affection.*[3]

Nor is familiarity a bar to affection, for the intimacies necessary to translation made Edward FitzGerald *doat* on the *Oedipus Coloneus, even more,* he confesses, than *before,* and, *so far from grudging the time and Eyesight* spent on the *Notes,* loved the book which *put both in request* as well as the *Dictionary* in which he had to *look out the words.*[4] There are some *knightly souls,* says Christopher Morley, *who even go so far as to make their visits to bookshops a kind of chivalrous errantry at large.* They seek not the volume they want but the volume that wants them: *Some wistful little forgotten sheaf of loveliness, long pining away on an upper shelf—why not ride up, fling her across your charger . . . and gallop away?*[5] After this manner that copy of the *Voyage dans un grenier* was *enlevé comme une jolie femme,* carried off like a pretty woman, to the consternation *des bibliophiles podagres et peu pressés,* from a sale at Morgand et Fatout, in the year 1878.[6] But no matter how you have gotten it, by capture, purchase or gift, it is yours to love in your own way, to use or misuse; you do not allow, says Gautier,[7] *à sa virginité le quart d'heure de grace, vous le touchez, vous le maniez, vous le trainez de votre table à votre lit, vous rompez sa robe d'innocence, vous déchirez ses pages.* Well may Emerson in general conclude that books take *rank in our lives with lovers and passionate experiences,*[8] for as men live for books so will they die for them, as Cassius Severus, an eloquent Roman, seeing his books burnt, exclaimed that by the same sentence he also should be condemned to be burnt alive.[9] Greater love hath no man.

IV. THE QUALITY OF BOOK-LOVE

Jean Joseph Rive[10] will have that a bibliophile is one who reads for pleasure; but he is opposed by Locker-Lampson,[11] who maintains that *your true bibliophile rarely reads anything: he contemplates, he examines bindings, criticizes illustrations, and scrutinizes title-pages or pagination.* Others, as G. H. Powell, have dilated upon the difference between reading and *the refined curiosities of the bibliophile,*[12] and Gleeson White,[13] in express words, affirms that your book-lover must gaze at books *mutely, with a satisfied joy in*

[1] *Letters to Three Friends.* 152.   [2] *C. E. Montague: A Memoir.* Elton. 7.   [3] Gosse, 'Lord de Tabley', *Critical Kit-Kats.* 191.   [4] *More Letters of Edward FitzGerald.* 85–6.   [5] 'On Visiting Bookshops', *Safety Pins.* Travellers' Lib. 34.   [6] Octave Uzanne, *Zig-zags d'un Curieux.* 210.   [7] Pref. *Les Jeunes-France.*   [8] *Society and Solitude.* (1870) 158.   [9] Montaigne, *Essays.* Ed. Seccombe. ii, 101.   [10] Qt. D'Israeli, *Cur. of Lit.*   [11] *My Confidences.* 216.   [12] Powell, *Excursions in Libraria.* Pref.   [13] *Book-Song.* Pref.

OF BIBLIOPHILY

being near enough to caress or abstain. A book need not even be *in a particular language, nor on a particular subject, to be the book of a book-lover.*[1] You love a book first because it is a book, however much you may particularize afterwards: *He loved a book because it was a book; he loved its odour, its form, its title.*[2] You love it inwardly and outwardly, soul and body. You fall in love with all its members: to do less, to occupy yourself principally with the outward parts of books, says Tenant de Latour, is to be *l'athée de la bibliophilie.*[3] You must love its inwardness, its character as well as its form. Charles Nodier loved books, but he was no *bibliomane ordinaire,* with him love was keen, active, persevering, passionate, and always directed and animated *par le goût le plus fin, le discernement le plus exquis et le plus délicat,* the finest taste and the most exquisite and delicate discrimination.[4] *You come, like other lovers, to feel an unreasoned sensuous thrill of joy at a word because it is just what it is;*[5] and you come, also, with no less delight to love a book's print, paper, form and dress. These are the true prognostics of the bibliophile, so that all true bookmen will approve Gleeson White's selection of Charles Lamb as his ideal bookman, for Lamb *adores not only their mental but their physical beauty,* he is *no mere æsthetic admirer content to 'worship from afar with distant reverence', but one who must fondle his treasures.*[6]

This opinion confutes at large those who would give bibliophily a purpose other than its name and character warrant, for true book-love passes the love of reading, truth, knowledge-seeking, without denying them. *It does not follow at all that a person devoted to reading is fond of books. It is often the other way: the most learned men, the most gluttonous of readers, may not have the smallest love for books.*[7] They know nothing of their value or how to treat them; using them for their *selfish purpose* and casting them aside as useless: *Ten people care for a book—but they are apostles. A thousand enjoy another book, but when they have sucked it on a hot afternoon, they have finished.*[8] I find Frederick York Powell a supporter of this idea in a reference to C. L. Dodgson (Lewis Carroll), whose library was in a constant state of change as his tastes and needs altered. *He had many of the rarer first editions of Tennyson, but he was never a bibliophile, and ignored all questions of original shape, keeping of covers, uncut paper, etc., and he bought no books except to read, and most of these, once read, he would get rid of at clearing-times.*[9]

Gosse suggests that *you must love books ere they seem books worthy to be loved;*[10] and George Moore, gloating as ever upon his own idiosyncrasy,

[1] H. P. du Bois, *Four Private Libraries of New York.* 116.   [2] Flaubert, *Bibliomania.* Trans. Koch. 11.   [3] Qt. Mouravit, *Le Livre et la Petite Bibliothèque d'Amateur.* 244.
[4] M. G. Duplessis, qt. Derome, *Les Editions Originales des Romantiques.* i, 196.
[5] C. E. Montague, *A Writer's Notes on His Trade.* 3.   [6] *Book-Song.* Pref.   [7] John Ferguson, *Some Aspects of Bibliography.* 3 and 4.   [8] Sir Walter Raleigh, *Letters.* 352.
[9] 'C. L. Dodgson', *Occasional Writings.* Vol. ii, 362, of *Life of Powell,* by Oliver Elton.   [10] *Library of Edmund Gosse.* Pref. xxii.

compares books to individuals: *You know at once,* he says, *if they are going to create a sense within the sense, to fever, to madden you in blood and brain, or if they will merely leave you indifferent, or irritable, having unpleasantly disturbed sweet intimate musings as might a draught from an open window.* He has many reasons for love, but he only loves *woman or book when it is as a voice of conscience, never heard before, heard suddenly, a voice* he is *at once endearingly intimate with. This announces feminine depravities in his affections,* but then, he confesses, *I am feminine, morbid, perverse; above all perverse, almost everything perverse interests, fascinates me.*[1] Leigh Hunt[2] loves an author the more *for having been himself a lover of books;* Mark Pattison testifies[3] that the *mechanical act of perusal gave him a sort of pleasure,* as a youth, but that *books, as books, irrespective of their contents,* were his *delight;* they offer, says another authority,[4] *something akin to the friendship of a charming and secretive woman.*

I for my part will subscribe that it is a passion, seeking no more advantage, no more reward, than its own satisfaction; *amare autem nihil aliud est, nisi eum ipsum diligere quem amas, nulla indigentia, nulla utilitate quaesita:*[5] to love is nought else than to hold in high esteem the object of your affection, free alike from compulsion and advantage. Most book-lovers acknowledge as much of themselves: *les bibliophiles trouvent du bonheur partout où l'on trouve des livres,*[6] find happiness wherever there are books. Nor is willingness to give high prices for books a symptom. *If a man gives a woman wealth it is only a sign of generosity; but if he give her his time it is a proof of his love.*[7] *Where my loved one is, there will my heart be also.* It needs no argument, and for my part I subscribe to it, and I reckon it a true and proper symptom when they *love an old volume for its own sake,*[8] as many have done and will do. In a phrase, they *fall in love,* and desire nothing better than to enjoy a favourite book like Scipio's captive maiden, according to one authority, *in deliciis amoribusque ab eo usurpatam.*[9]

But what of this? are we not all in love?[10]

I could cite many instances, and will do so in the extension of my discourse. I will here give only one testimony, which I take from the *Bibliophile's Almanack* for 1927: *My love of the 'Reliquiae Wottonianae' happened early, and at the moment of its unpremeditated birth it bore all the symptoms of authentic passion: it was sudden, excessive, and dogmatic;* it became *the one and only book, and if,* he continues, *as would seem inevitable, the heart has since been*

---

[1] *Confessions of a Young Man.* (1909.) 62.　[2] 'My Books'. *Essays.* Camelot Ed. 294.
[3] *Memoirs.* 37-8.　[4] Rosenbach, *Books and Bidders.* 34.　[5] Cicero, *De Am.* xxvii, 100.　[6] Jacob, *Ma République.* 57.　[7] Ninon de l'Enclos.　[8] Thomas Moult, 'Introduction', *Forty Years in My Bookshop.* W. T. Spencer.　[9] Aulus Gellius, *Noct. Att.* vii, 8.　[10] *Love's Labour's Lost.* iv, 3.

moved, sometimes lightly, at others profoundly, by this or that fair volume, the passing years have done no more than transmute the passionate bloom of adolescence into a patina of tenderness which must increase as well as endure in spite of time as well as because of time. Yet (to follow Lord Rosebery)[1] the *general love of books* may include *reading, buying, handling, and hunting them.* I would venture farther, and maintain that the very thought of them provokes ecstatic delight; to write of them is a joy, like writing a loveletter; Dominie Sampson, in *Guy Mannering*, entered the Bishop's books in the catalogue *in his best running hand, forming each letter with the accuracy of a lover writing a valentine.* Richard de Bury was so carried away with *ecstatic love* for books that *he resigned all thoughts of other earthly things.*[2]

Nulla tuum nobis subducet femina lectum;[3]

no woman shall filch thy place of love with me.

Bibliophily is its own reward like virtue, it has its own raptures like art, in which we are advised that not only *rapture suffices*, but that *the artist* (and I claim as much for the bibliophile) *has no more call to look forward than the lover in the arms of his mistress.*[4] Utility has small part in such love: *if they can avoid creating the impression that they regard their Library as a tool-house or workship, so much the better.*[5] Anatole France[6] discommends all purpose save love. Detractors have thought to confound bibliophiles by complaining that they never read their books; but one of them replied *and do you eat off your old china? You love them for their utility. Is that love? Does one love when one loves without disinterestedness? No! you have no fire and no joy and you will never know the delight of passing trembling fingers over the delicious grain of a morocco-bound volume.*[7] Yet, he discourses at large, *no true love without some sensuality;* he has known holy and saintly men look upon *books in mottled calf with concupiscence* and *finger fawn-coloured calf with voluptuousness;* and he has a memorable example of a canon of the Church of Rome, who with *amorous hand* caressed a fine copy in grained calf of the *Lives of the Fathers of the Desert*, which mine author reckoned a sin, and aggravated, moreover, in that it was a Jansenist book.[8] A more particular instance is recorded by Laurence Sterne,[9] wherein Mr. Shandy was so enamoured of his copy of *Bruscambille*, which he had just bought at a bookstall near Piccadilly for three half-crowns, that he solaced himself with it as, saith Sterne, *your Worship solaced yourself with your first mistress—that is from morning even unto night*, which supports Eugene Field, who holds that *no book can be appreciated until it has been slept with and dreamed over.*[10]

[1] *Appreciations and Addresses.* 165.   [2] *Philobiblon.* Thomas. 5.   [3] Tibullus, *Sulpicae Elegidia.* Loeb Ed. 337.   [4] Clive Bell, *Art.* 241.   [5] Augustine Birrell, *Ashley Lib. Cat.* Intro. ii, viii.   [6] *Garden of Epicurus.* 109.   [7] Anatole France, *Life and Letters.* Second Series. Trans. A. W. Evans. 60.   [8] *Ib.* 62–3.   [9] *Tristram Shandy.* III, ch. xxxv.   [10] *Love Affairs of a Bibliomaniac.* 31.

These passions are truly justified out of Merryweather,[1] where he records that the monkish librarians of the Middle Ages became great bibliophiles by being in such constant association with choice manuscripts that they acquired a *mania* for them. They became *lovers of musty parchments and cob-webbed chronicles* and what not; and he accounts it pleasing, as well he may, *to trace a deep book-passion growing up in the barrenness of the cloister.* He illustrates this point with the example of St. Dunstan (out of W. Malm., de Vita Dunst., ap. Leland, Script.; Strutt's Saxon. Antiq., etc.), who was so *passionately fond of books* that he does not hesitate *to proclaim him a bibliomaniac;*[2] and he goes on to record that Alcuin *sang the praises of his library in a tedious lay* (id. ch. viii, 116); Anselm stole away from Church dissensions to his favourite books, which he could scarce leave night or day; and Bede, Caedmon, Leofric, Prior Nicholas Hereford of Evesham, were all dear lovers of books. Richard de Bury, Bishop of Durham, illustrious author of the breviary of the bibliophile, *the Philobiblon,* had a passionate love of books, which throbbed with religious exaltation; he could not get enough of them, *iste summe delectabatur multitudine librorum,*[3] nor praise them enough; they were always with him, he formed a library in each of his palaces, *diversis maneriis,* and so engrossing his fancy that his dormitory was strewed with them, choice volumes in every nook and corner, *so that it was almost impossible to enter without stepping on them.*[4]

Many other bookmen in all ages have loved to have their books *en négligé;* as that famous bibliophile, Peiresc, whose dominant passion was his library: *books engrossed his house everywhere,—on shelves, on tables, on chairs, in 'nests' about the floor;*[5] and Lord de Tabley, in our own time, *belonged,* says Gosse,[6] *to a class of bibliophiles whose books lie strewn over sofas and armchairs, instead of being ranged in cases like jewels.* His servant came to look upon books as *personal enemies,* and when his master moved from Onslow Square *the man snorted with the joy of battle.* 'At last,' he said, 'I'll be even with them durned books.' And there are rough wooers, cave-men bibliophiles, heavy of hand, clumsy with them, as Dr. Johnson, who thumbed his pages, *soiled his folios,* yet, as Birrell holds, *no man of letters loved letters better than he. He knew literature in all its branches—he had read books, he had written books, he had sold books, he had bought books, and he had borrowed them. Sluggish and inert in all other directions, he pranced through libraries. He loved a catalogue; he delighted in an index.*[7]

Lord Rosebery records that Carteret was *strongly suspected* of bibliophily, for *classics were to be found in his dressing room.*[8] This is a true symp-

[1] *Bibliomania in the Middle Ages.* 1–16.   [2] *Ib.* 43–4.   [3] Wharton, *Angliae Sacra.* i, 765. Qt. Merryweather. *Op. cit.* 75.   [4] *Ib.*   [5] Dobson, *De Libris,* 252.   [6] *Critical Kit-Kats.* 192–3.   [7] 'Dr. Johnson', *Collected Essays.* i, 125.   [8] *Appreciations and Addresses.* 162–3.

tom, but only one of many; they must have them in all places; they cannot
live without them; they are ever thinking of them, their charm, rarity,
value, quality, condition; how they may enjoy them more, show them
off, care for them, brag about them; and they think about them with the
same delight with which men think upon their absent mistresses, for books
are a prime means of fulfilment, and when all the authorities have said
their say and cancelled out, as they so often do, the love of books remains
firmly implanted in the bookman, who loves himself through his books
finding himself in them, as lovers of all kinds and in all times have found
themselves in the beloved. *Love is the most subtle form of self-interest,*[1] however much lovers may seek to deny it, or circumvent it: *To love her for her
regard to me is not to love her, but myself.*[2] They look into a woman's eyes
perchance to find there, unconsciously, some image of themselves, and
not always unconsciously, for some peep knowingly. And so it is with
bibliophiles, who love not, as so many have argued, solely for the books,
but for themselves, books express the bookman and that is enough: *si
l'égoisme n'existait pas les bibliophiles l'auraient inventé,*[3] if egoism had not
existed bibliophiles would have invented it; and if they lose themselves in
books, as most of them would, 'tis, as in all other lovings, to find themselves in a greater, an illimitable essence, as when our poet Richard
Crashaw looked upon the book and picture of that seraphical Saint Teresa:

> O thou undaunted daughter of desires!
> By all thy dower of lights and fires;
> By all the eagle in thee, all the dove;
> By all thy lives and deaths of love;
> By thy large draughts of intellectual day,
> And by thy thirsts of love more large than they;
> By all thy brim-fill'd bowls of fierce desire,
> By thy last morning's draught of liquid fire;
> By the full kingdom of that final kiss
> That seized thy parting soul, and seal'd thee His;
> By all the Heav'n thou hast in Him
> (Fair sister of the Seraphim!)
> By all of Him we have in thee;
> Leave nothing of myself in me.
> Let me so read thy life, that I
> Unto all life of mine may die!

---

[1] Holbrook Jackson, *Platitudes in the Making.* 69. [2] Hazlitt, *Liber Amoris.*
[3] Cuvillier-Fleury, *Hist. Poét. et Rom.* ii, 188.

But this love of books is not to be comprehended in any bounds,

I have no mistress but my books,

sings one,[1] and most hold there's something in a book beyond all human delight: a magnetic virtue, a charming quality, an occult and powerful motive. Books command the heart and the head, and yet few can expound their love. Garrod has known men who have *lived all their lives with books*, but *never a one could discover* to him *what, in a book, are those qualities by which it is confidently pronounced good or bad.*[2] A book, says Douglas Jerrold,[3] is *the unfailing Damon to his loving Pythias*. Books are their devotion, their only joy and content. No happiness like it, no love more great. With some it is an act of adoration from which grosser contacts are removed. That lovers are mad, as Robert Burton thought,[4] no man would deny, but that bibliophiles can be both wise and loving together has much to support it, and I could (and shall) cite many proofs. Yet, methinks, this rapt contemplation of the externals of books is dotage and cousin german to mania, half-way to what Seneca calls *impotentem et insanam libidinem*, an impotent and raging lust; but I treat of this subject elsewhere.

---

[1] S. J. Adair FitzGerald, 'My Books', *Book-Song*. 49. [2] 'How to Know a Good Book from a Bad', *Profession of Poetry*. 254. [3] *Specimens of Jerrold's Wit*. [4] *Anat. of Mel.* (1904) i, 130.

Part XXXI

THE FIVE PORTS OF BOOK-LOVE

―――――――――――――――

I. HEARING

What sovereignty bibliophily hath, by many pregnant meanings and familiar examples may be proved, but first I would consider how far persons who so much admire as to dote upon books are to be explained, and how by what means books do produce this effect of love. 'Tis by all *the five ports of knowledge*[1] proper to love itself: hearing, seeing, smelling, tasting, and touching, diverse or together in one person. *Oh, delightful!* Hazlitt exclaims,[2] *to cut open the leaves* of a book, *to inhale the fragrancy of the scarcely dried paper, to examine the type*, and, I will add, to taste its new flavour with delicate anticipation, to feel its shape, smooth surface, and know it by touch, for each sense must concur to the perfection of this delight.

There is a grace cometh from hearing, as a moral philosopher informs us, as well as from sight,[3] and so the ear thrills to the rustle of the leaves and their resistance to the ivory paper-knife. Besides the waters of oblivion there is a fair place where storied silence breaks only to half-heard, familiar, but always new and strange communions. It is a sound heard almost without hearing, but more endeared because it pipes to the sensual ear love ditties of no tone laden with rare memories which of themselves are melodies. It is like the lisping of lake-waves, or the remonstrance of a shy stream at the overtures of the young wind when the morning or the evening stars sing together. It is the sound of all sounds the most companionable, this whispering of the leaves of books. You who love them have heard it in the quietness of your room, and you have been comforted; or, perchance, in the wizard silence of Bodley's Library at Oxford, where it has gone up to the painted beams as incense of sound; or in the echoing space of the vast rotunda of the cosmopolis of books in Bloomsbury; or in the Vaticano, or the Escurial, or the Bibliothèque Nationale. Most pleasing and most comfortable of sounds, so that book-lovers who hear it are made confident and rapt beyond themselves. Happy the man *qui scit jubilationem*, that knows this joyful music.

[1] Sir Thomas Browne, 'Garden of Cyrus', *Works*. Ed. Sayle. iii, 309.   [2] 'On Reading New Books', *Monthly Magazine*. July 1827.   [3] Piccolomineus, qt. Burton, *Anat. of Melan.* Bohn Ed. iii, 72. 'Gratia venit ab auditu aeque ac visu.'

II. SEEING

By sight: the eye betrays the soul, and is both active and passive in this business. It is an especial cause and instrument, both in the subject and in the object of all love. *I gazed at her, at first with that gaze which is not merely a messenger from the eyes, but in whose windows all the senses assemble and lean out, petrified and anxious, that gaze which would fain reach, touch, capture, bear off in triumph the body at which it is aimed, and the soul with the body.*[1] Books have a pleasing grace in this kind. *Ut vidi, ut perii!*[2] I saw, and was undone. Dibdin urges *every sober and cautious collector* not to risk the temptation of calling *only to look* at this or that book which the knowing bookseller advertises as *curious and rare*, for *when he views the morocco binding, silk water-tabley lining, blazing gilt edges; when he turns over the white and spotless leaves; gazes on the amplitude of margin; on a rare and lovely print introduced; and is charmed with the soft and coaxing manner in which 'leaf succeeds to leaf'—he can no longer bear up against the temptation,* and is like to be *led away by the passion which inflamed Berryer and Baillard.*[3] Fitzgerald[4] has record of a bibliophile who could not work out of the sight of books; Eugene Field thought an *Elzevir* one of the most *gladdening sights human eye* could rest upon;[5] another authority records that in the *contemplation* of a collection of works from the same press, *the hours fly wildly as if a furious god chased them with whips through the vast azure;*[6] and the *mere sight of Gibbon tuned Gissing's mind.*[7] Beauty is more beholden to Art than Nature, and stronger provocations proceed from outward ornaments than from such as Nature has provided. Bibliophiles are enamoured of the outward charms of books, for, as Propertius[8] holds, *ipse alimenta sibi maxima praebet amor*, love as a snowball enlargeth itself by sight. They delight to gaze in rapture, to dote upon them with their eyes:

> With wistful glance his aching eyes behold
> The Princeps-copy, clad in blue and gold,
> Where the tall Book-case, with partition thin,
> Displays, yet guards the tempting charms within.[9]

Almansa, in *Dibdin*,[10] *sat whole hours contemplating with rapture the sparkling radiance* of certain little volumes of Bodoni printed on vellum; Henry Drury adored with *rapture-speaking eyes* the *tall, wide, clean, brilliant, illum-*

---

[1] Proust, *Swann's Way*. Trans. Scott Moncrieff. i, 192–3.   [2] Virgil, *Eclogues.* viii, 41.   [3] *Bibliomania*. (1811) 687–9.   [4] *Book-Fancier*. 8.   [5] *Love Affairs of a Bibliomaniac*. 180.   [6] Henri Pène du Bois, *Four Private Libraries of New York*. 78.   [7] *Private Papers of Henry Ryecroft*. 36.   [8] iii, 21, 4. 'Love furnishes its own chief food.'   [9] Ferriar, *Bibliomania*. 3–4.   [10] *Bibliomania*. (1811) 697.

inated copy of the first Livy also upon vellum;[1] whilst Haslewood seemed *to hug the volumes* newly come from his binder, Charles Lewis, *as his eye sparkled upon their exterior splendour.*[2] They long to *ogle*[3] them. Over the Bishop's books, Scott records in *Guy Mannering,* the eye of Dominie Sampson *gloated with rapture;* Giacomo, in *Flaubert,* takes a favourite book and changes it from place to place and remains *for entire hours looking at its title and form,*[4] *devours it with his eyes,* looks at it and loves it as *a miser his treasure, a father his daughter, a king his crown.*[5] And the love-glances are returned, if Eugene Field's relation of his own experience be true: *When of a morning I awaken I cast my eyes about my room to see how fare my beloved treasures, and as I cry cheerily to them, 'Good-day to you, sweet friends!' how lovingly they beam upon me.*[6]

Many bibliophiles confess that when they come into the presence of their books they cannot hold off their eyes, but look wistfully and stead-fastly on them: overcome, entranced by such a sight. The exquisite copy of the Wetstein *Marot* in blue morocco, at the Beckford Sale, was *a sight to bring happy tears into the eyes of the amateur of Elzevirs,* for although it was not an Elzevir, it had an *exquisite delicacy of proportion, that lingered like music in the memory;*[7]

> Its burnished edge you eye with subtle glee,
> The dentelle borders and the slender bands.[8]

Coryat, in his *Crudities,*[9] records of such a one that the sight of a beautiful book printed at *Basil or Heidelberg makes him spinne; and at seeing the word Frankford or Venice, though but on the title of a booke, he is readie to breake doublet, cracke elbowes, and overflowe the roome with his murmure.*

It is not fair books alone which are Love's fowlers, those embroidered tomes in silk and velvet, or those rich volumes full of gold and jewels. Every book-lover admires his mistresses though they be deformed of themselves, ill-favoured, faded, frayed, foxed, flea'd, tattered carcasses; dirty, mouldy; they make as fair a show in their eyes, as much enamour as the rest. It is true that many prefer those fair sparkling volumes: crushed morocco, red, blue, green, purple, yellow, *vieux rose;* extra gilt, richly tooled, marbled end-papers, silk panels, etc. These of themselves are puissant enticers. But when they are added to a comely, well-composed character, the charm must needs be far more potent. And even when this inward quality is absent, those curious toolings, needleworks, variety of colours, purest dies, richest leathers, whitest vellum, fair paper, fine print-

---

[1] *Ib.* 182.   [2] Dibdin, *Reminiscences.* i, 418.   [3] Uzanne, *Book-Hunter in Paris.* 122. [4] *Bibliomania.* Trans. Koch. 10.   [5] *Ib.* 8–9.   [6] *Love Affairs of a Bibliomaniac.* 98. [7] Lang, *Books and Bookmen.* 10.   [8] Halkett Lord, *Book-Lore.* ii, 99.   [9] Qt. Dibdin, *Bibliomania.* (1811) 169.

ing, jewels, spangles, embroideries, shall make the veriest drab of a book adorable. A closer acquaintance is no impediment to this enjoyment of their outer aspect, for, as Dibdin maintains,[1] to know what books are valuable, what worthless; their *intrinsic and extrinsic merits*, rarity, beauty, and *particularities of various kinds;* and also *the estimation in which they are held by knowing men*, adds *a zest to the gratification we feel in even looking upon certain volumes.*

III. SMELLING

Although for the greater part this beauty be most eminent in the outer parts, yet those other qualities, as fragrance and taste, yield a most pleasing grace: like the gardens of Adonis, they invite both your seeing and your smelling, and are often sufficient to enamour, as well they may, *the sense of smell being more powerful to recall the ideas that have been associated with it than any other sense;*[2]

> Stronger than remembered looks,
> Nearer than old written words,
> Cling the loved old fragrances;
> At the matin time of birds,
> Giving birth to memories:
> Not one fancy perishes,
> Born before we woke to books.[3]

the reason being, as Dr. Oliver Wendell Holmes discovers, that *the ol-factory nerve is the only one directly connected with the hemispheres of the brain, the parts in which, as we have every reason to believe, the intellectual processes are performed;*[4] thus, as Southey records, the *atmospheric odour of antiquity, and books, is more grateful to the olfactories of a student than the fumes of any pastille.*[5] They dote upon this fragrance as upon a sweet-smelling flower or a delicate perfume: *Sweeter than thy unguents and cosmetics and Sabean perfumes is the smell of those old books of mine;*[6] they are so ravished by the fragrance of an old library, or even a single old book, that they are in like case with Fabullus, who was to dine with his friend Catullus, when, among other good things, there would be a perfume, *love's very essence, more delicious than love*, so that when he sniffed it he would pray the gods to make him all nose,

> Quod tu cum olfacies, deos rogabis,
> Totum ut te faciant, Fabulle, nasum.[7]

---

[1] *Bibliomania.* (1811) 31.   [2] Samuel Butler, *Life and Habit.* 219.   [3] Lionel Johnson, 'Incense', *Selections.* 52.   [4] *Autocrat of the Breakfast-Table.* (1902) 70.   [5] *The Doctor.* cxii.   [6] Eugene Field, *Love Affairs of a Bibliomaniac.* 61.   [7] *Catullus.* Loeb Lib. Ed. xiii, 19.

This is a true symptom of love, whether it is *the sexual significance of odour within the purely animal limit*, or the use of those *artificial perfumes* which have been most cunningly concocted, *to heighten the natural odour when it is regarded as attractive*, and *to disguise it when it is regarded as repellent*,[1] although, as many will agree with Remy de Gourmont, *la femme qu'on aime sent toujours bon*.[2] In this manner the fragrance of books recalls joys past and to come: *the body became adorned to the sense of smell just as by clothing and ornament it is adorned to the sense of sight*.[3]

More perpendicular to my argument is that influence of the odour of leather which Ellis clearly shows has ever been a concomitant of love, as in his instance of a lady[4] *entirely normal in sexual and other respects*, who was *conscious of a considerable degree of pleasurable sexual excitement in the presence of the smell of leather objects, leather-bound ledgers, etc.*, and that other case which he cites[5] out of *Salmuth*,[6] of a young girl of noble birth, in the seventeenth century, who experienced extreme pleasure in smelling old books; the fascination being not so much in the odour of the leather as in the mouldy smell of worm-eaten books themselves: *foetore veterum librorum, a blattis et tineis exesorum, situque prorsus corruptorum*. Thus the mustiness of old paper which might nauseate some rejoices the soul of the true bookman, as the bibliophile in *Fitzgerald*,[7] who, having read that Schiller always kept *rotten apples* in his study because their scent was beneficial to him, pointed to those bookshelves which held his oldest editions, and said: *These are my rotten apples*. But in most of my instances the aroma is pleasant as well as beneficent, as what seductive fragrance is not? When Charles Lamb entered the Bodleian for the first time, he seemed to *inhale learning walking amid* the *foliage* of so many eloquent books, *and the odour of their old moth-scented coverings is fragrant as the first bloom of those sciential apples which grew amid the happy orchard*.[8] Percy Fitzgerald himself recognized an agreeable *aroma* about the original editions of *Elia*;[9] Dibdin called those books he procured from Lincoln Cathedral his *Lincoln Nosegay*; Charles Dickens notes *the pleasant smell of paper freshly pressed*, which issued forth from a bookshop, awakening *instant recollections* of schooldays, and the *whiff of russia leather* from the rows of bound volumes suggested happiness;[10] James Russell Lowell *is at home wherever he smells the invigorating fragrance of russia leather*;[11] as in the poet,

[1] Havelock Ellis, 'Sexual Selection in Man', *Psych. of Sex*. iv, 91.   [2] *Promenades Philosophiques*. 3 Serie.   [3] Ellis, *op. cit*. iv, 91.   [4] *Ib*. iv, 101.   [5] *Ib*. iv. 101.n.   [6] *Observationes Medicae*. Centuria ii, 63.   [7] *Book-Fancier*. 8.   [8] 'Oxford in the Vacation', *Essays of Elia*.   [9] *Lamb*. Fitzgerald. 23.   [10] *Martin Chuzzlewit*.   [11] O. W. Holmes, *Autocrat of the Breakfast-Table*. (1902) 21.

With open nostrils from afar you scent
The faint aroma of the rich Levant;[1]

and Anatole France tells of an old Canon of the Church who, loving books
beyond all things, felt he was yielding too greatly to the things of this
world when he *breathed the perfume of a bookseller's shop on the Quai des
Grands-Augustins.*[2]

Thomas Rawlinson, the great collector, would *regale himself with the
sight and the scent of innumerable black-letter volumes,* arranged '*three deep*'
from the bottom to the top of his house;[3] Giacomo, in Flaubert's tale, breathes
the *venerable dust* of his *oldest* and *dirtiest* volumes with a *sweet and tender
delight.*[4] George Gissing knew every one of his books by its *scent;*[5] he had
but to put his *nose between the pages to be reminded of all sorts of things;* he
cannot open his Gibbon, which *he has read and read and read again for more
than thirty years, but the scent of the noble page* restores all *the exultant happiness* of the moment when he received it as a prize; and his *Great Cambridge
Shakespeare* has an *odour* which carries him yet farther back, for the copy
belonged to his father, who would take a volume down from its shelf and
permit him, as a child not old enough to read, *reverently to turn the leaves;
the volumes smell,* he recalls, *exactly as they did in that old time,* and *a strange
tenderness* comes upon him when he holds one of them in his hand. The
first scent of books[6] when newly received from the bookseller thrills him
as it thrilled Hazlitt.[7]

This fragrance creates longing, stimulates desire even, as some have
experienced, for the doctrines expressed in the book. Archbishop Parker,[8]
Queen Elizabeth's favourite prelate, records that *some men smelling the
printing* of his *Antiquity of the British Church,* were *very desirous cravers of
the same;* a statement which supports those who argue that the contents of
books themselves give off odours, both pleasant and unpleasant. C. E.
Montague *came to hate a bad sentence like a bad smell and to revel in a good one
as he might in a rose.*[9] Most bibliophiles are adept at *smelling out the odori-
ferous flowers of fancy.*[10] Richard le Gallienne finds *Marius the Epicurean*
sweet-smelling as sanctuary *incense;*[11] for Henri Pène du Bois the *Fleurs du
Mal* of Baudelaire *exhale intoxicating perfumes,* and the vignettes of the
eighteenth century are as *fragrant as the lily and the rose;*[12] but to show that
such smells are a matter of taste, Robert Buchanan stoutly gave out that
Baudelaire filled *the select salon of English literature with a perfume to which*

[1] Halkett Lord, *Book-Lore.* ii, 99.   [2] 'Bibliophilia', *Life and Letters.* Second Series.
Trans. Evans. 63.   [3] Dibdin, *Bibliomania.* (1811) 455.   [4] *Bibliomania.* Trans.
Koch. 11–12.   [5] *The Private Papers of Henry Ryecroft.* 30–1.   [6] *Private Papers of
Henry Ryecroft.* 44.   [7] Hazlitt, *Sketches and Essays.*   [8] *Life.* Strype. 415.   [9] *C. E.
Montague: a Memoir.* Elton. 7.   [10] *Love's Labour's Lost.* iv, 2.   [11] *Vanishing
Roads.* 267.   [12] *Four Private Libraries of New York.* 58, 86.

the smell of Mrs. Aphra Behn's books is savoury, and that of Catullus' 'lepidum novum libellum' absolutely delicious.[1] Arnold's *Light of Asia* not only enchanted Lafcadio Hearn, it *perfumed his mind as with the incense of a strangely new and beautiful worship.*[2] Eugene Field had a folio that smelt of the *sea* and *a staunch ship's hold,* a French book which gave off a *faint perfume* of *lily* and *asphodel,* a small Puritan volume which exhaled *wintergreen* and *peppermint,* and an *Izaak Walton* redolent of *buttercups* and *daisies* and *roses,* all of which and more he has celebrated in a song.[3]

Books, however, do not always smell sweet, as many stout moralists have maintained: even Coleridge asserts that the philosophers Hume, Locke, and Hobbes *stink worse than feather or assafœtida.*[4] But my business here is to associate the sense of smell with the body of the book rather than with its contents; and to indicate the rapture of the bibliophile in these inhalations, for *everything about a book smells sweet in his nostrils, from the leather of the binding to the print upon the page.*[5] A French authority[6] says that the development of this sense is the result of too much love of them as *material objects,* their form, weight, texture of paper, ease of opening. They seek out and revel in the fine fragrance of new books, the rich and distinctive *bouquet* of ripe old volumes, or the characteristic scent which in some indicates country of origin. It is a natural step from this state (if it is as superficial as he suspects) to *perfume them, when they had lost their odour,* to which I have said some things already.

IV. TASTING

Taste is proper to lovers, for love in itself is a kind of hunger,

> creature of poignant thirst
> And exquisite hunger,[7]

seeking ever the divine essence of the beloved, in which delicate pursuit taste is a chief instrument: *so many ways of tasting and adoring God,*[8] and as many of tasting and adoring books, for if, in the last resort, *taste,* as Poe believed, is the *sole arbiter* of poetry,[9] which forms but one part of literature, there needs no further proof of its arbitrament of the whole:

> Le goût n'est rien qu'un bon sens délicat;[10]

---

[1] *The Fleshly School of Poetry.* 21.   [2] *Life and Letters.* Ed. Bisland. i, 291.   [3] *Love Affairs of a Bibliomaniac.* 167.   [4] *Letters.* Ed. E. H. Coleridge. i, 358.   [5] Virginia Woolf, 'The Essays of Augustine Birrell', *Life and Letters.* July 1930.   [6] Valery Larbaud, *Transition.* Feb. 1929. 246.   [7] D. G. Rossetti, 'Bridal Love', *Poems.* (1870) 189.   [8] H. F. Amiel, *Journal.*   [9] 'The Poetic Principle', *Essays.*   [10] Chénier.

it is the common-sense of genius, Chateaubriand says,[1] and without it genius itself is but a sublime species of folly. It is therefore a necessary quality and naturally active among lovers, whether they love lightly or deeply, but most when passion deepens into ecstasy:

> Ah that my mouth for Muses' milk were fed
> On the sweet blood thy sweet small wounds had bled!
> That with my tongue I felt them, and could taste
> The faint flakes from thy bosom to the waist!
> That I could drink thy veins as wine, and eat
> Thy breasts like honey! that from face to feet
> Thy body were abolished and consumed,
> And in my flesh thy very flesh entombed![2]

There is as much variety as delight in the tastings proper to book-love, for *denique non omnes eadem mirantur amantque*,[3] all love not the same things, but in all it is a prime motive.

Many examples might I bring which for brevity I omit, further evidence being unnecessary in support of what is obvious; and I do so without fear of censure, as you will find much to this same end if you consult my chapter of the *Bibliophagi*.[4]

V. TOUCHING

I come, then, finally in this recital of the part played by the senses in bibliophily, to Touch, which the ancients believed to be the last and *most ignoble*[5] of them, perhaps because it is, as Aristotle records,[6] common to all save some *imperfect animals*. But in our time this would not be allowed, and the more discriminating would support Brillat-Savarin, who held that the *sense of touch* will *have its turn* and provide us with *a source of new modes of enjoyment*. What made this more probable was, he held, the fact that *tactile sensibility*, being confined to no *special part, can therefore be acted upon throughout the whole body*.[7] Touch, then, should be judged on its merits with the rest, for it may be exquisite in all men, as it is among the most admirable and illustrious of book-lovers, aiding them towards the perception of several otherwise unapprehended qualities in their adored treasures, for as the poet sings,

> Touch is understanding by relation,
> Touch is sympathy and so creation.[8]

[1] *Essai sur la Littérature.*   [2] Swinburne, 'Anactoria', *Poems and Ballads.* (1866) 69.
[3] Horace, *Epistles.* II, ii, 58.   [4] *Ante.* i, 187–218.   [5] Burton, *Anat. Melan.* (1904) i, 181.   [6] *On Memory.* Qt. Gellius, *Attic Nights.* vi. 6.   [7] *Physiologie du Goût.* Trans. Anderson. 7.   [8] Gordon Bottomley, 'A Hymn of Touch', *Chambers of Imagery.* 10.

Thus they achieve a peculiar, a rich sufficiency, an extraordinary delight, by stroking their books. The smooth back of a fair old volume is an irresistible temptation. They must touch, and, touching, gloat upon their happiness, as that old Canon in *Anatole France*,[1] who spent whole days on the Quai Voltaire, *taking delight* in such *pleasant touching*, or, in the other extreme, they long to hold and fondle a favourite all their lives.[2]

Arthur Symons was helped to a realization that prose *could be a fine art* by reading Pater's Studies in the *History of the Renaissance*, in its *first edition on ribbed paper. I have*, he tells, *the feel of its still in my fingers*.[3] That such men are conscious of the joys of this tactile sense I shall now demonstrate, for they not only long to be with their books, they must also fondle and caress them. *Oh that I could hug 'The gardin of Pleasance'*, '*French sonattis in writt'*, '*Recull de poesie'*, *etc.*, *breaks forth Atticus*;[4] and books yearn sometimes for the tender reciprocity, not often denied them: when I *take them from their places*, Eugene Field reports, *how tenderly do they respond to the caresses of my hands;*[5] *come, let me take thee from thy shelf*, he says to a favourite copy of *Walton* which he has *cherished full sweetly* for fifty years, *and hold thee lovingly in my hands and press thee tenderly to this aged and slowly-pulsing heart of mine!*[6]

> Oh friends, whom chance and change can never harm,
> Whom Death the tyrant cannot doom to die,
> Within whose folding soft eternal charm
> I love to lie.[7]

Floressas des Esseintes *fondled* reverently his copy of the *Satyricon* of 1585;[8] Librarian Jenkinson of Cambridge University *stroked* and *admired* a *Rushworth* which a young book-lover was carrying into the library;[9] *virtue passed through the hem of their parchment and leather garments whenever* James Russell Lowell *touched* his books, *as the precious drugs sweated through the bat's handle in the Arabian story*.[10] The very size of the first edition of the *Reliquiae Wottonianae*, I find in a confidence of mine own,[11] *was an invitation to caresses and those adorable little familiarities which are the prerogatives of the best-loved books. Possession*, Leigh Hunt argues,[12] is essential *to perfect the communion*, but *the mere contact is much, even when our mistress speaks an unknown language*. Petrarch could not read *Homer* in the original, but when the book is first printed in Italy he secures a copy and *in a transport* places it beside *Plato*, worshipping it as *an unknown god* and embracing

[1] 'Bibliophilia', *Life and Letters*. Second Series. Trans. Evans. 63.   [2] Flaubert, *Bibliomania*. Trans. Koch. 30.   [3] *Figures of Several Centuries*. 322.   [4] Dibdin, *Decameron*. iii, 245. n.   [5] *Love Affairs of a Bibliomaniac*. 98.   [6] *Ib*. 879.   [7] B. W. Proctor, *An Autobiographical Fragment*.   [8] Huysmans, *A Rebours*. 43.   [9] *Francis Jenkinson*. Stewart. 42.   [10] O.W. Holmes, *Autocrat of the Breakfast-Table*. (1902) 21.   [11] 'The Reliquiae Wottonianae', *Bibliophile's Almanack*. (1927) 7.   [12] 'My Books', *Essays*. Camelot Ed. 295.

it. He records a like habit in his friend Raymond Monet, who was *overjoyed* when Petrarch *placed some new book in his hands*; he would *clasp it to his bosom with a sigh*, and as lovers are exalted by contact with the beloved, so Raymond became happier by *the mere touch and sight of books*, and as he believed, *more learned*.[1]

Leigh Hunt is a conspicuous example of these intimacies, for he has these words of himself: *I delight to be in contact with them.* He loved the very *feel* of books; their closeness; he will press them, get close to them: *I like to lean my head against them:*[2]

> The fire-light flickers on the wall of books,
> While my dear father slumbers in its shade,
> And leaning as he sits, his head he's laid
> 'Gainst his beloved Spenser; and he looks,
> As though his mind through those delicious nooks
> Of Fairy-land with perfect Una stray'd,—
> List'ning to the lovely things she said
> In voice far sweeter than Spenserian brooks,[3]

and he is coy, casting sidelong glances, as though at shy nymphs: *I looked sideways at my 'Spenser', my 'Theocritus', and my 'Arabian Nights'; then above them at my Italian Poets; then behind me at my 'Dryden' and 'Pope', my romances, and my 'Boccaccio'; and on my left at my 'Chaucer'.*[4] And so doing he thought how natural it was for Charles Lamb to *kiss an old folio* as he once saw him kiss *Chapman's Homer*, which is not the only recorded demonstration of its kind, for Henry Crabb Robinson once saw Coleridge kiss the engraved title-page of his copy of *Spinoza*;[5] Benedetto Croce confesses[6] that when a youth he *kissed the pages* of Pellico's *Le mi prigioni, in an ecstasy of joy*; and a like affection was shown by Thackeray when, in the presence of Edward FitzGerald, he held a letter from Charles Lamb to his brows and ejaculated, *Saint Charles!* Nor have books been kissed only by bibliophiles. Vittoria Colonna kissed a neglected copy of *Dante*:

> And once, with pensive eyes and drooping head,
> Musing, Vittoria Colonna came,
> And touched my leaves with dreamy finger-tips,
> Lifted me up half absently, and read;
> Then kissed the page with sudden, tender lips,
> And sighed, and murmured one beloved name.

But this was not book-love.[7]

[1] Tatham, *Francesco Petrarca*. ii, 381.   [2] *Op. cit.* 287.   [3] Vincent Hunt. Qt. Blunden, *Leigh Hunt*. 310.   [4] Leigh Hunt, *op. cit.* 287.   [5] Crabb Robinson, *Diary*. i, 209.   [6] *An Autobiography*. Trans. R. G. Collingwood. (1927) 35.   [7] Caroline Wilder Fellows, *Book-Song*. 53,

When Johnson and Boswell visited William Henry Ireland, the forger of Shakespearian MSS., Boswell was so overcome with the sight of documents which he believed had been handled by Shakespeare that he knelt down and kissed them. Holy Books have been kissed in many ages, as a sign of truthfulness on taking oath. King Malcolm Canmore of Scotland, who could not read, showed so much reverence for the books beloved of his Queen, that he would often take them into his hands, fondle and kiss them.[1] In our own time William Morris confessed to so great a love for his own romance, *The Roots of the Mountains*, which he had caused to be printed finely in Caslon Old Face characters at the Chiswick Press, that *any day* he was *to be seen huggling it up*, and was *become a spectacle to Gods and men because of it*.[2] They cannot contain themselves in these extremes, they must ever be petting them, patting, stroking, feeling the smoothness of their covers; as Isaac D'Israeli[3] quotes out of Henry Rantzau, founder of a great library at Copenhagen, whose days were *dissolved in the pleasures of reading*:

> Salvete aureoli mei libelli
> Meae deliciae, mei lepores!
> Quam vos saepe oculis juvat videre,
> Et tritos manibus tenere nostris.
>
> Golden volumes! Richest treasures!
> Objects of delicious pleasures!
> You my eyes rejoicing please,
> You my hands in rapture seize!

Henry Bradshaw fondled the *caressing clasp*[4] of a rare volume, and when *early books and manuscripts* were to be moved to a new place in the Library at Cambridge *he carried them for the most part with his own hands*, as much from love as from fear that they might be hurt.[5] To see and touch the handwriting of some great man of the past, to hold in his possession a rare manuscript was for him a passionate experience.[6] He looked into the soul of his books and *loved to know something of the personal history of any volume which might come into his hands*.[7]

To turn over the pages of a book long coveted, to handle an unexpected find, to fondle a binding, to dust the edges, are exquisite joys in which the hand shares with the eye, exclaims Octave Uzanne;[8] and to hug under the arm a newly acquired book, he says, is an exquisite pleasure, the ecstasy and pride of possession. This is supported by Fontaine de Resbecq's[9] account of how he

[1] Madan, *Books in Manuscript*. 125.   [2] *Life*. Mackail. ii, 227.   [3] *Cur. of Lit*. i, 7–8.
[4] *Memoir*. Prothero. 326.   [5] *Ib*. 190.   [6] *Ib*. 331.   [7] *Ib*. 163.   [8] *Book-Hunter in Paris*. 101–11.   [9] Qt. Lang, *Books and Bookmen*. 14–15.

wooed and won his copy of the most desirable of all the Elzevirs, the famous old cookery book, *Le Pastissier François*. The event happened during a hunt for rare and fair copies *by the Pont Marie and the Quai de la Grève, the Pillars of Hercules of the book-hunting world*. He had scanned many boxes of volumes without a catch and was on the point of retiring from the chase when his attention was caught by *a small naked volume, without a stitch of binding*. He seized it, and to his delight recognized it as that famed Elzevir whose proportions are measured *as minutely as the carats of a diamond*. There was no indication of price on the box where the treasure was lying; and although the little book was unbound and neglected, it was wondrous sweet and clean within. 'How much?' he asked the *bouquiniste*. 'Six sous!' The happy hunter handed the money, *trembling a little* with excitement at his luck, and marched away *fondly embracing the beloved object of his search*. Dr. Rosenbach records[1] that when Mr. Harry B. Smith bought at auction the copy of *Queen Mab* with Shelley's inscription to Mary Wollstonecraft Godwin, an old bibliophile came up to him and, brushing tears from his eyes, asked *if he might merely hold the book in his hands for a moment*. Mr. Gladstone[2] *loved collecting, buying, handling books; a joy to him to arrange with his own hands the books in the library he had founded in memory of St. Deiniol*.

They all like to sort and arrange them. Gleeson White would *take pleasure* in selecting a place for a newcomer near by *kindred volumes*. He kept his favourites, and they were all favoured, free from *stain or scar*, handling his books, says York Powell,[3] *as a born lover should*. Spencer records that Andrew Lang turned the pages of *a treasured book with emotion*.[4] There were books of which George Gissing had *a passionate need*, books more necessary to him than *bodily nourishment: I could see them, of course, at the British Museum*, he confesses,[5] *but that was not at all the same thing as having and holding them, my own property, on my own shelf*. They cling passionately to them even when possession has reduced them to poverty: *still he caressed the cause of his ruin*, so there are those who *hug the very volumes of which they know they cannot afford the purchase-money*.[6] Like Virgil's shepherd,

Ut vidi, ut perii—ut me malus abstulit error!

one is not happy in books unless one loves to caress them,[7]

> The tender touches that I give,
> To every well-worn cover,
> And as I love you, friends of mine,
> I could not love a lover.[8]

---

[1] *Books and Bidders*. 40. [2] Lord Rosebery, *Appreciations and Addresses*. 150.
[3] Intro., *Cat. Lib. of Gleeson White*. 1899. x. [4] *Forty Years in My Bookshop*. 213.
[5] *Private Papers of Henry Ryecroft*. 33. [6] Dibdin, *Bibliomania*. (1811) 690. [7] Anatole France, *Life and Letters*. Second Series. 60. [8] Bessie Craigmyle, *Book-Song*. 30.

Their fingers *thrill to the touch of old vellum*, their eyes *light to the appeal of faded print*,[1] 'tis their only desire, they rave upon it. When Leigh Hunt spoke of being *in contact* with his books, he meant it *literally*:[2]

> How pure the joy, when first my hands unfold
> The small, rare volumes, black with tarnish'd gold![3]

Most of our bibliophiles are of his humour and opinion, they clamour for possession, *like to feel* their *darling books*[4] about them, *to be in the arms of our mistress Philosophy, rather than see her at a distance.*[5] And when Charles Lamb compiles his catalogue of the sweet things of life from which with the passage of time we must inevitably part, he does not forget his books: *and you, my midnight darlings, my folios! must I part with the intense delight of having you (huge armfuls) in my embraces?* And the books themselves are all the better for these familiarities. They like to be felt; bloom afresh, renew their vigour, are radiant, under the caressing touch of their lovers.

---

[1] *Portrait of a Scholar.* Chapman. 65.   [2] 'My Books', *Essays.* Camelot Ed.   [3] *Bibliomania.* Ferriar. 137–8.   [4] Merryweather, *Bibliomania in the Middle Ages.* 17.   [5] Leigh Hunt, *The Indicator.*

Part XXXII

BIBLIOPHILY TRIUMPHANT

———————————⬧◦⬧———————————

I. WEDDED TO BOOKS

Let us love books as we love love, *dum vires annique sinunt*,[1] while we are in the flower of years, fit for love, and while time serves,

> Gather ye rose-buds while ye may,
> Old Time is still a-flying:
> And this same flower that smiles to-day
> To-morrow will be dying.[2]

Volat irrevocabile tempus, time past cannot be recalled. But we need no such exhortation,

> Let me not to the marriage of true minds
> Admit impediments.[3]

We would be *wedded to books*, as Leigh Hunt advocates, and as Milton was *married to immortal verse*,[4] or that uxorious bibliophile, the Duke of Roxburghe, *whose passion*, saith Dibdin,[5] *evinced all the warmth of a lover, and all the fidelity of a husband*; and Southey, De Quincey declares,[6] *lived in his library, which Coleridge used to call his wife*, for, mine author[7] gives out, *he was by nature something of an old bachelor*, filling Greta Hall with *pretty articles—bijouterie*, etc., and cultivating *particularly elegant habits* (*Wordsworth called them finical*) *in the use of books*. We shall love them *with amorous precision*, as Robert Louis Stevenson notes[8] Hazlitt loved the *New Héloïse* at an inn at Llangollen, for we are the willing slaves of our collections as they are ours, we need them, they need us; and we shall love them forever, as Lionel Johnson his *Elia*:

> With, gentlest of the martyrs! *Lamb*,
> Whose lover I, long lover, am.[9]

---

[1] Ovid. A.A. ii, 669. [2] Herrick, 'To the Virgins, to make much of Time'.
[3] Shakespeare, *Sonnets*. cxvi. [4] *L'Allegro*. [5] *Reminiscences*. i, 361–2. [6] 'Literary Reminiscences', *Works*. ii, 312. [7] *Ib*. 317. [8] 'Walking Tours', *Virginibus Puerisque*. 257. [9] 'Oxford Nights', *Poetical Works*. 100.

Gissing devotes a whole chapter in *The Private Papers of Henry Ryecroft* to his love of *The Tempest*. *Live as long as one might*, it would be always the same *whilst one had strength to turn the pages and a mind left to read them*; love and reverence are increased by intimacy; *all its greatness and sweetness, all that incommunicable heritage for which men live and die*. It is a sweet bargain, and *notre innocente passion est une franc-maçonnerie*,[1] we know one another, whether our passion be innocent or not, *à mille ligues de distance, on sait le nom de celui-ci, de celui-là*, as when, he recalls, a Russian was presented to Sylvestre de Sacy and first recognized him by his wit, then by his books, *et la connaissance est faite*. We have but to observe their way with a book, their approach, behaviour, technique. You can *recognize a true bibliophile at a glance*, says Anatole France,[2] by his manner of touch: *The man who puts his hand on some precious, rare, lovable, or at the least, seemly volume, and who does not voluptuously pass a tender palm over its back, its sides, and its edges, that man never had the instinct that makes Groliers and Doubles.*

That this *literary voluptuousness*[3] is a true passion needs no controversy; and sure, I think it hath been ordered by God's especial providence, that in all ages there should be (as usually there is) a goodly company of bibliophiles who not only seek the tomes of their desire, but who open a *new catalogue*, as Leigh Hunt did, with all *the fervour of the first love*.[4] Dibdin, Merryweather, and some others, confused the love of books with bibliomania, as though there were no love but those aberrations which Krafft-Ebing discourses in his *Psychopathia Sexualis*. But it is improperly so called. It is a true and sane love, as I have said, and is opportunely named by our best authorities bibliophily. But it would be no over-seeming to put a more honourable title upon it, *amor nobilis*, as Savonarola styled *Heroical Love*, because noble men and women make a practice of it, and are so ordinarily affected with it, but not more noble than those who have been moved by bibliophily, as I have shown and none can disannul. Ferriar illustrates this point with many examples of the book-worthiness of the true bibliophile:

> For you the Monk illum'd his pictured page,
> For you the press defies the spoils of age;
> Faustus for you infernal tortures bore,
> For you Erasmus starved on Adria's shore.
> The Folio-Aldus loads your happy shelves,
> And dapper Elzevirs, like fairy-elves,
> Show their light forms amidst the well-gilt Twelves:

---

[1] Jules Janin, *Le Livre*. 17.   [2] *Life and Letters*. Second Series. 60.   [3] Leigh Hunt, *My Books*.   [4] *Monthly Repository*. (1837)

In slender type the Giolitos shine,
And bold Bodoni stamps his Roman line.
For you the Louvre opes its regal doors,
And either Didot lends his brilliant stores:
With faultless types, and costly sculptures bright,
Obarra's Quixote charms your ravished sight:
Laborde in splendid tablets shall explain
Thy beauties, glorious though unhappy Spain![1]

Yet because the necessary books are not at hand to every man, I will briefly touch upon what manner of man has been engendered by this humour, how affected and to what end.

II. OF BIBLIOPHILES

These illuminati, like poets and lovers, are born not made, indeed *you become less of a bibliophile the more you strive after that coveted title;*[2] nor are they to be reckoned of one breed: they are drawn from all classes, as the cream is separated and drawn from all the parts and constituent elements of the milk. Kings and princes, ministers of state, nobles of all degrees and nations, princes of the Church of Rome, and of our English Church, monks, priests, canons, prebendaries, etc., and clerks in holy orders of all manner and means; and the priests of other faiths, Mahommedan, Hebrew, Buddhist, and the like; sheiks, satraps, shereefs, pachas, nabobs, rajahs, etc.; students rich and poor; professors, doctors (divinity, medical, scientific, legal), barristers, attorneys, factors (in Scotland), authors, journalists, artists, teachers, dons, graduates and undergraduates; merchant princes, bankers, financiers, artisans, and manufacturers; rich and poor, noble and simple, each class, trade, profession, industry, estate, rendering tribute, supplying its quota, electing its candidates, unconsciously, unpretentiously, without fuss or show, by a natural selection, in which love, desire, passion (read more of this in Darwin, Huxley, Lamarck, Butler), play their part in the creation of a small old but ever new class, living apart, content in solitariness if needs be, but cognisant one of another, *en passant*, by signs, symptoms, indications, as among aristocrats, freemasons (as I have sufficiently shown).[3] But, unlike others, in that faculty of sufficiency in themselves and their all-satisfying passion, they do not gloom and glower like those who are solitary because unfavoured, and who are therefore resentful, splenetic, choleric, and dare not come abroad for fear of

[1] *Bibliomania*. 15–29.   [2] Gustave Mouravit, *Le Livre et la Petite Bibliothèque d'Amateur*. 120.   [3] 'The Origin of Species', *Ante*. i, 387–419.

rebuffs, but melancholize in corners, and keep in holes. Nor is their passion subject to fierce reactions, as concupiscence, *omne animal post coitum triste*; no after-effects, but a continuous glow of engendering warmth. And whensoever thou art thoroughly affected with this passion that sweetness will be thine, and thou wilt be among them, initiated by thine own fervent desire, nought else, pedigrees or credentials are unnecessary.

When bibliophiles are drawn from the loneliness of those Royal houses which stand apart from the commonalty, a *vita nuova* opens out for them. *The Stuarts were reading men; even Charles, Prince of Wales over the water, was a bibliophile. James I was a poet, James V was no better, James VI was a bookworm, and Charles I was a collector.*[1] King Alfred the Great became an *amator librorum* from the pages of *a richly illuminated* little book of Saxon poetry given him by the Queen-mother as *a reward for the facility with which he had mastered its contents.*[2] The Emperor Julian, even from a boy, he tells Ecdicius, Prefect of Egypt, had always *a violent passion for books*; and after the mob had murdered Georgius, Bishop of Alexandria, his love burst aflame for the good Bishop's books. He would have them at all costs, as any tyrant the desire of his eyes. He esteemed it *an unpardonable absurdity* that these treasures should belong to those *whose avarice cannot be satiated even with gold*; and he commands Ecdicius to secure the whole library of Georgius from his Librarian, with that functionary's freedom as his reward, *if he be diligent in this discovery*, but, on the other side, *let him know he shall not escape the Rack, if he prevaricates, or acts either maliciously or knavishly.*[3]

Some of the most stirring men of the world, *persons in the thick of business of all kinds, with the business of the world itself upon their hands*, have combined with their energies *the greatest love of books*[4] (for great geniuses have often been great lovers), as Lorenzo de Medici, who ruled a state, founded a library, and loved books. Many look forward to an old age devoted to them. Roger Ascham had a nostalgia for the quiet retreats of Cambridge: having *experience of life led at home and abroad*, and knowing what he could *do most fitly* and how he would *live most gladly*, he did well perceive there was *no such quietness in England, nor pleasure in strange countries, as even in St. John's College, to keep company with the Bible, Plato, Aristotle, Demosthenes and Tully.*[5] Such retreats from the tribulations and vanities of life have been sought by *wise and great men of all classes*, as the Diocletians of old and the Foxes and Burkes of nearer days. *The wish to possess a country house, a retreat, a nest, a harbour of some kind from the storms and even from the agitating*

---

[1] Lang, Intro., *Pleasures of Bookland.* Shaylor. xvi.　　[2] Merryweather, *Bibliomania in the Middle Ages.* 101–2.　　[3] *Letters of the Ancients.* Savage. 326–7.　　[4] Leigh Hunt, *Book for a Corner.* Intro.　　[5] From a Letter, 24.iii.1553. Qt. Saintsbury, *Letter Book.* 120.

pleasures of life, is as old as the sorrows and joys of civilization. The child feels it when he 'plays at house'; the schoolboy, when he is reading in his corner; the lover when he thinks of his mistress. Epicurus felt it in his garden; Horace and Virgil expressed their desire of it in passages which the sympathy of mankind has rendered immortal.[1] It was the end of all the wisdom of Shakespeare, who, it is said, retired to Stratford-on-Avon, and built himself a house, where he lived peacefully till he died.

III. THE UNDYING FLAME

But whether they retire from the busy world or not, their love continues: inborn and life-long. Robert Hoe said that *the love of books was born in him;*[2] and the book-passion *furnished the real occupation* of Gabriel Naudé's life.[3] 'Tis evident, even among booksellers, who often find the *dulcis odor libri* more grateful to their nostrils than the *dulcis odor lucri*, as George Nicol, bookseller to George III and the Duke of Roxburghe, who showed more interest in books than money, though a fortune could have been his for the gathering of it. *He always seemed to love his dusty retreat better than his boudoir-shop.*[4] Leigh Hunt had this *passion for books* more deeply than most. It formed the real business of his life, as it did that of Robert Southey, despite their indefatigable labours as men of letters, who saw so much of books, so many of them, for they were the raw material of their trade. What better evidence that it is a love without satiety, unchanging, indestructible! *Why, Montesinos* (who is Southey), asks the ghostly Sir Thomas More, in one of the *Colloquies*,[5] *with these books and the delight you take in their constant society, what have you to covet or desire? Nothing*, is the answer, *Nothing . . . but more books.* From an *unabating love of letters and perpetual occupation* with his studies, Huet derives benefits which he *regards as of the highest value*, because while so living he has *never felt that satiety of life, that weariness with all its objects, of which other persons are so often heard to complain.*[6] Crabb Robinson *fell in love* with Wordsworth's poems when they were first published; he became their *passionate lover*, and *fifty years* afterwards loved them *more* than he did at first.[7]

Such as these are bibliophiles, but they are married lovers. De Quincey called Southey's library his *wife*, and, adds Dowden,[8] *in a certain sense it was wife and mistress and mother to him.* Their presence and his enjoyment of

[1] Rosebery, *Appreciations and Addresses.* [2] *Essays and Verses about Books.* Beverley Chew. 99. [3] *Great Book-Collectors.* Elton. 183. [4] Dibdin, *Reminiscences.* i, 348. [5] Southey, *Sir Thomas More: Or Colloquies on the Progress and Prospects of Society.* xiv. 'The Library.' [6] *Memoirs of Huet.* Trans. Aikin. i, 15. [7] *Diary.* Third Edition. ii, 362. [8] *Southey.* Dowden. 103–4.

them were not his sole delight: *there was also the pursuit, the surprisal, the love-making or wooing. And at last in his hour of weakness, once more a little child, he would walk slowly round his library, looking at his cherished volumes, taking them down mechanically, and when he could no longer read, pressing them to his lips*, as Charles Lamb and Coleridge had done. All the joys of the lover were his when a new box of books arrived at Keswick. *O the joy of opening such a chest; of discovering the glorious folios; of glancing with the shy amorousness of first desire at title-page and colophon; of growing familiarity; of tracing out the history suggested by book-plate or autograph; of finding a lover's excuse for cropped margin, or water-stain, or worm-hole.*[1] All bookmen share his raptures, as Mark Pattison at his father's parsonage at Hauxwell, in north Yorkshire, when *the arrival of a new book in the house was the event of the week*. The reception of the parcel from the bookseller at Richmond provoked an *excitement* which he never forgot. He would walk *up and down the lane waiting for the butcher's cart, which acted as carrier for the village, snatch* up the parcel and *rush in with it*.[2]

Gissing[3] was overcome with joy at the thought of unpacking volumes which had been bought and not seen, and he, as he confesses, was no hunter of rarities, first editions, tall copies, etc. On such occasion when Southey had received the *bill of lading* of a recent acquisition from Verbeyst, of Brussels, he became lyrical. *By this day month they will probably be here*, exclaims this hungry lover, *then*, he continues, *I shall be happier than if his Majesty King George the Fourth were to give orders that I should be clothed in purple, and sleep upon gold, and have a chain upon my neck, and sit next him because of my wisdom, and be called his cousin*,[4] But all these lovers have acclaimed their books as riches, *above the price of rubies, treasures of great price*; when St. Jerome was given *twenty-five volumes of Origen in the martyr's delicate writing, he vowed he felt richer than if he had found the wealth of Croesus*.[5] Well may Austin Dobson sing:

> Brown books of mine, who never yet
> Have caused me anguish or regret,
> I love you. . . .[6]

IV. THE JEALOUS BOOKMAN

I may more appositely infer now that although bibliophiles are immune from many of the disabilities of sex-love, their familiar attendants are fears, jealousies, ficklenesses, exaggerations, estrangements, none the less.

[1] *Ib.* 105.   [2] *Memoirs.* 38.   [3] *Private Papers of Henry Ryecroft.* 44..   [4] *Southey.* Dowden. 104-5.   [5] Elton, *Great Book-Collectors.* 6.   [6] *Poetical Works.* 195.

No cause for surprise here, for all loves are love, however they differ in condition; so book-lovers have their temptations, and they toy with resistance and relish capitulation:

Let my temptation be a book.[1]

Books also must be wooed and courted; and, like women, Gautier observes,[2] *les uns ont de préfaces, les autres n'en ont pas*, some have prefaces, some have not; some surrender at once, others put up a determined resistance, but it is all the same *par la fin*, in the end. It is sad, he thinks, *triste et banal*, but better than if she threw herself at you like a wanton. Would you have a book more impudent than a woman, *et qu'il se livre à vous sans préliminaire?*

Dr. John North *courted, as a fond lover all best editions, fairest character, best bound and preserved.*[3] Dibdin once saw a copy of the *Acta Sanctorum* in Cochrane's bookshop which had been *courted in vain*. No less than *thirteen beneficed clergymen were in the habit of eyeing it askance, first taking up one volume then another*, but no *wooer's ardour* had the courage *to pop the question*.[4] Generally, however, passion overrules hesitation and the reason is carried hoodwinked to its destiny. *No man can have to do with books that presently he does not love them.*[5] They are tempted and fall, if fall it be; they fat themselves with future joys, as Turks feed themselves with an imaginary persuasion of a sensual Paradise, and as several pleasant objects diversely affect diverse men. To no purpose, then, to prescribe correctives, alteratives, cordials: they will go their way, seek their desire, so let those who dislike it howl for a season, it is all one. Let Passion have his course a while, he may burn his fingers, singe his wings, yet if he can learn he will learn; and 'tis a fit method, a very good means. But what have I to do with this? That which I aim at is to show you the progress of the burning book-love, to which the books themselves respond. *The motto of all books of original genius* is, says Birrell, *Love me or leave me alone.*[6] Dr. Adolphous Ward records that Jenkinson was *loved by his books*,[7] and Eugene Field relates[8] that *if I know one thing better than another I know this, that my books know me and love me.*

To epitomize, therefore, all this which I have hitherto said, here is a familiar example out of that eloquent bookman, George Gissing,[9] who was so enamoured that he was, he confesses, *guilty at times of mere self-indulgence* from glancing at a book and being *tempted* when he had not

[1] Eugene Field, in *Book-Song*. 53.   [2] Pref., *Les Jeunes-France*.   [3] Qt. Dibdin, *Bibliomania*. (1811) 410, from 'Life of Dr. John North', *North's Lives*. (1744) [4] *Bibliophobia*. 27.   [5] Field, *Love Affairs of a Bibliomaniac*. 154.   [6] 'Edward Gibbon', *Collected Essays*. i, 233.   [7] *Francis Jenkinson*. Stewart. 82.   [8] *Love Affairs of a Bibliomaniac*. 97–8.   [9] *Private Papers of Henry Ryecroft*. 33–4.

really craved for it. But if there are no cures for these bookish dilemmas, some authorities would take protective measures, as Jacob,[1] who invokes constabulary aid. Ought not the police, he asks, *empêcher ces immorales tentations qui renouvellent le supplice de Tantale, à chaque pas, dans les rues de Paris?*[2] But I am not of his opinion, for although some bibliophiles are too curious or too covetous, and others too amenable to temptation, they learn by experience. I am with William Blake in this matter, believing as I do that *he who desires, but acts not, breeds pestilence.*[3]

Fickleness often draws them from one book to another, as that fantastic bibliomane noted by Jacob who *n'adore ses livres que pour un temps*, gathering them together with enthusiasm, clothing them generously, maintaining them magnificently and honourably; then of a sudden love grows cold and weary, aversion sets in. *Adieu, gentes damoiselles!* The *Grand-Seigneur* is re-forming his harem! *Aux Circassiennes succéderont les Espagnoles, aux blanches Anglaises les négresses du Congo*, Spanish girls will take the place of Circassians, negresses of the Congo will replace the fair English; the *Grand-Seigneur* is selling his wives *à l'encan, mais demain il en achètera de moins jolies*, but they will have the charm *du caprice et de la nouveauté.*[4] The pursuit of variety, in some measure, is a condition of our lives as well as of our loves, and when gratified occasionally there is no harm in it; but habitual pursuit inflames the fever of living by stimulating appetite until it becomes unappeasable. In love, this is often a prime symptom of degeneration, and therefore more proper to bibliomania than to bibliophily, as that symptom of senility exhibited by Théophile Gautier when his book-love declined, and the only pleasure he could derive from books was in the cutting of the leaves with an ivory paper-knife: *c'est une virginité comme une autre, et cela est toujours agréable à prendre.*[5]

But, as in so many of the phenomena of our emotional lives, a hair divides the false and true, and sanity and insanity, goodness and badness, in their more subtle manifestations, differ in diagnosis with point of view. It would, for instance, be dangerous to give out whether the hero of Marcel Proust's *A la Recherche du Temps Perdu* was sane or insane in that vacillating love of his for Albertine, which so much recalls the phase of bibliophily which I have just pointed at. Such lovers as he and those bibliophiles who resemble him are fickle, perchance, because they seek in the beloved object something which cannot *in rerum natura* be there, and in order to give an intenser character to this search, whether the quality sought be there or not, the more sensitive of book-lovers may be endowed, as Proust's hero was, with *a supplementary sense of perception*, which

[1] *Ma République.* 15.   [2] 'Prevent these immoral temptations which renew the torture of Tantalus at every step in the streets of Paris.'   [3] *Marriage of Heaven and Hell.* [4] Jacob, *Ma République.* 54-5.   [5] Pref., *Les Jeunes-France.*

might help them to give a particular distinction to their books, as he was able to see in Gilberte more than was really there and, further, *to distinguish her in all her surroundings;*[1] for women and books are symbols of some exquisitely imagined bliss which remains exquisite, Heaven itself, because it cannot be captured or reached. Thus my Proustian lover declares[2] that the mistresses he has loved most passionately have never responded to his love for them. He claims that the love was genuine, since he *subordinated everything else to the need of seeing them,* of keeping them to himself and being distressed if he waited for them in vain, but more because they had *the faculty of arousing that love, of raising it to a paroxysm, than because they were its image.* When he saw and heard them, he could find nothing in them which resembled his love, and yet his sole joy lay in waiting for them, and seeing them. He believes, therefore, that, passing the promised pleasure in *the form of the woman, it is to those invisible forces which are attached to her that we address ourselves as to obscure deities*: the woman *puts us in touch and does little more.* As like as not, little more can be claimed for a book, and such infidelities as I have named become incidents in the pursuit of *invisible forces* and *obscure deities,* and not subjects of repentance, and I doubt not that bibliophiles (and other lovers) have indulged their presumed guilt so that they may taste the luxury of repentance and forgiveness: *Parce, precor, precor! Non sum qualis eram bonae sub regno Cinarae.*[3]

Dr. John Brown vowed, after some such infidelity, that he was going to *eschew all philandering* with *belles lettres.*[4] The learned and reverend Dr. Young, author of *Night Thoughts,* confessed to Samuel Richardson,[5] whether in stricken conscience for overmuch promiscuity or from a growing consciousness of the approach of old age and impotence, I know not, that *Clarissa* was to be his *last amour.* He was *tender of her welfare* and *sensible of her charms,* but *this amour* differed from *all the others in one respect: I should,* he admitted, *rejoice to have all the world my rivals in it,* which supports my suspicion of impotency. Of a like case, but from another cause, was Sir Walter Scott's reversion to barbaric custom when he sent a copy of *The Lady of the Lake* to Croker in that spirit, he is bold enough to confess, which prompted some ancient peoples to lend their wives to their friends. Scott does it willingly, *greatly to his relief; for never,* he allows, *was man bored of his wife as I am of the said 'Lady'.* Probably his boredom was a moral repulsion against incestuous practices, since he was the creator of the *Lady.*[6] Such examples are not common. Though bibliophiles have been active or passive in this business times out of number, they have rather given than

---

[1] *A la Recherche du Temps Perdu.* Trans. Scott Moncrieff, *Swann's Way.* ii, 273.
[2] *A la Recherche du Temps Perdu.* Trans. Scott Moncrieff, *Cities of the Plain.* ii, 348–9.
[3] Horace, *Odes.* iv, 1.   [4] *Letters.* 113.   [5] *Correspondence of Richardson.* Barbauld. ii, 18.   [6] *Croker Papers.* i, 32.

taken horns. They are over-suspicious, though willing enough to exhibit their treasures to friends, as when Pierre Deschamps, happening to be in St. Petersburg, knocked at Prince Galitzan's door: *Come in and welcome*, said the Prince, *Let me introduce you to my books!*[1] And they will even permit, on occasion, an embrace by way of salutation, or a caress of admiration, but for most part they

Dread the touch of aught but pious hands,[2]

and, for the matter of that, very few even of them. They can brook no rival, or endure any further participation, especially by letting the books out of their sight. Some are *incommunicative*, even on *the subject of their passion, to another not of the craft*,[3] and, says Christopher Morley, *there are even some perversions of passion by which a booklover loses much of his affection for his pet if he sees it too highly commended by some rival critic*, and jealously *indignant if he finds that anyone else has discovered the book.*[4] Such passionate ones look upon a willing lender of a book as no better than a wittol.

Isaac D'Israeli would seem to subscribe to the opposite of all this where he maintains that some collectors are subject to a species of exhibitionism, placing their fame on the *view* of a splendid library. They luxuriate in the thought of parading their books *arrayed in all the pomp of lettering, silk linings, triple gold bands and tinted leather*; but they are for sight, not touch, and they are *locked up in wire cases*, secure from the *vulgar hands* of the *mere reader; dazzling our eyes like Eastern beauties peering through their jalousies.*[5] But, at large, methinks, bibliophiles have little thought but for their own delight, even to the extent of denying a sight of them to their friends, fearing that the mere contact of a look might profane or corrupt, as Alexander when he forbade the beautiful wife of a vanquished foe to be brought to him, *ut eam ne oculis quidem suis contingeret*, lest he touched her with his eyes:[6]

Oh, I should bind this priceless prize
In bindings full and fine,
And keep her where no human eyes
Should see her charms but mine![7]

They have an eager desire to enjoy their books alone, to have them proper to themselves, and to take care lest any stranger should participate with them in their love, for as a recent observer reminds us, '*being in love*' *is a sensation which is essentially founded on an acute desire for possession, or, in*

[1] *Le Livre*. Janin. 17.   [2] Halkett Lord, *Book-Lore*. ii, 99.   [3] Tredwell, *Privately Illustrated Books*. 159.   [4] 'Visiting Bookshops', *Safety Pins*. Travellers Lib. 36. [5] *Cur. of Lit.* i, 14.   [6] Aulus Gellius, *Attic Nights*. vii, 8.   [7] Eugene Field, 'Bibliomaniac's Bride'. Qt. Pref., *Love Affairs of a Bibliomaniac*. vii.

happy cases, a deep satisfaction in possession;[1] for which reason the cautious bibliophile side-tracks possible depredations:

> Let me have books, and stores for one year hence,
> Nor make my life one flutter of suspense.[2]

But since they for the most part are polybiblous, these perturbations are limited. Leigh Hunt[3] was of this kind, and although he did not always act up to his fancies, it would be happy, he confessed, to have *exclusive possession of a book*, one's Shakespeare, for instance. *Think of the pleasure* he says, *of not only being with it in general, of having by far the greater part of its company, but of having it entirely to oneself*; of repeating to oneself *It is my property:*

> 'But mine, but mine,' so I sware to the rose,
> 'For ever and ever, mine,'[4]

of seeing it well dressed, purely to please one's own eyes, of wondering how any fellow could be so impudent as to propose borrowing it for an evening; of being at once proud of his admiration, certain that it was in vain, of the excitement, none the less, *of being a little uneasy* when he approached it *too nearly; of wishing it could give him a cuff on the cheek with one of its beautiful boards, for presuming to like its beauties as well as ourselves; of liking other people's books,* but not supporting *that they should like ours; of getting indifferent to it, and then comforting ourselves with the reflection that others are not so: though to no purpose; in short,* he concludes, *all the mixed transport and anxiety to which the book-wedded state would be liable; not to mention the impossibility of other people's having any literary offspring from our fair unique, and consequently of the danger of loving any compilations but our own.*

In the opposite extreme there are Lotharios among bibliophiles who are content to taste the varied luxury of temporary possession, flitting from flower to flower, enjoying what takes their fancy here and there, with no thought of permanence save in the memory of delicious experiences. Huet conceived an overwhelming desire to see and touch the famous *Garland of Julia*, which was then in the possession of the Duchess d'Uzez, and he expressed this wish to her so frequently that she at length *gratified* him *with the sight*. She locked him in her *cabinet* with the precious book for half a day, and when he was liberated he said he had *never passed a more agreeable afternoon.*[5]

---

[1] *The Technique of the Love Affair*. 44.   [2] Horace, *Epistles*. Trans. Conington. i, 18.
[3] Qt., *Book-Lovers' Anth.* 278–9.   [4] Tennyson, *Maud*.   [5] D'Israeli, *Cur. of Lit.* i, 434.

V. OF THE POLYBIBLOUS

Andrew Lang reports that there was once a bibliophile who claimed that *a man could only love one book at a time*, and he used to carry *the darling of the moment* in *a charming leather case*.[1] In support of this I may cite what Alexandre Dumas tells of the Marquis de Ganay, a roué of books, as amorous of them as any philanderer of the Regency is amorous of women; and his fidelity is as erratic as theirs. Whilst the book is a new toy he is the perfect knight; for a month none more faithful or so full of adoration. He carries it with him, introduces it to his friends, puts it under his pillow at night, and if he awakens before morning, he lights the candle and takes a peep at his treasure; but in a little while the affair ends, and he thinks of the favourite no more.[2] But such kinds are abnormal, most bibliophiles love more than one book at the same time. *Only in the East is man polygamous; nearly everywhere he is polybiblous—a creature of many books.*[3] However good it may be, as Dr. Donne advises, to

> prefer
> One woman first, and then one thing in her,[4]

no normal bibliophile is a monobiblist. *Here again*, Eugene Field advises,[5] *we behold advantage which the lover of books has over the lover of women. A genuine lover can and should love any number of books, and this polybibliophily is not to the disparagement of any one of that number.*

He may, as Dibdin suggests, be devoted to one book in *a union as close and honourable as that of wedlock*,[6] but that book would, as like as not, be no more than a favourite wife, one among many, for *a man's library*, as Emerson continues it, *is a sort of harem*, which many will support from observation and experience, as a correspondent of Hamerton, to whom the *reading of poetry* was *a service of Venus* and poetry itself a substitute for the harem.[7] Emerson goes farther when he gives out that, after the manner of those many-wived Moslems, *tender readers have a pudency in showing their books to a stranger.* Such pudency, perchance, is kin to that jealousy which Jacob will have is a symptom of bibliomania,[8] as well he may, for jealousy is generally morbid when it is not mad, and a well-known condition of erotomania. The library of *le bibliomane thésauriseur*, as he names him, is *un sérail où les eunuques même n'entrent pas*, a seraglio into which even

---

[1] *The Library.* Second Ed. 35.   [2] *Les Mariages du père Olifus.* Pref.   [3] Garrod, *Profession of Poetry.* 254.   [4] *Elegie.* xviii.   [5] *Love Affairs of a Bibliomaniac.* 18. [6] *Bibliomania.* (1811) 165. He knew such a case; the bibliophile was Haslewood, the book, Juliana Berners' *Bokys of Hauking and Hunting.* (1486)   [7] *Intellectual Life.* 44.   [8] *Ma République.* 50.

eunuchs may not enter. His pleasures are secret and solitary, *discrets, silencieux et ignorés*, and, regardless whether they are desirable to others, he will not permit even a friend *la vue d'une des maîtresses*, they are for himself alone, and he alone will feast his eyes upon them, caress them delicately, rejoicing in his solitary infatuation, and seeking to hide the existence of his treasures as if he had come by them unlawfully. Such precautions give wind to Nodier's rumour that *une bibliothèque de luxe est le harem des vieillards*, which reminds Gustave Mouravit of the anecdote of Cardinal Passionei, who, having permitted a visit to his library, asks the visitor whether the collection had aroused admiration. *Yes*, says he, *but if the library is beautiful, the librarian is rather ignorant. Sir*, quoth his Eminence, *my library is my harem, and I guard it with eunuchs.*[1]

The major number of bibliophiles are Don Juans carried headlong by their passion, and few are content with a few books any more than Coleridge was content with one of the Muses, but, as Hazlitt records, *flirted with all of them as with a set of mistresses*,[2] but in the end, as Don Juan, they

> Learnt how to live, then learnt to love the whole.[3]

Gibbon's library at Lausanne was his harem; *my Seraglio*, he commends,[4] *was ample, my choice was free, my appetite was keen.* Oliver Wendell Holmes[5] *must have his literary harem*, his *parc aux cerfs, where*, he confesses, *my favourites await my moments of leisure and pleasure*; they are scarce and precious editions, luxurious typographical masterpieces, pleasant storytellers and the like; *my Delilahs, that take my head in their lap; the books I love because they are fair to look upon*, prized by collectors, endeared by old associations, *secret treasures that nobody knows anything else about.* Possessing so charming a collection, we should, Leigh Hunt holds,[6] *be in the position of the Turks with their seraglios, which are a great improvement upon our petty exclusivenesses: nobody could then touch our Shakespeare, our Spenser, our Chaucer, our Greek and Italian writers.* They might look on the walls of our library and '*sigh and look, and sigh again*', but there would be no entering. He once was able to *glimpse the feelings* they might have in such circumstances when he was in the Library at Trinity College, Cambridge, and, the keeper being away, he was only able *to get a sight* of the manuscript of Milton's *Comus* through a *grille* of wire: *how we winked*, he confesses, and yearned, and imagined we saw a corner of the precious sheets, but to no purpose. The feelings, he concludes, were not very pleasant, but then *as long as they were confined to others, they would of course only add to our satisfaction.* There are books, in short, that he and others love for what O. W. Holmes calls *insufficient*

---

[1] *Le Livre et la Petite Bibliothèque d'Amateur.* 62–3.   [2] *The Spirit of the Age.*   [3] Flecker, 'Don Juan Disclaims', *Golden Journey.* 57.   [4] *Memoirs.* Ed. Hill. 234.   [5] *Autocrat of the Breakfast-Table.*   [6] Qt., *Book-Lovers' Anth.* 279.

reasons, which are the best of all reasons, since there is no reason in love, and which, therefore, as in all cases of true love, he means *to like and to love and to cherish till death do us part.* That bookcase of Delilahs, he concludes, *that you have paid wicked prices for, that you love without pretending to be reasonable about it, and would bag in case of fire before all the rest:*

> They dwell in an odour of camphor,
> They stand in a Sheraton shrine,
> They are 'warranted early editions'
> These worshipful tomes of mine. [1]

But his tastes differ from those of the luxurious autocrat with his Delilahs, our Laureate of Books being faithful to the old familiar favourites. [2]

No truer bibliophile than Alexander Smith, whose real favourites are not the books he visits in special occasions, but those worn by tender familiarity. They also live on a certain shelf and *are somewhat the worse for wear. Those of them which originally possessed gilding have had it fingered off, each of them has leaves turned down, and they open of themselves at places wherein he has been happy, and with whose every word he is familiar.* [3] *It is pleasanter*, Lamb advises Coleridge in the same strain, *to eat one's peas out of one's own garden, than to buy them by the peck at Covent Garden; and a book reads the better, which is our own, and has been so long known to us, that we know the topography of its blots and dogs' ears, and can trace the dirt in it to having read it at tea with buttered muffins, or over a pipe.* [4]

Charles Lamb loved *folios,* they were his *midnight darlings.* Dibdin was among *the old-fashioned fellows* who loved a *quarto, to the heart's core.* [5] But amplitude is not their sole concern: tastes vary, and if some are for Amazonian *folios,* and others love the plump and matronly *quarto,* some are all for height, and languish after tall *imperial octavos,* others cannot rest without bevies of slim *foolscap octavos.* Although *books* are Dr. Rosenbach's *real love,* he confesses [6] to certain infidelities, *flirtations* he calls them, with *pamphlets. The potentialities between slim covers play the devil with* his *imagination.* They *flaunt a certain piquancy* which he has *never been able to resist.* Others, as I have shown, and not a few, are wrought up with *those dear little dumpy 'twelves',* and there are some Don Juans, a lively crew, whose tastes are so catholic that they would encompass Leperello's scandalous census of his master's mistresses, if it were translated into an inventory of literary darlings.

---

[1] Austin Dobson, 'My Books', *Poetical Works.* 194.   [2] *Ante,* ii, 73.   [3] 'A Shelf in My Bookcase', *Dreamthorp.* 188.   [4] *Letters.* Ed. Lucas. i, 250-1.   [5] *Biblio-phobia.* 32.   [6] *Books and Bidders.* 13.

VI. HOW THEY WOULD DRESS THEM

They are as variable in their taste for their darlings' wardrobes, desiring them in all manner of covertures, *ex libidine*, according to taste; for they know how they respond to fine clothes, as he saith,[1] *ils aiment le luxe et le relèvent*. In all ages the passion for *the acquisition and enjoyment of books* hath been *the occasion of their lovers embellishing their outsides with costly ornaments*;[2] for, as Derome gives out,[3] *a man loveth his books as a lover loves the portrait of his mistress; and, like the lover, he loves to adorn that which he loves. He scrupulously takes care of the precious volume which has filled his heart with keen sensations of delight or sorrow, and clothes it in all the glories of gilded cloths and moroccos. His library is as resplendent with golden laces as the toilet of a favourite; and by their exterior appearance itself his books are worthy of the regards of consuls, as Virgil wished his own to be.*

The library of the Comte de Fortsas was *the Trianon of a book-lover, coquettish as the Queen's. A room the ceiling of which, in red morocco of the Levant, reproduces exactly the colour, harmonious lines, and lyrical flight into azure of a wing of a book bound for Grolier.*[4] Du Bois will have, further, that unless you stamp the books with the mark and character of your own personality, add to them a new splendour and a new beauty, you are no more than a collector. Into this class he boldly huddles such stars in the firmament of bookmen as Canevari, Maïoli, Grolier, De Thou, Spencer, Nodier, Didot, Brunet, and Brinley, who, he charges, *collected books like coins . . . indifferent to the latent life of them; and as they found them so they let them remain. Not a book of their libraries*, he says, *derived an advantage from having been in their possession*. If they bound them their bindings were merely *impersonally elegant marks of possession, uniform, invariable, inexpressive of the books they covered*. With the scorn of the romanticist he compares such libraries with the poetry of Delille, Parny, Michaud, Raynouard, Luce de Lancival, Delavigne, and Ponsard, of *that abolished pleiad*. He will not admit that they know the art of binding, or even that they are booklovers. Perhaps, he concludes, they were *lovers of bibliomania*. One bibliophile saw the light when these great collectors and bookmen were being exalted by the Didots. It was Charles Asselineau; and *he divined the art of forming a library because his mind, with regard to book-collecting as practised by others, was blank as a white page*. He was true, says mine author, to Ronsard's eloquent admonition in the *Abrégé de l' Art Poétique Français: You must have, in the first place, conceptions elevated, grand, beautiful, and not trailing on*

---

[1] 'They love luxury, and set it off', Octave Uzanne, *Zigzags d'un Curieux*. 205.
[2] D'Israeli, *Cur. of Lit.* i, 8.   [3] Qt. Fitzgerald, *Book-Fancier*. 306.   [4] H. P. du Bois, *Four Private Libraries of New York*. 103.

the ground.[1] All of which I quote to reveal how the romantic lover and the bibliophile are of imagination all compact, and not to set one kind of love against another. There is room for all; so back to my theme.

When Sydney Smith received a present of books from friends (*no very infrequent event*) he was *almost child-like in his delight, especially if the binding was gay*, and he would summon his daughter *to arrange and re-arrange them on the shelves, in order to place them in the most conspicuous situation.*[2] There are some bibliophiles who take a delight in associating their books with memories of other loves. Thus Eugene Field bound his *Béranger* in *dainty blue* with *border toolings* of *delicate tracings in white*, in tender memory of Fanchonette, who introduced him to the poet and who used to wear a *dainty blue gown* from which *the most immaculate of petticoats peeped out;*[3] his one regret was that Fanchonette was not a book but *a dainty, coquettish Gallic maiden.*[4]

And not only their outer clothing, but those within also they would have fine, and fair to look upon; *doublures* and panels of silk, or embossed and tooled leather stained with rich dyes or emblazoned with gold; decorated end-papers, margins, etc. They would mark their ownership with dainty labels, or *Book Plates*, of fanciful or eloquent designs. Gleeson White had a variety and *would choose out its appropriate book-plate, for each volume.*[5] Some, and not a few, care little if the dress of their books be mean or shabby, loving them more tenderly should they be in such poor condition. That Alexander Smith's favourites are *defaced and frayed* is *their pride and the best justification of their existence. Thay are tashed, as roses are, by being eagerly handled and smelt.*[6] Huet paid *little or no regard to elegance of bindings, which nicely* he *left to the luxury of financiers and farmers of the revenue;* he collected books *not for idle ostentation*, but for his *own use; cared little about keeping them unsoiled*, and marked the passages he liked or which required emendation at will.[7] But this is no sure sign of book-love, else what should we call those who like to see their favourites well and daintily clad, clean and in good repair? True book-love is careful and fastidious. Henry Bradshaw had *a horror of a dog's-eared page, or of a book carelessly cut*,[8] and he disliked *patched copies in gorgeous bindings.*[9] But for the most part a bibliophile is wrought up by the outward show of books: he develops an inexplicable excitement in their presence. They move him with strange perturbations, from which he would not be free, filling him with a desire to increase their beauty, to *charm* them *into perfection with passion in ecstasy.*[10]

---

[1] H. P. du Bois, *Four Private Libraries of New York.* 16-17.   [2] Holland, *Memoir.* i, 181.   [3] *Love Affairs of a Bibliomaniac.* 130.   [4] *Ib.* 103.   [5] F. York Powell, Intro. Cat., *Lib. of Gleeson White.* (1899) x.   [6] *Dreamthorp.* 18.   [7] *Memoirs.* Trans. Aikin. i, 52.   [8] Prothero, *Memoir of Bradshaw.* 3.   [9] *Ib.* 91.   [10] H. P. du Bois, *Four Private Libraries of New York.* 93.

But they are not all equally moved, or yet enamoured of unchanging beauties; and doubtless, were it possible, would deck their Enids variously, as Geraint loved

> To make her beauty vary day by day,
> In crimsons and in purples and in gems.[1]

Some, again, prefer the négligé of *boards*, others like their covers *limp*, uncorsaged, or the like; but most, and here is the greatest departure from the love of women, love them in old-fashioned styles, whether of the body, as printing and paper, or the clothing: it matters not so long as they are old; rich damask or brocade, calf or morocco, jewelled and bossed with ornaments and clasps of gold, silver and precious stones, and whether their cloths are worn or not, tattered and torn, blistered or frayed, it is all one, these, as I said just now, are reasons to love them the more. They are often aphrodisiacs, rousing the fiercest and the most hungry passions: you love them, fondle them, make much of them, *in spite*, Hippolyte Rigault[2] confesses, *of their poverty, as if they were clothed in gold and silk*. Perhaps it is, as Chapman[3] suggests, that *an old book will yield something of the treasure of its experience, something of the bloom of its youth*; giving more than youth can give in the stored-up impressions which only come from experience; so whether it be *imperfect, soiled, wormed, cropped, shabbily bound—all these things belongs to its years*.[4] Those who feel thus look upon the rebinding of an old book as an act of vandalism: *Would you tear off and cast away the covers which have felt the caressing pressure of the hands of those whose memory you revere?*[5]

To be desirable a book must have a past. When Coleridge and Hazlitt *found a little worn-out copy of the 'Seasons', lying in a window-seat* of the inn at Linton, Coleridge exclaimed, *'That is true fame!'*[6] To be adored books must have ventured through time and the perils of chance, for *they are love-letters that pass from hand to hand of a thousand lovers that never meet*.[7] *Books, like proverbs*, saith Sir William Temple,[8] *receive their chief value from the stamp and esteem of the ages through which they have passed*. Yet books are loved, and proverbs only, at best, respected, so we must look elsewhere for a reason. Love and esteem are not necessarily related—in bibliophily they more often come together than elsewhere—the admirable books are usually the most adorable. Some there are who affirm, with reason, that books long to be loved: *they betray no man and love their lovers*,[9] for they

[1] Tennyson, *Idylls of the King*. 'Enid.' 9–1po. [2] Qt. Octave Uzanne, *Book-Hunter in Paris*. 126. [3] *Portrait of a Scholar*. 65. [4] W. Carew Hazlitt, *Book-Collector*. 15–16. [5] Eugene Field, *Love Affairs of a Bibliomaniac*. 8. [6] Hazlitt, 'First Acquaintance with Poets'. [7] Richard Le Gallienne, *Prose Fancies*. 115. [8] *On Ancient and Modern Learning*. [9] G. S. Phillips, *Essays*.

are nothing until they have been *loved, and loved again*.[1] The love of old books is strong because it is reinforced by the love of all their lovers. A hundred love affairs have been distilled into the latest book-passion. *Nous le aimons pour leur antiquité même*, says Jules Janin, *et pour la rouille éloquente qui les pare*;[2] let the herd have its *fêtes*, its music, its *épouvantes de chaque jour*, its daily horrors, but *restons fidèles à ces belles choses antiques*,[3] let us be faithful to these beautiful old things; and with that we may leave these true lovers to the fondness of their own conceits, for I have said enough to prove that a book you love is a joy to your eyes at all times.

VII. THE WORLD WELL LOST FOR THEM

I would rather be a poor man in a garret with plenty of books than a king who did not love reading.[4] This is a sentiment which most true bibliophiles will uphold, even those austere philosophers whose minds might be their whole estate, as Plato, *a man of very slender means, but that nevertheless bought three books of Philolaus the Pythagorean for ten thousand denarii*,[5] which was a great sum, for even in those days popular authors could be bought for five or ten *denarii*; and Plato could not have had his desire but for the help of his rich disciple, Dion of Syracuse. Books are ever first among their desires. Erasmus was so enamoured of books that he said[6] *as soon as I receive any money, I shall first buy Greek authors, and afterwards some clothes*; the *earliest uses* Sydney Smith made of his increased wealth when prosperity finally came to him was to enlarge his library;[7] a large part of Shelley's *scanty income* was spent upon books, so that he always managed to form a library wherever he was;[8] Richard Le Gallienne *possesses a copy of Walton's Lives, that of Bishop Sanderson, with the author's donatory inscription to a friend upon the title-page. To keep this in his little library he has undergone willingly many privations, cheerfully faced hunger and cold rather than let it pass from his hand.*[9] Archbishop Fénelon would not exchange his *love of books* for all the *crowns and kingdoms of the Empire*;[10] Gibbon so prized his book-love as to reckon it *the pleasure and glory of his life*, which he would not *exchange for the wealth of the Indies*;[11] Magliabecchi *was content with frugal fare and frugal clothing, preferring the riches of a Library to those of house furniture;*[12] *tenui cultu: victuque contentus, quidquid ei pecuniae superaret in omnogenae*

[1] Ruskin, *Sesame and Lilies*. (1924) 55.   [2] 'For the eloquent rust which adorns them.' *Le Livre*. xxx.   [3] *Ib*.   [4] Macaulay.   [5] Aulus Gellius, *Attic Nights*. Loeb Ed. iii, 17.   [6] Qt. L. Johnson, *Post Liminium*. 164.   [7] Holland, *Memoir*. i, 240–1.   [8] Hogg, *Shelley*. London Lib. Ed. 360.   [9] *Compleat Angler*. (Reprint, 1896) Pref. v.   [10] Qt., *Book-Lover's Ench*. 101.   [11] *Autobiography*.   [12] Dibdin, *Bibliomania*. (1811) 160.

eruditionis libros comparandos erogabat, selectissimamque voluminum multi-
tudinem ea mente adquisivit, ut aliquando posset publicae utilitati dicari;[1] Anatole
France knew two old priests *who loved books and who loved nothing else in*
the world;[2] no such comfort as a sweet book,

> With pipe and book at close of day,
> O what is sweeter, mortal, say!
> It matters not what book on knee,
> *Old Izaak* or the *Odyssey.*[3]

Well may bookmen refuse to change fortunes with kings: they live for
their books. *No man ever lived so much with, and so entirely for his books* as
Douce.[4] None so merry, if they may thus quietly enjoy such company,
they are in heaven for a time and would be at all times had they their way,
for when they love books, all other things are importunate and burden-
some to them; as lovers and their lasses, *Tecum vivere amem, tecum obeam*
lubens, they would live and die with them alone: *O festus dies hominis!* O
happy night of tender companionship! Nor perturbations, nor doubts
afflict them, like those of Catullus towards one of his mistresses:

> Odi et amo. Quare id faciam, fortasse requiris.
> Nescio, sed fieri sentio et excrucior.[5]

> I hate, and yet I love thee too;
> How can that be? I know not how;
> Only that so it is I know,
> And feel with torment that 'tis so.[6]

And if they may not be with their books they are dejected in an instant,
and try most dolefully, as other lovers do.

> To entertain the time with thoughts of love,[7]

until they come to them again, *for a book at a touch pours its heart into our*
own.[8] Chao Shen-ch'iao, a famous Chinese magistrate, sold all his possessions to help the sufferers in a great famine, and when he was made Governor of Chehkiang his baggage consisted of *one load of books.*[9] Gabriel
Naudé passed all his life with books, sorting out those he had, lying in
wait for those he lacked; buying ceaselessly in France, Holland, Italy, England, mostly for others, but sometimes for himself when his patrons had

---

[1] Pref., *Bibl. Magliab.* A. Fossio. p. x. Qt. *Ib.* 160.   [2] 'Bibliophilia', *Life and*
Letters. Second Series. Trans. Evans. 60.   [3] Richard Le Gallienne, *Volumes in*
Folio. 87.   [4] Dibdin, *Reminiscences.* ii, 768.   [5] Catullus, 85.   [6] Cowley, 'Of
Solitude', *Essays.*   [7] Shakespeare, *Sonnets.* xxxix.   [8] Douglas Jerrold.   [9] Giles,
Chinese Biog. Dict. 76.

fallen upon evil days.[1] Other companionship they rarely need, even when their love turns to women, as it may do ('tis a common humour even of bibliophiles). Verbeyst, of Brussels, Southey's favourite bookseller, loved his books *only less than he loved his handsome and good-natured wife*.[2] There are many such, for books are the companions of lovers, married and unmarried. They cannot be tempted from them, even by love.

That Emperor Gordianus, whose *long life was innocently spent in the study of letters and the peaceful honours of Rome*, combined the domestic and the intellectual passions on a lavish scale: *Twenty-two acknowledged concubines, and a library of sixty-two thousand volumes, attested the variety of his inclinations, and from the productions which he left behind him, it appears that the former as well as the latter were designed for use rather than ostentation*.[3] Well may Edward FitzGerald exclaim: *Let Empires decline to such a tune!*[4] To come nearer home I may cite Cowley as typical of the rest of those who would combine love and books:

> Ah, yet, ere I descend to the grave,
> May I a small house and large garden have;
> And a few friends, and many books, both true,
> Both wise, and both delightful too!
>   And since love ne'er will from me flee,
> A mistress moderately fair,
> And good as guardian angels are,
>   Only beloved and loving me.[5]

And when they are bereft of the love of women they are not desolate so long as they may have their books. I need cite no further instance than that of the Duke of Roxeburghe, who found the transition from boudoir to library easy and comforting when he was denied, for political reasons, the hand of a princess to whom he had been affianced.[6]

Nor will preferment of any kind compass divorcement. *If the crowns of all the kingdoms of the Empire were laid down at my feet in exchange for my books*, says Fénelon, *I would spurn them all*.[7] There is a pleasant story to this purpose.[8] The learned John Wesselas loved books and despised riches and honours. When his friend and patron, Pope Sixtus IV, obtained the tiara, Wesselas visited him. The Pope asked him to name a wish he would have gratified. Wesselas desired copies of the *Bible* in Hebrew and Greek from the Vatican Library. The precious books were given to him. *But why*, asked

---

[1] Alcide Bonneau, Intro., *Avis pour Dresser une Bibliothèque*. Naudé. vi.   [2] Edward Dowden, *Southey*. 104.   [3] Gibbon, *Decline and Fall*. Everyman Ed. i, 171. He left three or four children by each concubine, and 'his literary productions were by no means contemptible'.   [4] *More Letters*. 13.   [5] 'The Wish.'   [6] Roberts, *Book-Hunter in London*. 52.   [7] Qt. Richardson, *Choice of Books*. 21.   [8] *Dict. Anec.* (1809) i, 188.

the Pope, *do you not ask for a Bishopric? Because*, said Wesselas, *I do not want one*. Books were his Bishopric, love of books enough. Nodier records[1] how Urbain Chevreau refused to be an Academician, or Secretary to Queen Christina of Sweden, because he preferred the company of his books: his books were his means of escape from the turmoil of the time. We are told, by another authority, that a doctor in Arabia refused an invitation to visit the Sultan of Bokhara, because he could not travel without his books, and their transport *would have required four hundred camels*.[2] And a notable citizen of London, Richard Smith, Roberts cites out of *Anthony à Wood*, was so *infinitely curious and inquisitive about books*, that in 1655 he gave up the position of Under-Sheriff, and a salary of £700 a year, *in order to devote himself entirely to book-hunting*,[3] If all cared less for wealth and prestige we should have much more content and quietness in our Commonwealth. Plenty of books and leisure for good reading, methinks, is a sufficient portion of itself, *beatus ille qui procul negotiis*, happy is he who is free from worldly cares, and he does well that will accept such a life. It was the counsel which the politic Cicero gave to his best friends, as it was the life he himself wished most to live. No less than this is implied in that remark of his when he longed to buy the books of Atticus: *If ever I do*, he said, *supero Crassum divitiis atque omnium vicos et prata contemno*, I shall be the richest of millionaires and shan't envy any man his manors and meadows.[4] Now go brag of thy money.

VIII. ON PARTING WITH BOOKS

Examples are common, how this love continues into old age, and what desolation supervenes on the forcible divorcement of the lover and his beloved. The prospect of parting with their books *adds a new pang to death;*[5] for they are his dear friends, and as Bacon expounds it: *Homo toties moritur quoties amittit suos*,[6] a man dies as often as he loses his friends. Eugene Field avows that if he lost his library and were unable to assemble another he would lay himself *down to die*, for he could not live without companionships which had grown as dear to him as *life itself*.[7] Fear of parting causes melancholy, desperation, and, more than metaphorically, sometimes it engenders death itself. I find an instance in *Gustave Mouravit*, who tells how *le bon Abbé Goujet* died of a broken heart when he was forced to sell his library,[8] and the Eltons[9] have another example in Samuel

[1] Qt. Derome, *Les Editions Originales des Romantiques*. (1887.) i, 215–16. [2] Qr. Elton, *Great Book-Collectors*. 10. [3] Roberts, *Book-Hunter in London*. 32. [4] *Letters to Atticus*. Loeb Ed. i, 13. [5] Fitzgerald, *Book-Fancier*. 7. [6] 'Ornamenta Rationalia'. *Moral and Hist. Works*. Bohn Ed. 192. [7] *Love Affairs of a Bibliomaniac*. 142. [8] *Le Livre et la Petite Bibliothèque d'Amateur*. 136. [9] *Great Book-Collectors*. 208.

Cromleholme, who had the best set of neatly bound classics in London. He was a great lover of his books, and *their loss hastened the end of his life;* as the good couple in Sir Henry Wotton's distich, which I may with reverence be permitted to paraphrase:[1]

> They first deceas'd: He for a little tri'd
> To live without Them: lik'd it not, and di'd.

When that diligent bookfellow, Sir Robert Cotton,[2] was accused of selling state secrets to Spain, excuses were found to close his library, and finally it was declared *contra bonum publicum* because of its political contents. That *tyranny*, said Sir Robert, *broke his heart*, and shortly before his death, in 1631, he told the Lords in Council that their action caused his *mortal malady*. Nor, as I have sufficiently shown,[3] can they bear to be separated from their books even in death: *Il faut quitter tout cela!*[4] exclaimed the aged Cardinal Mazarin, thinking himself alone in his famous library;[5] and I need do no more than add the story of Henri du Bouchet, who bequeathed his library to the Abbey of St. Victor-lez-Paris and asked to be buried among his books.[6]

Whether good bookmen suffer or not the misfortune of the loss of their treasures, they all contemplate the dispersion of them with anxiety. Huet was ever *greatly disturbed* by the thought that his library, *formed by so much labour and expense, the dearest solace and food of* his mind, *would hereafter be dispersed, in alleys and upon booksellers' stalls, and come into the hands of the ignorant and vulgar.*[7] *Whither are our treasurer to be scattered?* cries another,[8] *Will they find kind masters? or, worst fate of books, fall into the hands of women who will sell them to the trunk-maker? Are the leaves to line a box or to curl a maiden's locks? Are the rarities to become more rare, and at last fetch prodigious prices?* Those who are able to solve these problems he accounts unlucky, for they are *constrained to sell their libraries—an experience full of bitterness, wrath, and disappointment.* So I may conclude that it is best not to seek solutions, *nihil scire vita jucundissima,* 'tis the pleasantest life to know nothing; *iners malorum remedium ignorantia,*[9] ignorance is a poor remedy for such evils, for the same inconvenience may befall any of us. Adversity knows not discrimination, and as like as not those of us who begin by living for our books may end by living on them.

When adversity drove the learned William Roscoe, author of the *Life of Lorenzo de Medici,* to sell his books, he was inconsolable. *The parting,* as Washington Irving observes,[10] *touched upon his tenderest feelings and was the*

[1] *Reliquiae Wottonianae.* (1651.) 529.   [2] Elton, *Great Book-Collectors.* 117–18.
[3] 'The Twilight of the Bibliophile', *ante.* i, 283.   [4] 'Must I leave all these!'   [5] Qt.
Gustave Mouravit, *Le Livre et la Petite Bibliothèque d'Amateur.* 431.   [6] *Ib.* 419.
[7] *Memoirs.* Trans. Aikin. i, 52.   [8] Andrew Lang, *Library.* 15.   [9] Seneca, *Œdipus.*
515.   [10] *Sketch Book.*

only circumstance that could provoke the notice of his Muse. Roscoe consoled himself, as how many bereaved lovers have done before him, with the thought that he would meet the spirits of his *loved associates* in another world:

> For, pass a few short years, or days, or hours,
> And happier seasons may their dawn unfold,
> And all your sacred fellowship restore;
> When, freed from earth, unlimited its powers,
> Mind shall with Mind direct communion hold,
> And kindred spirits meet to part no more.[1]

William Beckford was more fortunate, for though *necessity forced him* to sell his pictures, he never till his death parted with a book.[2] *I have loved my books from my boyhood,* says Archbishop Le Tellier,[3] *and the taste has grown with age.* Parting is always sorrowful, whatever the age, and it is always their dread: *Though I can part with land,* Gibbon confessed,[4] *I cannot part with books;* it would have been easier to *repair* the loss of *acquaintances.*[5] *A day will come when you, my darling books! will be laid on the saleroom table,* Silvestre de Sacy fears, *and others will buy and possess you—persons, perhaps, less worthy of you than your old master.* Each book was dear to him, chosen one by one, gathered by the *sweat of his brow;*[6] as dear as friends, and selling them *as bad as losing friends, than which life has no worse sorrow.*[7]

Yet many are loth to part from their treasures even at the end, although they know that unless collections were dispersed collections could not be made. There is some folly in all this, for we are all in the same boat: it is *lex talionis,* tit for tat, and the nature of all things to part, and for some to benefit thereby. *Sic transit gloria mundi* might well be the motto of a history of book-collectors, for most of the collections of one generation of *genuine bookworms* are *scattered in the next by needy legatees.*[8] *The life of a library,* says Slater,[9] *is, as a rule, less than half that of a man,* and as volume is added to volume the closing scene of dissolution draws nearer and nearer: *the larger and more important a collection, the shorter its life,* so that, as Fitzgerald has it, many a bibliophile might look on an auction-room *as the scaffold whereon his darling 'hobby' will one day be done to death.*[10] Collecting is but *'writing in water', gathering for dispersion, heaping up only for scattering,* and the collector but *a bibliophilist Danaid, vainly filling his pitcher—the water running out at bottom!*[11] That a dispersal is a piteous sight few will deny, and it is hard, I confess, to see so many admirable libraries thus injured. Most

[1] Roscoe, 'On Parting with his Books', *Poems.* (1853.) 94–5. [2] Charles Whibley *Pageantry of Life.* 218. [3] *Great Book-Collectors.* Elton. 150. [4] *Autobiography and Correspondence.* (1869.) 337. [5] *Ib.* 27. [6] Qt., *Book-Fancier.* Fitzgerald. 1. [7] Andrew Lang, *Library.* 15. [8] Roberts, *Book-Hunter in London.* 25. [9] *Romance of Book-Collecting.* 162. [10] *Book-Fancier.* 222. [11] *Ib.* 2.

good bookmen will feel as Samuel Pepys[1] felt when he confessed to John Evelyn that the sale of Lord Maitland's collection, *which was certainly the noblest, most substantial and accomplished library that ever passed under the speare,* heartily grieved him *to behold its limbs, like those of the chaste Hippolytus, separated and torn from that so well chosen body.*

Some there be, and they are of the wiser sort, who cheat time and change by looking upon their collections as a trust to be handed on to State or College Libraries, and from this intention many such institutions have greatly benefited. Fearing, as I have shown, the ultimate scattering of his books into ignoble hands, and remembering the fate of the splendid library of James Augustus de Thou, which, in spite of its founder's efforts, was finally dispersed, Huet, after long consideration, devised a plan for keeping his own books together in perpetuity. He made over his library to the fathers of the *Professed House of Jesuits at Paris* on condition that he should enjoy the use of the books during his life, and that after his death they should neither be dispersed nor divided nor mingled with others, and that books taken out of the library should not be changed, or transferred from the place in which they were deposited, either for the purpose of lending, or of being more commodiously read or studied, or for any cause whatsoever. Should these conditions be violated, the donation should be void, and his heirs or their descendants have the right to reclaim the library.[2] But with all his care the tragedy of dissolution fell upon his collection, for seventy-one years later the society itself was dissolved and all its possessions were confiscated and sold.[3]

Samuel Pepys was more fortunate. He made such careful provisions for the preservation of his books *intire in one body, undivided unsold and secure against all manner of deminution damages and embesselments,*[4] that they have withstood the ravages of time, as so many bibliophiles can testify who have made the pilgrimage to Magdalene College, Cambridge, where they have feasted their eyes upon those books in the very presses and bindings which the loving care of Mr. Pepys and his nephew and penultimate heir, John Jackson, a good bookman also, provided for them. It is not, as we have seen, always sufficient protection for the integrity of a library that it should be bequeathed to some worthy institution, so to allay his fears our immortal diarist, who was not only a *very worthy, industrious and curious person,*[5] but shrewd as well, sought to secure his library against *the ordinary fate of such collections falling into the hands of an incompetent heir and thereby of being sold dissipated or imbezzled,* by offering it to one of two colleges *subject to the Annual visitation from the other and to the forfeiture*

---

[1] *Letters.*   [2] Huet, *Memoirs.* Trans. Aikin. ii, 357–8.   [3] Ibid., ii, 396. Note.   [4] 'The Will of Samuel Pepys', *Pepysiana.* Wheatley. (1899). 264   [5] John Evelyn, *Diary.* Globe Edn. 256.

thereof to the like possession and Use of the other upon Conviction of any breach of the said Covenant.[1] I wish there were more in our own times like him, or like Thomas J. Wise, who holds the *preservation* of his own collection to be a *national duty,*[2] and yet, for those reasons I have given, it is good that some desirable books should remain wild and fair game for the good bookman, so I welcome also those others who dream of an eternity of re-distribution for their books, as Dr. Anthony Askew, who would that *his treasures might be unreservedly submitted to sale, after his decease;* in which wish, saith Dibdin,[3] he was not *singular; many eminent collectors had indulged it before him:* and to his own knowledge *many modern ones still indulge it.* If, then, *literary stores which were accumulated in one deposit* are bequeathed *to persons ignorant of their value and incapable of using them,* by public sale they may once again come into *the hands of real lovers of books, and contribute to enrich a number of smaller collections.*[4]

Beverley Chew desired his beloved books *to pass after his death to those who would continue to cherish and care for them, and that they in their turn should transmit them to the booklovers of the future.*[5] Edmond de Goncourt dreaded the thought that his books and other works of art, which had been the joy of his life, should be consigned to the *cold tomb of a museum,* subject only to the *stupid glance of the careless passer-by,* and he provided in his will that they should be *dispersed under the hammer of the auctioneer,* so that the pleasure they had given him would be re-incarnate in some inheritor of his own taste. 'Tis a common dream, as the poet implies, when he hopes that his books, which he has loved so long, may escape *the shame and squalor of the stall; rather,* he sings,

> I trust your lot may touch
> Some Crocsus—if there should be such—
> To buy you, and that you may so
> From Croesus unto Croesus go
> Till that inevitable day
> When comes your moment of decay.[6]

You, perchance, think the same, and are composed, or find consolation by contemplating with Carew Hazlitt[7] for *how long a succession of holders the same beautiful or rare book has been a friend and a companion, a source of delight and pride,* and that even you are no more than *a temporary custodian and a trustee for others who shall come after* you.[8] When our great public

---

[1] 'The Will of Samuel Pepys', *op. cit.* 266.   [2] Richard Curle, *Ashley Lib. Cat.* Intro. i, 4.   [3] *Bibliomania.* (1811.) 515.   [4] John Aikin, M.D., Huet's *Memoirs.* ii, Notes 7, 395.   [5] *Essays and Verses about Books.* Chew. 99.   [6] Austin Dobson, 'The Collector to his Library', *Poetical Works.* 195.   [7] *Book-Collector.* 51.   [8] Slater, *Romance of Book-Collecting.* 93.

libraries have been furnished with representative collections, I hold this to be the better course, nay, it is the only one, the safest alternative to neglect and misusage, and in so generous a re-incarnation we shall find the greatest ease to be quiet and content with our mortal lot. And if few contemplate the fall of a great tree without regret, book-lovers may still exult, for *arbore dejecta qui vult ligna colligit*, when the tree falls everyone may gather wood. So whenever the parting comes, now or hence, console yourself: your library will *rise again to live once more*, not singly, maybe, but variously, under the protection of perennial lovers:

> Thus shall you live upon warm shelves again,
> And 'neath an evening lamp your pages glow.[1]

Our collections are like time: they will pass. We are no more, says Anatole France,[2] than children when they build castles on the seashore: *the tide sweeps away the sand castles, the auctioneer disperses the hoarded treasures*, yet what better can we do than *build sand castles at ten, and form collections at sixty? Better men than I have parted with their books*, says Edward Newton,[3] *better men, mind you, but none with a greater love than I; and if my present collection has to be jettisoned*, he bravely adds, *I'll at once begin collecting over again.* Book-love, I say again, lasts throughout life, it never flags or fails, but, like Beauty itself, is *a joy for ever:*

> Its loveliness increases; it will never
> Pass into nothingness; but still will keep
> A bower quiet for us, and a sleep
> Full of sweet dreams, and health, and quiet breathing.[4]

Therefore it may be said of every good bookman: *in finem*, he loves them to the end, as God is said to love man, not *in fine*, in the end, but *in finem*, to the end, and, as in the greater case, there is no higher testimony of an inexpressible love,[5] *ready to be any thing, in the extasie of being ever,*[6] for to love them to the end is to love them forever, beyond time and change; and I know of no more admirable and momentous commendation, and no more lively and tenacious note upon which to end this treatise.

FINIS

[1] Richard Le Gallienne.   [2] *Garden of Epicurus.* 109–10.   [3] *Magnificent Farce.* 59.
[4] Keats, *Emdymion.* 1–5.   [5] Donne, *Sermons.* 'Selected Passages.' L. P. Smith. 201–2.
[6] Sir Thomas Browne, *Hydriotaphia.* Chap. v.

EPILOGUE

There is now but to sum it all up. My task is done. A pleasant task, as I said at first, begun for mine own entertainment, and continued in that wise. It remains but to hem the end of my treatise that it ravel not out.

The sum of it all is: read what you like, because you like it, seeking no other reason and no other profit than the experience of reading. If you enjoy the experience it is well; but whether you enjoy it or not the experience is worth having. But I do not rule out reading with a more definite purpose, such as study or research. That which suits your purpose is best, for happiness, pleasure, joy, prefer to come unawares; they are shy of pursuit and resentful in captivity. And what is enjoined for reading is good also for collecting. Collect what you like, seeking neither profit nor applause. That is all.

A roundabout way to have achieved such concise axioms? True. But what would you? I set out to go round and about, and not to come to conclusions or even to make an end of so various a theme. I could have been more various and gone further, for there need be no end to the theme, and conclusions conclude nothing, as you may perchance have observed from my citations, which are alike only in their differences.

A treatise so whimsically set out must perforce stand or fall by its quality or power to interest or amuse. And what else should we demand of a book that is a book? For the rest, why read or collect books unless you have a mind to it? I do not advocate either. Most people have neither read nor owned books, yet they go on living. Go, then, choose your book and your time. There is no compulsion. Reading is not a virtue—unless the enjoyment be virtuous.

INDEX I

TO AUTHORS AND WORKS CITED

INDEX II

AUTHORS ETC. REFERRED TO IN TEXT

·N.B.—*The cross-references (in italic) are to Index I*